What They Said
in 1994

What They Said® In 1994

The Yearbook Of World Opinion

Compiled and Edited by
ALAN F. PATER
and
JASON R. PATER

MONITOR BOOK COMPANY

To

The Newsmakers of the World . . .

May they never be at a loss for words

Table of Contents

PART THREE: GENERAL

Preface to the First Edition (1969)

Words can be powerful or subtle, humorous or maddening. They can be vigorous or feeble, lucid or obscure, inspiring or despairing, wise or foolish, hopeful or pessimistic . . . they can be fearful or confident, timid or articulate, persuasive or perverse, honest or deceitful. As tools at a speaker's command, words can be used to reason, argue, discuss, cajole, plead, debate, declaim, threaten, infuriate, or appease; they can harangue, flourish, recite, preach, discourse, stab to the quick, or gently sermonize.

When casually spoken by a stage or film star, words can go beyond the press-agentry and make-up facade and reveal the inner man or woman. When purposefully uttered in the considered phrasing of a head of state, words can determine the destiny of millions of people, resolve peace or war, or chart the course of a nation on whose direction the fate of the entire world may depend.

Until now, the *copia verborum* of well-known and renowned public figures—the doctors and diplomats, the governors and generals, the potentates and presidents, the entertainers and educators, the bishops and baseball players, the jurists and journalists, the authors and attorneys, the congressmen and chairmen-of-the-board—whether enunciated in speeches, lectures, interviews, radio and television addresses, news conferences, forums, symposiums, town meetings, committee hearings, random remarks to the press, or delivered on the floors of the United States Senate and House of Representatives or in the parliaments and palaces of the world—have been dutifully reported in the media, then filed away and, for the most part, forgotten.

The editors of *WHAT THEY SAID* believe that consigning such a wealth of thoughts, ideas, doctrines, opinions and philosophies to interment in the morgues and archives of the Fourth Estate is lamentable and unnecessary. Yet the media, in all their forms, are constantly engulfing us in a profusion of endless and increasingly voluminous news reports. One is easily disposed to disregard or forget the stimulating discussion of critical issues embodied in so many of the utterances of those who make the news and, in their respective fields, shape the events throughout the world. The conclusion is therefore a natural and compelling one: the educator, the public official, the business executive, the statesman, the philosopher—everyone who has a stake in the complex, often confusing trends of our times—should have material of this kind readily available.

These, then, are the circumstances under which *WHAT THEY SAID* was conceived. It is the culmination of a year of listening to the people in the public eye; a year of scrutinizing, monitoring, reviewing, judging, deciding—a year during which the editors resurrected from almost certain oblivion those quintessential elements of the year's *spoken* opinion which, in their judgment, demanded preservation in book form.

WHAT THEY SAID is a pioneer in its field. Its *raison d'etre* is the firm conviction that presenting, each year, the highlights of vital and interesting views from the lips of prominent people on virtually every aspect of contemporary civilization fulfills the need to give the *spoken* word the permanence and lasting value of the *written* word. For, if it is true that a picture is worth 10,000 words, it is equally true that a verbal conclusion, an apt quote or a candid comment by a person of fame or influence can have more significance and can provide more understanding than an entire page of summary in a standard work of reference.

The editors of *WHAT THEY SAID* did not, however, design their book for researchers and scholars alone. One of the failings of the conventional reference work is that it is that it is blandly written and referred to primarily for facts and figures, lacking inherent "interest value." *WHAT THEY SAID*, on the other hand, was planned for sheer enjoyment and pleasure, for searching glimpses into the lives and thoughts of the world's celebrities, as well as for serious study, intellectual reflection and the philosophical contemplation of our multifaceted life and mores. Furthermore, those pressed for time, yet anxious to know what the newsmakers have been saying, will welcome the short excerpts which will make for quick, intermittent reading—and rereading. And, of course, the topical classifications, the speakers' index, the subject index, the place and date information—documented and authenticated and easily located—will supply a rich fund of hitherto not readily obtainable reference and statistical material.

Finally, the reader will find that the editors have eschewed trite comments and cliches, tedious and boring. The selected quotations, each standing on its own, are pertinent, significant, stimulating—above all, relevant to today's world, expressed in the speakers' own words. And they will, the editors feel, be even more relevant tomorrow. They will be re-examined and reflected upon in the future by men and women eager to learn from the past. The prophecies, the promises, the "golden dreams," the boastings and rantings, the bluster, the bravado, the pleadings and representations of those whose voices echo in these pages (and in those to come) should provide a rare and unique history lesson. The positions held by these luminaries, in their respective callings, are such that what they say today may profoundly affect the future as well as the present, and so will be of lasting importance and meaning.

ALAN F. PATER
JASON R. PATER

Beverly Hills, California

Editorial Treatment

ORGANIZATION OF MATERIAL

Special attention has been given to the arrangement of the book–from the major divisions down to the individual categories and speakers–the objective being a logical progression of related material, as follows:

(A) The categories are arranged alphabetically within each of three major sections:

Part one:	"National Affairs"
Part two:	"International"
Part three:	"General"

In this manner, the reader can quickly locate quotations pertaining to particular fields of interest (see also *Indexing*). It should be noted that some quotations contain a number of thoughts or ideas–sometimes on different subjects– while some are vague as to exact subject matter and thus do not fit clearly into a specific topic classification. In such cases, the judgment of the Editors has determined the most appropriate category.

(B) Within each category the speakers are in alphabetical order by surname, following alphabetization practices used in the speaker's country of origin.

(C) Where there are two or more quotations by one speaker within the same category, they appear chronologically by date spoken or date of source.

SPEAKER IDENTIFICATION

(A) The occupation, profession, rank, position or title of the speaker is given as it was *at the time the statement was made* (except when the speaker's relevant identification is in the past, in which case he is shown as "former"). Thus, due to possible changes in status during the year, a speaker may be shown with different identifications in various parts of the book, or even within the same category.

(B) In the case of a speaker who holds more than one position simultaneously, the judgment of the Editors has determined the most appropriate identification to use with a specific quotation.

(C) The nationality of a speaker is given when it will help in identifying the speaker or when it is relevant to the quotation.

THE QUOTATIONS

The quoted material selected for inclusion in this book is shown as it appeared in the source, except as follows:

(A) *Ellipses* have been inserted wherever the Editors have deleted extraneous words or overly long passages within the quoted material used. In no way has the meaning or intention of the quotations been altered. *Ellipses* are also used where they appeared in the source.

(B) *Punctuation and spelling* have been altered by the Editors where they were obviously incorrect in the source, or to make the quotations more intelligible, or to conform to the general style used throughout this book. Again, meaning and intention of the quotations have not been changed.

(C) *Brackets* ([]) indicate material inserted by the Editors or by the source to either correct obvious errors or to explain or clarify what they speaker is saying. In some instances, bracketed material may replace quoted material for sake of clarity.

(D) *Italics* either appeared in the original source or were added by the Editors where emphasis is clearly desirable.

Except for the above instances, the quoted material used has been printed verbatim, as reported by the source (even if the speaker made factual errors or was awkward in his choice of words).

Special care has been exercised to make certain that each quotation stands on its own and is not taken "out of context." The Editors, however, cannot be responsible for errors made by the original source, i.e., incorrect reporting, mis-quotations, or errors in interpretation.

DOCUMENTATION AND SOURCES

Documentation (circumstance, place, date) of each quotation is provided as fully as could be obtained, and the sources are furnished for all quotations. In some instances, no documentation details were available; in those cases, only the source is given. Following are the sequence and style used for this information:

Circumstance of quotation, place, date/Name of source, date:section (if applicable), page number.

Example: *Before the Senate, Washington, Dec.4/The Washington Post, 12-5:(A)13.*

The above example indicates that the quotation was delivered before the Senate in Washington on December 4. It was taken for *WHAT THEY SAID* from *The Washington Post,* issue of December 5, section A, page 13. (When a newspaper publishes more than one edition on the same date, it should be noted that page numbers may vary from edition to edition.)

(A) When the source is a television or radio broadcast, the name of the network or local station is indicated, along with the date of the broadcast (obviously, page and section information does not apply).

(B) An asterisk (*) before the (/) in the documentation indicates that the quoted material was written rather than spoken. Although the basic policy of *WHAT THEY SAID* is to use only *spoken* statements, there are occasions when written statements are considered by the Editors to be important enough to be included. These occasions are rare and usually involve Presidential messages and statements released to the press and other such documents attributed to persons in high government office.

INDEXING

(A) The *Index to Speakers* is keyed to the page number. (For alphabetization practices, see *Organization of Material*, paragraph B.)

(B) The *Index to Subjects* is keyed to both the page number and the quotation number on the page (thus, 210:3 indicates quotation number 3 on page 210); the quotation number appears at the right corner of each quotation.

(C) To locate quotations on a particular subject, regardless of the speaker, turn to the appropriate category (see *Table of Contents*) or use the detailed *Index to Subjects*.

(D) To locate all quotations by a particular speaker, regardless of subject, use the *Index to Speakers*.

(E) To locate quotations by a particular speaker on a particular subject, turn to the appropriate category and then to that person's quotations within the category.

(F) The reader will find that the basic categorization format of *WHAT THEY SAID* is itself a useful index, inasmuch as related quotations are grouped together by their respective categories. All aspects of journalism, for example, are relevant to each other; thus, the section *Journalism* embraces all phases of the news media. Similarly, quotations pertaining to the U. S. President, Congress, etc., are in the section *Government.*

MISCELLANEOUS

(A) Except where otherwise indicated or obviously to the contrary, all universities, organizations and business firms mentioned in this book are in the United States; similarly, references made to "national," "Federal," "this country," "the nation" etc., refer to the United States.

(B) In most cases, organizations whose names end with "of the United States" are Federal government agencies.

SELECTION OF CATEGORIES

The selected categories reflect, in the Editors' opinion, the most widely discussed public-interest subjects, those which readily fall into the over-all sphere of "current events." They represent topics continuously covered by the mass media because of their inherent importance to the changing world scene. Most of the categories are permanent; they appear in each annual edition of *WHAT THEY SAID*. However, because of the transient character of some subjects, there may be categories which appear one year and may not be repeated the next.

SELECTION OF SPEAKERS

The following persons are always considered eligible for inclusion in *WHAT THEY SAID*: top-level officials of all branches of national, state and local governments (both U.S. and foreign), including all United States Senators and Representatives; top-echelon military officers; college and university presidents, chancellors and professors; chairmen and presidents of major corporations; heads of national public-oriented organizations and associations; national and internationally known diplomats; recognized celebrities from the entertainment and literary spheres and the arts generally; sports figures of national stature; commentators on the world scene who are recognized as such and who command the attention of the mass media.

The determination of what and who are "major" and "recognized" must, necessarily, be made by the Editors of *WHAT THEY SAID* based on objective personal judgment.

WHAT THEY SAID IN 1994

Also, some persons, while not generally recognized as prominent or newsworthy, may have never-theless attracted an unusual amount of attention in connection with an important issue or event. These people, too, are considered for inclusion, depending upon the specific circumstance.

SELECTION OF QUOTATIONS

The quotations selected for inclusion in *WHAT THEY SAID* obviously represent a decided minority of the seemingly endless volume of quoted material appearing int he media each year. The process of selecting is scrupulously objective insofar as the partisan views of the Editors are concerned (see *About Fairness,* below). However, it is clear that the Editors must decide which quotations *per se* are suitable for inclusion, and in doing so look for comments that are aptly stated, offer insight into the subject being discussed, or into the speaker, and provide—for today as well as for future reference— a thought which readers will find useful for understanding the issues and the personalities that make up a year on this planet.

ABOUT FAIRNESS

The Editors of *WHAT THEY SAID* understand the necessity of being impartial when compiling a book of this kind. As a result, there has been no bias in the selection of the quotations, the choice of speakers or the manner of editing. Relevance of the statements and the status of the speakers are the exclusive criteria for inclusion, without any regard whatsoever to the personal beliefs and views of the Editors. Furthermore, every effort has been made to include a multiplicity of opinions and ideas from a wide cross-section of speakers on each topic. Nevertheless, should there appear to be, on some controver-sial issues, a majority of material favoring one point of view over another, it is simply the result of there having been more of those views expressed during the year, reported by the media and objectively con-sidered suitable by the Editors of *WHAT THEY SAID* (see *Selection of Quotations*, above). Also, since persons in politics and government account for a large percentage of the speakers in *WHAT THEY SAID*, there may exist a heavier weight of opinion favoring the philosophy of those in office at the time, whether in the United States Congress, the Administration, or in foreign capitals. This is natural and to be ex-pected and should not be construed as a reflection of agreement or disagreement with that philosophy on the part of the Editors of *WHAT THEY SAID.*

Abbreviations

The following are abbreviations used by the speakers in this volume. Rather than defining them each time they appear in the quotations, this list will facilitate reading and avoid unnecessary repetition.

AFI:	American Film Institute
AIDS:	acquired immune deficiency syndrome
ANC:	African National Congress
AT&T:	American Telephone & Telegraph Company
AWOL:	absent without leave
BBC:	British Broadcasting Corporation
BQ:	Bloc Quebecois
CD:	compact disc
CDC:	Centers for Disease Control
CD-ROM:	compact disc-read only memory
CEO:	chief executive officer
CIA:	Central Intelligence Agency
C.I.S.:	Commonwealth of Independent States
CNN:	Cable News Network
C-SPAN:	Cable-Satellite Public Affairs Network
CTB:	comprehensive (nuclear) test-ban treaty
DEA:	Drug Enforcement Administration
DOD:	Department of Defense
EPA:	Environmental Protection Agency
EU:	European Union
FAA:	Federal Aviation Administration
FBI:	Federal Bureau of Investigation
FCC:	Federal Communications Commission
FDA:	Food and Drug Administration
FMLN:	Farabundo Marti National Liberation Front
GAO:	General Accounting Office
GATT:	General Agreement on Tariffs and Trade
GDP:	gross domestic product

GM:	General Motors Corporation
GNP:	gross national product
GOP:	Grand Old party (Republican Party)
G-7:	Group of 7 industrial countries
HIV:	human immunodeficiency virus (AIDS virus)
HMO:	health maintenance organization
IBM:	International Business Machines Corporation
IMF:	International Monetary Fund
INS:	Immigration and Naturalization Service
IRA:	Irish Republican Army
J.F.K.:	John Fitzgerald Kennedy
KGB:	Soviet/Russian State Security Committee
L.B.J.:	Lyndon Baines Johnson
MBA:	Master of Business Administration
MFN:	most favored nation (trade status)
MGM:	Metro-Goldwyn-Mayer, Inc.
MIA:	missing in action
MRI:	magnetic resonance imaging
NAACP:	National Association for the Advancement of Colored People
NAFTA:	North American Free Trade Agreement
NASA:	National Aeronautics and Space Administration
NATO:	North Atlantic Treaty Organization
NBA:	National Basketball Association
NCAA:	National Collegiate Athletic Association
NEA:	National Endowment for the Arts
NFIB:	National Federation of Independent Business
NFL:	National Football League
NHL:	National Hockey League
NP:	nurse practitioner
NRA:	National Rifle Association
OAS:	Organization of American States
OECD:	Organization for Economic Cooperation and Development
OSHA:	Occupational Safety and Health Administration
PBS:	Public Broadcasting Service

PC:	personal computer
PLO:	Palestine Liberation Organization
POW:	prisoner of war
PQ:	Parti Quebecois
p.r.:	public relations
PRD:	Democratic Revolutionary Party
ROC:	Republic of China (Taiwan)
SAT:	Scholastic Aptitude Test
SBA:	Small Business Administration
SEC:	Securities and Exchange Commission
S&L:	savings-and-loan association
SSS:	Selective Service System
TV:	television
UAW:	United Automobile Workers of America
UN:	United Nations
UNPROFOR:	United Nations Protection Force
U.S.:	United States
U.S.A.:	United States of America
U.S.S.R.:	Union of Soviet Socialist Republics

Party affiliation of United States Senators, Representatives, Governors and state legislators:

D: Democrat
I: Independent
R: Republican

The Quote of the Year

There are two types of liberty: one, pre-critical, emotive, whimsical, proper to children; the other, critical, sober, deliberate, responsible, and proper to adults. Alexis de Tocqueville called attention to this alternative early in *Democracy in America;* and at Cambridge, Lord Acton put it this way: Liberty is not the freedom to do what you wish; it is the freedom to do what you ought . . . It is this second kind of liberty—critical, adult liberty—that lies at the living core of the free society. It is the liberty of self-command, a tolerable mastery over one's own passions, bigotry, ignorance and self-deceit. It is the liberty of self-government in one's own personal life. For how, James Madison once asked, can a people incapable of self-government in private life prove capable of it in public?

—MICHAEL NOVAK
Resident Scholar,
American Enterprise Institute.
Upon receiving 1994 Templeton Prize, May 5.

PART ONE

National Affairs

The State of the Union Address

Delivered by Bill Clinton, President of the United States, at the Capitol, Washington, D.C., January 25, 1994.

Mr. Speaker, Mr. President, members of the 103rd Congress, my fellow Americans:

I'm not at all sure what speech is in the Teleprompter tonight, but I hope we can talk about the state of the Union.

I ask you to begin by recalling the memory of the giant who presided over this chamber with such force and grace. Tip O'Neill liked to call himself a man of the House, and he surely was that. But even more, he was a man of the people, a bricklayer's son who helped to build the great American middle class. Tip O'Neill never forgot who he was, where he came from or who sent him here. Tonight he's smiling down on us for the first time from the Lord's gallery. But in his honor may we, too, always remember who we are, where we come from and who sent us here.

If we do that, we will return over and over again to the principle that if we simply give ordinary people equal opportunity, quality education and a fair shot at the American dream, they will do extraordinary things.

We gather tonight in a world of changes so profound and rapid that all nations are tested. Our American heritage has always been to master such change, to use it to expand opportunity at home and our leadership abroad. But for too long and in too many ways, that heritage was abandoned, and our country drifted.

For 30 years, family life in America has been breaking down. For 20 years, the wages of working people have been stagnant or declining. For the 12 years of trickle-down economics, we built a false prosperity on a hollow basis. Our national debt quadrupled. From 1989 to 1992 we experienced the slowest growth in a half-century.

For too many families, even when both parents were working, the American dream has been slipping away.

Accomplishments

In 1992, the American people demanded that we change.

A year ago, I asked all of you to join me in accepting responsibility for the future of our country. Well, we did. We replaced drift and deadlock with renewal and reform.

And I want to thank every one of you here who heard the American people, who broke gridlock, who gave them the most successful teamwork between a President and a Congress in 30 years.

This Congress produced a budget that cut the deficit by half a trillion dollars, cut spending and raised income taxes on only the wealthiest Americans. This Congress produced tax relief for millions of low-income workers to reward work over welfare. It produced NAFTA. It produced the Brady Bill, now the Brady Law.

And thank you, Jim Brady, for being here, and God bless you, sir.

This Congress produced tax cuts to reduce the taxes of 9 out of 10 small businesses, who used the money to invest more and create more jobs. It produced more research and treatment for AIDS, more childhood immunizations, more support for women's health research, more affordable college loans for the middle class, a new national service program for those who want to give something back to their country and their communities for higher education, a dramatic increase in high-tech investments to move us from a defense to a domestic high-tech economy.

This Congress produced a new law, the motor

voter bill, to help millions of people register to vote. It produced family and medical leave.

All passed, all signed into law with not one single veto.

These accomplishments were all commitments I made when I sought this office, and in fairness they all had to be passed by you and this Congress. But I am persuaded that the real credit belongs to the people who sent us here, who pay our salaries, who hold our feet to the fire.

Changing the Lives of Americans

But what we do here is really beginning to change lives. Let me just give you one example. I will never forget what the family and medical leave law meant to just one father I met early one Sunday morning in the White House.

It was unusual to see a family there touring early Sunday morning, but he had his wife and his three children there, one of them in a wheelchair. I came up, and after we had our picture taken and had a little visit, I was walking off, and that man grabbed me by the arm and he said, "Mr. President, let me tell you something. My little girl here is desperately ill. She's probably not going to make it. But because of the family leave law I was able to take time off to spend with her, the most important time I ever spent in my life without losing my job and hurting the rest of my family. It means more to me than I will ever be able to say. Don't you people up here ever think what you do doesn't make a difference. It does."

Though we are making a difference, our work has just begun. Many Americans still haven't felt the impact of what we've done. The recovery still hasn't touched every community or created enough jobs. Incomes are still stagnant. There's still too much violence and not enough hope in too many places. Abroad, the young democracies we are strongly supporting still face very difficult times and look to us for leadership.

And so tonight, let us resolve to continue the journey of renewal, to create more and better jobs, to guarantee health security for all, to reward work over welfare, to promote democracy abroad and to begin to reclaim our streets from violent crime and drugs and gangs, to renew our own American community.

Deficit, Spending, Taxes and Trade

Last year, we began to put our house in order by tackling the budget deficit that was driving us toward bankruptcy. We cut $255 billion in spending including entitlements and over 340 separate budget items. We froze domestic spending and used honest budget numbers.

Led by the Vice President, we launched a campaign to reinvent government. We cut staff, cut perks, even trimmed the fleet of Federal limousines. After years of leaders whose rhetoric attacked bureaucracy but whose actions expanded it, we will actually reduce it by 252,000 people over the next five years. By the time we have finished, the Federal bureaucracy will be at its lowest point in 30 years.

Because the deficit was so large and because they benefited from tax cuts in the 1980's, we did ask the wealthiest Americans to pay more to reduce the deficit. So on April the 15th, the American people will discover the truth about what we did last year on taxes. Only the top—yeah, listen—the top 1.2 percent of Americans, as I said all along, will pay higher income tax rates. Let me repeat, only the wealthiest 1.2 percent of Americans will face higher income tax rates and no one else will and that is the truth.

Of course, there were, as there always are in politics, naysayers who said this plan wouldn't work, but they were wrong.

In one year, with NAFTA, with GATT, with our efforts in Asia and the national export strategy, we did more to open world markets to American products than at any time in the last two generations. That means more jobs and rising living standards for the American people, low deficits, low inflation, low interest rates, low trade barriers and high investments. These are the building blocks of our recovery.

But if we want to take full advantage of the opportunities before us in the global economy, you all know we must do more.

As we reduce defense spending, I ask Congress to invest more in the technologies of tomorrow. Defense conversion will keep us strong militarily and create jobs for our people here at home.

As we protect our environment, we must invest in the environmental technologies of the future, which will create jobs. This year, we will fight for a revitalized Clean Water Act and a Safe Drinking Water Act and a reformed Superfund program.

And the Vice President is right. We must also work with the private sector to connect every classroom, every clinic, every library, every hospital in America into a national information superhighway by the year 2000.

Think of it, instant access. The information will increase productivity, will help to educate our children. It will provide better medical care. It will create jobs. And I call on the Congress to pass legislation to establish that information superhighway this year.

As we expand opportunity and create jobs, no one can be left out. We must continue to enforce fair lending and fair housing and all civil rights law because America will never be complete in its renewal until everyone shares in its bounty.

But we all know, too, we can do all these things, put our economic house in order, expand world trade, target the jobs of the future, guarantee equal opportunity. But if we're honest, we'll all admit that this strategy still cannot work unless we also give our people the education, training and skills they need to seize the opportunities of tomorrow.

Education and Employment

We must set tough world-class academic and occupational standards for all our children. And give our teachers and students the tools they need to meet them. Our Goals 2000 proposal will empower individual school districts to experiment with ideas like chartering their schools to be run by private corporations or having more public school choice, to do whatever they wish to do as long as we measure every school by one high standard: Are our children learning what they need to know to compete and win in the global economy?

Goals 2000 links world-class standards to grass-roots reforms, and I hope Congress will pass it without delay.

Our school-to-work initiative will for the first time link school to the world of work, providing at least one year of apprenticeship beyond high school. After all, most of the people we're counting on to build our economic future won't graduate from college. It's time to stop ignoring them and start empowering them.

We must literally transform our outdated unemployment system into a new re-employment system. The old unemployment system just sort of kept you going while you waited for your old job to come back. We've got to have a new system to move people into new and better jobs because most of those old jobs just don't come back, and we know that the only way to have real job security in the future, to get a good job with a growing income, is to have real skills and the ability to learn new ones.

So we've got to streamline today's patchwork of training programs and make them a source of new skills for our people who lose their jobs. Re-employment, not unemployment, must become the centerpiece of our economic renewal. I urge you to pass it in this session of Congress.

Welfare System

And just as we must transform our unemployment system so must we also revolutionize our welfare system. It doesn't work; it defies our values as a nation.

If we value work, we can't justify a system that makes welfare more attractive than work if people are worried about losing their health care. If we value responsibility, we can't ignore the $34 billion in child support absent parents ought to be paying to millions of parents who are taking care of their children. If we value strong families, we can't perpetuate a system that actually penalizes those who stay together.

Can you believe that a child who has a child gets more money from the Government for leaving home than for staying home with a parent or a grandparent? That's not just bad policy, it's wrong, and we ought to change it.

I worked on this problem for years before I became President—with other governors and with members of Congress of both parties, and with the previous Administration of another party. I worked on it with people who were on welfare, lots of them.

And I want to say something to everybody here who cares about this issue: The people who most want to change this system are the people who are dependent on it. They want to get off welfare, they want to go back to work, they want to do right by their kids.

I once had a hearing when I was a Governor and I brought in people on welfare from all over America who had found their way to work. And the woman from my state who testified was asked this question: "What's the best thing about being off welfare and in a job?"

And without blinking an eye, she looked at the 40 governors, and she said, "When my boy goes to school and they say what does your mother do for a living, he can give an answer."

These people want a better system, and we ought to give it to them.

Last year, we began this. We gave the states more power to innovate because we know that a lot of great ideas come from outside Washington, and many states are already using it.

Then this Congress took a dramatic step: Instead of taxing people with modest incomes into poverty, we helped them to work their way out of poverty by dramatically increasing the earned-income tax credit. It will lift 15 million working families out of poverty, rewarding work over welfare, making it possible for people to be successful workers and successful parents. Now that's real welfare reform.

But there is more to be done.

This spring, I will send you a comprehensive welfare reform bill that builds on the Family Support Act of 1988 and restores the basic values of work and responsibility.

We'll say to teen-agers: If you have a child out of wedlock, we'll no longer give you a check to set up a separate household. We want families to stay together.

Say to absent families who aren't paying their child support: If you're not providing for your children, we'll garnish your wages, suspend your license, track you across state lines, and, if necessary, make some of you work off what you owe.

People who bring children into this world cannot and must not walk away from them.

But to all those who depend on welfare, we should offer ultimately a simple compact: We'll provide the support, the job training, the child care you need for up to two years; but after that, anyone who can work must—in the private sector wherever possible, in community service if necessary. That's the only way we'll ever make welfare what it ought to be: a second chance, not a way of life.

I know it will be difficult to tackle welfare reform in 1994 at the same time we tackle health care. But let me point out I think it is inevitable and imperative.

It is estimated that one million people are on welfare today, because it's the only way they can get health care coverage for their children. Those who choose to leave welfare for jobs without health benefits—and many entry-level jobs don't have health benefits— find themselves in the incredible position of paying taxes that help to pay for health care coverage for those who made the other choice to stay on welfare. No wonder people leave work and go back to welfare—to get health care coverage.

Health-Care Reform

We've got to solve the health care problem to have real welfare reform.

So this year, we will make history by reforming the health care system. And I would say to you—all of you, my fellow public servants—this is another issue where the people are way ahead of the politicians. That may not be popular with either party, but it happens to be the truth.

You know the First Lady has received now almost a million letters from people all across America and from all walks of life. I'd like to share just one of them with you.

Richard Anderson of Reno, Nev., lost his job and with it his health insurance. Two weeks later, his wife, Judy, suffered a cerebral aneurysm. He rushed her to the hospital where she stayed in intensive care for 21 days.

The Andersons' bills were over $120,000. Although Judy recovered and Richard went back to work at $8 an hour, the bills were too much for them and they were literally forced into bankruptcy.

"Mrs. Clinton," he wrote to Hillary, "no one in the United States of America should have to lose everything they've worked for all their lives because they were unfortunate enough to become ill."

It was to help the Richard and Judy Andersons of America that the First Lady and so many others have worked so hard and so long on this health care reform issue. We owe them our thanks and our action.

I know there are people here who say there's no health care crisis. Tell it to Richard and Judy Anderson. Tell it to the 58 million Americans who have no coverage at all for some time each year. Tell it to the 81 million Americans with those pre-existing conditions. Those folks are paying more or they can't get insurance at all, or they can't ever change their jobs because they or someone in their family has one of those pre-existing conditions.

Tell it to the small businesses burdened by skyrocketing costs of insurance. Most small businesses cover their employees and they pay on average 35 percent more in premiums than big businesses or government.

Or tell it to the 76 percent of insured Americans, three out of four whose policies have lifetime limits, that means they can find themselves without any coverage at all just when they need it the most.

So if any of you believe there's no crisis, you tell it to those people because I can't.

There are some people who literally do not understand the impact of this problem on people's lives. And all you have to do is go out and listen to them. Just go talk to them anywhere in any Congressional district in this country. They're Republicans and Democrats and independents; it doesn't have a lick to do with party. They think we don't get it, and it's time we show them that we do get it.

From the day we began, our health care initiative has been designed to strengthen what is good about our health care system: the world's best health care professionals, cutting-edge research and wonderful research institutions, Medicare for older Americans. None of this, none of it should be put at risk.

But we're paying more and more money for less and less care. Every year fewer and fewer Americans even get to choose their own doctors. Every year doctors and nurses spend more time on paperwork and less time with patients because of the absolute bureaucratic nightmare the present system has become. This system is riddled with inefficiency, with abuse, with fraud and everybody knows it.

Health Insurance

In today's health care system, insurance companies call the shots. They pick whom they cover and how they cover them. They can cut off your benefits when you need your coverage the most. They are in charge.

What does it mean? It means every night millions of well-insured Americans go to bed just an illness, an accident or a pink slip away from having no coverage or financial ruin. It means every morning millions of Americans go to work without any health insurance at all, something the workers in no other advanced country in the world do. It means that every year more and more hardworking people are told to pick a new doctor because their boss has had to pick a new plan and countless others turn down better jobs because they know if they take the better job they'll lose their health insurance.

If we just let the health care system continue to drift, our country will have people with less care, fewer choices and higher bills. Now, our approach protects the quality of care and people's choices.

It builds on what works today in the private sector to expand employer-based coverage, to guarantee private insurance for every American. And I might say, employer-based private insurance for every American was proposed 20 years ago by President Richard Nixon to the United States Congress. it was a good idea then, and it's a better idea today.

Why do we want guaranteed private insurance? Because right now, 9 out of 10 people who have insurance get it through their employers. And that should continue. And if your employer is providing good benefits at reasonable prices, that should continue, too. That ought to make the Congress and the President feel better.

Our goal is health insurance everybody can depend on, comprehensive benefits that cover preventive care and prescription drugs, health premiums that don't just explode when you get sick or you get older; the power no matter how small your business is to choose dependable insurance at the same competitive rates governments and big business get today; one simple form for people who are sick, and most of all, the freedom to choose a plan and the right to choose your own doctor.

Our approach protects older Americans. Every plan before the Congress proposes to slow the growth of Medicare. The difference is this: We believe those savings should be used to improve health care for senior citizens. Medicare must be protected, and it should cover prescription drugs, and we should take the first steps in covering long-term care.

To those who would cut Medicare without protecting seniors, I say the solution to today's squeeze on middle-class working people's health care is not to put the squeeze on middle-class retired people's health care. We can do better than that.

When it's all said and done, it's pretty simple to me. Insurance ought to mean what it used to mean: You pay a fair price for security, and when you get sick, health care is always there, no matter what.

Along with the guarantee of health security, we all have to admit, too, there must be more responsibility on the part of all of us in how we use this system. People have to take their kids to get immunized. We should all take advantage of preventive care. We must all work together to stop the violence that explodes our emergency rooms. We have to practice better health habits, and we can't abuse the system.

And those who don't have insurance under our approach will get coverage, but they'll have to pay something for it, too. The minority of businesses that provide no insurance at all and in so doing shift the cost of the care of their employees to others should contribute something. People who smoke should pay more for a pack of cigarettes.

Everybody can contribute something if we want to solve the health care crisis. There can't be any more something for nothing. It will not be easy, but it can be done.

Now in the coming months, I hope very much to work with both Democrats and Republicans to reform a health care system by using the market to bring down costs and to achieve lasting health security. But if you look at history, we see that for 60 years this country's tried to reform health care. President Roosevelt tried. President Truman tried. President Nixon tried. President Carter tried.

Every time the special interests were powerful enough to defeat them. But not this time.

I know that facing up to these interests will require courage; it will raise critical questions about the way we finance our campaigns and how lobbyists yield their influence.

The work of change, frankly, will never get any easier until we limit the influence of well-financed interests who profit from this current system. So I also must now call on you to finish the job both houses began last year by passing tough and meaningful campaign finance reform and lobbying reform legislation this year.

You know, my fellow Americans, this is really a test for all of us. The American people provide those of us in government service with terrific health care benefits at reasonable cost. We have health care; it's always there. I think we need to give every hard-working, tax-paying American the same health care security they have already given to us.

I want to make this very clear. I am open—as I have said repeatedly—to the best ideas of concerned members of both parties. I have no special brief for any specific approach even in our own bill except this: If you send me legislation that does not guarantee every American private health insurance that can never be taken away, you will force me to take this pen, veto the legislation and we'll come right back here and start all over again.

But I don't think that's going to happen. I think we're ready to act now. I believe that you're ready to act now. And if you're ready to guarantee every American the same health care that you have, health care that can never be taken away, now—not next year or the year after—now is the time to stand with the people who sent us here. Now.

Foreign Affairs and the Military

As we take these steps together to renew our strength at home, we cannot turn away from our obligation to renew our leadership abroad. This is a promising moment. Because of the agreements we have reached this year—last year—Russia's strategic nuclear missiles soon will no longer be pointed at the United States nor will we point ours at them.

Instead of building weapons in space, Russian scientists will help us to build the international space station.

Of course, there are still dangers in the world: rampant arms proliferation, bitter regional conflicts, ethnic and nationalist tensions in many new democracies, severe environmental degradation the world over and fanatics [who] seek to cripple the world's cities with terror.

As the world's greatest power, we must, therefore, maintain our defenses and our responsibilities. This year we secured indictments against terrorists and sanctions against those who harbor them. We worked to promote environmentally sustainable economic growth. We achieved agreements with Ukraine, with Belarus, with Kazakhstan to eliminate completely their nuclear arsenals. We're working to achieve a Korean peninsula free of nuclear weapons. We will seek early ratification of a treaty to ban chemical weapons worldwide. And earlier today we joined with over 30 nations to begin negotiations on a comprehensive ban to stop all nuclear testing.

But nothing, nothing, is more important to our security than our nation's armed forces. We honor their contributions, including those who are carrying out the longest humanitarian airlift in history in Bosnia, those who will complete their mission in Somalia this year and their brave comrades who gave their lives there.

Our forces are the finest military our nation has ever had. And I have pledged that as long as I am President they will remain the best-equipped, the best-trained and the best-prepared fighting force on the face of the earth.

Last year, I proposed a defense plan that maintains our post-cold-war security at a lower cost. This year, many people urged us to cut our defense spending further to pay for other government programs. I said no.

The budget I sent to Congress draws the line against further defense cuts. It protects the readiness and quality of our forces. Ultimately, the best strategy is to do that. We must not cut defense further. I hope the Congress without regard to party will support that position.

Ultimately—ultimately the best strategy to insure our security and to build a durable peace is to support the advance of democracy elsewhere. Democracies don't attack each other; they make better trading partners and partners in diplomacy. That is why we have supported, you and I, the democratic reformers in Russia and in the other states of the former Soviet bloc. I applaud the bipartisan support this Congress provided last year for our initiatives to help Russia, Ukraine and the other states through their epic transformations.

Our support of reform must combine patience for the enormity of the task and vigilance for our fundamental interests and values. We will continue to urge Russia and the other states to press ahead with economic reforms, and we will seek to cooperate with Russia to solve regional problems while insisting that if Russian troops operate in neighboring states, they do so only when those states agree to their presence and in strict accord with international standards.

But we must also remember as these nations chart their own futures—and they must chart their own futures—how much more secure and more prosperous our own people will be if democratic and market reforms succeed all across the former Communist bloc.

Our policy has been to support that move, and that has been the policy of the Congress. We should continue it.

That is why I went to Europe earlier this month—to work with our European partners, to help to integrate all the former Communist countries into a Europe that has the possibility of becoming unified for the first time in its entire history—its entire history—based on the simple commitments of all nations in Europe to democracy, to free markets and to respect for existing borders.

With our allies, we have created a partnership for peace that invites states from the former Soviet bloc and other non-NATO members to work with NATO in military cooperation. When I met with Central Europe's leaders, including Lech Walesa and Vaclav Havel, men who put their lives on the line for freedom, I told them that the security of their region is important to our country's security.

This year we must also do more to support democratic renewal and human rights and sustainable development all around the world. We will ask Congress to ratify the new GATT accord. We will continue standing by South Africa as it works its way through its bold and hopeful and difficult transition to democracy.

We will convene a summit of the Western Hemisphere's democratic leaders from Canada to the tip of South America, and we will continue to press for the restoration of true democracy in Haiti.

And as we build a more constructive relationship with China, we must continue to insist on clear signs of improvement in that nation's human rights record.

We will also work for new progress toward the Middle East peace. Last year, the world watched Yitzhak Rabin and Yasir Arafat at the White House when they had their historic handshake of reconciliation. But there is a long, hard road ahead, and on that road I am determined that I and our Administration will do all we can to achieve a comprehensive and lasting peace for all the people of the region.

Now there are some in our country who argue that with the cold war [over,] America should turn its back on the rest of the world. Many around the world were afraid we would do just that.

But I took this office on a pledge that had no partisan tinge to keep our nation secure by remaining engaged in the rest of the world, and this year because of our work together—enacting NAFTA, keeping our military strong and prepared, supporting democracy abroad—we have reaffirmed America's leadership, America's engagement, and as a result, the American people are more secure than they were before.

Crime and Violence

But while Americans are more secure from threats abroad, I think we all know that in many ways we are less secure from threats here at home. Every day the national peace is shattered by crime. In Petaluma, Calif., an innocent slumber party gives way to agonizing tragedy for the family of Polly Klaas. An ordinary train ride on Long Island ends in a hail of 9-millimeter rounds. A tourist in Florida is nearly burned alive by bigots simply because he is black. Right here in our nation's capital a brave young man named Jason White, a policeman, the son and grandson of policemen, is ruthlessly gunned down.

Violent crime and the fear it provokes are crippling our society, limiting personal freedom and fraying the ties that bind us. The crime bill before Congress gives you a chance to do something about it, a chance to be tough and smart.

What does that mean? Let me begin by saying I care a lot about this issue. Many years ago when I started out in public life I was the Attorney General of my state. I served as the Governor for a dozen years. I know what it's like to sign laws increasing penalties, to build more prison cells, to carry out the death penalty. I understand this issue. And it is not a simple thing.

First, we must recognize that most violent crimes are committed by a small percentage of criminals, who too often break the laws even when they're on parole. Now those who commit crimes should be punished. And those who commit repeated violent crimes should be told when you commit a third violent crime you will be put away and put away for good. Three strikes, and you are out.

Second, we must take serious steps to reduce violence and prevent crime beginning with more police officers and more community policing. We know—we know right now that police who work the streets, know the folks, have the respect of the neighborhood kids, focus on high crime areas— we know that they are more likely to prevent crime as well as catch criminals. Look at the experience of Houston, where the crime rate dropped 17 percent in one year when that approach was taken.

Here tonight is one of those community policemen, a brave young detective, Kevin Jett, whose beat is eight square blocks in one of the toughest neighborhoods in New York. Every day he restores some sanity and safety, and a sense of values and connection to the people whose lives he protects. I'd like to ask him to stand up and be recognized tonight. Thank you, sir.

You will be given a chance to give the children of this country, the law-abiding working people of this country—and don't forget, in the toughest neighborhoods in this country, in the highest-crime neighborhoods in this country, the vast majority of people get up every day and obey the law, pay their taxes, do their best to raise their kids—they deserve people like Kevin Jett. And you're going to be given a chance to give the American people another 100,000 of them, well-trained, and I urge you to do it.

You have before you crime legislation which also establishes a police corps to encourage young people to get an education, pay it off by serving as police officers, which encourages retiring military personnel to move into police forces, an inordinate resource for our country. One which has a safe-schools provision which will give our young people the chance to walk to school in safety and to be in school in safety instead of dodging bullets. These are important things.

The third thing we have to do is to build on the Brady Bill, the Brady Law. To take further steps—to take further steps to keep guns out of the hands of criminals.

I want to say something about this issue. Hunters must always be free to hunt. Law-abiding adults should always be free to own guns and protect their homes. I respect that part of our culture; I grew up in it.

But I want to ask the sportsmen and others who lawfully own guns to join us in this campaign to reduce gun violence. I say to you: I know you didn't create this problem, but we need your help to solve it. There is no sporting purpose on earth that should stop the United States Congress from banishing assault weapons that out-gun police and cut down children.

Fourth, we must remember that drugs are a factor in an enormous percentage of crimes. Recent studies indicate, sadly, that drug use is on the rise again among our young people. The crime bill contains—all the crime bills contain more money for drug treatment for criminal addicts and boot camps for youthful offenders, that include incentives to get off drugs and to stay off drugs.

Our Administration's budget, with all its cuts, contains a large increase in funding for drug treatment and drug education. You must pass them both; we need them desperately.

My fellow Americans, the problem of violence is an American problem. It has no partisan or philosophical element. Therefore, I urge you to find ways as quickly as possible to set aside partisan differences and pass a strong, smart, tough crime bill.

But further, I urge you to consider this: As you demand tougher penalties for those who choose violence, let us also remember how we came to this sad point. In our toughest neighborhoods, on our meanest streets, in our poorest rural areas, we have seen a stunning and simultaneous breakdown of community, family and work—the heart and soul of civilized society.

This has created a vast vacuum which has been filled by violence and drugs and gangs. So I ask you to remember that even as we say no to crime, we must give people, especially our young people, something to say yes to.

Many of our initiatives from job training, to welfare reform, to health care, to national service will help to rebuild distressed communities, to strengthen families, to provide work. But more needs to be done. That's what our community empowerment agenda is all about, challenging businesses to provide more investment through empowerment zones; insuring banks will make loans in the same communities their deposits come from; passing legislation to unleash the power of capital through community development banks to create jobs; opportunity and hope where they're needed most.

Values

But I think you know that to really solve this problem we'll have to put our heads together, leave our ideological armor aside and find some new ideas to do even more. And let's be honest, we all know something else, too. Our problems go way beyond the reach of government. They're rooted in the loss of values, in the disappearance of work and the breakdown of our families and our communities.

My fellow Americans, we can cut the deficit, create jobs, promote democracy around the world, pass welfare reform and health care, pass the toughest crime bill in history and still leave too many of our people behind. The American people have got to want to change from within if we're going to bring back work and family and community.

We cannot renew our country when, within a decade, more than half of the children will be born into families where there has been no marriage. We cannot renew this country when 13-year-old boys get semiautomatic weapons to shoot 9-year-olds for kicks. We can't renew our country when children are having children and the fathers walk away as if the kids don't amount to anything. We can't renew the country when our businesses eagerly look for new investments and new customers abroad but ignore those people right here at home who would give anything to have their jobs and would gladly buy their products if they had the money to do it.

We can't renew our country unless more of us, I mean all of us, are willing to join churches and the other good citizens, people like all the—like ministers I've worked with over the years or the priests and the nuns I met at Our Lady of Help in East Los Angeles or my good friend Tony Campolo in Philadelphia. Unless we're willing to work with people like that, people who are saving kids, adopting schools, making streets safer. All of us can do that. We can't renew our country until we realize that governments don't raise children, parents do.

Parents who know their children's teachers and turn off the television and help with the homework and teach their kids right from wrong. Those kind of parents can make all the difference. I know, I had one.

And I'm telling you we have got to stop pointing our fingers at these kids who have no future and reach our hands out to them. Our country needs it, we need it, and they deserve it.

And so I say to you tonight, let's give our children a future. Let us take away their guns and give them books. Let us overcome their despair and replace it with hope. Let us by our example teach them to obey the law, respect our neighbors and cherish our values.

Let us weave these sturdy threads into a new

American community that can once more stand strong against the forces of despair and evil, because everybody has a chance to walk into a better tomorrow.

Americans Facing Challenges

Oh, there will be naysayers who fear that we won't be equal to the challenges of this time. But this misreads our history, our heritage, even today's headlines. All of those things tell us we can and we will overcome any challenge.

When the earth shook and fires raged in California, when I saw the Mississippi deluge the farmlands of the Midwest in a 500-year flood, when the century's bitterest cold swept from North Dakota to Newport News, it seemed as though the world itself was coming apart at the seams. But the American people? They just came together. They rose to the occasion, neighbor helping neighbor, strangers risking life and limb to save total strangers, showing the better angels of our nature.

Let us not reserve the better angels only for natural disasters, leaving our deepest and most profound problems to petty political fighting.

Let us instead be true to our spirit, facing facts, coming together, bringing hope and moving forward.

Tonight, my fellow Americans, we are summoned to answer a question as old as the Republic itself: What is the state of our Union? It is growing stronger, but it must be stronger still. With your help and God's help it will be.

Thank you, and God bless America.

The American Scene

Isabel Allende
Chilean author

1

One of the characteristics of [U.S.] culture is that you can always start again. You can always move forward, cross a border of a state or a city or a county, and move West, most of the time West. You leave behind guilt, past traditions, memories. You are as if born again, in the sense of the snake: You leave your skin behind and you begin again. For most people in the world, that is totally impossible . . . In the United States, the fact that you can start again gives a lot of energy and strength and youth to this country. That is why it's so powerful in many ways, and so creative. However, it has the disadvantage of loneliness, individuality carried to an extreme, where you don't belong to the group and where you can just do whatever you want and never think of other people. I think that's a great disadvantage—a moral and spiritual and ethical disadvantage.

Interview, California/
Mother Jones,
Sept.-Oct.:21.

Margaret Atwood
Canadian author

2

The United States has promoted individualism so much that the responsibilities of giving to a community, and vice versa, have been trampled by rampant individualism. Canada hasn't gone in the direction of extreme individualism: *my* mortgage; *my* bank account; no pies when I hurt my leg, and I won't bring pies to you. Americans tried to weld some sort of fellow feeling in all of this— to shed their ethnic roots and be part of an American identity but, paradoxically, an individual. Community as once proposed meant all Americans. That was the myth. All were not included in it.

Interview/Mother Jones,
May-June:22.

William J. Bennett
Former Secretary of Education
of the United States

3

[On the renewed national interest in traditional and family values]: Why did it come back? Because that's what it's all about. The question I'd get asked was: "What's going on with America? Are our wheels coming off? Are we losing this great republic? Is it getting nasty and mean and brutal and coarse, and can we get it back?"

The New York Times,
11-22:(C)18.

4

[On the "trashiness" of American culture]: I'm worried because of the barbarism that the culture can lead to. If you look at some rap videos, they're barbarous . . . We know what happens to children with a steady diet of this sort of thing, particularly when they aren't offered—as an alternative— things which are good, positive and uplifting. We've seen a phenomenal increase in social pathologies—crime, broken families and so on. There are a lot of things going on here, but one of them is a culture that's become increasingly trashy.

Interview/
Newsweek, 12-26:112.

George Bush
Former President of the United States

5

We no longer fear another superpower. We no longer worry about a Berlin Wall that divides the free West from the brutalized East. We no longer live each day with the threat of a nuclear holocaust . . . But we've got to turn our attention, then, to the equally devastating threats in our own homeland, because here lurk the old enemies of the human spirit—bitterness, bigotry, despair . . . As President, I anguished each day about how to fill the hollows in America's soul. And if as President I had the power to give just one thing to the

(GEORGE BUSH)

nation, it would have been the return to an inner moral compass, nurtured by the family and valued by the community.

At Colby College commencement/
USA Today, 6-8:(A)11.

Bill Clinton
President of the United States

1

Our problems go way beyond the reach of government. They're rooted in the loss of values and the disappearance of work and the breakdown of our families and our communities. The American people have got to want to change from within if we're going to bring back work and family and community.

State of the Union address,
before a joint session of Congress,
Washington, D.C., Jan.25/
Los Angeles Times, 1-26:(A)18.

2

We cannot survive as a people if our children cannot grow up safe and free from fear in good schools, on safe streets, doing wholesome, constructive things. We talk a lot in the country about our rights, and our rights as Americans are the most important thing to us. But the thing that makes our rights work is the right of the community to exist and the responsibilities of citizens to help them exist.

Speech at housing project,
Chicago, Ill., June 17/
Los Angeles Times, 6-18:(A)21.

3

I think there is too much cynicism and too much intolerance. But if you look at the information [people] get, if you look at how much more negative the news reports are, how much more editorial they are and how much less direct they are, if you look at how much of talk radio is just a constant, unremitting drumbeat of negativism and cynicism . . . I don't think the American people

are cynical, but you can't blame them for responding that way . . . You know, I just got back from Normandy [France] celebrating the 50th anniversary of D-Day, and when I stood on the Normandy beaches and when I saw all those rows of crosses there, it occurred to me that those people did not die so the American people could indulge themselves in the luxury of cynicism; and frankly, that's just what it is.

Broadcast interview
St. Louis, Mo., June 24/
The New York Times, 6-25:10.

4

Leaders and people can make a difference, and not just the President but the other great institutions of society. What kinds of leaders are in Congress? What do they do and say? What is the role of the American press? What does it do and say? Does it feed on the fears and cynicisms of the American public? Or does it basically proceed in challenging us to do better? History proceeds in cycles to some extent, but also every time is different, and the outcome is not foreordained. I mean, it really does make a difference who's there and what they do.

Interview, Washington, D.C., August/
American Heritage, December:121.

5

Whenever we move from one historic era into another—at the end of World War I, at the end of World War II, moving into the Cold War, now at the end of the Cold War, moving toward the 21st century—our people are filled with a mixture of hope and concern. Almost every American is genuinely concerned about something now, whether it's their economic circumstances, their health care, insecurity over crime, concern about what's happening to the fabric of our society with so many children being born out of wedlock and so many families breaking down. There's something gripping the concern of most Americans.

News conference,
Washington, D.C., Aug. 3/
The New York Times, 8-4:(A)10.

William Ferris
Director, Center for the Study of
Southern Culture,
University of Mississippi

1

I think one of the aspects about the South is its accessibility culturally, the fact that we are not dealing with large urban worlds. We have a rural world that's family-related. It's also a society that has known defeat and poverty and illiteracy. It's a Third World culture in many ways, not the high-tech, progress-related cosmos that America projects in its public image . . . [There] will always be a kind of two-way street that we are living on in the South: the Americanization of Dixie and the Southernizing of the nation. This in many ways has been part of our world from the very beginning, with figures like Thomas Jefferson, who so significantly shaped our nation's future. Southern worlds, from country music and blues and rock 'n' roll to Faulkner to politics, are significant to the nation's identity. We've always been what Vann Woodward has called a counterpoint to the American experience. While the nation has aspired to financial achievement and progress, the South has stood apart in many ways. And yet emerging from the South we see the quintessential images of corporate America: Coca-Cola, CNN, Federal Express, Holiday Inn, Wal-Mart. These are Southern-bred institutions that symbolize not so much the South as America.

Interview/American Heritage,
July-Aug.:72,75.

Geoffrey Garin
Democratic Party consultant

2

What people believe is, as a country, we've lost sight of the fundamentals and spent too much time arguing about the exceptions to the rules, rather than the rules themselves . . . People feel the reason we are in trouble with our values is the failure to insist on standards.

Los Angeles Times, 8-8:(A)5.

Newt Gingrich
United States Representative, R-Georgia;
Speaker of the House-designate

3

A society which punishes violence and a society that is emphatic about right and wrong tends to have less sickness and less violence. [Since the 1950s, the U.S. has become] a culture which is extraordinarily tolerant of violence, with a situation-ethics morality, in which your immediate concern about your personal needs outweighs any obligation to others.

Interview, Nov. 9/
The New York Times,
11-10:(B)3.

4

If, by moral tone, you mean voluntary school prayer, the bulk of Americans are for it; if, by moral tone, you mean punishing violent criminals the first time they're violent, the majority of Americans are for it; if, by moral tone, you mean teaching the truth about American history, teaching about the Founding Fathers and how this country came to be the most extraordinary civilization in history, the vast majority of Americans are for it. There's only a very small counter-culture elite, which is terrified of the opportunity to actually renew American civilization.

News conference, Nov. 9/
The New York Times,
11-10:(B)3.

5

It is impossible to maintain civilization with 12-year-olds having babies, with 15-year-olds killing each other, with 17-year-olds dying of AIDS and with 18-year-olds getting diplomas they can't even read.

Before Washington Research Group,
Washington D.C., Nov. 11/
Newsweek, 11-28:34.

(NEWT GINGRICH)

1

[On the new Republican majority in Congress starting in 1995]:I think we're in [the Franklin Roosevelt] tradition. I think we want to say to the nation that we have nothing to fear but fear itself, that we can reach out together as a family, all Americans, and we can dramatically improve our quality of life, the economic opportunity and the safety of virtually every American between now and the year 2000 . . . The real success [for Republicans] isn't a Republican re-election. The real success isn't even a balanced [Federal] budget. The real success is no law. The real success is the morning we wake up on a Monday and no child has been killed anywhere in America that weekend, and every child is going to a school their parents think is worth attending, and across the country there is a smaller, more customer-friendly government doing what governments should do, and every American has a chance to create a job or find a job, and across the planet freedom is winning and civility and decency are driving barbarism out of our lives.

Before fellow Republican
members of the House,
Washington, D.C., Dec. 5/
The New York Times, 12-6:(A)1.

Barry Glassner
Chairman, department of sociology,
University of Southern California

2

[There is a] uniquely American phenomenon of "the cult of the average person" . . . Why do people watch Phil Donahue and Geraldo and all those other talk and tabloid [TV] programs? A big part of it is that the people on those shows are portrayed as average, except for the one special thing that got them on TV. People identify with that . . . Nothing is more fundamental to the American mythology than the concept that anyone can be anything.

Los Angeles Times, 2-17:(A)18.

Patricia Gober
Professor of geography,
University of Arizona

3

Today [in the U.S.], a couple is less likely to move, since the move would disrupt both the man's and the woman's work. And if a couple owns a house [as more do than in the past], the possibility of moving becomes even more distant . . . In the United States, moving up has been synonymous with moving on. High levels of mobility have traditionally been linked with an innate restlessness, thirst for change, drive for innovation and dynamism in American culture . . . Even though Americans are risk-takers, even though they have always sought out new opportunities, new places, new people, the forces working against mobility today are too profound.

The Christian Science Monitor,
1-13:4.

Daniel S. Goldin
Administrator, National Aeronautics
and Space Administration of the United States

4

This nation used to take risks and it used to have long-term vision that spanned decades. Then we lost that vision. We stopped investing in the future . . . Since the early '70s, we've been a risk-averse society.

USA Today, 7-20:(A)6.

Jared Hazleton
Director, Center for Business and
Economic Analysis, Texas A&M University

5

[On the Texas economy]: Texas now looks like the rest of the country so much more than we ever did before. We're unique, maybe, because we're a younger and growing population, more ethnic; but if you look at our economy, can you really tell when you leave Dallas and go to Los Angeles? We like to think of ourselves as different. We cling to those myths. But I think, by and large, they are gone . . . If you do make your for-

(JARED HAZLETON)

tune in Texas anymore, you'll do it largely by getting into high tech, not in the oil business. All you'll get from that anymore are people making small fortunes out of the large fortunes their daddies left them.

The Washington Post,
4-4:(A)10.

Peter Jennings
Anchor, "World News Tonight,"
ABC-TV

1

[Americans have a unique] hunger to identify with personalities, larger-than-life personalities especially. No country in the world is so driven by personality as this one . . . Our political campaigns, largely at the behest of the media, have been covered like sports contests, and sports is another personality-driven facet of our national life . . . Our greatest export is culture. Our culture is Hollywood; Hollywood is built on personalities.

Interview/
Los Angeles Times, 2-17:(A)18.

Lee Kuan Yew
Former Prime Minister of Singapore

2

As an East Asian looking at America, I find attractive and unattractive features. I like, for example, the free, easy and open relations between people regardless of social status, ethnicity or religion. And the thing that I have always admired about America, as against the Communist system, I still do: a certain openness in argument about what is good or bad for society; the accountability of public officials; none of the secrecy and terror that's part and parcel of Communist government. But, as a total system, I find parts of it totally unacceptable: guns, drugs, violent crime, vagrancy, unbecoming behavior in public—in sum, the breakdown of civil society. The expansion of the right of the individual to behave or misbehave as he pleases has come at the expense of orderly society.

Interview/Foreign Affairs,
March-April:111.

Martha Minow
Professor of law,
Harvard University

3

I think one of the negative aspects of the dominance of legal and political ideology in the binding of Americans to one another is that it tends to use individual liberty as the organizing framework rather than a notion of responsibility of duty. I don't think it has to, and I think in other periods of American history, there has been a greater informal culture of responsibility and duty rhetoric. Yet, if you look simply at the language of the political documents, it's not there. So wherever a sense of duty came from, it wasn't written down, and it hasn't been transmitted as well as some of the other aspects of our Constitutional heritage . . . I think it is fair to say that the framers of the Constitution felt strongly that duty and loyalty and commitment and responsibility were crucial aspects to the pursuit of happiness, the same way they believed that maintaining one's family in safety and security were crucial to the pursuit of happiness. Again, they didn't write that down. I guess I think it is important to rescue and revitalize those unwritten aspects of our traditions alongside the written aspects.

Interview/
Humanities, Sept.-Oct.:50.

George J. Mitchell
United States Senator, D-Maine

4

We're the most fortunate people ever to have lived, to be Americans, citizens of the most free, the most open society in all of human history. I consider myself especially fortunate. My mother was an immigrant, my father the orphan son of immigrants. They had no education, but they dedicated their lives to the education of their children . . . They taught me that, in America, there's no limit to how far you can go if you get a good education and you're willing to work hard.

Address to Maine voters
after announcing he will retire
after his current term, March 4/
Los Angeles Times, 3-5:(A)16.

Walter F. Mondale
United States Ambassador to Japan

1

[On his meetings with young Japanese]: They want to come to the Unites States, go to school and so on, but they fear for their lives and their safety . . . The lack of safety in the streets [of America] really causes them to question whether we're falling apart.

At National Press Club,
Washington, D.C./
Los Angeles Times, 9-8:(A)5.

Michael Olivas
Immigration-law specialist,
University of Houston

2

Our immigration policy shows our country at its absolute best—its generous impulses, its willingness to absorb so many people—and simultaneously shows us at our worst—our xenophobia, our fear of people of color and people from the Third World.

U.S. News & World Report,
9-12:8.

John Ricard
Auxiliary Roman Catholic Bishop,
Baltimore, Md.;
Chairman, Domestic Policy Committee,
National Conference of Catholic Bishops

3

Culturally, we [in the U.S.] are condoning and putting up with far too much in our media, our general approach to living and the way we relate to one another. We've gotten so far afield from a clear sense of what is right and wrong, that there are principles and values that are transcendent and that are absolutely right and wrong.

The New York Times, 11-26:9.

Benjamin Spock
Author; Former pediatrician

4

[On the problems that negatively impact American society today]: Instability of marriage and the family; cruel competitiveness in business, sports and education; racial and ethnic divisiveness; materialism running rampant, with no spiritual or ethical values to offset it; increasing violence; a coarsening of our attitudes toward sex; lack of high-quality day care; an educational system that spews out children with no skills, no goals and no preparation for productive, satisfying lives. Tote it up and you have a picture of a society speeding downhill.

Interview, Maine/
Los Angeles Times, 8-31:(E)1.

Pete Wilson
Governor of California (R)

5

[On illegal immigrants in the U.S.]: We are a state [California] and nation of immigrants, proud of our immigrant traditions . . . But we, as a sovereign nation, have a right and an obligation to determine how and when people come into our country. We are a nation of laws . . . The United States already accepts more legal immigrants into our country than the rest of the world combined . . . There is a limit to what we can absorb, and illegal immigration is now taxing us past that limit.

Before Town Hall,
Los Angeles, Calif./
Los Angeles Times, 5-2:(A)3.

Harris Wofford
United States Senator,
D-Pennsylvania

6

[Supporting the idea of a national-service program for young people]: I would love to see service—whether community service or service overseas—as a common expectation for young people, a routine rite of passage. Citizenship is as impor-

(HARRIS WOFFORD)

tant as anything our young people will learn, and the best way to learn citizenship is by doing it . . . I include military service and paid national service. I don't favor a "draft"—a *requirement* that all young people give a year or more of service at home or abroad—but I do favor a strong *ask* . . . The actual work that's accomplished is a good thing, of course; but it goes beyond that. If this idea is to work the way it should, it's absolutely crucial that it involve the college-bound as well as the non-college-bound, black and white and brown, rich and poor, city and suburb. This is a chance for us to get serious about *"E pluribus unum."*

Sept. 9/The Washington Post,
9-12:(A)23.

Flip Benham
Executive director,
Operation Rescue
(anti-abortion organization)

1

[On the use of Federal forces to protect abortion clinics from anti-abortion activists]: It is a sad commentary that our Federal government would send marshals to protect facilities where innocent children are killed. The abortion clinic has become the most sacred, protected shrine in our nation.
Christianity Today, 9-12:57.

2

[Criticizing the killing of abortionists by anti-abortion activists]: One does not overcome the horrible murder of little boys and girls waiting to be born by murdering other people. One never has the right to take upon himself the role of judge, jury and executioner.
Christianity Today, 9-12:57.

Harry A. Blackmun
Associate Justice,
Supreme Court
of the United States

3

[On the 1973 *Roe v. Wade* Supreme Court decision supporting abortion rights, which he as a Justice voted for]: Roe against Wade hit me early in my tenure on the Supreme Court. And people forget that it was a 7-2 decision; they always typify it as a "Blackmun opinion." But I'll say what I've said many times publicly: I think it was right in 1973, and I think it is right today. I think it's a step that had to be taken as we go down the road toward the full emancipation of women.
News conference
announcing his retirement,
Washington D.C., April 6/
The New York Times,
4-7:(A)12.

Julian Bond
Civil-rights activist

4

Surveys of public opinion demonstrate with crushing frequency that many members of the diminishing American majority believe racial minorities are less worthy than themselves of inclusion into the national community, their cries for justice easily dismissed as special pleading from disgruntled and non-competitive complainers. On the other side, years and years of endless pleas for justice, turned aside time and again, have produced a reaction among many of the dispossessed that argues for an end to unanswered cries for inclusion, and a voluntary return to the separate but equal world that many imagine existed years ago.
At Loyola Marymount University,
March 18/Los Angeles Times,
3-25:(B)2.

Freeman Bosley, Jr.
Mayor of St. Louis, Mo.

5

[On his city's voluntary school-desegregation busing program]: It costs $75-million a year for these kids to ride the yellow bus. After 10 years, I have serious reservations about the impact the program is having. I think we need to take another look at it . . . Our schools and our communities are more segregated right now than they were in 1960. So what are we doing? In the interest of saying that they are doing something about integration, people have just put the car on cruise control, and they're just sitting back going for a ride . . . So why are we doing it [busing]? We're doing it because people say that we shouldn't have separate but equal [schools], and I agree. We're doing it because people say there ought to be greater interaction between the races, and I agree. But you don't achieve that by pushing kids to go to school together. You achieve that by integrating housing patterns.
The Christian Science Monitor, 5-16:11.

Ellen Bravo

Executive director, 9 to 5,
the National Association
of Working Women

1

One reason women earn so little money compared with men is that most women and men don't do the same job. And the jobs women do pay less, mainly because women do them. Unfortunately, not all women's groups have seen this as a women's issue.

U.S. News & World Report,
3-28:50.

Joseph Broadus

Professor of law,
George Mason University

2

[Homosexuals have] unjustly played the victim card to advance. [Homosexuals are] an elite whose insider status has permitted it to abuse the political process in search, not of equal opportunity, but of special privilege and public endorsement.

Before Senate Labor Committee,
Washington, D.C./
Christianity Today, 9-12:60.

Judie Brown

President, American Life League

3

[Criticizing the recent clearing of the way for U.S. importation and testing of the French abortion pill, RU-486]: This chemical effectively kills children who live in the womb and is not safe for the mother, according to many scientific reports . . . The Clinton Administration is so dedicated to killing human beings who live in the womb that they are now prepared to jeopardize the lives of those babies' mothers as well.

May 16/Los Angeles Times,
5-17:(A)17.

Gro Harlem Brundtland

Prime Minister of Norway

4

[Criticizing the Catholic Church's stand against abortion and its negative reaction to a proposed international agreement on women's reproductive health care and curbing population growth]: Morality becomes hypocrisy if it means accepting mothers' suffering or dying in connection with unwanted pregnancies and illegal abortions and unwanted children . . . I have tried in vain to understand how the term "reproductive health care" can be read as promoting abortion as a means of family planning. Rarely if ever have so many misrepresentations been used to imply a meaning that was never there in the first place.

At United Nations Conference on Population
and Development, Cairo, Egypt, Sept. 5/
The New York Times, 9-6:(A)1,6.

Lonnie Bunch

Assistant director for curatorial
affairs, National Museum of
American History

5

America is great, but one reason is because we have struggled with issues of race, and that has enlarged our ideas about citizenship, liberty and notions of fairness.

Los Angeles Times, 8-2:(H)3.

Benjamin F. Chavis, Jr.

Executive director, National
Association for the Advancement of
Colored People

6

[On criticism of the NAACP for inviting controversial U.S. Islamic leader Louis Farrakhan, whom many accuse of being anti-Semitic, to one of its summit meetings]: Never again will we allow any external forces to dictate who we can meet with. Never again. Never again. We have locked arms, and our circle cannot be broken.

At NAACP summit meeting, Baltimore, Md.,
June 14/Los Angeles Times, 6-15:(A)17.

(BENJAMIN F. CHAVIS, JR.)

1

[On suggestions that the NAACP's association with Nation of Islam leader Louis Farrakhan would alienate many Jews who see Farrakhan as anti-Semitic]: We welcome the continued support and involvement of our Jewish sisters and brothers in the life and totality of the NAACP. At the same time, we would hope that Jewish leaders would not see our attempt to bring unity within our community as being oppositional to the Jewish community. I don't define black unity as being anti-Jewish. And we would hope that Jewish leaders would not misunderstand what we're attempting to do.

Interview/USA Today, 7-7:(A)11.

2

One of the most pressing issues [for blacks] is the need for economic empowerment. So much of the deprivation and degradation that exists within the African-American community exists within a broader context of economic inequality. The extent to which we become more economically empowered is the extent to which we can reduce some of the very real problems that are now emerging almost to crisis proportions within our community.

Interview/USA Today, 7-7:(A)11.

Bill Clinton
President of the United States

3

If democracy is the involvement of all of our people, if it is making strength out of our diversity, if we want to say to the people in the troubled areas of Europe: "Put your ethnic hatreds behind you. Take the differences—the religious differences, the racial differences, the ethnic differences—of some of your people, and make them a strength in the global economy," surely we must do the same here.

*Marking the birthday
of the late civil-rights leader
Martin Luther King, Jr.,
Howard University, Jan. 17/
The New York Times, 1-18:(A)10.*

4

[On abortion]: When I was a young man, I think I just automatically assumed that life began at birth. In the last seven or eight years, however, I've spent an enormous amount of time thinking about this—about the biological reality of how people are formed, about what point in time the various functions develop in an unborn child, about whether it would ever be possible to go beyond the viability tests to make any more sophisticated judgment about personhood—which is really a spiritual determination and not a biological determination . . . The truth is, no one knows when the spirit enters the body. I have . . . read all the scriptural verses cited as authority for the abortion-is-murder thesis, as well as all those verses cited on the other side—what the root words mean and all that stuff. It's a much graver issue to me now. I think having a child made it so. Abortion has now moved beyond the point of serious argument to a shouting match. A lot of pro-lifers in the Christian community think it's self-evident and not even worth discussing [whether] the Bible clearly says the spirit enters the body at the point of conception . . . I've heard it argued by dedicated Christian theologians both ways . . . My position has always been that abortion should be safe, legal, and rare.

*Interview, Washington, D.C./
Christianity Today,
4-25:29.*

5

A lot of us who were Southerners, who grew up in the South, really knew better. We knew that segregation was wrong, and we knew that, those of us who were white, that we were being deprived of the opportunity to know people, to share their feeling, to share their life experiences, to share their music, their culture, to deal with people. We were just being cut off.

*At Rev. Dr. Martin Luther King Jr.
Middle School, Beltsville, Md.,
May 17/The New York Times,
5-18:(A)10.*

(BILL CLINTON)

1

Being deaf or having any disability is not tragic, but the stereotypes attached to it are tragic. Discrimination is tragic. Not getting a job or having the chance to reach your God-given potential because someone else is handicapped by prejudice or fear is tragic. It must not be tolerated because none of us can afford it. We need each other, and we do not have a person to waste.

At Gallaudet University
commencement/
USA Today, 5-19:(A)13.

2

[On the controversy over his position on homosexual rights, including the right to serve in the military]: The way it was reported and the way it was talked about was all in screaming matches, where everybody had a temperature of 105—on both sides. Everybody's neck was bulging. Steam was coming out of everybody's ears . . . My belief is that most of us in a democracy should be judged based on what we do, not what we say; how we behave toward one another, not who we are inside. And if you follow the rules and you serve your country and you pay your taxes, you ought to be able to live up to the fullest of your capacities. I do not believe, therefore, that my position is self-evidently heathen on this issue.

To religion journalists,
Washington, D.C., Oct. 3/
The New York Times, 10-4:(A)11.

Hillary Rodham Clinton
Wife of President of the United States
Bill Clinton

3

[Saying much of the criticism of her is because she is a woman]: I think that the viciousness of some of the attacks—going all the way back to the [1992 election] campaign and the Republican Convention—is because people don't know what to make of women, not just me. There are still so many stereotypes around. What I have

said for years and years is that I just want to live my life the way that I believe is right for me. I want every woman to have the same opportunity. I do not prejudge any other woman's choices. I have dear friends who have made every choice available to modern women, from being full-time homemakers to being full-time unmarried career women. What I wish for them is what I wish for every young girl: that their life choices give them the satisfaction and the happiness that comes from leading an integrated life. So I am who I am, and I know that is a red flag for some who are in the right wing who have different views about a woman's appropriate role in life.

Interview/People, 4-11:41.

Ellis Cose
Author; Essayist,
"Newsweek" magazine

4

I don't think we have trouble talking about race. I think we have trouble talking about it *intelligently* . . . We tend to talk in stereotypes, or in sound-bites, or from behind huge defenses we've erected . . . People don't see the same reality. You almost get into this caricature of a conversation. You have whites going through all kinds of contortions trying to prove that they aren't racist . . . that what you think is racist isn't racist. And then you have blacks going through the opposite sort of dance . . . So you have people who . . . connect with somebody of another race as a *representative* as opposed to as a person.

Interview/
Los Angeles Times, 3-3:(E)1.

Joycelyn Elders
Surgeon General
of the United States

5

[On anti-abortion groups that criticize her stand on abortion]: Groups that were fighting me so hard knew I was not advocating abortion. They talked about my being for abortion as a way to

(JOYCELYN ELDERS)

attract attention. I very much support condoms in schools, which I've never denied, but that's about preventing pregnancy, not about abortion. Those against me thought the only way to prevent birth was to have an abortion. But if you prevent pregnancy, then abortion is a non-issue . . . I'm a firm believer in choice [on abortion]. I can't make the decision to abort for you. I don't know what decision I'd make if it were my 12-year-old daughter who was pregnant. I don't know what decision I'd make for myself. It's the kind of decision you can't make until you're in the situation.

Interview,
Washington, D.C./
Cosmopolitan, April:126.

1

[Saying homosexuals should not be denied admission into the Boy Scouts]: I don't feel that policy-makers and decision-makers should worry about anyone's bedroom but their own . . . I also think girls who are lesbians should be allowed to join the Girl Scouts. None of us is good enough to make decisions about other people's sexual preferences.

Interview/
USA Today, 6-2:(A)6.

Louis Farrakhan
Spiritual leader,
Nation of Islam
in the United States

2

The truth of the matter is, whites are superior. They are not superior because they are born superior. They are superior because they have the ruling power, that God has permitted them to rule. They have had the wisdom and the guidance to rule while most of the dark world or the darker people of the world have been, as they have called it, asleep. Now it's the awakening of all the darker

people of the world, and we are awakening at the level that the white world is now beginning to decline . . . But to tell the truth, to tear down the mind built on a false premise of white supremacy, that is nothing but proper because that will allow whites to relate to themselves as well as to other human beings as human beings.

Time, 2-28:24.

Wanda Franz
President, National Right to
Life Committee

3

[Saying that her organization, though anti-abortion, opposes violence against abortion clinics and doctors]: We are a pro-life organization, and we are concerned to protect life. We are opposed to having our members engage in any kind of illegal activity. This is just one . . . peripheral issue that involves a very small proportion of fringe people who have nothing to do with the mainstream pro-life movement.

U.S. News & World Report,
11-14:50.

Ruth Bader Ginsburg
Associate Justice, Supreme Court
of the United States

4

When fathers take equal responsibility for the care of their children, that's when women will truly be liberated. I was so pleased to see that there are indeed men who are doing a parent's work, men who do not regard that as strange . . . Women will have truly equal opportunity when men accept responsibility for raising children to the same extent that women do. Is that an impossible dream? I don't think so.

Interview/
The New York Times,
1-7:(B)13.

Al Gore
Vice President
of the United States

1

[On U.S. policy for the upcoming UN population conference in Cairo]: The United States has not sought, does not seek and will not seek to establish any international right to abortion.

At National Press Club,
Washington, D.C./
U.S. News & World Report,
9-12:55.

Orrin G. Hatch
United States Senator, R-Utah

2

[Criticizing recent Congressional approval of legislation making Federal crimes of certain activities at abortion clinics by anti-abortion activists]: It's about punishing purely civil, peaceful disobedience for a cause that is not . . . "politically correct." I think we're starting something here that could really end up hurting this country.

May 12/The Washington Post,
5-13:(A)8.

John Higham
Historian, Johns Hopkins University

3

I don't regard assimilation as something static. I see assimilation as one side of what I call pluralistic integration. Assimilation counterbalances the differentiating forces in our history. When we badmouth assimilation, we're failing to appreciate that it goes on at all levels of life. People are constantly moving out of one class and becoming assimilated into another. Ethnic groups are changing their boundaries. People of Hispanic descent, for example, are trying to assimilate to one another in order to become more than Dominicans, Cubans and so on, and therefore acquire a larger and more powerful identity. They might not make it. Assimilation doesn't always work. But it's part of change. And it's part of change that is exceedingly impor-

tant in a society that has to be bound together in the presence of such extraordinary heterogeneity as we have . . . I mean that we want and need a society that is integrated but yet provides space for an appreciation of differences.

Interview/Humanities,
Jan.-Feb.:41.

Freeman Hrabowski
President, University of Maryland,
Baltimore County

4

[Saying many black males are discouraged by other black males from doing well in school]: Often boys who do well in school are laughed at, looked down upon, ridiculed and embarrassed for doing well, They are told they are acting white when they earn A's . . . We as a society do not encourage young African-American males who want to do well in academics . . . Our children don't see examples of brainy young black males whom they want to emulate. All they see are [basketball star] Michael Jordan and [entertainer] Michael Jackson. We have a responsibility to find ways of helping our young males feel good for doing well in school.

Interview/The Washington Post,
3-21:(A)8.

Edward M. Kennedy
United States Senator, D-Massachusetts

5

[Supporting recent Congressional approval of legislation making Federal crimes of certain activities at abortion clinics by anti-abortion activists]: This law will protect women, doctors and other health personnel from the tactics of violence and intimidation that have closed clinics and restricted access to health care across this country. Congress sends a clear message today to those who would break the law that no matter which city or town they target, their tactics of force and threats will be met with one standard of law.

May 12/The Washington Post, 5-13:(A)1.

Coretta Scott King
Widow of the late civil-rights
leader Martin Luther King, Jr.

1

[On the Martin Luther King Jr. Day holiday]:
Today, unfortunately, too many Americans perceive the King holiday as an African-American
holiday. Our goal is to change this to help them
understand that the King holiday is an American
holiday . . . We have made great progress with the
King holiday, but it is not where it should be. We
want the King holiday to become a time for every
American to make a contribution, however small,
to help alleviate such conditions as hunger,
homelessness and illiteracy, to fight drugs, gangs,
crime and violence in all forms.

Los Angeles Times, 1-13:(A)5.

Frances Kissling
President, Catholics
for a Free Choice

2

[Criticizing the influence of the Vatican in its
denunciations of liberal views on abortion and family planning at the current UN population conference in Cairo]: How come a country [Vatican City],
a so-called country, that is in essence 800 square
acres of office space in the middle of Rome, that
has a citizenry that excludes women and children,
seems to attract the most attention in talking about
public policy that deals with women and children?

At United Nations
Conference on Population
and Development, Cairo, Egypt,
Sept. 7/Los Angeles Times,
9-8:(A)15.

William Kristol
Chairman, Project for the
Republican Future

3

[Criticizing 1973's Supreme Court *Roe v.*
Wade decision supporting abortion rights]: The
issues raised by *Roe v. Wade* aren't going to go

away, though they may continue to take new forms.
For conservatives, it represents a high-water mark
of a certain kind of imperial liberalism, of judges
taking these powerfully personal issues out of the
hands of the voters.

The Washington Post,
4-7:(A)10.

Renato R. Martino
Roman Catholic Archbishop and
chief Vatican delegate to the United
Nations Conference on Population
and Development

4

[A declared worldwide] concept of a "right
to abortion" would be entirely innovative in the
international community and would be contrary
to the constitutional legislative positions of many
[countries], as well as being alien to the sensitivi-
ties of vast numbers of persons, believers and un-
believers alike.

At United Nations Conference
of Population and Development,
Cairo, Egypt, Sept. 7/
Los Angeles Times, 9-8:(A)1.

Janet McKay
President, Mills College

5

[On the advantages of an all-women's college
such as Mills]: We are a long way from economic
and gender equity in our society, and there are more
women than men going to college now. But women
who graduate from college still have the same lifetime earning capacity as men who graduate from
high school. What we have now is a system that
allows educational opportunities for women, but
not economic opportunities . . . We market the
value of the classroom experience for women at a
woman's college, and it is an asset, especially for
women who are a little bit more mature.

Interview, Oakland, Calif./
The Christian Science Monitor,
7-12:13.

Ian McKellen
British actor

1

There have always been gay playwrights. Very few of them have written about being gay. The first one to do it was Christopher Marlowe . . . But throughout the 17th, 18th, 19th and 20th centuries, gay playwrights like Oscar Wilde and Noel Coward never acknowledged in their work that they had ever fallen in love with another man. That's the cruelty of society's repression—that people as independent and spirited as they were didn't dare speak openly about themselves and their work. And it's only very, very, very recently this has happened. There are still famous playwrights alive that don't want to be identified as gay and disguise their sexuality not only in public interviews but in writings.

Interview, New York, N.Y./
Los Angeles Times,
6-26:(M)3.

Kate Michelman
President, National Abortion
and Reproductive Rights
Action League

2

[On 1973's Supreme Court *Roe vs. Wade* decision supporting abortion rights]: It was probably the most important decision affecting women and their role, their autonomy, their dignity. Laws against abortion were the last bastion of reproductive control that the state has over women. Giving that control to women, letting them make decisions without government intrusion, played a central role in our ability to win equality and respect . . . It challenged the deeply held views of what women were able to do. And you saw more women going to college, delaying marriage, starting careers, having their children later in life. *Roe* had an incredible impact on our lives.

The Washington Post,
4-7:(A)10.

Martha Minow
Professor of law,
Harvard University

3

In American history, there has been a continual struggle between groups and among groups to define a place of privilege and a place of exclusion, and in part to define who is American by reference to who's not American. Yet there's been a shifting definition of the in and the out, the boundaries. Sometimes it's ethnicity, sometimes language, sometimes it is national origin . . . Often [it is] religion. Sometimes skin color, which is really quite a different category. Sometimes it is just shared historical experience: Did you live through the blizzard of 1978? One of the hopeful signs for me is this very mutability in the categories. It is not as though it is always the same categories.

Interview/Humanities,
Sept.-Oct.:48.

Don Nickles
United States Senator, R-Oklahoma

4

[Criticizing legislation that makes it a Federal felony for pro-life activists to engage in many kinds of anti-abortion protests at abortion clinics]: This nation has a history of tolerance for non-violent civil disobedience. We have always recognized the close association between peaceful civil disobedience and political speech, which is clearly one of the most highly protected rights within our Constitution. All groups that engage in peaceful sit-ins and similar activity should be treated in an evenhanded manner, regardless of the motivation of those engaged in this conduct. But this bill does not do that. [Instead,] the real target is thought, not behavior.

The New York Times,
5-13:(A)12.

Eleanor Holmes Norton
Delegate to the U.S. House of
Representatives from the
District of Columbia (D)

1

[On the current murder case against black former football star O.J. Simpson]: For many blacks, every black man is on trial. O.J. Simpson has become the proxy not because the black man is a criminal but because the black man is increasingly seen as a criminal by virtue of his sex and color.

Time, 8-1:25.

Karen Nussbaum
Director, Women's Bureau,
Department of Labor
of the United States

2

[On a new government survey showing working women still have concerns about discrimination in the workplace]: The concern about discrimination and equal pay surprised me. The popular wisdom had been that we don't talk about things that way anymore, but clearly it is the way women talk about it. I was also surprised by the consensus that emerged. We tend to think of training as a blue-collar issue, child care as a low-income issue, the glass ceiling as something professional women care about and discrimination as a concern for women of color; but each of these issues cut across all the lines.

The New York Times, 10-15:8.

John Cardinal O'Connor
Roman Catholic Archbishop
of New York, N.Y.

3

[Criticizing those who murder abortionists, even though he himself is against abortion]: If anyone has an urge to kill an abortionist, let him kill me instead. That's about as clearly as I can renounce such madness.

Newsweek, 8-15:17.

Major R. Owens
United States Representative, D-New York

4

Responsible African-American leadership should cease the pursuit of total unity within the black community. We must leave the 10 percent who advocate hatred and violence and let them march off to their own destruction.

Feb. 2/The Washington Post, 2-3:(A)16.

Bob Packwood
United States Senator, R-Oregon

5

[On charges against him of sexual harassment made by several women]: Some men are suave as Cary Grant and others have the motor skills of Quasimodo. If you approach a woman and she rebuffs you, and you say that's it and you're a gentleman—you don't pursue her simply because you made an approach to her, even if unartful— are you guilty [of sexual harassment]? The thing that intrigues me most is the way the women's groups look for a way to absolutely excoriate me and [at the same time] look for some way to attempt to exonerate the President [Clinton, who is also being charged by a woman with sexual harassment].

Broadcast interview/
"This Week With David Brinkley,"
ABC-TV, 5-8.

Deval Patrick
Assistant Attorney General-designate,
Civil Rights Division, Department of
Justice of the United States

6

The Civil Rights Division must move firmly, fearlessly and unambiguously to enforce the anti-discrimination laws . . . [and take] the lead in shaping policies and lawsuits that promote the notion of an inclusive democracy.

At Senate Judiciary Committee
hearing on his nomination,
Washington, D.C.,
March 10/The Washington Post
3-11:(A)23.

49

(DEVAL PATRICK)

1

The interest of the United States is integrating the workforce. We do not support quotas, [but] affirmative action is a different animal.

Sept. 6/Los Angeles Times,
9-7:(A)4.

Colin L. Powell
General, United States Army (Ret.);
Former Chairman,
Joint Chiefs of Staff

2

There is great wisdom in the message of self-reliance, of education, of hard work, and of the need to raise strong families. There is utter foolishness, evil and danger in the message of hatred, or of condoning violence, however cleverly the message is packaged or entertainingly it is presented. We must find nothing to stand up and cheer about or applaud in a message of racial or ethnic hatred.

At Howard University
commencement/
USA Today, 9-30:(A)6.

3

[Advising young blacks not to let racism be *their* problem]: Let it be a problem to someone else. You can't change it. Don't have a chip on your shoulder, and don't think everyone is staring at you because you're black . . . Let it drag *them* down. Don't use it as an excuse for your own shortcomings.

Newsweek, 10-10:26.

Hugh B. Price
President, National Urban League

4

Race is [still] very much a factor in American life . . . The pattern of discrimination against African-American [job] applicants persists to this day. It's true in lending practices. It's true in housing. So, yes, racism is still abroad in the land. It is sub-

tler and less pervasive than before, but it is still a factor in American life.

Interview,
New York, N.Y./
Los Angeles Times,
7-3:(M)3.

5

Yes, racism is still abroad in the land. Even so, we must not let ourselves and, especially, our children, fall into the paranoid trap of thinking that racism accounts for all that plagues us. [The goal should be] to help dependent people become independently productive . . . We African-Americans who have made it must tithe with our time and, more importantly, our money, to see to it that those of our children whom the civil-rights movement hasn't touched also have a real chance to succeed.

At National Urban League
convention, Indianapolis, Ind.,
July 24/USA Today, 7-25:(A)2.

Ann W. Richards
Governor of Texas (D)

6

If there is one single thing that holds [women] back at the higher levels—that keeps us from being more than tokens or exceptions that do nothing to break the strength of the old rules—it is our reluctance to face the reality of money. In politics, money must be raised. You have to work hard to raise it. It is no different than getting money for a car, or money for a house. Or money to start your own business. You've got to be willing to do the heavy lifting and the decision-making and earn or raise the money to do it. You've got to be willing to take charge of your life and responsibility for yourself. That is the only way you will be able to please yourself in the long run, and the only way you can be sure you did not cheat yourself along the way.

At 50th anniversary meeting
of Texas Girls State,
Austin, Texas, June 20/
The New York Times, 6-25:15.

Thomas P. Schneider
United States Attorney
for Milwaukee, Wis.

1

[On his decision to prosecute a group of demonstrators arrested in Milwaukee under new legislation that makes it a Federal felony for anti-abortion activists to block access to abortion clinics]: Women and doctors cannot be free to choose in private, when a small minority uses force to deny them their legal and Constitutional rights. I respect the rights of those who disagree with the Constitution and the law. They are free to work to change the law by petitioning their representatives, by speaking freely and openly of their position, and by publicly gathering and peacefully protesting to express their views. However, there is no right to intimidate patients, to threaten doctors, or to obstruct free access to medical clinics.

June 6/The New York Times,
6-7:(A)8.

Louis Sheldon
Presbyterian minister;
Chairman,
Traditional Values Coalition

2

[On his organization's stand against homosexuality]: We are here at the capital because the churches sent us here. We stand upon the principles of Judeo-Christian values and beliefs. And there is no way we are going to say that homosexuality is viable . . . Anytime you say that it's viable and that's a valid alternative, that's promotion. You don't want to tolerate sin. You don't want to tolerate perversion. I'm not saying that you've got to have the state adopting theological statements—absolutely not. But what the Bible teaches in morals and in behavior is relevant to public policy. And there are millions of people who are holding to that firm belief.

Interview, Washington, D.C./
The New York Times,
12-19:(A)8.

Eleanor Smeal
President,
Feminist Majority Foundation

3

[On the recent clearing of the way for U.S. importation and testing of the French abortion pill, RU-486]: This milestone victory will significantly increase abortion access and fundamentally reshape abortion debate by finally providing American women with the only known form of early abortion.

May 16/Los Angeles Times,
5-17:(A)17.

Gloria Steinem
Author; Women's-rights
advocate

4

We [women] are trying hard to redefine power, to control our own lives, not other people's. [But] I do worry about some women in power. The root of the problem is their self-hatred. Women were raised to think of themselves as inferior; then these women [in power] see themselves as exceptions. From that self-hatred, they put other women down. I do worry that some women running for [political] office will do us in.

At question-and-answer event,
Washington, D.C./USA Today,
5-16:(D)4.

Randall Terry
Founder, Operation Rescue
(anti-abortion organization)

5

[Criticizing President Clinton's signing of legislation making it a Federal felony for pro-life activists to engage in certain types of protests at abortion clinics]: Everybody in America can protest except when we try to protect babies. If Bill Clinton had signed a bill like this in the 1960s, there never would have been [civil-rights] sit-ins at lunch counters in the South.

Washington, D.C./
Los Angeles Times, 5-27:(A)20.

Richard A. Viguerie
Chairman, United Conservatives

1

[The] abortion [issue] changed politics for-ever—Republican as well as Democrat. Hard as it is to believe, [former Presidents] Richard Nixon and Dwight Eisenhower probably never had to say what they thought about abortion; but after [the Supreme Court's *Roe v. Wade* decision supporting abortion rights] Ronald Reagan and George Bush [who were Presidents after the decision] had to change their positions to survive. Same with the Democrats: [Civil-rights leader] Jesse Jackson changed his mind because you could no longer play on the national scene as a Democrat if you are pro-life.

The Washington Post,
4-7:(A)10.

George C. Wallace (*D.*)
Former Governor of Alabama

2

The New York Times, the Eastern establish-ment newspapers, never did understand that seg-regation [in the South] wasn't about hate. I didn't hate anybody . . . When I was young, I used to swim and play with blacks all the time. You find more hate in New York, Chicago and Washington, D.C., than in all the Southern states put together . . . Segregation was wrong. But I didn't bring seg-regation about. It was there when I got to the Governor's office. It's gone, and I'm glad it's gone. It's so much better to see people together the way they are now.

Interview, Montgomery, Alabama/
The New York Times, 2-11:(A)9.

Maxine Waters
United States Representative,
D-California

3

[On some blacks' dissatisfaction with Presi-dent Clinton's policies]: Everybody is anxious to get along with the President. But when I endorsed him [during his election campaign], I knew it wouldn't be a love-fest. I want to handle [differ-ences] as diplomatically as possible, but I have to be true to my philosophy and my constituency, and I think that speaks to where the [Congressional] Black Caucus is now.

Los Angeles Times,
2-9:(A)5.

William Waybourn
Executive director,
Gay and Lesbian
Victory Fund

4

[Applauding President Clinton's stand against anti-homosexual ballot initiatives in local and state elections]: I think it's clear: There are two Presi-dent Clintons and you've seen them both. The political Bill Clinton realizes he's going to catch a lot of heat for this, but the personal Bill Clinton understood it was the right thing to do . . . What-ever in political capital it will cost him, he's let his true feelings be known.

Feb. 15/The Washington Post,
2-16:(A)7.

Christine Todd Whitman
Governor of New Jersey (R)

5

I believe in promoting women. I believe that women need to have a place at the table. We need more female voices. But I'm not out to run gov-ernment as a woman or for women. I don't think most women want that . . . I'm uncomfortable with any kind of label. It just doesn't fit. It raises ex-pectations on both sides. If you say you're a femi-nist, people expect that you're going to do a lot of aggressive changes of policy. I say, just do it and let people decide what you are.

Interview, Trenton, N.J./
Vogue, August:176.

Marshall Whittman
Legislative director,
Christian Coalition

1

[Criticizing 1973's Supreme Court *Roe v. Wade* ruling supporting abortion rights]: [That] single issue speaks to a whole range of concerns about the lack of traditional values. In our view, that 1973 decision was the most visible of a whole range of societal constraints being removed. And so it has brought together a lot of people who would never have had anything to do with each other before; evangelical Protestants coming together with Roman Catholics and even some Orthodox Jews.

The Washington Post, 4-7:(A)10.

Roger Wilkins
Professor of history
and American culture,
George Mason University

2

Black people are aggrieved in this country, and the lower down the socioeconomic-power levels you go, the more they feel put upon. But by tapping into that sense of injustice, someone can hit a deep political well that extends from the bottom up to the top of the black community.

Los Angeles Times, 9-15:(A)22.

Wendy Wright
Communications director,
Operation Rescue
(anti-abortion organization)

3

[On her group's response to a Supreme Court ruling allowing the Federal racketeering law to be used against abortion protesters who block entrances to abortion clinics]: We will continue our activities that save lives. For us, this is the same old thing. For years, we've faced massive lawsuits and horrendous jail sentences. But we're accountable to God, not to the government. And as long as people believe it's right to save unborn children, they'll be willing to pay the price.

Interview,
Melbourne, Fla., Jan 24/
The New York Times, 1-25:(A)10.

Commerce • Industry • Finance

Nancy Adler
Professor of management,
McGill University (Canada)

1

[On a new trend toward posting managers overseas to gain experience in the foreign marketplace]: The maxim [*used* to be] that the best place to get international experience was standing next to the globe in the CEO's office [at the U.S. headquarters].

U.S. News & World Report,
10-31:94.

Robert E. Allen
Chairman, American Telephone
& Telegraph Company

2

[Saying changes in business, particularly communications businesses, are happening fast]: I thought divestiture [at AT&T] was a major change. But what's happening now, what's happened the last couple of years—I really think you'd have to question the sanity of anybody who says they know how it's going to come out and what their particular company is going to look like.

Interview, Basking Ridge, N.J./
USA Today, 3-15:(B)1.

John C. Bogle
Chairman, The Vanguard Group,
investments

3

A major reason for the remarkable growth in the mutual-fund industry has been the diverse classes of financial assets to which its principles have been successfully applied.

Time, 3-14:49.

Lawrence Bossidy
Chairman, AlliedSignal, Inc.

4

[On the recent increase in corporate mergers and takeovers]: It's an inevitable situation. With the competitive scene as it is, big is back. That doesn't mean big can't be nimble, but you need scale. I think that drives it. Too, I think the financing makes more sense; a lot of these have been stock swaps instead of cash and debt. I think you'll see more of it. Everybody is trying to get into areas of excellence, and get out of areas that are suboptimal. I don't see us getting into the financing frenzy that we saw in the 1980s. Every year there'll be a number of combinations that occur like we see now.

Interview, July 18/
USA Today, 7-19:(B)4.

5

The most important ingredient [for customers], when all is said and done, is lower price, lower cost to them. We're in a world that buys on cost. Quality and distribution [ability] are a given. If you don't have those, you don't play. You've got to have world purchasing scale; you've got to have good designs. It's easier to discuss than it is to execute.

Interview, July 18/
USA Today, 7-19:(B)4.

Nicholas F. Brady
Chairman, Darby Advisors, investments;
Former Secretary of the Treasury
of the United States

6

The trend to global investing is not only the most significant trend for the next year but for the next five years. I think it is at least the equivalent of the industrial revolution. Those financial markets that understand the enormous change that computers and technology have made and organized their societies to accommodate that change are going to be the winners.

Interview/
The New York Times,
1-3:(C)30.

Charles Bunstine II
Chief operating officer,
Barney's New York,
clothing store

1

What's happening with retail sales is that fashion over the past few years hasn't been the driving force of consumption. [Customers] are very much interested in real pricing. They've learned that they can wait around for sales.
U.S. News & World Report,
11-14:104.

Bill Clinton
President of the United States

2

[On the new wave of corporate mergers]: There are two ways in which mergers can be not in the interest of the people of the United States. First is if they violate our antitrust laws, that they do significant damage to the competitive environment. And our Administration has tried to reinvigorate the Antitrust Division of the Justice Department to a significantly higher level than in the last two Administrations. Secondly is if there is some illegal erosion of the rights and interests of the stockholders of these companies or their workers or others who have legal rights that are being undermined. That is within the jurisdiction of the Securities and Exchange Commission. I would be glad to ask them to look into these things more than I'm sure they already are.
News conference,
Washington, D.C., Aug. 3/
The New York Times, 8-4:(A)11.

Richard Cortese
Securities administrator, State of Vermont;
Chairman, investment company
sales practices committee,
North American Securities
Administrators Association

3

There are now more than 4,000 mutual funds, and they are becoming ever more "cutting edge," ever more exotic, ever more specialized. But sig-

nificant numbers of people have moved to mutual funds from bank savings instruments and other government-insured strategies. That tells you that we're dealing with a large element that is less sophisticated than might have been the case a few years ago.
The New York Times, 8-9:(C)2.

Tony DeGregorio
Executive vice president,
TBWA Advertising

4

If there's [an advertising] philosophy I adhere to, it's entertaining consumers. Because if people don't remember you, it doesn't matter how marvelous your strategy is.
Interview, New York, N.Y., June 29/
The New York Times, 6-30:(C)6.

Barry Diller
Chairman, QVC, Inc.

5

I do believe that the acceleration of daily life, this confusing mad rush to get ahead of the future, is eroding our ability at the most critical time to gather together the building blocks to do the real and necessary work of new product creation. It used to be that there was a cadence, a rhythm to things. It would take a reasonable length of time to play out the analysis and the understanding to incubate.
At American Magazine Conference,
Laguna Niguel, Calif., Oct. 24/
The New York Times,
10-25:(C)18.

Robert Eaton
Chairman, Chrysler Corporation

6

[On the current increase in the number of corporate mergers]: Throughout all of U.S. industry, and particularly in the automotive sector, the trend is clearly toward reducing the number of suppliers you want to do business with.
Time, 8-15:29.

Philip Feigen
Securities regulator,
State of Colorado

1

[On the lack of adequate government regulation of the mutual-fund industry]: It's a world where the cops are in Ford Escorts and everybody else is driving a Ferrari. You're just not going to catch many crooks . . . Right now, millions of people are giving their money to mutual funds in the blind faith that somebody out there is watching out for them. All the focus groups, all the surveys, all the studies show you the same thing: You cannot find substantial numbers of people who read and make their investment decisions based on those tomes that mutual funds call prospectuses.

The New York Times,
8-9:(A)1,(C)2.

Richard Fisher
Chairman, Morgan Stanley Group,
investment bankers

2

Globalization is the most important trend in our business, but it is still being vastly underestimated even though it's been a factor for more than 10 years . . . We've discovered that we must be strong not only in London and Tokyo but everywhere, because we never know where the other side of a transaction may be. Two years ago, I would not have believed that substantial money would be flowing into Pakistan or Turkey.

U.S. News & World Report,
3-28:62.

Jeffrey E. Garten
Under Secretary of Commerce
of the United States

3

A unique thing about investment banking [as a career] is that it allows for multiple roles. You are not penalized in your career for taking strong public [political] positions that may or may not be consistent with the flow of [your business] deals.

The New York Times, 8-2:(A)11.

Gerry Greenwald
Chairman, United Airlines

4

[Saying many companies have downsized too much over the past several years]: I think there's been too much cutting back . . . You can't ultimately save your way to heaven . . . You've got to spend some money to make money.

USA Today,
7-22:(A)11.

Samuel Hayes
Professor of finance,
Harvard University

5

[Saying corporate downsizing, mergers, etc. over the past number of years have been positive occurrences]: Our competitiveness in the global economy today can be attributed in large part to the restructurings that began in the 1980s. There's no question that this has, on balance, been a good thing.

Los Angeles Times,
7-15:(A)24.

Edward C. Johnson III
Chairman, Fidelity Investments

6

People are very high on Southeast Asia stocks. But those stocks are more volatile than American stocks. They're just like small companies on the NASDAQ market here. When there is any kind of fear, the prices can drop very quickly. People should look at these stocks as being the high-risk part of their portfolio. Looking at it long term, it's probably very attractive. Short term, there are risks. How much is the Hong Kong market down since the beginning of the year? *Only* 15 or 20 percent?

Interview/Newsweek,
3-14:46.

Kim Chulsu
Minister of Trade, Industry and
Energy of South Korea

1

Surely international commerce is one of the most humanizing of man's activities. It can sublimate conflict into competition, teach tolerance of other cultures and ways of life, promote the peaceful uses of science and technology, and, of course, raise the living standards of all who are touched by it. It is hardly coincidental that the world's great port cities, past and present, have usually been the most cultured and cosmopolitan and—in the broadest sense, liberal—of their time and country.

At Dickinson College, May 19/
The Wall Street Journal, 5-25:(A)14.

Lee Kun Hee
Chairman, Samsung Group (South Korea)

2

Upgrading the quality of one's personal life is the beginning of quality management and production. Only those who can play hard can work hard, too.

Interview/World Press Review,
October:35.

Arthur Levitt, Jr.
Chairman, Securities and Exchange
Commission of the United States

3

[Asking Congress to increase his agency's budget]: The resources requested in the budget are absolutely critical for the agency. Without the increases, the agency cannot meet its mandate of protecting investors and enforcing the nation's securities laws . . . Unfortunately, as investors are entrusting more and more of their savings . . . to mutual funds, the SEC's resources to regulate and inspect those funds have lagged far behind . . . The SEC is a profit center for the Federal government. The Commission strongly supports the creation of a self-funding mechanism.

Before Senate subcommittee, Washington, D.C.,
May 5/Los Angeles Times, 5-6:(D)3.

4

I sold an awful lot of municipal bonds when I was a broker. I know that many retail investors don't know what they are buying, or the fortunes of the issuer of the bond or the incentives the broker gets. I want to put more light on this process and bring the municipal markets into the 20th century before we enter the 21st.

The New York Times,
10-25:(C)1.

David A. Levy
Director, Jerome Levy Economic Institute,
Bard College

5

Business investment decisions are very different from the way in which economists generally describe them. In reality, investment is far more a strategic rather than a financial decision.

The Washington Post,
2-7:(A)4.

Deryck Maughan
Chief executive, Salomon Brothers
(U.K.), investment bankers

6

American firms are succeeding because the home market has been competitive. Wall Street has a risk-seeking, high-return, entrepreneurial mindset.

U.S. News & World Report,
3-28:62.

Merton Miller
Professor of finance,
University of Chicago

7

[On the riskiness of dealing in derivatives]: It's still possible to lose money in all the old familiar ways . . . But derivatives are a novelty item. And the very notion that some of it is done by computer has an ominous ring to it.

Los Angeles Times, 5-12:(A)10.

Kevin J. Murphy
Associate professor,
Harvard Business School

1

I would love to see us get to a place where the typical [corporate] executive has a very low base salary and very high performance-based compensation. Executives should be able to send their kids through college, to afford the mortgage on one or both houses, and to buy new cars every once in a while. But if you look at the level of cash compensation now, there's lots of room to play with. We can go almost across the board and reduce salaries and bonuses by 50 percent, replaced by options or restricted stock or some other type of vehicle. We can reduce salary and even give the executive 150 percent of that salary reduction in options—and make everyone better off.

Panel discussion/
The Wall Street Journal,
4-13:(R)12.

Ralph Nader
Lawyer; Consumer advocate

2

[On consumer rights]: What we want to do in the future is to have group buyers and group complaints . . . A company can cheat people in huge volumes—with telephone charges that include 30 percent and 40 percent surcharges. So a class-action suit is the best to combat this unfairness.

Interview/
The Christian Science Monitor,
1-25:14.

Dan Nagy
Director of career services and
placement, Fuqua Graduate School of
Business, Duke University

3

[On the importance, in today's international marketplace, for managers to accept overseas postings]: The length of assignments is shorter than before, maybe one year versus three years. But companies expect their best people to move anywhere in the world, not just once but several times.

U.S. News & World Report,
10-31:98.

Albert Nicholas
Chairman, Nicholas Fund

4

When Nicholas Fund became public, there were only about 400 mutual funds. Today there are over 5,000. That has made money managers subject to a lot of short-term considerations. Some use gimmicky investments, like initial public offerings or derivatives, hoping to prop up their short-term return. Or they'll grab "momentum stocks" as they rise, even though those stocks can blow up as they get over-priced. You can get badly burned chasing whatever is hot today. We advise investors to take a long-term view. If we perform, we'll get money. If we don't perform, we won't get money—and we won't deserve any.

Interview/Newsweek, 10-10:52.

Michael Novak
Resident scholar, American
Enterprise Institute

5

[Capitalism] is competitive by design, to prevent the growth of monopolies that would allow one person or a few to exercise disproportionate economic power. Unfortunately, it has many other checks and balances that make it difficult for a corporation to survive. We do regulate very intently. But please notice that the whole concept for democratic capitalism requires a three-sided system. The economic system is regulated not only by the political system and the rule of law and its regulations, but also by a moral cultural order, religious principles, and by custom and convention. They limit what is good behavior and mark off what is bad behavior. So there are multiple sources of criticism of business activities. Business is a serious moral activity, and it plays an exceedingly important moral role for the United States.

Interview/
Christianity Today, 10-24:30.

Kevin O'Leary
President,
SoftKey International, Inc.

1

I think there's a fundamental shift going on in the [computer] software business. It's not about technology anymore. It's about marketing, merchandising, brand management and [store] shelf space . . . In the cat-food business, that's all that matters. And in the software business, that's all that matters.

The Christian Science Monitor,
5-13:8.

Ross Perot
Industrialist; 1992 independent
Presidential candidate

2

When you compete [in the business world], keep in mind [that in the beginning] my little company had to compete against IBM. We were the Bad News Bears; they were the New York *Yankees.* Never forget . . . when you go out there with no money in your pocket, brains and wits will beat money 10 times out of 10. Beat 'em with brains and wits . . . A small, high-talent team will beat an army anytime.

At Boston University commencement/
USA Today, 6-8:(A)11.

Cassandra M. Pulley
Deputy Administrator,
Small Business Administration
of the United States

3

I think one of the problems for us is a lack of understanding on the part of our customers or potential customers of what the SBA is. I think a lot of people believe that since it's a government program, they're entitled to whatever we do because they are taxpayers, or because we've got some grant or giveaway program. That really isn't

the case. The agency over time will increasingly become a wholesaler. We provide guarantees to other financial institutions that make the loans— whether they're commercial banks, whether they're small-business or specialized small-business investment companies, or whether they're community-development corporations that provide longer-term financing for capital and equipment. The SBA is getting out of the direct-loan business, so that the criteria you have to meet as a borrower are primarily those of another intermediary. The reality is that the money the SBA uses is taxpayer money, and we have a fiduciary responsibility to get that money back, if at all possible.

Panel discussion/
The Wall Street Journal,
6-22:(Suppl.)18.

Jane Bryant Quinn
Financial columnist

4

One of the best ways to learn about investing is to lose some money. You can read up on investments all you want, but ultimately you have to lose money and analyze what you did wrong and try not to do it again.

Working Woman,
September:31.

Janet Reno
Attorney General
of the United States

5

[Saying banks should not pass by minority areas when marketing their services]: To shun an entire community because of its racial makeup is just as wrong as to reject an applicant because they are African-American . . . We don't want banks to make bad loans; we want them to make fair loans.

Aug. 22/USA Today,
8-23:(B)1.

WHAT THEY SAID IN 1994

James S. Riepe
Managing director,
T. Rowe Price Associates,
investments

1

I think one of the ironies of investing . . . is that the basics are so simple. They've been unchanged in my 25 years in the business and probably in 50 years. If you had to pick the single most overlooked basic, it's probably the time horizon. People do not perceive how long the future is until they need to tap their long-term savings. And the volatility of the markets over longer timeframes really disappears, just as bad events get smaller in our own memory as time goes on. The unchallengeable evidence is that if you're willing to take a little more risk of short-term volatility, and invest in stocks, you're going to get higher returns over the long term.

Interview/
The Wall Street Journal,
12-9:(R)22.

Felix G. Rohatyn
Senior partner,
Lazard Freres & Company,
investment bankers;
Chairman,
Municipal Assistance Corporation
of New York

2

[On the risks in buying derivatives]: There's a whole different world in off-balance-sheet transactions that are potentially quite dangerous if people don't know what they're doing and a chain of financial commitments breaks down. These are interlocking commitments of trillions of dollars. As long as they remain solid and stable, everything is fine. But what do you do if something goes wrong?

Time, 4-11:30.

Richard Russell
Financial analyst;
Editor, "Dow Theory Letters"

3

A bear [stock] market can't be reversed by a news event, a Presidential promise or a Congressional edict. It has to play itself out.

Newsweek, 4-11:48.

Roger Servison
Managing director,
Fidelity Investments

4

The 90-point drop [in the stock market] has become a fairly routine event. Most investors would be well advised to screen out or ignore swings in the market.

Newsweek, 12-5:47.

Nan Sheppard
Manager of global human resources,
General Electric Medical Systems

5

[In today's international marketplace,] someone who doesn't have a global outlook and a willingness to tackle an overseas posting isn't going to continue to be promoted, period.

U.S. News & World Report,
10-31:94.

Muriel Siebert
President, Muriel Siebert & Company,
securities brokers;
First woman to buy a seat on the
New York Stock Exchange.

6

You can make money two ways in the stock market. You can either trade stocks, meaning that you buy and sell them all the time, or you can buy stock in a good-quality company and then sit on your rear end. That's what I do.

Working Woman,
September:31.

Hedrick Smith
Journalist

1

[Saying U.S. companies and analysts should focus on long-term rather than short-term performance]: In Germany you *cannot* report [a company's] quarterly performance. You must only report annual performance. In fact, some of the German companies that have thought about listing themselves on the American stock exchange refused to list themselves because they're afraid that if they have to make quarterly reports it will change the mentality of their corporate leadership . . . [In the U.S.,] maybe executive bonuses have got to be built more toward long-term performance rather than short-term performance . . . [And] we've got to re-educate some Wall Street analysts. I remember reading not too long ago a story in *The New York Times* quoting several analysts about Motorola's having a bad quarterly performance. And the story went on to indicate that Motorola was deliberately setting aside more money during [that] quarter for long-term investments than they had in the previous quarter. So you could *see* why their performance was down. Well, I think it's time for people to start pointing their fingers.
Interview/American Way,
1-4:47,48.

Hans Stoll
Director,
Financial Markets Research Center,
Vanderbilt University

2

The United States is the dominant financial market in the world. We lead the world in stock-market electronic systems. Our financial products are dominant. And we are the biggest exporter of trading systems.
The Christian Science Monitor,
8-24:10.

Jurgen Strube
Managing board chairman,
BASF A.G. (Germany)

3

The challenge [in running a large corporation] is to create a climate in which change is not seen as threatening. We have to make sure that in the heads and hearts of our colleagues the will to change is there. And we do have to change. The old ways of doing things sometimes are completely unsuited to today's global economy. We have to be much more flexible, more efficient and more in tune to our customers' needs now.
The New York Times, 4-9:17.

Richard Thaler
Professor of economics,
Cornell University

4

We over-explain the stock market. If [the market crash of] October '87 taught us anything, it's that movements in the stock market are not all explainable.
Newsweek, 4-11:47.

Esteban E. Torres
United States Representative,
D-California

5

[On pending legislation that would require credit bureaus to correct errors in their consumer credit files sooner than before and hold those reporting erroneous material to the bureaus legally responsible for such reporting]: [This bill] may be the most important consumer legislation considered by Congress this year . . . Our country has changed dramatically . . . and the present state of technology and the volume of credit transactions have rendered the [current 24-year-old Fair Credit Reporting Act] dangerously ill-equipped to meet the needs of today's consumer. We can no longer tolerate a system that denies employment to workers, prevents families from purchasing a mortgage or ruins thousands of credit histories because of errors in their files.
Los Angeles Times, 6-14:(D)1.

Ted Turner
Chairman,
Turner Broadcasting System

1

I've said for years that I would like to buy a [TV] network . . . I would like to have a [movie] studio. In fact, I'd like to have three or four studios and all four TV networks. And I'd like to have all the newspapers and magazines. I'd like to own the BBC, too—[but] it's not for sale; it belongs to the British people. I'd like to own General Motors and General Foods, while we're talking about it. And let's not forget Coca-Cola and Delta Airlines— two companies I can see out the window [here in Atlanta]!

Interview, Atlanta, Ga./
Los Angeles Times,
4-3:(Calendar)82.

Abraham Zaleznik
Former professor,
Harvard Business School;
Authority on executive compensation

2

[On the idea that corporate executives should take a 50 percent cut in salary in exchange for other incentives and performance-based compensation]: I wouldn't do that. The reason is the need to keep focused on long-term development of the corporation. If people start playing around with the annual return, they may take certain kinds of impulsive actions and risks that are just not wise to do. They could become traders, managers of portfolios, instead of managers or leaders of a business.

That would be most unfortunate. It's the "churning" mentality. If chief executives figure they've got to start doing things because you increase the odds of this pot of gold at the end of the rainbow, that would be a dreadful thing.

Panel discussion/
The Wall Street Journal,
4-13:(R)12.

Alfred M. Zeien
Chairman, Gillette Company

3

The most important decision that I made was to "globalize" [products]. We decided not to tailor products to any marketplace, but to treat all marketplaces the same. And it worked in most countries . . . I did not find foreign countries "foreign." They have distinctive characteristics, but they are not foreign. When people shop, they do not think very differently than Americans.

Interview, Boston, Mass./
The New York Times, 1-3:(C)3.

Arthur H. Zeikel
President, Merrill Lynch Asset
Management

4

Mutual funds have gained such wide acceptance by individuals because they realize it has become increasingly difficult to pick stocks and bonds on their own in today's highly complex investing environment.

Time, 3-14:47.

Crime • Law Enforcement

Richard Aborn
President,
Handgun Control, Inc.

1

[Applauding the passage by Congress of legislation banning private ownership of certain types of assault weapons]: I think we've finally convinced our supporters that these are political movements, not just grass-roots efforts. For years, we've [gun-control advocates] had overwhelming support in the polls. But Congress wouldn't vote for us, because gun-control advocates were soft. Our supporters have learned they have to write, call, lobby, do the talk shows . . . In this era of perception, getting [the previously passed Brady gun-control bill] through was tremendously important. It showed we could win. Everybody said Brady was the icebreaker. It turned out to be the floodgates.

The Washington Post,
5-7:(A)1.

Perry Anderson
Commissioner of Police
of Cambridge, Mass.;
Former Chief of Police
of Miami, Fla.

2

If you look at the troublemakers, you'll find it's a small group committing many crimes. We're not talking about people who make a mistake on a Saturday night. We're talking about incorrigibles with proven track records. We can't overlook racism. We can't ignore rehabilitation. But some harsh method must be used against this group, because we have blood on our streets and playgrounds.

Interview/
USA Today, 1-6:(A)6.

Michael A. Andrews
United States Representative,
D-Texas

3

[Supporting proposed legislation to ban ownership of certain assault-type weapons by private individuals]: I have always believed in the old Texas saying that gun control means steady aim. At the same time . . . I am convinced that if we limit the availability of military-style assault weapons, we will be taking a meaningful step toward improving the safety of our streets without trampling on our Constitutional rights . . . Who can, in good conscience, defend such weapons as appropriate for hunters or sportsmen? Anyone that needs a 20-round clip of high-velocity ammunition to fell a duck or deer needs to look into taking up golf.

Los Angeles Times,
5-5:(A)28.

Ronald Angelone
Director, Department of Prisons
of Nevada

4

[Supporting the "three strikes and you're out" bill, recently approved by the U.S. Senate, which would impose mandatory life sentences for repeat felons]: Are [those who are against the bill] saying that we should release violent criminals because we don't want to hold them in prison through life's stages? This law will hinder criminals because a large percentage of violent crime is committed by the same individuals over and over again . . . [But] I don't believe any prison system can rehabilitate people. Just by capturing more people on the streets is not going to stop crime. We have to go back to the roots of crime in communities if we want to see crime rates go down.

The Christian Science Monitor,
2-23:7.

Maryanne Trump Barry
Judge, United States District Court
for the District of New Jersey

1

[Arguing against such proposals as "three strikes and you're out" that would mandate life imprisonment for those committing three serious felonies]: [Mandatory sentences such as] three strikes [are] totally inconsistent with any fair or rational sentencing scheme. The individual defendant isn't considered, nor are the facts of the situation.

Interview, March 16/
The Washington Post,
3-17:(A)10.

Lloyd N. Bentsen
Secretary of the Treasury
of the United States

2

[Proposing to reduce gun sales by cutting the number of gun dealers through an increase in the Federal gun-dealers' license fee]: To sell liquor in the five boroughs of New York, it costs $5,200 for a three-year license. To teach Spanish and history ... it costs $200 for a teacher's certificate. But to sell guns in New York, it's only $66 a year. That isn't just ridiculous. That goes all the way to reckless.

Jan.4/USA Today,
1-5:(A)2.

Joseph R. Biden, Jr.
United States Senator, D-Delaware

3

[Supporting proposals to allow death-row inmates to challenge their sentences on grounds of racial bias]: As we expand the death penalty, we just want to make sure we do not slip into some bad old habits ... of having a different standard when we apply it to black folk than we do to white folk.

Before the Senate, Washington, D.C.,
May 6/The Washington Post, 5-11:(A)4.

4

[Supporting President Clinton's proposed anti-crime bill]: As much as anything I have ever voted on in 22 years as a United States Senator, I believe passage of this legislation will make a difference in the lives of the American people.

Before the Senate,
Washington, D.C., Aug 22/
Los Angeles Times, 8-23:(A)4.

Steven Bishop
Chief of Police of Kansas City, Mo.

5

We must clearly articulate that more police does not equal less crime. But adding more police officers is an absolute necessity for community policing. Violent crime has escalated beyond our ability to respond.

U.S. News & World Report,
6-27:34.

Bruce Blakeman
Republican Party
public-opinion analyst

6

If you ask people how to fix the crime problem, you will get at least a plurality saying that it is the breakup of family and [the] single-parent family [that needs to be dealt with]. You will get more people saying that you can solve the problem by parents taking control of their kids than by locking [criminals] up.

Los Angeles Times, 8-1:(A)24.

David Boaz
Executive vice president,
Cato Institute

7

[Criticizing a proposed crime bill because it contains restrictions on personal freedom]: Congress acts as if it has no responsibility to act within the Constitution. They figure the Constitution is a problem for the courts, not them.

USA Today, 5-13:(A)10.

Carl T. Bogus
Visiting professor,
Rutgers Law School;
Adviser, Violence Policy Center

1

The system of Federal licensure of gun dealers is a national scandal. There are more Federally licensed gun dealers than gas stations in this country, and the gas stations are far more rigorously regulated and monitored.
The New York Times, 6-6:(C)11.

Boutros Boutros-Ghali
Secretary General
of the United Nations

2

Organized crime has become a world phenomenon. In Europe, in Asia, in Africa and in America, the forces of darkness are at work and no society is spared . . . Transnational crime undermines the very foundations of the international democratic order. Transnational crime poisons the business climate, corrupts political leaders and undermines human rights. [The mafias of the world are] veritable crime multinationals.
At United Nations conference
on crime, Naples, Italy, Nov. 21/
The New York Times, 11-22:(A)4.

Michael Box
Alabama State Representative (D)

3

[Criticizing a proposed Federal crime bill that would require states to meet certain Federal standards or risk losing Federal anti-crime aid]: The idea of the Federal government trying to determine on a national scale how crime and punishment should be dealt with on a state level because it makes some Congressman feel good is repugnant to us [in the states]. We'll take a very close look at this before we buy into it.
At National Conference
of State Legislatures,
New Orleans, La., July 28/
The Washington Post, 7-29:(A)11.

Bill Bradley
United States Senator, D-New Jersey

4

So often, Americans on the one hand seem catatonic in the face of [criminal] violence and, on the other hand, ready to entertain the most radical solutions to stop violence. Unless we have a way to tell whether what we're doing is working, people will assume the worst and we will be caught in a spiral of extreme measures, perhaps endangering our rights permanently. We cannot simply replace a violent society with a repressive one.
Before National Press Club,
Washington, D.C., May 11/
The New York Times, 5-12:(A)10.

Stephen G. Breyer
Judge, United States Court of
Appeals for the First Circuit;
Associate Justice-designate,
Supreme Court of the United States

5

[On capital punishment]: It seems to me that the Supreme Court has considered that matter for quite a long time in a large number of cases. And, indeed, if you look at those cases, you will see that the fact that there are some circumstances in which the death penalty is consistent with the Cruel and Unusual Punishment Clause of the Constitution is, in my opinion, settled law. At this point, it is settled.
At Senate Judiciary Committee
hearing on his nomination,
Washington, D.C., July 12/
The New York Times, 7-13:(A)8.

Lee P. Brown
Director, White House Office of
National Drug Control Policy;
Former Commissioner of Police of
New York, N.Y.

6

[On whether now-illegal drugs should be legalized as a way to cut down on crime]: That's an

WHAT THEY SAID IN 1994

issue that's being proposed by some respectable people, and I often tell them that they're very sincerely wrong. First, we've got to ask some basic questions: What do we want to legalize—LSD, PCP, heroin, cocaine, crack cocaine? And two, we have to look at the cost of legalization. We know that legalizing drugs would result in more drug use, more crime and violence, more spouse and child abuse, and higher health-care costs.

Interview/
USA Today, 6-30:(A)11.

William F. Buckley, Jr.
Political commentator;
Host, "Firing Line," PBS-TV

1

[Capital punishment] is the supreme sanction that validates the concern we hold for human life.
Broadcast debate, Bard College/
"Firing Line," PBS-TV, 7-1

George Bushnell
President-elect,
American Bar Association

2

I personally favor decriminalization of all drugs. [If government sells and regulates drugs,] it takes the profit out of it, which in turn reduces the attractiveness of drug activity among kids. One of the main reasons for crime is that people need money to bug the stuff.
USA Today, 6-28:(A)2.

Bill Clinton
President of the United States

3

[On the current proposed crime bill]: [It will give police officers] the tools you need to do your job. This is not a partisan issue or a sectional issue or a racial issue or an income issue. If anything

should truly make us a United States of America, it should be the passionate desire to restore real freedom to our streets.
At ceremony honoring police officers,
Washington, D.C., April 14/
The New York Times, 4-15:(A)12.

4

The crime rate overall in our country has pretty well leveled off, but it's still going up among young people. Young people are the principal perpetrators of violent crime. Young people are also the principal victims of violent crime . . . I have to tell you, no matter what we do with the laws, we have to have a change in the behavior and attitude and feeling among young people all across this country.
At youth forum sponsored by MTV,
Washington, D.C., April 19/
The New York Times, 4-20:(A)8.

5

When people enter this country illegally and commit crimes while they are here, it is not fair to ask the states to bear the entire costs of their imprisonment.
Statement asking Congress
for $350-million in aid to help states
pay for such imprisonment, April 22/
The Washington Post, 4-23:(A)10.

6

[On the difficulty he is having in rounding up enough votes in Congress to pass legislation banning private ownership of many kinds of assault-type weapons]: It's amazing to me that we even have to have this debate. I mean, how long are we going to let this go on? I'm sorry to be so frustrated. But sometimes it seems that the President's job ought to be dealing with things that are not obvious. I mean, at least health care is a complex subject; it's obvious we need to do something about it, but it's complicated . . . [But as for assault-type weapons,] I have heard people with a

(BILL CLINTON)

straight face saying, well, there are some adults that like to go target practice with these things. Well, they need [instead] to read a good book. Or take up bowling.

Speech to law-enforcement officials,
Washington, D.C., May 2/
The New York Times, 5-3:(A)10.

1

[Supporting the crime bill now before Congress]: We have a chance to pass the toughest, smartest crime bill in the history of the United States after six years of bickering over it. Let me remind you of what that bill will do. It will put 100,000 police officers on the streets of our communities, a 20 percent increase. It will make three strikes and you're out [for repeat felons] the law of the land. it will ban deadly assault weapons and hand-gun ownership by minors. It will provide tougher sentences for violent criminals and more prisons to put them in. And we've listened to police, prosecutors and community leaders who tell us that they need much more for prevention programs to give our young people something to say yes to as well as something to say no to. Believe it or not, there are still special interests here in Washington trying to derail this crime bill. But we're fighting them, and the American people will win this fight, too.

News conference,
Washington, D.C., Aug. 3/
The New York Times,
8-4:(A)10.

2

[Criticizing the House's vote against considering his crime bill]: Under any circumstances I would be disappointed if the House of Representatives turned its back on the toughest and largest attack on crime in the history of our country at a time when the American people say it is the most important issue to them. But is especially disheartening to see 225 members of the House participate in a procedural trick orchestrated by the Na-

tional Rifle Association, then heavily, heavily, pushed by the Republican leadership in the House and designed with only one thing in mind, to put the protection of particular interests over the protection of ordinary Americans . . . Well, tonight a majority of the House attempted to take the easy way out, but they have failed the American people. And now I say to them, the easy way out is not an option. Fear and violence, especially among our children, will still be there tonight when they go home to bed. So I want them to come back tomorrow and the day after that and the day after that, and to keep coming back until we give the American people the essential elements of this crime bill.

News conference,
Washington, D.C., Aug. 11/
The New York Times,
8-12:(A)8.

3

[Criticizing House members who voted against having his crime bill considered]: The American people have said over and over [that crime] is their first concern, If we can't meet this concern, there is something badly wrong in Washington . . . Yes, it was a defeat yesterday, and I feel terrible about it. But this morning I woke up feeling good because that's a vote I'd much rather be on the losing wide of than the winning side. I am glad I will never have to explain to my wife, my daughter, my grandchildren and the people who sent me to Washington why I did something like what was done to the American people [in the house] yesterday.

Before National Association
of Police Organizations,
Minneapolis, Minn., Aug. 12/
The New York Times, 8-13:1,8.

4

[On his signing of the crime bill which was finally passed by Congress]: For six years, Washington debated a crime bill without action while more and more children died and more and more children became criminals and foreclosed a productive life for themselves. Today, at last, the wait-

(BILL CLINTON)

ing ends. Today the bickering stops, the era of excuses is over, the law-abiding citizens of our country have made their voices heard.

At signing of the bill,
Washington, D.C., Sept. 13/
Los Angeles Times, 9-14:(A).

Robert K. Corbin
President,
National Rifle Association

1

[Criticizing gun-control proposals aimed at reducing violent crime]: Did drug laws reduce the use of drugs and the amount of drugs coming into this country? A criminal is a criminal. A criminal doesn't obey any law. What makes you think he is going to obey a little gun law? . . . [Gun-control advocates] lie. They said: "All we want is the Brady Bill and a waiting period [for gun purchase]." And then, after it passed, they say it's just the beginning, the camel's nose under the tent and "we're coming after all your guns." So why should we compromise? Let *them* compromise once in a while . . . About 70 million law-abiding citizens own 200 million guns in this country. Less than 3/10s of 1 percent of those 70 million misuse them. And if 99.77 percent don't misuse them, why do you want to punish them? Criminals are the problem, not the law-abiding gun owner.

Interview, Phoenix, Ariz./
Los Angeles Times, 5-18:(E)4.

Tom Cross
Illinois State Representative (R)

2

[On a trend toward treating young criminals as adults when they commit serious crimes]: We have a different juvenile offender than we had 30 years ago. When you have drive-by shootings tak-

ing place and 15-year-old kids selling cocaine, those guys—or girls—are in a different category than those who have busted a window or stolen hubcaps.

The Christian Science Monitor,
5-19:2.

Mario M. Cuomo
Governor of New York (D)

3

[Supporting "three strikes and you're out" laws that mandate life imprisonment for those who commit three serious felonies]: Violence and crime have taken on a terrible urgency and we are determined to move quickly and decisively to protect our people. In baseball, it's three strikes and you're out. Here [in the law], it's three strikes and you're in, for life.

State of the State address,
Albany, N.Y./The Washington Post,
1-24:(A)1.

Alfonse M. D'Amato
United States Senator, R-New York

4

[Criticizing proposed legislation that would allow black death-row inmates to challenge their sentences as being based on racism]: This proposal is nothing more than an exercise in political correctness being injected into our legal system. It has nothing to do with guilt or innocence and it is absolutely intended to do away with the death penalty.

USA Today, 5-13:(A)10.

5

[Criticizing President Clinton's proposed anti-crime bill, sung to the tune of *Old MacDonald*]: President Clinton had a bill, E-I-E-I-O. And in that bill was lots of pork, E-I-E-I-O.

Before the Senate,
Washington, D.C./
Newsweek, 9-5:21.

Denton Darrington
Idaho State Senator (R)

1

[Criticizing a proposed Federal crime bill that would require states to meet certain Federal standards or risk losing Federal anti-crime aid]: We think we [in the states] are quite capable of writing our own criminal codes without the Federal government telling us what we have to do to get their money. This will be a drain on our budgets because we'll have to provide prison space, policemen and additional prosecutors.

*At National Conference
of State Legislatures,
New Orleans, La., July 28/
The Washington Post,
7-29:(A)11.*

Scott Decker
*Chairman,
criminal-justice department,
University of Missouri, St. Louis*

2

The pattern of homicide has changed. The decreasing age of both offenders and victims is the most profound change in homicide rates since World War II . . . All of the indicators in the demographics [that point to a percentage increase in the 15-19 age group by 2005] are supporting the contention that homicide is only going to increase.

The New York Times, 1-1:7.

Phil Donahue
Television talk-show host

3

[Saying TV should be allowed to broadcast executions]: Television has as much right to be [at an execution] as it does at a four-alarm fire . . . This irrevocable, powerful act of the state is mandated by the people, it's paid for by the people and it is most certainly the business of the people.

Newsweek, 6-27:13.

Marian Wright Edelman
*President,
Children's Defense Fund*

4

[On the increase in arrests of children committing crimes with guns]: Our worst nightmares are coming true. After years of epidemic poverty, joblessness, racial intolerance, family disintegration, domestic violence and drug and alcohol abuse, the crisis of children having children has been eclipsed by the greater crisis of children killing children.

*Jan. 20/The Washington Post,
1-21:(A)3.*

Joycelyn Elders
*Surgeon General
of the United States*

5

I want to make it as hard as possible [to own guns]. I support a total ban on handgun ownership for anyone under 18. Uzis should be absolutely banned from entering this country. Automatic weapons of any kind should not be for sale in America. For that matter, toy Uzis should not be available for kids, either. There would be a minimum seven-day waiting period between applying for a gun permit and obtaining a gun . . . Nobody with a criminal record would ever be allowed to buy a gun. All assault weapons would be banned, completely. And everybody who still possesses a gun license would receive mandatory education and training by professionals on how to handle a gun. After all, I can't drive my car until I pass a test proving I know how to handle a car. Gun owners would have to be evaluated by how they scored on their written and firing tests, and have to pass the tests in order to own a gun. And I would, as I say, tax the guns, bullets and the license itself very heavily.

*Interview/Mother Jones,
Jan.-Feb.:56.*

Dianne Feinstein
United States Senator, D-California

1

It's extraordinarily difficult to get [gun-control] legislation passed, and that's because there is a certain degree of fanaticism within the NRA. But at some point . . . you simply have to conclude that the rights of the many come before the rights of the few.

USA Today, 1-24:(A)9.

Daniel L. Feldman
Chairman, Correction Committee,
New York State Assembly

2

The only rational approach is to use prison space far more efficiently than we have been doing. We should be locking up violent criminals far longer than we are doing . . . rather than locking up so many street dealers of drugs who are instantly replaceable.

Los Angeles Times, 1-25:(A)24.

James Alan Fox
Professor of criminology,
Northeastern University

3

Criminals keep up with trends, too. We all take advantage of new technology; there's no reason to expect they wouldn't.

USA Today, 4-1:(A)2.

Louis J. Freeh
Director,
Federal Bureau of Investigation

4

[Criticizing rivalry between the FBI and the Drug Enforcement Administration]: The American people don't want to hear about two bureaucrats fighting over jurisdiction, who gets credit for a case or who was there first. They just don't want to hear it, and I don't want to hear it. [There have been] more than a couple of instances [in which FBI and DEA field offices] are not only not cooperating, but [are] not telling each other what they were doing in their areas. I just can't think of a more dysfunctional or more dangerous method of operation. It's to the point where we could conceivably be buying and selling drugs to each other through our informants and witnesses, and there's a potential there for people getting killed.

Interview/Los Angeles Times,
6-15:(A)1,36.

5

[On the FBI's offering assistance to Russian authorities to crack down on the increasing crime in that country]: We're here to protect democracy [in Russia] . . . I'm not willing to ignore Russian organized crime the way we ignored La Cosa Nostra for 50 years.

Moscow, Russia/
Newsweek, 7-25:28.

Richard H. Girgenti
Director, Division of
Criminal Justice Services
of New York State

6

[On the "three strikes and you're out" concept in which those who habitually commit serious crimes would be put in prison for life]: We believe there are certain people, because of the need to protect society, who have really forfeited their right to be in the community. The second thing is that you will have an impact in that these people will not be able to go out and commit additional crime. Will that cause a decrease in crime statistics? I doubt it. But will it take some of the most serious habitual criminals off the street? Absolutely.

The New York Times,
1-25:(A)16.

Rudolph W. Giuliani
Mayor of New York, N.Y.

1

Police officers have to play the role primarily of preventing crime. Social-services aspects that were kind of added on to community policing, some of that has to be done but can't become a primary focus of all the police aspects in the neighborhood. The police officer's there to make sure the burglary doesn't take place, the robbery doesn't take place, a person can walk along the street safely.

News conference,
New York, N.Y., Jan. 24/
The New York Times,
1-25:(A)16.

Phil Gramm
United States Senator, R-Texas

2

[Attorney General Janet Reno is] a very sweet lady, [but she should not be Attorney General because she cares] more about day care than . . . about violent crime. I believe some people should have that priority, but I do not believe they should be Attorney General of the United States . . . I wish more people would call me sweet . . . In fact, of all the Cabinet officials, I like her personally better than any of the rest. The point is, maybe a person with her perspective should be head of Health and Human Services. But I want the chief law-enforcement official of the country to be more concerned about prosecuting criminals than about child care . . . [Child care is] an important part of the [crime-prevention] puzzle, but it [should not be] her part of the puzzle.

To reporters and before
Republican National Committee,
Washington, D.C., Jan. 21/
Los Angeles Times,
1-22:(A)23.

Marcia Greenfield
Administrative assistant,
Crime Prevention Committee,
Minnesota State Senate

3

[Arguing against the "three strikes and you're out" proposal that would mandate a life sentence for repeat felons]: Why would you want to put a third-time barroom brawler in prison and run the risk of [having to let] out a first-time rapist? We want to have the flexibility to toughen penalties as we see fit, depending on the record of the offender.

The New York Times,
5-10:(A)14.

Frank Hall
Director,
Department of Corrections
of Oregon

4

[Criticizing the "three strikes and you're out" bill, recently approved by the U.S. Senate, which would impose mandatory life sentences for repeat felons]: In Oregon, we refer to this proposal as the corrections full-employment bill. In reality, there is no magic bullet, no single solution to the problem. And if the Federal government goes in this direction, we will end up running geriatric facilities for people who are long past the point in their lives when they are a threat to the community . . . We need balance, prisons for people who are a threat to the community, and intermediate sanctions and other ways of holding lesser offenders accountable while leading them back into the community under strict supervision. We need more funds to expand drug and alcohol programs, too. But we shouldn't continue to build these incredibly expensive prisons which we then have to maintain.

The Christian Science Monitor,
2-23:7.

Ronald Hampton
Executive director,
National Black Police Association

1

[Saying that, for the most part, there are enough police officers, but they should be trained and used to better advantage]: We need to focus on what police do, not how many of them are doing it. If I take a hundred thousand new police officers and put them through the present induction program, most of them won't end up on the street and they won't bring their heads with them if they get there. If we don't first change the philosophy of policing in this country, whatever police officers we add will fall into the black hole that exists in every police department.

The Atlantic Monthly, May:112.

Orrin G. Hatch
United States Senator, R-Utah

2

[Criticizing President Clinton's proposed anti-crime bill]: A vote for this bill is a vote to spend literally billions of dollars in 1960s-style social-spending boondoggles.

Before the Senate,
Washington, D.C., Aug. 22/
Los Angeles Times, 8-23:(A)4.

Philip B. Heymann
Former Deputy Attorney General
of the United States

3

[Saying there is too much politics in drafting Federal anti-crime bills]: It's become too easy to pretend we're going to solve this [crime] problem with a set of remedies that look good for the first 15 seconds you look at them and very bad when you get to half a minute. If we didn't have a terrible problem to deal with, this would be funny . . . Politics has overwhelmed serious debate.

To reporters, Washington, D.C.,
Feb. 15/The Washington Post,
2-16:(A)1.

4

Crime is one of the great political issues in most Western democracies. It generally breaks down along partisan lines. We're seeing a time when it's being handled in a non-partisan way [in the U.S.], with both parties competing to be as firm and tough on crime as they can be. I don't have any objection to that, but you can't be the toughest and the smartest. President Clinton said he wanted to be tough but smart. If you want to be decently smart and exercise some common sense, you can't be tougher than anybody who's competing for toughness. The toughest guy will say [to criminals], "One strike, and you're out." Or the toughest guy will say, "Build 10 times more prisons." So the difficult trick is how to be smart as well as tough in a political environment that rewards toughness more than smartness. The reason for that is it takes a little while to explain why one thing's smart and the other thing isn't. It doesn't take any time at all to explain why one thing's tougher than the next.

Interview,
Washington, D.C./
Los Angeles Times,
2-20:(M)3.

Eric H. Holder, Jr.
United States Attorney
for the District of Columbia

5

What I hope to do is broaden the scope of this job so that we try to take meaningful prevention activities that deal with the problems that breed crime—poverty, illiteracy and unwed births. I think too often law-enforcement people focus on the enforcement side and don't deal with the prevention side. And unless you do both, how are you ever going to ever really get a handle on the crime problem?

Interview/
Ebony, September:136.

Steny H. Hoyer
United States Representative,
D-Maryland

1

[Supporting the proposed "three-time loser" legislation that would require life imprisonment for repeat violent felons]: Those individuals who have been convicted of three separate violent crimes have forfeited their rights to be members of our society. They should be off our streets, in jail, forever, never to plague us again.
Los Angeles Times,
1-25:(A)24.

R. William Ide
President,
American Bar Association

2

It's understandable that Congress wants to be seen as tough on crime in a political year . . . But Federalization of crimes that belong in state jurisdictions is posturing and not a long-range solution to violent crimes . . . Violent crimes is a community problem that must be solved through community involvement.
To law-enforcement specialists,
Washington, D.C., Jan. 26/
Los Angeles Times, 1-27:(A)12.

Jesse L. Jackson
Civil-rights leader

3

[On black-on-black violence]: This is an American crisis. If whites shoot blacks, we [blacks] want to riot. If blacks shoot whites, whites want revenge and capital punishment. But if black shoots black, no one cares. There's a permissiveness that is unacceptable.
Interview/USA Today,
1-6:(A)6.

Oliver J. Keller
Former President,
American Correctional Association

4

Many of the people who wind up with mandatory [prison] sentences are small-time drug dealers who are taking up valuable prison space. This country has been on a prison-building binge for over 20 years, and if that were the answer [to crime], we'd be crime-free by now.
Los Angeles Times, 1-25:(A)24.

Dean Kilpatrick
Director, Crime Victims Research
and Treatment Center, Medical
University of South Carolina

5

[On violent crime in society]: There is the feeling that no place is safe. The crime and the fear of crime has pushed the boundary of safety further and further back and brought the danger zone much closer.
The Washington Post, 1-3:(A)1.

Edward I. Koch
Former Mayor of New York, N.Y.

6

[On capital punishment]: There are certain crimes that are so heinous, so egregious, so violent that your soul calls out for punishment of death.
Broadcast debate, Bard College/
"Firing Line," PBS-TV, 7-1.

Louis F. Kosco
New Jersey State Senator (R)

7

[Saying concerns that a proposed "three strikes and you're out" bill—which would mandate life imprisonment for those convicted of three or more violent offenses—would cost the state too much money are irrelevant]: Each time they go through the revolving door, repeat offenders cost

(LOUIS F. KOSCO)

the state a great deal in legal and parole expenses. And we must take into account the economic and social costs society incurs with each new offense perpetrated by repeat offenders.

The New York Times, 5-13:(A)1.

Wayne LaPierre
Executive vice president,
National Rifle Association

1

[Criticizing attempts to ban private ownership of certain types of assault weapons]: The "good guns" they don't want to ban and the guns they want to ban all fire the same. None fires any faster, none makes any bigger holes, none shoot any harder, none make any bigger noise.

Broadcast interview/
"Meet the Press," NBC-TV, 5-1.

Jack Levin
Professor of sociology and criminology,
Northeastern University

2

[On the high level of violent crime in the U.S. compared with Canada]: Let's face it; we have a culture of violence in the United States that Canada does not have. We have the murder of the week; you [in Canada} have the murder of the year.

The Washington Post, 1-7:(A)15.

Dan Lungren
Attorney General of California

3

As we pursue even tougher policies aimed at criminals—and we do so without apology—I will also continue to push our societal response to crime in a comprehensive context. We must lead . . . away from a culture of violence to a culture of hope and civility where the rights of every person are respected.

News conference,
Sacramento, Calif., March 7/
Los Angeles Times, 3-8:(A)18.

4

It's easy to talk on crime . . . And this [election] year, nearly everybody will do it. Watch the actions of your elected officials and see if it matches with their tough talk.

June 10/Los Angeles Times,
6-11:(A)22.

Nora Manella
United Stated Attorney
for Los Angeles, Calif.

5

[As a criminal,] you certainly want to [commit crime] in a major metropolitan center where the prosecutors are spread the thinnest. If you do, then you get away with it.

USA Today, 6-22:(A)7.

Marc Mauer
Spokesman, Sentencing Project

6

[Criticizing a Federal "three strikes and you're out" bill mandating life in prison for committing three violent felonies]: The Federal role in responding to violence is limited. This creates false expectations. People hear about all these Federal crime initiatives and then they are frustrated when they don't work.

The Washington Post,
2-22:(A)4.

Tanya K. Metaksa
Chief lobbyist,
National Rifle Association

7

[Criticizing Congressional passage of legislation banning private ownership of certain types of assault weapons]: Basically, this was a political fight that had nothing to do with the issue of crime. We were fighting not just the Congress, but the President [Clinton] as well. They not only twisted arms, they broke them.

The Washington Post, 5-7:(A)8.

Kweisi Mfume
United States Representative,
D-Maryland

1

[On the changes he and others have been able to make to President Clinton's proposed anti-crime bill]: We were able to take a crime bill that was absolutely punitive in nature and put into it billions of dollars in [crime-] prevention money to assist in giving hope and opportunity and options to the young people of our communities. It is a bill that began with no reference to weapons that now includes, for the first time in our nation's history, a ban on assault weapons . . . More than anything else, it carries the shape of not just six months of effort but six months of activism and assertiveness . . . It is not the end-all . . . but it is a worthwhile beginning, because prevention now is part of our discussion. When we talk about crime, it is [now] not all about punishment.
Interview, Washington, D.C./
Los Angeles Times,
8-21:(M)3.

2

Because we continue to take discretion away from judges through the use of mandatory minimum sentences and other measures, we give young people sentences that you can't change and that take away any possibility for them to be redeemed, because they're going into an institution that doesn't provide rehabilitation services. I am as outraged as anybody on the matter of crime. But I am also concerned that we remember that everybody who commits a crime is not unredeemable. If that were the case, we would not have some of the people now in professional positions who run our society.
Interview/Essence,
September:88.

Robert H. Michel
United States Representative,
R-Illinois

3

[Supporting a ban on the private ownership of assault-type weapons]: They may have their place in wartime, but certainly not on our streets in peacetime. When our police need to increase their firepower so that they can match the firepower of criminals, it is time to ban assault weapons.
May 5/The Washington Post,
5-6:(A)22.

Milton Morris
Vice president,
Joint Center for Political
and Economic Studies

4

[On how to deal with violent crime in the black community]: Everything we see in the black community right now is on the level of exhortation. But in terms of what do we do in policies, strategies and programs, I don't see anything yet. And the truth is it's tough and difficult to find solutions. All the solutions before us are either Draconian, prison-oriented types of measures or the kind of costly long-term violence-prevention efforts that I don't think the society right now has the patience or the will to take on.
At conference on crime
in the black community,
Washington, D.C., Jan. 7/
The New York Times, 1-8:8.

Norval Morris
Professor, University of
Chicago Law School

5

[Saying increasingly large Federal involvement in trying to control crime is not desirable]: This stuff is just ludicrous. I think the bottom line is that the assumption that the Federal government

(NORVAL MORRIS)

handles crime matters better than the states is an assumption that's believed only within the [Washington] beltway.

U.S. News & World Report,
3-28:35.

Carole Moseley-Braun
United States Senator, D-Illinois

1

[Supporting legislation that would allow black death-row inmates to challenge their sentences as being based on racism]: This bill simply gives those sentenced to death the same opportunity to present a discrimination claim as someone who was turned down for an apartment.

USA Today, 5-13:(A)10.

2

We should treat youngsters differently from how we treat older criminals. but when it is precisely because of those exemptions that we make for juveniles that violent crimes have risen at such an exponential rate, we have to begin to realize this does not work as well as we had intended. On the other hand, to the extent that our youngsters have more access to guns, less opportunity and more hopelessness, they are disproportionately affected. But that is a function of the environment, and we can't fix societal problems with criminal law.

Interview/Essence,
September:86.

Dee Dee Myers
Press Secretary to President
of the United States Bill Clinton

3

Crime is something that I think affects almost every other issue. It certainly affects health care. It affects welfare reform. It affects the state of the economy. It is both a legislative issue and an issue of the country's spirit.

Jan. 28/The New York Times, 1-29:8.

Gail Nayowith
Executive director,
Citizens' Committee for Children,
New York, N.Y.

4

[Arguing against proposals to toughen penalties for young criminals]: There is a very dearly held belief that we can use the criminal-justice system to reduce juvenile crime. But, in fact, it hasn't worked. The Juvenile Offender Law passed in the 1970s was an attempt to get tough, to treat some youths like adults. But that law has not reduced juvenile crime. In fact, juvenile crime has increased . . . Not every kid needs to be locked up. We [now] have detention and probation. That's about it. There should be a wider range of sanctions.

June 20/The New York Times,
6-21:(A)16.

Kristen Rand
Counsel, Violence Policy Center

5

Toasters, teddy bears, trucks, or guns—which product is virtually unregulated? The answer, surprising to most people, is guns. The conclusion of our study, "Cease Fire," is that the time has come to hold the gun industry to the same standards we apply to manufacturers of lawnmowers and [toys]. The result would be a significant reduction in firearms violence . . . [We] call for a ban on the sale of new handguns because the risks associated with these products far outweigh any benefits.

Feb. 17/
The Christian Science Monitor,
2-23:6.

6

[On the 19 assault-type weapons banned in President Clinton's proposed anti-crime bill]: It would be problematic to ban a list of just 19 weapons, or any other specific number, for that matter. No matter how many weapons you ban by name, there are more out there with the same characteristics . . . [But] the bottom line is that these [19]

(KRISTEN RAND)

weapons were designed for military and law-enforcement use and then brought into civilian manufacture. The military and law-enforcement agencies came up with these designs to make them better for combat and riot control. If the changes are only cosmetic, why are these weapons better for military and law-enforcement use? There's obviously some value that makes them appropriate for those uses, and that's what makes them inappropriate for civilian use.

The Washington Post, 8-13:(A)8.

Charles B. Rangel
United States Representative,
D-New York

1

[On violent crime by inner-city youth]: I'm a decorated combat soldier and I can testify that animals, especially humans, fear death. But not these young men. There's never been anything like it in combat or among the gangsters in the Roaring Twenties. There's a total lack of fear of police or incarceration. The reason is simple: What difference does it make? These kids don't know anyone who's gotten out of the inner city. Even if you're straight, there are no jobs. These kids have a choice between making a little money and making tons dealing drugs. But these young drug dealers can't even count the money they make! They can't launder money. They can't buy a decent suit, find a restaurant that serves a decent meal or make a reservation to Europe. Money is a symbol of success, but they're so poorly educated they don't even know what to do with it other than get gold teeth and gold chains and baggy pants.

Interview/USA Today, 1-6:(A)6.

Peter Reinharz
Chief Prosecutor, Family Courts
of New York, N.Y.

2

[Supporting proposals to toughen penalties for young criminals]: [The proposals] add a modicum of common sense to a juvenile-justice system that seems to run on chaos. Most of the things they're changing haven't been changed since 1962 when the Family Court was established. We're not dealing with the same kind of kids as in the '60s. We're not dealing with stealing hubcaps, breaking bottles and standing around on street corners. What we're dealing with now are felony offenders. We're dealing with armed offenders. We're dealing with dangers. And the first obligation of the criminal-justice system is to protect the people out there. The present system doesn't do that.

June 20/The New York Times,
6-21:(A)16.

Janet Reno
Attorney General
of the United States

3

If we're ever going to stop violence in America, we're going to have to stop it in the home. Today's violence is the legacy of three decades of neglect of our children.

Newsweek, 8-15:47.

Mimi Rose
Chief, Family Violence
and Assault Unit,
District Attorney's Office
of Philadelphia, Pa.

4

When women call the police [because of domestic violence], they don't call because they want to prosecute. They are scared and want the violence to stop. Ten days later, when they get the subpoena to appear in court, the situation has changed. The idea of putting someone you live with in jail becomes impossible . . . We need to rethink what we're doing. Prosecution isn't a panacea. It's like a tourniquet. We put it on when there is an emergency and we keep it on as long as necessary. But the question is, then what?

Newsweek, 7-4:32.

Marvin Runyon
Postmaster General
of the United States

1

[On recent acts of violence at post offices]:
You hear a lot about violence in the post office
because there's a post office in every city. And if a
postal worker, a retired postal worker, a fired postal
worker or the spouse of a postal worker does something [violent against the post office], it comes out
"post office." It just gets reported that way. I don't
think that the Postal Service, as a company of
700,000 career employees, is as bad as other companies. There is violence in this country. There is
violence in the workplace. It's something that this
country needs to fix.

Interview/
USA Today, 3-7:(A)13.

Charles E. Schumer
United States Representative,
D-New York

2

[On the difficulty in passing anti-crime legis-
lation]: The left wants prevention and no punishment. The right wants punishment and no prevention. The consensus of the House is to do both,
prevention and punishment. The question is finding the proper balance.

The Washington Post,
1-24:(A)4.

3

[On the difficulty in passing an anti-crime
bill]: The crime bill shows what's wrong with
American politics. It shows how people's desires
don't translate into action; it shows how image
often supersedes substance; and it shows how different people's values become more important than
the actual legislation itself.

Interview/
The New York Times,
3-14:(A)10.

4

[Republicans] have a strategy to create
gridlock [in passing a crime bill]. They don't want
to see a Democratic Congress passing and a Democratic President signing a good, fair crime bill.

March 24/USA Today,
3-25:(A)3.

5

If you look particularly at the state level, violent repeat criminals are not punished enough. The
average murderer is sentenced to 17 1/2 years but
serves six. The average rapist is sentenced to 10
years but serves about three and a half. The average mugger is sentenced to five years and serves
little more than one. I, on the other hand, don't
think we should be putting first-time drug offenders in jail for five years. It's a waste of resources
. . . I support the death penalty for the [drug] king-
pin, the guy at the top; but I don't think you should
throw a drug offender in jail for five years, and let
a mugger out after a year.

Interview, Washington, D.C./
Los Angeles Times 5-8:(M)3.

6

[On the recent passage by the House of legislation, which he supported, banning private ownership of certain kinds of assault-type weapons]:
It's in between symbolism and a panacea, a cure-
all. It will do some good . . . The ban actually is
going to save lives. There is also some symbolic
value. The symbolism is that the NRA [which is
against the ban] can be beaten, that members [of
Congress] can stand up to the NRA . . . It speaks
not so much that the NRA is weakening but the
opposing forces are stronger. A member of Congress has and still does pay a price for voting
against the NRA. But now a member pays a price
for voting *with* the NRA, too. In many districts,
the price is higher when a member votes with the
NRA than against the NRA. The public is outraged [about gun violence].

Interview, Washington, D.C./
Los Angeles Times, 5-8:(M)3.

(CHARLES E. SCHUMER)

1

[On the comprehensive crime bill now before Congress]: Any member who stands against this crime bill will do so at his own peril. This is one of the few times politics and substance collide.

USA Today, 8-3:(A)2.

Bret Schundler
Mayor of Jersey City, N.J.

2

[On existing regulations, Federal mandates, binding arbitration and other rules which he says hinder cities from reforming their police departments]: Our crime problem would be greatly reduced if cities weren't blocked from effectively managing their police departments. Most Mayors won't publicly speak the truth, but privately many tell me the most effective way to reduce crime is to reform Federal and state labor laws.

The Wall Street Journal,
9-7:(A)12.

Thomas J. Scotto
President, National Association
of Police Organizations

3

[Criticizing House members who voted against having President Clinton's crime bill considered]: This action can only be described as an assault on the law-enforcement community. Without the aid and resources contained in this bill, we will be forced to continue [to] fight the war on crime with limited manpower, substandard equipment and outdated laws.

At National Association
of Police Organizations
convention, Minneapolis, Minn.,
Aug. 12/The New York Times,
8-13:8.

Bob Scully
Executive director,
National Association
of Police Organizations

4

[Carjacking is] part of a trend of more violence in relation to crime. Years ago, the person [stealing your car] would be happy just to get the car and would want to avoid confrontation. Now violence seems to accompany crime more. There is an element of people out there who just don't care.

The Washington Post, 4-2:(A)1.

Brian Sheridan
Deputy Assistant Secretary
for Drug Enforcement,
Department of Defense
of the United States

5

[On the scaling-back of the military's efforts to fight drug trafficking]: We are not backing away. What we are doing is fine-tuning the whole effort. We had a program that was fat, that was unfocused and that had no major goals or objectives. Now it's lean and can be more effective again . . . Somewhere along the line, people began to think that if the military gets into the act, we will stop the flow of drugs into the United States flatly. That is not going to happen. We can help law-enforcement agencies. But demand for drugs is too high.

Los Angeles Times, 4-2:(A)14.

Wesley Skogan
Professor of political science
and urban affairs,
Northwestern University

6

[On serious crime committed by juveniles]: It's a combination of bravado, hopelessness, access to firepower and the allure of the drug market.

USA Today, 7-25:(A)1.

D. Brooks Smith
Judge, United States
District Court for the
Western District of Pennsylvania

1

Can anybody sincerely look back over the last 10 years and honestly say that the increase in Federal prosecutions has resulted in a dramatic drop in crime? We've seen dramatic increases in the number of prison cells, but what else do we have to show for it?

U.S. News & World Report,
3-28:37.

Andrew L. Sonner
State's Attorney for
Montgomery County, Md.

2

[Criticizing the proposed "three-time loser" legislation that would require life imprisonment for repeat violent felons]: It hasn't been shown in the last 12 years that imprisoning more people is solving our [crime] problem. There's a huge price tag on it, and you can't build these prisons overnight . . . We'll be getting a lot of punishment out of it but not much crime prevention.

Los Angeles Times, 1-25:(A)24.

Dewey R. Stokes
President,
Fraternal Order of Police

3

Every time a police officer dies in the line of duty, it strikes at the heart of society.

USA Today, 5-13:(A)3.

Randolph Stone
Director, Mandel Legal Aid Clinic,
University of Chicago Law School

4

There is a distressing trend to make the juvenile justice system more like the adult criminal-justice system, to make it more of a punitive model. The rationale seems to be to treat children more like adults because of the perception that they are just little criminals. There is little recognition that it is essentially an adult responsibility when kids are engaging in crimes.

The Christian Science Monitor,
5-19:2.

Jerome Storch
Professor of law and police science,
John Jay College of Criminal Justice

5

[On domestic violence]: There's this thing in the back of the [cops'] mind that it's "a domestic matter," not criminal activity . . . If there's a minor assault, are you going to make an arrest just because it's "a domestic crime?" Then if you take it to court and the judge says, "This is minor," it's dismissed. If you place mandates on the police [to take domestic violence more seriously], you must place them [also] on the courts.

Newsweek, 7-4:32.

Clarence Thomas
Associate Justice,
Supreme Court of the United States

6

An effective criminal-justice system—one that holds people accountable for harmful conduct—simply cannot be sustained under conditions where there are boundless excuses for violent behavior and no moral authority for the state to punish. If people know that they are not going to be held accountable because of a myriad of excuses, how will our society be able to influence behavior and provide incentives to follow the law? How can we teach future generations right from wrong if the idea of criminal responsibility is riddled with exceptions and our governing institutions and courts lack moral self-confidence? A society that does not hold someone accountable for harmful behavior can be viewed as condoning—or even worse, endorsing—such conduct.

Before Federalist Society
and Manhattan Institute,
Washington, D.C., May 16/
The Wall Street Journal, 5-26:(A)14.

Jeremy Travis
Deputy Commissioner
of Legal Matters, New York (N.Y.)
Police Department

1

[On plans to expand and make easier the use of police officers to control public nuisance matters such as panhandling, graffiti, street prostitution, noise, etc.]: What I see as the significance of this strategy is we are empowering precinct commanders to take aggressive and sustained action against a persistent quality-of-life condition and in many ways the prostitution initiative is emblematic of that policy. In quality-of-life [matters], the effective response is a sustained response.

New York, N.Y., July 5/
The New York Times,
7-6:(A)13.

Vaughn R. Walker
Judge, United States District Court
for the Northern District of California

2

[Saying currently illegal drugs should be decriminalized]: I make no bones about my personal view that the best course of action for us to take is exactly the same course of action we took after Prohibition [of alcohol], and that is decriminalization . . . (As a judge,] when you're called upon to impose extremely lengthy sentences [for drug offense], you begin to ask yourself whether what you are doing makes any sense.

Interview, San Francisco, Calif./
The New York Times, 3-4:(B)16.

Pete Wilson
Governor of California (R)

3

For some vicious criminals, three strikes [three violent felonies and they're sentenced to life in prison] is two too many. For those who commit forcible rape, who molest a child, or devastate a community through arson, the first offense should be the last . . . [And] we cannot let criminals out

early because they've done a good job folding shirts in the prison laundry.

State of the State address,
Sacramento, Calif., Jan. 5/
USA Today, 1-6:(A)3.

Jay Winsten
Associate dean,
Harvard School of Public Health

4

[On the increase in violent crime among young people]: Yesterday's adolescent fist fight is today's adolescent shootout. Yesterday's black eye and injured pride is today's gaping exit wound with massive injuries. It's casting a pall of fear over the lives of American children.

The New York Times, 5-16:(C)11.

Tom Wyld
Spokesman, National Rifle Association

5

[Criticizing a proposed ban on assault-type weapons, which he says are not all that different from many hunting and target-shooting guns]: You can take a duck gun or a deer gun or any pistol and fire a lot of shots in rapid succession, or you can do the same with an assault-type weapon. The real question is not about guns but whether or not you're a criminal on the loose.

The New York Times, 5-5:(A)14.

Lewis Yablonsky
Professor of sociology and criminology,
California State University, Northridge

6

[On new technological devices, such as robots, designed to help police fight crime with less risk to themselves]: Police officers tend to be more rigid, especially as they get older, in terms of innovation. [But] most cops don't want to shoot or get shot . . . I think that the more mechanical intervention we can develop, the better.

Los Angeles Times, 7-23:(A)25.

Edwin Zedlewski
Economist,
National Institute of Justice

1

[On chronic repeat offenders]: We know these people exist, but we are terrible at guessing who these people are. For every one person you lock up, you may miss one. Some of the worst repeat offenders are smart enough to avoid the system and never get caught. It is extraordinarily difficult to separate these people out.

The Washington Post,
1-24:(A)4.

Les Aspin
Secretary of Defense
of the United States

1

We've made historic progress in opening up opportunities for women in all of the [military] services. Expanding the roles for women in the military is the right thing to do, and it's also the smart thing to do.

News conference,
Washington, D.C., Jan. 13/
The New York Times,
1-14:(A)10.

Norman R. Augustine
Chairman,
Martin Marietta Corporation

2

[On the idea that, with the cutbacks in military spending, defense-industry firms should look for other lines of business to go into]: I'm not the least bit optimistic about the future success of the defense industry moving far afield from the things it does best. Just as you wouldn't expect the world's foremost maker of toothpaste to be able to put a man on the moon, why should we expect companies that put spacecraft on the moon to be able to sell toothpaste?

August/
Los Angeles Times,
9-1:(D)1.

3

[On consolidation and mergers in the defense industry due to government defense-spending cuts]: Three full factories are better than six that are half full . . . These are Darwinian times in our industry. The failure to change is the failure to survive.

U.S. News & World Report,
9-12:74.

Martin Binkin
Analyst, Brookings Institution

4

[On recent incidents of "friendly-fire" accidents and other scandals in the armed forces]: I will admit things haven't been going the military's way since the Persian Gulf war. If there is a problem, it's human error . . . There is the possibility that military personnel tend to be more distracted these days.

USA Today, 4-15:(A)3.

Dennis C. Blair
Rear Admiral, United States Navy

5

When the [military] budgets come down, it makes us more inventive. The trouble is that, with a few exceptions, we don't reward efficiency and innovation. We haven't institutionalized it.

The New York Times,
7-5:(A)7.

Harold Blot
Lieutenant General,
and Chief of Aviation,
United States Marine Corps

6

[Lamenting cutbacks in Marine Corps flight training due to budget constraints]: Aviation is a very perishable skill. You have to fly or you lose that skill.

U.S. News & World Report,
10-10:35.

Jeremy M. Boorda
Admiral, United States Navy;
Commander, Southern Forces,
North Atlantic Treaty Organization

7

Forces won't stay ready if you deploy them too much [in peacetime]. Six months is an arduous amount of duty; it's a long time away from home if you have a family.

U.S. News & World Report,
2-28:38.

WHAT THEY SAID IN 1994

Jeremy M. Boorda
Admiral, United States Navy;
Chief of Naval Operations

1

[Arguing against the downsizing of the Navy, given its responsibilities around the world]: We had a tactic that said if we get little real quick, we will be able to keep the money [for research and development of future Naval equipment]; and even though we will have some pain today as we are getting littler, the gain we will have in the not-too-distant future is worth it . . . [But] given these risks [hot spots around the world where the Navy has been required to dispatch ships], it is time for us to go back and look and make sure that we do not get too small so that we drive our people and ships too hard.
Interview/The New York Times,
11-15:(A)10.

Arthur Cebrowski
Vice Admiral, United States Navy;
Director, Command, Control,
Communication and Computers,
Department of Defense
of the United States

2

[Saying battlefield information technology will become more and more important as the size of the military shrinks]: Many of us are convinced that the information domain is the future battlefield. These are things you must do if you're going to get smaller.
U.S. News & World Report,
10-24:37.

Bill Clinton
President of the United States

3

One of the deepest transformations within the trans-Atlantic community over the past half-century occurred because the armed forces of our respective nations trained, studied and marched through their careers together. It is not only the compatibility of our weapons, but the camaraderie of our warriors that provide the sinews behind our mutual-security guarantees and our best hope for peace.
Speech, Brussels, Belgium,
Jan. 9/The New York Times,
1-10:(A)4.

4

[On his ordering the continuation of draft registration]: While tangible military requirements alone do not currently make a mass call-up of American young men likely, there are three reasons I believe we should maintain both the SSS and the draft registration requirement. [First, registration serves as] a hedge against unforeseen threats and is a relatively low-cost "insurance policy" against our underestimating the maximum level of threat we expect our armed forces to face. [Second, ending registration now] could send the wrong signal to our potential enemies who are watching for signs of U.S. resolve. [Third, it is important] to maintain the link between the all-volunteer force and the society at-large. The armed forces must also know that the general population stands behind them, committed to serve, should the preservation of our national security so require.
May 18/Los Angeles Times,
5-19:(A)21.

5

[On his being Commander-in-Chief of the armed forces even though he never served in the military and successfully sought to avoid the draft during the Vietnam war]: President [Ronald] Reagan didn't have conventional military service in World War II. And it didn't stop him from being an effective Commander-in-Chief. [Most Americans] were united in what we thought about World War II . . . We were divided in what we thought about Vietnam.
Voice of America radio interview,
May 27/USA Today,
6-3:(A)4.

(BILL CLINTON)

1

[Saying he wants to increase military spending by $25-billion over the next six years]: I have pledged that . . . our military will remain the best-trained, best-equipped, the best fighting force on earth. We ask much of our military, and we owe much to them.

Speech, Washington, D.C./
USA Today, 12-2:(A)2.

Eliot Cohen
Military historian,
Advanced School of
International Studies,
Johns Hopkins University

2

[On the recent "friendly-fire" shooting down of two U.S. helicopters by U.S. warplanes on patrol over Iraq]: If you have forces operating intensively with live ammunition, with complex systems, [when] there's adrenalin flowing, then this sort of thing is going to happen and you shouldn't expect anything different.

U.S. News & World Report,
4-25:28.

Walter Cronkite
Former anchor, CBS News

3

[On news coverage of the military during wartime]: I do not agree, necessarily, with my colleagues who are all for live battlefield coverage, now that we have the capability in television. I don't think that's practical. You've got to have military security. I can't imagine having a live camera behind our own lines transmitting to a satellite that can be intercepted. What might appear to be innocent to a civilian cameraman could be terribly interesting to the opposing general. I think we must have censorship. But what must be provided are facilities for the press to be present at all times, under all circumstances. Then the material that the press gathers goes through a censoring process.

And if that is operating efficiently and well, and with proper civilian monitoring, there's no reason material can't be released almost simultaneously with the shooting. But we've got to have the record.

Interview, New York, N.Y./
American Heritage,
December:50.

Ronald V. Dellums
United States Representative,
D-California

4

[Calling for a smaller military budget]: Do we need the forces to fight and win two wars simultaneously on two fronts? Is that more a political statement than a military reality? There can still be [an economic] "peace dividend." The question is whether we have the political will to do it.

The New York Times,
2-8:(A)13.

Robert J. Dole
United States Senator, R-Kansas

5

The one place [President Clinton] has cut [the budget] drastically is precisely the wrong place: national security—slashed to the lowest levels since before Pearl Harbor. History tells us, and many of us know firsthand, that America cannot afford to have a hollow military.

Broadcast address to the nation,
Washington, D.C., Jan. 25/
Los Angeles Times, 2-26:(A)18.

Newt Gingrich
United States Representative,
R-Georgia

6

[On the recent incident in which U.S. fighters mistakenly shot down two U.S. helicopters over Iraq]: It's a symptom I think of the decay that has set in because the Clinton defense budgets are sim-

(NEWT GINGRICH)

ply much too low for the kind of activities that his Administration seems to want to go on all over the planet. As the force shrinks, we've got to be more careful with how you use it. How many of these flights do they think they can make simultaneously?

USA Today, 4-15:(A)3.

Patrick Glynn
Scholar,
American Enterprise Institute

1

[Criticizing Senator Jesse Helms's remark that President Clinton is not up to being Commander-in-Chief]: That's a mistake. You may dislike Clinton, you may hate Clinton. But he is the Commander-in-Chief and there is a real limit as to how far you want to go to weaken a President. He still has to conduct foreign policy. He still may have to order troops into battle.

Nov. 18/The New York Times,
11-19:9.

Barry M. Goldwater
Former United States Senator,
R-Arizona

2

The thing that worries me [about the military] right now is [President] Clinton. I don't think he understands the military. And I don't think the people around him understand the military. And evidently, they have no real compunction against cutting the military . . . If a country wanted to go to war with us, we better be ready, because we might not win the next war. It worries the hell out of me.

Interview, Phoenix, Ariz./
The Washington Post,
7-28:(C)2.

John Harbison
Aerospace-industry specialist,
Booz, Allen & Hamilton

3

[On whether the sweeping Republican Congressional victory in the just-held national elections will affect defense spending]: The forces driving down the defense budget transcend politics. The world is the same as it was yesterday [before the election]; the threat is the same as it was yesterday. The most immediate impact of the change will not be on the budget but as [Congressional] committee heads change. Agendas will change and decisions may be delayed during the transition.

Nov. 9/The New York Times,
11-10:(C)4.

Richard D. Hearney
General and Assistant Commandant,
United States Marine Corps

4

[On the future of high technology in the armed forces]: The technology needs to be transferred down to the individual soldier, sailor and marine. We are going to have to concentrate on *them*, not just this high-tech "I can see everything within the 200-mile-by-200-mile-area." One, I do not know whether that is achievable. I also do not think we could pay for it even if it were achievable.

The New York Times,
12-12:(A)8.

Jesse Helms
United States Senator,
R-North Carolina

5

[On whether he thinks President Clinton is "up to the job" of being Commander-in-Chief]: You ask an honest question; I'll give you an honest answer. No, I do not. And neither do the people

(JESSE HELMS)

in the armed forces . . . Just about every military man who writes to me [says President Clinton is not fit for the job].

Broadcast interview,
Washington, D.C./
"Evans & Novak,"
CNN-TV, 11-18.

1

[Saying President Clinton has angered many servicemen because of his military policies]: Mr. Clinton better watch out if he comes down here [to North Carolina's military bases]. He'd better have a bodyguard.

Broadcast interview,
Washington, D.C./
"Evans & Novak,"
CNN-TV, 11-18.

John D. Holum
Director, Arms Control and
Disarmament Agency
of the United States

2

[Saying President Clinton's decision to extend the U.S. nuclear-weapons test moratorium into next year is a way to encourage other countries to join in a test-ban treaty]: A CTB will strengthen the global norm against the proliferation of nuclear weapons. It will also constrain the qualitative development of nuclear weapons in nuclear-weapons states and help to limit further nuclear-weapons capability in proliferant states.

The Washington Post,
3-16:(A)16.

3

Dangers from chemical weapons are aggravated by the production and potential proliferation of ballistic missiles that can hurl a chemical-weapons warhead hundreds of miles. [Chemical weapons are called] the poor man's nuclear bomb. [And] unlike the nuclear threshold, the chemical-weapons threshold has proved all to easy to cross.

At Congressional hearing,
Washington, D.C., March/
The Washington Post,
4-11:(A)20.

Andrew F. Krepinevich
Director,
Defense Budget Project

4

[Criticizing Chief of Naval Operations Admiral Jeremy Boorda's desire to curtail the downsizing of the Navy's fleet]: Boorda is robbing from the future to cover the near term. You have a Navy that is talking about adding ships to its base. Meanwhile, the Defense Department admits it has a budget shortfall of somewhere between $40-billion to $50-billion for the next five years, and others say the shortfall is even larger.

The New York Times,
11-15:(A)10.

Clyde MacDonald
Legislative Consultant,
Task Force on Defense Conversion,
California State Assembly

5

[On the defense industry's attempts to convert to other businesses because of government military-spending cuts]: Converting to a new industry is very difficult. You have to determine a need, develop a market . . . What are you going to do, compete with Toyota [or] go up against Dow Chemical?

The Christian Science Monitor,
2-17:8.

Angela Manos
Major, and strategist
for the Chief of Staff,
United States Army

1

Women are part of the Army now . . . When people see we want to do our jobs, don't want any preferential treatment, we're part of the team.
USA Today, 7-28:(A)11.

Merrill A. McPeak
General and Chief of Staff,
United States Air Force

2

[Saying he has doubts about the U.S. military currently having sufficient resources to fight and win two simultaneous wars]: I have a tough time thinking we could fight two Koreas or two Vietnams in the middle years of this decade . . . There is a risk factor.
March 15/The Washington Post,
3-16:(A)6.

Donald Nelson
Former Chairman,
War Production Board
of the United States (1942-1944)

3

The American war-production job [in World War II] was probably the greatest collective achievement of all time. It makes the seven wonders of the ancient world look like the doodlings of a small boy on a rainy Saturday afternoon.
Time, 6-13:48.

William A. Owens
Admiral, United States Navy;
Vice Chairman, Joint Chiefs of Staff

4

[On cut-backs in defense spending]: Elements of our military are being particularly pressed because of real-world contingencies and crises . . . We have commitments for forces in the event we

have a full-blown major regional contingency, so you have to keep those forces in mind as you make commitments [to] these various [small] crises around the world.
Interview/
U.S. News & World Report,
7-25:22,23.

5

[Calling for the development of more high technology for the armed forces]: It is not, as some people think, just a bit of software here or a little bit of communications here. It is the system of systems that can come together in about 5 to 10 years.
Interview/
The New York Times,
12-12:(A)8.

William J. Perry
Secretary of Defense
of the United States

6

[On the idea that when U.S. military force is used, it should be applied overwhelmingly, or it should not be used at all]: I support that point of view, but that's not a full answer to the question. You can still entertain, and indeed we have entertained, in every war we've fought since the Second World War, limited political objectives . . . Therefore, you have to tailor your military power to achieving those objectives.
Interview/
The Washington Post,
4-7:(A)8.

7

[On the assignment of women on board the aircraft carrier *Dwight D. Eisenhower*]: It's past the experiment stage. It's working, and it's working well . . . I commend each of [the crew] for your maturity, your competence and your can-do attitude in tackling this truly historic first. You have set high standards for all of those who follow you

(WILLIAM J. PERRY)

... There's no reason why [assigning women] can't be done, and indeed it will be done, on board all the other surface ships of the Navy.

To crew on board the Eisenhower,
June 26/Los Angeles Times,
6-27:(A)12.

1

[On "prepositioning," a strategy that calls for military equipment and supplies to be already in position in an area of possible combat so that personnel can be dispatched there quickly in the event of an emergency]: Prepositioning works. It is the key to the ability to respond rapidly with ground combat forces.

News conference,
Camp Doha, Kuwait, Oct. 15/
The Washington Post,
10-17:(A)11.

Patricia Schroeder
United States Representative,
D-Colorado

2

[Saying she is disappointed in the lack of more serious punishment for those involved in the Navy's 1991 Tailhook sex scandal]: I am very troubled. I think the message of this is justice in the Navy is for the Admirals, by the Admirals and of the Admirals.

Broadcast interview/
"MacNeil-Lehrer NewsHour,"
PBS-TV, 2-15.

John M. Shalikashvili
General, United States Army;
Chairman, Joint Chiefs of Staff

3

[On the accidental shooting down of two U.S. helicopters by American fighters patrolling over Iraq]: This loss cuts deeper, for this tragedy touches the very fabric of our institution [the military], an institution whose code, whose passion is to take care of each other and to protect each other from any danger. And when that goes wrong, as it did 11 days ago, our hearts are doubly heavy and our grief especially deep.

At memorial service,
Fort Myer, Va., April 25/
The New York Times,
4-26:(A)16.

4

[Urging the U.S. to sign the Chemical Weapons Convention that would abolish such weapons, saying it would not leave the U.S. vulnerable in that area]: The U.S. military's ability to deter chemical weapons . . . will be predicated upon a robust chemical-weapons defense and the ability to rapidly bring to bear superior and overwhelming military force.

Before Senate Armed
Services Committee,
Washington, D.C., Aug. 11/
The Washington Post,
8-12:(A)34.

5

[On the use of the armed forces for foreign humanitarian missions]: We have to be very careful that we don't prepare our [military] for humanitarian operations instead of taking the time to prepare to be first and foremost solders, sailors, airmen who are the best at fighting this nation's wars. Because I think then we would be doing a great disservice to this country. Then, in *addition* to that, we must train them to participate in these humanitarian and peacekeeping operations.

Interview/
USA Today, 8-31:(A)11.

6

[Saying his job requires that he be apolitical]: I really try to be and I try not to put myself in a position where someone could say, "Gee, there's a political general." I think I get paid for provid-

(JOHN M. SHALIKASHVILI)

ing the best possible military advice, making sure we do the right things, not because politically they are palatable.

Interview,
Washington, D.C./
USA Today, 9-23:(A)2.

1

[On U.S. military readiness]: We're stretched, but we are not stretched too thin. You have to look at what we are doing in Haiti and how well we are doing it, and that speaks to our readiness and capability. You have to carefully analyze how rapidly and how professionally we moved in response to [Iraqi President] Saddam Hussein's [recent] actions . . . We are better off today in command, control and communications than we were [during 1991's Persian Gulf war]; we are better off in the intelligence field than we were then; we are even better off in strategic lift so we can deliver the forces quicker. I think we are a more capable force, pound for pound, man for man, woman for woman. And we will remain so as long as we still continue to attract and retain the same top-quality men and women that we have with us today.

Interview/
U.S. News & World Report,
10-24:34.

2

[On joint operations among the military services]: We have for the longest time thought of jointness as working the seams between services. That is, if you have a Marine force here and an Army force next to it, there's a joint between the two. And we thought that jointness was really ensuring that we minimize the friction in that joint. But there is a next level of jointness . . . what we saw in our [current] Haiti operation, some of the innovative things, like being able to put infantry brigades on aircraft carriers, which applies only in certain situations, or, for instance, joint medical

systems. A year ago, certainly at the time of [1991's Persian Gulf war], we couldn't even have begun to think like this. It would have been unthinkable.

Interview/
U.S. News & World Report,
10-24:34.

Gordon R. Sullivan
General and Chief of Staff,
United States Army

3

[On concern that the increasing use of the U.S. armed forces in foreign peacekeeping and aid missions will adversely affect their ability as a military fighting force]: We have to strike a balance [between training for war and being used in other activities]. I feel that tension. Everyone has to recognize that the ultimate purpose of the Army is to fight and win the nation's wars.

Interview/
The Washington Post,
7-29:(A)29.

John Taylor
Senior vice president,
Center for Strategic and
International Studies

4

[Criticizing Senator Jesse Helms's remark that President Clinton is not up to being Commander-in-Chief]: Bill Clinton is still our President. He is still our Commander-in-Chief. If you want to go after the policies of the planning, fine. But to go public and to say our President is not fit to be the Commander-in-Chief, I take great exception to that. This man is our President. This nation must have a national-security policy and strategy, and we should not try to undercut it for domestic political reasons.

Nov. 18/
The New York Times,
11-19:9.

John Welch
Vice president for programs,
Electric Boat Division,
General Dynamics Corporation

1

[On the downsizing of defense-industry companies]: The defense industry is going through what the rest of American industry had to go through a decade ago to compete. Only we're not competing with the Japanese. The competition is for dollars in the defense budget.

U.S. News & World Report,
6-27:49.

C.W. "Bill" Young
United States Representative,
R-Florida

2

[Saying U.S. military forces are being committed to too many "peacekeeping" operations around the world]: During the first week of the [current] Haiti operation, I went to Haiti. We were quite surprised to learn how many times these [American troops] had been deployed in one part of the world or another. We feel very strongly about American troops just being given to the United Nations. UN officers do not have near the knowledge or experience in military situations.

USA Today, 12-2:(A)10.

The Economy • Labor

George Ackerloff
Economist,
University of California,
Berkeley

1

The old-style economics is the standard story of perfect competition. The new style of economics makes you focus very heavily on imperfections in markets and their consequences.

The New York Times,
2-9:(C)12.

William T. Archey
Senior vice president for policy
and Congressional affairs,
United States Chamber of Commerce

2

Congress approved NAFTA only because large numbers of small-business owners worked hard to make it unmistakably clear that the agreement was essential to their future competitiveness. Not many issues in the [Chamber of Commerce's] long history have enjoyed as much grass-roots support as NAFTA.

Nation's Business,
January:24.

Richard K. Armey
United States Representative, R-Texas

3

If you want to encourage investment, you do that better by making the tax code neutral rather than coming in the back door and taxing consumption.

USA Today, 11-11:(B)6.

Haley Barbour
Chairman,
Republican National Committee

4

Some people act as if cutting [government] spending is easy. Cutting spending is hard. Cut-

ting spending is harder than raising taxes, because every appropriation has a constituency. Sure there will be battles over spending cuts [in the upcoming Republican-controlled Congress], over how much, over what to cut.

USA Today, 11-18:(A)4.

Kleber Beauvillain
Director,
Hewlett-Packard (France)

5

I think we could phase-in the four-day [work] week, but only if we work more each day. And we would have to be able to make Saturday or Sunday a workday once every three or four months. With that system, everyone would come out ahead. For the customer, the company would be open most of the time. The employee would get three rest days a week and, therefore, a better quality of life. But it's not by reducing time on the job that you attack unemployment. The countries where people work the most hours are the countries that have the least unemployment. The more you work, the more you sell, the more you create jobs. So the problem is not working less but working better.

Interview/
World Press Review,
February:42.

Lloyd N. Bentsen
Secretary of the Treasury
of the United States

6

[On the recent increase in interest rates by the Federal Reserve]: I do have concern for the long-term rates if they continue to climb because those could have an effect on interest-sensitive businesses. I hope that doesn't happen . . . We don't want to experience what happened in the [George] Bush administration, when twice they thought they were out of the recession—and they were not. [But] we cannot sustain what we saw in the fourth

(LLOYD N. BENTSEN)

quarter [of 1993] with a 7 percent growth rate. You had to moderate that . . . or inflation would get out of hand.

To reporters,
Washington, D.C., May 9/
The Washington Post,
5-10:(A)6.

1

The 1992 election hinged on one major issue, and that was the economy, so I'm here with charts to give you the report card. By any standard, this economy is doing well, and we're doing it with inflation under control.

Economic briefing for reporters,
Washington, D.C., July 14/
Los Angeles Times, 7-15:(D)2.

2

[We in the Clinton Administration are} talking about having a responsible [tax-reduction] program, a paid-for program, and not one penny of increase in that [Federal budget] deficit. We've come too far in this budget-deficit-cutting to let the next [Republican-led] Congress turn back and start cooking the books. The President wants to make things fair without cooking those books, and that's the way to do it.

Dec. 16/The New York Times,
12-17:1.

3

[On the Clinton Administration's economic program]: We had a great product. But we were lousy salesmen.

U.S. News & World Report,
12-19:26.

Owen F. Bieber
President, United Automobile Workers
of America

4

[Criticizing the practice of companies permanently replacing striking workers]: To say "per-manently replace"—you might as well say you don't have the right under law to strike, when you have a situation with a shortage of jobs and a large unemployment pool.

Interview, Detroit, Mich./
The New York Times,
1-1:19.

Nancy Birdsall
Executive vice president,
Inter-American Development Bank

5

Growing [economic] inequality isn't a necessary byproduct of [a country's economic] success. If you have the right policies—such as heavy emphasis on universal education—you can have higher growth and lower inequality.

The New York Times, 1-8:17.

Alan S. Blinder
Member,
Council of Economic Advisers
to President of the
United States Bill Clinton;
Vice Chairman-designate,
Federal Reserve Board

6

There is simply no good reason to push the economy beyond its normal capacity and into the inflationary zone; any job gains we enjoyed in the short run would be balanced by job losses later.

At Senate
Banking Committee hearing
on his nomination,
Washington, D.C., May 6/
The Washington Post, 5-7:(C)1.

7

[The economy] is not too hot, not too cold, sort of just right . . . When the [Federal Reserve] is thrust into fine-tuning [the economy], as we are now, and when there are uncertainties, as there are now, you ought to be cautious about how you pull the levers.

Interview, Aug. 2/
USA Today, 8-3:(B).

Norbert Blum
Minister of Labor and
Social Affairs of Germany

1

The cycles of [technological] innovation [in the workplace] become shorter and shorter. Therefore, we have lifelong learning [for employees]. I think it is a false belief that well-trained and qualified people are not endangered by unemployment. In all our jobs we have to be very flexible, and we should be ready to retrain at any time. Retraining is the duty of management.

At international jobs seminar,
Detroit, Mich./
The New York Times, 3-16:(C)2.

David L. Boren
United States Senator, D-Oklahoma

2

A little over a year ago, I think we made a tragic mistake in this country by passing the budget of the United States government for the first time in modern memory totally along a party-line vote—51 votes in the Senate and a tie-breaking vote, all from one party [the Democrats]. The same happened in the House of Representatives. And what a tragedy that is for the country, because . . . the need to bring down the deficits of this country will take a long, sustained joint partnership on the part of all the American people. While we have made some progress toward getting the deficit down, the job is far from over. The [Clinton] Administration's own figures indicate that with additions to the deficit that are anticipated under the budgets we have passed, shortly into the next century we will reach the point in which all of the private savings, 100 percent of the private savings in this country, will be used just to pay the interest on the national debt. That will mean that our economic growth in this country is imperiled and our future will be subject to the decisions of investors in other countries, not in this country.

Before the Senate,
Washington, D.C., Aug. 11/
The New York Times, 8-12:(A)11.

Michael J. Boskin
Professor of economics,
Stanford University;
Former Chairman,
Council of Economic Advisers
to the President of the
United States (George Bush)

3

[Criticizing President Clinton's economic program]: This is the mirror image of Reaganomics. In 1981, [then-President Ronald] Reagan tried to cut taxes to put pressure on Congress to reduce spending. Now, in 1994, Clinton is trying to build new programs into the budget that ultimately Americans will get hooked on, will require new spending and will put pressure on Congress to raise taxes.

Los Angeles Times,
1-29:(A)16.

4

The [President] Clinton budget plan has almost nothing to do with the [current economic] recovery. Clinton inherited an economy doing much better than many people realized and certainly better than what he let on during the [1992 Presidential-election] campaign.

Los Angeles Times,
1-29:(A)16.

Lawrence Bossidy
Chairman, AlliedSignal, Inc.

5

[On the passage of NAFTA earlier this year]: It's too early to declare victory, but we know it's a big success. The auto exports they said would occur have happened. There's a lot of export business. The trade surplus is up. I don't think there's any question but that it's a good thing. It also will be interesting to get the rest of Latin America in that category. It will take some time, but I think it will happen.

Interview, July 18/
USA Today, 7-19:(B)4.

Stephen G. Breyer
Judge,
United States Court of Appeals
for the First Circuit;
Associate Justice-designate,
Supreme Court of the United States

1

I wrote a book review not too long ago in which I tried, because it was written about the economics of AIDS . . . [to explain there's] an important difference between what you might call classical economic regulation, like airlines or trucks, and the regulation involving health, safety and the environment. And I said, "As to the first, trucking, airlines, it isn't really surprising that economics may help; it isn't the whole story, but it tells a significant amount of the story because our object there is to get low prices for consumers, and maybe economics can help us." [But] when you start talking about health, safety and the environment, the role is much more limited, because there no one would think that economics is going to tell you how much you want to spend helping the life of another person. If in fact people want to spend a lot of money to help save earthquake victims in California, who could say that was wrong? And what I ended up there saying is that in this kind of area, it's probably John Donne, the poet, who has more to tell us about what to do than Adam Smith, the economist. That's a decision for Congress to make reflecting the values of people.
At Senate Judiciary Committee
hearing on his nomination,
Washington, D.C., July 12/
The New York Times, 7-13:(A)8.

George Bush
Former President
of the United States

2

[On NAFTA, which originated in the Bush Administration, and was recently passed during the current Clinton Administration]: NAFTA was our baby. Clinton, once he got through trying to get by the [anti-NAFTA] labor and environmental

crowd, worked like hell for it. Give him credit. But it was our deal.
Interview, Houston, Texas/
Time, 3-28:32.

Robert C. Byrd
United States Senator, D-West Virginia

3

[On new proposals by Republicans and Democrats to cut taxes]: [The] drag racing by both parties in an effort to cross the tax-cut finish line first with the most is disheartening and will, I fear, result in a demolition derby.
The New York Times,
12-20:(A)14.

Ron Carey
President, International
Brotherhood of Teamsters

4

My predecessors backed anti-union, reactionary [U.S] Presidents like [Richard] Nixon and [Ronald] Reagan and [George] Bush in hopes those Presidents would keep those former union presidents out of jail. That didn't work for long. But my administration didn't need or want such help. We supported the Democrat, [President] Bill Clinton, along with the rest of organized labor, because he is at least trying to do more for workers and unions. I appreciate the story that asking working people if they were better off after four years under Bush is like asking whether the chickens are better off under the leadership of [fast-food chicken mogul] Colonel Sanders. We are no longer going to be chickens.
Interview/Los Angeles Times,
7-17:(M)3.

5

I was elected because our members were sick of corruption—which is what the average person walking down the street thinks when you say Teamster. I've established an ethical-practices committee that investigates members' complaints

(RON CAREY)

of corruption. I've put more than 30 locals in temporary trusteeship so the members could help correct wrongdoing and undemocratic practices. That should help change the public's view of us. But my opponents don't seem to want that. They want this union back so bad they could care less if they destroy the union in the process.

Interview/Los Angeles Times,
7-17:(M)3.

John H. Chafee
United States Senator,
R-Rhode Island

1

It's far more traumatic to go to a radical revision in a tax system than to stick with what you've got.

U.S. News & World Report,
12-12:48.

Bill Clinton
President of the United States

2

[On his Administration's plans for retraining the unemployed to help them get jobs]: The unemployment-insurance system was designed, and functions primarily, as a system for helping tide people over until they get their old jobs back. But the old jobs aren't coming back, even though we're in a [economic] recovery.

At "What's Working"
employment conference,
Washington, D.C./
The Christian Science Monitor,
2-4:1.

3

[On his new Federal budget, which was just submitted to Congress]: If the Congress adopts it, it will keep the deficit coming down, it will keep interest rates down, it will send a clear signal to the Fed [-eral Reserve] and to the rest of the world

that we mean business and that the investment climate will continue. These lower interest rates, if they can be maintained, will save over $20-billion in deficit in the next year's budget alone and over $150-billion in the next five years.

To business people,
Houston, Texas, Feb. 7/
The New York Times,
2-8:(A)12.

4

A lot of the opposition to NAFTA really had nothing to do with the terms of the agreement, but instead had to do with the incredible anxiety that working people felt [because they believed] that their jobs and their incomes and their families weren't really all that important to their employers.

Presenting Malcolm Baldrige
National Quality Award,
before executives and employees
of Eastman Chemical Co.
and Ames Rubber Corp.,
Washington, D.C./
Nation's Business, March:8.

5

In every wealthy country now, there is difficulty creating new jobs. In every advanced economy now, there are problems regarding work with higher wages, year in and year out, and many, many people are stuck with wages that do not go up, even when they work harder. And we are looking for answers to unlock this.

Detroit, Mich., March 13/
The Washington Post, 3-14:(A)7.

6

We have to restore confidence in people that if they do acquire the skills they need and help their country move forward, they'll be rewarded, not punished. We have got to make our people believe that productivity can be a source of gain, not pain. Throughout the whole 20th century, every time we had productivity in one area that meant that fewer people could do more work in that area,

(BILL CLINTON)

technological changes were always creating more jobs in another area. That is still true today, but the problem is there has been an explosion of productivity in manufacturing and now it's in the service industry. There is a great insecurity that productivity, for the first time, may be a job threat, not a job creator.

At international jobs conference,
Detroit, Mich., March 14/
The New York Times, 3-15:(C)5.

1

Let us begin by recognizing the fundamental reality that private enterprise, not government action, is the engine of economic growth and job creation. Our vision of the good society depends as much on a thriving private sector as anything else.

At international jobs conference,
Detroit, Mich., March 14/
The Washington Post, 3-15:(D)6.

2

Too many Republicans would say that free trade today always equals economic growth. Well, it can, but only if we have a comprehensive national strategy to promote that kind of growth. Some Democrats would say that free trade today always equals exporting jobs and lowering wages. Well, it sure can if you don't have a comprehensive economic strategy to maintain a high-wage, high-growth economy.

Speech/The Atlantic Monthly,
May:76.

3

[Approving the Federal Reserve's recent increase in interest rates]: After all, what we want for America is steady, sustained growth, where we get more jobs and we keep them for as long as possible. We don't want to put the American people on another rollercoaster where they go way up and then they turn around and go way down. If we can keep steady, sustained growth, that's what we want. And I think that's where we are now.

Interview, Washington, D.C.,
May 18/Los Angeles Times,
5-19:(A)16.

4

We have to move from coping with [economic] crises to planning for prosperity. In other words, we have to lay the foundation for the 21st-century economy, one in which change will be the order of the day, and the real question will be whether change is our friend or our enemy . . . For a decade, [the U.S.'s] out-of-control budget deficit robbed us of the standing to press our [foreign] partners to act. Well, now, instead of having the biggest deficit in the G-7, we have the smallest.

At U.S. Dept. of Commerce,
Washington, D.C., July 5/
The New York Times, 7-6:(A)5.

5

We are about now a year from the time when Congress passed our economic recovery plan. I remember then that our opponents said if that plan passed, the sky would fall, unemployment would go up, the [Federal budget] deficit would explode. Well, they were wrong. Look at the facts: We cut $255-billion in spending, raised tax rates on only 1.2 percent of the wealthiest Americans, cut taxes for 15 million working families of modest incomes, made 90 percent of our small businesses eligible for a tax cut and 20 million Americans eligible to refinance their college loans at lower interest rates. Now the deficit is going down three years in a row for the first time since Harry Truman was President. We've got almost 4 million new jobs, very low inflation, a 1.5 percent drop in unemployment. There were other skeptics later who said the sky would fall if we passed the North American Free Trade Agreement. They, too, were wrong. We can see this year that automobile sales, for example, to Mexico are growing at five times the rate of last year, and our trade with Mexico is grow-

(BILL CLINTON)

ing more rapidly than that with any other country. And while I know an awful lot of people are still hurting, the road ahead looks good. According to *Fortune* magazine, for the first time in a decade, all 50 states will expand their private economies next year. Let me say that again: For the first time in a decade, all 50 states will experience economic growth next year.

News conference,
Washington, D.C., Aug. 3/
The New York Times, 8-4:(A)10.

1

When the Federal Reserve raised [interest] rates this week, the Chairman, Mr. [Alan] Greenspan, said that he thought that this would be sufficient for a time [to head off inflation]. The truth is that our economic strategy has produced more rapid growth than they [the Federal Reserve] thought it would and then we thought it would. We are even doing better than we thought we would. We've got over four million jobs already in the last year and a half, and we've got rapid growth in the economy, dramatic new investments in the private sector, so they [the Federal Reserve] are worried about inflation. When it is apparent to me that the drag on the economy will be more about slowing the economy down than stopping inflation, I will do what I can to influence that [interest-rate] policy. But I think my policy of letting [the Federal Reserve] do their job and having me do mine has worked out rather well.

News conference,
Washington, D.C., Aug. 19/
The New York Times,
8-20:10.

2

[On the pending new GATT trade initiative which the Senate will vote on in a couple of months]: Every serious economic study of GATT has estimated that it will create hundreds of thousands of high-paying American jobs over the next decade and ultimately add between $100 [-billion] and $200-billion to our [GDP] every single year.

At U.S. Treasury Department,
Washington, D.C./
Los Angeles Times, 9-30:(A)20.

3

For too many of our people, [foreign] trade still appears to be a gale-force wind [threatening U.S. jobs]. [But] if we continue to work together on this trade issue . . . we can agree on ways to help all our people make their way in the new global economy . . . [GATT] is the key link to free trade, more open society and economic growth all around the world. For the United States, it means both free and fair trade.

At Georgetown University,
Nov. 10/USA Today 11-11:(B)6.

4

I ran for President to restore the American dream and to prepare the American people to compete and win in the new American economy. For too long too many Americans have worked longer for stagnant wages and less security. For two years, we pursued an economic strategy that has helped to produce over five million new jobs. But even though the economic statistics are moving up, most of our living standards aren't. It's almost as if some Americans are being punished for their productivity in this new economy. We've got to change that. More jobs aren't enough; we have to raise incomes.

Broadcast address to the nation,
Washington, D.C., Dec.15/
The New York Times, 12-16:(A)12.

Stan Collender
Director of Federal budget policy,
Price Waterhouse, CPA's

5

[On the use of euphemisms by government officials to describe economic policies the public might not like to hear]: The politics of the [Federal] budget are so difficult because nobody wants

(STAN COLLENDER)

to call a spade a spade or admit to a tax increase or a spending increase. That is why we have all these euphemisms and budget sleight-of-hand . . . People here in Washington who follow these things know what they are, but the regular voter—the ordinary citizen who doesn't follow it day to day—can be easily fooled . . . Where the Republicans never liked to admit to higher taxes, the Democrats have to find new ways to describe spending increases without admitting what they are doing.

Los Angeles Times, 3-27:(D)2.

Richard T. Curtin
Director of survey on consumer confidence conducted by Consumer Research Center, University of Michigan

1

There was a time last year when people were very apprehensive that we would slip back into recession, and that apprehension is [now] gone, although no one is expecting a boom or the prosperity that existed in earlier times. Now when our confidence index rises, it does so on the expectation that the economy will continue to expand in the style of this decade, which means slowly . . . People clearly have a different point of reference. This is a new age of diminished expectations, and in the context of diminished expectations, we are in a relatively positive period. The indexes reflect that optimism, but no one expects a quick and substantial return to the good times people enjoyed in the past.

The New York Times, 3-30:(C)2.

Robert DiClemente
Economist, Salomon Brothers, investment bankers

2

Job growth beyond 200,000 a month is a trajectory that will blow us through full employment. Bondholders ask, "What is your job growth forecast; how do you see it for the next few months?"

If you tell them 250,000 a month, they walk away saying there is going to be trouble with inflation. They are not thinking of it as jobs, but as more income, more spending, more demand for scarce resources, more [economic] overheating.

The New York Times, 5-24:(C)6.

Robert J. Dole
United States Senator, R-Kansas

3

[Arguing against a proposed bill that would ban employers from hiring permanent replacements for striking workers]: The bottom line is that our system of collective bargaining has worked well for over half a century, and continues to work well today. But by eliminating the risk factor from strikes, this bill presents employers with an untenable Hobson's choice: shut down the business— close down the factory—or accede to the union's demands, whether those demands are reasonable or not.

Los Angeles Times, 7-13:(A)15.

Stuart E. Eizenstat
United States Ambassador to the European Union

4

In this vast, globalized and fiercely competitive [international] market, where workers are hungry for jobs, those countries which work the longest and hardest will do the best in the long run. If competitiveness is out of line in one place, products will be sourced somewhere else.

The Wall Street Journal, 9-30:(R)4.

James Galbraith
Economist, University of Texas

5

[On the Federal Reserve's increasing interest rates]: [The Fed's actions amount to] a very large tax increase on the middle class. The Fed has offered nothing in the way of a coherent explanation for what they're doing.

U.S. News & World Report, 5-30:47.

(JAMES GALBRAITH)

1

[On the "soft-landing" approach of the Federal Reserve gradually increasing interest rates to head off inflation while keeping the economy afloat]: There is no historical evidence that a [soft landing] will work. There is no case in which the policy was tried and there was a nice tapering off in inflation and a long period of uninterrupted, steady growth. Each time, we got a recession first and a drop in inflation later.

U.S. News & World Report,
8-29:46.

John Kenneth Galbraith
Economist

2

The lesson of the whole post-Keynesian world is that governments are now responsible for economic performance. Any notion that poor performance can't be remedied by the state is a reversion to 19th-century attitudes, which I'm not prepared to accept.

Interview/Mother Jones,
March-April:36.

Richard A. Gephardt
United States Representative,
D-Missouri

3

Having a fetish about a balanced [Federal] budget doesn't reach our primary goal. The balanced budget is not what we seek . . . Our ultimate goal is economic success and happiness on the part of our people. And if the balanced budget each year would serve that goal, then I'd be for it. I don't think it does. I think the American economy sometimes requires an unbalanced budget.

Interview, Washington, D.C./
The Christian Science Monitor,
2-7:8.

4

[Comparing President Clinton's tax-reduction plan with that of the incoming Republican majority in Congress]: What is remarkable is the sharp contrast between the President's agenda—fighting

for working families—and the Republican agenda: forcing more deficit-busting, trickle-down tax cuts for the wealthy.

Dec. 16/The New York Times,
12-17:9.

Henry B. Gonzalez
United States Representative, D-Texas

5

[Criticizing the latest increase in interest rates instituted by the Federal Reserve]: Is the Fed acting in the national interest or chasing its long-held dreams of zero inflation to the detriment of American taxpayers? Once again, [Fed Chairman Alan] Greenspan and the Federal Reserve have mugged America.

Aug. 16/Los Angeles Times,
8-17:(A)24.

Robert Gordon
Economist, Northwestern University

6

The [current increase in consumer and business] borrowing is a sign that people are relaxing and the expansion will stay for a while. And it is a sign that people in most of the country, while they might not be getting raises, are no longer so worried about losing their jobs. That's more important.

The New York Times, 8-3:(C)1.

Al Gore
Vice President of the United States

7

[Saying future trade negotiations should include questions of worker well-being]: The United States realizes that many countries fear that folding labor standards into the world trade context exposes their exports to potential forms of concealed trade restrictions. The United States will resist any effort to convert the issue of improved labor standards into a form of protectionism.

At meeting of Uruguay Round
of General Agreement on Tariffs
and Trade, Marrakesh, Morocco,
April 14/The New York Times,
4-15:(C)1.

Phil Gramm
United States Senator, R-Texas

1

[Saying the current upswing in the economy was under way long before President Clinton took office and therefore he should not be taking credit for it]: In considering President Clinton's gusher of praise for his economic record, we should remember that no modern President's economic program has required less than 18 months to have an impact on the economy.

> *Feb. 14/Los Angeles Times,*
> *2-15:(A)14.*

Alan Greenspan
Chairman, Federal Reserve Board

2

Inflation tends to surface rather late in the business cycle and hence is not a good leading indicator of emerging troubles. By the time inflation pressures are evident, many imbalances that are costly to rectify have already developed and only harsh monetary therapy can restore the financial stability necessary to sustain [economic growth].

> *Before Congressional*
> *Joint Economic Committee,*
> *Washington, D.C., Jan. 31/*
> *The New York Times, 2-1:(C)1.*

3

[On the possibility of the Federal Reserve raising interest rates to head off future inflation]: Such an action would not be taken in order to cut off or limit the economic expansion, but rather to sustain and enhance it. [Because] by the time inflation pressures are evident, many imbalances that are costly to rectify have already developed and only harsh monetary therapy can restore the financial stability necessary to sustain growth. This situation, regrettably, has arisen too often in the past.

> *Before Congressional*
> *Joint Economic Committee,*
> *Washington, D.C./*
> *USA Today, 2-7:(B)2.*

4

Overall . . . this looks like a well-balanced economy. This is looking to me as good as I've seen an economy evolving in a balanced form in a very long period of time. The economy is moving at a fairly respectable pace . . . It could go on for quite a long period of time, provided that inflationary imbalances don't emerge.

> *Before Senate Banking Committee,*
> *Washington, D.C., May 27/*
> *Los Angeles Times, 5-28:(D)1.*

5

[Saying the Federal Reserve will raise interest rates if there is sufficient threat of inflation]: We are looking at a complex economy with a rate of growth which has been extraordinary. If we are simmering down to more long-term, sustainable levels [of growth], that is all to the good. We're trying to get an economy which is balanced over time.

> *Congressional testimony,*
> *Washington, D.C., July 20/*
> *Los Angeles Times, 7-21:(A)16.*

6

Information on [company] behavior and signals from financial and commodity markets may warn about the development or easing of [economic] bottlenecks sooner than . . .unemployment, national income, prices or . . . monetary aggregates.

> *Congressional testimony/*
> *U.S. News & World Report,*
> *8-29:45.*

7

[Saying he does not agree with those who say the U.S. economy's susceptibility to inflation has lessened sufficiently enough to preclude further interest-rate increases by the Federal Reserve]: There is a significant element of truth in these arguments, but these developments are evolutionary, working slowly and incrementally over time. If we ignore experience, we would be taking un-

(ALAN GREENSPAN)

acceptable risks of higher inflation, economic and financial instability and ultimately subpar economic performance over time.

Before Congressional
Joint Economic Committee,
Washington, D.C., Dec. 7/
The New York Times, 12-8:(C)13.

David Halberstam
Pulitzer Prize-winning author
and journalist

1

The country is in the midst of profound economic change. We're going from an essential blue-collar economy and relative easy affluence to a time where we're in an international economy and the blue-collar jobs are disappearing, and where in many homes there is more anxiety, and more and more the middle class depends on education. These are changes that have been going on for decades, but the political consequences are just beginning to surface.

Nov. 9/The New York Times,
11-10:(B)5.

David Hale
Senior economist,
Kemper Financial Services

2

This is the first time since the outbreak of World War I that every nation on this planet has a capitalist economic system or a market-oriented economy whether in place or about to happen. But because of that [and the need for capital that goes along with it], we'll probably have [here in the U.S.] much higher interest rates over the next two or three years.

Time, 8-1:46.

Amos Ilan
Manager of economic trends,
Port Authority of New York
and New Jersey

3

[Saying that while the economy is improving and unemployment in general is going down, a new wave of corporate mergers and restructuring is resulting in more layoffs]: [The irony is that] the two trends are occurring at the same time. The business cycle is working. The economy is starting to pick up. But continued restructuring is taking place, in part because of new business opportunities, which leads to new job losses.

The Christian Science Monitor,
2-25:11.

Edward C. Johnson III
Chairman, Fidelity Investments

4

[On Federal Reserve Chairman Alan Greenspan's recent decision to raise short-term interest rates]: I think Greenspan did the right thing. The question is whether he did it at the right time. Some might say he did it too soon. The rest of us might say he did it later than he should have. I would have been more likely to have criticized him for being too late, rather than too early. I think it has been evident for a while that business has turned around. Easy money is like pouring gasoline on fire. In the beginning, it's wonderful—it makes you warm. But if it starts burning the whole building down, you pay the price later on. But mind you, greater minds than I, with a lot more power, don't agree.

Interview/
Newsweek, 3-14:46.

Mickey Kantor
United States Trade Representative

5

[On those in the European Union who are against the U.S. get-tough policy on trade with Japan and who criticize it as "managed trade"]:

(MICKEY KANTOR)

It's interesting that there have been some voices in the Union that have said our approach is "managed trade." First of all, I'm not sure what managed trade is. Is managed trade when you have a voluntary restraint on automobiles and trucks at 16 percent in Europe, including transplant production? No, because the Europeans did it . . . When *they* do it, that's protecting their markets and making sure it's fair. When *we* do it—the largest open market in the world, who led Bretton Woods and GATT, have kept their markets open since the Second World War, who've led global growth, who have a President [Clinton] who made sure there was an Uruguay Round [of trade negotiations], who made sure there was a NAFTA, who made sure we're trying to open up Japanese markets—*that's* not good enough!

> *At trade conference sponsored by*
> *Economic Strategy Institute,*
> *Washington, D.C., March 9/*
> *The New York Times, 3-10:(C)1.*

1

[On U. S. trade negotiations with Japan]: We have suffered for decades because the American people have not been convinced that Washington will stand up for their interests, especially in trade. And, fairly or unfairly, Japan has become the test case for that view. It is critical that we develop the trust of the American people that what we are doing in pushing for freer trade and more open markets is in their economic interests.

> *Interview, Washington, D. C.,*
> *Oct. 2/The New York Times,*
> *10-3:(C)8.*

Lawrence Katz
Chief Economist,
Department of Labor
of the United States

2

I think we [the U.S.] have traditionally had a system [of unemployment benefits] that gave work-ers a relatively short period of benefits and then allowed them to fall off a cliff; while the Europeans had a system that ignored people for two years or more while they were getting benefits, and they were out of the workforce for such a long period of time that it became difficult for governments to help them readjust. Now, I think all of us recognize the need to find a third way, that we all need to develop early-intervention programs that help get people training and job-placement quickly to keep them employable.

> *Detroit, Mich./*
> *Los Angeles Times, 3-17:(A)9.*

Irwin L. Kellner
Chief economist, Chemical Bank,
New York, N.Y.

3

[Saying the Federal Reserve, worried about future inflation, has raised interest rates too much]: The level of the long-term [Treasury bond] rate is a drag on economic growth. The real world wonders what the Fed has been smoking. Businesses are not raising selling prices, consumers are refusing to pay higher prices and people are worried about their jobs.

> *U.S. News & World Report,*
> *5-30:46.*

Lane Kirkland
President, American Federation
of Labor-Congress
of Industrial Organizations

4

[Saying American business' support of continued MFN trade status for China is for its own self-interest]: I do not believe that American corporations give a tinker's damn about jobs in the United States, and any representations they make about their deep and dying concerns over American jobs ought to be taken with a ton of salt. It's quite clear that the soft underbelly of freedom, American corporate enterprise, is doing its level best to serve the interests of the dictators and the

(LANE KIRKLAND)

totalitarian regime in China . . . There are lobbyists lobbying hard on China's behalf for the sake of their own narrow pocketbook interests and for the right to continue to abuse and exploit labor.

News conference, April 13/
Los Angeles Times, 4-14:(A)7.

1

Just about every major social problem we have today—from our soaring crime rate and the decay of our urban areas to the rise of poverty and homelessness—can be traced to one factor: the decline in the number of decent-paying, entry-level jobs for people of limited skills. Those jobs used to offer immigrants and disadvantaged Americans a ladder up into the middle class—jobs that paid enough for them to raise families and send their kids to college. Today, however, economically disadvantaged Americans have little choice but to accept work, when they can find it, from the expanding sector of employers who have concocted every conceivable method of keeping wages down and workers powerless. And it's all in the name of "competitiveness."

At bakery, confectionery
and tobacco workers convention,
Las Vegas, Nev., July 21/
The Washington Post,
7-28:(A)30.

2

We insist that there are no jobs which natural law ordains as inherently poorly paid and devoid of benefits or security. Before trade-unionism brought civilization to the mines and mills of America, those jobs were just as cheap and just as bad as those in what is now called the "low-paid service sector." Not management enlightenment but trade-unionism made the difference.

At bakery, confectionery
and tobacco workers convention,
Las Vegas, Nev., July 21/
The Washington Post,
7-28:(A)30.

William Klinefelter
Chief lobbyist,
industrial-union department,
American Federation of
Labor-Congress of
Industrial Organizations

3

[Supporting a proposed bill that would ban employers from hiring permanent replacements for striking workers]: This goes right to the heart of what the trade-union movement is all about. This issue is such an emotional one for our members because almost all of them have been on strike at one time or another in their lives.

Los Angeles Times,
7-12:(A)10.

Richard L. Lesher
President, United States
Chamber of Commerce

4

[Applauding the Senate defeat of a proposed bill that would have prevented employers from hiring permanent replacements for striking workers]: This is a major blow to organized labor. [If the legislation had passed, it] would have destroyed the balance of power that has existed for more than 50 years between labor and management.

July 12/Los Angeles Times,
7-13:(A)1.

John Lewis
United States Representative,
D-Georgia

5

[Arguing against a Constitutional amendment requiring a balanced Federal Budget]: We don't want people [in Congress] to get into the habit of voting for [such an amendment]. We shouldn't hide behind the Constitution. If we want to balance the budget, we should have the courage to just do it.

The Washington Post,
3-10:(A)29.

Enrique M. Loaeza
Mexican Consul General
in Los Angeles, Calif.

1

We strongly reject the notion that Mexican immigrants are driven to come [to the U.S.] to have children and to gain access to primary education, emergency health care and citizenship. The demand [in the U.S.] for low-cost labor brings immigrant workers seeking better incomes for their families.

May 26/Los Angeles Times,
5-27:(A)3.

William A. Lovett
Professor,
Tulane University Law School

2

[Arguing against the U.S. joining the new GATT world-trade agreement]: This thing has no flex for the U.S., but everybody else gets lots of flex. It's criminal negligence—dumb, dumb, dumb.

Newsweek, 11-28:40.

Roy MacLaren
Minister of Trade of Canada

3

The great flaw of NAFTA—the black hole at its center—is the continuing absence of a common set of trading rules and procedures that would define a permissible [government] subsidy and establish a harmonized competition policy to replace anti-dumping actions. Anti-dumping is incongruous in a free-trade area. It essentially depends on border controls. But in a free-trade area, there are no commercial borders.

Interview/
The Wall Street Journal,
10-28:(R)12.

Sean McAlinden
Labor economist,
University of Michigan

4

GM won't hire [new workers] because if the market goes into the tank and they've hired 7,000 workers, that could cost them an arm and a leg. [Because of the terms of the current UAW contract,] jobs in the auto industry are basically jobs for life.

The Christian Science Monitor,
9-28:2.

Marvin Miller
Former executive director,
Major League (baseball)
Players Association

5

[On the use of mediators to try to end strikes]: It's hard to estimate [the contribution of a mediator) unless you're at the table, unless you see who the mediator is and what he knows, how he operates. You can make some generalization [that] a mediator is most helpful when the issues are complex and the parties have gotten too close to view them from a different angle. The mediator is least helpful when the parties themselves understand the issues thoroughly and are still at loggerheads.

Aug. 14/USA Today, 8-15:(C)4.

Lawrence Mishel
Co-author, "The State of Working
America 1994-95," sponsored by
Economic Policy Institute

6

Since 1987, inflation-adjusted wages have fallen every year. That includes several years before the recession, the recession and the economic recovery. So this is not cyclical. And it's not caused by technology. If it were, wages of skilled technical workers would have risen. But they've fallen, although not as much as the wages of unskilled workers. The rise of part-time and temporary employment has led to a long-term erosion in ...

wages and opportunities for training and advancement. And don't forget about the vast expansion of low-wage, service-sector employment the past few years. Also, 25 percent of the wage drop is due to the sharp [real] drop in the minimum wage, which has not kept pace with inflation.

Interview/
USA Today, 9-2:(B)3.

Michael Novak
Resident scholar,
American Enterprise Institute

1

The existence of poverty raises systemic questions, such as, How does a nation's economic system contribute to its degree of indigence? In one sense, one of the poorest places on earth is Hong Kong. It has almost no natural resources; it's only a rock. It has a location and a harbor, but because of the structure of its laws and its taxing system, it has become one of the beehives of entrepreneurial activity. The movement of very poor people out of poverty occurs quite rapidly in Hong Kong. And at one point, its gross domestic product was a sizable proportion of the entire product of the People's Republic of China. We've learned that peoples who have very few natural resources but who organize themselves well and have a favorable system of entrepreneurship, invention and organization are able to raise the standard of living in a very short time.

Interview/
Christianity Today, 10-24:30.

David R. Obey
United States Representative,
D-Wisconsin

2

[On the proposed Federal budget, which would necessitate cutting programs and spending]: Due to the current financial constraints, the light at the end of the tunnel [for many Americans] will be turned off until further notice.

May 12/The Washington Post,
5-13:(A)8.

Paul Ostermann
Economist,
Sloan School of Management,
Massachusetts Institute
of Technology

3

[On large job cuts that are continuing at major companies]: AT&T and the other phone companies can't lay off people indefinitely. But when the phone companies stop, then the banks start in and then the retailers do it. The staff cuts migrate from industry to industry and that is why the layoff announcements feel to the public like they are going on indefinitely.

The New York Times,
3-22:(C)4.

Bob Packwood
United States Senator, R-Oregon

4

I'm not even going to consider what tax cuts we're going to do until I see spending cuts that will match them. I am not going to support any tax cuts that are going to widen the deficit, period. I just don't want to see us once again send out tax cuts with a lick and a promise and a hope that the spending cuts are coming later. We somehow never quite seem to get to them.

Broadcast interview/
"Meet the Press,"
NBC-TV, 12-18.

Leon E. Panetta
Director, Federal Office
of Management and Budget

5

If we want to stay on the [Federal budget] deficit-reduction track that we're now embarked on, we've got to begin to address [certain] areas, particularly health care, because health care is the largest culprit in the entitlement programs right now in terms of being out of control.

Feb. 7/The New York Times,
2-8:(A)12.

Ross Perot
Industrialist;
1992 independent
Presidential candidate

1

[Supporting a proposal that Congress be allowed to cut government spending more quickly through bypassing the committee system and having individual members propose cuts in any program]: We have to go through this process, unfortunately, because there's no discipline on spending. We still think that we are the last superpower, that we have all the money in the world. We don't like to look at the instrument panel and see that we're running out of fuel.

News conference,
Washington, D.C., April 21/
The Washington Post,
4-22:(A)22.

Kevin P. Phillips
President, American Political
Research Corporation

2

The structure of an advanced economy has to include a substantial middle class. But you could have a situation where you have the top 4 or 5 or 6 percent with a very disproportionate amount of income, and another 20 or 30 percent that approximate the typical view of the middle class, and then 60 percent below the rest. One of the worst things the United States faces is that it can't generate many more of the jobs that used to enable people with high-school diplomas to become part of the blue-collar middle class. Export industries are succeeding only where they can pay reasonably skilled labor $8 or $9 an hour for jobs that used to pay $13 or $14 an hour, plus benefits. The blue-collar middle class is disappearing.

Interview/
Mother Jones,
March-April:36.

Clyde V. Prestowitz, Jr.
President,
Economic Strategy Institute

3

In the past, we could always fix domestic economic problems by priming the pump with some deficit spending, but [President] Clinton can't do that anymore. So the only place he can go is to the trade side. Clinton now has to deal with Japan to address his domestic problems. Stimulating [Japanese] demand [for U.S. products] is now more important than ever for getting growth here.

The New York Times, 2-11:(A)7.

Robert B. Reich
Secretary of Labor
of the United States

4

[On the Clinton Administration's plans to retrain the unemployed to help them get jobs]: One of the primary goals of unemployment reform or changing the unemployment system into a re-employment system . . . is to help people get the next job, not just pay them while they wait for the old jobs to come back.

The Christian Science Monitor,
2-4:1.

5

[Comparing the employment situation in Europe and Japan with that in the U.S.]: There's a great deal to learn from one another. Their job growth has not been very healthy, although those who have jobs have seen wage increases of very healthy proportions. The United States is almost the mirror image. Over the past 15 years, we've created a lot of new jobs, but . . . a majority of Americans have seen their wages stagnate or decline and many of their benefits disappear. The underlying question is: Are we condemned to choose between these two alternatives, neither of which is very appealing? . . . There may be another alternative . . . Some would say that in Europe and Japan they've done a much better job bringing the bottom two-thirds of their populations

(ROBERT B. REICH)

up to a high minimal level of competence in education and training and skills. Some would say that in the United States, our strength is our labor market mobility, the dynamism and change that our markets allow.

Los Angeles Times, 3-14:(A)16.

1

[Calling for legislation to reform government-guaranteed corporate pension plans, many of which are under-funded]: There is no reason to panic now, but legislation is necessary if we are to avoid a crisis in the future. [Potential taxpayer liability from under-funded plans] is a serious problem and it's growing worse. I don't want to get into scaremongering by comparing this to the S&L crisis, but we need to get a handle on this to get it under control.

Los Angeles Times, 5-12:(A)10.

2

In a seeming paradox of today's economic news, financial markets fret that unemployment is too low to contain inflation, even while 8 million American workers remain jobless . . . [But] there is no fixed number of good jobs to be parceled out, nor any natural limit to the ingenuity of the human mind and the new products and services it can concoct.

Before Center for National Policy,
Washington, D.C., Aug. 31/
Los Angeles Times, 9-1:(A)27.

Robert D. Reischauer
Director,
Congressional Budget Office

3

[Saying the Federal budget deficit is under control and being reduced]: The dramatic improvement is largely the result of the enactment [of President Clinton's economic plan]. The difficult step taken by the President and the Congress in adopt-

ing a major deficit-reduction package last August seems likely to achieve the desired outcome—significantly lower deficits than were projected a year ago.

Before Senate Budget Committee,
Washington, D.C., Jan. 27/
Los Angeles Times, 1-28:(A)21.

Alice M. Rivlin
Director, Federal Office
of Management and Budget

4

[On President Clinton's low public-approval ratings despite improvements in the economy]: I find this as hard to understand as anybody else. When you think back to what was happening in the economy two years ago, or less, the projections then were very gloomy. We were facing rising [Federal budget] deficits, a very sluggish economy, very little job growth, [and] a very high unemployment rate. Now that has turned around. The deficit's coming down very substantially and faster than we thought it would . . . Unemployment is back down; we created a lot of jobs. It's hard to see why this hasn't gotten more favorable attention.

Interview, Washington, D.C./
The Christian Science Monitor,
8-16:4.

Stephen Roach
Chief economist,
Morgan Stanley & Company,
investments

5

What we're seeing is really a two-tiered labor market. The low-wage tier is responding to the pickup in the economy the old-fashioned way by adding new employees. But the high-wage tier is still generating its growth through boosting productivity rather than boosting the number of employees.

The Washington Post,
5-7:(A)9.

Robert E. Rubin
Chairman, White House
National Economic Council

1

We've cut our budget deficit, created 3.5 million new jobs in the last 18 months, held inflation below 2.5 percent, and we've got a couple of good years' growth ahead of us.

Newsweek,
7-11:32.

Anthony Rucci
Executive vice president
of merchandising,
Sears, Roebuck & Company

2

[On his company's recent cutting of many jobs]: We are asking a fundamental question: Are our workers adding value? When you wade into this area of what can we do to add value, a whole world opens up . . . The bulk of the cutbacks were in administration and we are now down to where we think we want to be. We might even add salespeople on the floor at our stores, if revenue continues to show double-digit increases. But one thing I can tell you: There is a very strong commitment to get rid of needless staff work, tasks that don't add value; and that will continue.

The New York Times,
3-22:(C)4.

Ron Schreibman
Economist, National Association
of Wholesale Distributors

3

I'm trying to worry [about inflation]. But I can't find much to worry about. Inflation is the rhinoceros in the room that everyone fears but no one can locate.

April 12/
Los Angeles Times,
4-13:(D)2.

Allen Sinai
Economist,
Lehman Brothers, investments

4

We are entering the best part of the business cycle now, with more jobs, improved wages, better profits, and an expansion that is well entrenched . . . Main street America is cooking.

The Washington Post,
5-7:(A)9.

Hedrick Smith
Journalist

5

[The Japanese are] concerned with essentially having very fierce [economic] competition, having price competition, and having the market—up to a point. But at some point they begin to say, "Hey, those of us who are competing with each other need to collaborate." Either with the government's help or the government's encouragement or just on their own, because over the long run, there's going to be a better standard of living, there's going to be more jobs and more economic power for all of them together. If you put Americans in that circumstance, they'd say, "Hey, wait a minute, that's wrong. You're interfering with the market." Neither Germany nor Japan trusts the market to do as well for all of society, or even most of society, as we do.

Interview/
American Way, 1-4:44.

Gene Sperling
Deputy Assistant to President
of the United States
Bill Clinton for Economic Policy

6

I don't think that anybody can say with scientific precision what is the exact rate of unemployment that starts to lead to an acceleration in inflation. But I think our view is that whatever that rule is, our goal should be to lower it, through increasing the productivity of workers and the efficiency with which they move from job to job. I believe that over the long run, financial markets will come to recognize this.

The New York Times,
5-24:(C)1.

Joseph Stiglitz
Member, Council of Economic
Advisers to President of the
United States Bill Clinton

1

The key to economics is problems of information—who knows what—and these problems of information are core to our understanding of all our institutions.

Interview/
The New York Times, 2-9:(C)12.

Peter Sutherland
Director General,
General Agreement on
Tariffs and Trade

2

The transformation of the world we've seen the last five to 10 years [with the collapse of Communism] has resulted in an addition to the free-market population of the world of about 3 billion people. Now, if we just want to keep unemployment in the developing countries at the same level it is now, over the next 30 years we'll have to provide a number of additional jobs in those countries that's equivalent to the current populations of Europe and North America combined. Trade is a critical issue in generating jobs.

USA Today, 6-27:(B)4.

Lester Thurow
Professor of economics,
Massachusetts Institute of Technology

3

This time we didn't have a recession. We had something more fundamental. In the 1980s, we had a speculative bubble followed by a financial crash.

Right now, we're cleaning up the mess and working off the excesses, which is different than a classic recovery. This is not the Great Depression, but some historian might call it the Great Stagnation, because on a worldwide basis we've already had five years of a growth rate of 1.5 percent or less . . . If you ask what will be the effect of $500-billion worth of deficit reduction, the answer is that it will slow down the economy. Income tax is going up on wealthy individuals, and we're cutting government spending. How does that create jobs? If anything, it subtracts jobs and lowers wages.

Interview/Mother Jones,
March-April:34,35.

Michael Traugott
Political scientist,
University of Michigan

4

[On President Clinton's low public-approval ratings despite improvements in the economy]: I have a suspicion that citizens are getting conflicting measures through the media and their personal contacts. The gross economic data are generally good, but [company] downsizing may have cost some friends and neighbors their jobs. The literature suggests that people are responding more to [these kinds of] concerns about others than their own circumstances.

The Washington Post, 8-9:(A)8.

Laura D'Andrea Tyson
Chairman, Council of
Economic Advisers to
President of the United States
Bill Clinton

5

A persistent and unresolved . . . [Federal budget] deficit is widely agreed by economists to be a problem. If debt is growing relative to the growth of the economy as far as the eye can see, that is clearly an unsustainable path.

The Washington Post,
2-7:(A)4.

(LAURA D'ANDREA TYSON)

1

Most of the increase in unemployment that occurred between 1989 and 1993 was due to the slowdown in the growth rate of the economy, rather than any structural changes. In other words, there's a fairly significant cyclical component to the unemployment of the last few years. It's true that the United States has too high a level of what you might call "cyclically insensitive" unemployment. If we got the economy back on an expansion path of 3 percent a year, we might bring unemployment down to 5.5 percent . . . The real problem for the economy is to generate attractive employment alternatives so that people can move from industries with increasing unemployment to new industries with new technologies. If the economy is doing well, then the jobs will create themselves. Structural and technological change will generate new demands, which will generate new jobs and higher wages.

Interview/Mother Jones,
March-April:33.

2

The income of the unskilled is falling in absolute and relative terms, and that suggests that the only long-term solution, given the technological changes [in the workplace], is targeting programs on the unskilled and revamping education and training with regard to the unskilled.

At international jobs seminar,
Detroit, Mich./
The New York Times,
3-16:(C)2.

3

I came to this conference [on jobs attended by the G-7 nations] thinking that the United States lagged behind Europe and Japan in the way we handled transitions from school to work and the way we dealt with retraining and re-employment. But one thing I've learned is that the pace of technological change has been so swift in the last few years that even the Europeans are being forced to rethink the way they handle these issues.

Detroit, Mich./
Los Angeles Times, 3-17:(A)9.

4

The economy's news continues to be good, and it's news that suggests the economy is on an investment-led expansion. [That's positive because business investment in equipment and buildings] contributes to current economic strength, since it is a form of spending. It adds to contemporary growth. But unlike other forms of spending that only add to contemporary growth, investment spending also adds to future growth because it builds capacity for the future.

Interview/USA Today,
8-3:(B)2.

5

Among economists there is a view . . . that trade liberalization is like a bicycle. As long as it's going forward, it's fine. If you stop, it falls down. You need something that liberalizes trade, that pushes open markets. It is very important for the [Clinton] Administration to make sure that the GATT issue stays in people's minds.

Interview/USA Today,
8-3:(B)2.

6

If the economy were in trouble right now, I am sure that there would be a lot of observation to the effect that the Clinton Administration strategy was totally responsible. So in a sense I feel like I should start by saying I will take as much credit—we will, the President will, the Administration will—take as much credit for the current good situation, as I'm sure many of you would cast blame on the Administration if the economy were not performing well.

News conference,
Washington, D.C., Aug. 4/
The New York Times,
8-5:(C)1,5.

(LAURA D'ANDREA TYSON)

1

It is not the case that we in Washington can freely act to do things which are fiscally irresponsible, because the result of that will be not just in domestic financial markets, but in global financial markets. Two constraints will provide discipline—the discipline of the voter and the discipline of the market.

Dec. 16/The New York Times,
12-17:8.

J. Antonio Villamil
President,
Washington Economics Group,
Miami, Fla.;
Former Under Secretary
of Commerce of the United States

2

It's very wrong to center U.S. trade policy on trade balances only, because imports reflect the decisions of consumers and corporations. We should not be in the business of setting market-share arrangements and quantitative targets.

Interview, Feb. 14/
USA Today, 2-15:(B)2.

Paul A. Volcker
Former Chairman,
Federal Reserve Board

3

[Supporting the Federal Reserve's recent increase in interest rates as a way to dampen possible future inflation]: I don't think that it is surprising that the Fed took some modest steps . . . to remind everyone that they are still alive. But it is not fair to call [the steps] a real tightening as much as a move away from easy money.

To business people,
Amsterdam, Netherlands,
March 23/USA Today,
3-24:(B)1.

S. Linn Williams
Former Deputy
United States
Trade Representative

4

[On trade sanctions imposed on foreign companies because of their alleged unfair trade practices]: There's a school of thought that sanctions are effective for maybe six months and, after that, the company against which the sanctions are applied figures out a way to do business around them.

Los Angeles Times,
2-15:(D)2.

David Wyss
Economist, DRI/McGraw-Hill

5

Because our [U.S.] economy has done so much better than foreign economies, we have been gaining market share. But the problem is that there are [shrinking] markets. If customers are not buying, businesses are not selling, no matter how good the prices are.

U.S. News & World Report,
7-25:43.

Janet L. Yellen
Member-designate,
Federal Reserve Board

6

I agree with the Fed's [recent] decision to reduce monetary stimulus [raise interest rates]—before the emergence of obvious inflationary pressure—in order to avoid over-shooting the natural rate [of economic growth]. On the other hand, the appropriate amount of tightening involves some guesswork and it is difficult to know whether the actions that have been taken thus far will prove sufficient to prevent overheating, insufficient to the task at hand or possibly excessive.

At Senate Banking Committee
hearing on her nomination,
Washington, D.C., July 22/
The New York Times, 7-23:17.

Robert Albright
Chairman, Council for
International Activities,
Educational Testing Service

1

A lot of the education reform in the future will be driven by economic pressures and the ability of corporate leaders to employ a work force that is diligent, productive and inventive . . . Much of the demand to study other [of the world's educational] systems is based on the concerns of business leaders. I'm not so sure that educational leaders on their own would have come up with the notion of studying other educational systems [for ideas].

The Christian Science Monitor,
9-7:9.

Philip Altbach
Professor of education,
Boston College

2

American educators are always looking over our shoulders so we can know where we are [in relation to other countries] and then can benchmark ourselves. The same is true of many other countries. The European Union countries now do a lot more comparison [of education systems] between their nations . . . You can get insight from other countries, but direct applications of educational innovations are not generally very successful. It's difficult to incorporate what we learn [from other nations] because of drastic differences [in systems]. But some ideas can be shared and borrowed.

The Christian Science Monitor,
9-7:8.

William J. Bennett
Former Secretary of Education
of the United States

3

The moral education of our children is the first priority of a nation. We're not just talking about learning subjects here, about history or calculus — whatever. In the education of our children, we're involved in nothing less than the architecture of souls.

At Oregon State University/
Vanity Fair,
August:142.

C. Diane Bishop
Superintendent
of Schools
of Arizona

4

[On Arizona's plan to institute state-administered competency tests for high-school students before they are allowed to graduate]: Statewide tests will judge every student by the same standard. The message now is that the state doesn't care anymore how many students graduate each year. We want them to be able to read, write and have a knowledge of math, science and social studies.

The Christian Science Monitor,
2-25:4.

William Cleveland Bosher, Jr.
Superintendent
of Public Instruction
of Virginia

5

The best decision-making takes place at the local school level. The state's role should be to develop . . . standards statewide and a set of assessment tools that tell us how close we are to meeting those goals, and then leave the issue of curriculum . . . and methods to the local school systems.

Interview,
Richmond, Va./
The Washington Post,
3-10:(Va.)1.

Ernest L. Boyer
President,
Carnegie Foundation for
the Advancement of Teaching

1

[On the increasing Federal role in education]: If I had ever whispered "national standards" [as is now being proposed by the Clinton Administration], I think I would have lost my job [as Commissioner in the 1970s]. We bent over backwards 15 years ago so that no one would think we were interfering [with state and local control of education]. Within a decade, we have gone from this preoccupation of local control to national standards. There is no turning back.

The New York Times,
3-30:(B)7.

2

[On college presidents]: Today, they are faced with reconciling forces that are unreconcilable in the absence of new priorities in higher education . . . [And] they are too busy minding the store, or they have so many constituents to please and are under so much pressure to raise money, that they cannot afford to speak out [on the issues of the day]. It's a matter of grim survival for many presidents today.

U.S. News & World Report,
12-12:82.

Michael Casserly
Executive director,
Council of the Great City Schools

3

[On the poor physical condition of many city school buildings]: You've got facilities that most adults would never think of working in themselves, and buildings that send clear signals to kids about how they're valued. Certainly, Congress wouldn't work in facilities like that . . . There are some beautiful schools in this country. But the schools that are in terrible shape, particularly those in the cities, are a downright scandal.

USA Today, 7-19:(D)2.

Bill Clinton
President of the United States

4

College tuition should be tax deductible. Just as we make mortgage interest tax deductible because we want people to own their own homes, we should make college tuition deductible because we want people to go to college. Specifically, I propose that all tuition for college—community college, graduate school, professional school, vocational education or worker retraining after high school—be fully deductible, phased up to $10,000 a year for families making up to $120,000 a year. Education, after all, has a bigger impact on earnings and job security than ever before. So let's invest the fruits of today's [economic] recovery into tomorrow's opportunity.

Broadcast address to the nation,
Washington, D.C., Dec. 15/
The New York Times,
12-16:(A)12.

Ramon Cortines
Chancellor, New York City
Public School System

5

[On national education standards being proposed by the Clinton Administration]: This legislation will make a difference. Once you have a curriculum framework, it helps us understand where we are going and that we are going to be responsible for what students know and what they are able to do.

The New York Times,
3-30:(B)7.

Walter Cronkite
Former anchor, CBS News

6

I'm not happy with the way history has ever been taught, in any class I ever went to. I mean, history is the drama, for heaven's sake, of human existence. And history is the story of people, and how they coped, how they met problems, and of

(WALTER CRONKITE)

the competition between them, the rivalries between them. With all the emotions—jealousy, hate, love. And it's never taught this way. It's taught in this dull rote—dates and places. People never come alive. All these people lived dramatic lives. Every history lesson, every hour in history class, ought to be a terribly exciting lecture on the lives and loves of these peoples. And their personalities. Because the personalities of these leaders, and of those who sought to be, is what affected history. But we don't learn it that way, and as a consequence history is a course that most people hate in school. It's just a shame.

Interview, New York, N.Y./
American Heritage,
December:50.

Terry Dozier
Adviser to U.S. Secretary
of Education Richard W. Riley;
Former teacher

1

[On the Clinton Administration's Goals 2000 legislation, aimed at setting objectives to be met by the nation's schools by the turn of the century]: As a teacher, I always hoped I was expecting what I should of my students, but I really had absolutely nothing to judge that by. I think this [legislation] will help all of us to have a benchmark by which we can measure how we're doing compared to what the rest of the nation and the world expect their students to know and be able to do.

The Christian Science Monitor,
4-11:14.

Ken Ducote
Director of facility planning,
New Orleans (La.) Public Schools

2

[On the deterioration of many public-school buildings around the country due to tight school budgets]: Imagine if you were on the school board

and you were faced with [either] closing schools, increasing teacher-student ratios, cutting athletics or putting off maintenance. Which one of [those] things would you do?

U.S. News & World Report,
9-12:80.

Flora Mancuso Edwards
President,
Middlesex Community College
(New Jersey)

3

[On her college's new policy of "guaranteeing" to employers the ability of its graduates]: It's the same thing as a warranty on a product. We warranty the expertise of our students to be absolutely fit for the purposes for which the education was intended.

The New York Times,
11-26:9.

Jon Ericson
Professor of speech communications,
Drake University

4

[Saying college sports departments can put pressure on professors to pass a failing student for the sake of the school's athletics program]: When a teacher has a jock who's failing his course, he's sure to hear from someone at the athletic department. The guy will say, "He is a nice kid who wants to make something of himself. Can't you be caring, understanding, sensitive? Don't you like sports? Are you a racist? Give him a break and pass him. Who'll it hurt?" It's hard not to give in to that, especially when you feel you're alone. But let's put the shoe on the other foot. What do you think Rudy Washington [Drake's basketball coach] would say if I told him I had a very good student who wasn't much of a basketball player, and hadn't much time for practice, but needed an ego boost, and would just love to play for Drake against Iowa State? I think he'd tell me to get lost, and be justi-

(JON ERICSON)

fied in doing so. He has high standards and sticks to them. Yet college-athletic people everywhere think nothing of asking profs to do that very thing.

Interview/
The Wall Street Journal,
9-9:(A)12.

Dianne Feinstein
United States Senator,
D-California

1

[On her not supporting a ballot proposition in California that calls for denying many social services, such as education, to illegal immigrants and their children]: I don't believe we want our teachers or doctors to be INS agents. As I read the initiative, every teacher, if they suspected a student was here illegally, would have to report that student. Now, think about how you do this. You do it by accent, by skin color. And I do not believe that this is what our teachers should be doing with their time. I think whatever time they have should be focused on teaching. I also believe that school is a very good thing for kids, and if you take kids out of school, they then become fodder for gangs, for drug activity, for other problems, because most of these kids are very poor.

Interview/
Los Angeles Times,
10-30:(M)4.

William D. Ford
United States Representative,
D-Michigan

2

Congress has nothing to do with the question of home schooling. It's none of the Federal government's business how the states regulate compulsory school attendance.

Before the House,
Washington, D.C., Feb.24/
The New York Times, 2-25:(A)10.

James O. Freedman
President, Dartmouth College

3

Hearing a physician say the dread word "cancer" [Freedman has lymphatic cancer] has an uncanny capacity to concentrate the mind. That is what liberal education does, too. When the ground seems to shake and shift beneath us, liberal education provides perspective, enabling us to see life steadily and see it whole. It has taken an illness to remind me, in my middle age, of that lesson.

At Dartmouth College
commencement, June/
The New York Times, 7-6:(A)12.

Derek Gandy
Director of minority recruitment,
Yale University

4

[On recent acts of violence on college campuses]: One thing is for certain: People are getting shot in the city, in the innocent suburban schools and in the cornfield schools. They are getting shot everywhere these days. I think society in general has become more violent. We look at college and try to make it different from the real world. It's not different from the real world.

The Washington Post,
2-15:(A)1.

Milton Goldberg
Executive director,
National Education Commission
on Time and Learning

5

[Saying the school day and year in the U.S. are too short]: For over a decade, education-reform advocates have been working feverishly to improve our schools. But . . . if reform is to truly take hold, the six-hour, 180-day school year should be relegated to museums—an exhibit from our education past.

The Christian Science Monitor,
5-5:2.

Sheldon Hackney
Chairman, National Endowment
for the Humanities
of the United States

1

The boundaries between [academic] disciplines are becoming blurred. We've reached the point in the study of American history where you can't tell the difference between what the sociologists, the political scientists and the historians are doing.

The New York Times,
3-23:(B)8.

Martha Harron
Member,
Quality Education Network
(Canada)

2

You start to feel as though your child is a computer into which the primary schools are placing a stupidity virus.

World Press Review,
August:5.

John Higham
Historian,
Johns Hopkins University

3

Multiculturalism [in education] is used in all kinds of different ways. For a great many people, it means a wider recognition and appreciation of the different endowments that young people bring to the classroom . . . What I call academic multiculturalism is an ideology of minority rights that pays no attention to majorities. It's a belief that equality can be advanced by maximizing the cohesiveness and the power of particular groups, particular minority groups, if they will stand together, if they ally themselves with one another. So academic multiculturalism I would define as a belief in and an effort to propagate the idea of alliance between a particular set of disadvantaged elements.

Interview/Humanities,
Jan.-Feb.:6.

David Honeyman
Associate professor
of education,
University of Florida

4

A small town has as much trouble building one new school as an urban community has building 25.

U.S. News & World Report,
9-12:80.

Reed E. Hundt
Chairman, Federal
Communications Commission

5

The [developing] telecommunications networks have the ability to revolutionize education. They have the ability to break through classroom walls and connect all the kids to all the great libraries, to all the great educational opportunities. I was a schoolteacher for a couple of years and it was a tragedy that the kids in my classroom didn't have access to enough books, much less access to the world outside. So our job is to help make sure the networks get into the classrooms.

Interview/USA Today,
3-21:(A)11.

Tom Ingram
President, Association of
Governing Boards of
Universities and Colleges

6

[On the decrease in funds available for universities]: The amount available for public and tax-supported or- assisted universities has undergone substantial shrinkage. In private education, there is a strong resistance [from consumers] to pay more, and charitable contributions have leveled off to make up the difference between college tuition and costs.

The Christian Science Monitor,
5-23:13.

Augusta F. Kappner
Assistant Secretary for
Vocational and Adult Education,
Department of Education
of the United States

1

[Supporting Federal funding of a job-training program for high school students who do not plan to attend college]: The days were when a young person in Pittsburgh could drop out of school, go to a steel mill and get a good job. Those jobs aren't available anymore. Young people don't see the connection between learning in high school and what lies ahead for them in the job market.

Interview, Washington, D.C.,
April 22/The New York Times,
4-23:9.

Elizabeth Kennan
President,
Mount Holyoke College

2

After the Ivy Leagues and other colleges went coed in the 1970s, there was an expectation that the world of equality had come [for women students], that there would be a level playing field for men and women in education. But in fact, the stereotypes have not been broken. The millennium has not come for women's education in a coeducational setting.

The New York Times,
1-15:1.

Edward M. Kennedy
United States Senator,
D-Massachusetts

3

[On the Federal government's Goal's 2000 program, which aims at setting national educational standards and providing Federal funds to aid states in implementing educational plans]: In the years ahead, Goals 2000 will be regarded as a turning point in American education. Parents and local communities will finally be able to know what every student should learn in core subjects like English, history, mathematics and science . . . We

all wish that we could do more. But education is primarily a state and local responsibility, and our hope is that this Federal contribution will provide the much-needed seed money essential to enable local efforts to flourish to improve the nation's schools.

Los Angeles Times,
3-26:(A)18.

Hilton Kramer
Editor, "The New Criterion"

4

The great mistake is to identify public intellectuals with academics. Most of the most-serious intellectual discourse for some years has not come out of the academy. The academy is intellectually dead.

The New York Times,
8-9:(A)13.

Howard Lappin
Principal,
James A. Foshay Middle School,
Los Angeles, Calif.

5

[On the new California open-enrollment system in which parents may choose to which public high school to send their children, and which has caused many high schools to advertise for students]: This is the new age of advertising and marketing—some people think that those are dirty words, but we are going to market our little school. It's time that schools realize we are living in the real world and we better start doing this.

Los Angeles Times,
5-12:(A)1.

Valerie Lee
Professor of education,
University of Michigan

6

[On the policy of some community colleges of "guaranteeing" to employers the ability of their graduates]: My guess is they're trying to build

(VALERIE LEE)

credibility with the general public, to say that the community college has some value. They have served so many needs, and some people have come to believe that when you serve that many needs, you serve no needs.
The New York Times,
11-26:9.

Sanford Levinson
Professor, University of
Texas Law School
1

[On the mixing of and crossover between academic disciplines]: Literary scholars now recognize that there is no such thing as the rock-hard meaning of language, and legal scholars see that there is no particular way of thinking like a lawyer, and so they both look around for other takes and interesting juxtapositions.
The New York Times,
3-23:(B)8.

Altaf Malik
Operator of a chain of schools
for girls in Pakistan
2

When you educate a male, you educate an individual. When you educate a female, you educate a family.
Los Angeles Times,
4-12:(H)5.

Susan Molinari
United States Representative,
R-New York
3

[On a bill she is sponsoring aimed at combating educational bias against girls in public schools]: At a time when [America's] economic competitiveness depends on the recruitment of qualified engineers, scientists and entrepreneurs—teachers, almost without realizing it, treat girls differently, and unconsciously veer them away from these important career choices.
The Christian Science Monitor,
3-31:2.

Diane S. Ravitch
Former Assistant Secretary for
Educational Research and Improvement,
Department of Education
of the United States
4

[Saying a House bill aimed at combating educational bias against girls in public schools is unnecessary]: Twenty years ago, you could have made an argument for this bill with a tremendous amount of evidence. [But] today, when you have women dominant in higher education, it's kind of ridiculous . . . Women are now 55 percent of all undergraduates and 59 percent of all master's-degree candidates. Is it that we want women to be 70 percent of all undergraduates and 90 percent of all master's-degree candidates?
The Christian Science Monitor,
3-31:2.

Robert B. Reich
Secretary of Labor
of the United States
5

The evidence from recent history and from other industrialized countries suggests the old saying is true: What you earn will continue to depend on what you learn. Starting this fall, 20,000 [American] young people will enter national service, earning money they can apply to a college education. But it's dangerous for a four-year college [degree] to be what divides the winners from the losers in the workforce.
Interview/USA Today,
9-2:(B)3.

C. Duncan Rice

Vice chancellor,
New York University

1

If you think of a university in traditional American terms as an agency where you teach the young and do basic research in a highly formal sense, you're probably not doing enough to serve the society that pays a great deal of money for us.

The New York Times,
8-9:(A)13.

Richard W. Riley

Secretary of Education
of the United States

2

When I talk to teachers, it has been my observation that they don't talk to me about their pay or their long hours or the difficulty of their jobs. They talk to me about the fact that they can't get parents to help them with the education of their children. That is a real problem in American education . . . [The] Goals 2000 [plan] is the answer to that. It is a way that each school can develop their own systemic reform—which means parents are involved in it. Each person can begin by working with their own children every night—and take a special interest in what is happening in their school and what their teacher is telling them and develop respect for teachers and schools and learning. Every parent can do that.

Interview, Washington, D.C./
Los Angeles Times, 2-13:(M)3.

3

If contracting out [by schools to private-sector businesses] for services means better, more-successful action going on in the classroom and money is gravitating toward the classroom where the teaching and learning is better, then it makes sense to look at that. But if it is some way for a company to make money and that is the purpose of it, that doesn't appeal to me from an educational standpoint.

Interview/Nation's Business,
March:31.

4

[On the Federal government's Goals 2000 program, which aims at setting national educational standards and providing Federal funds to aid states in implementing educational plans]: Goals 2000 will lead to the establishment of voluntary national standards. They will be guides for parents and teachers and communities to judge the quality of their schools. [Today], we want our schools to be excellent, but we don't know exactly what that means.

Los Angeles Times,
3-26:(A)18.

5

[On a childhood book that helped shape his life]: A biography of Thomas Jefferson. Jefferson linked democracy to educational progress and opportunity. I still believe quality education is the key to our success as a democratic nation.

U.S News & World Report,
4-25:(A)7.

6

All the [education] reforms in Washington will not matter a great deal unless parents are parents and give their children the love of learning.

Announcing results of
"1992 Writing Report Card,"
Tubman Elementary School,
Washington, D.C., June 7/
The Christian Science Monitor,
6-10:3.

7

[Saying recent improvements in math and science test scores by U.S. elementary- and secondary-school students is encouraging but not fast enough for today's world]: Holding our own in the Information Age is simply not enough. We live in an unprecedented era of new knowledge, and our children must be prepared for the future.

To reporters,
Washington, D.C., Aug. 17/
Los Angeles Times,
8-18:(A)15.

(RICHARD W. RILEY)

1

[Saying parents can help children to read and write better]: Children who read and are read to, who see their parents read, who have a variety of reading materials in the home and who write letters or notes at home, read and write better.

U.S. News & World Report,
8-29:12.

Dana Rohrabacher
United States Representative,
R-California

2

[On criticism of him in Congress for sponsoring legislation that would require public schools to ascertain and report the number of illegal immigrants in attendance as a way to crack down on such aliens]: The flood of illegal aliens is breaking the bank . . . and we have to get control of it. It is essential to know how much it is costing to educate illegal aliens . . . If I were to even suggest that someone had Communist sympathies because he opposed something I was pushing, the reaction [in Congress] would be outrage . . . Yet we have to sit here for hours listening to people calling us Nazis because they oppose doing anything about this [illegal-alien] issue. To say we can't take care of everybody is not being mean-spirited. We just don't have the money to provide free education and other services to everybody in the world who comes here illegally.

Washington, D.C., March 3/
Los Angeles Times, 3-4:(A)30.

Andy Rooney
Correspondent,
"60 Minutes," CBS-TV

3

We're desperately short of people who actually know how to do anything. Would it be demeaning or a waste of your education for someone who graduated with honors from Gettysburg [College] to build houses for a living? . . . An education is good for its own sake—not necessarily

because you use it to make money. An education is a lifelong comfort to anyone who has one, and there's no reason an educated person shouldn't make a living with his hands. The notion that someone who works with his hands isn't also working with his head is wrong. It's possible to work with your head without moving a muscle, but it's not possible to work with your muscles without using your head, too.

At Gettysburg College
commencement/
USA Today, 6-8:(A)11.

Bob Schaeffer
Public-education director,
FairTest

4

[Advice to students taking the SAT]: Understand that this is a game. The name of the test *should* be something like "How Well Students Fill In 138 Ovals." But if the game is going to count, learn how to play. And keep in mind that the test is not a thermometer that accurately measures intelligence, ability or capacity to do college work. You're much more than your score, and many colleges understand that. Besides, every fall, there are still colleges advertising to attract freshmen. If you're a high-school graduate with a tuition check, you'll get into some college somewhere.

Interview/
U.S. News & World Report,
10-17:89.

Bret Schundler
Mayor of Jersey City, N.J.

5

Some of the people in Jersey City say, "Do you think about running for higher office?" I say, "No, no, no, no." What I want to do is be remembered in history someday for doing school choice in Jersey City. Let's see a poor child in Jersey City literally look at the best public schools in America and choose between them. And do so without increasing taxes by one penny.

Interview/
The New York Times, 2-9:(A)8.

Judith R. Shapiro
Provost,
Bryn Mawr College;
President-elect,
Barnard College

1

I don't think the reason you have a women's college is because women think differently from men, but rather that women need a place that belongs to them. The surrounding society is not one where the sexes are equal. Women's colleges are places that are first and foremost committed to the welfare and progress of women students.

Interview,
New York, N.Y., March 21/
The New York Times,
3-22:(A)13.

Theodore R. Sizer
Professor of education,
Brown University;
Director, Coalition
of Essential Schools

2

To me, [school reform] means reform of schools when 50 of us get together with a bunch of kids to try to help them learn. But other people, they will say, "Should we have an elected or an appointed school board?" "Should we have vouchers?" Most of the howling and screaming is about this kind of thing, and not so much gets done for the kids. They figure out what's right for the grown-ups. We have a long history of using children to meet our social problems . . . Our assumption has got to be that [school improvement] is never going to be unsolvable—because to say that problems in schools are unsolvable is far too despairing. In the richest nation in the world, that is not a silly statement.

Interview/
Providence, R.I./
Los Angeles Times,
1-12:(E)3.

3

Democracy depends upon devoted and informed citizens. And the secure future of a decent America depends upon schools which prepare such citizens.

Los Angeles Times,
1-12:(E)3.

Sherwood Small
Chairman,
honorary degree committee,
Clark University

4

The choice of a [college's] commencement speaker is important because it positions the school in the public mind and also because it's the last thing the students will remember about the school.

The New York Times, 5-21:6.

Franklin L. Smith
Superintendent of Schools
of the District of Columbia

5

[On his plans to hire private tutors to teach about-to-graduate high-school students to read better]: It's ridiculous to have these students graduating [with fourth-grade reading skills]. I have to stop the bleeding. This will give those youngsters who have slipped through the cracks an opportunity to be successful . . . All I'm trying to do is teach people to read.

The Washington Post,
5-6:(A)1.

Gary Watts
Director of a school
innovation center,
National Education Association

6

[Criticizing state or national standardized school testing of students]: If the purpose of a test is to show, after the fact, what the student has done, then it doesn't matter. [But] a good testing system

(GARY WATTS)

doesn't do that. A good testing system has a diagnostic component.

The Christian Science Monitor,
2-25:4.

Charles Willie
Professor of education
and urban studies,
Harvard University

1

While "magnet schools" were wonderful educational innovations, they were unfair. The overwhelming majority of people could not be accommodated in them. There simply were not enough resources to establish magnet schools for everybody.

The Christian Science Monitor,
5-16:11.

James Winn
Director,
Institute for the Humanities,
University of Michigan

2

[On the mixing of and crossover between academic disciplines]: Many scholars have come to believe that the narrow approaches to a subject have been pretty much played out, and so they have begun to look elsewhere. If the English scholar looks to anthropology, say, he can come up with a striking new set of questions to address.

The New York Times,
3-23:(B)8.

The Environment • Energy

Cecil D. Andrus
Governor of Idaho (D);
Former Secretary of the
Interior of the United States

1

[Saying U.S. Interior Secretary Bruce Babbitt has been trying to iron out differences between Western states and the Clinton Administration over the Administration's policy of increased land-grazing fees and regulations]: That poor devil has worn out three pairs of airplane wings and nine pairs of shoe leather to turn this around. Although if they had done this right the first time around, they wouldn't have had to do this.

Interview/
Nation's Business, July:36.

Bruce Babbitt
Secretary of the Interior
of the United States

2

[On improving the national-park system]: Our first mission is to protect park resources. Under my watch, the National Park Service is not going to be in the hotel business. And . . . roads can be the enemies of national parks . . . National parks are not about entertainment. That's for Disney, Warner Brothers and others. If you want to play golf, watch people feeding bears or see a nighttime firefall . . . that's fine. Just don't expect to do it in a national park.

Speech at start of
National Park Week,
Philadelphia, Pa., May 23/
USA Today, 5-24:(A)9.

Alicia Barcena
Executive Director, Earth Council
(UN-sponsored Costa Rican-based
environmental organization)

3

Ten years ago, development was synonymous with growth, size and quantity. Big dams, resorts

or cities were the name of the game. But that model didn't work as we thought it would. Poverty, unemployment and other problems are worse than ever. All this happened as we liquidated our natural capital, the environment.

Los Angeles Times,
1-18:(H)4.

Max Baucus
United States Senator,
D-Montana

4

For years now, there has been in essence a religious war between the business community and the environmental community . . . It seemed like you were either for the environment or for the economy . . . [But] the American people want us to take a practical, common-sense approach to our environmental problems.

Washington, D.C., May 19/
Los Angeles Times,
5-20:(A)14.

Kent Briggs
Senior fellow,
Center for the New West,
Denver, Colo.

5

[Saying Westerners are not happy about the Clinton Administration's attempts to change national policy on mining, logging, water and land-grazing fees in their part of the country]: [In the West,] there's a respect for the culture of the rural areas, and that's why I think [the Administration] ran into a buzz saw. The Administration is seen as elite and effete, insular and insolent . . . What will finally shake out is going to be the failure of the so-called new politics of the new West.

The Christian Science Monitor,
11-2:3.

Lester Brown
President, Worldwatch Institute

1

I personally do not think we are ever going to get close [to a world population of 10 billion]. Ecosystems are already starting to break down . . . Achieving a humane balance between food and people now depends more on family planners than on farmers.

Before Senate Appropriations
Committee, Washington, D.C./
U.S. News & World Report,
9-12:57.

Carol M. Browner
Administrator,
Environmental Protection Agency
of the United States

2

If you look at labor laws at the turn of the century, and the conditions that people worked under, people began to say, "This is not humane. We can't continue to treat people this way. To treat *children* this way." And yet the people who talked about making changes were . . . told they would be the death knell of American business. I don't think there's anyone who would suggest we should go back to where we were. And I think that 30 or 40 years after the beginning of environmental protection, we will be in the same place. People will say, "That's right. That's what government does for us."

Vogue, January:65.

3

[On a plan to look at pollution on an industry-by-industry basis]: The old piecemeal approach, where the [EPA's] air office looks at air pollution, the water office looks at water pollution, and so on, doesn't work for me as a regulator, and it doesn't work for you [business people].

At town hall meeting at
U.S. Chamber of Commerce,
Washington, D.C./
Nation's Business, February:7.

4

[Saying urban rivers, such as the Anacostia in Washington, D.C., should be revived after years of pollution]: Rivers like this used to be cities' cultural centers, but now they're just dead. Our cities can no longer make use of these rivers. People can't swim in them; they can't fish from them; they can't come down and spend an afternoon on their banks. The nation's urban communities deserve to have their lakes and rivers back.

Washington, D.C./
Los Angeles Times,
4-28:(A)5.

Fidel Castro
President of Cuba

5

I tell you that capitalism has no future. Capitalism has destroyed in 100 years almost all the oil that it took millions of years to create. What would happen if every Indian, every Eskimo had a car to drive?

To visiting Americans,
Havana, Cuba/
Vanity Fair, March:133.

Bill Clinton
President of the United States

6

[Announcing U.S. trade sanctions against Taiwan in response to that country's refusal to stop sales of parts from tigers and rhinoceroses]: This is the first time any country has acted on the international call for trade sanctions to protect endangered species, but if the illegal trade in rhinos and tigers is not eliminated, these species could be extinct in five years. The world must know that the United States will take strong actions to protect the earth's natural heritage.

April 11/
The New York Times,
4-12:(C)1,

WHAT THEY SAID IN 1994

(BILL CLINTON)

1

Since the first Earth Day 24 years ago, our nation has been on a journey of national renewal. But as long as 70 million Americans live in areas where the air is too dangerous to breathe, as long as half our rivers and lakes are too polluted for fishing and swimming, as long as people in our poorest communities face terrible hazards from lead paint to toxic waste dumps . . . our journey is far from finished.

Speech, Washington, D.C.,
April 21/The Washington Post,
4-22:(A)3.

Larry E. Craig
United States Senator, R-Idaho

2

[Criticizing the Clinton Administration's policies of increased land-grazing fees and regulations in the West]: When you have a government whose policies drive you toward a zero-tolerance, politically correct environment, and you have an Administration that is almost gleeful in enforcing those policies, you find that in the hinterland some people are likely to get trampled on.

Nation's Business, July:36.

Daniel Dreyfus
Director of Civilian Radioactive
Waste Management,
Department of Energy
of the United States

3

[Despite being scientifically sound,] I don't think deep-seabed disposal [of nuclear waste] is [politically] viable, because what goes on in the environmental business is not susceptible to logic or reason. It's a state of mind—anyone who forgets that is whistling Dixie.

U.S. News & World Report,
11-7:66.

Thomas Eisner
Evolutionary biologist,
Cornell University

4

[Criticizing a court ruling that allows destruction of the surrounding habitat of a protected endangered species]: I find it totally absurd to conclude legalistically that the Endangered Species Act did not mean to include habitat. This [court ruling] says that you can build on either side of an eagle's nest as long as you don't build right on top of the eagle.

The New York Times,
11-22:(B)12.

Scott Fenn
Director,
Environmental Information Service,
Investor Responsibility
Research Center

5

Environmental performance benchmarking is rapidly becoming a vital component of the total quality management efforts of major corporations.

The Christian Science Monitor,
1-12:18.

George Frampton
Assistant Secretary for Wildlife,
Department of the Interior
of the United States

6

[On plans for the Endangered Species Act to now focus more on regional habitats and species rather than specific species]: The Endangered Species Act now is involving us in a whole different generation of problems, which have to do with regional habitat fragmentation. You simply can't do regional habitat protection one species at a time.

The New York Times,
6-30:(A)8.

Kathryn S. Fuller
President,
World Wildlife Federation

1

[Supporting new U.S. trade sanctions against Taiwan in response to that country's refusal to stop sales of parts from tigers and rhinoceroses]: The U.S. has taken a critical first step, but we have a long way to go before we can declare victory for rhinos and tigers. Sanctions on Taiwan must lead to significant and lasting progress in curbing smuggling in that country. In addition, China and other countries with serious wildlife smuggling problems must remain under continued scrutiny to insure that they are taking effective actions.

April 11/The New York Times,
4-12:(C)6.

Sherri Goodman
Deputy Under Secretary for
Environmental Security,
Department of Defense
of the United States

2

My job is to look at our [military] facilities and try to find ways they can use alternative-fuel vehicles and anti-pollution devices, and ways to get rid of ozone-polluting substances. Besides the environmental considerations, I'm also looking out to see that the Department gets the best value for the money it spends . . . I think it speaks well of this [Clinton] Administration that it created this office in the largest Federal agency in the country and gave it the kind of responsibilities it has. It shows how significant the Administration regards environmental policy.

The Washington Post,
3-3:(A)27.

Al Gore
Vice President
of the United States

3

[Ecologically,] we are in an unusual predicament as a global civilization. The maximum that

is politically feasible, even the maximum that is politically imaginable right now, still falls short of the minimum that is scientifically and ecologically necessary . . . Part of the secret to bringing about necessary change is understanding the lulls when the public's concern is beneath the surface . . . It's inevitable that some combination of events will produce a new surge of public concern. Outside of the public view there's an enormous amount going on. I'm eager to talk about it, but unlike the Senate, there's an inverse relationship between progress and publicity.

Interview/Vogue,
January:65,66.

Tom Graff
Lawyer,
Environmental Defense Fund

4

[Increased competition in the utility business,] in the long run, is likely to be positive for both the economy and the environment. [But alternative-energy firms could be at risk in a deregulated [market if consumers look only for the lowest price]. It's one thing to go to a local grocer and buy a head of lettuce that's free of pesticides. But electricity is kind of a generic product. You're not getting a better type of electricity from your renewable resource, even though you may feel better about how it's generated.

Los Angeles Times,
4-21:(D)4.

Hillel Gray
Co-author of report on
toxic-chemical accidents,
sponsored by Environmental
Law Center and U.S. Public
Interest Research Group

5

[On toxic-chemical accidents]: The fires, explosions and toxic-gas releases endanger people from all walks of life, from factory workers, firefighters and truck drivers to schoolchildren . . .

(HILLEL GRAY)

We're being daily besieged by a barrage of accidents involving toxic chemicals that cause cancer, birth defects, reproductive disorders and ecological damage.

Aug. 18/USA Today,
8-19:(A)3.

James Hartung
Director, Port of Indiana

1

The time has come for environmentalists and "developmentalists" to stop fighting through the media and start communicating with each other face to face with a very clearly structured agenda for progress.

The Christian Science Monitor,
3-14:13.

Michael Huffington
United States Representative,
R-California

2

People or flies. People or fairy shrimp. People or rats. These are not hard choices . . . I say it's time we focus less on saving endangered species and more on saving endangered jobs.

Los Angeles Times,
9-29:(A)21.

Charles Jordan
Director, Parks and Recreation
Department of Portland, Ore.

3

[On his city's aggressive policy of conserving and creating urban parks and other green and open spaces]: We're anticipating another half million people [in Portland] in the next 20 years. We're trying to ensure that our legacy is no less than our inheritance here, and so we're trying to set aside those special places right now . . . Urban areas have been a tough nut to crack. Public officials

must have the intestinal fortitude to set aside areas . . . They have to be visionary. You can always get rid of land, but you can't always recapture it.

The Christian Science Monitor,
2-8:10.

Peter L. Kelley
Director of communications,
League of Conservation Voters

4

[Criticizing the "Sportsmen's Caucus," a group made up of U.S. Congressmen who wish to further the interests of sports hunters and fishermen]: Typically, the Caucus is terrible. They're the kind that put on plaid shorts on Election Day and pretend they're environmentalists, then go back to Washington and vote against the environment the rest of the time.

Los Angeles Times,
3-16:(A)13.

Jim Maddy
President,
League of Conservation Voters

5

[Saying environmentalists have scaled back their expectations of aggressive environmental legislation coming out of the Clinton Administration and Congress]: The best we can do is prevent the Congress from weakening the Clean Water Act, prevent this Congress from weakening Superfund, prevent this Congress from weakening the Safe Drinking Water Act, and prevent this Congress from weakening the Endangered Species Act.

The New York Times,
3-30:(A)10.

Maher Mahran
Minister of Population of Egypt

6

[On the importance of all countries being involved in controlling population growth]: We all

(MAHER MAHRAN)

live in one boat. No country can withdraw, set itself aside; and those who do this are defeatists.

At a meeting of
Arab organizations/
Time, 9-12:56.

Jim Makris
Director, Office of
Preparedness and Prevention,
Environmental Protection
Administration of the
United States

1

[On toxic-chemical accidents]: There are a lot
of chemicals and a lot of accidents, but there also
are a fair number of checks that have prevented us
from having a major disaster in the U.S. Zero accidents is the goal, but I don't know if we'll achieve
that in our lifetime.

Aug. 18/USA Today,
8-19:(A)3.

Sylvia Marcos
Mexican
women's-rights advocate

2

Poor women [in under-developed countries]
are being blamed for the over-population of the
world and the ecological crisis, but we are very
clear that we don't accept that blame. A U.S. child
will spend and consume so much more than a child
born in Mexico. There's no comparison in the
impact on the environment . . . We don't want the
rich countries telling us how many babies to have,
but we don't want the church or our own government imposing that on us either.

The Christian Science Monitor,
9-7:9.

Thomas McGuane
Author; Board member,
American Rivers and
Craighead Wildlife Institute

3

I just happen to be obsessed with rivers, fix-
ated on rivers. [Water is] our internal environment
as well as our external environment. We're defined
by rivers . . . [But] like so many environmental
things that are right in our faces, rivers have come
in for extensive neglect . . . We know that aquatic
species are going extinct at twice the rate of ter-
restrial species, which substantiates our views that
rivers are collecting the negative effects of human
impact.

Interview/
USA Today, 2-23:(D)4.

George Miller
United States Representative,
D-California

4

[Criticizing Interior Secretary Bruce Babbitt
for capitulating to livestock interests in forming
new grazing regulations for Federal lands]:
Babbitt's been negotiating with people who never
had any intent of accepting any compromise. They
[the Clinton Administration] have got to take stock
of who it is they've been doing business with. The
grazing and timber and mining and water barons
do not go quietly. They really have no interest in
change.

Interview/
The Washington Post,
3-8:(A)3.

Donald O. Mitchell
Economist, International Bank
for Reconstruction and
Development (World Bank)

5

Meeting the world's food requirements during the 21st century should be increasingly easy if
past trends in production and consumption con-

(DONALD O. MITCHELL)

tinue. World food production has more than kept pace with population growth, and rates of growth of food production show few signs of slowing.

At International Food Policy
Research Institute,
Washington, D.C./
The Washington Post,
2-28:(A)3.

David Ozonoff
Director of environmental health,
Boston University School
of Public Health

1

[[Saying the safety of public water systems around the country has deteriorated]: People are committing an act of faith when they turn on their tap. The only thing standing between most people and waterborne disease is . . . good luck.

USA Today, 7-28:(A)5.

Bob Packwood
United States Senator,
R-Oregon

2

[Saying the new Republican majority in the next Congress can push through changes softening the Endangered Species Act]: We now have the votes to change [the law] so people count as much as bugs.

USA Today, 12-2:(A)1.

Per Pinstrup-Anderson
Director,
International Food Policy
Research Institute

3

[On the increases in food-crop yields that have compensated for increases in the world's population]: The *only* reason we've had these large yield increases is that we've made large investments in

the past. It's been fine up until now only because people with foresight did the right thing.

U.S. News & World Report,
9-12:60.

Carl Pope
Executive director, Sierra Club

4

Much as we [environmentalists] might like to be able to move a positive agenda by inspiring people, providing good ideas, working with enlightened and sympathetic people in the [Clinton] Administration and Congress, the ground rules of the game remain that in order to actually move environmental legislation, those [in government] who oppose it must feel pain. And they must feel pain where they care about it, which is back home [in their states and districts].

The New York Times,
3-30:(A)10.

Lewis T. Preston
President, International Bank
for Reconstruction and
Development (World Bank)

5

People-first environmentalism must have a strong focus on cities, because that is where the majority of the world's population is going to be living. Anyone who has visited a large city in the developing world has a sense of the scale and complexity of the issues involved.

At conference at
National Academy of Sciences,
Washington, D.C./
The Washington Post, 9-26:(A)3.

Melanie Rowland
Environmental lawyer,
University of Washington

6

[Arguing against weakening of laws protecting endangered species]: The importance is that we are driving so many [species] to extinction. We

(MELANIE ROWLAND)

don't know the significance of any one. We get all this stuff for free from nature. As we unravel it, we don't know what we're doing.

USA Today, 12-2:(A)2.

Nikki Roy
Analyst,
Environmental Defense Fund

1

We're always sending the message that your air problem is separate from your water problem, which is separate from your waste problem, which is separate from your worker-safety problem—the message that environmental protection can and should be split apart into different pieces. But if you're interested in pollution prevention, you need to think of all these things at the same time.

Los Angeles Times, 8-2:(A)5.

Ismail Serageldin
Vice president for
environmentally sustainable development,
International Bank for Reconstruction
and Development (World Bank)

2

The massive growth in the numbers of [the world's] urban poor, combined with the lack of urban planning on sanitation, air pollution, water supply and transportation, is what is making the environmental problems so intractable.

The Washington Post,
9-26:(A)3.

Stephen Smith
Executive director,
Tennessee Valley Energy
Reform Coalition

3

Nuclear power is really too costly to continue in its present form. As other energy options become more cost-effective, the financial risks . . .

associated with nuclear power are going to make it a less attractive option. Many utilities have already identified that.

The Christian Science Monitor,
12-14:8.

Gus Speth
Director, United Nations
Development Program

4

Sustainable [environment-preserving] development is the *sine qua non* of the new world order. Sustainability is now essential to achieve all of the major international goals of the United States or any other country—peace, democratization, disease control, migration control, environmental protection and population stabilization.

Los Angeles Times, 1-18:(H)1.

Jack Ward Thomas
Chief, United States Forest Service

5

[On balancing the interests of the environment with the interest of jobs that might be adversely affected by environmental legislation]: Human pain versus risk to the environment is one of the great philosophical arguments of our time. I don't think we can avoid the pain. But we can make things easier. Compassion for the plight of those affected and a helping hand are part of the President's (Clinton) plan.

Interview/People, 4-18:64.

Russell Train
Former Administrator, Environmental
Protection Agency of the United States

6

If you have to single out the one biggest threat facing humanity, it's population control. We didn't have to face it before. Politically, it's very difficult. The pressure of population converts forests to fields.

Interview/The Washington Post,
9-12:(D)3.

Government

Douglas Applegate
United States Representative,
D-Ohio

1

[On his decision not to seek re-election to the House]: The institution is changing and it is time for younger people to take the reins of government and lead us into the next century. I would further suggest that other older members of Congress consider this, as well.

Jan. 3/The Washington Post,
1-5:(A)13.

Richard K. Armey
United States Representative,
R-Texas

2

Government is too big, and in its excessive size does too much of the wrong things in the wrong way. Fat weakens muscle.

Interview, Washington, D.C./
The New York Times,
12-6:(A)11.

3

The government's dumb. No one spends another person's money as wisely as he spends his own.

U.S. News & World Report,
12-12:52.

4

I'm amused that [I've gotten] credit for doing the impossible. That shows you how impossible things are around here [in Washington]— when the impossible is the most doable.

U.S. News & World Report,
12-12:53.

Cass Ballenger
United States Representative,
R-North Carolina

5

[Supporting the so-called "A to Z" proposal, which would permit members of Congress to by-

pass House committees and take their Federal budget-cutting plans directly to the House floor]: A to Z is untraditional. But we have all seen where traditional methods take us: straight into debt.

May 4/Los Angeles Times,
5-5:(A)17.

Paul Begala
Political Adviser to President
of the United States Bill Clinton

6

[On charges that President Clinton doesn't have enough women in key White House positions]: It seems like only yesterday that [conservative commentator] Rush Limbaugh and the hot-air boys were attacking Clinton for having too many minorities. He has always picked the best people for the job and sometimes the very best people happen to be people of color or women. Sometimes they're not.

USA Today, 10-5:(A)9.

William J. Bennett
Former Secretary of Education
of the United States

7

We need to take functions away from the Federal government and return them to state and local levels. Government programs are always more effective when they are administered locally. [For example,] if the people in the state of California want bilingual education and they vote for it, then let them have it. But there is no reason [for Washington] to impose absurd uniform standards about bilingual education.

USA Today, 11-18:(A)10.

J. Christian Bollwage
Mayor of Elizabeth, N.J.

8

The attitude at both the national and state level is, "Let's cut income taxes!" There's no regard for

(J. CHRISTIAN BOLLWAGE)

the [local] governments below them. We're the only ones left who *have* to provide services.

Newsweek, 12-5:28.

David L. Boren
United States Senator, D-Oklahoma

1

[Criticizing the defeat of legislation that would have reformed the way Congress operates]: Our [public-] approval rating is down to 14 points. Are we going to wait to do something until not a single soul in America trusts us?

The New York Times,
10-1:1.

2

[On his decision not to run for another Senate term, but to instead become a university president]: I decided, at the end of the day, if I put in a 12-hour day as president of the University of Oklahoma, I would feel I had done something more constructive, more effective, more important to the country, really, in terms of results, than if I had put in 12 hours a day mainly arguing, not solving problems, but mainly arguing with my colleagues in the Senate.

Interview, Norman, Okla./
The New York Times,
11-17:(A)13.

Stephen G. Breyer
Judge, United States Court of
Appeals for the First Circuit;
Associate Justice-designate,
Supreme Court of the United States

3

There's a [property-] takings clause in the Constitution. It doesn't mean that people's clothes and toothbrushes are somehow at stake and could be swept away randomly. What it means is that the Constitution, which is a document that basically wants to guarantee people rights that will enable

them to lead lives of dignity, foresees over the course of history that a person's right to speak freely and to practice his religion is something that is of value, is not going to change. But one particular economic theory or some other economic theory is a function of the circumstances of the moment, and if the world changes so that it becomes crucially important to all of us that we protect the environment, that we protect health, that we protect safety, the Constitution is not a bar to that, because its basic object is to permit people to lead lives of dignity.

At Senate Judiciary Committee
hearing on his nomination,
Washington, D.C., July 12/
The New York Times, 7-13:(A)8.

William E. Brock III
Former United States Senator,
R-Tennessee

4

[On his decision to run for U.S. Senator from Maryland]: I've had some very good friends, Democrats and Republicans in the Congress, who have asked me if I've lost my mind. They say, "This is a mean place; it's not a happy place; it isn't as much fun as it used to be." I was talking to [Senator] Jack Danforth. He said, "I love you for doing it, but I can't imagine why you'd want to."

The New York Times,
4-4:(A)8.

Kathleen Brown
State Treasurer of California;
Candidate for the Democratic
nomination for Governor
of California

5

[Referring to the past Administrations of her father Pat and brother Jerry, both California Governors]: [In her father's time in the 1960s,] when you saw some problems, you built. [But] the old ways of my father just won't work because of limited resources. [In the 1970s and early 1980s, when

(KATHLEEN BROWN)

her brother was in office,] he focused on the power of ideas. Ideas could change things. That isn't what's going to do it now. [Today, you must] figure out what works and get it done.

Interview/
Newsweek, 4-11:28.

George W. Bush
Governor-elect of Texas (R)

1

My priority is for Texans to be running Texas. And I hope that that's the message that comes out of Congress. We're pretty good at what we do in Texas, and we like to be left alone by the Federal government as much as possible.

News conference,
Williamsburg, Va., Nov. 20/
The New York Times,
11-21:(A)14.

Robert C. Byrd
United States Senator,
D-West Virginia

2

Clearly the Senate is not what it once was. It isn't the institution, but those of us who make up the institution. We don't have the same inspiration, the same goals, the same motivation. Most important today is the 20-second sound bite, making of the headlines. It is not as uplifting as it once was.

Interview/
The New York Times, 3-3:(A)8.

Becky Cain
President,
League of Women Voters

3

[Arguing against term limits for members of Congress]: We already have term limits. They're called elections.

USA Today, 6-21:(A)1.

Thomas Carper
Governor of Delaware (D)

4

Governors, from both parties, want fewer Federal mandates [on states]. But I hope the new Republican majority [in Congress] will not give programs back to the states without including funds for the new responsibilities . . . The Clinton Administration was able to reduce the [Federal budget] deficit without leaving states holding the bag.

USA Today, 11-18:(A)10.

Bill Clinton
President of the United States

5

I like the job [of being President] . . . The bad days are part of it. I didn't run to have a pleasant time; I ran to have the chance to change the country. And if the bad days come with it—that's part of life, and it's humbling and educational. It keeps you in your place.

Newsweek, 1-31:15.

6

When people turn on television and they see their national government, what do you inevitably see? People with words, using extreme words to characterize conduct or activity or positions. The other politicians do it, the media do it; always trying to twist it like taffy to the nth degree. I've had older members of the Congress tell me just in the last week how much meaner and partisan and negative the national arena is.

At Brooklyn (N.Y.) College,
March 10/The Washington Post,
3-11:(A)11.

7

Compromise [in government] is very often given a bad name in popular circles today. And yet our system was set up to mandate compromise in ways that most governmental democracies weren't. We don't have a parliamentary system, for example, where the President is the leader of the party in Congress, where if people want to stay

(BILL CLINTON)

in the party and have positions, then they have to vote party line . . . The whole essence of democracy is that people are given limited power, and others have power, and you have to work together to get something done. And the idea is that nobody is the sole repository of complete wisdom. But in the world we're living in—instantaneous news coverage, snap judgments, everybody looking for an angle—compromise is more difficult, because the minute you begin serious negotiation, there's this the-sky-is-falling effect that sometimes takes over the reporting of it to imply that something dishonorable is going on. But in our Constitution, compromise is written in as a virtue, not a vice.

Interview, Washington, D.C.,
August/American Heritage,
December:121.

1

[Saying he has difficulty getting his positions across to the people because of the filters of his critics and the news media]: Sometimes I think the President, when I look at it, is least able to communicate with the American people because of the fog that I have to go through to reach them.

To religion journalists,
Washington, D.C., Oct. 3/
The New York Times,
10-4:(A)11.

2

[On the sweeping Republican Congressional victory in the just-held national elections]: The American people sent us [Democrats] here to rebuild the American dream, to change the way Washington does business, to make our country work for ordinary citizens again. We've made a good start . . . [But] there has been too much politics as usual in Washington, too much partisan conflict, too little reform of Congress and the political process. And though we have made progress, not enough people have felt more prosperous and more secure, or believe we were meeting their de-

sires for fundamental change in the role of government in their lives . . . I will do everything in my power to reach out to the leaders and the members of this new Congress. It must be possible to make it a more effective, more functioning institution. It must be possible for us to give our people a government that is smaller, that is more effective, that reflects both our interests and our values . . . [The public is] still not sure that we understand what they expect the role of government to be. I think they want a smaller government that gives them better value for their dollar, that reflects both their interests and their values, that is not a burden to them but that empowers them. That's what I have tried to do, but I don't think they believe we're there yet by a long shot.

News conference,
Washington, D.C., Nov. 9/
The New York Times,
11-10:(B)8.

3

I know some people just want to cut the government blindly, and I know that's popular now, but I won't do it. I want a leaner, not a meaner, government that's back on the side of hard-working Americans, a new government for the new economy, creative, flexible, high quality, low cost, service oriented, just like our more innovative private companies.

Broadcast address to the nation,
Washington D.C., Dec. 15/
The New York Times,
12-16:(A)12.

Hillary Rodham Clinton
Wife of President of the
United States Bill Clinton

4

[On suggestions that, as First Lady, she has been given too much policy making authority, such as her leading the health-care reform task force]: People have been doing that to women in this position since Martha Washington. I was not the first to testify before a Congressional committee; I was

(HILLARY RODHAM CLINTON)

not the first to be criticized by the press; I was not the first to have issues that I was involved in questioned or attacked. I look at what was said about Eleanor Roosevelt. There's always the possibility that no matter what you do you're going to be criticized. I do think that the fact that I am involved in an issue of such magnitude [health care] with so many interests at stake has raised the visibility of my role and has caused some to question it for their own purposes.

Interview, Washington, D.C./
Newsweek, 3-21:35.

1

[On criticism that she has not been accountable to the press, the public or government agencies despite her involvement in formulating health-care reform policy and despite controversies about her finances and the Whitewater scandal]: I think I have been held accountable. I don't know how many press interviews and press conferences I have held around the country, but if we were to add them up, there would be probably hundreds in the last year. So I feel very accountable. I think everyone who works in the White House is here because the President chose us. He is the only person that is here on his own merits; everybody else has been chosen by him and works for him. I think we are all accountable, and I don't mind that at all. And I have certainly tried to be available. Sometimes it's a little funny to me that I can travel all over the country and speak to thousands of people and answer hundreds of press questions and do dozens of live TV interviews, but because I haven't done it in Washington, it doesn't count. I don't understand that attitude.

Interview/People, 4-11:40.

2

[On her being an activist First Lady]: I came to this role having worked my entire life. I mean, I started working in the summers when I was 13. I always worked. I worked through college. I worked through law school. That's what I did. And

after I married, I continued to work. And after my daughter was born, with the exception of the four months I took off for maternity leave, I worked. And I think that, having been independent, having made decisions, it's a little difficult for us as a country, maybe, to make the transition of having a woman like many of the women in this room sitting in [the White House]. So I think that the standards and, to some extent . . . the expectations and the demands have changed, and I'm trying to find my way through it and trying to figure out how best to be true to myself and how to fulfill my responsibilities to my husband and my daughter and the country.

News conference,
Washington, D.C., April 22/
Los Angeles Times, 4-23:(A)25.

3

Government, alone, cannot solve our problems, but government, as a partner with us, can move us a very far way down the road of beginning to deal honestly with our problems and being able to make progress together. If, for an instant, you doubt our ability to change, to make progress, to build a more economically productive, socially just, politically productive and morally right society, think about places like South Africa and hear what [new South African President] Nelson Mandela said.

At University of Illinois
at Urbana-Champaign
commencement/USA Today,
5-19:(A)13.

4

[On being involved in the Federal government]: I can see how you can become so captured by the system that you live or die by what people say about you, and I'm trying to avoid that . . . You know, I really do take each day at a time . . . You could drive yourself crazy if you were somebody who couldn't let go of responsibilities around here, because there's more than you could ever get done.

Interview, Washington, D.C./
Working Woman, June:42.

GOVERNMENT

(HILLARY RODHAM CLINTON)

1

[On suggestions that she is too influential or powerful for her position]: Much of the influence that First Ladies have exercised in the past has been extremely private and totally unaccountable. Nobody had any idea what she was saying to him [the President] about anything. My belief is that each woman has to fashion this undefined role for herself—and maybe at some point a man will have to do the same. I have always been an up-front person. I have always felt that public policy was important, and that we could make a difference, whether my husband was Governor or President, and this is how I have conducted myself.

Interview, Washington, D.C./
Vanity Fair, June:108.

2

It is only in the last 20 or 30 years that we've gotten two extreme views of government, I think, neither of which is very helpful. One is that government is evil and incompetent and always messes up. Well, the National Institutes of Health, the National Park Service, Social Security and Medicare are evidence that that's not necessarily true, right? And the other view is that government can solve all people's problems. Well, if you look at the breakdown of the social fabric in America in the last 30 years, it's obvious no government program can fix all that.

Interview, Washington, D.C.,
August/American Heritage,
December:123.

3

Unfortunately, we're living in a time when it is increasingly difficult, if you're in public life, to get your side of the facts out, because unless it is sensationalistic, or about conflict, it isn't considered very newsworthy. That's been frustrating. And that gets me back to the era that we're in. I worry very much about how we keep a democracy going when people don't know who to believe, when

they think everybody's in it for themselves, when they don't think there's any objective facts out there.

Interview, Washington, D.C./
Ladies' Home Journal,
November:274.

Tony Coelho
Former United States Representative,
D-California

4

[Arguing against term limits for members of Congress]: A constituency has a right to elect their representative for as long as they want. [Term limits would] eliminate much of the knowledge and experience in Congress and, in effect, turn over power to staff, to lobbyists and to the press. I don't think that's where the power should be.

Interview, Washington, D.C./
The Wall Street Journal,
2-3:(A)15.

5

Congress has become stagnant; it hasn't grown with the changes that have occurred in society . . . They have created more power centers and with them more opportunities for gridlock. These are not only legislative centers but you then get the law firms, the lobbyists and all the industries that then fit in with them.

Interview, Washington, D.C./
The Wall Street Journal,
2-3:(A)15.

William E. Colby
Former Director of
Central Intelligence
of the United States

6

[Saying the decision by Bobby Ray Inman not to accept the nomination for Defense Secretary illustrates how some people don't want to subject themselves to the accusations and personal investigations that go with the process]: Somewhere

137

(WILLIAM E. COLBY)

underneath in him he was very unhappy with the idea of getting booted about in public. When I was nominated to be Director of Central Intelligence, they put posters all over town saying what a terrible war criminal I was. It seems to me when you go into something like this, you [should] expect to get kicked around.

The New York Times,
1-20:(A)10.

Mario M. Cuomo
Governor of New York (D)

1

I laugh about the labels: Democrats, Republicans, conservatives, liberals. That you talk about in [election] campaigns. You don't *govern* that way.

Speech to bankers,
Saratoga Springs, N.Y./
The New York Times,
6-30:(C)19.

John C. Danforth
United States Senator, R-Missouri

2

In the House, Republicans are treated like dogs. And when people are treated as dogs, they start biting back. That's happened in the House, and then as House Republicans got elected to the Senate, they brought the same combativeness with them.

Interview, St. Louis, Mo./
The Christian Science Monitor,
11-21:12.

John Dean
Former Counsel to the President
of the United States (Richard M. Nixon)

3

You can't believe how much time a White House will spend on things they are publicly very

nonchalant about. They spend much more time than they would ever admit . . . and that's not governing.

Interview,
Washington, D.C./
USA Today, 8-5:(A)4.

Vic Fazio
United States Representative,
D-California

4

[On the House's passage of a bill aimed at requiring lobbyists to disclose contacts with members of Congress and which prohibits them from buying meals, gifts, etc. for members]: This [bill] is an important step, not because I believe there is a widespread problem in this institution, but because there is a perception that highly paid lobbyists wine and dine members of Congress into supporting whatever cause they promote. Every member . . . came here for a reason. No one came here for a free lunch.

Washington, D.C., March 24/
Los Angeles Times,
3-25:(A)23.

Dianne Feinstein
United States Senator,
D-California

5

Californians want less government, a government that places a higher priority on individual responsibility and less emphasis on tax-supported solutions. They want fewer Federal mandates and impositions, whether the issue is welfare or water policy, endangered species or education, health care or human resources. They want tough enforcement of tough laws on crime and immigration. And, finally, no more new taxes.

News conference declaring victory
in the recent California
U.S. Senate election,
San Francisco, Calif., Nov. 18/
The New York Times, 11-19:8.

Marlin Fitzwater
Former Press Secretary to former
Presidents of the United States
Ronald Reagan and George Bush

1

[Saying independent counsels investigating possible Presidential wrongdoing can actually be beneficial to the White House]: [The independent investigation] was crucial to us during [the] Iran-contra [scandal]. Although there was some initial to-ing and fro-ing over who knew what when, essentially the White House was able to take the position from that point on that this was all being investigated by the independent counsel, which relieved them from the obligation of answering any questions [publicly]. It's an enormous asset.

Los Angeles Times, 1-13:(A)18.

Thomas S. Foley
United States Representative,
D-Washington;
Speaker of the House

2

[On the public's negative opinion of Congress]: You've got a tremendous public disinformation program going about the Congress. It's not a conspiratorial thing. It's just [that] it suits a number of different organizations and entities in the country to characterize the Congress in a very, very negative way. [But] the public reaction to this is still to have a very high degree of confidence in their *own* member [of Congress] . . . But everybody's guy can't be okay and the whole thing bad . . . How do you explain it?

The Washington Post, 1-25:(A)4.

3

[Criticizing the so-called "A to Z" proposal, which would permit members of Congress to by-pass House committees and take their Federal budget-cutting plans directly to the House floor]: I think this is the most poorly thought out proposal for the consideration of public policy that I have seen in many years, and maybe the worst one ever in terms of consideration by the House.

May 4/Los Angeles Times,
5-5:(A)17.

4

[On criticism of Congress]: There has been some tendency . . . to denigrate the institution itself by its own members. I think that is unfortunate, because it has led many people to have a loss of confidence, a loss of respect for the institution that is their body more than any other place in our public life, the place where their hopes and concerns, their opinions and their values are carried forward.

News briefing, Washington, D.C./
U.S. News & World Report,
12-12:34.

5

If I had one sort of compelling concern in the time that I have been Speaker in particular, but previous to that as well, it is that we not idly tamper with the Constitution of the United States.

News briefing, Washington, D.C./
U.S. News & World Report,
12-12:34.

Robert M. Gates
Former Director of
Central Intelligence
of the United States

6

[On accusations made against, and personal investigations of, those nominated for high government positions]: Everybody talks about thick skin and thin skin, but I have served six Presidents and have been in this town 28 years and I don't know anybody who is thick-skinned when it comes to an attack on personal reputation, character and integrity.

The New York Times, 1-20:(A)10.

Fred Gebler
President,
American League of Lobbyists

7

[Criticizing pending legislation that would restrict members of Congress' acceptance of

(FRED GEBLER)

meals, travel and other gifts from lobbyists, and saying many members are already shunning such "freebies"]: It's already having a chilling effect [on lobbying efforts]. Members [of Congress] are still coming [to events], but such that they give their remarks and depart. If there's a meal, they just have a cup of coffee. We [lobbyists] feel we should not be targeted as a class of citizens.

The Christian Science Monitor,
6-15:2.

David R. Gergen
Counsellor to President
of the United States Bill Clinton

1

[Defending the Clinton Administration practice of using non-government aides and advisers who do not have to meet security and conflict-of-interest regulations and who are not accountable the way official government employees are]: If the President didn't reach out to people, critics would say he is isolated. There is a tremendous value to a President in reaching beyond government.

U.S. News & World Report,
3-28:28.

Alfred Gilchrist
Legislative director,
Texas Medical Association

2

Relationships [between interest groups and their Congressmen] are more important than anything else in this business. When they're developed with a strong sense of trust, Congressmen tend to rely on them. On close calls, when a committee is marking up a bill in closed doors and a bad amendment comes up, you hope the member with strong local relationships will say, "Mr. Chairman, that's not the way to go."

The Washington Post,
3-8:(A)6.

Newt Gingrich
Unites States Representative, R-Georgia

3

I've spent much of my career reporting accurately on a Congress that's worthy of being despised.

Los Angeles Times,
10-3:(A)1.

Newt Gingrich
Unites States Representative, R-Georgia;
Speaker of the House-designate

4

[On the sweeping Republican Congressional victory in the just-held national elections]: The first thing we're [Republicans] going to do is keep our word. We said, the very first thing we'd do on opening day [of the new Republican-controlled Congress] is pass the Shays Act to apply to the Congress every law that applies to the rest of the country. We're going to do it. We're going to keep our word. And we're going to invite everybody in America to watch us on C-SPAN that day, and to see that we actually do what we promised to do. The first thing we're going to do, frankly, is offer to work with the Democrats to re-establish the kind of openness that [the late House Speaker] Sam Rayburn had in a different era. [Current House Republican leader] Bob Michel has often talked about a time when you could amend on the floor, when you could really craft legislation, a very much more collegial House than the one that has gradually become more bitter and more partisan. I think we have a chance to recreate that kind of environment.

Broadcast interview/
"Morning News,"
CNN-TV, 11-9.

5

The experiment we've had with professional politicians and professional government has failed. We've discovered that you can't hire people to think about your government and society and then walk off and let them do it.

USA Today, 11-18:(A)10.

(NEWT GINGRICH)

1

When you see a large government bureaucracy, is it an inevitable relic of the past that can't be changed? Or is it an opportunity for an extraordinary transformation to provide better services and better opportunities at lower cost—exactly what every major corporation is going through.

*Before fellow Republican members
of the House, Washington, D.C.,
Dec. 5/The New York Times,
12-6:(A)10.*

2

[On the new Republican majority in Congress starting in 1995]: We're not going to change America in Washington, D.C. We're going to change America one individual at a time, one family at a time, one neighborhood at a time, one church or synagogue at a time, one voluntary organization at a time, one private business at a time, and then one local government, one school board, one city council, one state legislature. And, yeah, Congress and the President are going to have a role to play in all this. But we're not going to get through these changes if we [Republicans] think we can hire a bunch of professional bureaucrats, but *ours* will be smarter; if we think that *our* professional politicians hiding in rooms are better than the Democrats' professional politicians hiding in rooms.

*Before fellow Republican members
of the House, Washington, D.C.,
Dec. 5/The New York Times,
12-6:(A)10.*

Rudolph W. Giuliani
Mayor of New York, N.Y.

3

[Saying the Federal government should cut the red tape on money it gives to cities]: If you let us spend the money more in the way that we want to spend the money, we can actually spend less more effectively.

*The Christian Science Monitor,
11-21:3.*

Doris Kearns Goodwin
Historian, Biographer

4

[On being the wife of the President of the United States]: One of the peculiarities of the role [of First Lady] is that you make what you want of it. You choose what constituencies to represent. [Current First Lady Hillary Rodham Clinton] could have chosen civil rights or something like that. She chose policy analysis; very important and valuable—good for her— but not the kind of choice that develops constituencies that stick with you.

Working Woman, June:84.

5

[On the sweeping Republican Congressional victory in the just-held national elections]: The time has come for those who still believe, as most Democrats do, that the government has a positive role to play in the lives of the people to re-define what that role is, and to communicate that definition with a passion and a conviction that the Republicans seem to have evoked in their call for no government or less government or smaller government.

*Nov. 9/The New York Times,
11-10:(B)4.*

Al Gore
Vice President of the United States

6

[On President Clinton's directive that government agencies improve their services to the public]: In the past we have designed programs and systems to satisfy bosses. Now, the boss [President Clinton] is telling us to design programs and systems that satisfy the customer. That is the critical difference.

*Presenting the National Performance
Review Hammer Award
to the Veterans Affairs
New York City regional office,
New York, N.Y., March 11/
The Washington Post,
3-14:(A)17.*

(AL GORE)

1

[On the Clinton Administration's proposals to implement changes in several Federal agencies as a cost-saving measure]: I know that you are all aware that we gave serious consideration to totally eliminating each of these agencies. In these cases, the President and I were convinced that the re-invention and reform option was preferable. But over the next several months we will be looking at every other agency and program, asking the direct question, "Do we really need this agency; do we really need this program; is there a better way to do it; is there an opportunity here to give middle-class Americans a break?"

Press briefing,
Washington, D.C., Dec. 19/
The New York Times,
12-20:(A)14.

Billy Graham
Evangelist

2

Few events touch the heart of every American as profoundly as the death of a President. For the President is our leader, and every American feels he knows him in a very special way, because he hears his voice so often, sees him on television, reads about him in the press. And so we all mourn his loss and feel that our world is a bit lonelier without him.

At burial ceremony for the late
President Richard Nixon,
Yorba Linda, Calif., April 27/
Los Angeles Times, 4-28:(A)12.

Fred Grandy
United States Representative, R-Iowa

3

[On the mood of the voters in this year's national elections]: They are torn between their addiction to "bacon" and their aversion to "pork."

U.S. News & World Report,
11-14:39.

Mark Green
Public Advocate of New York, N.Y.

4

You can't have a democracy without citizenship. We brag we're the world's greatest democracy, yet proportionately fewer of us vote than the citizens of France, England, Nicaragua, Israel . . . The problem is that it's not enough for a citizen to vote every two or four years and pay his or her taxes, and then bellyache in-between. On their side, government officials have to have an interactive relationship with citizens.

Interview, New York, N.Y./
Lear's, March:16.

Paul Hillegonds
Michigan State Representative (R)

5

[Saying state governments may have gone too far in implementing tougher ethical standards for their legislators]: My attitude has changed. I now believe you can get too involved in reform. The more detailed you get, the more change there is, the more the public and the press will focus on the negative . . . I'm wary of going too far.

The Christian Science Monitor,
8-3:4.

Bob Inglis
United States Representative,
R-South Carolina

6

Asking an incumbent member of Congress to vote for term limits [for members of Congress] is a bit like asking the chicken to vote for Colonel Sanders.

U.S. News & World Report,
12-12:39.

John R. Kasich
United States Representative, R-Ohio

7

[On the new Republican majority in Congress beginning next January]: Our goal will be to shrink

(JOHN R. KASICH)

the size and scope and influence of the Federal government and respond directly to what the people have been saying. We're a group of supply-siders who also happen to be deficit [-reduction] hawks. What we really want to do is complete the [former President Ronald] Reagan agenda. And the Reagan agenda is you give people incentives and you also reduce the size and scope of government.

USA Today, 11-18:(A)4.

David Keene
President,
American Conservative Union

1

[On Democratic Congressional staff who will lose their jobs as a result of the sweeping Republican victory in the recent national elections]: Washington is a company town, and this is the equivalent of Boeing closing down in Seattle.

U.S. News & World Report,
11-21:34.

Edward M. Kennedy
United States Senator,
D-Massachusetts

2

[On being a Senator]: When you're a Presidential contender, you always get more attention around here but less credibility. When you're not, you get more credibility but less attention. That's always been the classic commentary.

Interview/Esquire,
September:129.

Bob Kerrey
United States Senator, D-Nebraska

3

[Federal bureaucracy] is the most formidable enemy of all sometimes.

Time, 9-12:39.

Michael Kinsley
Senior editor, "The New Republic";
Co-host, "Crossfire," CNN-TV

4

You have to be really thick-skinned to be a politician. Anyone who would really put themselves through this must be so twisted by ambition that they probably shouldn't be running our lives. They have a need for approval. When you vote for someone, you have to go into the voting booth and make a physical gesture of approval. I think [politicians] are victims of loving mothers.

Interview, Chevy Chase, Md./
Vanity Fair, November:80.

Tom Korologos
Washington lobbyist;
Former official in the
Administration of former
President of the United States
Richard M. Nixon

5

Washington is [like] Salem [Mass., during the witch hunts]. If we're not lynching somebody 24 hours a day in this wretched town, we're not happy.

Newsweek, 3-21:27.

Patrick J. Leahy
United States Senator, D-Vermont

6

[On Senate Majority Leader George Mitchell's decision not to run for re-election to the Senate this fall]: I would not be surprised if there was a frustration [on his part] with the Senate. There are too many Senators who forget that the Senate is supposed to be the conscience of the nation, and there are too many Senators who act as if they never want to take a position that would jeopardize them from owning a seat for life. George Mitchell put principal above political expedience.

March 4/
The Washington Post,
3-5:(A)4.

Mike Leavitt
Governor of Utah (R);
President, Republican
Governors Association

1

[We in the states are] balancing budgets, we're reforming welfare, we're fixing health care, we're dealing with crime. Our message will be to Congressional leaders, people of this country: Give us the ball and get out of the way. We [not the Federal government] can solve these problems.

News conference,
Williamsburg, Va., Nov. 20/
The New York Times,
11-21:(A)1.

Carl M. Levin
United States Senator, D-Michigan

2

[On legislation by the Senate to limit perks and gifts its members may receive]: A reasonable case can be made that [members' privileged airport] parking helps us perform our duties [in a timely manner]. [But] for me, the gifts don't help us perform our duties . . . and I don't think it's related to our performance of duties to spend three days at a golf tournament [paid for by special interests].

Interview/
The Washington Post,
5-9:(A)8.

Charles Lewis
Executive director,
Center for Public Integrity

3

[On the Clinton Administration's practice of using non-government aides and advisers who do not have to meet security and conflict-of-interest regulations and who are not accountable the way official government employees are]: You have an adjunct kind of shadow government that is exploiting a gray area. They will do whatever they need to do to help [President Clinton] and to also re-

main robust in the private sector. There is this yuppie arrogance: "We're the good guys, don't bust our chops."

U.S. News & World Report,
3-28:28.

4

[On his organization's study that shows many former members of Congress keep funds left over from campaign contributions for themselves]: The American people are deeply suspicious of Congress, and there is a persistent perception out there that individual elected officials are out of touch with ordinary, everyday citizens . . . and worse, that they are principally interested in feathering their own nests. I must say that the findings of this study don't exactly bolster our confidence in Congress.

To reporters/
The Christian Science Monitor,
7-1:3.

Joseph I. Lieberman
United States Senator, D-Connecticut

5

What happens here [in Congress] is transparent to most people. It's a meaningless tit-for-tat [political] tug of war. And that's clearly part of why the public is so frustrated and angry with us.

U.S. News & World Report,
11-14:40.

Frank Luntz
Republican Party
public-opinion analyst

6

[Saying Republicans, who had a sweeping Congressional victory in the recent national elections, should not now change their stand away from the idea of terms limits for members of Congress]: Any Republican who thinks they can now switch their position on term limits will not learn of their mistake until [the elections of] November 1996, but they will learn it at that time. I hope they see the seriousness of the public on term limits.

USA Today, 12-2:(A)7.

Sandy Maisel
Professor of government,
Colby College

1

[On the problems of a Senate Majority Leader]: The Senate is a very tough place to lead. You've got a hundred millionaires and egomaniacs, a bunch of them running for re-election . . . and you've got rules which are stacked against you.
USA Today, 9-9:(A)4.

John McCain
United States Senator, R-Arizona

2

[Saying Senate filibusters should not keep that body from adjourning on time]: Most Americans want us to get out of town. They think we have done enough harm.
Newsweek, 10-17:23.

Eugene J. McCarthy
Former United States Senator,
D-Minnesota

3

[President] Clinton should give up being Governor of the United States, which he ran for, and be President. Crime control and welfare reform and education are state and local problems. Do something about basic disorders in society, like debt and jobs. Fire the Rhodes and Yale and Oxford scholars and everyone from Arkansas [in the Administration]. You can't run the country with a clique.
Interview/Mother Jones,
Nov.-Dec.:51.

Mark Mellman
Democratic Party
public-opinion analyst

4

[On public cynicism toward government]: In Washington, we distinguish between Republicans and Democrats. [But] in the real world, it is "the politicians" against "the rest of us."
U.S. News & World Report,
10-24:63.

Robert H. Michel
United States Representative,
R-Illinois

5

[On his advice to Republicans who will take over Congressional leadership positions in 1995 as a result of the Party's recent sweeping national elections victory]: I didn't crave power when I was leader [of the minority for 14 years; he recently announced his retirement]. I don't know if it would have changed if I were Speaker [of the House]. I just hope it doesn't go to our newly elected leaders' heads. There's always a danger in clawing at power because power corrupts and absolute power corrupts absolutely . . . Over-playing your hand in the majority can lend itself to the minority in justifying itself in really sticking it to you.
Interview/
The New York Times,
11-26:9.

Abner J. Mikva
Chief Judge,
United States Court of Appeals
for the District of Columbia;
Counsel-designate to
President of the United States
Bill Clinton

6

[On his soon-to-be post of White House Counsel]: The Presidency is not an empty vessel; a real-live person with human needs and concerns occupies the office. A White House Counsel can represent the person while recognizing that the lawyer's ultimate loyalty is to the office [of the Presidency]. Occasionally, there may be a conflict between the office and the person, and in those cases my top responsibility will be to the country.
Interview, Aug. 12/
The Christian Science Monitor,
8-16:3.

George J. Mitchell
United States Senator, D-Maine

1

[On his decision to leave the Senate, where he is Majority Leader]: One of the baseball-team owners approached me and said, "If you become Baseball Commissioner, you're going to have to deal with 28 big egos [the team owners]," and I said, "For me, that's a 72 percent reduction!"

Newsweek, 5-16:19.

2

[On the Senate]: This is the world's champion forum for nit-picking, second-guessing and should-have dones.

Washington, D.C., Sept. 21/
The New York Times,
9-22:(A)8.

W. Henson Moore
Former Deputy Chief of Staff
to the President of the
United States (George Bush)

3

[On the absence of many women in the President's inner circle of advisers]: Formulas [for increasing diversity] don't necessarily give you good judgement and formulas don't give you people who do the job right. Usually the inner circle in any White House is very small and to ever have that truly be diverse is probably not realistic.

USA Today, 10-5:(A)9.

Daniel Patrick Moynihan
United States Senator, D-New York

4

[On the Senate Finance Committee, which he chairs]: This is a committee that has its own rhythm, and when we do something it's real. We try to talk it out and talk it out and talk it out til we're ready, and we try to be as near bipartisan as we can.

Interview,
Washington, D.C., June 28/
The New York Times, 6-29:(A)1.

Patty Murray
United States Senator,
D-Washington

5

I know the women in the Senate are being watched—not just on Capitol Hill but across the nation—by a whole generation of women who want to know if we can succeed. I think we really feel the pressure of that, which is why we're so supportive of each other and work together to make sure we all succeed, because quite frankly, if we don't, there's a whole generation behind us who will take forever to get in here.

Interview/Cosmopolitan,
October:219.

Dee Dee Myers
Press Secretary to President
of the United States Bill Clinton

6

[On a suggestion that personal friendships protect certain White House officials from dismissal by President Clinton or his wife Hillary]: Nobody's bulletproof in this White House. Every single person here serves at the pleasure of the President. It's a tough neighborhood.

Newsweek, 3-14:19.

7

There is an institutional cynicism that causes reporters to question everything the President says, and the motives of everything the President and his Administration try to accomplish. I think that is troubling. I don't think anything is ever taken at face value. The press never accepts at face value that the President is taking a certain action because he wants to create jobs or because he believes that it is in the best interests of the American people or that he is genuinely committed to making life better for people. There is a relentless search for motives, bad actions, insincerity. This is a generation weaned on Watergate, and there is no presumption of innocence and no presumption of good in-

(DEE DEE MYERS)

tentions. Instead, there is a presumption that, without relentless scrutiny, the government will misbehave.

Interview, Washington, D.C./
Los Angeles Times, 3-20:(M)3.

Ralph Nader
Lawyer; Consumer advocate

1

I'm flexible. But in Washington you don't usually have the luxury of dealing in shades of gray. The issues are black and white . . . No honest person can differ.

Newsweek, 8-22:40.

Verne Newton
Director, Franklin D. Roosevelt
Presidential Library

2

[On current First Lady Hillary Rodham Clinton's activist involvement in her husband's Administration]: It may not be possible after Mrs. Clinton for any First Lady to accept a lesser role. I don't think many women would accept that—and for all we know, the next President could be a woman. The point is, she has historically altered the role. All things are possible.

Working Woman, June:84.

Jim Nussle
United States Representative,
R-Iowa

3

[On the new Republican majority's intention to downsize the operations of the House]: We [the House] have an office of typewriter repair. We've got an office of the clocks. We've got an office of the bells . . . Every morning, every office is delivered a bucket of ice. Why is it done? Well, it's always been done that way . . . [But now] we have a mandate to fulfill from the voters to change busi-

ness-as-usual in Washington. The trains have to run on time [when the Republican majority takes over] on January 4.

USA Today, 11-17:(A)5.

Norman J. Ornstein
Fellow,
American Enterprise Institute

4

[The hardest thing in a legislature is] forming a majority—taking a series of disparate, independent and strong-minded individuals with varied interests to represent, pulling them together to a common purpose and then getting them to vote for that common purpose.

The New York Times,
6-1:(A)13.

5

Ideally, you want Congress to be a variegated group, people with diverse life experiences. You lose something if personal wealth becomes a criterion.

Time, 6-20:36.

Leon E. Panetta
Director, Federal Office
of Management and Budget

6

[Saying the management and the budget operations of his office sometimes work at cross purposes]: Generally, each kind of lets the other do their thing, and they don't really work together in terms of implementing the decisions. There is oftentimes conflict. I mean, what will happen is that management will implement, try to implement, a certain policy through the agencies, and it may very well contradict what is being done on the budget side, in terms of providing resources.

Interview/
The Washington Post,
3-10:(A)19.

Timothy J. Penny
United States Representative,
D-Minnesota

1

[Saying he will not run for re-election]: After 10 years in Congress, it is evident to me that far too many politicians end up staying far too long . . . My family, my friends, my roots call me home.
USA Today, 10-5:(A)11.

Jody Powell
Former Press Secretary
to the President of the United States
(Jimmy Carter)

2

There is so much going on in any White House on virtually any given day that there is always a certain amount of chaos. People are always short of time and under pressure, and you're always understaffed. Communications are frequently hurried and cryptic or elliptical.
USA Today, 7-28:(A)9.

Janet Reno
Attorney General
of the United States

3

To get along in Washington, you should . . . try to keep your feet on the ground . . . and not let five different people who have five different ideas about what you should do pull you in so may different directions that you aren't the person you really are.
Interview/Vanity Fair,
April:175.

Marvin Runyon
Postmaster General
of the United States

4

We've got to change the way we do business . . . in the Postal Service. We have lots of competitors out there . . . We have been the information superhighway of this country for over 200 years, and the only thing changing that is electronics. We used to have 100 percent share of first-class mail. Today, we have about 60 percent. There are predictions that say we'll have 35 percent by the year 2000. That's a big hit. So we're working on products to replace that.
Interview/USA Today,
3-7:(A)13.

Patricia Schroeder
United States Representative,
D-Colorado

5

Things are a little more colorful here [in Congress for women members]. We've gotten better committee assignments for women than ever before. But we're still very marginal . . . Anybody who's ever studied institutions knows that you need a critical mass—about 35 percent—before you can really do anything. We're up five percent to 10 percent. With all the women around here, we still don't have a full committee chairman. I was a full committee chairman [of the Select Committee on Children, Youth and Families] for about nine months; then they abolished the committee.
Lear's, January:54.

Donna E. Shalala
Secretary of Health and
Human Services of the United States

6

In this [Clinton] Administration, there are so many women at high levels that you literally can move a major policy issue all the way to the President's desk without ever touching a male's hands.
At celebration of the first year
in office of top-level female
Administration appointees,
Washington, D.C., Feb. 8/
The Washington Post,
2-10:(C)2.

Patricia R. Sher
Maryland State Senator (D)

1

We [in government] do the hard things in the second and third year of a term. In election years, we pass a lot of fluff to make ourselves look good.
The Washington Post,
4-11:(A)1.

Alan K. Simpson
United States Senator, R-Wyoming

2

[On the public's attitude toward Congress]: There's an attitude out there in the public which is more volatile than anything I've ever seen. They don't trust us . . . They're fed up.
USA Today, 1-24:(A)9.

Yvonne Sims
Community-forum moderator,
Kettering Foundation

3

[Saying public dialogue on important issues is the essence of democracy]: Polls and surveys do not substitute for my interacting with you. You don't have a democracy when you have one person's opinion. You may have paradise, but you don't have a democracy.
The Washington Post,
4-25:(A)17.

Frederick T. Steeper
Public-opinion analyst

4

[On the possibility of having more "direct democracy," in which the public uses today's technologies to vote on issues, thereby bypassing representative democracy as typified by Congress and local governments]: We need to rethink the whole idea of indirect [representative] democracy that we've been committed to for 200 years. The problem with direct democracy was logistical, not philosophical. But with the information technol-

ogy we have now, there's no reason why the whole people cannot "meet" electronically and decide public issues.
News conference sponsored by
Americans Talk Issues Foundation,
April 19/The Washington Post,
4-25:(A)17.

Mike Synar
United States Representative,
D-Oklahoma

5

[On Senate filibusters]: In the past, the filibuster was used sparingly. Now not only is it used a lot, but just the threat of it being used has made it harder for us to deal with issues that are vital.
Los Angeles Times, 8-31:(A)5.

Tommy G. Thompson
Governor of Wisconsin (R)

6

[On the relationship he sees between state Governors and the new Republican-controlled Congress]: They're eager to cooperate with us [Governors]. And that is such a change of philosophy and common courtesy that we've been asking for for so long. And it is really refreshing to go to Washington and have somebody come in and say, you know, they'll listen to us . . . Each of us in our own way have gone to Washington on bended knee, to kiss the ring, to get a waiver in order to do something. All we're saying now is we don't want to have to go through the mating dance.
News conference,
Williamsburg, Va., Nov. 20/
The New York Times,
11-21:(A)14.

George Voinovich
Governor of Ohio (R)

7

The partisanship is out of hand in Washington. The President [Clinton] uses it as an excuse

149

(GEORGE VOINOVICH)

sometimes, but there's not enough sitting down with your opponents and getting the job done. That's what people want.

U.S. News & World Report,
10-31:56.

Malcolm Wallop
United States Senator, R-Wyoming

1

[Criticizing strict legislation by the Senate to limit perks and gifts its members may receive]: [The public will not be impressed by] a Senate that says we cannot trust ourselves. Lawyers have taken over the concept of life int he Senate . . . and it is killing the effective creativity of this body.

The Washington Post, 5-9:(A)1.

Craig A. Washington
United States Representative, D-Texas

2

[Saying he tries to work in the interest of those individuals and organizations that help him at re-election time]: It's human nature that you should be grateful to people who help you in your time of need. When my constituents are equally well served by either side, I support those who support me.

Interview/The Washington Post,
3-8:(A)1.

Vin Weber
Republican Party strategist;
Former United States Representative,
R-Minnesota

3

[On the idea of downsizing government, which was favored by the Republican Party in its sweeping Congressional victory in the recent national elections]: Nobody ever again will be able to run on re-establishing a Federal agency to solve a problem.

U.S. News & World Report,
11-21:46.

Fred Wertheimer
President, Common Cause

4

[On ethics scandals in Congress]: There is a clear environment up there [on Capitol Hill] that the rules aren't to be enforced. It does enormous damage to the institution [of Congress] because it allows lowest-common-denominator ethics to set the public standard for the institution.

Los Angeles Times, 6-2:(A)12.

5

We have a corrupt system, a system where large sums of [election-] campaign contributions can be given to members of Congress by people trying to influence their decisions. Washington lobbyists and special interests finance the lifestyles of members of Congress. The system breeds public cynicism. Washington is the last holdout against the idea that fundamental change must be made in the way business is done in this town. It can't hold out forever. Its time is coming.

Interview, Washington, D.C./
U.S. News & World Report,
10-24:20.

Christine Todd Whitman
Governor of New Jersey (R)

6

I hope that the legislature, that [the new Republican-controlled] Congress, understands that what got everyone elected this year was fiscal issues; that the people want to see less government, less taxing, less spending by the government, and that's where we put our emphasis.

Broadcast interview/
"Meet the Press," NBC-TV, 11-20.

Pete Wilson
Governor of California (R)

7

We [Governors] believe the states that we have been privileged to govern are just that. They are sovereign, proud states of the United States. They are not colonies of the Federal government.

News conference,
Williamsburg, Va., Nov. 20/
The New York Times, 11-21:(A)1.

Law • The Judiciary

Eleanor Dean Acheson
Assistant Attorney General
of the United States

1

[Saying the Clinton Administration has chosen many women and minorities in its Federal judgeship appointments and that there are no political ideology tests]: We have not seen a tension between excellence and diversity . . . We have a very rich field to pick from . . . We are seeking people who have intellectual ability and energy, people who are interested in the law and have a good judicial temperament. There are no litmus tests.

Los Angeles Times,
1-11:(A)11.

2

[Disputing charges that the pace of Clinton Administration appointments to fill Federal judgeship vacancies has been too slow]: I absolutely, aggressively disagree. Critics have no clue as to the process and how incredibly important it is to be deliberate . . . People used to say there was a tension between excellence and diversity. We haven't found that at all. Across the board, we have had some excellent candidates to work with.

USA Today, 6-27:(A)2.

Cory M. Amron
Lawyer; Chairman,
Commission on Women
in the Profession,
American Bar Association

3

Nationally, client development [at law firms]—especially in these economic times—has become absolutely crucial. Where once you could be just a good lawyer and progress within your firm, today there is an inordinate emphasis placed on the clients you can bring to the firm. The firms see that as their lifeblood.

Los Angeles Times,
3-10:(D)4.

Nan Aron
Director,
Alliance for Justice

4

Since 1990, the [U.S.] Supreme Court has lost its three most passionate voices for justice: William J. Brennan, Jr., Thurgood Marshall and Harry A. Blackmun [all of whom have retired]. We need a [new] Justice [to] carry on their vision . . . and help resurrect the Court as promoter of the rights of and liberties of ordinary people.

Los Angeles Times,
7-12:(A)12.

Jimmy Banks
Executive director,
Texans for
Judicial Election Reform

5

[Criticizing the current system of judges having to raise large sums of campaign money to run in judgeship elections]: Judicial fund-raiding leads to the appearance of impropriety, and sometimes it leads to actual corruption in the administration of justice.

The Christian Science Monitor,
8-22:13.

Robert S. Bennett
Lawyer;
Former Special Counsel
to the U.S. Senate
Ethics Committee

6

[As a lawyer,] you can't just be an ass-kicker. And you can't be a cheerleader. And you can't walk around saying the sky is falling. It's a real people business. You have to bring the defendants—and their families, too—you have to bring them through.

Vanity Fair,
August:86.

Anne K. Bingaman
Assistant Attorney General,
Antitrust Division,
Department of Justice
of the United States

1

[Saying women lawyers in the Federal government have more flexibility to be involved in their family life than they do in private practice]: Society has not evolved to the point where young husbands take as much responsibility for children as young women. Young women get caught in the dilemma of raising families and may drop out of private practice. There are trade-offs. We have brilliant lawyers here [in the Federal government] who work very hard, sometimes around the clock. But there are times when they can leave at 5 p.m. That almost never happens in private practice.

The Washington Post,
7-28:(A)13.

Harry A. Blackmun
Associate Justice,
Supreme Court
of the United States

2

[On serving on the Supreme Court, from which he is about to retire after 24 years]: It's been a great ride . . . Most of the time it isn't much fun . . . But it's a fantastic, intimate experience.

Newsweek, 4-18:17.

Stephen G. Breyer
Judge,
United States Court of Appeals
for the First Circuit;
Associate Justice-designate,
Supreme Court of the United States

3

If I were to pick out one feature of the academic side of my life that really influenced me especially, I think it would be this: The opportunity to study law as a whole helped me understand that everything in the law is related to every other

thing, and always, as Holmes pointed out, that whole law reflects not so much logic as history and experience.

At Senate
Judiciary Committee hearing
on his nomination,
Washington, D.C., July 12/
The New York Times,
7-13:(A)8.

4

Academic lawyers, practicing lawyers, government lawyers, judges in my opinion have a special responsibility to try to understand how different parts of [the] seamless web of the law interact with each other and how legal decisions will actually work in practice to affect people and to help them . . . I believe that law must work for people. That vast array of Constitution, statutes, rules, regulations, practices, procedures—that huge, vast web—has a single basic purpose. That purpose is to help the many different individuals who make up America from so many different backgrounds and circumstances, with so many different needs and hopes. Its purpose is to help them live together productively, harmoniously and in freedom. Keeping that ultimate purpose in mind helps guide a judge through the labyrinth of rules and regulations that the law too often becomes, to reach what is there at bottom: the very human goals that underlie the constitutions and the statutes that Congress writes.

At Senate
Judiciary Committee hearing
on his nomination,
Washington, D.C., July 12/
The New York Times,
7-13:(A)8.

5

Law requires both a heart and a head. If you don't have a heart, it becomes a sterile set of rules removed from human problems, and it won't help. If you don't have a head, there's the risk that in trying to decide a particular person's problem in a case that may look fine for that person, you cause

(STEPHEN G. BREYER)

trouble for a lot of other people, making their lives yet worse. It's a question of balance.

*At Senate
Judiciary Committee hearing
on his nomination,
Washington, D.C., July 13/
The New York Times,
7-14:(A)10.*

1

[In law,] consensus is important, because law is not theoretical; law is a set of opinions and rules that lawyers have to understand, judges have to understand them, lower-court judges have to understand them, and eventually the labor union, the business, small businesses, everyone else in the country has to understand how they are supposed to act or not act according to law.

*At Senate
Judiciary Committee hearing
on his nomination,
Washington, D.C., July 13/
The New York Times,
7-14:(A)10.*

Steven Brill
*Chief executive officer,
Court TV*

2

[On the possibility that Judge Lance Ito will disallow Court TV's cameras in the courtroom during the upcoming controversial murder trial of former football star O. J. Simpson]: I'm confident that when Judge Ito contrasts what's gone on with cameras outside the courtroom with what's happening with cameras inside the courtroom in this case and all the others we've covered, he'll see we're part of his solution, not part of his problem.

*Oct. 3/
The New York Times,
10-4:(A)8.*

Willie Brown
*Speaker of the
California State Assembly*

3

[On his proposed bill to prohibit witnesses in high-profile criminal cases from selling their stories or interviews to the news media]: A witness who tells the truth, but admits to being paid for his story, may lose credibility in the eyes of the jury. A witness who has lied in order to get a $100,000 or $1-million fee, on the other hand, could compromise the entire proceedings. In criminal cases, where the life and liberty of a defendant are at stake, such practices should not be permitted. I am not barring [witnesses] from saying things. I am barring them from being paid for it. They can still talk to the press, but they can't make a deal.

*News conference,
Sacramento, Calif., July 26/
Los Angeles Times,
7-27:(A)3.*

Bill Clinton
President of the United States

4

[On retiring U.S. Supreme Court Justice Harry Blackmun]: Justice Blackmun's identification was firmly and decisively with the ordinary people of this country, with their concerns; and his humanity was often given voice not only in majority [Court] opinions but in his dissents . . . I can only say that every one of us who serves in any capacity in public life would do very well by the people of the United States if we could bring to our work half the integrity, the passion and the love for this country that Justice Blackmun has given us on the United States Supreme Court for 24 years—and I thank him very much.

*News conference,
Washington, D.C., April 6/
The New York Times,
4-7:(A)12.*

(BILL CLINTON)

1

[On criticism that he is taking too long to nominate a replacement for retiring Supreme Court Justice Harry Blackmun]: I think one of the benefits and perhaps one of the burdens the American people got when I was elected President is that I believe I know a lot about this issue and I care a lot about it. I used to teach Constitutional law. This is not a decision I can defer to aides. So I am going to attempt to do what I did last time, even against all the pressure of time deadlines; and that's to make a really good decision that I feel good about . . . On these matters, I tend to keep my own counsel more than on other things. I think it is the right thing to do. It is one of the few things that the President just does on his own—of course, ultimately, with the advice and consent of the Senate—and I'm going to do my best to do a good job with it.

News conference,
Washington, D.C.,May12/
The New York Times
5-13:(A)12.

2

I believe a President can best serve our country by nominating a candidate to the Supreme Court whose experience manifests the qualities in a Justice that matter most: Excellence. Excellence in knowledge, excellence in judgment, excellence in devotion to the Constitution, to the country and to the real people. It is a duty best exercised wisely and not in haste.

Announcing
his nomination
of Stephen Breyer
for the Supreme Court,
Washington, D.C.,
May 13/
The New York Times,
5-14:10.

Alan M. Dershowitz
Professor of law,
Harvard University Law School

3

The American public has a love/hate relationship with lawyers. The problem is, it sometimes loves the wrong lawyers and hates the wrong lawyers. When a lawyer helps bring about the release of somebody who many people may think is guilty, he or she is *immediately* subject to criticism. Defense lawyers . . . ought to be our heroes—the ones who take on the establishment and the ones who do the thankless work of representing people on death row, in mental hospitals, aliens seeking to come into the United States—because these lawyers shake up the system. They are the current-day gladiators, the people about whom Shakespeare wrote . . . when he writes about the people who were on the front line, in the days of *Macbeth* or in the days of *Hamlet*. Today Shakespeare would be writing about these lawyers. Because when he said, "The play is the thing," today the trial is the "thing." Today the trial is the international drama.

Interview/
"Interview" magazine,
September:119.

Helen E. Freedman
Justice, New York
State Supreme Court

4

[On a trend among juries to not side with plaintiffs as often as they used to in suits against deep-pocket insurance companies, and, when they do, the awards are not as high as they used to be]: I've seen a kind of conservatism among jurors, and you get defendants' verdicts that you might not have a few years ago. Jurors say they're very concerned about the high verdicts you read about in the newspaper—though they don't ever hear about the verdicts for the defendant—and they're very concerned about the high costs of health care and insurance.

The New York Times,
6-17:(B)13.

Stephen Gillers
Professor of legal ethics,
New York University
Law School

1

Lawyers can seek help wherever they find it, so long as the lawyer makes the ultimate judgment about how to try a case. He can consult with psychologists or sociologists or even a tarot-card reader.

Newsweek, 8-22:29.

Ruth Bader Ginsburg
Associate Justice,
Supreme Court
of the United States

2

[On what makes a good judge]: It's important to be secure in your own judgment, to be ready to make decisions and not look back. Some of the best legal minds are not the best judges because they're constantly rethinking a position and won't let an opinion go. A judge should have the attitude, "I can resolve this as well as, or probably better than, the next person. I'm as comfortable as one should be making the decision, and I'm not going to worry about it constantly after I've make it."

Interview/
The New York Times,
1-7:(B)13.

Robert Hirschhorn
Lawyer; Jury consultant

3

[On sequestering of juries in long trials, such as the forthcoming murder trial of former football star O. J. Simpson, which could take six months]: Sequestering is a fancy word for prison. You're talking about separating these people from their families for a good three to six months minimum. They're going to miss Thanksgiving, Christmas, birthdays, anniversaries. I think it's cruel and unusual punishment.

USA Today, 9-2:(A)3.

4

[On prospective jurors who have made up their minds about a case before the trial starts]: These black-and-white thinkers are power brokers on a jury. I don't want to eliminate them if they are for us. Most lawyers think it's only the well-educated, coat-and-tie jurors who will run the jury. But our experience shows that's not true. These people are like Henry Fonda in the movie *Twelve Angry Men*, who started as a lone holdout on the jury and ended up persuading everyone else.

The New York Times,
11-29:(B)8.

Lance A. Ito
Judge, Superior Court,
Los Angeles, Calif.

5

In criminal court, you're dealing with adults who have lifestyles and patterns that are established. With juveniles [in juvenile court], you have the ability to intervene. You have the potential to make a positive change in people's lives. That's not always the case in adult criminal cases.

Los Angeles Times,
7-23:(A)19.

Steve Johnson
Executive producer,
Court TV

6

Trials have a beginning, middle and end. There are two opposing, often antithetical, views. People are required to tell the truth, they are questioned by two sides, and then a bunch of people vote. It's always about law and justice. It meets Aristotle's view of the structure of drama.

Emmy, August:60.

Anthony M. Kennedy
Associate Justice,
Supreme Court
of the United States

1

[Criticizing the idea of mandatory minimum sentences for many Federal crimes]: I think I am in agreement with most judges in the Federal system that mandatory minimums are an imprudent, unwise and often unjust mechanism for sentencing.

Before House
Appropriations subcommittee,
Washington, D.C., March 9/
The New York Times,
3-10:(A)14.

Harold Hongju Koh
Professor of international law,
Yale University

2

[On Supreme Court Justice Harry Blackmun, who recently announced his decision to retire after 24 years on the Court]: This is a guy who came to the Court thinking it was the role of the Court to defer to government. But as he read the cases, he realized that all government wasn't good and there was a lot of suffering. In a series of cases, he began siding with the outsiders: women facing tough choices on abortion, the gays, the aliens.

The Washington Post,
4-7:(A)10.

William Lasser
Political scientist,
Clemson University

3

[On suggestions that President Clinton appoint a Hispanic to fill the seat on the U.S. Supreme Court soon to be vacated by retiring Justice Harry Blackmun]: It's a political judgment Clinton will have to make. A Hispanic Justice would have great symbolic value, but you can't satisfy every constituency on a nine-member body.

U.S. News & World Report,
4-25:12.

Dan Lungren
Attorney General of California

4

[Saying some TV talk shows, such as the one hosted by Oprah Winfrey, may be creating sympathy for those accused of crimes by focusing on how they may have been mistreated when young or suffered other abuse]: I call it the Oprahization of the jury pool. It's the idea that people have become so set on viewing things from the Oprah view, the Geraldo view or the Phil Donahue view that they bring that into the jury box with them. And I think at base much of that tends to say, "We don't hold people responsible for their actions because they've been the victim of some influence at some time in their life."

Time, 6-6:30.

Robert M. Mallano
Presiding Judge,
Superior Court
of Los Angeles, Calif.

5

Lawyers were asked [in a recent study] what attribute they thought was most important in a judge. The majority said decisiveness. That's the nature of our role . . . You can't stop the trial and do an hour's research every time there is an objection. You'd never get done.

Interview/
Los Angeles Times,
7-13:(B)3.

Abner J. Mikva
Chief Judge, United States
Court of Appeals for the
District of Columbia;
Counsel-designate to
President of the United States
Bill Clinton

6

The best thing that a lawyer can do is to give a client good preventive advice before problems arise. It's always more difficult when a lawyer is

(ABNER J. MIKVA)

called in to help resolve a controversy that is already raging.
Interview, Aug. 12/
The Christian Science Monitor,
8-16:3.

Barry Nace
President, Association of
Trial Lawyers of America
1

The only "litigation explosion" is in lawsuits by businesses against other businesses. The number of product-liability and medical-malpractice suits has actually declined in recent years. The so-called litigation explosion is a figment either of poor research or of intentionally misleading reports by groups like the Manhattan Institute, which is funded and controlled by big business.
The Christian Science Monitor,
1-25:11.

Roberta Cooper Ramo
President-elect,
American Bar Association
2

Domestic violence is treated in a criminal court. We've got juvenile courts that deal with children. We have totally unrelated family courts that deal with things like divorce and child-custody issues. It's possible for all three courts to be dealing with the same family and never know what [the others are doing]. If we could put the criminal-, juvenile-, and family-court issues all in the same place, we'd be far more likely to get a solution . . . In a lot of courthouses, district attorneys and judges have no idea that somebody's been arrested for the same thing 84 times. So we want to make sure that all the judges and the prosecutors know when there are multiple offenses from the same person, for when the same family has a whole series of things going on, that all that information is there.
Interview/
USA Today, 8-8:(A)11.

Joe Saltzman
Professor of journalism,
University of Southern California
3

[On the gavel-to-gavel TV coverage of the preliminary hearing on the murder charges against former football star O. J. Simpson]: This is the ideal of a public trial. This is great for democracy. All the camera does is let more citizens see the event. Whether or not it changes what happens in the courtroom, I don't think so . . . I actually think it makes everybody involved act in a higher way.
USA Today, 6-30:(A)3.

Brian Shenker
Editorial director,
Jury Verdict Research
4

[Saying juries are not siding with plaintiffs as often as they used to in suits against deep-pocket insurance companies, and when they do the awards are not as high as they used to be]: There's been such a campaign by the insurance industry, [and] by people like [former Vice President] Dan Quayle, saying these big awards are killing our society. People see this in the media, and when they get on juries they think, "I'm not going to contribute to this."
The New York Times,
6-17:(A)1.

Mark Silverstein
Political scientist,
Boston University
5

[On Presidential appointments to the Supreme Court]: Years ago, the assumption was that the President could appoint whoever he wanted to, within reasonable bounds. Now the rule seems to be: "We have to pick someone who can get through" [the confirmation process] . . . Now politics defines who is on our courts. I don't think that's so bad in a democracy.
Los Angeles Times,
7-18:(A)5.

Larry Sipes
President, National Center
for State Courts

1

For the vast majority of us, justice is sought not at some remote Federal courthouse but at the county seat, in a state or local courthouse. That's really the place you most often end up when bumping into the legal system, whether it be traffic cases, divorces, disputes over a will, kids in trouble.

The Washington Post,
1-1:(A)4.

Jerry Spence
Lawyer

2

My experience is that jurors want to hear a complete story about what happened. When I make an opening statement, I always do it as a story. At that point, about 85 percent of jurors will come to a conclusion in that case. But you had better be able to prove your story, because if jurors who believed you find out you haven't told the whole story, then they turn against you. Jurors ought not to be criticized for making up their minds so early on the basis of a story, because people have an immense ability to hear what rings true.

The New York Times,
11-29:(B)8.

Hilton L. Stein
Lawyer

3

[On his specialty of suing other lawyers in malpractice cases]: This [kind of] practice is hell. The lawyers we sue all take it very personally; they're angry and nasty. Other lawyers think we're scum; even judges look on us disfavorably . . . I found the cover-up of [legal] malpractice; I found lawyers doing whatever they could to hide their errors from their clients and defeat legitimate claims. I frankly think there's an epidemic of legal malpractice in this country.

Interview/The New York Times,
8-5:(B)13.

Paul Thaler
Director of journalism and media,
Mercy College (Dobbs Ferry, N.Y.)

4

[On allowing television in the courtroom]: One of the dangers of a televised trial is we believe what we are seeing is the truth, that television images don't lie. [But] I think there can be very deceptive angles. The lighting, the editing and the juxtaposition of images play an important part in what our understanding of the event is.

USA Today, 8-10:(A)9.

Clarence Thomas
Associate Justice,
Supreme Court of the United States

5

[On suggestions that he, a black Supreme Court Justice, has sold out to the white establishment]: I am not an Uncle Tom . . . I'm going to be here [on the Court] for 40 years. For those who don't like it, get over it.

Newsweek, 11-7:21.

6

[Saying elite law schools neglect teaching of the basics, and thus their students are not ready for the reality of the legal system they find after graduation]: Young law-school graduates are often shocked to learn that much of the law is already settled and it is only their job to apply it to a new set of facts before them. [Elite law schools] neglect to teach that law is an art, a craft, and not an adjunct to fancy theories or a means for political and social revolution.

At Samford University/
USA Today, 11-18:(A)3.

Frank Tuerkheimer
Professor of law,
University of Wisconsin;
Former United States Attorney

7

[On the current murder case against former

(FRANK TUERKHEIMER)

football star O. J. Simpson]: If you look historically at prosecutions against people who are public figures, the conviction rate is lower . . . Jurors
are more willing to find a reasonable doubt in
people who are more famous.
USA Today, 6-30:(A)3.

Kim McLane Wardlaw
Partner, O'Melveny & Meyers,
attorneys at law;
President, Women Lawyers
Association of
Los Angeles (Calif.)

1

Women [lawyers] have made a lot of progress
[in law firms], especially in clear issues such as
part-time work and maternity-leave policies and
in areas of sexual harassment. But it's a cup half-
empty, half-full . . . Women [lawyers] are increasingly welcomed [in law firms] as "minders" and
"grinders," but not as "finders" [of new business
and clients]. Unfortunately, the "finders" are the
ones who have the most power, prestige and standing in the profession, so we're still behind in obtaining this power.
March 9/
Los Angeles Times,
3-10:(D)1.

Frances Zemans
Executive vice president,
American Judicature Society

2

Merit selection is the best way to ensure independent and qualified judges committed to applying the law.
The Christian Science Monitor,
8-22:13.

Politics

Lamar Alexander
Former Secretary of Education
of the United States

1

[On the Christian Coalition's influence in the Republican Party]: The concerns expressed by the Christian Coalition are no different from those I've heard from other Americans. The question for us as Republicans is how we can give voice to those concerns without coming across as intolerant or angry or threatening.

Interview/Time, 9-26:35.

Roger C. Altman
Deputy Secretary of the
Treasury of the United States

2

[On suggestions that he was not truthful in Senate testimony last February regarding Treasury Department contacts with the White House about investigations of the Whitewater scandal]: Mr. Chairman, I do not have perfect recall, and I may have heard or understood questions in a way that was not intended by the Senator asking the question. If I did so, I sincerely apologize to all members of the Committee. But I do want to be clear. In no way did I intend to mislead or not to provide complete and forthright answers.

At Senate Banking Committee
hearing on the
Whitewater scandal,
Washington, D.C., Aug. 2/
The New York Times,
8-3:(A)1.

Richard K. Armey
United States Representative,
R-Texas

3

[Saying the Republicans, who will control the new House beginning next January, will not seek vengeance on the Democrats, who he says treated Republicans badly in the past]: You cannot get ahead while you are getting even. It's a waste of time, it's a waste of other people's resources, it's not an honorable thing to do.

Nov. 14/
The New York Times,
11-15:(A)12.

4

[On the sweeping Republican Congressional victory in the recent national elections]: We didn't win power; we gained responsibility. We do not view ourselves as a temporary strike force. We view ourselves as a permanent presence.

At Conservative Leadership
Conference, Dec. 3/
The New York Times,
12-6:(A)11.

Ted Arrington
Political scientist,
University of North Carolina

5

[On why the Democratic Party is losing Southern voters]: These folks [in the South] like manliness and guns. They don't like [President] Clinton because he doesn't seem too manly. He lets his wife [Hillary] do too much.

Newsweek, 11-21:33.

Jim Bacchus
United States Representative,
D-Florida

6

[On the current Congressional hearings into the Whitewater scandal]: The Republicans have committed the ultimate political sin in Washington—they have no news [in pressing the Whitewater issue]. After all the predictions, after all the press conferences, after all the dire warnings [about Whitewater], this was much ado about not very much.

Los Angeles Times,
8-2:(E)6.

Douglas Bailey
Republican Party strategist

1

[President Clinton] is like the moth and the candle. He gets as close as he can to the flame. But he's got energy and commitment and is an incredible salesman, and in that sense he's [former President Ronald] Reagan-esque. The passion is certainly there. But the way he likes to get close to the flame, God knows what might happen down the road.

Los Angeles Times,
2-28:(A)18.

2

[On cover-ups of potential political scandals]: I don't believe I have ever had a conversation with a candidate or a campaign where I didn't start by saying: "Look, whatever the truth is, once the subject has been raised in any way, you have to make the assumption that it is going to come out. Now, do you want it dragged out piece by piece and make you look like a fool and a liar? Or do you want to have it come out all at once and have you look like just a fool? If it comes out all at once, chances are people will be forgiving. If you drag it out, people never forgive." What is amazing is how many otherwise good and sensible people may understand that advice but simply ignore it.

Los Angeles Times,
3-7:(A)11.

Howard Baker
Former United States Senator,
R-Tennessee

3

[On the sweeping Republic Congressional victory in the just-held national elections]: The country is in gentle rebellion, and I think it has been now for the last two or three election cycles. By that I mean the long-term rising of the anger. People are focusing their anger right now on a few specific things, but mostly they are just express-

ing their dissatisfaction with the existing order. I don't know where they are going, and I don't think they know where, either. But what frightens me is that if we do not address their feelings, they may develop a tendency to savage our institutions.

Nov. 9/
The New York Times,
11-10:(B)4.

Richard Hugh Baker
United States Representative,
R-Louisiana

4

[The current Congressional hearings into whether Treasury officials improperly advised the White House about investigations into the Whitewater scandal may simply show that] good judgment got clouded in the heat of the moment, and some folks stretched beyond a reasonable line of proper conduct . . . [At issue may be that White House aides tried] to preclude finding out what happened [between the White House and Treasury]. Isn't it always the way? The cover-up is worse than the crime.

USA Today, 7-28:(A)9.

Haley Barbour
Chairman,
Republican National Committee

5

[On Democrats' contention that the Whitewater scandal, and the alleged possible involvement of President Clinton and his wife, is being pushed by Republicans for political gain]: The Democrats have this fraudulent defense that it's all being stirred up by the Republicans. [But] when *The Washington Post, L.A. Times* and *New York Times* dig all this stuff up, they can't say it's Republicans doing it.

Denver, Colo., March 10/
Los Angeles Times,
3-11:(A)18.

(HALEY BARBOUR)

1

[Saying the Republican Party should not be torn apart over the abortion issue, because abortion is not as important to voters in an election as some people think]: If we let abortion be the threshold issue of Republicanism, we need our heads examined . . . I don't think it's the party-splitting issue that some in the media like to write about, and that the Democrats are down on their knees praying for.

The Christian Science Monitor,
3-16:12.

2

[Saying Republicans should be cautious in how they pursue the Whitewater scandal and the alleged possible involvement of President Clinton and his wife]: We don't want to aid the Democrats in their fraudulent defense that this [the Whitewater investigation] is a Republican plot. I subscribe to Napoleon's old adage: Never interfere with your enemy while he's in the process of destroying himself.

USA Today, 3-25:(A)4.

3

In [Congressional] district after district, you see Democrats in relatively conservative and moderate districts who are choosing not to run for re-election. And I think one of the reasons is that they have been so pressured to support their Party and not to let this President [Clinton] fail, and are being called on to vote against their own views and the views of their constituents.

The New York Times,
5-21:8.

4

[On industrialist Ross Perot, who ran for President as an independent in 1992 and who some say cost then-President George Bush re-election and permitted Bill Clinton to be the victor]: If Ross Perot were to run [again in 1996], it would be the greatest threat to electing a Republican candidate, and sending President Clinton back to Arkansas.

Look at the people who voted for Ross Perot the last time. They agree with Republicans . . . on most issues.

USA Today, 6-14:(A)10.

5

[On the effect of President Clinton's low poll ratings on the forthcoming off-year elections]: Democrats are running from Clinton like scalded dogs.

Time, 9-12:40.

Marion Barry
City Councilman,
and former Mayor,
of Washington, D.C.

6

[On his running again for Mayor of Washington, after having left that office two years ago and served jail time for cocaine possession]: It's like a prizefighter. You get knocked down and you just know you can't win if you get up, so why get up? You've got to have a winning attitude . . . Most people who go through what I've gone through don't come back. Either they just wallow in their own self-pity or they're in jail or dead or in the hospital.

Los Angeles Times,
9-1:(A)5.

Paul Begala
Political Adviser to
President of the
United States Bill Clinton

7

[On President Clinton's agreeing to a special counsel being appointed to investigate suggestions that he might have been involved with the Whitewater scandal]: It's a recognition of the reality of the way the political culture works that people who haven't done anything wrong have to call for a special investigation of themselves. You can make me accept it, but you can't make me like it.

Jan. 12/Los Angeles Times,
1-13:(A)18.

(PAUL BEGALA)

1

[Saying the Clinton Administration doesn't fit as smoothly into the Washington culture as did past Administrations]: Any institution, and you can call political Washington an institution, is always going to act in its own interests and be suspicious of outsiders. I think there is a great deal of prejudice showing here from, let us say, the sort of people who refer to Washington as "this town."

The New York Times,
3-15:(A)10.

2

[On the political turmoil that has rocked the Clinton Administration]: The good ship Clinton, although it might tilt this way or that way or get tossed about in a storm and maybe have a deckhand getting seasick and even occasionally a man overboard, is setting sail and getting us there.

USA Today, 7-28:(A)9.

William J. Bennett
Former Secretary of Education
of the United States

3

[Saying the Democratic Party and the Clinton Administration have begun espousing issues and policies that have traditionally been the province of the Republican Party]: We [Republicans] once were found and now we're lost. If somebody takes your ideas, begins to sound like you and tries to implement them, the only possible response is to say, "This is a very good thing. Well done."

Newsweek, 2-7:20.

Lloyd N. Bentsen
Secretary of the Treasury
of the United States

4

[On suggestions that Treasury Department officials may have breached ethical standards in their contacts with the White House regarding

criminal investigations involving the Whitewater scandal and President and Mrs. Clinton]: We turned the Treasury Department inside out to find every scrap of paper and every record that might conceivably have some bearing on this issue. [Based on what independent inspectors found,] I can reasonably conclude that the conduct of the people working here . . . did not, I repeat, did not, violate the standards of ethical conduct for Executive Branch employees.

News conference,
Washington, D.C., July 31/
Los Angeles Times,
8-1:(A)4.

5

[On suggestions that Treasury Department officials may have had improper contacts with the White House regarding investigations into the Whitewater scandal and possible connections with President and Mrs. Clinton]: I've been in public service for nearly 30 years. I've seen everything from the McCarthy hearings to Watergate, Iran-contra, the Church committee, all of it. What you have here in a unique confluence of circumstances that, when you strip away all the rhetoric, resulted in actions that broke no criminal law, did not violate the ethics rules and did not in any way affect the Madison [Whitewater] case.

At Senate Banking Committee
hearing on the
Whitewater scandal,
Washington, D.C., Aug. 3/
Los Angeles Times,
8-4:(A)12.

Michael Beschloss
Historian

6

[On the sweeping Republican Congressional victory in the just-held national elections]: Tuesday was potentially one of the most important days in 20th-century political history. It could mean that the Republicans definitively become the majority party in this country. It could mean that we are

(MICHAEL BESCHLOSS)

headed back into a period of Congressional dominance and Presidential weakness such as we had in the late 19th century.

Nov. 9/
The New York Times,
11-10:(A)1.

Merle Black
Political scientist,
Emory University

1

[On the possibility of Republican victories in this fall's Congressional elections in Southern districts now held by Democrats]: If the Republicans pick up 10 Southern seats, it would not only put them in a position where they can better check the [President] Clinton agenda in Congress, but it would also help to reshape the national Republican Party in a Southern, very, very conservative direction.

The New York Times,
5-21:1.

Morton C. Blackwell
Member,
Republican National Committee

2

[On the increasing clout of politically active Christians]: Time was when Christian activists compared voter registration to church rolls, and that was it. Now they hold seminars on public relations, precinct organization, soliciting funds and election law. Christians are much more politically sophisticated than they were a decade ago. This is a big project, and it takes time.

The New York Times,
5-5:(A)15.

John A. Boehner
United States Representative,
R-Ohio

3

[On the new Republican majority in Congress starting in 1995]: We have to set the agenda now. We have to bring bills to the floor and get them passed. We never had to do this stuff as a minority. We just had to anticipate, react—and lose.

The New York Times,
12-17:8.

David L. Boren
United States Senator,
D-Oklahoma

4

The real anger in this country comes from the [political] center. The people in the center are disenfranchised, and they're feeling more and more cut off from both [the Republican and Democratic] parties as [those parties] become more extreme. The people hate partisanship, and meanwhile Congress has become more and more partisan . . . I think there's a great likelihood that there will be a centrist independent political movement in this country. I think there's a great likelihood that there will probably be a centrist independent President in this country in the next 10 years.

Interview, Norman, Okla./
The New York Times,
11-17:(A)13.

Lawrence Bossidy
Chairman, AlliedSignal, Inc.

5

[On the Clinton Administration]: They tackled a lot of issues that hadn't been tackled—health care, welfare reform. Certainly, he [Clinton] could have walked away from [supporting] NAFTA. He's not going to walk away from GATT, either. I've been [praising] the courage needed to take on these issues. On the other hand, I think it's turned into a real smorgasbord now. I don't think anybody knows what he really is going to stand for. I

(LAWRENCE BOSSIDY)

think the Administration has something to do with the drift in the stock market. I think there's a lack of confidence. You juxtapose this Administration with the [Ronald] Reagan Administration, where the guy [Reagan] had three things that he was interested in. This Administration has 100 things and it is interested in doing all of them. If you ask the question, which [Administration] does the American public feel more comfortable in, it's the former.

Interview, July 18/
USA Today 7-19:(B)4.

John B. Breaux
United States Senator,
D-Louisiana

1

[On the sweeping Republican Congressional victory in the just-held national elections]: We're in the same position in [the new] Congress as the last Congress. Nobody [neither party] has 60 votes in the Senate. We [Democrats] can veto things, and they [Republicans] can't override them. They can block anything we want to pass. It's a recipe for gridlock.

Interview, Nov. 9/
The New York Times,
11-10:(B)2.

Alan Brinkley
Professor of history,
Columbia University

2

[On the sweeping Republican Congressional victory in the just-held national elections]: The Republican Party in particular has not in recent years had much of a positive agenda. It seems to want power to prevent things from happening instead of to do things. The benefit for the Republicans is that nothing will happen in the next two years that they don't want to happen. It's hard to imagine that they're going to be able to transform government. But they've got all sorts of opportu-

nities to produce embarrassments for the Clinton Administration.

Nov. 9/
The New York Times,
11-10:(B)4.

Edmund G. "Jerry" Brown, Jr.
Former Governor
of California (D)

3

[President] Clinton was elected in a manner that made inevitable his failure. He ran a deceptive and hypocritical campaign . . . He's been abandoned and can't call upon people who want change because his pact with the Devil has destroyed him. He sold out his constituents by abandoning single-payer health care. He's nowhere in campaign reform, having caved in to the same corrupt interests. His China policy is a complete betrayal. It's not easy to take a populist position, but if you don't, you might as well be a Republican.

Interview/
Mother Jones,
Nov.-Dec.:54.

George Bush
Former President
of the United States

4

[On his keeping a low profile on political affairs since he left the Presidency]: some day I may have more to say publicly, but I try not to lecture our President [Clinton], try not to criticize the President. Before events in Haiti—it was kind of the exception that proved the rule—I spoke out on Haiti. Other than that, I recognize that he's got a very difficult job. Try to let other loyal opposition spokesmen do the heavy lifting on that. And they're doing a good job in my view. I don't crave the limelight. I don't go to Washington. Very seldom go the New York.

Interview,
Guatemala City, Guatemala,
Oct. 2/The New York Times,
10-4:(A)12.

Mike Casey
Spokesman,
Democratic Congressional
Campaign Committee

1

[On predictions of possible Republican victories in this fall's Congressional elections in Southern districts now held by Democrats]: The silver lining [for Democrats] in the South is that the Republican Party continues to lurch to the right. And if it keeps on lurching, it's going to leave the bulk of voters who are moderate, mainstream voters uncomfortable with their agenda.

The New York Times,
5-21:8.

Bill Clinton
President of the United States

2

[On his possible involvement in the Whitewater scandal]: There is no credible evidence and no credible charge that I violated any criminal or civil Federal laws eight or nine years ago, when most of these facts that are being bandied around are discussed. I mean, this is really about a real-estate investment I made almost 16 years ago now that lost money and sputtered to a not-successful conclusion—several years ago. So there is no analogy [to the Watergate scandal of the 1970s], except an hysteria that they can gin up around it. That's why I say I have been forthcoming; I will continue to be forthcoming. You're going to be confident in the way we handle this. There will not be a cover-up; there will not be an abuse of power in this office. And there is no credible charge that I violated any law, even way back in the Dark Ages—or years ago when this happened. And I just would remind you, I was Governor of [Arkansas] for 12 years; there was never a hint of scandal in my Administration.

News conference,
Washington, D.C.,
March 7/
The New York Times,
3-8:(A)12.

3

[On questions about his wife Hillary's possible involvement in the Whitewater scandal]: I can tell you this: I believe I'm a better authority than anybody else in America on my wife. I have never known a person with a stronger sense of right and wrong in my life—ever. I could cite you chapter and verse over 20 years-plus now that I have known her when it would have been very easy for her to take a shortcut, to take an easy way out, to do something else, when she has unfailingly done the right thing. And I do not believe for a moment that she has done anything wrong . . . If everybody in this country had a character as strong as hers, we wouldn't have half the problems we've got today.

News conference,
Washington, D.C., March 7/
The New York Times,
3-8:(A)12.

4

[Criticizing Republicans for being destructive and obstructive in dealing with his Administration]: [Why] are we confronted in this Administration with an opposition party that just stands up and says, no, no, no, no, no, no, no, no, no? [As a Democratic Governor of Arkansas,] I constantly sought [Republican Presidents] out, engaged them in debate, offered to work with them . . . I never did them the way they are doing us in Washington, D.C., today. It is wrong. And it is not good for the United States of America . . . This overriding, intensely personal, totally political, devoid-of-principle attack is not good for the country and is inconsistent with the tradition of Abraham Lincoln and Teddy Roosevelt.

At Democratic Party
fund-raising dinner,
Boston, Mass., March 14/
USA Today, 3-15:(A)5.

5

[On the Whitewater scandal and his alleged possible involvement]: I know that many people around America must believe that Washington is

(BILL CLINTON)

overwhelmingly preoccupied with the Whitewater matter. But our Administration is preoccupied with the business we were sent here to do for the American people. The investigation of Whitewater is being handled by an independent special counsel whose appointment I supported. Our cooperation with that counsel has been total. We have supplied over 14,000 documents, my tax returns dating back to 1978, and made available every Administration witness he has sought. I support the actions of the House and the Senate clearing the way for hearings at an appropriate time that does not interfere with [special counsel Robert] Fiske's responsibilities, and I will fully cooperate with their work as well . . . Tomorrow I will make available my tax returns dating back to 1977 when I first held public office. Cooperation, disclosure and doing the people's business are the order of the day.

News conference,
Washington, D.C.,
March 24/
Los Angeles Times,
3-25:(A)18.

1

By common consensus, we had the most productive first year of a Presidency last year of anyone in a generation.

News conference,
Washington, D.C.,
March 24/
Newsweek, 4-4:19.

2

[On suggestions that his explanations about the Whitewater scandal sound evasive]: Can I answer every question that anybody might ever ask me about something that happened 10, 15, 17 years ago on the spur of the moment and have total recall of that while trying to be President? No sir, I cannot.

Newsweek, 4-25:19.

3

[On the late President Nixon]: Oh, yes, he knew great controversy amid defeat as well as victory. He made mistakes and they, like his accomplishments, are part of his life and record. But the enduring lesson of Richard Nixon is that he never gave up being part of the action and passion of his times.

At burial ceremony for Nixon,
Yorba Linda, Calif., April 27/
Los Angeles Times,
4-28:(A)12.

4

[Saying the press is paying too much attention to the Whitewater scandal and his alleged possible involvement]: I'm at a loss to explain [the press's attitude] . . . I have been astonished by the feeding frenzy around it and the whole "trust" thing. I think part of it is the presumption—maybe rooted in past experiences with past Presidents— that the President has always done something that justifies removing him from office and that the President's a liar . . . Nothing you do really counts unless you find something bad about the President.

Interview,
Washington, D.C./
Esquire, May:44.

5

[Criticizing the raising of questions about his character, his alleged womanizing and his alleged possible involvement in the Whitewater scandal]: [I am the target of the] constant politics of diversion and division and destruction . . . I think I've been subject to more assault than any President. But we'll have an election in 1996, and I wish that we could just all settle down and be Americans for a while and work on our problems, and then evaluate me based on the job I do.

At Rhode Island
"town-hall meeting,"
May 9/
The Christian Science Monitor,
5-11:10.

WHAT THEY SAID IN 1994

(BILL CLINTON)

1

[On the scandals over his past financial dealings and possible extra-marital affairs]: [A President] has very little protection against people who wish in an organized way to pillory or vilify the President. And so, the only protection is, it seems to me, to keep working and keep taking on the tough challenges and to demonstrate to the best of your ability who you really are to those people. I don't think that it requires a great perception to conclude that a lot of the motivation for this is to deprive me of my voice.

Interview,
Washington, D.C., May 18/
Los Angeles Times, 5-19:(A)16.

2

[On criticism of him by the so-called "religious right" or "Christian conservatives"]: I have bent over backwards as a Governor and as a President to respect the religious convictions of all Americans. I have strong religious convictions myself. But that is different, that is very different from what is going on when people come into the political system and they say that anybody that doesn't agree with them is Godless, anyone who doesn't agree with them is not a good Christian, anyone who doesn't agree with them is fair game for any wild charge, no matter how false, for any kind of personal, demeaning attack. I don't suppose there's any public figure that's ever been subject to any more violent personal attacks than I have, at least in modern history, anybody who's been President. And that's fine; I deal with them. But I don't believe that it's the work of God . . . I think that evangelical Christians should be good citizens, should be involved in our politics. They can be Republicans or Democrats. They can do whatever they want. But remember that Jesus threw the money changers out of the temple; he didn't try to take over the job of the money changers.

Broadcast interview,
St. Louis, Mo., June 24/
The New York Times,
6-25:10.

3

I know everything I do as President isn't popular. But I'll tell you what: I show up for work every day and I ask people to face real problems.

At National Council of
La Raza convention,
Miami, Fla., July 18/
Los Angeles Times,
7-19:(A)14.

4

[On his low approval rating in public-opinion polls]: When people have these balances going on, hope or fear, it is sometimes difficult to get through with the hope and the progress. I can't worry about that. All I can do is show up for work here every day and . . . try to make this the home office of the American Association for Ordinary Citizens. And if I keep doing that, I think that the future will take care of itself. My only concern is to continue to be able to be effective, and that's what I will work for.

News conference,
Washington, D.C., Aug. 3/
The New York Times,
8-4:(A)10.

5

[On the current Congressional hearings into the Whitewater scandal, in which he may be possibly involved]: I've watched none of these hearings; I've not kept up with them. I've been working on jobs, and health care, and the crime bill, and peace in the Middle East, and doing the things I was hired to do by the American people . . . I welcome this investigation. And it will vindicate what I have been saying all along [that he did nothing improper in Whitewater].

News conference,
Washington, D.C., Aug. 3/
Los Angeles Times, 8-4:(A)12.

6

[On his political problems with Congress and the public]: I believe what I have to do is to keep trying to change things [for the better in the U.S.].

(BILL CLINTON)

Any time you try to provoke as much change as I have, you are going to have resistance, and you will be criticized. Is it more difficult that I had [only] 43 percent of the vote [in the 1992 election]? Perhaps it is. But I think you can make another argument, which was that 62 percent of the American people voted for fundamental change [by not voting for incumbent President George Bush].

News conference,
Washington, D.C., Aug. 19/
The New York Times,
8-20:10.

1

[On the sweeping Republican Congressional victory in the just-held national elections]: With the Democrats in control of both the White House and the Congress, we were held accountable [in the elections] yesterday, and I accept my share of the responsibility in the result of the elections. When the Republican Party assumes leadership in the House and in the Senate, they will also have a larger responsibility for acting in the best interest of the American people. I reach out to them today and I ask them to join me in the center of the public debate where the best ideas for the next generation of American progress must come. Democrats and Republicans have often joined together when it was clearly in the national interest . . . [But] I don't believe the American people were saying, "We're sorry [that under the Democrats] the deficit has been reduced; we're sorry the size of government has been reduced; we're sorry you've taken a tough stand on crime; we're sorry you're expanding trade." I don't believe that. I don't think they were disagreeing with a lot of the specifics. I do think they still just don't like it when they watch what we do up here [in Washington], and they haven't felt the positive impact of what [we Democrats have] done. And since I'm the President, I have to take some responsibility for that.

News conference,
Washington, D.C., Nov. 9/
The New York Times,
11-10:(B)8.

2

[Addressing Democrats in the aftermath of the sweeping Republican Congressional victory in last month's national elections]: I ask you now once again to think about what your responsibility is . . . What is your responsibility? It's to join me in the arena—not in the peanut gallery, in the arena—and fight, and roll up your sleeves, and be willing to make a mistake now and then, be willing to struggle, be willing to debate and enjoy this.

Before Democratic
Leadership Council,
Washington, D.C.,
Dec. 6/
The New York Times,
12-8:(A)1.

3

[On the sweeping Republican Congressional victory in last month's national elections]: That's the thing I regret about this election more than anything else: All the people who are working harder for lower wages and less security than they were 10 years ago, they're the people I ran to help. All the people who are trying to follow the rules—and are sick and tired of people benefiting who don't, who take advantage of the system whether they're rich or poor or somewhere in-between—those are the folks that the Democratic Party ought to be championing and the ones who will ultimately benefit if we stay on the right course. Well, we did a lot of things that they didn't like very much—especially after it got explained to them, as we say at home. I think I was right when I opposed discrimination and intolerance, but a lot of folks thought I was just more concerned about minorities than the problems for the majority.

Before Democratic
Leadership Council,
Washington, D.C.,
Dec. 6/
The New York Times,
12-8:(A)15.

Hillary Rodham Clinton
Wife of President of the
United States Bill Clinton

1

[On the Whitewater scandal and the alleged possible involvement of her and her husband]: We have been candid all the way through this. We made an investment decision that lost money. We did the best we could, always, to be as straightforward on this as we could, based on what we knew. We have fully cooperated with the grand jury, with the special counsel; we have been more than open and candid. We have not denied any documents; we have claimed no privilege. But for years, now, we've been asked questions that we don't know the answers to. We did not run the company [involved in the Whitewater affair], we did not make its decisions, we did not have its documents or its records. So we could not answer many of your [the press's] questions anyway. We did the very best we could with what we knew.

Interview, March 12/
Time, 3-21:38.

2

[On her reluctance to supply material and to publicly answer questions about the Whitewater scandal]: I have a big thing about [privacy]. I really have been pulled kicking and screaming to the conclusion that if you choose to run for public office you give up any zone of privacy at all. I get my back up every so often about even having to answer questions that I don't think are in any way connected with the fact that my husband is in public life. That's what's going to be concluded about all this—people are going to spend millions and millions of dollars [investigating Whitewater] and they're going to conclude [only that] we made a bad land investment.

Interview, Washington, D.C./
Newsweek, 3-21:35.

3

[On questions about her success in commodity trading in the late 1970s and early 1980s in light of her and her husband's criticism of specu-

lators and investors in the '80s being greedy types]: I think it's a pretty long stretch to say that the decisions that we made to try to create some financial security for our family and make some investments come anywhere near there. I don't think you'll ever find anything that my husband or I said that in any way condemns the importance of making good investments and saving or that in any way undermines what is the heart and soul of the American economy, which is risk-taking and investing in the future.

News conference,
Washington, D.C., April 22/
The New York Times,
4-23:34.

4

[On accusations impugning the character of her and her husband involving past financial dealings and his alleged infidelity]: It is very hard, when people lie about you and attack you, not to feel anger. I have struggled with this, because there's no human being who, if he were walking down the street and someone shouted an insult at him or got in his face and said terrible things about him, would not respond. Bill and I are in this position where it's apparently fair for people to say anything they want about us, but we have to rise above it. If we act human, which is to say we resent it, we get angry about it—that somehow diminishes us. I find that very difficult to understand. So I am trying very hard to come to grips with that . . . I don't like people impugning my motives and saying bad things about me.

Interview,
Washington, D.C./
Vanity Fair, June:107.

5

[On accusations impugning the character of her and her husband involving past financial dealings and his alleged infidelity]: I understand the dilemma I'm in, but I can't answer every one of these terrible crackpot vicious rotten stories, and I don't think I should have to: I think we have so severely undermined the capacity of the country

(HILLARY RODHAM CLINTON)

to make decisions, because we tear everybody down . . . I sure think we're headed for disaster [in this country]. I just think that everybody who is doing this stuff has to understand that if you make money off of or gain political advantage out of deliberate malicious falsehoods, you are building on very shaky foundations, and I think our country deserves better than that . . . There's a lot at stake here, far beyond what happens to Bill and me. If we've proved nothing else, we've proved we are resilient. We know how to fight; we can take these people on. I'm not worried about that. I just don't want to have to compete in that arena. This stuff means nothing in the life of the country. What we ought to be hearing about is what kind of health-care system we're going to have. We are challenging established interests.

Interview, Washington, D.C./
Vanity Fair, June:159.

1

What I do not like is the amount of hatred that is being conveyed and really injected into our political system . . . This personal, vicious hatred that for the time being is being aimed at the President and, to a lesser extent, myself, is very dangerous for our political process. Those encouraging it should think long and hard about the consequences of such encouragement. We have to draw the line on violence and protests that incite violence.

Interview,
Washington, D.C., Aug. 9/
The Washington Post,
8-10:(A)5.

2

[Saying much of the public hostility toward her is due to her activism as First Lady]: A friend told me I've turned into a gender Rorschach test. People are not really often reacting to me so much as they are reacting to their own lives and the transitions they are going through. [For instance,] if somebody has a female boss for the first time, and

they've never experienced that—well, maybe they can't take out their hostility against her so they turn it on me . . . Men often talk to me and say I've made a difference in their daughters' lives or their wife has gone back to school. Or sometimes they come up and criticize me because their wife has decided to go back to school. I've been brought into people's kitchen-table conversations over whether or not someone's wife should go back to school. If the wife says, "Well, Hillary Clinton has a good education," all of a sudden it's my responsibility. So a husband who is not happy about that is not going to be happy with me.

Interview, Washington, D.C./
The Wall Street Journal,
9-30:(A)1.

Tony Coelho
Former United States Representative,
D-California

3

[Election] campaigns have become a full-time business. You set up the mechanism to have full-time media people and others. They are engaged year-round; that means you raise enough money to pay them all year. The cycle just goes on and on. Also, it's like health care in that every new fandangle thing that comes along politically your consultant wants to try. You don't need it, but you're afraid the other side will have it. And it just keeps driving costs up.

Interview, Washington, D.C./
The Wall Street Journal,
2-3:(A)15.

V. B. Corn
Ohio state director,
United We Stand America

4

[On industrialist Ross Perot, who founded United We Stand America]: Mr. Perot is no doubt our founding father. Mr. Perot is our national spokesman. Mr. Perot provides us national lead-

(V. B. CORN)

ership. But the true strength of this organization is not going to be based on the popularity of Mr. Perot. The true strength of the organization is going to be based on the members and what the members do out in their districts.

The Washington Post,
2-7:(A)7.

Bruce Crippen
Montana State Senator (R)

1

[On the sweeping Republican victory in the recent national elections]: Republicans in this state and nationally have always been painted as the big-business, cigar-smoking, back-room bully boys, insensitive to the needs of education, to the needy. This is going to be an opportunity to disprove that.

The New York Times,
11-12:8.

Michael Cromartie
Senior fellow,
Ethics and Public Policy Center

2

[On the "religious right," which has come under political attack]: These people aren't Birchers or followers of the [Ku Klux] Klan. They are people of generally conservative outlook who are deeply concerned about what's happening to the culture. They want a place at the table. They want to be part of the pluralistic experiment.

U.S. News & World Report,
7-18:18.

Mario M. Cuomo
Governor of New York (D)

3

You ask me kind of broadly what was [my] greatest accomplishment [in 11 years as Governor]. It was resisting the temptation to put my ego before the agenda and say: "I will do something

to let them remember me for all time. I will build myself a pyramid of accomplishment."

Interview, Albany, N.Y./
The New York Times,
1-5:(A)12.

4

[Comparing his low poll ratings with those of former President George Bush, saying both he and Bush were blamed for poor economic conditions beyond their control]: If everything is good and you're in place, you're a George Bush with a 90 percent [approval] rating because you just beat Saddam Hussein [in 1991's war against Iraq]. But if you're there when everything goes bad, you're George Bush with a 29 percent rating because they just announced that my brother-in-law has been fired and he's coming to live with me. And that's called unemployment, and you've got to blame somebody.

Speech to bankers,
Saratoga Springs, N.Y./
The New York Times,
6-30:(C)19.

5

[President Clinton] has the most extraordinary record for achieving things that has not been appreciated. I think I know why: When you get something done, you don't let it sink in and exploit it. Let the people know what you've done.

While campaigning
for re-election, Oct. 17/
The New York Times,
10-18:(A)18.

6

[Criticizing proposals made by the new Republican majority in Congress, which will take office in 1995]: In the end, behind nearly every one of the Republican proposals lurks the same harshness and negativity. And I think we need better from our leaders than to have them distill

(MARIO M. CUOMO)

our worst instincts and then bottle the bitter juices and offer them back to us as a magic elixir.

Before National Press Club,
Washington, D.C., Dec. 15/
The New York Times,
12-17:16.

Lloyd N. Cutler
Counsel to President
of the United States
Bill Clinton

1

[On the plethora of accusations and allegations of wrongdoing that have been made against President Clinton]: These attacks have reached a level of invective and viciousness that is unparalleled. There are a great many people who would like to bring President Clinton down who will stop at practically nothing.

At Congressional
Whitewater hearings,
Washington, D.C., July/
U.S. News & World Report,
8-8:30.

2

[Saying there was nothing wrong with Treasury Department officials notifying the White House about investigations touching on the Whitewater scandal, which allegedly may involve President and Mrs. Clinton]: [It is not improper] when your superior is the President of the United States, who has to deal with press queries and carry on his job. He needs to know when either important people in his Administration or he himself is, are or may be under some form of criminal or other investigation. That doesn't mean he should interfere with the investigation, but he needs to know to perform his job.

At House Banking Committee
hearing on the
Whitewater scandal,
Washington, D.C., July 26/
The Washington Post,
7-28:(A)16.

Alfonse M. D'Amato
United States Senator,
R-New York

3

[On whether there has been any change in the White House since Leon Panetta's recent appointment as Chief of Staff]: Nope. I still think they're a bunch of jackasses trying to plan things to appear better politically instead of dealing with substantive problems.

USA Today, 7-15:(A)6.

John C. Danforth
United States Senator,
R-Missouri

4

Democrats have tended to become more hard-edged liberals and the Republicans more hard-edged conservatives . . . I think the American people are somewhere in the middle. Not to say that the entire political spectrum isn't covered by the American people; it certainly is. But the center of gravity is somewhere in the middle, and that center has not held in Congress.

Interview, St. Louis, Mo./
The Christian Science Monitor,
11-21:12.

Sam Dash
Former Chief Counsel,
Senate committee investigating
the Watergate scandal
in the 1970s

5

[On whether calls for Congressional hearings into the Whitewater scandal, and the alleged possible involvement of President Clinton, are appropriate]: We have a democracy. The ultimate sovereign is the people. And Congress is the agency that is given the power and the right and the duty to inform the public on how the government's working . . . So I see no problem, by the way, in Congress holding hearings. I think it was a reasonable request on the [Whitewater] Special

(SAM DASH)

Counsel's part, and I think Senator [Alfonse] D'Amato and the other members of Congress [who have called for hearings] have acted responsibly.

Broadcast interview/
"Good Morning America,"
ABC-TV, 3-10.

Nathan Deal
United States Representative,
D-Georgia

1

[On the possibility of Republican victories in this fall's Congressional elections in Southern districts now held by Democrats]: There is a real danger that if we [Democrats] lose the South, then that's enough to swing the balance of power [in Congress]. And it would be very difficult for the Party to ever reclaim it.

The New York Times,
5-21:1.

Robert J. Dole
United States Senator,
R-Kansas

2

[Saying he is beginning to take steps toward a possible run for President in 1996]: Whether or not I [run], you've got to be prepared. If you're going to get into this thing, you ought not wait until after next year. If you wait until you decide to do it, you may be behind the curve. I've had that happen to me.

Interview, June 14/
The New York Times,
6-15:(A)1.

Terry Eastland
Authority on the Presidency,
Center for Ethics
and Public Policy

3

[On President Clinton]: His model isn't re-

ally J.F.K. but L.B.J. There's a big speech—and a big bill for every problem.

Newsweek, 8-29:26.

4

[Democrats] used the "sleaze factor" to tar the [Ronald] Reagan Administration, but more people in this [Democratic Clinton] Administration are subject to investigation than any since the later part of the [Richard] Nixon years.

USA Today, 10-5:(A)9.

J. James Exon
United States Senator,
D-Nebraska

5

[On the sweeping Republican Congressional victory in the just-held national elections]: [Democrats should] not give up on all their fundamental principles and not roll over and play dead, but [should] recognize that people have elected the Republicans the majority. I hope Democrats won't fall into the trap of using the filibuster to get even.

USA Today, 11-11:(A)3.

Lauch Faircloth
United States Senator,
R-North Carolina

6

[On the Whitewater scandal, and the alleged possible involvement of President Clinton and his wife]: [Attorney General Janet] Reno was here November 7 and I asked her very straightforward to appoint an independent investigator to take a look at it. She was quite adamant in her statement that she was handling it, she would decide when to appoint an investigator, and that the buck stopped with her. I was really impressed by what she had to say, but I find out three months, or two and a half months, later that she decides that she needs to appoint an investigator when the "investigatees" [Clinton and his wife] say it is fine to appoint somebody to investigate [them]. She [Reno] never moved until the President said, "Yes,

(LAUCH FAIRCLOTH)

it looks like now we better appoint an investigator." And up she comes with an investigator.

At Senate Banking Committee
hearing on the nomination
of Ricki Tigert to be
Chairman of the FDIC,
Washington, D.C., Feb. 1/
The Wall Street Journal,
2-3:(A)14.

Diego Fernandez (de Cevallos)
National Action Party
nominee for President of Mexico

1

Political exposure is like exposure to the sun: Half an hour can be good, but if you expose yourself too much, you can get burned.

Interview,
Mexico City, Mexico, July 24/
The New York Times,
7-27:(A)3.

Thomas S. Foley
United States Representative,
D-Washington;
Speaker of the House

2

There's a segment of the Republican Party that is essentially pragmatic, I would say more philosophical than political. There is an element—I'm not trying to say things that sound like a slam, I think they're true—there are elements in the Republican Party in the House whose primary attitude toward a lot of these issues is a political one: how to defeat [President] Bill Clinton, how to embarrass Bill Clinton. And there's enormous anger, *enormous* anger, directed at the Republican moderates who joined with us [Democrats] on the crime bill.

Interview,
Washington, D.C., Aug. 23/
The Christian Science Monitor,
8-24:2.

3

[Saying the Democrats failed to communicate their accomplishments, which led to the sweeping Republican Congressional victory in the just-held national elections]: If the public believes the deficit is going up when it's going down, that we are in a recession when in fact we've added millions of new jobs, that's a problem of perception. But perception is reality in this day of politics.

Interview, Nov. 8/
The New York Times,
11-10:(B)3.

4

[On his recent loss in his bid for re-election to the House]: All of those who are in public life know that elections are about decision, and when you have the honor of being elected, and I have had that 15 times in my Congressional career, you know also that the public is entitled and will inevitably perhaps make a decision not to return you to office. And I respect that decision.

News briefing,
Washington, D.C./
U.S. News & World Report,
12-12:34.

Al From
President, Democratic
Leadership Council

5

[On President Clinton's low public-approval ratings]: He got captured by the Washington-Capitol Hill Democratic Establishment. and until he breaks that yoke, he won't pull out of [his slide].

U.S. News & World Report, 8-29:31.

6

Our great hope was that [President] Bill Clinton, governing as a New Democrat, would stop the realignment [in the country toward the Republican Party]. Unfortunately, the fact that Clinton is perceived as an Old Democrat seems to have accelerated it.

Newsweek, 10-31:33.

Geoffrey Garin
Democratic Party consultant

1

[On the future of President Clinton, in the wake of the sweeping Republican Congressional victory in last month's national elections]: I think the next four to six months are crucial for him and will be determinative in a lot of ways. It's crucial for him to be in charge of his own destiny. The period right now is really not about explaining what happened, but about understanding what happened and moving forward—smartly.

The New York Times,
12-8:(A)15.

David R. Gergen
Counsellor to President of the
United States Bill Clinton

2

[Criticizing those who are pursuing an investigation into the Whitewater scandal and the alleged possible involvement of President Clinton and his wife]:There is a cannibalism that's loose in our society in which public figures, such as the Clintons, could try to come to this town and do something good for the country and then they get hammered away even though they're trying to do the right thing. Yesterday, as the President goes home to bury his mother, to have the political opposition on the warpath [about Whitewater], hammering away, raises all sorts of questions about what has happened in this town. Where is the decency we once had?

Broadcast interview/
"Today" show,
NBC-TV, 1-7.

3

[Saying President Clinton's charisma accounts in part for the hatred many people feel for him]: I don't think it's totally coincidental that the two [most recent] Presidents who have been shot— [John F.] Kennedy and then [Ronald] Reagan— were both charismatic figures on television. I think that they somehow draw people out in a different way . . . And people have been out in Arkansas to "get" Bill Clinton for a long, long time, and we all know that.

Interview,
Washington, D.C.,
March 17/
Los Angeles Times,
3-18(A)15.

4

[Saying the current Whitewater scandal, which some say may involve President Clinton, and the Watergate scandal of the 1970s cannot be compared]: [Watergate] was a very traumatic period in the lives of a lot of us there, and we made some egregious mistakes, as you all know, some of which involved the use of institutions in violation of the law. [But in Whitewater, there has been] no credible allegation of wrongdoing [by Clinton].

Interview,
Washington, D.C.,
March 17/
Los Angeles Times,
3-18:(A)15.

5

[On the Whitewater scandal and the alleged possible involvement of President Clinton]: There were so many questions at [Clinton's] press conference last week on Whitewater, and so few on policy, our hope was to say, "Look, we're going to deal with Whitewater and be as responsive, cooperative as possible." But at the same time, it's important to get on with the rest of the [President's] agenda. That's what the country wants. That's what the country expects . . . I don't think we will ever have time, nor should we spend time, going back and resurrecting everything that may have happened [regarding Whitewater] 15 years ago.

To reporters,
Washington, D.C.,
March 30/
The New York Times,
3-31:(A)8.

Newt Gingrich
United States Representative,
R-Georgia

1

[On President Clinton's reluctance to release documents about the Whitewater scandal, which he may be linked to]: To have the White House going to the Justice Department to apparently collude together to get a subpoena so the American people can't see the documents—there's something a little bit sick about that kind of approach.

Broadcast interview/
"Today" show, NBC-TV, 1-6.

2

[Saying President Clinton is wrong to blame Republicans for keeping the Whitewater scandal alive]: [If President Clinton believes the Republican Party caused his Whitewater problems,] then he has a very big problem engaging reality . . . The worst thing he's doing in terms of the country and his Presidency is not the "politics of personal destruction" [as Clinton accused the Republicans of pursuing]; it's the politics of self-destruction. It is not the politics of [Republican] partisanship; it is the politics of [Clinton's] self-deception.

News conference, March 15/
The Washington Post,
3-16:(A)2.

3

[Criticizing the fact that the same lawyer, Robert Bennett, who is involved with President Clinton's scandal problems, also is involved with Congressman Dan Rostenkowski's Federal fraud scandal case]: Clearly, when you have the President's lawyer negotiating with the Justice Department over a national health-care leader [Rostenkowski], the American people have some cause to wonder what's going on . . . What we're concerned about is some sort of strange plea-bargaining taking place in which political pressure could be brought to bear. You can't have one of the most powerful members of the House having the same lawyer as the President at this critical moment being involved in a plea bargain and not

say anything about it. This is a very serious matter of public ethics and it needs to be dealt with in a manner that restores public confidence, not undermines it further.

May 24/
Los Angeles Times,
5-25:(A)4.

4

[On President Clinton's chances for re-election in 1996]: In these days of television, cycles are about 90 days long. I think if Clinton has a good 90-day cycle in '96 before election day, he will be re-elected. If he doesn't, he won't.

Interview/
The Christian Science Monitor,
8-30:19.

5

[With the Clinton Administration,] you have the most ethics problems since Warren Harding. You have an Administration that is to the left of [1988 Democratic President nominee Michael] Dukakis. You have a level of confusion greater than that of [former President] Jimmy Carter. All in one Administration. Now, in that setting, why would the country be happy?

Interview/
The Christian Science Monitor,
8-30:19.

6

[Saying his dream is a Republican majority in the House of Representatives]: To truly achieve the level of change we want [for the country], we have to have control. I very, very much want to have the Ways and Means Committee holding hearings on [Republican Congressman] Dick Armey's flat-tax [proposal]. I very much want to have the Budget Committee insisting on the replacement of the [government's] socialist accounting system with a free-market model . . . I very much want the Judiciary Committee to have a hearing on school prayer in every state in the union in the first six months of next year. I don't think anybody should think that we're going to be happy if

(NEWT GINGRICH)

we get 25 [additional seats in the forthcoming national elections]. Until we get control, we don't have control.

Los Angeles Times,
10-3:(A)11.

Newt Gingrich
United States Representative,
R-Georgia;
Speaker of the House-designate

1

[Saying President Clinton is in reality a follower of the views of liberal former Senator George McGovern]: That is honestly who he is. He's a very smart, very clever tactician whose core system activity is a combination of counter-culture and McGovern. He has McGovern's Texas director; he and his wife [First Lady Hillary Rodham Clinton] were counter-culture at Yale; and why wouldn't you accept that they really are who they are? Their problem is, that is a contradiction with the vast majority of Americans. So you have this constant internal stress, and what the American people were saying [in the just-held elections which put Republicans in charge of both houses of Congress] is "Enough."

Interview, Nov. 9/
The New York Times,
11-10:(B)3.

2

[On the sweeping Republican Congressional victory in the just-held national elections]: As you know, we had a "contract" with Americans that we put in *TV Guide* a couple weeks ago. It's a clear document that was designed to be torn out as a full-page ad so people could keep it. And on January 4 [when the Republicans take over the House and Senate leadership], they [the public] could literally watch us keep our word on C-SPAN. And I think we are bound, to some extent, by the contract. But within that framework, we'd like to work with the President [Clinton] and find some common ground—welfare reform, line-item veto,

strengthening families—things that he has said he believes in, and see if we can't put some of them front and center in a bipartisan way, so that we can actually get some things signed into law . . . We actually hope to be more open with the Democrats than they have been with us [Republicans] in the 16 years I've served.

Broadcast interview/
"Morning News,"
CNN-TV, 11-9.

3

[On the sweeping Republican Congressional victory in the just-held national elections]: Everybody who wants to change Washington and who wants to dramatically change the Federal government should be very happy we've arrived. Everyone who wants to protect the old order should be frightened.

USA Today, 11-11:(A)3.

4

I want to draw a distinction between two words. [As the new Speaker of the House,] I am very prepared to *cooperate* with the Clinton Administration. I am not prepared to *compromise*. On everything on which we can find agreement, I will cooperate. On those things that are at the core of [the Republican] Contract [With America], on those things which are at the core of our philosophy and on those things where we believe we represent the vast majority of Americans, there will be no compromise.

Before Washington
Research Group,
Washington, D.C., Nov. 11/
The New York Times,
11-12:9.

Benjamin Ginsberg
Specialist in elections and
political parties,
Johns Hopkins University

5

[On the current fractious campaign for this fall's Virginia U.S. Senate election]: Virginia is at

(BENJAMIN GINSBERG)

an advanced stage of what's going on in politics throughout the country. Parties mean less and less, and each so-called party is breaking up into various wings.

Los Angeles Times,
5-5:(A)5.

Rudolph W. Giuliani
Mayor of New York, N.Y.

1

[Upon paying the 15-cent clerk's fee to take the Mayoral oath of office, comparing it with the cost of his two Mayoral election campaigns]: The [15 cents] is all it costs to become Mayor of New York City. Of course, there was that 9 million [dollars] and the 5 million before that.

New York, N.Y./
Newsweek, 1-10:19.

2

I think I know some Republicans that are going to vote for [Democrat] Mario Cuomo [for re-election as New York Governor] this year, except they feel, because they're so tied into partisan politics, they can't tell you the truth about it. It's kind of circumlocutous, but I think that's one of the reasons why people are so turned off about politics today. Because we don't act like we're real people.

News conference
announcing his decision,
as a Republican,
to endorse Democrat Cuomo,
New York, N.Y., Oct. 24/
The New York Times,
10-25:(C)23.

3

[On his being a Republican and recently supporting the Democratic candidate for New York Governor, and Republican Los Angeles Mayor Richard Riordan recently supporting the Democratic candidate for U.S. Senate from California]: Dick Riordan and I analyze things very much the

same way, which is that we realize that we have to put the good of our city ahead of blind party loyalty. If we can, in any way, consistently support our Party, consistent with the interests of the city, then we'll do that, even if you have to give the benefit of the doubt to your Party . . . But when there is a wide discrepancy, as the one that I faced between [Democrat] Mario Cuomo and [Republican] George Pataki, you have to do what is best for your city. I assume the same thing is true with Dick Riordan.

Interview, New York, N.Y./
Los Angeles Times,
11-13:(M)3.

Ira Glasser
Executive director,
American Civil Liberties Union

4

[Saying President Clinton cannot be counted on to support liberal and civil-liberties causes]: He seems unwilling to stake out a principled position and defend it . . . We're telling [liberals] we have to defend our principles ourselves, because the people who are supposed to be our political friends in office have turned out to be accomplices of our adversaries.

The New York Times,
11-28:(A)8.

John Glenn
United States Senator, D-Ohio

5

[On Senators having to raise money for re-election campaigns]: It's gotten so gosh-darned expensive to campaign that you have to work every day for six years to raise enough money to run for re-election. If you haven't come into someone's home via television, you're not going to get their vote. So here we are, spending an inordinate amount of time each day, not doing the people's business but just raising money.

Interview, Washington, D.C./
Mother Jones, Sept.-Oct.:30.

(JOHN GLENN)

1

[On Democratic Party relations with the Republicans following the sweeping Republican Congressional victory in just-held national elections]: The big unknown is whether this anti-Democratic, scorched-earth, political demolition derby we've been in for the last six months is going to continue, or do we really work together.

USA Today, 11-11:(A)3.

Doris Kearns Goodwin
Historian, Biographer

2

[On the public hostility to First Lady Hillary Rodham Clinton]: When a First Lady is speaking out and is independent and powerful, there is some strain in the country that is touched forever. [The late President] Franklin Roosevelt would get letters saying, "Can't you muzzle that wife of yours?" or "Can't you at least chain her up?" [But despite the similarities,] there seems to be an anger toward Hillary that wasn't even present toward Eleanor [Roosevelt]. Because [Eleanor] was so far ahead of her time, she wasn't representing, as Hillary is, the change that is taking place in this country between men and women . . . There is an anger in the criticism of Hillary that has got to mean it is not only about her, because otherwise it doesn't make sense.

The Wall Street Journal, 9-30:(A)1.

3

[On the sweeping Republican Congressional victory in the just-held national elections]: Somehow, the Republicans have captured that insurgent feeling against all politicians in general. And now it's their turn to try to prove that their solutions for the complex problems of America—the balanced budget, lower taxes, somehow magically reducing the deficit, and welfare reform and harsher measures on crime—will actually work rather than just being a rallying call for discontent.

Nov. 9/The New York Times, 11-10:(B)4.

Al Gore
*Vice President
of the United States*

4

[On the Whitewater scandal and the alleged possible involvement of President Clinton]: [The Republicans have pursued Whitewater out of] political panic [because] everything's beginning to go right with the economy. They're going into an election year. They haven't been able to sustain any attacks on President Clinton's policies; the country's turning round; the President's doing a fantastic job. And so [the Republicans are] going after him personally.

*Broadcast interview/
"Face the Nation,"
CBS-TV, 1-9.*

5

[Calling for a Democratic Party victory in the forthcoming national elections]: Let us be clear about the fact that America [faces] a choice. We've made a good start. We're moving in the right direction. Are we going to continue moving forward, or call a halt to the progress and take a radical right-wing U-turn back to the [1980s] trickle-down Reaganomics approach that almost bankrupted this country and caused those two deep recessions, the worst since the Great Depression?

*Campaigning for New York
Governor Mario Cuomo,
Freeport, N.Y., Oct. 17/
The New York Times,
10-18:(A)18.*

Bob Graham
United States Senator, D-Florida

6

[Saying it is hard these days for Democratic Party members of Congress to disassociate themselves from an unpopular national Democratic Party and an unpopular President Clinton]: We used to be able to separate ourselves from our "national" Party. But politics has been McDonaldized, and the President is Ronald McDonald.

Newsweek, 10-10:30.

Phil Gramm
United States Senator,
R-Texas

1

[Criticizing President Clinton's handling of an investigation into the Whitewater scandal]: Let's not forget that [former President] Richard Nixon turned a third-rate burglary into a Constitutional crisis by not leveling, by interfering in the [Watergate] investigation. I think the President [Clinton] is getting deeper into a hole. If the President continues to have officials of the regulatory agencies over to the White House to brief staff [on the investigation], if the President continues to have White House counsels interfere in investigations, that can quickly become obstruction of justice if you're not careful about it.

Broadcast interview/
"This Week With David Brinkley,"
ABC-TV, 3-6.

2

I have found that [political] opponents never resort to name-calling and personal attacks when they are winning the debate, only when they are losing it.

Aug. 9/The Washington Post,
8-10:(A)5.

Fred Grandy
United States Representative,
R-Iowa

3

The problem is hypocrisy. We [Republicans] spend half our time criticizing the Democrats and the other half imitating every move they make.

U.S. News & World Report,
12-5:50.

Charles E. Grassley
United States Senator, R-Iowa

4

[Saying Republicans should not oppose Oliver North, their Party's controversial U.S. Senate nominee from Virginia]: The bottom line is that there have been a lot of nuts elected to the United States Senate.

Newsweek, 6-20:19.

Mark Green
Public Advocate
of New York, N.Y.

5

There's a bill in Washington that's been going nowhere—the campaign finance reform bill—because the only people who vote on it are members of the incumbent party, who got there by the old rules and don't want any new rules. So we have a real gridlock. There's no gridlock yet on health-care reform, on trade relations. But there is on democracy.

Interview, New York, N.Y./
Lear's, March:16.

Stanley B. Greenberg
Chief public-opinion analyst
for President of the
United States Bill Clinton

6

[On subpoenas issued to Clinton Administration staffers regarding the Whitewater scandal]: The subpoenas brought something understandable into this. Before that, [Whitewater] was very complicated and potentially very old, not something [the public] wanted to see get in the way of the people's agenda. The subpoenas brought an immediacy and something real. It has the potential to change the issue, but I don't think we yet know whether it's going to have a substantial effect.

The Washington Post,
3-11:(A)11.

7

[On the sweeping Republican Congressional victory in the just-held national elections]: The Republicans will make a very big mistake if they interpret this election as having settled the Clinton Presidency. The forces at work that threw [the

(STANLEY B. GREENBERG)

Republicans] out in [the] 1992 [election] are still at work in '94. [Now] the Democrats were seen to be in power, which is why they paid the price.

Nov. 9/
The New York Times,
11-10:(B)1.

1

[On the sweeping Republican congressional victory in the recent national elections]: The Republicans will try to say this election is a repudiation of where the President is trying to take the country. But I think this is a condemnation of the ugly process needed to bring about change. Voters have no confidence that either party knows where to take the country.

U.S. News & World Report,
11-21:50.

Lee H. Hamilton
United States Representative,
D-Indiana

2

[On the Iran-contra scandal of the 1980s]: The complexity of Iran-contra should not obscure the facts of what happened. As a small group of [U.S.] government officials decided they knew what was right for the United States, they kept it secret from the Congress; they showed disdain for the law and acted totally in conflict with the Constitution.

The New York Times,
1-19:(A)27.

Jean E. Hanson
General Counsel,
Department of the Treasury
of the United States

3

[Denying suggestions that she violated legal or ethical rules regarding notification to the White House that President and Mrs. Clinton may be objects of an investigation into the Whitewater

scandal]: I am aware that others' recollections [of what happened] differ from my own. I do not question the good faith of anyone who has a differing recollection. Most importantly, I think these differences in recollection are irrelevant. What matters is that each of the events in which I was a participant pursued legitimate objectives and was appropriate. Despite differences in recollections, no one to my knowledge intended to do, or did, anything wrong or unethical.

At Senate Banking
Committee hearing on
the Whitewater scandal,
Washington, D.C., Aug 1/
The New York Times,
8-2:(A)1.

Mark O. Hatfield
United States Senator, R-Oregon

4

[On issues such as school prayer, a balanced-budget amendment and term limits for Congress that Republicans talked about in their recent sweeping national-elections victory]: These are all symbols, and the Republicans will beat the drums and get a lot of pizzazz going because they have fed the public a line about these things. But to present them as if they are the answers and solutions to our problems is just phony.

Interview, Portland, Ore./
The New York Times,
11-26:8.

Stephen Hess
Senior fellow, Brookings Institution

5

[On President Clinton]: He procrastinates, and things catch up with him. He'll let something slide, and then he throws the energy, the intellect and the power of the Presidency into it. It's been a high-wire act for one and a half years.

The New York Times,
7-27:(A)17.

(STEPHEN HESS)

1

[On President Clinton's political and administrative troubles]: As someone who cares about the authority of the Presidency—whoever has the job—I can barely stand to watch him. He seems intent on trying to undermine his own power.

Newsweek, 8-29:25.

2

[On the possibility that former Joint Chiefs of Staff Chairman Colin Powell, a black, will run for President]: He hasn't been a "black leader." He's been a leader who is black. So he hasn't brought all of the feelings one way or the other that come with the issue of civil rights and race . . . Powell is a very skilled politician. You don't get to be Chairman of the Joint Chiefs of Staff without knowing the Byzantine world of [military] politics and Administration partisan politics . . . He'll still have to go through the same obstacle course everyone else who wants to be President has to. It's very arduous and long [and] there are lots of places to fall over the cliff.

USA Today, 9-30:(A)6.

Peter Hoagland
United States Representative,
D-Nebraska

3

[Saying President Clinton is a liability for Democrats such as himself who are running for re-election this fall]: [He is] an enormous liability. I'm like a scuba diver carrying two to three times as much weight as normal.

U.S. News & World Report,
9-12:53.

Eric H. Holder, Jr.
United States Attorney
for the District of Columbia

4

[Announcing the indictment of U.S. Representative Dan Rostenkowski on 17 counts involv-

ing abuse of office]: The allegations contained in today's indictment represent a betrayal of the public trust for personal gain. In essence, this indictment alleges that Congressman Rostenkowski used his elective office to perpetrate an extensive fraud on the American people. The wrongful expenditure of taxpayer dollars by and at the behest of Congressman Rostenkowski rolls into the hundreds of thousands of dollars. This is not, as some have suggested, a petty matter. But in a larger sense, the true cost of such corruption by elected officials cannot be measured solely in dollar amounts, no matter how high this total. Rather, the cost of such misconduct must also be measured in terms of the corrosive effect it has on our democratic system of government and on the trust our citizens have in their elected officials. Let me be clear. Historically and presently, the vast majority of the members of Congress have been and are decent and honorable public officials who work incredibly hard and follow all of the rules. These women and men are as appalled by such acts of corruption as anyone else. But the criminal acts of a few feed the cynicism which increasingly haunts our political landscape. It causes too many of our citizens to assume that all persons in public life are motivated by greed and self-interest and to succumb to the defeatist notion that we must resign ourselves to the fact that a certain level of political misconduct is a way of life. I reject that notion that there is an acceptable level of corruption. As a society, we must be committed to a policy of zero tolerance when it comes to official misconduct. Otherwise, its corrosive effect will undermine the very principles upon which the nation stands. Therefore, today's indictment of Congressman Rostenkowski should stand as a firm and solemn reminder that the Department of Justice has an unwavering commitment to hold accountable all those who engage in corruption—regardless of their political position, regardless of their political party and regardless of their political power.

News conference,
Washington, D.C., May 31/
The New York Times,
6-1:(A)12.

Robert D. Holsworth
Political scientist,
Virginia Commonwealth University

1

[On this year's Virginia U.S. Senatorial nominations of Democrat Charles Robb and Republican Oliver North, both of whom are seen by many as being too politically controversial]: The parties are finding it difficult to nominate candidates that are not leaving them vulnerable to attacks on their flanks. This campaign in Virginia really shows the fracturing of the political party system, and I don't think this is the only time we're going to see this.
The New York Times,
6-15:(A)38.

Michael Huffington
United States Representative,
R-California

2

[On the forthcoming 1994 national elections, in which he is running for U.S. Senator from California]: I see this as a turning-point election. There will be a sea-change if people like myself and [Massachusetts Republican candidate] Mitt Romney get elected to the United States Senate. We're a new breed of politicians, because we are citizen-politicians. We don't want to stay [in Washington] forever, but to go there to change things, and then return home to the state from which we were elected.
Interview/Los Angeles Times,
10-30:(M)5.

3

[On his spending $28-million of his own money on his unsuccessful U.S. Senate election campaign]: It was very worth it.
Newsweek, 11-28:23.

Henry J. Hyde
United States Representative,
R-Illinois

4

[On Republicans' pursuit of the Whitewater scandal and the alleged possible involvement of President Clinton]: You have to remember the position that all Republicans have been in for 12 years, where we were investigated [by Democrats], sometimes frivolously. If we get a chance to point a finger, why, it requires a saintlessness that is superhuman, supernatural to act with restraint.
Newsweek, 3-21:27.

Patricia Ireland
President, National Organization
for Women

5

[Saying that, following 1973's Supreme Court *Roe v. Wade* ruling supporting abortion rights, that issue became a coalescing force for anti-abortion conservatives of various kinds to rally around]: The more traditional conservative figures . . . zeroed in on abortion as a way to bring normally disparate groups together in a conservative coalition. Southern evangelicals joined a coalition with urban ethnics, galvanizing around this emotional issue and, ultimately I think, led the way to a [Ronald] Reagan Presidency.
The Washington Post,
4-7:(A)10.

Jesse L. Jackson
Civil-rights leader

6

[On the possibility that retired Joint Chiefs of Staff Chairman Colin Powell, a black, will run for President]: He is exalted as a symbol, much as [former football star] O. J. Simpson was, because he isn't threatening to whites. He's seen [that way] because he's never been a combatant in America's race wars. But he hasn't transcended race. No black can transcend race. That's ridiculous.
Newsweek, 10-10:24.

Sherry Bebitch Jeffe
Political analyst,
Claremont Graduate School

7

[On political candidates who are wealthy enough to finance their own campaigns]: Some-

(SHERRY BEBITCH JEFFE)

thing strange is going on. Voters used to be scorn-
ful of candidates who bankrolled their own campaigns. Now they see a candidate's own funds as
the only clean money left in politics.

USA Today, 10-5:(A)2.

Don Johnson
United States Representative,
D-Georgia

1

[On whether he would invite fellow Democrats President Clinton and Vice President Gore
to campaign for him in the forthcoming election,
given Clinton's low poll ratings]: Only if they are
coming down to endorse my opponent.

Time, 9-12:28.

Paula Corbin Jones
Former Arkansas state employee

2

[On her sexual-harassment suit against President Clinton for an incident she said took place
when he was Governor of Arkansas]: [The American people] don't know until they are in my shoes.
I don't know if people can imagine a strange person . . . plus being the Governor, dropping his pants
[in a hotel room]. It's like being raped mentally.
He's responsible . . . If he's found guilty and if
that's what he has to pay, to not be President anymore, I guess that's his way of paying for what
he's done.

Interview, Washington, D.C./
USA Today, 6-17:(A)2.

Nancy Landon Kassebaum
United States Senator, R-Kansas

3

[The religious right] has taken over a lot [of
the Republican Party] in Kansans, including my
own county organization. Part of the problem is
that moderates aren't willing to work in the

trenches, while the Christian conservatives have
gone door to door and worked hard and won control fair and square. My hat's off to them for that.

Los Angeles Times,
7-28:(A)19.

David Keene
President,
American Conservative Union

4

[Saying recent sweeping Republican election
victories may bring out more potential candidates
to run for President in 1996 against incumbent
Democrat Bill Clinton]: If politicians are like any
animal, they're like piranhas. And there's blood in
the water.

U. S. News & World Report,
11-21:52.

Jack Kemp
Former Secretary of
Housing and Urban Development
of the United States;
Former United States
Representative, R-New York

5

We've [Republicans] got to repeal the old
Southern strategy of the 1960s and 1970s. We need
a new strategy based on asking black and minority men and women to vote Republican—and give
them a reason to vote Republican.

Time, 9-26:36.

Bob Kerrey
United States Senator,
D-Nebraska

6

[On the sweeping Republican Congressional
victory in the recent national elections]: This election was a severe, sharp and obvious repudiation
of the President [Clinton]. We [Democrats] are on
the wrong side of many important issues.

The New York Times,
11-21:(A)14.

Michael Kinsley
Senior editor,
"The New Republic";
Co-host, "Crossfire,"
CNN-TV

1

Democrats went through this period where they nominated these purists [for President]—[Michael] Dukakis, [Jimmy] Carter, [Walter] Mondale sort of—and kept losing elections. So they finally decided that what we really need is a smart, ruthless, media-savvy candidate—not a purist. Finally they decided, "We gotta get down and dirty, the way the Republicans do." And that was right—so you've got [President] Bill Clinton, who's not pure in his approach to politics and not completely financially pure, either . . . If you want somebody who's tough, who can really play the game, then he's not going to be a morally perfect human being.

Interview, Chevy Chase, Md./
Vanity Fair, November:86.

Henry A. Kissinger
Former Secretary of State
of the United States

2

[On former President Richard Nixon, who recently died]: So let us now say goodbye to our gallant friend. He stood on pinnacles that dissolved in the precipice. He achieved greatly and he suffered deeply. But he never gave up.

Eulogy at Nixon's burial/
Newsweek, 5-9:15.

William Kristol
Chairman, Project for
the Republican Future

3

[Criticizing President Clinton's performance in office]: He deserves credit for working with Republicans on NAFTA. Otherwise, he has raised taxes, imposed some new unfunded mandates, and his centerpiece domestic policy proposal, health-care reform, is in total collapse. [And it's] no surprise a Democratic President and a Democrat-controlled Congress could pass a few pieces of standard Democratic legislation.

USA Today, 5-13:(A)4.

4

In an era where everyone is suddenly talking about virtue, it's useful to be reminded that our politicians are not saints. As Samuel Johnson said, "When people start speaking of honor, I count my spoons."

The New York Times,
9-16:(A)8.

5

[On the new Republican majority in Congress in 1995]: It's important [for us Republicans] not to depend on [Democratic Party] scandals to do our work for us. We have a chance to win a huge ideological victory. We could blow it, but the New Deal era is over and the opportunity is there for a long-term reshaping of American politics.

Interview/
USA Today, 12-9:(A)8.

Celinda Lake
Democratic Party
public-opinion analyst

6

[President] Clinton has carried a permanent negative with him throughout his term of office. That [negative] group has had an intensity and verbalization few Presidents have seen.

U.S. News & World Report,
11-7:37.

Richard D. Lamm
Director, Public Policy Institute,
University of Denver;
Former Governor of Colorado (D)

7

[On former President Richard Nixon, who recently died]: There are really two Richard Nixons.

(RICHARD D. LAMM)

There is the paranoid politician, a man who picked at every sore he could find on the body politic. And there in the same body was this overarching geopolitical thinker. You've got to find a way to weigh them together.

Los Angeles Times,
4-24:(A)14.

Jim Leach
United States Representative,
R-Iowa

1

[I] believe that, just as it's insufficient for a conservative to advocate family values and not to have a good family life, it's insufficient for a liberal to advocate compassionate programs and not live an ethical life. There is hypocrisy in both instances.

Interview, Coral Gables, Fla./
The Washington Post,
1-11:(B)2.

2

[On the Whitewater scandal and the alleged possible involvement of President Clinton]: I don't think there's anything really big at the end of the tunnel. I think there's something very symbolic, and I've recently been talking about the Shakespearean analogies of whether it's much ado about nothing or something rotten in the Ozarks. It may be a little bit of each. But I see nothing that isn't beyond very serious embarrassment. And I don't know of an issue that could be more readily put behind than this one. And in many ways the bigger story has become not what's an issue in the past but how they're handling it in the present.

To reporters,
Washington, D.C., Jan.11/
The Christian Science Monitor,
1-12:6.

3

[On the Whitewater scandal and the alleged possible involvement of President Clinton when

he was Arkansas Governor]: Whitewater is about conflicts of interest . . . involving a real-estate investment in which one-half of a partnership put in substantially more resources than the other half. They also involve the intermixing of taxpayer-guaranteed resources with a private venture, to the potential advantage of a public official. That is what makes the circumstances a public rather than simply a private interest. It should be stressed that on the public record is the fact that a failed savings and loan infused far more capital into Whitewater than then-Governor [Clinton]. In a nutshell, you have a conflict of interest in multithousand-dollar proportions which may have contributed to multimillion-dollar losses for the taxpayer when the S&L subsequently failed—due, in part, to its investment in Whitewater and other real-estate ventures of quasi-similar composition . . . My own sense is that what you have here is an issue of public ethics that deserves being raised— and then deserves being resolved. All the [Republicans] ever requested almost five months ago was for a hearing on the subject. If that hearing had occurred, that would have been a one-to-three-week issue. As it worked out, the [Administration] decision to deny public accountability piqued public interest, and particularly press interest, and the issue escalated . . . It's one of the reasons why I have repeatedly suggested that, with full public disclosure and full accountability, I am more than willing—in fact, I am quite eager—to bring this issue to resolution. It's my view that accountability is in order, but that a Constitutional crisis is not.

Interview, Washington, D.C./
Los Angeles Times,
4-3:(M)3.

4

[Saying it was improper for Treasury Department officials to notify the White House about investigations touching on the Whitewater scandal, which may involve President and Mrs. Clinton]: It was unethical for the Department of the Treasury to inform the White House of these criminal referrals and unethical for a lawyer at the

(JIM LEACH)

White House [Presidential Counsel Lloyd Cutler] either to inform the President or see that the President was provided information about these referrals . . . No American . . . including the President of the United States, is entitled to insider information on the development of criminal referrals that may relate to that individual.

At House Banking Committee hearing on the Whitewater scandal, Washington, D.C., July 26/ The Washington Post, 7-28:(A)16.

1

[On the Whitewater scandal and the alleged possible involvement of President Clinton]: [It is a picture of] me-generation ethics [in which the Administration conspired with Congressional Democrats to hide] full disclosure . . . and mislead the public. [Whitewater is] about the arrogance of power. It is a metaphor for privilege, for a government run by a new political class which takes short cuts to power with end-runs of the law.

At House Banking Committee hearing on the Whitewater scandal, Washington, D.C., July 26/ Los Angeles Times, 7-27:(A)10.

Charles Lewis
Executive director,
Center for Public Integrity

2

[On the recently established defense fund for President Clinton and his wife Hillary, which was set up to collect contributions to help them pay the costs associated with private legal actions being taken against them]: They're doing a tin cup for Bill and Hillary, and, any way you cut it, it's unprecedented and it's not pretty.

Newsweek, 7-11:13.

G. Gordon Liddy
Radio talk-show host;
Former U.S. Treasury
Department official

3

[On political strategy for the Christian Coalition]: Emulate even more of the old Communist Party tactics! They had "sleeper agents," agents of influence . . . If you have someone widely known as a Christian, it may be difficult to get that person into an administrative position [in government]. If that person is not constantly trumpeting his Christianity . . . you can get them in there. At a key moment, you can cast a key vote, and the other side doesn't know what happened to them! . . . [Jews] are inherently conservative. You don't want to alienate them and frighten them by saying, "This is, by God, a Christian country" . . . Remember, you need all the allies you can get. Your enemies are many and we are still few.

At Christian Coalition convention, Washington, D.C., Sept. 16/ The Washington Post, 9-19:(D)6.

Nita M. Lowey
United States Representative,
D-New York

4

[On new Republican House Speaker-to-be Newt Gingrich]: Newt . . . is determined to remake the House in his own image. If he thinks he won a mandate [because of the sweeping Republican Congressional victory in the recent national elections] to pursue a narrow, partisan agenda, he's mistaken. I don't think [people] voted for a bomb-throwing, McCarthyite witchhunt.

USA Today, 11-11:(A)3.

Frank Luntz
Republican Party
public-opinion analyst

5

The current [political] structures are shattering; 1996 may be the last election in which parti-

(FRANK LUNTZ)

san affiliation counts for much. The only people left who express strong party loyalty are those over 55. Few under 32 have allegiances at all.

Newsweek, 7-18:38.

1

[On United We Stand America, the political organization founded by industrialist and 1992 independent Presidential candidate Ross Perot]: United We Stand is basically ineffectual in most places. Maine, Florida, parts of Texas, parts of Michigan, it might count for something. But what you have here is like an iceberg; what's interesting is the 85-90 percent below the surface, the people no longer personally loyal to Ross Perot, no longer active, if they ever were, in the organization, but still profoundly committed to his issues.

The New York Times,
9-6:(A)1.

Frank Mankiewicz
Former Press Secretary
to the late Attorney General
of the United States
Robert F. Kennedy

2

[On former President Richard Nixon, who recently died]: I thought he had lower self-esteem than any other successful American politician. He was the Willy Loman [a character in the play *Death of a Salesman*] of American politics. "Attention must be paid." Remember where Willy talks about a salesman—clearly it's himself—and he says, "He was liked, but he wasn't *well* liked." I think there was a lot of that in Nixon. I never knew anybody who said, the way people would say, "I'm a [John Kennedy] man" or "I'm a [Ronald] Reagan man" —I don't think anybody ever said, "I'm a Nixon man."

The Washington Post,
4-25:(B)8.

Thomas E. Mann
Director
of governmental studies,
Brookings Institution

3

[On President Clinton's low public-approval ratings despite improvements in the economy]: It is truly staggering the mismatch between the public perceptions of the government and the Administration's handling of the economy and the objective news on the economy. It is one of the biggest mysteries of this Administration.

The Washington Post,
8-9:(A)1.

Will Marshall
President,
Progressive Policy Institute

4

[On the possibility of President Clinton being challenged by other Democrats for the Party's 1996 Presidential nomination]: The Democratic landscape is not exactly peopled by giants right now.

U.S. News & World Report,
12-26:24.

Mary Matalin
Host, "Equal Time," CNBC-TV;
Former deputy
campaign manager
for former President
of the United States
George Bush's 1992
re-election campaign

5

[Running election campaigns] is a weird occupation. You need a combination of experience, which requires age, and the energy of a 28-year-old. You only have a couple of peak years where the energy and experience dovetail.

Interview/
Working Woman,
August:74.

189

George S. McGovern
Former United States Senator,
D-South Dakota

1

[On the sweeping Republican Congressional victory in the just-held national elections]: One of the basic problems is that while the people in the top 20 percent of the American public are benefiting from the growth in the economy . . . for everyone else, 80 percent of the public, including the middle class, are not doing as well as they were a few years ago. We are told the election is going to result in less government and reduced spending, except for the military, and in tougher stands on welfare, and so on. Even some tax reduction. But I don't think that addresses the problem that I have just described. And my guess is that if that is the direction we go in, that the Republican time will come [to lose an election] in a couple of years down the road.

Nov. 9/
The New York Times,
11-10:(B)4.

Thomas F. McLarty III
Chief of Staff to
President of the United States
Bill Clinton

2

[On the Whitewater scandal and the alleged possible involvement of President Clinton]: Whitewater may be like sinuses: You're not going to be fully able to cure it in a short period of time. It's going to come and go.

Interview,
Washington, D.C., March 30/
The New York Times,
3-31:(A)8.

Harry McPherson
Former Counsel to the
President of the United States
(Lyndon B. Johnson)

3

[Saying President Clinton has little choice, in today's political climate, but to move to the right politically]: If he goes too far, he loses the true [liberal] believers, the people who run phone banks and lick stamps. But the fact is that there's really no one out there carrying the flag for liberalism anymore. The shock troops of the poverty program are gone; [labor] unions [are] smaller and less effective; same for the big civil-rights groups. The old coalition isn't big enough to win anymore. So whatever base he risks alienating, he has no choice but to try to add to it by moving right.

The New York Times,
12-15:(A)12.

Patrick McSweeney
Chairman,
Republican Party of Virginia

4

[On the controversy over Oliver North's running for the Virginia Republican nomination for U.S. Senate, in view of his connection with the Iran-contra scandal a number of years ago]: People are tired of the same old thing [from their candidates]. They really do believe in their frustration that this kind of politician [North] can make things change. They want someone who will not be sucked into the vortex.

Los Angeles Times,
5-5(A)5.

Ellen Miller
Executive director,
Center for Responsive Politics

5

[On total public financing of election campaigns]: Achieving this goal will require jumping the enormous hurdles of public cynicism and suspicion toward politics and politicians. Public-interest groups have failed to make the case that today's cost of private financing of elections is far, far higher than the cost of a system of total public financing.

Mother Jones,
Jan.-Feb.:21.

George J. Mitchell
United States Senator,
D-Maine

1

Clearly, Republican obstructionism has been a major factor in this Congress, a desire on their part to prevent action and then go to the people and say, "Look, there was no action." That is to say, benefit from the very obstructionism in which they engaged.

Interview/
USA Today, 10-5:(A)6.

Daniel Patrick Moynihan
United States Senator,
D-New York

2

[Saying President Clinton should release all documents relating to the Whitewater scandal in order to avoid the appearance of a cover-up]: Presidents can't be seen to have any hesitation about any matter that concerns their propriety. And this is an honorable man . . . He has nothing to hide . . . Or nothing should be hidden. And everything, I'm sure, will be understood—excepting if there is that old phrase . . . "stonewall."

Broadcast interview/
"Meet the Press,"
NBC-TV, 1-9.

Dawn Clark Netsch
State Comptroller of Illinois;
1994 Democratic nominee
for Governor of Illinois

3

[Saying her being a woman running for Governor has not helped her candidacy]: Nobody is really paying much attention. Maybe it's our fault for not having made more of it. But if you beat everybody over the head with it constantly, then is sounds as if you're saying people should vote for you just because you're a woman.

Interview, Chicago, Ill./
The New York Times,
10-3:(A)1.

Lyn Nofziger
Former Special Assistant for
Political Affairs to the
President of the United States
(Ronald Reagan)

4

[On President Clinton's political skills and speech-making ability]: He's like down-home folks, and he's always talking in terms of helping people. [Former President Ronald] Reagan was always pretty self-deprecating, which people appreciated; but Clinton's every bit as good, and he's smoother at kidding himself without it appearing contrived.

Los Angeles Times,
2-28:(A)18.

Grover Norquist
President,
Americans for Tax Reform

5

The tax issue is the critical divide between the [Democratic and Republican] parties. That's the centerpiece. The Republican Party is saying, "No more money and power to Washington; turn off the spigot." And the Democratic Party is saying, "No, no; more money and power."

The New York Times,
11-22:(C)18.

Oliver L. North
Lieutenant Colonel,
United States Marine Corps (Ret.);
Candidate for the
1994 Republican nomination
for U.S. Senator from Virginia

6

[On suggestions that his involvement in the Iran-contra scandal of the 1980s makes him unfit for the office of Senator]: Most people don't give a rat's patootie.

Newsweek, 2-7:15.

191

Michael Novak
Resident scholar,
American Enterprise Institute

1

[On the reasons for his changing his political views from left to right]: It was seeing many things that I had supported with enthusiasm, like domestic social-welfare programs, turn to ash. Since it seemed to me that what it meant to be on the left was to think as clearly as one could and to take responsibility for one's decisions, I thought we should take responsibility for our mistakes and make corrections. I was astonished when many people on the left did not follow me. It turned out that many people made a big investment in where they were, and they didn't want to move, and they didn't like taking criticism . . . [To many people on the left,] if you move from the right to the left in this country, that's called growth; [but] if you move from the left to the right, that's called treason. So many people who are afraid of being called names hide their real opinions and pretend to be more on the left than they are.

Interview/
Christianity Today,
10-24:31.

Jim Nussle
United States Representative,
R-Iowa

2

[Saying the Republican takeover of the House leadership next January will be more of a "transformation" than a transition]: Transition would be when you trade keys—you give me your keys, I'll give you my keys. Transformation is really a redesign and renewal of the administrative and legislative processes. [The process, which he will be in charge of, will be] like building a rocket ship while it's taking off.

The New York Times,
11-15:(A)1.

Norman J. Ornstein
Fellow,
American Enterprise Institute

3

The relationship between [President] Clinton and the Democrats [in Congress] is going to be a love-hate relationship in many ways. It's in their interest to pass a substantial part of Clinton's program. But the closer you get to the [fall 1994] election, the more they'll want to step aside from anything controversial.

USA Today, 1-24:(A)9.

Leon E. Panetta
Chief of Staff to
President of the United States
Bill Clinton

4

[Criticizing Newt Gingrich, who will be the new House Speaker, for saying that as much as a fourth of President Clinton's White House staff has used illegal drugs in recent years]: He's Speaker of the House of Representatives. Words matter. And he's no longer just the minority whip in the House of Representatives; he's not the editor of a cheap tabloid; he's not just an out-of-control radio talk-show host. He's Speaker of the House of Representatives, and he's got to learn to behave as the Speaker of the House of Representatives.

News briefing,
Washington, D.C., Dec. 5/
The New York Times,
12-6:(A)1.

Bill Paxon
United States Representative,
R-New York; Chairman, National
Republican Congressional Committee

5

[In Congress,] you can't make policy unless you have the votes. At the same time, if you focus just on elections without good policy, you'll fail also. That's the problem of the Democrats. For the

(BILL PAXON)

last 20 years, they have been running the House without much of a philosophical rudder.

The New York Times,
11-15:(A)11.

Timothy J. Penny
United States Representative,
D-Minnesota

1

[On the sweeping Republican Congressional victory in the just-held national elections]: Except for a handful of issues, the liberals are going to be in the wilderness.

USA Today, 11-11:(A)3.

Michael Pertschuk
Director, Advocacy Institute

2

[On the sweeping Republican Congressional victory in the recent national elections]: The mood of the liberal groups is hardly gleeful right now. But the silver lining in this disaster is that the ability to alarm and motivate contributors [to liberal causes] has grown enormously.

The New York Times,
11-28:(A)8.

Kevin P. Phillips
President, American Political
Research Corporation

3

Unfortunately for [President] Clinton, he may have to be the President who proves the [political] system doesn't work very will. Does the party system produce Presidents who can lead? Should we have votes of no-confidence on a leader? There may have to be a major upheaval in electoral and party systems, and the Clinton Administration may be the catalyst for that. We need to face up to the fact that [the 1992 Presidential election should not have consisted of] a fellow from Arkansas

[Clinton] running against a preppy [then-President George Bush] who wouldn't know a cash register from a lobster.

Interview/Mother Jones,
Nov.-Dec.:54.

John J. Pitney, Jr.
Political scientist,
Claremont McKenna College

4

[On the fragmentation of U.S. politics]: It's been true of almost every other area in American life. Big structures have broken down. Our grandparents thought there were only three flavors of ice cream: vanilla, chocolate and strawberry. We demand more choices.

Newsweek, 7-18:38.

Colin L. Powell
General,
United States Army (Ret.);
Former Chairman,
Joint Chiefs of Staff

5

I think there is a possibility of a third [political] party in '96 . . . It would be wonderful.

U.S. News & World Report,
11-28:47.

Dan Quayle
Former Vice President
of the United States

6

[On President and Mrs. Clinton]: What they have is a moral certitude that what they say—and, more important, what they do—is morally right. Therefore, "You in the press, in Congress, really ought to bug off; you don't have any right to question what I'm doing because I am morally correct." That kind of arrogance is something people can detect, and is very harmful.

Interview/
The New York Times,
4-26:(A)15.

(DAN QUAYLE)

1

[On whether the media ridicule he endured when he was Vice President will follow him if he enters politics again]: No way! Absolutely no way! Serious journalists cannot write that garbage again. They can't do it. It's not true. It's not fair. And they know it. No. No way.

Interview/
The Washington Post,
5-10:(B)1.

2

[Saying he has tried to find out why he was the subject of ridicule by the media throughout his Vice Presidency]: I wanted the media to talk about me and about themselves to try to answer the question I've asked all along—"How did this happen?" . . . Basically, the answer came back that once the first impressions were formed, the media liked the caricature. I learned how critically important first impressions truly are in politics.

People, 5-16:50.

Nancy Reagan
Wife of former President
of the United States
Ronald Reagan

3

[On Virginia Republican U. S. Senate candidate Oliver North, who was involved in the Iran-contra scandal during the Reagan Administration]: Ollie North has a great deal of trouble separating fact from fantasy. He lied to my husband. He lied about my husband. He kept things from him that he should not have kept from him. That's what I think of Ollie North.

Speech,
New York, N.Y./
Newsweek, 11-7:21.

Ronald Reagan
Former President
of the United States

4

We [his Administration in the 1980s] brought America back bigger and better than ever. I believe history will record our era as one of peace and global prosperity. However . . . the [Democratic] Party will never forgive us for our success and are doing everything in their power to rewrite history. They were claiming [the 1980s] was a decade of greed and neglect . . . I don't know about you, but I'm getting awfully tired of the whining voices from the [Clinton] White House these days.

At celebration of his 83rd birthday
sponsored by Republican
National Committee,
Washington, D.C., Feb. 3/
USA Today, 2-4:(A)4.

5

[Saying Democratic President Clinton is trying to appropriate themes and issues that have traditionally been Republican]: After watching the State of the Union address the other night, I'm reminded of the old adage that imitation is the sincerest form of flattery. Only in this case, it's not flattery, but grand larceny—the intellectual theft of ideas you and I recognize as our own.

At celebration of his 83rd birthday
sponsored by Republican
National Committee,
Washington, D.C., Feb. 3/
The Washington Post, 2-5:(G)8.

Ralph Reed, Jr.
Director, Christian Coalition

6

Social change proceeds in America with deliberate and slow steps. Our desire to restore the centrality of the family will take place over decades, not years. The mistake that frankly the religious conservative movement made in the early 1980s with [former President Ronald] Reagan, and the gay-rights movement made with [President]

(RALPH REED, JR.)

Clinton, was: "Okay, we won. Now we want, in turn, our entire agenda legislated immediately."
The New York Times,
11-22:(C)18.

Dan Rostenkowski
United States Representative, D-Illinois

1

[On his just being re-elected despite allegations against him of corruption]: Politics is not a profession that rewards purity or perfection.
Victory statement,
Chicago, Ill., March 15/
Los Angeles Times, 3-16:(A)1.

2

[Arguing against Congressional hearings on the Whitewater scandal and the alleged possible involvement of President Clinton]: I do not believe there should be a Congressional investigation into the Whitewater situation. Such a probe would be a serious mistake that would impede the legitimate investigations that are already in progress. It is clear that those who want a Congressional investigation are making a partisan effort to divert public attention from Bill Clinton's substantive successes. I'm confident that the voters are too smart to fall for such a cheap and transparent ploy.
March 17/The Washington Post,
3-18:(A)9.

3

[On his being indicted on 17 criminal counts involving fraud and other misconduct in office]: I will be vindicated! I will fight these false charges and will prevail! I will wash away the mud that has been splattered upon my reputation. Some ask, "How could you have done these things?" The answer is simple: I didn't do them.
After his arraignment,
Washington, D.C., June 10/
The New York Times,
6-11:1.

Henry Ruth, Jr.
Former Special Prosecutor
during the Watergate
scandal of the 1970s

4

[Criticizing the Clinton Administration and its advisers for not being more cooperative in the Whitewater scandal]: It is kind of baffling how very smart people and supposedly smart lawyers come to Washington and think they can manage the news. They invariably find out they can't, and in trying to unsuccessfully manage the news, they do a great disservice to their bosses.
Los Angeles Times, 3-7:(A)11.

Larry J. Sabato
Professor of government,
University of Virginia

5

[On this year's U.S. Senate race in Virginia, which may have two candidates linked to ethics scandals, Republican Oliver North and Democrat Charles Robb, running against each other as their parties' nominees]: This is the most bizarre race in the state's history. To have two scandal-ridden candidates is a breakdown of Virginia's norms.
Time, 4-18:40.

Michael J. Sandel
Professor of government,
Harvard University

6

[On the sweeping Republican Congressional victory in the just-held national elections]: This election was haunted by the fear that we are losing control of the forces that govern our lives, that the moral fabric of community is unraveling around us, and that our political institutions are unable to respond . . . The next two years are likely to deepen these frustrations. Democrats and Republicans will struggle to avoid being held responsible for the likely impasse, so as not to be the target of the next round of voter wrath. But if the deeper problems go unaddressed, and if disen-

(MICHAEL J. SANDEL)

chantment is compounded by economic downturn, darker scenarios become imaginable. There is the danger that the politics of protest may find its next expression in the "man on horseback," an authoritarian figure who offers a way beyond impasse, above politics, and beyond the messy, often frustrating restraints of constitutional government.

Nov. 9/
The New York Times,
11-10:(B)5.

Rudolf Scharping
Leader, Social Democratic Party
of Germany

1

You cannot make politics without hope. But it must be a realistic horizon of hope.

Newsweek, 1-31:46.

Steven E. Schier
Professor of political science,
Carleton College

2

[On the controversy in the Republican Party about the increasing strength of what is being termed the religious right]: This division within the Party could be the roadblock to long-term Republican dominance of national politics. People are being brought into the Party with a narrowly defined religious mission. When you start talking from a Biblically influenced agenda, that is quite alien to the swing voters.

The New York Times,
6-3:(A)8.

Dan Schnur
Spokesman for Governor of
California Pete Wilson (R)

3

The strength of the Republican Party has always been our ability to come together despite our

internal differences, and in [the] 1992 [national elections] we forgot that. We acted like Democrats and we got our clocks cleaned. Nobody wants a repeat of that, so we're all working harder than ever to keep this Party united.

Los Angeles Times,
2-26:(A)25.

Richard C. Shelby
United States Senator,
R-Alabama

4

[On his decision to switch from Democrat to Republican]: I thought there was room in the Democratic Party for a conservative Southern Democrat such as myself. But I can tell you, there is not.

U.S. News & World Report,
11-21:40.

Mark A. Siegel
Former executive director
of the Democratic Party;
Former political aide to former
President of the United States
Jimmy Carter

5

The political talent of this [Clinton] White House is clearly at a higher level than what we saw in the previous Democratic White House [during the Carter Administration], but the political decision-making process seems to be less structured. Clearly, Hamilton Jordan was in charge of politics at the Carter White House. He frequently made the wrong calls, but he was always making the calls. Here [in the Clinton White House], there is not one central focus to the process.

The New York Times,
2-22:(A)12.

Richard Norton Smith
Director, Ronald Reagan
(Presidential) Library

1

Presidential libraries are not built to the egos of Presidents but to the egos of Presidents' friends and particularly their wealthy friends.
The Washington Post,
4-25:(A)4.

Darry Sragow
Democratic Party strategist

2

[On California Republican Governor Pete Wilson's successful election campaigns]: I always picture the Wilson operation stepping out in the path of the opponent and throwing a bag of marbles in the opponent's path. The opponent has to dance on the marbles and invariably skips, falls and is immediately set upon by a host of Wilson operatives who emerge from the woods. They just sit on the opponent until the end of the campaign.
The New York Times,
7-2:8.

3

Voters' impressions of a candidate are based on a lot of bits of information that are perceived visually. I don't want to put ideas in anybody's head, but if you had a picture of your opponent as a flower child looking hippie-ish, that could be very powerful [negatively].
Los Angeles Times,
8-5:(A)1.

George Stephanopoulos
Senior Adviser to President
of the United States Bill Clinton

4

The only way to resolve the problem of politics—which is that sometimes you have to do bad things for a good end, or that you have to get dirty hands—is that you have to know when to leave. And that there have to be certain things that you're going to leave over; that you'll know that it's unsustainable over the long haul. Now, the question is, what is the long haul and how do you know when you're not doing what you thought you're supposed to be doing? I don't know, but you just have to keep asking the question.
Vanity Fair,
March:185.

5

[Criticizing Republicans for pushing the Whitewater scandal as a way to discredit President Clinton]: The Republicans can't run on the economy. They can't run on health care. They can't run on welfare, and they can't run on crime. So they're going to try to exploit this [Whitewater] issue. We shouldn't help them by making mistakes [in the way the Administration handles Whitewater]. That's our fault.
Broadcast interview/
"This Week With
David Brinkley,"
ABC-TV, 3-6.

6

[On the Clinton Administration's political problems]: One of the lessons we [in the Administration] all learned is that coming to Washington, coming to the White House, as in no other place, the personal is the political. We've come to deeply understand that over the last year, and that has been one of the toughest realities for us to deal with.
The New York Times,
3-15:(A)10.

7

[On President Clinton's accomplishments]: That's what keeps us going. In the end, that really is how the people are going to judge him ... Whatever [his critics] say, whatever the right wing will do, they can't take away the real accomplishments. They can't make the [Federal budget] deficit bigger, they can't take jobs away, they can't put assault weapons back on the street.
USA Today, 5-13:(A)4.

WHAT THEY SAID IN 1994

Robert S. Strauss
Former chairman,
Democratic National Committee

1

I was a young man during [the late President Franklin] Roosevelt's time, but I can tell you [President] Clinton's political detractors dislike him with even more intensity than they disliked Roosevelt. They say [Clinton] doesn't deserve the Presidency. The hatred has moralistic and militaristic dimension. And they can't stand for him to succeed. When he pulled off the Saudi plane deal, it drove his enemies crazy. They said, "The son of a bitch ought to be a salesman; that's all he can do." They terribly resent his wife [Hillary] being involved in the Administration, and they direct a lot of venom and fire at her.

Interview/
Los Angeles Times,
2-28:(A)18.

Fred Thompson
United States Senator,
R-Tennessee

2

[On the sweeping Republican Congressional victory in the last month's national elections]: Those of us who just came to town don't claim to have all the answers. But . . . we know why you sent us here: to cut big government down to size, to turn Congress around, and to set our country in a new direction. We campaigned on these principles, and now we're going to do something that has become all to unusual in American politics: We're going to do exactly what we said.

Broadcast address to the nation,
Washington, D.C., Dec. 15/
USA Today, 12-16:(A)4.

Martin J. Wattenberg
Professor of political science,
University of California, Irvine

3

[On the Republican Mayors of New York and Los Angeles endorsing the Democratic candidates for Governor and U.S. Senate respectively in their states in the forthcoming national election]: [These out-of-party endorsements] show that the Republicans aren't as cohesive as they might sometimes seem, particularly on New Right issues. [It is] also symptomatic of the fact that parties can't control their nominations.

The New York Times,
11-1:(A)11.

Stephen Wayne
Political scientist,
Georgetown University

4

[President] Clinton needs to stand for something . . . The sense you get is of a President who blows with the wind.

The Christian Science Monitor,
8-24:6.

Harris Weinstein
Former General Counsel,
Federal Office of
Thrift Supervision

5

[On the controversy over whether current Treasury Department officials improperly notified the White House about investigations touching on the Whitewater scandal, which allegedly may involve President Clinton]: [When I was in government,] it was certainly always my understanding and my practice to treat the existence of a criminal referral as highly confidential. It was my understanding that no one identified in a criminal referral as a possible witness would be alerted except by the U.S. Attorney's office for what the investigating lawyer thought was an appropriate investigative purpose.

The Washington Post,
7-28:(A)16.

Fred Wertheimer
President, Common Cause

1

We believe the public record makes clear that there have been widespread abuses by members of Congress of the statutory prohibition of the conversion of campaign funds to personal use. The burden of proof should be placed on the candidate.

Before Federal
Election Commission,
Washington, D.C., Jan. 12/
The Washington Post,
1-13:(A)25.

2

[Criticizing the fact that the National Policy Forum, an offshoot of the Republican Party, can receive large donations that are not subject to Federal regulations because it says it is a non-profit, non-political organization]: The danger here is that it creates a new way to evade the Federal campaign-finance laws and allow national parties to raise unlimited amount of undisclosed contributions from special interests who have a stake in government decisions. The notion that a political party engaged in partisan politics can have an arm that is not engaged in politics is simply not credible.

The New York Times,
4-1:(A)9.

3

[Blaming Congressional Republicans and Democrats as well as President Clinton for failure to pass a campaign-finance reform bill this year]: [Republicans, who] have not opposed and obstructed every serious effort to clean up the corrupt campaign-finance system for the past 20 years; [the House Democratic leadership, which] inexcusably delayed and delayed and delayed; [and the President, who] never made campaign-finance reform a priority.

Sept. 30/
The New York Times,
10-1:1.

Darrell West
Political scientist,
Brown University

4

There's still a lot of evidence that negative [political-campaign] advertising works. In a race where both candidates are going negative, it's harder for voters to find someone to blame.

The Washington Post,
9-26:(A)7.

Paul M. Weyrich
Conservative analyst

5

It is not a crime to vote for somebody less than perfect. Often you can get more out of somebody that is traumatized by a close election, that needs your help. It's worth electing even one of the turkeys if you have enough schwack with them that you can get 'em to work right.

At Christian Coalition conference,
Washington, D.C., Sept. 16/
The Washington Post,
9-19:(D)6.

Ralph Whitehead
Professor of journalism,
University of Massachusetts,
Amherst; Democratic Party
political analyst

6

For the first time in Massachusetts political history, this [year's U.S. Senate race] will not be a [re-election] cakewalk for [Senator] Ted Kennedy. It doesn't mean he'll lose, but he will not have the margin of comfort that he's enjoyed in the past . . . In this state in the 1990s, the ideal candidate is a newcomer to politics, 45 to 50 years old, without any skeletons in his closet, a record of entrepreneurial success in the private sector, socially liberal, fiscally conservative. A critical mass of the voters are either like that themselves or aspire to that role.

The New York Times,
6-4:7.

Christine Todd Whitman
Governor of New Jersey (R)

1

We've [Republicans] got to understand what it takes to win nationally, and that's why . . . it may take another year like '64 to really convince [Republicans] that extremism, as perceived or real, is not going to win. It cannot win nationally . . . The trouble with it is that as you look at people like the religious right . . . they can only win in caucuses and they can only win in conventions and platform committee meetings. That's where they can concentrate their forces . . . We're going to have to be very careful as we move forward to ensure that the public knows there's a lot more to the Republican Party than that.

Interview,
Washington, D.C., July 11/
Los Angeles Times,
7-12:(A)4.

David C. Wilhelm
Chairman,
Democratic National Committee

2

[Saying Democratic Congressional candidates in this fall's elections should not be afraid of running on President Clinton's record, even though in some quarters Clinton is perceived as being unpopular]: Democrats should run as Democrats . . . [They should be] proud [creating] 3 million jobs, [and should not] pretend as if you were in a different party or your President was somebody else.

May 25/Los Angeles Times,
5-26:(A)33.

3

[On the sweeping Republican Congressional victory in the just-held national elections]: Well, we made history last night. Call it what you want:

an earthquake, a tidal wave, a blowout. We [Democrats] got our butts kicked. We're bruised and battered, but we're still standing.

Nov. 9/The New York Times,
11-10:(B)5.

4

[On the recent national elections in which the Republicans gained control of both the House and Senate]: You can't look at these midterms and not admit that, at a very basic level, it is a referendum on governing. We [Democrats] were the majority party, we had our chance, and I think the American people see that we didn't come through on certain things.

Broadcast interview/
"CBS This Morning,"
CBS-TV, 11-9.

5

[On President Clinton's re-election chances for 1996, in light of the sweeping Republican Congressional victory in the just-held national elections]: Two years is an eternity in politics, and Bill Clinton didn't get the name Comeback Kid by accident. Uniting behind a [Presidential] candidate is going to be a tough balancing act for a GOP that is badly divided along ideological lines.

USA Today,
11-11:(A)11.

Richard Wirthlin
Republican
public-opinion analyst

6

[Activist First Lady Hillary Rodham Clinton] is viewed as aggressive, effective and able to get things done, which are pluses. But they turn into negatives, because she is not the President.

Newsweek, 7-11:18.

Richard K. Armey
United States Representative,
R-Texas

1

Entitlement spending is partisan pork. It's the politics of greed wrapped in the language of love, and [the late Democratic President] Lyndon Johnson taught it to his Party.

U.S. News & World Report,
12-12:53.

Victor Ashe
Mayor of Knoxville, Tenn.

2

Everyone favors welfare reform. We, as Mayors, have to deal with third- and fourth-generations on welfare. But [reform] needs to be implemented in a way that makes sense and doesn't leave the burden sitting on the city streets.

The Christian Science Monitor,
11-21:3.

Bill Ayres
Director, World Hunger Year

3

People saw the homeless as temporary when it really began in the recession years of the [former President Ronald] Reagan years. Millions of people reached out with shelters and food banks, but after a few years the homeless didn't go away. Now you hear about "compassion fatigue," and that the homeless are a nuisance.

The Christian Science Monitor,
5-24:3.

Warren E. Barry
Virginia State Senator (R)

4

[On the influx of illegal immigrants to the U.S. and the Federal mandates that require states to provide social services to those immigrants]: There's a silent invasion going on, and nobody's doing anything about it. We used to be the country of golden opportunity, but we are now the country of the golden goose. There are simply limits to what we can absorb.

The Washington Post,
4-25:(A)1.

William J. Bennett
Former Secretary of Education
of the United States

5

Supporters of the welfare state seem to talk like they have a monopoly on compassion. Well, they don't. The measure of real compassion is to make that sacrifice [of one's own time or money]. The cynical approach is to write the [government] check.

At seminar on welfare,
Los Angeles, Calif., Sept. 13/
Los Angeles Times, 9-14:(A)3.

Jared Bernstein
Economist,
Economic Policy Institute

6

Conservatives talk about family values. Sure, they want women to stay home and look after their children—unless, of course, they're talking about women on welfare, and then they're supposed to get out and get a job. The level of hypocrisy is enough to make you sick.

World Press Review,
June:35.

Douglas Besharov
Resident scholar,
American Enterprise Institute

7

From the President on down, there has been an amazing shift in attitude [toward the welfare system]. Today everyone recognizes that dealing with births out of wedlock is the central issue of

(DOUGLAS BESHAROV)

welfare reform, so much so that the President's [Clinton] draft plan [on welfare reform] makes dealing with illegitimacy the Number 1 priority.

Time, 6-20:27.

Dan Bloom
Senior research associate,
Manpower Demonstration
Research Corporation

1

[On a program designed to help absent fathers who are delinquent in child-support payments find employment or better-paying jobs so they can afford to make the payments]: There's usually a knee-jerk reaction to this group—the notion that there's no use designing a program for them because they won't come. But this is actually a very diverse population, and while there are some who won't accept responsibility, there are some who are capable of responding to intervention.

Interview/
The Washington Post,
2-11:(A)3.

Mary Brosnahan
Executive director,
Coalition for the Homeless
(New York, N.Y.)

2

[On homeless people]: As we entered the second decade of this crisis, we stopped seeing them as people in pain. We started seeing them as fixtures, like mailboxes and lamp posts. After 12 years, there are more homeless than ever out there.

The New York Times,
2-25:(A)15.

George Bush
Former President of the United States

3

I firmly believe that the biggest danger to us is the disintegration of the American family. I talked about it in [his unsuccessful re-election campaign in 1992]. Single biggest thing, the decline of the family. We were written off as rabid right-wingers [for saying so]. [Now President] Clinton goes and gives a speech in the South, a good speech [saying what Bush said about the family], and people say, "Ain't it wonderful he's putting focus on the family." And I'm glad he is. But you know, as I look at society, we're far worse off in that regard.

Interview,
Houston, Texas/
Time, 3-28:32.

Henry G. Cisneros
Secretary of Housing and
Urban Development
of the United States

4

Homelessness has become a structural problem in America: chronic, continuous, large-scale, complex.

The New York Times,
2-17:(A)1.

5

[On President Clinton's proposal to improve the Department of Housing and Urban Development]: The President gave us a direct order. He said: "Change. And if you can't change, then we have to consider either dismantling this agency or eliminating it outright." There's something about the prospect of elimination that focuses your attention like few other prospects in government, and I suspect that's one answer of why we advanced these [changes] at this time . . . Many aspects of this Department are simply indefensible. We cannot maintain public housing as we have for the last generations and cannot allow landlords, for example, to keep people in slum conditions because the government provides them a check that enables them to do that.

Dec. 19/
The New York Times,
12-20:(A)14.

Bill Clinton
President
of the United States

1

To all those who depend on welfare, we should offer ultimately a simple compact: We'll provide the support, the job training, the child care you need for up to two years; but after that, anyone who can work must.

State of the Union address,
Washington, D.C., Jan. 25/
Newsweek, 2-7:17.

2

[On absent parents who fail to pay child support]: If you're not providing for your children, we'll garnish your wages, suspend your license, track you across state lines and, if necessary, make some of you work off what you owe. People who bring children into this world cannot and must not walk away from them.

State of the Union address,
Washington, D.C., Jan. 25/
Los Angeles Times,
6-11:(A)17.

3

[Addressing inner-city students]: I'm trying to do everything I can to give you more hope and more possibility for the future. But I can't lead your life for you. Every day *you* have to decide whether to be on time or not, whether to attend classes, whether to take drugs, whether to do your homework. And I'll be honest with you: The very best thing you can do to stay out of poverty is to make up your mind to wait to have a baby till you're old enough to take care of it and until you're married. You young men who get a girl pregnant and just walk away from her—you know it's wrong. It'll haunt you and stay with you all your life.

At Kramer Junior High School,
Washington, D.C., Feb. 3/
Christianity Today,
4-25:28.

4

[On his welfare reform plan]: Most Americans believe that working, even if it's in a subsidized job, is preferable to just drawing welfare and not working. I made that clear all along, that if we're going to end welfare after a two-year period, people had to be able to work. And if there was not work in the private sector, then we'd [government] have to create the jobs. Second, I think that this bill, plus the earned-income tax credit, plus providing health-care coverage to people in low-wage jobs, will dramatically undermine the whole basis of dependency. Finally, we go after what is the real source of this problem, which is the inordinate number of out-of-wedlock births in this country. I think all these things put together give us a real chance to end welfare as we know it . . . In the long run, the expenditures we make [in reforming the welfare system] will be more than repaid by people who move into the workforce and stay there for a lifetime instead of coming back on welfare. And if we can change the value system of the society toward more work and responsible parenting, the savings are going to be enormous. Many of them can't even be calculated in terms of how many more successful children you're going to have who don't drop out of school and don't get in trouble.

Interview,
June 10/
Time, 6-20:28.

5

There's no greater gap between our good intentions and our misguided consequences than you see in the welfare system. We have to restore faith . . . in certain basic principles that our forebears took for granted—the bond of family, the virtue of community, the dignity of work.

Speech,
Kansas City, Mo.,
June 14/
USA Today,
6-15:(A)10.

Hillary Rodham Clinton
Wife of President
of the United States
Bill Clinton

1

[On whether she likes the idea of condom distribution in schools]: No, I'm not comfortable with that. I would much prefer that every child be given appropriate guidance and discipline so that was never an issue. But I also think that it is a problem that has to be addressed in certain parts of the country where, for whatever reasons, family and religion have failed to do their jobs.

Interview,
Washington, D.C./
Newsweek, 10-31:25.

2

We need in these next months to come up with a decent welfare-reform proposal that will move people from welfare to work but which will recognize that there are some skills and some training and some child-care and health needs that will have to be met. Unless we want to see literally thousands and thousands of people on our streets and seeing the unbelievable and absurd idea of putting children into orphanages [as suggested by House Speaker-designate Newt Gingrich] because their mothers couldn't find jobs.

Before
New York Women's Agenda,
New York, N.Y., Nov. 30/
The New York Times,
12-1:(A)11.

Mario M. Cuomo
Governor of New York (D)

3

[Criticizing Republican social-welfare proposals]: We [Democrats would] rather preserve a family than build an orphanage. We believe that we're too good as a people to seek solutions by hurting the weakest among us—especially our children. And at our wisest, we believe that we [Americans] are all in this together.

Before National Press Club,
Washington, D.C., Dec. 15/
The New York Times,
12-17:16.

David Elkind
Professor of child study,
Tufts University

4

One thing about contemporary society is that we've lost control of the information flow our children get. In the past, parents could monitor the movies kids saw, the magazines and newspapers that came into the house. Now with TV, children get information they never would have had before. So we have to do more both to prepare them and to help them deal with what they've seen—like a body being dragged through the streets of Mogadishu [Somalia] on the TV, or a homeless person on the street where they walk. We should give children a healthy respect for the world out there, but focus on the good things as well as the negative ones.

Interview/Newsweek, 1-10:50.

David T. Ellwood
Assistant Secretary
for Planning and Evaluation,
Department of Health
and Human Services
of the United States

5

[On reforming the welfare system to include limits on how long recipients can receive welfare payments]: In some ways, the notion that welfare should be transitional is as old as recorded history. The reason time limits are important is that we are in the wrong business. We have a welfare system that is basically in the check-writing business. The culture of welfare offices is entirely focused on getting people in, asking them lots of difficult, painful questions . . . then they write them out a check. Time limits say to the people in the system, the workers as well as the recipients, that

(DAVID T. ELLWOOD)

this will ultimately come to an end. This is transitional. At some point, the expectation is you are going to have to go to work . . . In Washington, people get very preoccupied with passing a bill and getting a law in place when, in fact, the critical thing is what will have to happen at the street level, what will happen in every city, in every county, in every local office. How do we take a [welfare] system that has, for 60 years, been in the check-writing business, that doesn't really try at all to help people help themselves—and turn it around and focus it on really helping people get a paycheck? That's going to be extraordinarily tough. The real hard work won't be passing [a welfare-reform] bill—although that will be plenty hard; it will be then making something really work, so that, in the end, this system really is about helping people go to work and really encouraging and expecting responsibility.

Interview, Washington, D.C./
Los Angeles Times,
7-24:(M)3.

Stacy Furukawa
Author of a U.S. Census Bureau
report on families

1

With more and more women bearing children out of wedlock, along with high divorce rates, more children than ever are spending at least part of their childhoods in single-parent families or other alternative family situations.

Aug. 29/Los Angeles Times,
8-30:(A)1.

John Kenneth Galbraith
Economist

2

We have a lot of well-off people whose personal comfort is threatened by government action. I would hope that there were a few people whose compassion and sympathies would extend to the

unfortunate and who would be willing to accept affirmative government and what it can do for all those who are less fortunately situated. Once the great dialectic was capital versus labor. Now it's the conflict between the comfortable and the deprived. And the comfortable see government as the threat because it is the only hope for the deprived.

Interview/Mother Jones,
March-April:38.

Newt Gingrich
United States Representative,
R-Georgia;
Speaker of the House-designate

3

It is impossible to take the Great Society structure of bureaucracy, the redistribution model of how wealth is acquired and the counter-culture values that now permeate how we deal with the poor, and have any hope of fixing things. They are a disaster. They have ruined the poor. They create a culture of poverty and a culture of violence. And they have to be replaced thoroughly from the ground up.

Before Washington
Research Group,
Washington, D.C., Nov. 11/
The New York Times,
11-12:9.

4

The most powerful single moment I've had since becoming Speaker-elect was breakfast . . . the other day with two members of the [Congressional] Black Caucus. One of them said to me, "Don't assume that we're liberal." He said when you walk into a first-grade class and you realize by the time they are 25, one out of every four boys will be dead or in prison . . . He said, "I will try virtually anything to save their lives." It was one of the most humbling and emotionally shattering moments I've had in years, because [of] the pain in this member's entire being as he talked about the funerals he's gone to for 10-, 11-, 12-year-olds.

(NEWT GINGRICH)

He said, "Don't assume that we're not going to work with you [the new Republican-controlled House]. We'll work with anybody who gives us a chance to save these children."

At Conservative
Leadership Conference,
Washington, D.C., Dec. 2/
The Wall Street Journal,
12-7:(A)18.

1

[On those who criticize his suggestion that orphanages could be used to house children of parents who can't take care of them]: I don't understand liberals who live in enclaves and safety who say, "Oh, this would be a terrible thing; look at the Norman Rockwell family that would break up." [But] the fact is, [today] we are allowing a brutalization and a degradation of children in this country, a destructiveness. We say to a 13-year-old drug addict who is pregnant, you know, "Put your baby in a dumpster, that's okay, but we're not going to give you a boarding school, we're not going to give you a place for that child to grow up" . . . Wouldn't it have been better for those mothers to have known, "Here's an 800 number I can call. Here are people who want children to take care of, and I don't have to dump them in a trash dumpster."

Broadcast interview/
"Meet the Press,"
NBC-TV, 12-4.

2

[We should] have a discussion about definitions. When you see a person without money, are they victims or are they opportunities for a better future? Are they people to have care-taking or are they people who in fact if you care for them you can give them a helping hand and change their lives? Which are we looking at?

Before fellow Republican
members of the House,
Washington, D.C., Dec. 5/
The New York Times,
12-6:(A)10.

Michael Huffington
United States Representative,
R-California

3

[Saying government should turn over the welfare problems to the private sector to solve]: I firmly believe that if we allow people to keep more of what they earn [through tax reduction], they will begin taking responsibility for each other again. My critics say that is unrealistic. Well, I don't agree. I am an optimist. I believe in the basic goodness of people. I believe that if we give every American an incentive to give their time, their energy, their resources to help their fellow man, they will rise to the challenge.

To black entrepreneurs,
San Diego, Calif./
Los Angeles Times,
8-19:(A)22.

4

[Supporting a ballot proposition in California that calls for denying many social services to illegal immigrants]: I decided to vote for it because illegal immigrants are breaking the law by coming across the border, and the law must be upheld. We also need to send a message to Washington, D.C., that the people of California are fed up with paying $3-billion a year in services to illegal immigrants that are mandated on us by Washington. If it passes, which I think it will, it will send a message to the Clinton Administration that the time has come for the Federal government to pick up its responsibility . . . The obligation to provide children with education and so forth is that of the home country [of the illegal immigrants]. It's clear that those countries are shirking their duty. But there's no reason that this country should have an open border to 5 billion people around the world who might want to come here.

Interview/
Los Angeles Times,
10-30:(M)5.

Jesse L. Jackson
Civil-rights leader

1

We now have a generation of 15-year-old mothers, 28-year-old grandmothers and 48-50-year old great-grandmothers—three generations of children without fathers or jobs. Many of these youths have never been taught the Ten Commandments or what we know as moral values. They didn't do well in school and have never had jobs. For many of them, jail is a step up. Once they're in jail, they are free of drive-by shootings, it's warm in the winter and cool in the summer, and there's organized recreation, adult supervision, quality medical care. A society that has more faith in locking up children than building them up is approaching spiritual death.

Interview/Essence,
September:88.

Judith Jones
Director, National Center
for Children in Poverty,
Columbia University

2

[Saying the government should spend more on health and education programs to help children in poverty]: No matter what Administration it is [in Washington], they tell us there are insufficient resources. Yet anytime there is a disaster, we always find millions of dollars to fix it. It's a question of priorities.

The Christian Science Monitor,
1-27:2.

Penelope Leach
British psychologist

3

[Supporting Sweden's system of allowing parents of young children up to 18 months leave from work at 90 percent of pay]: I think it's clear that we [in other countries] could do it, and it's absolutely clear that at this moment nobody wants to. People don't really believe that what happens to children in their first years matters really much. I don't think people see that half the problems we've got—school failure, truancy, behavior problems—are due to the bad time children are having. A lot of people will just keep their heads down and do the best for themselves.

Interview,
London, England/
USA Today,
2-28:(D)4.

Patrick J. Leahy
United States Senator,
D-Vermont

4

[Arguing against the idea of states paying cash to recipients instead of food stamps]: Providing cash instead of coupons will increase the number of hungry children in America. I am worried that food-stamp cash-out will leave poor families even poorer. I am worried that landlords will just raise rents, knowing that their tenants have additional cash.

Before the Senate,
Washington, D.C.,
July 19/
Los Angeles Times,
7-20:(A)8.

Joseph I. Lieberman
United States Senator,
D-Connecticut

5

[Saying the Federal poverty measure should take into account cost-of-living differences among the states]: States like Connecticut, where the cost of living is high, get fewer Federal dollars than they deserve because cost differences are ignored. Other states, where the cost of living is low, get more than they deserve.

The New York Times,
8-5:(A)7.

207

Joseph Marinan
Mayor of Meriden, Conn.

1

[On his policy of cutting his city's social services for the poor]: The poor in this community were not born or brought up or educated here. You can come here to work, play and learn, but there's no free ride in the city of Meriden anymore.

Newsweek, 9-15:38.

Will Marshall
President,
Progressive Policy Institute

2

[Criticizing the idea of some conservatives that government should turn over the welfare problem to the private sector to solve]: The private sector is not ready to absorb the 14 million people on welfare. Our social structures would be overwhelmed. What's wrong with the conservative approach is that there is no transition from the current system to the wonderful world where private security and philanthropy pick up the slack.

Los Angeles Times,
8-19:(A)22.

John McCain
United States Senator,
R-Arizona

3

[Supporting the idea of states being able to pay cash to recipients instead of food stamps]: The Senate should embrace and encourage rather than prohibit state and local initiatives that will better serve needy Americans and help break the grinding cycle of poverty and dependence . . . I know that some advocates do not like the idea of cash-outs and wage subsidies because they fear that poor families will not or cannot make the proper spending choices if empowered to do so. To me, this kind of paternalism is at the core of our troubled welfare system.

Before the Senate,
Washington, July 19/
Los Angeles Times,
7-20:(A)8.

Dowell Myers
Demographer,
University of Southern California

4

The current [Federal] poverty measure is indefensible. It doesn't show what's happening to real people in real places. Rents in the Northeast and in California are more than twice as high as rents in Southern and Plains states. It costs much more to live in a high-rent state than in a low-rent state. But the poverty index doesn't make any distinction.

The New York Times,
8-5:(A)7.

Douglas Nelson
Executive director,
Annie E. Casey Foundation

5

We can no longer be surprised by the terrible outcomes experienced by young people who grow up in environments where violence and teenage pregnancies are more prevalent than high-school diplomas and good jobs.

The Christian Science Monitor,
4-25:28.

Michael Novak
Resident scholar,
American Enterprise Institute

6

[In the U.S., the poor] alone have been singled out for a socialist system that makes them totally dependent upon the state for their health care, for their housing, for their food stamps, for their income. And it demands of them, until now, nothing in return. They are excluded from the land of the free and the home of the brave and made to subsist as serfs or even slaves in a kind of Federal plantation system. This has debilitating effects on their morale and their sense of themselves. All of this grew out of the good intentions of [the late] President Lyndon Johnson's Great Society. I was one of those who strongly supported the welfare

(MICHAEL NOVAK)

programs of the 1960's, but I didn't tell anybody then that if you support this program, crime will rise by 500 percent in the next 30 years and illegitimacy will go from 6 percent to 30 percent, and to 44 percent among the poor. I didn't tell you that the program costs would go from $10-billion a year to $310-billion. None of us anticipated those developments. But what we put into place had consequences far different from those that we hoped for, and it is simply a matter of responsibility now to take note of those consequences and to correct them.

Interview/
Christianity Today,
10-24:31.

Kate O'Beirne
Vice president,
Heritage Foundation

1

Illegitimacy is now on center stage. We've moved way beyond work requirements [for mothers to receive welfare payments]. Even if Washington could effectively impose a real work requirement—and that's a big if—American children are not well served by a working matriarchy. Families have got to be put back together.

U.S. News & World Report,
11-28:49.

John Parry
Chief of staff,
commission on mental
and physical disability law,
American Bar Association

2

[On the trend toward making it easier to force the mentally ill into hospitals against their will]: Broadening the commitment laws is bad in terms of policy and bad in terms of Constitutional prin-

ciples. The gut reaction is to solve the problem of homeless mentally ill by putting people back in institutions, instead of providing a more humane life for these people. But given the resources that we have and given what institutions are able to do, it is not a good idea to put more people into institutions.

Los Angeles Times,
8-18:(A)14.

Ross Perot
Industrialist;
1992 independent
Presidential candidate

3

We've given out a lot of free social candy over the last 20 years. Most of it didn't taste good when the people got it. And you who had jobs paid a huge price for it.

Before
United We Stand America,
Dallas, Texas, Feb. 4/
The Washington Post,
2-5:(A)5.

Howard Peters III
Director of Corrections
of Illinois

4

The reality is that most violence happens among people that know each other. It occurs more often in family units. We have to help young people, beginning in the first grade, to learn to resolve conflict without violence. What families did for each other in the past they aren't doing anymore because of the deterioration of the family. If society doesn't have children who are healthy and whole in the first grade, then we are likely to continue making a new crop of prison inmates.

The Christian Science Monitor,
2-23:7.

Jon Pynoos
Associate professor
of gerontology,
Andrus Gerontology Center,
University of
Southern California

1

Our nation has not yet faced the issue of seeing all older Americans as productive . . . In the future we will have many more people who have successfully aged, and we need to figure out how to make use of what they have to offer.

The Christian Science Monitor,
3-18:1,18.

Robert Rector
Senior policy analyst,
Heritage Foundation

2

Nothing could be worse than the current [welfare] system. The current system has already pulled the family apart. The system treats having a child out of wedlock as a favored lifestyle that's deliberately subsidized by the government. Nothing could be more harmful than that.

Time, 6-20:30.

Robert B. Reich
Secretary of Labor
of the United States

3

[Saying many employers are not keeping up with pension-funding payments]: Promises are being broken. The longer we wait . . . the more people will be hurt . . . Year after year, the gap between pension promises and pension assets has widened. This chronic under-funding can undermine our retirement system.

Before House Education
and Labor Subcommittee,
Washington, D.C.,
July 19/
Los Angeles Times,
7-20:(A)8.

Uwe E. Reinhardt
Professor of
political economy,
Princeton University

4

Americans are unusually charitable when they can see the target. Americans are less charitable when they don't know the target, because they think [their money] will never reach it. We don't have that faith anymore. Some feel our public programs feed the horses—the middle class that leeches off the trough—to feed the birds [the poor], with the birds getting only the pickings. It is that suspicion that makes a people I consider one of the most decent in the world look so stingy. If we trusted the process more to use our tax money honorably, we would be more generous.

Interview,
Washington, D.C./
Modern Maturity,
Nov.-Dec.:67.

Stanford G. Ross
Former Commissioner,
Social Security Administration
of the United States

5

The long-term deterioration in the Social Security retirement trust fund is a serious concern. When combined with the long-term financial imbalance in Medicare, it suggests that we need to take a serious look at the long-term financing of these programs.

Interview/
The New York Times,
4-12:(A)8.

Bret Schundler
Mayor of Jersey City, N.J.

6

We are destroying human spirits and souls when we create a [welfare] system which is focused totally on the elimination of deprivation, instead of a system which encourages autonomy,

(BRET SCHUNDLER)

encourages people to develop their skills, encourages people to live lives of disciplined virtue . . . [Under the current system,] we're mandating virtue, but paying for vice.

Christianity Today,
6-20:45.

Donna E. Shalala
Secretary of Health
and Human Services
of the United States

1

[Saying the Ronald Reagan and George Bush Administrations cut too much from social services]: It's going to take us a long time to rebuild, in fundamental rights, in programs for the poor, the disadvantaged and kids. [But] we've [the Democrats] waited 12 years to get back here [to the White House], with a lot of pent-up optimism and energy. It's just exploding.

Interview/
Harper's Bazarre,
July:37.

James Skillen
Director,
Center for Public Justice

2

Government should be doing more, not less, to fight hard-core poverty; but it should be doing so by working to strengthen and hold accountable the primary and secondary institutions of society, especially families, rather than by taking on poor people as its own clients while allowing more immediate institutions and relationships to disintegrate or perpetuate irresponsibility.

Christianity Today,
6-20:45.

Martin Slate
Executive Director,
Pension Benefit Guarantee
Corporation of the
United States

3

[Saying many employers are not keeping up with pension-funding payments]: Companies can utilize credits and offsets and set actuarial assumptions so that contributions are minimized. Fully within the law, many employers have been able to make little or no pension contributions, even though their plans are severely under-funded.

Before House Education
and Labor Subcommittee,
Washington, D.C.,
July 19/
Los Angeles Times,
7-20:(A)8.

James P. Steyer
President, Children Now

4

Today, there are 14 million children who live below the poverty line and nearly twice that many just above the poverty line. Children are the poorest group in America.

Feb. 28/
Los Angeles Times,
3-1:(A)19.

Daniel H. Weinberg
Chief of Income and
Poverty Statistics,
Census Bureau
of the United States

5

With the [Federal] poverty [level], you are trying to measure who doesn't have the resources to purchase the necessities of life. If those cost less in Mississippi than in New York City, we should take account of that.

The New York Times,
8-5:(A)7.

Cornel West
*Professor of religion
and director of Afro-American
studies program,
Princeton University*

1

I think it's very important to keep in mind that we've got 18 percent of people in America in the labor force who are working poor, which means that they are working hard, they're disciplined, they're sacrificing, and yet they still find themselves on the bottom. They exemplify the Protestant ethic at its height, much more so, probably, than many in the corporate world.

*Interview/
Humanities,
March-April:5.*

David Willetts
Member of British Parliament

2

The paradox at the heart of the debate about the welfare state [is that] we provide money to people in need so they can afford to participate in the life of society. But if they become dependent on state finance, they may not be really integrated into society.

*The Christian Science Monitor,
11-2:2.*

Pete Wilson
Governor of California (R)

3

[On the costs of illegal immigrants]: In Washington, illegal immigration is too often viewed as simply a matter of politics. But out in the states, illegal immigration [is] a matter of how well we can educate our children, whether or not we can keep dangerous criminals off the streets, and how we'll provide health care to those who can't afford it.

*The Christian Science Monitor,
4-21:3.*

4

[Saying the Federal government—because of its responsibility for keeping out illegal immigrants and its mandates on states to provide social services when illegals get in—should pay the costs of those services, which are now assumed by states as required by Federal law]: If the Federal government were held accountable, they would quickly discover that the cost of ignoring the real and explosively growing problem of illegal immigration is far greater than the cost of fixing it . . . No one [should condemn] the illegal immigrants. It is those in Washington that we should condemn.

*Speech, Los Angeles, Calif.,
April 25/
Los Angeles Times,
4-26:(A)3.*

Jeff Bobeck
Lobbyist, American Automobile
Manufacturers Association

1

[On a new law requiring new cars to have stickers showing the amount of foreign parts used in their manufacture]: We think the law will shed new light. It will help consumers who have become confused about where their cars are built. It's information they can use or choose to ignore.
The Christian Science Monitor,
9-21:4.

Carol M. Browner
Administrator,
Environmental Protection Agency
of the United States

2

[On developing mass-transit systems]: It's not as simple as making a system that moves you from point A to point B. There's a subsystem that makes that system work: sidewalks; minivans if it's pouring rain; a little grocery store on the corner so that if you're walking home you can grab a gallon of milk. If you don't have that kind of community development, people aren't going to get on that transportation system.
Vogue, January:66.

David Davis
Editor, "Automobile" magazine

3

[On the new crops of U.S. small cars]: They're really good, really modern cars. We're finally reaching the point with this model-year where you have a legitimate reason not to buy Japanese.
Time, 9-12:58.

Thomas M. Downs
President, Amtrak

4

[Saying Amtrak service has deteriorated and more government funding is necessary]: We are now, as America's railroad, promising a service we can't deliver. We're selling disappointment at the same time we're selling transportation. My fear is that this is the precise formula that 30 years ago led to the rapid decline and near demise of rail passenger service in the country.
Before House Appropriations
Subcommittee on Transportation,
Washington, D.C., March 17/
The Washington Post,
3-18:(A)1.

Al Gore
Vice President
of the United States

5

[On a Clinton Administration proposal to take the air-traffic-control system away from the FAA and establish a government corporation to run air-traffic control]: The plan to establish an air-traffic-control corporation is a model of our reinventing-government effort. The plan will cut red tape and make it easier to procure the most up-to-date equipment. By improving working conditions through the use of updated equipment, the plan allows air-traffic employees to focus on the business of ensuring safer air travel for everyone.
The Washington Post,
5-2:(A)11.

Walter Huizenga
President,
American International Automobile
Dealers Association

6

[Criticizing a new law requiring new cars to have stickers showing the amount of foreign parts used in their manufacture]: The law is ridiculous. It's very cleverly written and designed to exaggerate the domestic content of the Big Three [U.S. car manufacturers]. It's a "Buy America" bumper sticker disguised as consumer information.
The Christian Science Monitor,
9-21:4.

Herbert D. Kelleher
Chairman, Southwest Airlines

1

[On the economics of the airline industry]: If [aviation pioneers] Wilbur and Orville [Wright] were alive today, Wilbur would have to fire Orville to reduce costs. A turnaround in the economy would not cure the ills that beset the industry. This industry never achieves even the average profit margin for U.S. industry as a whole in the best of times, despite the fact that it's a very risky industry. It should have a higher net profit margin if the more the risk, the more the reward.

At National Press Club,
Washington, D.C., June 8/
USA Today, 6-9:(B)2.

John Norquist
Mayor of Milwaukee, Wis.

2

Whereas highways tend to spread the economy over more landscape and waste land, and spread jobs farther and farther away from those who need them, high-speed rail tends to concentrate the jobs, save energy, be more efficient, and reinforce the value of cities.

The Christian Science Monitor,
6-17:4.

James L. Oberstar
United States Representative,
D-Minnesota

3

[Criticizing a Clinton Administration proposal to take the air-traffic-control system away from the FAA and establish a government corporation to run air-traffic control]: This is just the wrong course and it would take years to recover from it . . . Shake up the agency; don't dismember it . . . There has been no effort to fix what is there while proposing radical surgery. Will they just fire people? This is terribly disruptive. [The proposed corporation] is being designed to serve the interests of airlines. In hard times, they may push to cut fees, to cut the number of controllers. That could lead to . . . precariousness for safety.

The Washington Post,
5-2:(A)11.

Brian O'Neill
President, Insurance Institute
for Highway Safety

4

[On increasing consumer demand for automobile safety devices]: It used to be a longstanding myth in Detroit that nobody was interested in hearing about safety. Now they are all scrambling to add safety devices . . . There is more awareness on the part of the public that you are no longer in total control of your own destiny on the highway. There are some collisions you cannot avoid no matter how good a driver you are.

USA Today,
8-16:(B)1,2.

Federico F. Pena
Secretary of Transportation
of the United States

5

The aviation [manufacturing] industry is critical to our country. It contributes $80-billion a year to our economy. It plays a significant role in perhaps the world's largest industry . . . the $3-trillion global travel and tourism industry.

The Christian Science Monitor,
1-20:8.

6

[On the Clinton Administration's new regulations mandating random tests for alcohol use by transportation workers whose jobs involve the safety of passengers]: We are working to insure that when you board the subway, or a plane, a train or a bus, those responsible for your safety will have strong incentives to be sober and fit for duty.

Feb. 3/
The New York Times,
2-4:(A)11.

David Schulz
Director,
Infrastructure Technology Institute,
Northwestern University

1

It will be excruciatingly difficult to build new airports or expand existing [ones] well into the next century . . . We're going to have to figure out ways to move people between cities that are 250 to 400 miles apart on the surface, and high-speed rail appears to me to be clearly the most attractive alternative . . . The public sector and private sector need to partner up, each doing what it does best.

The Christian Science Monitor, 6-17:4.

PART TWO

International

Kenneth Anderson
Lecturer, Harvard University
Law School

1

I believe that there are moments when it is appropriate, just, right and defensible for one political community [country] to come to the aid of another country without any national-interest calculation at all, out of pure altruism, on exclusively moral grounds. These moments are limited and . . . require extraordinary political leadership. [The current ethnic war in] Bosnia, I would argue, is such a case.

Panel discussion,
Washington, D.C./
January:59.

Christopher Andrew
Authority on foreign intelligence,
Cambridge University (Britain)

2

[On perceived weaknesses in the U.S. CIA] The CIA has been far, far better than the [Russian] KGB. We are talking about weaknesses within a system that have been vastly superior to its opposition.

U.S. News & World Report,
7-4:42.

Kofi A. Annan
Undersecretary General
of the United Nations
for Peacekeeping Operations

3

Frankly, if the response [support] of governments remains the way it is today, we couldn't get another [UN peacekeeping] operation off the ground . . . Look at Georgia. They want a peacekeeping force of 2,500 to 3,000. But Russia is the only country willing to send troops, and who is going to pay for them? And if the peace talks in Lusaka go well between the factions in the Angola civil war, the [UN] Security Council will prob-

ably want us to get more involved there as well . . . We've had promises from Muslim countries [regarding the war in Bosnia]. The problem is to get them there quickly because they lack equipment . . . We can't get [the UN] troops because we haven't got the money to pay for them or the staff to manage them. And poorer countries can't afford to contribute if they have to pay themselves . . . [But] peacekeeping is always cheaper than war.

Interview,
United Nations, New York/
The New York Times,
3-4:(A)5.

4

We are encountering considerable difficulties in finding well-trained and equipped [peacekeeping] troops for the assignments that the [UN Security] Council has given us. This is partly due to perceived dangers the governments see associated with these operations, which are supposed to be peacekeeping but . . . where there's really no peace to keep . . . Here I am looking at situations like [the current conflicts in] Bosnia and Rwanda. I think that, as hesitant as everybody is about going in, nobody says don't do anything. And yet, when you turn around and ask, "How many troops would you give?"—each one is prepared to volunteer the other person's army, the other country's army and, if necessary, to make some financial contribution. It's a problem that we need to try and resolve quickly.

Interview,
United Nations, New York/
Los Angeles Times,
6-19:(M)3.

5

I often feel that we [UN peacekeepers] are not judged fairly. The goal posts have shifted, and we are held up to unrealistic tests and then condemned. If indeed the international community wants to roll back an aggressor, you don't put in peacekeepers. [But] peacekeeping works where you have a clear mandate, a will on the part of the

(KOFI A. ANNAN)

people to make peace. The inspiration for acceptable and viable peace can only spring from the leaders and the people in the country.

Interview/
The New York Times,
12-5:(A)6.

James A. Baker III
Former Secretary of State
of the United States

1

[Criticizing U.S. President Clinton's handling of foreign policy]: We have a situation where promises are unkept; we have a situation where policy flip-flops debase the currency of United States credibility . . . [And] the United States President should never, never, never threaten the use of force unless he is prepared to follow up. [Clinton views foreign policy through] this exclusive prism of domestic politics.

At Republican
foreign-policy forum,
Washington, D.C., July 27/
The New York Times,
7-28:(A)4.

Doug Bandow
Former Special Assistant to
the President of the United States
(Ronald Reagan)
for Policy Development

2

[Arguing against U.S. acceptance of the Law of the Sea Treaty]: Why do we need all this burdensome bureaucracy in the first place? When I was looking at this [in the 1980s], there were all these awful predictions of shootouts on the high seas if we didn't have a convention, none of which has happened. This is a solution in search of a problem.

The Washington Post,
7-29:(A)3.

Douglas J. Bennett
Assistant Secretary of State
of the United States

3

[On the fiftieth anniversary of the Dumbarton Oaks conference, which laid the groundwork for the creation of the United Nations]: Fiftieth anniversaries invite celebration. But let us not celebrate an illusion that the Dumbarton Oaks institutions . . . will spontaneously regenerate and start serving mankind as the founders intended. Without a fresh interpretation of the forces driving today's world, and without a fresh infusion of vision and commitment, the Dumbarton Oaks institutions may be overwhelmed by forces already loose in the world.

At meeting marking the anniversary,
Washington, D.C./
Los Angeles Times, 5-14:(A)2.

Sandy Berger
Deputy Assistant to President
of the United States Bill Clinton
for National Security Affairs

4

[On how the sweeping Republican Congressional victory in the just-held national elections will affect American foreign policy]: There's no Republican or Democratic answer to the security issues that we face in the world. There are American issues and American approaches.

Interview/
USA Today, 11-11:(B)6.

Boutros Boutros-Ghali
Secretary General
of the United Nations

5

[The UN is] in a period of transition, and the world hasn't decided yet what will be the new rules of the game. The member states haven't decided whether they really want a strong United Nations . . . The United Nations is not able to do a huge peace-enforcement operation. This is the lesson of the last two years. If it is traditional peacekeep-

(BOUTROS BOUTROS-GHALI)

ing or something in-between, with 5,000 soldiers, or 10,000 observers, we can do it. But if you move to a peace-enforcement operation of tens of thousands, we don't have the capacity.

Interview/
The Washington Post,
1-5:(A)24.

1

We must accept that in certain operations we [the UN] will not be successful. And the fact you are not successful in a certain operation must not be an obstacle to additional operations all over the world. It is like going to a hospital. You cannot say, "I don't want to take this case." There is a moral responsibility. The *raison d'etre* of this organization is to help member states solve peacefully their internal disputes and their international disputes.

News conference,
United Nations, New York,
May 25/Los Angeles Times,
5-26:(A)6.

2

[On UN peacekeeping operations around the world]: The member states are fatigued. When I was elected in 1991, we thought the UN would be able to solve all the world's problems with a few thousand troops. Suddenly we discovered that rather than one or two operations, we had 17; rather than a few thousand, we needed 70,000 soldiers; rather than spending $600-million for the peacekeeping, we needed $4-billion. We discovered that instead of a few accidents, every month a few peacekeepers are killed. All these factors create a kind of despair and hopelessness: Why must we intervene? We will never be finished . . . The U.S. also has the special responsibility of being a superpower. If you want to play a role in international affairs, you must get involved in the security of the world. You have a responsibility belonging to the family of nations. We all have a responsibility; we are in the same boat.

Interview, July/Time, 8-1:37.

3

[Saying countries are reluctant to intervene in foreign conflicts or humanitarian situations now that the Cold War is over]: We are confronted with 10 or 20 situations. To solve them costs only 2 or 3 percent of what the Cold War cost. But there is not the political will to do so.

Interview/
Newsweek, 8-8:27.

Lakdhar Brahimi
United Nations
Special Representative
for Haiti;
Former Foreign Minister
of Algeria

4

Diplomacy is at its very, very best in preventive diplomacy. The best that can happen to you is that no one notices what you do. And since nobody sees anything, why should anyone say thank you? When a problem appears, then you have failed.

Interview/
Los Angeles Times,
9-29:(A)10.

Zbigniew Brzezinski
Counsellor, Center for Strategic
and International Studies
(United States); Former Assistant to
the President of the United States
(Jimmy Carter) for
National Security Affairs

5

[On whether former U.S. President Jimmy Carter, who has recently sometimes acted as a negotiator in foreign crises, is operating as a "shadow State Department" in the Clinton Administration]: You can't be a shadow of something that casts no shadow.

Newsweek, 10-3:29.

George Bush
Former President
of the United States

1

[Criticizing U.S. President Clinton for a lack of leadership in foreign affairs]: If I'd have sat around and waited for somebody else to decide [what to do when Iraq invaded Kuwait in 1990], Saddam Hussein [of Iraq] would have been in Riyadh [Saudi Arabia] now, and we'd be paying $10 a gallon for gasoline.

USA Today, 2-11:(A)11.

Emilio J. Cardenas
Argentinean Ambassador/
Permanent Representative
to the United Nations

2

If you look at the [UN] Security Council resolutions in the last two or three years, you will find that, in almost every crisis, we insist—sometimes apparently out of the blue—on preserving the sovereignty and territorial integrity of the state [over the rights of minorities and ethnic groups pushing for independence]. We went as far recently in making that point about Iraq, where we believe that you should protect the Shias and Kurds without breaking the national identity—providing that the country respects diversity . . . We talk less and less about self-determination, because of the fear of secession. We talk more and more about the need to protect minorities inside the state.

Interview/
The New York Times,
12-26:5.

Jimmy Carter
Former President
of the United States

3

[On dealing with dictators]: Quite often . . . these little guys, who might be making atomic weapons or who might be guilty of some human-rights violation or whatever, are looking for some-

one to listen to their problems and to help them communicate.

Newsweek, 10-3:21.

4

[On those in the U.S. Clinton Administration who criticize Carter's visits with foreign leaders to try to end crises, even though he may go with Clinton's blessings]: I need to know frankly what is it about the Carter Center [his public-policy organization] that displeases people. What can I do to alleviate their displeasure? Because it's certainly to our disadvantage to have to come back from a crisis like [Haiti] or the one in North Korea where war was imminent and find to my amazement that what we've done is considered by some people inappropriate . . . I feel, as a former President, that my obligation for accommodating feelings can be restricted just to President Clinton. If he says, "Jimmy," or "President Carter, you're authorized to do this; we know it might be fraught with the likelihood of failure; it's a last-minute chance," I make clear that I have adequate instructions and I go and carry out those instructions. There may be times when some of his subordinates don't know what his instructions are. I don't really know the identity of people that are most adamant against the role we play.

Interview, Atlanta, Ga./
Newsweek, 10-3:37.

Dick Cheney
Former Secretary of Defense
of the United States

5

I've been struck in recent years, and especially in the last few months, by the extent to which we've turned inward as a nation . . . Bottom line is there isn't anybody else other than the United States to do what we've done over the last 50 years. No other nation has the moral authority, has the trust, has the leadership capacity to do what we've done.

At Pennsylvania State University
commencement/USA Today,
5-19:(A)13.

(DICK CHENEY)

1

[Criticizing U.S. President Clinton's handling of foreign policy]: Optimism, confidence and an understanding of power will be badly needed by the time Clinton ends his term in 1996. The American people need leaders who are not afraid to engage the rest of the world and do not tremble.

At Republican foreign-policy forum,
Washington, D.C., July 27/
The New York Times,
7-28:(A)4.

2

[Discounting the idea that strong U.S. actions somewhere in the world will send a signal to discourage bad behavior somewhere else]: I never thought our resolve in getting [Iraqi President] Saddam [Hussein] out of Kuwait [in 1991] would deter the Serbs in Bosina or the coup that overthrew [Haitian President Jean-Bertrand] Aristide. It doesn't work that way unless, like [current U.S. President] Clinton, you talk loudly about using force and then fail to follow through. When you project weakness consistently, you do embolden bad guys. But standing up for a truly vital interest, as we did in the [Persian] Gulf [in 1991], has never had much of a deterrent effect elsewhere, even during the Cold War.

Time, 9-19:34.

Warren Christopher
Secretary of State
of the United States

3

[On U.S. President Clinton's foreign-policy priorities]: First, economic security . . . Second, effectively dealing with Russia and the newly independent [former Soviet] states. Third, the expansion of NATO. Fourth, dealing with Asia and especially China and Japan. Fifth, the Middle East. And sixth, global issues such as [nuclear] non-proliferation and population and human rights . . . That's what the President thinks is important. He's made more progress on the first of those priori-

ties, economic security, than probably any President in history . . . What may have gotten out of focus is the amount of headline time that was devoted to these issues because of the instantaneous communication of images around the world.

Interview, Jan. 5/
USA Today, 1-6:(A)15.

4

Probably the most useful thing I can do as Secretary of State is to assist the President [Clinton] in adapting and renewing the trannational institutions that were created after World War II. We established this marvelous set of institutions— NATO, the World Bank, the IMF, OECD—which has so much to do with the prosperity that we've enjoyed over the last 50 years. These other problems—like Bosnia, Haiti, and so forth—are very important, but the larger responsibility I feel I have is to be helpful to the President to try to adapt these institutions to our times . . . We need to set up these transnational institutions because so many of the problems we now face are transnational problems. Environmental degradation, over-population, refugees, narcotics, terrorism, world crime movements and organized crime are worldwide problems that don't stop at a nation's borders. So I try to remember our broader responsibilities, even though, on a day-to-day basis, obviously we're very much taken up with more immediate difficulties.

Interview/
"Interview" magazine,
November:74.

5

[Saying that, despite the sweeping Republican Party Congressional victory in the recent U.S. national elections, foreign leaders understand that President Clinton, a Democrat, still runs American foreign policy]: These are all men in political life themselves. And they know about elections and about things going up and down. They understand that the President of the United States is our key foreign-policy spokesman, that he has tremendous foreign-policy powers.

Broadcast interview/
CNN-TV, 11-14.

Tansu Ciller
Prime Minister of Turkey

1

The Cold War is over and the Berlin Wall is down. [Islamic] fundamentalism is the challenge for the next decade. But we should not look at fundamentalism as only an Islamic threat because similar extremism can again emerge in Europe. The main thing is not to build new walls. Turkey is the only democratic, secular country in the Islamic world. It could serve as a bridge between the two sides.

Interview, Ankara, Turkey/
U.S. News & World Report,
6-6:52.

Bill Clinton
President of the United States

2

[On the CIA]: Every morning, the President begins the day asking what happened overnight—what do we know, how do we know it. Like my predecessors, I have to look to the intelligence [community] for the answers to those questions . . . Even now this new [post-Cold War] world remains dangerous and, in many ways, more complex and more difficult to fathom. We need to understand more than we do about the challenges of ethnic conflict, militant nationalism, terrorism and the proliferation of all kinds of weapons.

Before CIA employees,
Langley, Va., Jan. 4/
The Washington Post,
1-5:(A)13.

3

[On the death of former President Richard Nixon]: It's impossible to be in this job without feeling a special bond with the people who have gone before. And I was deeply grateful to President Nixon for his wise counsel on so many occasions on many issues over the last year. His service to me and to our country during this period was like the rest of his service to the nation for nearly a half-century: He gave of himself with intelligence and devotion to duty, and his country owes him a debt of gratitude for that service. We face today a world of increasingly uncertain and difficult challenges. But it is a world of great opportunity in no small part because of the vision of Richard Nixon during a particularly difficult period of the Cold War. He understood the threat of Communism, but he also had the wisdom to know when it was time to reach out to the Soviet Union and to China. All Americans, indeed all people throughout the world, owe him what he regarded as the ultimate compliment: He was a statesman who sought to build a lasting structure of peace.

April 11/
Los Angeles Times,
4-23:(A)23.

4

The end of the [U.S.-Soviet] superpower standoff lifted the lid from a cauldron of long-simmering hatreds [around the world]. Now the entire global terrain is bloody with such conflicts, from Rwanda to Georgia [in the former Soviet Union]. We [the U.S.] cannot solve every such outburst of civil strife or militant nationalism simply by sending in our forces. We cannot turn away from them; but our interests are not sufficiently at stake in so many of them to justify a commitment of our folks.

At U.S. Naval Academy
commencement, May 25/
Los Angeles Times,
5-26:(A)14.

5

[On whether criticism of his handling of foreign policy weakens him when he travels overseas]: No. Unless you say the test ought to be whether or not I've solved every problem that exists in the world . . . One of the problems is that neither I nor anyone else have succeeded in simple clear terms in explaining the post-Cold War world in a way that enables people to say . . . here's what the big objectives are.

Voice of America radio interview,
May 27/USA Today,
6-8:(A)4.

(BILL CLINTON)

1

[On suggestions that he might replace members of his foreign-policy staff because of public uneasiness with his handling of international affairs]: We've got delicate negotiations in the Middle East right now. The Secretary of State [Warren Christopher] is involved in that and China. And the last thing in the world I need to be doing is to be considering changing my team. What I need to be doing is considering changing whatever it is that is not inspiring people's confidence in me and, if we've made some mistakes, we need to fix it. That's what I'm working on. [If we do] a better job of communicating our foreign policy, [Americans will be] much more understanding of what I'm trying to do and that will give me the flexibility I need.

Interview,
Washington, D.C.,
May 27/
Los Angeles Times,
5-28:(A)20.

2

No country is immune to people who run [for high public office] making extreme statements trying to divide people, trying to, in effect, play on both the economic frustrations and the social and moral frustration that people feel in all countries where there is both economic stagnation and social disintegration. People everywhere yearn for a certain sense of order and discipline and hopefulness about the daily conditions of life. And when those things are under stress, every political system will be vulnerable to people who try to play on fears and to divide people.

News conference,
Rome, Italy,
June 2/
Los Angeles Times,
6-3:(A)6.

[Saying the U.S. desire to promote democracy in the world must be tempered by what America can actually accomplish]: The 20th century proved that the forces of freedom and democracy can endure against great odds. Our job is to see that in the 21st century these forces triumph . . . [But] there are good reasons for the caution that people feel. Often the chances for success, or the costs, are unclear . . . The problem is deciding when we must respond, and how we shall overcome our reluctance. This will never be easy; there are no simple formulas.

At United Nations, New York, Sept. 26/The
Christian Science Monitor, 9-28:7.

Ronald V. Dellums
United States Representative,
D-California

4

We [the U.S.] are the last great superpower—we should be walking gently in the world.

At Congressional Black Caucus
Foundation dinner,
Washington, D.C., Sept. 17/
The Washington Post,
9-19:(D)6.

Robert J. Dole
United States Senator, R-Kansas

5

The bottom line is that America, under the Clinton Administration, is abdicating American leadership at the United Nations, at NATO and around the globe. Unfortunately, our image and position abroad is on the same downward spiral as during the [former President Jimmy] Carter years, when the United States was feared by none, respected by few and ignored by many.

At Conservative Political
Action Conference,
Washington, D.C., Feb. 10/
The Washington Post,
2-11:(A)14.

William J. Durch
Senior associate,
Henry L. Stimson Center
(United States)

1

[On recent UN peacekeeping operations]: This is where the UN has really been handed too much. These disasters [local conflicts where UN peacekeeping forces are sent in] are political in nature, and when the UN goes in, you inject yourself into an ongoing war. At the same time, you try to pretend you are impartial. But if you don't come down on those who perpetuate the war, you might actually extend it.

Interview/
The New York Times,
12-5:(A)6.

Jan Eliasson
Undersecretary General
for Humanitarian Affairs
of the United Nations

2

[The UN must] adhere strictly to the guiding principles of humanity, neutrality and impartiality. Once those principles are compromised, our legitimacy and utility are at risk.

Speech/
The Washington Post,
1-5:(A)24.

Jean Bethke Elshtain
Political philosopher,
Vanderbilt University
(United States)

3

[On U.S. foreign policy under President Clinton]: The word "doctrine" implies a comprehensiveness for which we're not prepared. We haven't begun to take the measure of the post-Cold War world. After World War II, we were able to talk about a Truman Doctrine, but that's because it was easier then to perceive our interests and concerns . . . All [Clinton] and [his] advisers have been

able to come up with is "enlargement"—and that's a nostrum, not a strategy. Of *course* America is in favor of the expansion of democracy and free markets. It's like saying the Pope ought to be Catholic.

Panel discussion,
Washington, D.C./
Harper's, January:58.

David R. Gergen
Counsellor to President
of the United States Bill Clinton;
Special Adviser-designate
to the President and
Secretary of State
of the United States

4

[On his new upcoming role at the State Department]: The President outlined a role that he wanted filled—to be one of his principal advisers at the table, helping him as he thought through the options on foreign policy, as he tried to integrate his foreign policy and tried to communicate it. He told me today: "When we first started talking to you about foreign policy, I often asked you about the communications part of it. But more recently I've turned to you more and more often to hear your views on substance. And I'd like you to be there for both full time."

Interview,
Washington, D.C., June 27/
The New York Times,
6-28:(A)8.

Newt Gingrich
United States Representative,
R-Georgia

5

[In foreign affairs,] there's a level of sloppiness about this [U.S. Clinton] Administration that's scary. Even when they do the right thing, they do it badly . . . It's like following along behind somebody who is going through a store knocking things

(NEWT GINGRICH)

over. [But no one] in either party has articulated a vision of what America's role in the new world is.

Interview,
Washington, D.C. May 18/
The Christian Science Monitor,
5-19:3.

Barry M. Goldwater
Former United States Senator,
R-Arizona

1

[On President Clinton's handling of foreign policy]: I worry about it because he doesn't know a goddamn thing about it. We don't *have* any foreign policy . . . The best thing Clinton could do . . . is to shut up.

Interview, Phoenix, Ariz./
The Washington Post,
7-28:(C)2.

Al Gore
Vice President
of the United States

2

There is a great temptation in all our nations to focus only on our own problems. But my message today . . . is very simply this: In order to be strong at home we must engage abroad as well. We must work with other nations to get the world economy growing and open foreign markets. We must engage with other nations to lock in the end of the Cold War.

Speech,
Milwaukee, Wis., Jan. 6/
USA Today, 1-7:(A)4.

Bob Graham
United States Senator,
D-Florida

3

The intelligence community as we know it has grown up largely during and since World War

II. In those periods, we had a clear, identifiable enemy. Today, the world is different, and our intelligence needs are different. Yet, my sense is the agencies haven't come to full grips with that reality.

USA Today, 7-15:(A)5.

James Grant
Executive Director,
United Nations Children's Fund
(UNICEF)

4

In Bosnia, Somalia, Sudan and Angola today, the so-called legal government and the rebel governments acquiesce in [international] relief efforts. This is a mammoth shift from five years ago. Before Sudan, hundreds of thousands of children died in civil wars in Angola and Mozambique. The world did not respond [with relief efforts] because they were in a no-man's land. But we have not yet crossed that divide on the use of *force* for humanitarian ends. This is all a new frontier, with no historical precedent . . . As long as large numbers of people are dying, particularly children, whose lives could be saved by humanitarian action without great risk of death to the aid-givers, the new morality will say we must respond.

Interview/
U.S. News & World Report,
8-22:13.

Stanley B. Greenberg
Chief public-opinion analyst
for President
of the United States
Bill Clinton

5

[Americans] are looking for an exit [from foreign-policy adventures]. They turned the channel when the Berlin Wall came down, and after all the years of sacrifice from the Cold War, they are largely turning the channel [away from the ethnic conflict in] Bosnia . . . What is interesting is how little foreign-policy events seem to be linked to

WHAT THEY SAID IN 1994

(STANLEY B. GREENBERG)

[U.S. President] Clinton's overall job performance approval rating. After [the U.S. involvement in] Somalia, Clinton's foreign-policy rating dropped 20 points, but his job performance rating only budged a couple points.

Los Angeles Times,
7-25:(A)15.

Fred Greenstein
Presidential scholar,
Princeton University

1

In foreign policy, it's important to present a firm image. With [U.S. President] Clinton, it's like blobs of mercury; he's all over the place.

Los Angeles Times,
5-26:(A)5.

Dick Greenwald
President,
Ocean Mining Associates

2

[Arguing against U.S. acceptance of the Law of the Sea Treaty]: It's an extremely complex treaty with a lot of bureaucracy and social policy that is adverse to private enterprise. It's been reduced in complexity, but it's still a treaty based on socialist models. We will carry on urging the [U.S.] Senate not to give assent.

The Washington Post,
7-29:(A)3.

Lee H. Hamilton
United States Representative,
D-Indiana

3

The criticisms that are made [about U.S. President Clinton's handling of foreign policy] are that he has backtracked on positions he took in the [1992 election] campaign, that he has flip-flopped, that he's not able to articulate an overall vision for

American foreign policy. I think there is some validity to each of these. In general, I think he has the policies right. But his challenge is to sort out the U.S. role in the world and talk to the American people about it, and he hasn't done that yet . . . The President has gotten into trouble in places like Haiti, Bosnia and Somalia where he has not precisely defined American national interests beforehand. He never gave a speech on Somalia until he had decided to withdraw. He has never tried to define American interests in Bosnia so far as I know. In Haiti, he has begun to do it, but he needs to do more.

Los Angeles Times,
8-1:(A)10.

David Hannay
British Ambassador/
Permanent Representative
to the United Nations

4

Five years into the post-Cold War era, I think we've all learned that the UN is fairly indispensable. At the same time, there is no lack of disasters and problems. So that means that it's the UN with all its warts, or it's the law of the jungle.

The New York Times,
12-5:(A)6.

Tom Harkin
United States Senator,
D-Iowa

5

[Criticizing U.S. President Clinton's handling of foreign policy]: If we dawdle, if we equivocate any longer and if this President doesn't stand up forthrightly and put some backbone behind our policy, then I don't see how we're ever going to stand for human rights and democracy anywhere else in the world.

April/
Los Angeles Times,
5-28:(A)20.

Bruce Hoffman
Co-director,
Center for Terrorism
and Conflict Studies,
St. Andrew's University
(Scotland)

1

Terrorism is never a direct line. It is wheels within wheels, shadows overshadowing other shadows.

Los Angeles Times,
8-1:(A)6.

Kim R. Holmes
Vice president and director
of foreign-policy and defense studies,
Heritage Foundation

2

The essential division in the debate over American foreign policy has always been between a national-interest approach and a humanitarian approach. We Americans find it difficult to navigate between those two poles, because we confuse our national interest with humanitarian concerns . . . You can't get a consensus behind a strategy totally devoid of national interest. Not only that; I also think such a strategy is morally corrupt. The American government is elected to represent the interests and values of the American people. To pretend that foreign policy can operate without regard for our self-interest is a breach of the social contract between the U.S. government and the American people . . . That's precisely the problem with elevating any humanitarian principle to a foreign-policy goal: As soon as you state it, you have to start issuing exceptions. In foreign policy, you have to abandon the world of pure moral ideas, where consistency is effortless, for the practical world of international relations, where hypocrisy comes easy. The difference between what we say and what we do is that the former is unlimited and the latter is not.

Panel discussion,
Washington, D.C./
Harper's, January:59,60.

Oleg Kalugin
Former Director
of Foreign Counterintelligence,
KGB (Soviet security police)

3

[On the recent revelation that a CIA employee, Aldrich Ames, had been working as a spy for Russia]: The CIA had for many years spies inside the Russian and Soviet intelligence organization. So now we're even. Why make all this noise and fuss about it?

U.S. News & World Report,
3-7:30.

Henry A. Kissinger
Former Secretary of State
of the United States

4

What [today's] balance of power says is that we are trying to arrange an international order in which disagreements . . . do not threaten the overall system . . . You do this by making it difficult for any nation or group of nations to achieve preponderant power.

At National Press Club,
Washington, D.C./
The Washington Post,
4-11:(B)4.

5

In the conduct of foreign policy, [the late U.S. President] Richard Nixon was one of the seminal Presidents. He came into office when the forces of history were moving America from a position of dominance to one of leadership. Dominance reflects strength; leadership must be earned. And Richard Nixon earned that leadership role for his country with courage, dedication and skill.

At burial ceremony for Nixon,
Yorba Linda, Calif.,
April 27/
Los Angeles Times,
4-28:(A)12.

(HENRY A. KISSINGER)

1

It's one thing to talk about the enlargement of democracy [around the world], but in foreign policy the problem is what are you going to do about it, how much are you willing to pay for it, and what is the operational method for carrying it out.

At forum on foreign policy
sponsored by the
Republican National Committee,
Washington, D.C., July 27/
Los Angeles Times,
7-28:(A)20.

Harold Hongju Koh
Professor of international law,
Yale University

2

We [in the U.S.] have a 21st-century foreign policy operating with a 19th-century apparatus. As a result, we have these cycles. First, the President does anything he wants in foreign policy. Then there is an attempt by Congress to rein in his power. That leads to a period of micromanagement by Congress. And then we return to the President acting unilaterally.

Los Angeles Times,
1-19:(A)27.

Everett Carll Ladd
Professor of political science,
University of Connecticut;
President, Roper Center for
Public Opinion Research

3

Foreign policy is not just about foreign affairs; it's also an opportunity for the President [of the U.S.] to display leadership capabilities in the one arena in which he can do so with fewest challenges. We have loads of evidence that people form impressions of Presidents by what they see of them on the world stage.

Los Angeles Times, 5-26:(A)5.

Anthony Lake
Assistant to President
of the United States
Bill Clinton for
National Security Affairs

4

[Saying that, with the end of the Cold War, it has become more difficult for a U.S. President to justify to the people the use of military force abroad]: It is a tremendously difficult thing to work through. [For earlier Presidents,] it was much easier to gain an American national consensus ... behind the use of force because you had a Cold War context in which to place it. The nature of the debates was simpler.

Los Angeles Times,
8-1:(A)10.

Patrick J. Leahy
United States Senator,
D-Vermont

5

Spying is a fact of life in international relations. Rivals do it to us; friends do it to us; we do it to them.

U.S. News & World Report,
3-7:30.

Lee Kuan Yew
Former Prime Minister
of Singapore

6

I think the best way forward is through the United Nations. It already has 48 years of experience. It is imperfect, but what is the alternative? You cannot have a consortium of five big powers lording it over the rest of mankind. They will not have the moral authority or legitimacy to do it. Are they going to divide the world into five spheres of influence? So they have to fall back on some multilateral framework and work out a set of rules that makes it viable.

Interview/Foreign Affairs,
March-April:122.

(LEE KUAN YEW)

1

With few exceptions, democracy has not brought good government to new developing countries. Democracy has not led to development because the government did not establish stability and discipline necessary for development.

Los Angeles Times,
5-28:(A)14.

Slaven Letica
Professor of political science,
Zagreb University (Croatia)

2

I worked at the United Nations for five years, so I'm familiar with its institutional mentality. It is lazy, bureaucratic and institutionally stupid. The people who take part in these [UN peacekeeping] missions learn to accommodate the local suffering. They have to develop this indifference as a survival strategy, because they are nice young people who cannot really do anything to help. Their preoccupation becomes that of any other job—getting by, getting a paycheck, achieving career advancement.

Los Angeles Times,
6-22:(A)8.

Edward Luck
President,
United Nations Association
of the United States

3

[Saying the U.S. and the UN have lately not seen eye-to-eye on their roles in the world]: The United Nations has become a symbol of activist internationalism at a time when the United States would like the world to go away. The Secretary General [Boutros Boutros-Ghali] is to trying to expand his role at a time when the United States would like him to be quiet. He has become the nagging voice in the middle of the night . . . It's as if the stars are crossed. We have an activist Secretary General with a lot of ideas and a [U.S. Clinton]

Administration with a minimalist foreign policy that does not want to be reminded about what goes on in the world.

Interview/
Los Angeles Times,
4-2:(A)9.

4

[On UN Secretary General Boutros Boutros-Ghali]: The Secretary General has thought more about his role than any other Secretary General. He has a pretty coherent idea of what he wants to do. But he shouldn't preach about it. He pays too little attention to the political nuances of how and when something is said.

Interview/
Los Angeles Times,
4-2:(A)9.

Michael Mandelbaum
Professor of American foreign policy,
School of
Advanced International Studies,
Johns Hopkins University
(United States)

5

This [U.S. Clinton] Administration has a problem with [foreign] intervention. It wants to do good around the world, mostly for humanitarian reasons . . . But the American people, who were willing to shed blood in the Cold War when it was a form of self-defense, aren't convinced that they want to shed blood in a series of what appear to be humanitarian causes.

Los Angeles Times,
8-1:(A)10.

Will Marshall
President,
Progressive Policy Institute

6

[On U.S. foreign policy under President Clinton]: I would agree that the international picture is just too inchoate for something as rigid as a

(WILL MARSHALL)

"Clinton Doctrine." But I would argue that [President Clinton has] already articulated a general foreign-policy framework—elevating commerce to a strategic interest, revamping our military to meet new threats, and reinforcing the global movement toward democracy and markets. [He *has*] a policy; it's just that the problems cropping up in the daily headlines don't fit neatly into it.

Panel discussion,
Washington, D.C./
Harper's, January:58.

1

Who defines a nation's [foreign-policy] interests? My problem with foreign-policy realists is that they arrogate to themselves the ability to divine the nation's true interests. But the national interest is a complex calculation, done by the American people, of values and costs, not an abstract and theoretical truth. If the American people want to intervene [somewhere] on humanitarian grounds, a President would be hard-pressed not to listen . . . I don't think there has to be a solid substratum of interests on which to base each policy. If the American people think that we should intervene to prevent mass slaughter in Bosnia, fine. That's a worthy and enlightened impulse. But in each case, we have to calibrate the costs.

Panel discussion,
Washington, D.C./
Harper's, January:61.

Eugene J. McCarthy
Former United States Senator,
D-Minnesota

2

[Saying U.S. President Clinton should replace Secretary of State Warren Christopher]: Get a new Secretary of State instead of a direct descendant of [former Secretaries of State] John Foster Dulles by way of Dean Rusk and Cyrus Vance. It's like a biblical succession. Democrats retreat to the foreign-policy establishment and it goes nowhere.

Interview/
Mother Jones, Nov.-Dec.:51.

Mitch McConnell
United States Senator,
R-Kentucky

3

[On U.S. foreign aid]: We send money to countries where government policies actually defeat the prospects for real economic growth. It's in our interest to facilitate the transition to free markets, not to subsidize failures . . . U.S. foreign aid must better serve U.S. foreign-policy interests. Somehow along the way over the last 33 years of this program, the connection between U.S. aid and U.S. interests seems to have been lost.

Before the Senate,
Washington, D.C., Dec. 12/
The New York Times,
12-13:(A)4.

Dave McCurdy
United States Representative,
D-Oklahoma

4

[Criticizing U.S. President Clinton's handling of foreign policy]: We have conducted ourselves abroad with an unsteady hand. In [the ethnic conflict in] Bosnia, blustery [U.S.] rhetoric faded into reluctant diplomacy . . . On North Korea, we have been anything but decisive.

Before Commonwealth Club,
San Francisco, Calif., April/
Los Angeles Times, 5-26:(A)5.

Donald McHenry
Former United States Ambassador/
Permanent Representative
to the United Nations

5

If we [the U.S.] don't want to be the policeman of the world, and we don't want to take criticism for the failure of action in places like Somalia or Bosnia, then we have to come up with some kind of credible international force as an alternative . . . We are going to have to play a major role. But to the extent the operation is seen as an Ameri-

(DONALD McHENRY)

can operation, we will be the ones embroiled in political difficulties when they arise, whether internationally or locally.

Los Angeles Times,
3-4:(A)16.

John McNeill
Chairman, Task Force on the Law
of the Sea Treaty,
Department of Defense
of the United States

1

[Supporting U.S. acceptance of the Law of the Sea Treaty]: As the Navy of the future evolves, it's far preferable to have a common understanding in a legal document. This will promote global stability and fix the rules.

The Washington Post,
7-29:(A)3.

Gary Milhollin
Director, Wisconsin Project
on Nuclear Arms Control
(United States)

2

[Criticizing the U.S. Clinton Administration's lifting the ban on American companies selling high-tech equipment to former U.S. Cold War enemies]: It is a fantasy to think that you can ship strategic computers to places like China and Romania and not have them end up in places like Iran [which remains on the U.S. no-sales list]. This means that every bomb and missile maker in the world will save time and money by using what are practically the most powerful U.S. computers available. The happiest people in the world tonight are in Pakistan, India and North Korea [which also remain on the U.S. no-sale list], because they can now obtain, through front companies, computer power that previously was beyond their wildest dreams.

The New York Times,
3-31:(C)4.

Walter F. Mondale
United States Ambassador
to Japan

3

[On the advantages of being Ambassador to Japan]: When Washington is awake, I am asleep. And even better, when I am awake, Washington is sleeping.

Newsweek, 9-19:19.

Aryeh Neier
President, Open Society Fund;
Former executive director,
Human Rights Watch;
Former executive director,
American Civil Liberties Union

4

[A U.S. President can't ignore] the importance of leadership [in foreign policy]. Just because the current President [Clinton] tends to follow public opinion doesn't mean that's the way it has to be. When the Marshall Plan was proposed in 1947, it was supported by only 10 percent of the American people. But the President [Harry Truman] led the public, through argument, to see that the Marshall Plan was in their self-interest. My premise—that what's needed is a statement of principles—is based on the idea that there is no fixed set of national interests.

Panel discussion,
Washington, D.C./
Harper's, January:59.

Richard M. Nixon
Former President
of the United States

5

I did something [during a recent visit to] Russia that no one has ever done, something that I've not done in my 10 visits to the Soviet Union: I met with every opposition leader. I covered everybody. It is very important in a democracy not to just meet the leaders in power.

News conference,
Kiev, Ukraine, March 16/
Los Angeles Times, 3-17:(A)4.

Robert B. Oakley
Former United States
Special Envoy to Somalia;
Former U.S. Ambassador
to Somalia

1

[On the possibility of foreign peacekeeping forces being sent to Rwanda to try to stop the civil war, as were sent to Somalia in 1992-93]: Somalia showed just how difficult and dangerous the mission of saving a country can be. The international community is not disposed to deploying 20, 40, 60,000 military forces each time there is an internal crisis in a failed state.

The New York Times,
4-15:(A)3.

Ichiro Ozawa
Chief strategist for Japanese
Prime Minister Tsutomu Hata

2

The only nation, while maintaining a high level of living standards, that can guarantee its own security by itself is the United States. Other countries can't. Therefore, the others must cooperate with the United States and other countries to maintain one another's security. That is the only way.

Tokyo, Japan, June 14/
Los Angeles Times,
6-15:(A)6.

Chris Padilla
Manager of government affairs,
American Telephone
& Telegraph Company

3

[Supporting the U.S. Clinton Administration's lifting the ban on American companies selling high-tech equipment to former U.S. Cold War enemies]: This is a blockbuster announcement for the American telecommunications industry and for AT&T. What the Clinton Administration has done is open up huge new markets for American companies in the former Soviet Union and China by removing export restrictions that were outdated, and in the light of the end of the Cold War, no longer necessary. For AT&T, we estimate that over the next three or four years, we will have increased sales of at least $500-million as a result of this announcement.

March 30/
The New York Times,
3-31:(A)4.

William J. Perry
Secretary of Defense
of the United States

4

We should be careful to only use [force] and threaten to use it in areas where we are confident we can be effective. No empty threats.

U.S. News & World Report,
3-28:34.

Guy Pfeffermann
Chief economist,
World Bank's International
Finance Corporation

5

[Saying the trend toward privatization of government entities has attracted huge amounts of foreign private investment]: For the first time in the post-World War II history, foreign direct investment alone exceeds all official aid. But why is the world privatizing? The theory is that it's more efficient. [But it is also that] countries are privatizing because they need the revenues. They can no longer sustain the costs.

The Christian Science Monitor,
10-26:7.

Robin Renwick
British Ambassador
to the United States

6

What we [in the West] have learned is that we can't accomplish much unless we are united.

(ROBIN RENWICK)

Also, that we can't end all conflicts [in the world]. We have to choose what we do and then sustain it. This has been the difficulty in Somalia and Bosnia because vivid television coverage portrays terrible situations in various parts of the world with the message: "You, the West, must do something about it." But when you send people, as you [the U.S.] did to Somalia, and the mess goes on, the effect can be the opposite: "What on earth are we doing in the middle of this mess?" Television helped to push the U.S. into Somalia and then helped to push you out.

Interview, Boston, Mass./
The Christian Science Monitor,
6-10:6.

Peter Rodman
Adviser on foreign policy
to several U.S. Presidents

1

The best form of multilateralism sometimes requires unilateral assertions of leadership.

U.S. News & World Report,
10-31:52.

James R. Schlesinger
Former Secretary of Defense
of the United States;
Former Director of
Central Intelligence
of the United States

2

[Saying U.S. President Clinton's recent handling of situations in Haiti, Iraq, North Korea and his forthcoming visit to the Middle East may have given him a boost in the public's perception of how he deals with foreign policy]: It's a lot better carpentry, but it's not yet solid architecture. They are disposing of some of the problems that have been around since the [1992 Presidential election] campaign; with others, like Korea, they have kicked the can down the road.

The New York Times,
10-22:5.

Raymond Seitz
United States Ambassador
to the United Kingdom

3

[On the foreign-policy responsibility of the U.S. President]: There are certain things only a President can do. You really can't subcontract foreign policy. You just can't. To approach it by saying, "You take care of this, Warren [Christopher, Secretary of State], I'm busy over here," just doesn't work. It's the nature of the Presidency. It's all going to end up on his desk.

Interview, London, England/
U.S. News & World Report,
5-9:14.

4

There is no substitute for conceptual, analytical thinking, the serious identification of American foreign-policy interests and some sense of their priorities and interrelationships. We haven't gotten very far on that score . . . We really need to involve ourselves [in the world], to be active and to be seen to be actively engaged, understanding, attentive, responsive rather than fitful. Because we come across now as fitful . . . There's no confidence in Europe that the [U.S. Clinton] Administration, or the United States, has adapted to the big changes in the world, identified what is important and what is not important and what the priorities are, and can come up not with positions but with policies . . . We will be condemned to use our power clumsily until we have a much clearer sense of what we want.

Interview, London, England/
U.S. News & World Report,
5-9:14.

5

[Foreign policy] is not something we Americans come to naturally. Therefore you can only do it with leadership. And that means only from the Oval Office [of the President]. But a President will almost always have to go against the political grain to conduct a foreign policy that is understood and accepted by the people. Basically that means him

(RAYMOND SEITZ)

saying, "This is the national interest. It's not this or that state or this or that ethnic group" . . . I'm not naive. I know different pressures act on any President. But if a President makes his foreign-policy decisions solely on the basis of votes, it is bound to be erratic foreign policy. Bound to be.

Interview/
U.S. News & World Report,
5-16:38,39.

John M. Shalikashvili
General, United States Army;
Chairman, Joint Chiefs of Staff

1

With the end of the Cold War, billions of the world's citizens, most of them having never known freedom, are suddenly free to choose their own governments, to embrace the prosperity that comes from free markets, and to find new ways to create world peace. For the first time in my life, the world is not divided into armed camps on the verge of a conflict that would threaten our very existence . . . And while dangers abound . . . it is a remarkably better and more hopeful world than ever in the history of mankind.

At Bradley University
commencement/
USA Today, 5-29:(A)13.

Robert W. Tucker
Foreign-policy specialist,
Johns Hopkins University
(United States)

2

[U.S. President] Clinton is caught in a [foreign-policy] dilemma of his own making. He came into office intending to concentrate on domestic affairs . . . but he made a lot of commitments on foreign policy during the [1992 election] campaign, on Bosnia and Haiti and other issues. And he wanted to fulfill them without the use of American military power. He has developed something

new under the sun: the idea of bloodless war. The only problem is that it doesn't exist.

Los Angeles Times,
8-1:(A)10.

Stansfield Turner
Former Director
of Central Intelligence
of the United States

3

The greatest value of the CIA is that it is not associated with a policy-making body of government.

USA Today, 7-15:(A)5.

Pete Wilson
Governor of California (R)

4

[On illegal immigration to the U.S. from Mexico]: Throughout all of its history, the [U.S.] Border Patrol had been grossly under-staffed. Man for man, woman for woman, they are terrific—they do a great job. They cannot, however, be expected to succeed against overwhelming odds. If Congress has one-tenth the guts of illegal immigrants seeking to enter this country, they will admit that they have to do what is exclusively their responsibility—they have to provide the Border Patrol with . . . the necessary resources that will let them do the job.

News conference, El Paso, Texas/
The Washington Post, 5-2:(A)17.

5

Morally and legally, it is exclusively a Federal obligation to secure the border against illegal immigration. Immigration is a Constitutionally assigned Federal responsibility. Only the Federal government, the Administration and the Congress have jurisdiction. Only they can really deal with this. And they have failed to do so.

Interview/
Nation's Business,
December:31.

Timothy E. Wirth
Under Secretary of State
of the United States

1

A government which is violating basic human rights should not hide behind the defense of "sovereignty."

U.S. News & World Report,
9-19:26.

R. James Woolsey
Director of Central Intelligence
of the United States

2

We [in the CIA] can only conduct covert action pursuant to a formal Presidential finding that is transmitted in proper fashion, in a timely way, to Capitol Hill. This whole business of taking action politically or economically or with propaganda or with supporting some group with arms transfers such as the *mujahideen* in Afghanistan—that whole side of the Agency, covert action, is way, way down compared to what it was back during the 1980s. There will not be any free-lancing during this [Clinton] Administration by anyone on that dimension. If the President signs a finding that instructs us to undertake some sort of covert action and it's properly transmitted to the Hill, then we'll do it. But over 99 percent of the intelligence-community effort these days is in the business of intelligence collection and analysis and not in the business of covert action.

Interview, Washington, D.C./
Los Angeles Times, 1-2:(M)3.

3

There is no single approach [to intelligence gathering today]. Spies tip off satellites, and satellites tip off spies . . . Spies are, and I think always will be, essential, particularly in trying to get at the intentions and plans of really closed regimes and organizations.

Time, 3-7:36,37.

4

I am not worried in a fundamental sense [about the future of the CIA]. All responsible decision-makers in Congress and elsewhere understand that we need a CIA. And we need one that functions well . . . I'm confident that any fair-minded observer who has all the information will rather rapidly come to the conclusion that the country badly needs the CIA to deal with such matters as: proliferation of weapons; mass destruction; terrorist groups abroad; understanding rogue states such as Iraq, Iran, North Korea; helping understand where major countries whose future is somewhat uncertain, such as Russia and China, [are] going; their politics, economics and military program. All of these things are important to the future and present security of the United States.

Interview/
USA Today, 10-6:(A)2.

5

After 19 months [as CIA Director], I'm developing a pretty good interior network of people [in the CIA] who talk to me frankly . . . I very much believe something [the late] Admiral [Hyman] Rickover once told me: "Always use the chain of command to issue orders, but if you use the chain of command for information, you're dead."

Interview, Langley, Va./
Newsweek, 10-10:34.

Africa

Kofi A. Annan
Undersecretary General
of the United Nations
for Peacekeeping Operations

1

[On the massive refugee, disease and starvation problem in and near Rwanda resulting from the ethnic war there]: The [world's] response has fallen woefully short of needs. There is nothing the United Nations needs that its member states do not already possess and could provide if the necessary political will existed.

The Washington Post,
7-29:(A)30.

Derek Auret
Deputy Director General for Africa,
Foreign Ministry of South Africa

2

Perhaps the best chance [for the economies of South Africa and other African countries] is in coming together around common economic objectives and achieving collective economic growth, which will lead to all the benefits that this government would like to see accrue to South Africans [and to] all southern Africans. South Africa cannot be an island of prosperity in a sea of poverty.

Pretoria, South Africa/
Los Angeles Times,
6-3:(A)5.

Andre Azoulay
Chief economic adviser
to Moroccan King Hassan II

3

It's no accident that [Morocco] was chosen as the place to sign history's most important agreement between rich and poor nations [the recent international trade treaty]. Morocco is the natural bridge between the Western and Islamic worlds, a relationship that will be crucial in the years to come.

The Washington Post,
5-9:(A)10.

Roelof F. Botha
Foreign Minister of South Africa

4

[On the current unrest in Lesotho]: What we want to see in Lesotho is what we want to see in our own country—that fair elections can be carried out and the results kept in place. If we sit here with little countries on our border playing yo-yo, what does the future hold for us?

The New York Times,
1-25:(A)2.

Boutros Boutros-Ghali
Secretary General
of the United Nations

5

[On the mass killings taking place in Rwanda]: All of us are responsible for this failure. It is a genocide which has been committed. More than 200,000 people have been killed, and . . . the international community is still discussing what ought to be done. I have tried. I have been in contact with different heads of state and begged them to send troops . . . Unfortunately, let us say with great humility, I failed. It is a scandal. I am the first one to say it. And I am ready to repeat it.

News conference,
United Nations, New York,
May 25/Los Angeles Times,
5-26:(A)6.

Ronald H. Brown
Secretary of Commerce
of the United States

6

We believe that a democratic [non-apartheid] South Africa will promote peace and prosperity in the entire southern Africa region while simultaneously advancing American interests by expanding the market for U.S. goods and services, even as we create jobs in South Africa through the purchase of increasingly available and sophisticated exports. We intend to forge a partnership

(RONALD H. BROWN)

between our two countries that is long-lasting and mutually beneficial.

> *At Howard University,*
> *Washington, D.C., April 25/*
> *The Washington Post,*
> *4-26:(A)10.*

1

[Saying foreign aid is not the key to South Africa's post-apartheid economic future]: It will be the private sector that drives the economic recovery in South Africa. Salvation is not going to come from an aid policy. Salvation is going to come from increasing investment and trade.

> *At Howard University,*
> *Washington, D.C., April 25/*
> *The Christian Science Monitor,*
> *4-27:4.*

Mangosuthu Gatsha Buthelezi
President, Inkatha Freedom Party
of South Africa;
Chief of the Zulu people

2

My Party is committed to a federation [in South Africa]. The issue that would make it easier for us to participate [in the forthcoming South African elections] is if the powers that regions have were not taken over by the National Assembly, which emasculates the federal idea [of regional autonomy] completely. You see, the government of KwaZulu [his area] is a regional government dealing with people on a regional basis. And I am the inheritory leader of those people. Among the Zulu people I hold the position of the traditional prime minister of the king. Those positions are not affected by the outcome of elections. So long as the Zulu people are here, clearly I will still have a role to play in this country.

> *Interview,*
> *Ulundi, KwaZulu, South Africa/*
> *"Interview" magazine,*
> *June:72.*

Frank C. Carlucci
Former Secretary of Defense
of the United States

3

[On the ending of the U.S.-UN peacekeeping and humanitarian mission in Somalia, which began 14 months ago]: It will clearly influence and make the United States more reluctant about decisions to undertake missions of this kind elsewhere in the world . . . In terms of the humanitarian mission, I'd say it achieved its initial purpose. But when the mandate changed to nation-building—an impossible task, especially for a multilateral organization [like the UN]—I'd have to give it an "F."

> *Los Angeles Times,*
> *3-4:(A)16.*

Michael Chege
Kenyan scholar,
Harvard University (United States)

4

[On Nelson Mandela, who is about to become South Africa's first black President]: Look at the statesmanship and superiority of leadership that Nelson Mandela and people like [South African Archbishop] Desmond Tutu have shown. That's something that gives heart to an awful lot of us . . . If Nelson Mandela does make democracy work in South Africa, with a great deal of decentralization and autonomy for minorities, be they Zulus or whites, it will be a moral that will challenge arguments for dictatorship in the rest of the continent.

> *The Washington Post,*
> *5-6:(A)32.*

Bill Clinton
President of the United States

5

[On the now-ending U.S. military role in trying to establish peace in strife-torn Somalia]: The American people have been very generous with their money and with their support. We have lost

(BILL CLINTON)

some of our most precious resources—[the lives of] our young people—in Somalia because of the nature of the conflict. And I think we have done our job there and then some . . . There are civil wars in a lot of countries in this world [where] we have not made anything like the effort we've made in Somalia . . . If you go back to 1992, this whole mission was billed as a humanitarian mission, and the first time [then-U.S. President George] Bush spoke with me about it, he said he thought maybe [the U.S. troops] would be out before I was inaugurated or by the end of January [1993]. And what we learned from that, of course, is that—at least in the case of Somalia and many other cases— you can't have a humanitarian mission divorced from the political problems of the time. The people in Somalia were starving not because there was no food that could be given to them. They were starving because of the political and military conflicts consuming the country.

To reporters,
Washington, D.C., March 9/
Los Angeles Times,
3-10:(A)4.

1

[Announcing a U.S. aid package for the new black-led South African government]: We have important interests at stake in the success of South Africa's journey. America must be a new and full partner with that new government, so that it can deliver on its promise as quickly as possible.

At White House ceremony,
Washington, D.C., May 5/
The Washington Post,
5-6:(A)16.

Frederik W. de Klerk
President of South Africa

2

[On his efforts the past several years to bring about the end of apartheid in his country]: Looking back, I wouldn't have done any of the fundamental things I did differently. I achieved thus far almost all of the goals which I set for myself within

these past four years. I would hope that history would recognize that I, together with all those who supported me, have shown courage, integrity, honesty at the moment of truth in our history. That we took the right turn.

Interview/Time, 1-3:57.

3

[On the ending of apartheid in South Africa and the forthcoming free elections, both of which he supported]: There is no other option for South Africa . . . The tension is high, but if we hadn't done what we'd done, then I'm convinced that maybe before the end of 1990, the whole of South Africa would have been in flames.

Interview/
U.S. News & World Report,
4-25:59.

4

[On the ending of apartheid in South Africa]: As in America, in the hearts and minds of many people racism is a fact . . . That, you cannot legislate away. To change, that means basically a change of heart, and that needs religious efforts, it needs strong political leadership and guidance, it needs top management in business to show strong leadership. It is a reality, which we say in South Africa must be overcome.

Interview/
U.S. News & World Report,
4-25:59

5

[Acknowledging the victory of Nelson Mandela's ANC in the just-held South African elections, the first in which blacks have been able to participate]: Mr. Mandela has walked a long road and now stands at the top of the hill. A traveler would sit down and admire the view. But a man of destiny knows that beyond this hill lies another and another. The journey is never complete. As he contemplates the next hill, I hold out my hand in friendship and in cooperation.

Pretoria, South Africa, May 2/
The New York Times, 5-3:(A)5.

(FREDERIK W. DE KLERK)

1

[On the forthcoming government of Nelson Mandela, who will become South Africa's President following the just-held elections, the first in which blacks have been able to participate]: We must insure that we adopt the right approaches in the economic and social spheres. We need a strong and a vibrant economy based on the tried and tested principles of free enterprise. Only then can we insure that we will generate the wealth which we need to address the pressing social needs of large sections of our population. We must insure that social services are affordable, caring and effective. I will be in a good position in the government of national unity to promote these objectives. I will not be there at the whim of any person or any party, but in my own right as the representative of many millions of South Africans. Just as we could not rule South Africa effectively without the support of the ANC and its supporters, no [ANC] government will be able to rule South Africa effectively without the support of the people and the institutions that I represent.

Pretoria, South Africa, May 2/
The New York Times, 5-3:(A)5.

Alison DesForges
Africa specialist,
Human Rights Watch

2

Rwanda depends on foreign aid for 60 percent of its annual budget. That's a hell of a lot of foreign influence on what happens in Rwanda.

U.S. News & World Report,
9-19:52.

Atef Mohamed Ebeid
Minister of the Business Sector
of Egypt

3

[On Egypt's relations with Libya, which many regard as an outlaw nation]: [We are at a] relaxed time in our relationship. You can't afford to have a neighbor that doesn't like you.

Interview, Washington, D.C./
U.S. News & World Report,
10-31:66.

Al Gore
Vice President of the United States

4

[New South African] President [Nelson] Mandela's moral authority and the moral authority of the United States over a long period of time can perhaps create a whole greater than the sum of its parts in our efforts to promote reconciliation in places like Angola, Mozambique, even Rwanda.

To reporters,
Johannesburg, South Africa,
May 10/
The Washington Post,
5-11:(A)26.

Cyril Goungounga
Deputy, National Assembly
of Burkina Faso

5

It's a mistake [for African countries] to copy Western democracies because it's artificial. Look at the U.S. You elect a President. He's in office for four years, eight years. Then he's out. That's what the Constitution says. We have a Constitution too. But it doesn't work. It's just a piece of paper. Because we have two civilizations here. The Western one on top where everything is fine and differences are submerged in talk of national unity. And a parallel one underneath, an African one where ethnic groups are a reality.

Interview/
The New York Times,
6-21:(A)6.

Reed E. Hundt
Chairman,
Federal Communications Commission
(United States)

6

There are more telephones in Tokyo than there are in all of Africa. Africa's inability to grow economically is directly related to its lack of a telecommunications infrastructure.

Los Angeles Times,
3-17:(D)2.

Alain Juppe
Foreign Minister of France

1

[On the Islamic unrest in Algeria]: We are not supporting this or that regime in Algeria, and I must insist on this point. Our only interest in Algeria is democracy, and when I speak of democracy, I address fanatics of [the Islamic Salvation Front] who violate it as well as those who see total repression [of Islam] or total security as the only solution to the drama Algeria is living through.

French broadcast interview,
Dec. 25/
The Christian Science Monitor,
12-28:3.

Sylvie Kinigi
Former Prime Minister
of Burundi

2

[On the current ethnic unrest in Burundi]: We entered into democracy [following independence from Belgium in 1962] without having the means of dealing with it. The process was too rapid. There was no time to form political leaders. So parties formed on the simple criteria of ethnicity. With Rwanda [which is now experiencing a bloody ethnic war], we have in common inexperience in democracy and ineptness in managing power.

The New York Times,
4-26:(A)6.

Alain Lamassoure
Minister for European Affairs
of France

3

There might be 10 good reasons for [France] not intervening [in the ethnic war in Rwanda]. The one essential reason *for* doing so is that a whole people is in the course of dying.

U.S. News & World Report,
7-4:52.

Tom Lantos
United States Representative,
D-California

4

[Criticizing the failure of the world to take sufficient action against Libya for its alleged role in the 1988 bombing of a Pan American World Airways flight over Scotland]: I find it absolutely unconscionable that 189 Americans are dead, and almost six years after the event nothing effective has been done to bring the perpetrators to justice.

U.S. News & World Report,
10-31:71.

Tom Lodge
Political scientist,
University of the Witwatersrand
(South Africa)

5

[On pledges by the new South African government of President Nelson Mandela to increase salaries and other expenditures to civil servants in the former homelands and to expand the military by adding former ANC guerrillas into the ranks]: Even before Nelson Mandela has opened his mouth, we have a government that's practically increased by 50 percent the expenditure on salaries. That's not a good start for a government committed to fiscal austerity, to increased social spending and to luring foreign investors.

Los Angeles Times,
5-24:(H)4.

Nelson Mandela
President, African National Congress
(South Africa)

6

[On negotiations for a post-apartheid South Africa]: There is no question of compromising on majority rule. But there has been a demand for federalism. The regions can draw up their own constitutions. They can make their own laws and impose taxation. We did not agree with this. But we felt that in order to bring everybody on board, we should make certain compromises.

Interview/Time, 1-3:57.

(NELSON MANDELA)

1

[On the current elections in South Africa, the first to include all races, in which his ANC is expected to win]: Even if we may emerge with a landslide victory, we have to be very careful and not create the fear that the majority is going to be used for the purpose of coercing minorities to accept the policy of a particular party which has emerged victorious.

Interview, April 29/
The New York Times,
4-30:5.

Nelson Mandela
President-elect of South Africa

2

[On his victory in the just-held elections in South Africa, the first in which blacks have been able to participate]: We [the ANC] have emerged as the majority party on the basis of the program which is contained in the reconstruction and development program. There we have outlined the steps that we are going to take in order to insure a better life for all South Africans . . . And I appeal to all the leaders who are going to serve in this government to honor that program and to go there determined to contribute toward its immediate implementation. If there are attempts on the part of anybody to undermine that program, there will be serious tensions in the government of national unity . . . It is a program which was developed by the masses of the people themselves in people's forums. It has been accepted by state corporations, by government departments, by business, academics, by religious leaders, youth movements, women's organizations. And nobody will be entitled to participate in that government of national unity to oppose that plan.

Victory statement
following the elections,
Johannesburg, South Africa,
May 2/
The New York Times,
5-3:(A)5.

[On his winning South Africa's just-held elections, the first in which blacks were able to participate]: I am your servant. I don't come to you as a leader, as one above others . . . Leaders come and go, but the organization [the ANC] and the collective leadership that has looked after the fortunes and reversals of this [anti-apartheid] struggle will always be there. And the ideas I express are not ideas invented in my own mind. They stem from our fundamental policy document, the Freedom Charter, from the decisions, resolutions of the national conference and from the decisions of the national executive committee [of the ANC]. That is the nature of our organization. It is not the individuals that matter; it is the collective leadership which has led this organization so skillfully.

Victory statement
following the elections,
Johannesburg, South Africa,
May 2/Ebony, August:29.

4

I am neither [a socialist nor a capitalist]. I have never advocated socialist views. There is a clause in [South Africa's new] Freedom Charter which says that the wealth beneath the soil shall be the property of the people. That is the principle which we find in places like Canada and Australia. It is true that we [in the ANC] advocated some form of nationalization because we said we'd nationalize the banks, we'd nationalize monopolies. That was ideological. But because of the criticism we got, we shifted our position . . . We make no distinction among the conservatives who believe in the capitalist system and those who believe in the Communist Party, no distinction whatsoever. [Communists] hold a position as members of the ANC. They are loyal to its policy, its code of conduct, to its regulations and to its discipline.

Interview/
Newsweek,
5-9:36.

Nelson Mandela
President of South Africa

1

[On his becoming South Africa's first black President]: We have, at last, achieved our political emancipation. We pledge ourselves to liberate all our people from the continuing bondage of poverty, deprivation, suffering, gender and other discrimination. The time for healing of the wounds has come. The moment to bridge the chasms that devide us has come. The time to build is upon us.

Inaugural address,
Pretoria, South Africa, May 10/
The Christian Science Monitor,
5-11:1.

2

Never, never . . . shall it be that this beautiful land [South Africa] will again experience the oppression of one [race] by another and suffer the indignity of being the skunk of the world.

USA Today, 5-13:(A)13.

3

There are major areas of desperate need in our society. As a signal of its seriousness to address this, the government will, within the next hundred days, implement various projects under the direct provision of the President . . . Children under the age of six and pregnant mothers will receive free medical care in every state hospital and clinic where such need exists. Similarly, a nutrition feeding scheme will be implemented in every primary school where such a need is established . . . A program is already being implemented to electrify 350,000 homes during the current financial year. A campaign will be launched at every level of government, a public-works program designed, and all efforts made to involve the private sector, organized labor, the civics and other community organizations, to rebuild our townships, restore services in rural and urban areas, while addressing the issue of job creation and training especially for our unemployed youths.

Before South African Parliament,
Cape Town, South Africa,
May 24/Ebony, August:29.

4

As we take our rightful place among the nations of Africa, South Africa commits itself to join our neighbors in rising to the challenge represented by a growing affliction known as Afro-pessimism—loss of confidence in our continent's capacity to overcome under-development and declining standards.

At World Economic
Forum conference,
Cape Town, South Africa/
The Christian Science Monitor,
6-13:3.

5

A hundred days after our inauguration, our overwhelming impression of our reality is that our nation has succeeded to handle its problems with great wisdom. We have a government that has brought together bitter enemies into a constructive relationship. Our Parliament and Cabinet have properly focused on the task of reconstruction and development. And we have a government that is in control and whose programs are on course.

Before South African Parliament,
Cape Town, South Africa,
Aug. 18/Los Angeles Times,
8-19:(A)4.

6

[Calling on South African labor unions to end strikes, which he says scare foreign investors away from the country]: You still have this question of populism—"Let the workers strike!" They say, "We want only investors who will invest at all costs." I'm trying to warn against that type of thinking. That is irresponsible. We [the country's black majority] must move from the position of a resistance movement [against the now-outlawed apartheid] to one of builders.

Interview enroute from
Pretoria to Cape Town,
South Africa, Sept. 8/
The New York Times,
9-12:(A)1.

(NELSON MANDELA)

1

[On the recent end of apartheid in South Africa and his being elected that country's first black President]: It surely must be one of the ironies of the age that this august assembly [the UN] is addressed for the first time in its 49 years by a South African head of state drawn from among the African majority of what is an African country . . . It is indeed a most welcome thing that this august organization will mark its 50th anniversary next year with [South Africa's] apartheid system having been vanquished and consigned to the past. That historic change has come about not least because of the great efforts in which the UN engaged to ensure the suppression of the apartheid crime against humanity. The millions of our people say thank you, and thank you again, that the respect for your own dignity as human beings inspired you to act to insure the restoration of our dignity as well.

At United Nations,
New York, Oct. 3/
The New York Times,
10-4:(A)3.

2

We [in South Africa] talk of fiscal discipline, waste and inefficiency of the [former] apartheid regime. In fact, there is no fiscal discipline in the [now-ruling] ANC; there is waste and inefficiency in the ANC. We must never forget the saying that power corrupts. Freedom-fighters of yesterday have become part of the government without any idea of leadership. They have forgotten the people who put them into power.

At ANC conference,
Bloemfontein, South Africa/
The Christian Science Monitor,
12-23:6.

Tei Mante
Director, African office,
World Bank's International
Finance Corporation

3

Today you won't find a single African head of state who stands on a podium and declares: "I'm a Marxist." Instead, all the talk is about floating currency, private enterprise, and getting hold of capital.

The New York Times,
6-20:(A)1.

Donald McHenry
Former United States
Ambassador/
Permanent Representative
to the United Nations

4

[On the ending of the U.S.-UN peacekeeping and humanitarian mission in Somalia, which began 14 months ago]: Somalia was set up for failure by the terms of reference. Anyone who was naive enough to believe we could go in and simply feed people and then pull out was fooling themselves. To follow that course would have ensured the same conditions that forced us to go in would reoccur.

Los Angeles Times,
3-4:(A)16.

Robert Menard
Director, Reporters
Without Frontiers

5

[On the reluctance of foreign journalists to cover the conflict in Algeria because of the risks involved]: The first reason is fear. It would be a colossal risk for any editor to send a reporter to Algeria. For working journalists, Algerians and foreigners alike, the place is 100 times more dangerous than Bosnia or Rwanda. Going there is like playing Russian roulette with a journalist's life. Most editors are reluctant to make this decision.

The New York Times,
12-28:(A)3.

Dominique Moisi
Deputy director,
Institute for International
Relations (France)

1

The main impact of the violence in Algeria in France is to encourage an obsession with security. The French are puzzled by the Algerian quagmire. There is a feeling that there is very little we can do to affect events there. So we try to limit the impact of immigration, terrorism, [Islamic] fundamentalism reaching significant segments of the Algerian population in France. Toward that end, there is not one French policy toward Algeria, but many.

The Christian Science Monitor,
12-27:7.

Jonathan Moyo
Director, Ford Foundation's
international affairs
and governance programs
(Kenya)

2

The passing away of apartheid [in South Africa] will also be accompanied by the passing away of those African leaders who stayed in power because there was an enemy [apartheid] next door. The one leader who has really tried to champion this and make an issue of it is Zimbabwe's [President] Robert Mugabe. He made political capital out of apartheid. [Mugabe] thrives on enemies, [and with the end of apartheid,] I think it's fair to say that Mugabe's days are numbered.

The Washington Post,
5-6:(A)32.

3

[Comparing formerly white-ruled South Africa with the current conflict-ridden situation in Rwanda]: The cruelty of the system of oppression is the same. When you set one group above another and close all channels of political expression, you sow the seeds of eruption further down the line. The difference is, South Africa underwent a process of managed change. It started in 1986. If they had suddenly lifted the lid off back then, people would have been slaughtering each other too. That's what happened in Rwanda—it was too much too quickly for a system that had been totally closed. Today the one-party structure is ending all over Africa and people demand elections within 21 days. The South Africa experience [of ending apartheid] teaches us it should be done gradually by people of vision, allowing the structures to evolve and preaching values of tolerance the whole way . . . No country in Africa since the winds of change started blowing four years ago has really achieved democracy. The triggering of change has led to political liberalization but not to democracy. Democracy is much more far-reaching. It requires change in institutions. They have to become strong and competing and they have to recognize each other's legitimacy. That's far down the line. Who knows how far it really is?

Interview/
The New York Times,
6-21:(A)6,7.

4

The leadership of Africa today is in a state of deep-seated bewilderment. Everywhere there is a vacuum. We need ideas, but who is going to produce them? The scholars haven't. They sound worldly, but they have not yielded usable or intelligible policies, and the universities and research centers of yesterday have collapsed. The entrepreneurs? They're despised by people as collaborators with the West and have never developed a sensible business culture. All three groups—political, academic, business—are bewildered, and even the Africans themselves seem to think this is a hopeless continent.

Los Angeles Times,
6-27:(A)9.

Makau Mutua
Kenyan attorney; Projects director,
Human Rights Program,
Harvard Law School
(United States)
1

[Saying African countries' borders were set arbitrarily by Europeans in the 19th century]: You have a bunch of land masses which were bounded for the expediency of European expansion. Almost none of these became viable states.

Newsweek, 8-1:32.

Richard Newcomb
Director,
Office of Foreign Assets Control,
Department of the Treasury
of the United States
2

[Criticizing countries that permit Libya to make investments within their borders]: Governments that allow [Libya] to make these kinds of investments . . . are fueling the pot of this renegade nation.

U.S. News & World Report,
10-31:59.

Eugene Nyati
Director,
Center for African Studies
(South Africa)
3

[On the effect on other African countries of the end of apartheid and the start of full democracy in South Africa]: There are many people in Africa who are clearly very nervous. We [South Africa] are bigger. We are stronger. And once you are powerful, it doesn't matter if you are a white or black government. You sometimes have a tendency to take advantage of weaker people.

Los Angeles Times,
4-21:(A)12.

Robert B. Oakley
United States
Special Envoy to Somalia;
Former U.S. Ambassador
to Somalia
4

[On the ending of the U.S.-UN peacekeeping and humanitarian mission in Somalia, which began 14 months ago]: We need greater selectivity and care in defining missions and to make sure they're finite . . . Somalia was the first test for UN leadership in these kinds of crises of failed states, and it over-reached. The objective in Somalia became too encompassing and too intrusive and more than the United Nations could handle.

Los Angeles Times,
3-4:(A)16.

Joe Oloka-Onyango
Lecturer,
Makerere University (Uganda)
5

[On Ugandan President Yoweri Museveni]: Museveni has been a boon and a bane, larger than life. No other person could have done [for Uganda] what he has done. My problem [with him] is sustainability. The institutional basis for stability has not been created. If Museveni were to disappear, a lot that is positive would collapse. It's too close to a one-party system. It's a slippery slope. At some point diminishing returns are going to set in. Museveni must recognize the point at which it's time to let go.

Interview, Kampala, Uganda/
The Atlantic Monthly,
September:30.

Rakiya Omaar
Co-director,
African Rights (Britain)
6

[On the effect on other African countries of the end of apartheid and the start of full democracy in South Africa]: Many Africans, myself included, have been impatient for South Africa to become [free] because its plight has for so long been an excuse for other African leaders to deflect attention from the continent's other problems. South Africa was, morally, a black and white issue. But criticizing [dictators like former President Ibrahim] Babangida in Nigeria or [Hastings Kamuzu] Banda in Malawi was considered interference. We don't want African leaders and institutions to have any more excuses.

Los Angeles Times,
4-21:(A)12.

Cyril Ramaphosa
Secretary general,
African National Congress
(South Africa)

1

[On South African President Nelson Mandela]: He eats like a President, he walks like a President, speaks like a President. I am one of the lucky few who have seen him sleep—and he even sleeps like a President.

The Christian Science Monitor,
12-23:7.

Alberto Bento Ribeiro
Angolan Ambassador-designate
to Zimbabwe

2

[On the end of apartheid in South Africa and the current free elections there]: If it goes badly in South Africa, it will be a disaster for all of us [in Africa]. We have shown that elections and democracy are not the entire solution. That's the trouble— the West thinks it's a magic wand that will solve everything. We're watching South Africa closely. [Current President Frederik W. de Klerk and ANC leader Nelson Mandela] have to keep dancing, but not rock-and-roll. It must be a tango.

The New York Times,
4-30:5.

Randall Robinson
Executive director,
TransAfrica
(United States)

3

South Africa has, because of apartheid, a disproportionate section of its population living in a kind [of] extended despair: 50 percent unemployment, 80 percent or so illiteracy, 7 million of 28 million black South Africans living in corrugated lean-to shanties. A whole generation of young people is out of school because of the political situation. There is no health care in the black community to speak of. All of these are systemic, far-reaching social problems that have given rise to much of the violence that we have seen.

Interview/
USA Today,
4-21:(A)13.

Salim Ahmed Salim
Secretary General,
Organization of African Unity

4

Colonial education, limited to training very low functionaries, did not prepare the African for the eventual assumption of leadership and management of the affairs of a modern state.

World Press Review,
July:22.

Amos Sawyer
Former President of Liberia

5

[On the current civil war in Liberia]: Things have deteriorated to the point where what we are seeing emerge nowadays are sub-warlords, each of whom is a law unto himself. If we don't arrest the situation quickly, we will soon be back to where we were at the end of the 19th century, when this country was a stage for roving tribal gangs that fought back and forth for territory.

The New York Times,
10-22:6.

Desmond M. Tutu
South African
Anglican Archbishop;
Winner,
1984 Nobel Peace Prize

1

[On his just having voted in South Africa's first non-racial elections]: I am about two inches taller than before I arrived. It's an incredible experience, like falling in love.

Newsweek, 5-9:34.

2

[On the recent post-apartheid elections in South Africa in which, for the first time, blacks were allowed to vote]: What should have been a secular event became a religious occasion. Even secularists found themselves saying things like "It was a miracle." For many, it was a transforming experience. People emerged from the polling booth different than they went in. It restored dignity to black South Africans, and it gained whites a new sense of relief from the burden of guilt they had been carrying. All of us found ourselves walking tall, with an incredible pride in being South African.

Interview/
American Way, 10-1:58.

Faustin Twagiramungu
Prime Minister of Rwanda

3

[Saying his new Administration will proceed with war-crimes trials against those suspected of being involved in genocide during the current ethnic conflict in Rwanda]: We are not going to wait for long for an international tribunal to be held. It can take more than three years for the United Nations to organize an international tribunal, and people will think we are playing around here . . . I'm not a lawyer, but I think if you kill, you simply kill. The people involved in giving orders are just as guilty as the people killing. There are no clean people involved in massacres.

Aug. 2/The New York Times,
8-3:(A)1.

4

[On the ethnic conflict in his country which has claimed hundreds of thousands of lives]: I am personally fed up. I am sincerely fed up for not having a future for my children, for the people from my generation or for the people of the generations to come. A child who is 7 years old now can live maybe 60 years. When they are 67 years old, they will still remember what has happened in this country. Just imagine a whole generation that for about a half century is going to remember this. What do we do for people to forget? I think that we can only start by teaching children that we are one people.

Interview, Kigali, Rwanda/
The New York Times,
8-12:(A)4.

Wilhelm Verwoed
Former professor of geology,
Stellenbosch University
(South Africa);
Son of former South African
Prime Minister Hendrik Verwoed

5

[On white South Africas' attitude toward the ending of apartheid in their country]: There is a serious split that cuts across families; it's the kind of thing that happens in civil wars. Maybe it's not so bad. It shows people think for themselves, which you can't say for some of the black population. There the strongest wins, the law of the jungle abides.

U.S. News & World Report,
4-25:62.

Kojo Yankah
Deputy Minister
of Information of Ghana

6

[On his government's control of Ghana's broadcasting media]: This government is fully committed to freedom of expression. But for our purposes, at this moment, radio and television

(KOJO YANKAH)

should serve as the forum for a discussion of our development needs. I am afraid that our society is not as stable as some others, and we could have disorder as a result of the misuse of this resource.

The New York Times,
12-26:6.

I. William Zartman
Director of African studies,
School of Advanced
International Studies,
Johns Hopkins University
(United States)

1
[On South Africa's economic outlook as it changes from apartheid to a freely elected, majority-ruled system]: The new, legitimate government is in danger of losing its legitimacy because it cannot live up to the expectations that have been raised. The South African economy is weak and artificial. What looked like good free enterprise . . . was heavily supported by the state, by state ownership and state subsidies. It has been dependent upon cheap [black] labor, but the labor will get much more expensive. It is as if you took two-thirds of the society and let them out of prison and dumped them on the job market. They have no money, they have no housing, and the state is now responsible for them.

Los Angeles Times,
3-9:(D)3.

The Americas

Sergio Aguayo
President, Mexican Academy
of Human Rights

1

[On the forthcoming Mexican national elections]: People who are saying these are going to be truly democratic elections are confusing the start of this process with the end. It is as though at the moment of *Brown v. the Board of Education of Topeka* [desegregation court case in the U.S.], they were saying that segregation was over.

The New York Times,
8-19:(A)1.

Hattie Babbitt
United States Ambassador to,
and President
of the Permanent Council of,
the Organization
of American States

2

[On the recent assassination of Luis Donaldo Colosio, the leading candidate for President of Mexico]: The fundamental *raison d'etre* of the OAS is to be supportive of representative democracy. To have a candidate in a [Presidential election] race assassinated is a special affront to the solidarity the countries of the hemisphere are now expressing [for democracy].

March 24/
Los Angeles Times,
3-25:(A)6.

Miguel Antonio Bernal
Professor,
University of Panama

3

[On his country's taking in of a number of the world's deposed leaders who are forced to flee their homelands]: Our country is being used as a wastebasket for the political toxic waste of the world.

Newsweek,
10-24:21.

Lawrence Bossidy
Chairman, AlliedSignal, Inc.
(United States)

4

[On South America's market potential]: I maintain a healthy skepticism. I was in Brazil 25 years ago, and I was uncertain it was going to be a wonderful economic place. It never has been.

Interview, July 18/
USA Today, 7-19:(B)4.

Jimmy Carter
Former President
of the United States

5

[On the current elections in Panama, of which he is an official observer]: Five years ago [when the U.S. invaded Panama to capture its strongman, Manuel Noriega], we left Panama distressed that an opportunity for peaceful, democratic change was aborted. Today, we return confident that the Panamanian people will have the chance that was denied them by General Noriega—to fulfill the democratic right to choose their next leaders.

Panama City, Panama, May 8/
The Washington Post,
5-9:(A)10.

Fidel Castro
President of Cuba

6

It's not my fault that I haven't died yet. It's not my fault that the [U.S.] CIA has failed to kill me! . . . My vocation is the revolution. I am a revolutionary, and revolutionaries do not retire . . . I feel like it all began yesterday. You could say that from the time I was 19 years old I have been engaged in an intense struggle. For 48 years. And in spirit I feel just like I did when I began. Some people say I am stubborn, but in reality I have been tenacious, persistent. I think that if I could live my life over again, I would do things the same way.

Interview, Havana, Cuba/
Vanity Fair, March:130.

251

(FIDEL CASTRO)

1

[Criticizing U.S. actions over the years in the Americas]: Decade after decade, century after century, we have been going from slogan to slogan, from deceit to deceit. There have also been wars, interventions and territorial conquests at the expense of our America. What, then, can we expect from that invariably expansionist, selfish and hegemonic force?

At Ibero-American Summit,
Cartagena, Colombia, June 14/
Los Angeles Times, 6-15:(A)10.

2

[On Cubans who flee their country to try to get to the U.S.]: If we are to talk about solutions, we must speak, among other things, of a solution to the United States embargo against Cuba. They want to strangle us, starve us and kill us with disease. Does this or does this not force illegal departures?

News conference,
Havana, Cuba, Aug. 5/
The New York Times, 8-20:9.

3

This country [Cuba] can only be ruled by the revolution. If this country explodes, the headaches for the United States will be inconceivable. The country will be ungovernable for 100 years. Cuba could become a huge center of drug trafficking. We are prepared to be flexible and constructive. But also, people are willing to fight. No one should think we are just going to sit down and accept the destruction of our country. We are willing to talk, but we are also willing to resist and put up a struggle. Nothing that has to do with the sovereignty of the country can be negotiated. We hope the United States understands that. The United States would never accept another country dictating steps it should take. We are not going to renounce the conquests of the revolution.

Interview, Havana, Cuba/
U.S. News & World Report
9-26:57.

4

[On Cuban relations with the U.S.]: We are not going to negotiate the normalization of our relations on the basis of concessions. The United States did not blockade South Africa. It does not blockade Saudi Arabia, where [a] few rich families own all of the wealth. The United States does not dictate political conditions to China. It does not dictate political conditions to Vietnam. Why does it have to dictate political conditions to us?

Interview, Havana, Cuba, Dec. 11/
The New York Times, 12-13:(A)8.

Eugenia Charles
Prime Minister of Dominica

5

[On her decision to trade with Cuba, despite U.S. objections]: I have always said that I'll do business with the devil if it will buy products and put money in the hands of my people. I told the Americans, "I'm not even going to discuss the matter with you, because I can sell my soap to Cuba. You're not buying a bar of my soap in America, and my people deserve to sell their soap so that they can make some money." I'll trade anywhere in the world where I can get money for my farmers.

Interview/
Essence, September:73.

Gregorio Rosa Chavez
Salvadoran Roman
Catholic Bishop

6

[On the forthcoming Presidential election in El Salvador, the first such free peacetime election in that country in 64 years]: These elections open a new chapter in El Salvador's dramatic history. It has been a history marked by injustice, marginalization and much blood, a history that must be changed . . . The biggest challenges facing the winner are carrying out the peace agreements [with the former rebels] fully; consolidat-

(GREGORIO ROSA CHAVEZ)

ing democracy; giving the poorest hope and dignity; and making justice available to all.

Broadcast homily, April 24/
The Washington Post,
4-25:(A)10.

Warren Christopher
Secretary of State
of the United States

1

[On criticism that the U.S. is not very much concerned with repression in Cuba anymore, despite a recent massacre at sea of Cubans by their government]: We're proceeding to carry out the Cuban Democracy Act, which is one of the most severe sets of sanctions that there is on the books anyplace. This is a relationship between the [U.S. Clinton] Administration and Congress, which is a very determined one . . . But it certainly is a problem that gnaws at us continuously, and this recent reminder is one of the brutal character of that regime and the need to seek a replacement of that present regime and hopefully a return to the democratic days of Cuba.

Before House
Foreign Affairs Committee,
Washington, D.C., July 28/
The Washington Post, 7-29:(A)24.

Bill Clinton
President of the United States

2

I think our security is caught up in whether the people in this hemisphere are moving toward democracy and open markets and observation of the rule of law . . . We know that many of our democracies are fragile, but we're moving in the right direction. We don't want to see Latin America take one more wrong turn. We're moving right; we want to stay right. And I think that is profoundly important to us.

News conference,
Washington, D.C., Aug. 3/
Los Angeles Times, 8-4:(A)12.

I support the [economic] embargo [against Cuba] and I support the [U.S.] Cuban Democracy Act, which was passed in 1992. And I do not believe we should change our policy there. The fundamental problem is democracy is sweeping the world; democracy and freedom are sweeping our hemisphere. In the Caribbean alone and in Central and South America, in all of this region, there are only two countries now not democratically governed with open societies and open economies. The real problem is the stubborn refusal of the [Cuban President Fidel] Castro regime to have an open democracy and an open economy, and I think the policies we are following will hasten the day when that occurs.

News conference,
Washington, D.C., Aug. 19/
The New York Times,
8-20:10.

4

[On the current flow of Cubans trying to get to the U.S. on rafts and home-made boats]: The people leaving Cuba will not be permitted to come to the United States. They will be sent to safe havens . . . The people who reach here will be apprehended and will be treated like others. Their cases will be reviewed, and those who qualify can stay, and those who don't will not be permitted to. [Cubans] will now [be] treated like others who come here [rather than receiving preferential treatment as in the past] . . . As to whether it is immoral [to do this], I just would say it is my belief that the American people, and that the Cuban-American people, and the people of Florida, but the people of the entire United States, do not want to see another Mariel boatlift [of Cuban immigrants that took place in 1980]. They do not want to see [Cuban President Fidel] Castro able to export his political and economic problems to the United States. Now, that is what is plainly being set up. We have gone through that once. [In 1980,] we had 120,000 people sent to this country as a deliberate attempt— not because they themselves wanted to flee—they were encouraged to flee; they were pushed out.

(BILL CLINTON)

We had [Cuban] jails open, we had [Cuban] mental hospitals open, all in an attempt to export all the problems of Cuba to the United States. We tried it that way once. It was wrong then and it's wrong now, and I'm not going to let it happen again.

News conference,
Washington, D.C., Aug. 19/
The New York Times,
8-20:10.

Alfredo Cristiani
President of El Salvador

1

[Criticizing pending U.S. aid cuts to Central American countries]: We are critical of the fact that the United States is more worried about Europe than about what happens in its own yard. They could take $1-billion from Egypt and Israel for Central America, and it would be a better investment.

Interview,
San Salvador, El Salvador,
March 9/
The Washington Post,
3-11:(A)20.

2

[On his country's forthcoming elections, in which the FMLN, the former rebel group, will take part]: For us, these elections are the consolidation of democracy. The FMLN will be inside the system, acting within the system. They have become the second [-largest] political force; they will have important participation in the assembly and municipalities. If they were anything, they were politicians, an armed political party that should have done this long ago [instead of engaging in the civil war of the 1980s].

Interview,
San Salvador, El Salvador,
March 9/
The Washington Post,
3-11:(A)20.

Hector Dada
Salvadoran political scientist

3

[On irregularities in the recent elections in El Salvador that prevented many people from voting]: Salvadorans trusted that the international community was going to guarantee the rules. The lesson was that without a [strong] civil society, you cannot have free, democratic elections. These elections laid bare the real problem: You have to build democratic structures in order to guarantee elections . . . People value democracy more if they have elected their closest leader, the one they can see and greet on the street. People have the idea these elections were not clean, and that does not help build democracy.

Los Angeles Times,
3-28:(A)8.

Robertson Davies
Canadian author

4

[Comparing Canada with the U.S.]: The myth of America is a very powerful one and one that we in Canada look toward with envy. You [in the U.S.] have your heroes. You have your great men of the past. You have your myth of tradition, of the conquering of the West, and the pioneer life and the gold-rush life and all that sort of thing, which is enormously romantic. And nations feed on the romantic tradition. We [Canada] don't go for heroes. As soon as a man begins to achieve some sort of high stature, we want to cut him down and get rid of him, embarrass him.

Interview,
Toronto, Canada/
The New York Times,
12-15:(A)4.

Lincoln Diaz-Balart
United States Representative,
R-Florida

5

[Addressing U.S. Secretary of State Warren Christopher]: I must admit that I found it unfortu-

(LINCOLN DIAZ-BALART)

nate and somewhat objectionable that in your formal statement you omitted Cuba from your survey of the world's trouble spots even though . . . just two weeks ago one of the most brutal massacres in the history of the 35-year-old [Cuban President Fidel] Castro regime occurred [at sea] less than 90 miles from our shores . . . Would you not agree, sir, that—due to the continued omission of Cuba from the elemental survey of the trouble spots of the world—there seems to be no choice but for those who want to see Cuba free . . . to intensify [their] militancy [in order that] not only the [U.S. Clinton] Administration, but some of the national media, will pick up Cuba on its radar screen?

At House Foreign Affairs
Committee hearing,
Washington, D.C., July 28/
The Washington Post,
7-29:(A)24.

Denise Dresser
Mexican political scientist

1

[On the current Indian revolt in the southern Mexican state of Chiapas]: [President Carlos Salinas de Gortari] was leaving office unscathed, going down as the great modernizer of Mexico, and then Chiapas shows that his whole strategy may have been flawed. Salinas was creating a two-tiered country of the haves and have-nots. I think he made the conscious decision to propel half of Mexico into the First World, even if that meant propelling the other half into the Fourth World . . . Now he's confronted with his Achilles' heel.

Interview/
Los Angeles Times, 1-6:(A)8.

Michel Dupuy
Heritage Minister of Canada

2

[Criticizing the U.S. domination of media in Canada]: Let us get one thing clear. We must bring back [Canadian] culture to the forefront of

society's concerns, for it is essential to our identity . . . and our independence.

Before Canadian Parliament,
Ottawa, Canada/
The Christian Science Monitor,
12-23:1.

Guillermo Endara
President of Panama

3

[Criticizing how the U.S. treated his country during negotiations for an agreement, now cancelled by Panama, that called for Panama to accept up to 10,000 refugees fleeing from Haiti]: [The U.S.] scolded us as if we were little children. They tried to intimidate us and pressure us, when we were simply trying to do them a favor. Instead of treating us like friends, they treated us like enemies.

Interview, July 7/
Los Angeles Times,
7-8:(A)1.

Eduardo Frei
President of Chile

4

[Supporting the idea of a Latin American free-trade zone]: If we look at the world economy today, Latin America confronts three blocs—Europe, NAFTA and the Pacific. Our union is fundamental.

At Latin American
trade conference,
Cartagena, Colombia/
The New York Times,
6-17:(C)2.

Dan Goure
Analyst, Center for Strategic
and International Studies
(United States)

5

[On the idea of a U.S. naval blockade around Cuba to prevent refugees from fleeing that coun-

(DAN GOURE)

try to the United States, a blockade that could also cut off world trade with Cuba]: The risk is that [the U.S. would] be creating the same sort of problem in Cuba that has resulted [from the U.S. embargo against Haiti]—that the embargo creates such pressure on the economy [of those countries] that people will want to leave all the more. It didn't work the first time, so why would you want to repeat it? [The U.S. Clinton Administration] would be buying themselves an explosion—and nobody wants that.

Los Angeles Times,
8-23:(A)24.

Daniel Johnson
Premier of Quebec,
Canada

1

[Arguing against the idea of Quebec independence from Canada]: As we become citizens of the world, it seems to me wrong that we should put up new borders, new frontiers, and reduce ourselves to a smaller geographic entity.

Inaugural address,
Quebec City, Canada,
Jan. 11/
The Washington Post,
1-12:(A)13.

Rowland Lorimer
Director,
Canadian Center
for Studies in Publishing

2

There is not a very strong libertarian streak in Canadian society. If anything, Canada defines itself against the United States by its lack of libertarianism. We have a positive attitude toward public enterprise. We believe the state *can* act on behalf of society as a whole.

The Washington Post,
1-31:(A)13.

Roy MacLaren
Minister of Trade
of Canada

3

[On U.S. restrictions on wheat imports from Canada]: In trade policy, what has Canada done wrong? If you could answer me that question, I think I could begin to understand why the U.S. is imposing on itself these limitations on Canadian wheat that is merely entering the U.S. to fill a market vacuum, and which benefits the U.S. consumer. There is no trade principle that we are violating. We are trading openly and fairly in the U.S. market. This is a direct contradiction of the commitments under the [NAFTA] free-trade agreement. We are offering grain to the U.S. consumer. If they want the grain, they pay a fair price. Our grain reaches the U.S. market, and for our trouble we are told that it is unacceptable. I have to assume that this is their response to the demands of local interests in the Dakotas and Montana as the price of their support in other areas of public policy.

Interview/
The Wall Street Journal,
10-28:(R)12.

John F. Maisto
United States
Ambassador
to Nicaragua

4

[Saying the U.S. will cease its interference in Nicaragua's political affairs now that democracy there has taken root and the Cold War is over]: There is no real security threat to the United States in this part of the world [anymore], and that's what I find fascinating, and that's why we can get back to the real roots of U.S. values in foreign policy.

Interview,
Managua, Nicaragua/
The New York Times,
2-10:(A)8.

Preston Manning
Leader,
Reform Party of Canada

1

[On his party's opposition to the Bloc Quebecois party in the Canadian Parliament and their common opposition to the ruling Liberal Party]: I would hope this new Parliament will not be a contest between the BQ and ourselves, but between our vision of a new federalism and the Liberals' view of an old federalism. That would be a far more constructive debate since it would present the country with new options as we approach the 21st century.

Interview/
The Christian Science Monitor,
1-19:2.

Carlos Saul Menem
President of Argentina

2

[On the new Southern Cone South American Common Market, economically uniting Argentina, Uruguay, Brazil and Paraguay]: Free trade can solve an infinity of problems that have dragged us [four nations] down far more that a century.

Interview/
The Christian Science Monitor,
12-21:4.

Alfredo Molano
Colombian anthropologist

3

Colombia is a strangely paradoxical country. A great portion of public opinion, and the government, is against drug trafficking from a legal point of view, and from a moral point of view. But economically, it fills the pockets of many people—not just the rich but the poor too. In spite of everything, the cultivation and trafficking [of narcotics] has provided the country with certain economic stability. Therein lies the ambivalence.

Los Angeles Times,
7-8:(A)8.

Ambler H. Moss
Director, North-South Center,
University of Miami

4

[In the past, Latin American countries] were all expanding state enterprises, raising barriers against imports, nationalizing American companies and blocking American investment. Today, the typical Latin American head of state is a salesman. They are all here [at Miami's Summit of the Americas] hustling business for their countries.

Interview, Miami, Fla./
The New York Times,
12-12:(A)4.

Jayson Myers
Chief economist,
Canadian Manufacturers
Association

5

[On the Canadian economy]: What's happening in Canada overall is that manufacturing is being driven as a part of an integrated overall North American market. If exports were flat, then Canada would be in recession right now. . . . Because it's a branch in a larger North American market, Canada hasn't been able to retain or attract the level of investment we would want to see to give an additional boost to manufacturing capacity. Future jobs are not in the existing capacity but in new production—and you're not seeing that being built here.

The Christian Science Monitor,
9-7:4.

David P. O'Brien
Chairman, PanCanadian
Petroleum, Ltd.

6

[On the Canadian province of Alberta's independent, western spirit]: Alberta swaggers less than [the U.S. state of Texas], but within the Canadian context it is certainly the hottest province in terms of free enterprise.

The Washington Post,
2-4:(A)21.

Andre Ouellet
Foreign Minister of Canada

1

[On Canada's decision to provide $1-million in aid to Cuba, ending a 16-year moratorium on such transactions]: The Cold War is long over. The people of Cuba are suffering from food shortages brought on by economic crises, and Canadians want to help them.

To reporters,
Ottawa, Canada, June 20/
Los Angeles Times,
6-21:(A)4.

Leon E. Panetta
Chief of Staff to President
of the United States Bill Clinton

2

[On Cuban President Fidel Castro's recent decision to allow Cubans to leave the country for the U.S., which has resulted in an immigration problem for the United States]: [A U.S. naval blockade is] obviously one of the options that we would look at in the future as we see whether or not Castro begins to make some legitimate movements toward democracy . . . We have got to continue to put pressure on Castro because the problem here is not the problem of refugees, it's not the problem of migrants, it's the problem with the Castro regime.

Broadcast interview/
"This Week With David Brinkley,"
ABC-TV, 8-21.

Jacques Parizeau
Premier-elect of Quebec, Canada

3

[On the election victory of his Parti Quebecois, which wants Quebec to separate from Canada]: We want to become a normal people and a normal country. Together, regardless of where we come from . . . we now begin a new chapter in our history.

Victory speech, Sept. 12/
The Christian Science Monitor,
10-3:9.

Ernesto Perez Balladares
Candidate for President of Panama

4

[On Panama's Democratric Revolutionary Party, the PRD, which he represents in his running for President of Panama in the current elections]: I understand it is difficult for many Americans to understand that a Party that was demonized in 1989 [when the U.S. invaded Panama to capture strongman Manuel Noriega], that was the political arm of a man portrayed as the anti-Christ [Noriega], is going to win [the current elections]. But the PRD before 1984 had nothing to do with what Noriega made it by 1989. It is diametrically opposed.

Interview/
The Washington Post,
5-9:(A)10.

Maurice Pinard
Professor of sociology,
McGill University (Canada)

5

[On the recent provincial-election victory of the Parti Quebecois, which wants to separate Quebec from the rest of Canada]: The PQ won a victory, it's in power, but certainly not the victory the polls predicted and the victory they wanted. If they can't win an election with more than 45 percent of the vote, how can they win a referendum [on Quebec separation from Canada]? It seems to me they're in real trouble on that.

Sept. 13/
Los Angeles Times,
9-14:(A)4.

Janet Reno
Attorney General
of the United States

6

[Criticizing Cuban President Fidel Castro's recent encouragement of Cubans to flee their country on small boats to head for the U.S.]: To divert the Cuban people from seeking a democratic

(JANET RENO)

change, the government of Cuba has resorted to the unconscionable tactic of letting people risk their lives by leaving in flimsy vessels through the treacherous waters of the Florida Straits. An uncontrolled exodus from Cuba will do nothing to address Cuba's internal problems. The solution to Cuba's problems is rapid, fundamental and far-reaching political and economic reform.

News conference,
Washington, D.C.,
Aug. 18/
The New York Times,
8-19:(A)10.

Roberto Robaina (Gonzalez)
Foreign Minister of Cuba

1

[On the increasing number of Cubans trying to flee to the U.S.]: If the United States is worried and wants to solve the problem, it is not enough just to keep Cubans from arriving. What promotes the exits . . . is the [U.S.] economic blockade imposed against our country. That's the bottom of the problem.

Newsweek, 8-29:24.

Ernesto Samper
President of Colombia

2

We have combatted—and we will continue to combat—drug trafficking because of our conviction, because of the serious damage that it has done to Colombian society . . . My government will be as bold and resolute in the eradication of illicit crops and the persecution of drug traffickers as it will be categorical in demanding effective action by [drug-consuming] nations in reducing demand and controlling money laundering.

Inaugural address,
Bogota, Colombia, Aug. 7/
Los Angeles Times,
8-8:(A)6.

Margaret E. Scranton
Political scientist and
authority on Panama,
University of Arkansas
(United States)

3

[On the scheduled turn-over of the Panama Canal by the U.S. to Panama by 1999]: This is Panama's historical moment. Panama must rise to the occasion. If they botch this, they will never forgive themselves, and the world community will never forgive them. The Panama Canal [would] become an interesting historical artifact, like the pyramids, like the dinosaurs.

Los Angeles Times,
6-6:(A)13.

Peter Smith
Authority on Mexico,
University of California,
San Diego

4

[On the forthcoming Presidential elections in Mexico]: These will be the most important, most contested, most transparent, most democratic, most observed, most judged and most criticized elections in Mexican history.

The Christian Science Monitor,
8-17:10.

Joaquin J. Vallarino
Chairman, Panamanian
Presidential commission drafting
a transitional plan
for managing the Panama Canal
when control passes from
the U.S. to Panama by 1999

5

[On skepticism about Panama's ability to run the Canal]: Many things were done badly . . . [on] both sides. The Panamanians themselves have doubts. They are frightened. But it is perfectly within the capacity of Panamanians [to manage the Canal], as long as it is not politicized.

Los Angeles Times,
6-6:(A)13.

Ernesto Zedillo (Ponce de Leon)
President of Mexico

1

The well-being of the Mexican family is in fact the central objective of my economic policy proposal. Until now, the well-being of the population has suffered from a lack of real economic growth and the concentration of wealth. Until very recently, the economy was stagnant and the population was growing, so we were trying to distribute the same size pie among more and more people. We now must make that pie grow faster than the population, so that there is real growth in wages and income.

Interview/
The New York Times,
12-1:(C)5.

2

[On his plan to share the power of Mexico's Presidency with the Mexican Congress]: I have decided that the power of the Presidency cannot and should not be an omnipotent power, an omniscient power, nor an omnipresent power. With this act, we start a new, different relationship between the legislative and executive powers of this country. I respect the autonomy of legislative power.

Before
Mexican Chamber
of Deputies,
Mexico City, Mexico/
The Christian Science Monitor,
12-28:19.

THE CRISIS IN HAITI

All of the quotations in this section relate to the situation in Haiti, whose elected President, Jean-Bertrand Aristide, was overthrown in a military coup in 1991 and who went into exile in the United States. This year, in response to increasing numbers of Haitians fleeing that country for the U.S. in flimsy boats and rafts to escape the ruling military junta, U.S. President Clinton threatened an American invasion of Haiti to oust the junta and restore Aristide. At the last moment, on September 18, a negotiated agreement was worked out for the junta to step down. And the invasion became a peaceful U.S. military landing.

Madeleine K. Albright
United States Ambassador/
Permanent Representative
to the United Nations

1

[On the UN vote to authorize an invasion]: [The message to junta leader Lt. Gen. Raoul Cedras is,] You can depart voluntarily and soon, or you can depart involuntarily and soon. The sun is setting on your ruthless ambition.
July 31/The Washington Post,
8-1:(A)1.

Jean-Bertrand Aristide
Exiled former President of Haiti

2

[Criticizing the U.S. policy of returning Haitians who flee their country by sea to escape the repression there]: The death toll rises weekly as those who support democracy in Haiti are murdered, tortured or forced to flee the repression that has gripped our country. When citizens of Haiti take to the seas to flee that repression, they are met by a floating Berlin Wall [of U.S. ships] that forces their return to the very captors they have fled.
Feb. 8/The Washington Post,
2-9:(A)17.

3

[On attacks by his opponents on his character and mental stability]: I am at peace with my consciousness. When you hear the voice of the nation, the huge majority [of Haitians] saying you are right, you feel natural. As a psychologist, I know that when people attack you, they use lies . . . But I know these things are not true. I am at peace . . . When I see character assassination, I don't pay attention.
Interview, Washington, D.C./
Current History, March:111.

4

[Criticizing the U.S. for not doing more to help the Haitian people and oust the military regime]: Every day [in Haiti], people are murdered, and pigs are eating their corpses. How many murders does it take to create a holocaust?
News conference,
Washington, D.C., April 21/
The Washington Post,
4-22:(A)37.

5

[Supporting the possible U.S. military intervention]: The action could be a surgical move to remove the thugs within hours. Once we do that,

(JEAN-BERTRAND ARISTIDE)

we could have the international community in the country within the framework of agreements we have already signed. Not in the framework of a military intervention . . . If I could do it alone, I would. If the United States could do it alone, they would. But we have to go together.

Interview,
Washington, D.C., June 2/
The New York Times,
6-3:(A)4.

1

Never, never, never would I agree to be re-stored to power by [a U.S.] invasion [of Haiti].

Newsweek, 7-18:47.

2

[On his exile in the U.S.]: The Presidency and exile have been a lesson for me. I learned that I am a leader, but also a statesman with grave responsibilities. It is easier to be a leader than a negotiator. It is easier to lead the Haitian people in Haiti than to represent them before the world community.

Interview/Time, 9-26:31.

3

[On U.S. officials who say he is intransigent when they try to help him in his desire to return to Haiti as President]: When I tell them I want justice for my people above all, they look at me as though I'm crazy. But that is the one thing I keep in my mind all the time. Idealism is a little bit alien to them.

Time, 9-26:32.

4

[Addressing U.S. President Clinton on the recent forcing from power by the U.S. of the Haitian junta, which will allow Aristide to return as

President]: Once again, the people of Haiti thank you for the leadership that you have demonstrated. You just said "bonne chance" [good luck] to Haiti, and we say "thank you so much."

At ceremony marking
his leaving for Haiti,
Washington, D.C.,
Oct. 14/
The New York Times,
10-15:4.

James A. Baker III
Former Secretary of State
of the United States

5

[Criticizing the U.S. Clinton Administration's handling of the situation in Haiti]: With Haiti, the Administration seems to have changed policies more often than most of us change our shirts—and it's July in Washington.

At forum on foreign policy
sponsored by the
Republican National Committee,
Washington, D.C., July 27/
Los Angeles Times,
7-28:(A)20.

6

[Saying the U.S. should support Jean-Bertrand Aristide, but that the U.S. should not invade Haiti to restore him to power]: [Those] who urge walking away [from him] because Aristide isn't our kind of democrat are wrong. If supporting democracy is a cornerstone of our foreign policy, which it is and should be, then you can't treat what democracy produces as a fruit salad, taking a raisin here while rejecting a pecan there. The test should be whether Aristide was chosen in a free and fair election. He was. Supporting him therefore is an American interest. [But] it isn't an interest that justifies war.

Time, 9-19:34.

Haley Barbour
Chairman,
Republican National Committee
(United States)

1

[On a possible U.S. invasion]: The overwhelming majority of Americans do not want the U.S. to invade Haiti. There is no good public-policy reason to invade Haiti. The U.S. has no national-security interest in Haiti. There is no excuse for invading Haiti. If they [the U.S. Democratic Party] think invading Haiti is going to help them politically, they need to rethink that position.

Los Angeles Times,
9-16:(A)9.

George Bush
Former President
of the United States

2

Aristide has proved to be totally unable to help facilitate his own return. He has been unwilling to compromise, and in attacking President Clinton's policies he is attacking those who have been trying to help him . . . We must never waver in our support for democracy. As President I felt that the way to support democracy in Haiti was to insist on the return of Aristide to power. Given recent events and Aristide's demonstrated instability, the time has come to break the linkage.

Interview/
The Christian Science Monitor,
5-4:9.

Jimmy Carter
Former President
of the United States

3

[On the just-reached agreement between Haiti's ruling military junta and a U.S. negotiating team, of which he was part, that calls for the junta to step down, thus averting a U.S. invasion of the island to remove the junta by force]: The key to our success, to the extent that it is success-

ful, was the inexorability of the entry of the forces into Haiti, and we spent the first hours of discussion with [Haiti's] military leaders to convince them that this was going to happen, it would be with an overwhelming capability and that the schedule was set and that we had no intention or authority to change the schedule. And it was that inevitability that was a major factor in their decision [to step down]. Another one, I should hasten to say, was their quandary about what to do that was right and honorable. Haiti is one of the proudest nations I have ever seen—because of their long history and because of the turmoil in which they have often lived. And it was difficult for Haitian military commanders to accept the proposition that foreign forces could come on their soil without their fighting. But we all worked to convince them that this was the best thing to do for their country and for their people.

News conference,
Washington, D.C., Sept. 19/
The New York Times,
9-20:(A)10.

Raoul Cedras
Lieutenant General,
Haitian Armed Forces;
Leader of military junta ruling Haiti

4

[On the possibility of a U.S. invasion]: If you intervene, it will mean bloodshed on both sides . . . Every [military] barracks [in Haiti] is filling up with young people who are fighting to sign up and get training because they know they must defend their country. It's not a matter of General Cedras. It's not a matter of Aristide. The matter is to defend Haiti.

U.S. broadcast interview/
Los Angeles Times,
8-8:(A)8.

5

[If the U.S. invades,] first you will have the resistance of the people, and then you will have a massacre, starting with a civil war. We have no

(RAOUL CEDRAS)

desire to kill Americans, but that is not the problem. We have the duty to defend our country. We are going to fight. A solution cannot be imposed [on] this country. What I'm interested in is not only the end of this crisis; it's the future of Haiti.

Interview/
The New York Times,
9-16:(A)6.

Dick Cheney
Former Secretary of Defense
of the United States

1

[Arguing against a possible U.S. invasion]: Why would we want to invade Haiti? And what are we going to do with it once we've got it? [Haiti] represents no significant threat to our interest nor is it an asset to U.S. policy.

At Republican
foreign-policy forum,
Washington, D.C., July 27/
The New York Times,
7-28:(A)4.

Warren Christopher
Secretary of State
of the United States

2

Our interests in Haiti are very strong ones. It is in our own back yard. Stability in the Caribbean and in the region really is dependent upon not having elected leaders overthrown by an illegitimate group of thugs.

Before Senate
Foreign Relations Committee,
Washington, D.C., June 30/
Los Angeles Times,
7-1:(A)14.

3

[On the current sanctions against Haiti being used to try to remove the military junta]: I think we need to see if the sanctions won't work. The new, enhanced sanctions have only been in effect for a limited period of time. Clearly nobody thinks the use of [U.S. military] force is the most attractive action [to oust the junta] . . . It may come to that, but [U.S. President Clinton] has not made that decision. He is continuing to go forward with the [sanctions], trying to put the maximum amount of pressure on the illegal government.

Jerusalem, Israel, July 19/
Los Angeles Times,
7-20:(A)1.

4

For 200 years, Haiti had totalitarian or repressive regimes. In 1990, for the first time in their 200-year history, they had a free and open election. They chose a President—[Jean-Bertrand] Aristide—who won by more than two thirds of the votes. The United States was very supportive of that election; we sent monitors and it was really an election that we took a lot of pride in. So it was especially sad for us when, a few months later, the elected government was overthrown by a military regime. This was condemned at the time by [U.S. President George] Bush and Secretary of State [James] Baker; and that produced a period in which the United States, both that Administration and this [Clinton Administration], did everything it could by way of diplomatic steps and sanctions and so forth to try to restore the democratic regime. The stakes are very high for us in Haiti, and we have many important interests there. Perhaps the most important to me is our interest in the promotion of democracy in this hemisphere. Only two countries in this hemisphere are not democratic [Haiti and Cuba], but many, many countries in both Central and South America, and in the Caribbean, are really fragile democracies. If we were to show that we are willing to stand by and permit a military regime to overthrow this democracy [in Haiti] and do nothing about it, I think it would have bad ramifications.

Interview/
"Interview" magazine,
November:73.

Bill Clinton
President of the United States

1

[On U.S. asylum policy toward Haitians fleeing their country on makeshift boats]: I have become increasingly concerned that Haiti's declining human-rights situation may endanger the safety of those who have valid fears of political persecution, who flee by boat, and who are then returned to Haiti, where they are met at the docks by Haitian authorities before they can be referred to in-country processing [by U.S. officials in Haiti]. Therefore, I have decided to modify our procedures. We will continue to interdict all Haitian migrants at sea, but we will determine aboard ship or in other countries which ones are bona fide political refugees. Those who are not will still be returned to Haiti, but those who are will be provided refuge. We will also approach other countries to seek their participation in this humanitarian endeavor.

May 8/
The New York Times,
7-6:(A)4.

2

Let me remind you all of what our interests are [in Haiti]: We have Americans living and working there, several thousand of them. We have a million Haitian-Americans in this country who have family and friends there. We have an interest in promoting democracy in our hemisphere. We have an interest in stabilizing those democracies that are in our hemisphere. For the first time ever, 33 of the 35 nations in the Caribbean and Central and South America are governed by popularly elected leaders, but many of those democracies are fragile. As we look ahead to the next century, we need a strong and democratic Latin America and Central America and Caribbean with which to trade and grow. So those are our fundamental interests.

News conference,
Washington, D.C., Aug. 3/
The New York Times,
8-4:(A)10.

3

[Saying the U.S. will invade Haiti to remove the military junta there if they will not leave of their own accord]: Haiti's dictators, led by General Raoul Cedras, control the most violent regime in our hemisphere. For three years they have rejected every peaceful solution that the international community has proposed. They have broken an agreement that they made to give up power. They have brutalized their people and destroyed their economy. And for three years we and other nations have worked exhaustively to find a diplomatic solution, only to have the dictators reject each one. Now the United States must protect our interests; to stop the brutal atrocities that threaten tens of thousands of Haitians; to secure our borders [from Haitian refugees]; and to preserve stability and promote democracy in our hemisphere; and to uphold the reliability of the commitments we make and the commitments others make to us . . . The message of the United States to the Haitian dictators is clear: Your time is up. Leave now or we will force you from power.

Broadcast address to the nation,
Washington, D.C., Sept. 15/
The New York Times,
9-16:(A)5.

4

[On the just-reached agreement between Haiti's ruling military junta and a U.S. negotiating team that calls for the junta to step down, thus averting a U.S. invasion]: In the end, two things led to the agreement [that the junta] leave. The first was this delegation's appeal to the Haitians to do the right and honorable thing for their own people in accordance with United Nations Security Council resolutions. The second was the clear imminence of military action by the United States. This is a good agreement. It will further our goals in Haiti. [Junta leader General Raoul] Cedras and the other leaders will leave power no later than October 15th. After three years and a series of broken promises, American steadfastness has given us the opportunity to restore Haiti's democratically elected government and President Aristide . . .This

(BILL CLINTON)

[U.S. military] mission [in Haiti] will be limited in time and scope. It is clearly designed to provide a secure environment for the restoration of President Aristide and democracy, to begin the work of retraining the police and the military in a professional manner and to facilitate a quick handoff to the United Nations mission so that the work of restoring democracy can be continued, the developmental aid can begin to flow, Haiti can be rebuilt and, in 1995, another free and fair election for President can be held.

News conference,
Washington, D.C., Sept. 19/
The New York Times,
9-20:(A)10.

1

[On whether it is necessary for the President to obtain consent of Congress to engage U.S. forces in foreign military action—such as the current mission in Haiti, for which he did not get Congressional consent]: With regard to the consent of Congress, I think that every President and all my predecessors in both parties have clearly maintained that they—by [the] Constitution—did not have to have Congressional approval for every kind of military action. I obviously think the bigger and more prolonged the action, the better it is to have Congressional approval. If you look at the pattern of my two immediate predecessors [George Bush and Ronald Reagan], there was Congressional approval sought [by Bush] in the Desert Storm [1991's Persian Gulf war] operation, where there was a five-and-a-half-month buildup and a half a million troops on the other side. [But] there was not Congressional approval in advance of [Bush's] actions in Panama and [Reagan's in] Grenada. So I think that we will have to take that on a case-by-case basis. In terms of popular approval, the American people, probably wisely, are almost always against any kind of military action when they first hear about it, unless our people have been directly attacked. And they have historically felt that way;

and obviously at the end of the Cold War, they may be more inclined to feel that way. The job of the President is to try to do what is right.

News conference,
Washington, D.C., Sept 19/
The New York Times,
9-20:(A)10.

2

[On the recent forcing from office by the U.S. of the Haitian junta]: Let's look at what has happened in the last four weeks. We have restored democracy, the military dictators have stepped down, the military dictators have left Haiti. President Aristide is rebuilding his government, the economy is beginning to be rebuilt, people are being put to work at rebuilding the country. This is a signal triumph for the [U.S.] men and women in uniform who are down there [in Haiti] and the work that they have done. And it is a very important lesson in what can be done to promote democracy and to end human-rights abuses.

News conference,
Washington, D.C., Oct. 21/
The New York Times,
10-22:4.

Charles David
Former Foreign Minister of Haiti

3

[On Aristide's forthcoming return as President]: [He] knows nothing about administration. He can exploit the problems of this country, but he can't solve them.

U. S. News & World Report,
10-24:54.

Robert J. Dole
United States Senator, R-Kansas

4

[Arguing against a possible U.S. invasion]: Before invading Haiti, the [Clinton Administration] has checked in with the United Nations Security Council, but I would also hope they check in with Congress. International support is fine, but

(ROBERT J. DOLE)

it is no substitute for the support of Congress and the American people . . . There is no emergency in Haiti requiring the dispatch of American troops.

Washington, D.C., Aug. 1/
Los Angeles Times,
8-2:(A)8.

Victor Flores (Olea)
Mexican Ambassador/
Permanent Representative
to the United Nations

1

[Arguing against a possible U.S. invasion]: There are not sufficient elements to justify the broad use of force and even less to give across-the-board [UN] authorization for the actions of poorly defined multinational forces.

At United Nations,
New York, July 31/
Los Angeles Times,
8-1:(A)14.

Steven Forester
Attorney,
Haitian Refugee Center
(United States)

2

[Criticizing the U.S. policy of turning away Haitian boat people trying to land in the U.S.]: There should be no more repatriations to Haiti and no more interdictions at sea [by the U.S. Coast Guard]. To send terrified people back to Haiti at a time when the streets [there] are littered with bodies of victims of the military is like sending Jews back to Nazi Germany.

Miami, Fla., April 22/
The New York Times,
4-23:4.

Bob Graham
United States Senator,
D-Florida

3

[On the possibility of a U.S. invasion]: The best solution, of course, would be if they [the Haitian military leaders] would just salute and march off to wherever old dictators go. But it's not likely to happen. The choices will be surrender or invasion, and given the choices, I think we should invade . . . If word gets out that the United States is not committed to protect democracy in Haiti, we will see a rash of threats to new democracies in the rest of the Western Hemisphere.

Newsweek, 7-18:46.

4

[Saying it is important that the U.S. not allow the ruling military junta in Haiti to stay in power]: When it appears as if the democracies are willing to accommodate and placate a dictatorship, it emboldens other dictatorships. I believe that one of the reasons [Cuban President Fidel] Castro picked August of 1994 to open the floodgates again [and allow Cubans to flee toward the U.S.] . . . is in part because he observed what we have thus far failed to do in Haiti.

USA Today, 9-9:(A)5.

William H. Gray III
United States Special Envoy
for Haiti

5

[On the newly increased U.S. sanctions on Haiti aimed at forcing the military dictatorship there to step down]: We believe these sanctions can work, just as sanctions worked in South Africa, once the coup leaders see that we are serious about enforcing them. Most of these actions have been in effect for less than four weeks. Before May 21 [when earlier UN sanctions were in effect], you didn't have any real sanctions. So it's too early to tell what the substantive impact [of these new sanctions] is . . . But already, we have seen some people rush to get out of Haiti and others rush to ship

WHAT THEY SAID IN 1994

(WILLIAM H. GRAY III)

money and packages to their families in Haiti. So
they are having both a physical and psychological
impact.

Interview,
Washington, D.C./
Los Angeles Times,
6-15:(A)12.

1

[Criticizing suggestions that the U.S. should
not become involved in Haiti to reinstate Aristide
as President]: Democracy is not me sitting here
telling the people of another country—who [in
1990] had a free and fair election and 70 percent
voted one way [for Aristide]—that they didn't
know what they were doing. I find it interesting
that we want to apply all these new different standards of democracy to other countries that we
would not tolerate here [in the U.S.], nor would
we tolerate in any Western industrialized world.
The real question is, are we going to nurture democracy? I think our job in foreign policy ought
to be, where we can, to make a difference. The
difference between [the conflict in] Bosnia and [the
situation in Haiti] is that we can make a difference
[in Haiti].

Interview, July 19/
USA Today,
7-20:(A)11.

Judd Gregg
United States Senator,
R-New Hampshire

2

[Arguing against a U.S. invasion]: As far as I
can see, there is no [U.S.] national interest in Haiti.
If the United States wants to invade Haiti for immigration reasons [to stem the flow of Haitians
fleeing their country for the U.S.], why not invade
Mexico [to stop illegal Mexican immigration to
the U.S.]? If we want to invade Haiti for democratic reasons, why not invade Cuba?

Newsweek, 7-18:47.

Alcee L. Hastings
United States Representative,
D-Florida

3

[Supporting the use of force by the U.S. to
oust Haiti's ruling military junta]: We should stabilize Haiti or we'll have to stabilize [fleeing]
Haitians in Miami, Washington and elsewhere. It's
different from [the war in] Bosnia. The folk aren't
leaving Bosnia and coming here. Haitians are leaving and coming to Florida, and it affects our
schools, our hospitals, our jails.

The Washington Post,
5-6:(A)14.

Jesse Helms
United States Senator,
R-North Carolina

4

[Arguing against a possible U.S. invasion]: I
don't believe that there is any vital national interest or strategic reason for the United States to risk
even one life of one American service person to
restore Aristide to power. If we do invade, and
that first body bag comes out, that's when all hell
is going to break loose [in the U.S. against that
policy].

At Senate Foreign Relations
Committee hearing,
Washington, D.C., June 30/
Los Angeles Times,
7-1:(A)14.

5

[Saying President Clinton should not have sent
U.S. troops into Haiti]: They ought never to have
been sent in there in the first place. I don't think
it's been a successful operation [keeping the peace
after the junta left and Aristide returned]. And furthermore, I think it's disgraceful that we have U.S.
troops collecting garbage in Haiti.

Broadcast interview,
Washington, D.C./
"Evans & Novak,"
CNN-TV, 11-18.

Emile Jonassaint
President of Haiti

1

[Criticizing a possible U.S. invasion]: The battle of Haiti is being prepared. We shall fight it with all our strength and all the means at our disposal . . . Here we are at a point where war is openly declared on a state threatening no one, nor international peace and security. Today Haiti, tomorrow what other sovereign state?

Broadcast address,
Port-au-Prince, Haiti,
Aug. 1/
The New York Times,
8-2:(A)3.

Henry A. Kissinger
Former Secretary of State
of the United States

2

[Arguing against a possible U.S. invasion]: I do not favor a military invasion, because I can't describe the threat Haiti presents to the United States.

At Richard Nixon
Presidential Library,
Yorba Linda, Calif.,
July 20/
Los Angeles Times,
7-21:(A)18.

Raymond Lafontant
Executive director,
Association of Haitian Industries

3

The real economic problems of Haiti are so profound that we need more than infrastructure, more than even reorganizing. We need assistance in organizing a civil society.

U.S. News & World Report,
10-24:55.

Georges Leger
Former Haitian Ambassador
to the United States

4

[Criticizing U.S. policy toward Haiti's military dictatorship]: People are laughing at the Americans because they have been so inconsistent. Nobody believes in any of this [U.S. threats against the military leaders] anymore. If [President] Clinton had sent in a few Marines earlier on, that would have been the end of it, but they never wanted to grab the bull by the horns and tell [Haitian leader General Raoul] Cedras enough is enough.

The New York Times,
4-1:(A)4.

Robert Malval
Acting Prime Minister of Haiti

5

[Saying Haitian military government leader General Raoul Cedras should resign or face being removed by force by a possible U.S. invasion]: He thinks he can outsmart the world. I got news for him. He will be forced to resign without amnesty and he must bear in mind he will have the fate of [former Panamanian leader Manuel] Noriega [who was ousted and captured in a U.S. invasion several years ago] . . . When the people who are maintaining order are promoting disorders, there is no other choice [but U.S. invasion] . . . There is nothing [else] left.

Interview, Port-au-Prince, Haiti/
USA Today, 6-7:(A)4.

Michael Mandelbaum
Professor of American foreign policy,
School of Advanced International Studies,
Johns Hopkins University (United States)

6

[On the possibility of a U.S. invasion]: The whole issue of military intervention is more difficult since the end of the Cold War . . . and the generals in Haiti know that. It doesn't help that

(MICHAEL MANDELBAUM)

we pulled out of Somalia. Neither does it help that half the [U.S.] Congress and half the country don't want to intervene . . . And it doesn't help that our interest in Haiti is not as clear as it could be . . . The American public has been willing to shed blood if it had something to do with self-defense. But that rationale is gone now . . . There's an argument that can be made now that invading Haiti would be good for U.S. credibility. But how important that credibility is depends on what the stakes are . . . And since the Cold War, the stakes just don't seem as big as they used to be.

Los Angeles Times,
7-8:(A)11.

1

Looking beyond the immediate issue of [President] Clinton's credibility, invading Haiti doesn't have anything to do with U.S. vital interests as traditionally defined. This kind of intervention makes sense only as a prelude to a 5- to 10-year exercise in nation-building—in trying to straighten Haiti out and make it a stable and viable country. But I don't think the American public, in its present inward-looking mood, is prepared to accept that . . . [If the U.S. does invade, there would be] 10 scary minutes, the actual invasion; 10 easy weeks, the immediate, self-congratulatory aftermath; and 10 very difficult years, making Haiti into a modern state.

Interview/
The Washington Post,
9-12:(A)14.

Kweisi Mfume
United States Representative,
D-Maryland

2

[Criticizing U.S. President Clinton's changing policies on how to deal with Haiti]: [Washington cannot] continue a back-and-forth, up-and-down, in-and-out policy on Haiti and expect to have any measure of respect in the world community.

Newsweek, 7-18:46.

Sam Nunn
United States Senator,
D-Georgia

3

Returning one man [Aristide], even though elected and even though he certainly should and will be returned, is not democracy. Democracy involves institutions. Democracy involves an elected parliament. I hope the focal point of our foreign policy can be, in addition to returning President Aristide, free and fair elections of a parliament. Democracies don't work unless minorities are protected. In Haiti today, when you lose an election, there is a fear of the minority that they may lose their lives. That fear has to be dealt with through a parliamentary election and protection under the Constitution with an independent judicial system. So this is going to be the challenge ahead for the Haitian people.

News conference
upon returning from Haiti
as part of a U.S. delegation
that negotiated
the stepping-down of the junta,
Washington, D.C.,
Sept. 19/
The New York Times,
9-20:(A)10.

David R. Obey
United States Representative,
D-Wisconsin

4

[Saying the U.S. should invade Haiti to oust the military leaders]: [We should get rid of] that useless, sick, poor excuse for a government. Haitians are being ground up like hamburger because the clowns who run that government don't know how to behave like adults. [Haiti] isn't a country anymore, it's a condition.

At House Foreign Operations
Subcommittee hearing,
Washington, D.C., April 14/
USA Today,
4-15:(A)4.

Leon E. Panetta
Chief of Staff to
President of the United States
Bill Clinton

1

The arguments [for a U.S. invasion] are there. A military dictatorship in our back yard, impacting clearly on our policies . . . affecting not only U.S. citizens but a huge number of Haitian refugees impacting on policies of our country. So for all those reasons, it is a matter of national interest in the United States.

Interview,
Washington, D.C., Aug. 1/
Los Angeles Times,
8-2:(A)1.

Evans Paul
Mayor of
Port-au-Prince, Haiti

2

The root problem in Haiti, despite its poverty, is political and not economic. The problem is the minority wants to own everything. There is no negotiation. In Haiti, those with power refuse to negotiate, and without negotiations we cannot do anything.

The Washington Post,
9-19:(A)18.

3

[On Aristide's forthcoming return as President]: Even if one doesn't like Aristide, one is obliged to work with him. Even if Aristide doesn't like others, he'll be obliged to work with them. We are in a country where everything is polarized [and many politicians] are opportunists. But sometimes you need opportunists to permit you to implement your program. I think that if we have to make an alliance with the Devil, we do it for the well-being of the country.

Interview/
U.S. News & World Report,
10-24:55.

Donald M. Payne
United States Representative,
D-New Jersey

4

[On the U.S. Congressional Black Caucus, of which he is a member, and its stand on possible U.S. military intervention in Haiti]: We have not been, generally speaking, a group that supported gun-barrel diplomacy. But we are seeing a changing world. I don't think any of the members of the Caucus initially supported military intervention and there are still some who oppose it. But I do think the majority of the members are slowly moving toward the point where it might be the only solution at the present time.

The New York Times,
7-14:(A)6.

Lawrence Pezzullo
Former United States
Special Envoy to Haiti

5

[On a CIA report that says Aristide is a psychotic]: What I saw was not a psychopathic maniac but a rigid, narrow person who does not have the courage to make decisions and is incapable of compromise.

Newsweek, 9-19:37.

Colin L. Powell
General, United States Army (Ret.);
Former Chairman,
Joint Chiefs of Staff

6

[On the just-reached agreement between Haiti's ruling military junta and a U.S. negotiating team, of which he was part, that calls for the junta to step down, thus averting a U.S. invasion]: [We conveyed] to the Haitian leaders the inevitability of the arrival of U.S. forces and [encouraged] them to cooperate so that arrival would take place in a peaceful way. And I think the role that I may have played with some effect is to appeal to their sense of what is right and what is wrong at

(COLIN L. POWELL)

this particular point in their history. And we had long and painful conversations, and there was a lot of emotion in the room, but we kept coming back to that point: What is best for the people of Haiti? What is best for the future of Haiti? And at the end of the day, that worked.

News conference,
Washington, D.C., Sept. 19/
The New York Times,
9-20:(A)10.

Dan Quayle
Former Vice President
of the United States

1

[Criticizing President Clinton for considering using U.S. military force]: He is responding to the left wing of the [U.S.] Democratic Party. When you're President of the United States, you cannot govern by emotion, especially in foreign policy . . . This is life or death . . . This is [deciding] whether we're going to risk American men and women serving our country, to return Aristide to power . . . If Bill Clinton uses the military, he feels perhaps this solves some of his domestic [political] problems . . . If he invades, it's going to dominate the news for weeks, and perhaps months. It is wrong.

To reporters,
Washington, D.C., May 13/
The Christian Science Monitor,
5-16:7.

Roberto Robaina (Gonzalez)
Foreign Minister of Cuba

2

[Criticizing the current U.S. military mission in Haiti aimed at ousting the military junta and restoring Aristide to power]: The cannons of the invaders and the boots of the foreign occupants were the ones that installed in Haiti the dictatorships of this century and trained and supported

those who are still tyrannizing their people. How then can we trust that they will encourage democracy in the future? The evils of the Third World are not resolved through [foreign] military occupations, which are just used to serve selfish interests.

At United Nations,
New York, Oct. 3/
The New York Times,
10-4:(A)3.

Brent Scowcroft
Former Assistant to the President
of the United States
(Gerald Ford and George Bush)
for National Security Affairs

3

[Arguing against a possible U.S. invasion]: Let's go back and focus on democracy [for Haiti], not on Aristide . . . Let's organize new elections [and] start over again. We've done our best. The UN vote [authorizing an invasion] shows that the world is less than enthusiastic about what we want to do. There's even less enthusiasm in Latin America. Therefore, we need to take a different course [than an invasion].

Interview,
Washington, D.C., Aug. 2/
The Christian Science Monitor,
8-3:3.

John M. Shalikashvili
General, United States Army;
Chairman, Joint Chiefs of Staff

4

[Saying he believes Haitian military leader Lt. Gen. Raoul Cedras will leave Haiti as a result of the recent U.S. military intervention]: I cannot see how, with such animosity toward Cedras and [his] no longer having the protection of the tough military and oppressive police, how he imagines that he will live in that country when it's free and when people will remember all that he was responsible for . . . I would be hard pressed to imagine that a

(JOHN M. SHALIKASHVILI)

single American soldier would be asked to risk his life to protect General Cedras.

Broadcast interview/
"Face the Nation,"
CBS-TV, 9-25.

Robert G. Torricelli
United States Representative,
D-New Jersey

1

[Arguing against a possible U.S. invasion]: We're all sympathetic with the restoration of democracy in Haiti. But I cannot for the life of me see how this becomes the responsibility of the United States.

Los Angeles Times,
9-16:(A)9.

James A. Traficant
United States Representative,
D-Ohio

2

[Saying Aristide should show more gratitude than he has about the recent U.S. deployment of forces to Haiti to oust the military junta there and reinstall Aristide]: While America is spending a half a billion dollars over there to help straighten out Haiti, we have 40 million Americans without health care. American workers are absolutely worried about their next paycheck, how they are going to pay their mortgage off. I say enough is enough. Maybe Congress should hand Aristide an

M-16 [rifle] and have him take care of business for himself.

Before the House,
Washington, D.C./
The New York Times,
9-22:(A)9.

Robert White
President,
Center for International Policy
(United States)

3

[The Clinton Administration] can't walk away from Aristide. But they can't move forward because they are not willing to say "or else" to the [Haitian] military. The administration is like a deer caught in the headlights.

U.S. News & World Report,
2-28:22.

R. James Woolsey, Jr.
Director of Central Intelligence
of the United States

4

Haiti is a country wherein there has been and continues to be a lot of violence. I think if you and I had sitting here before us all of the work that we had done on Haiti, and you look at some of the possible strongmen down there, and some of their behavior and conduct in the past, both you and I would agree that, as individuals, a national policy for the United States of supporting President Aristide—who has been elected by two-thirds of the people of Haiti—was a reasonable policy.

Interview, Washington, D.C./
Los Angeles Times, 1-2:(M)3.

Asia and the Pacific

Askar Akayev
President of Kyrgyzstan

1

[On independent Kyrgyzstan, which used to be a Soviet republic]: We in Kyrgyzstan have already achieved certain successes in pouring the foundation for democratic society, the purpose of which is to defend mankind, his integrity, his freedom and his interests.

The Christian Science Monitor,
5-4:14.

Ronald Aqua
Vice President,
U.S.-Japan Foundation

2

[On the U.S. Clinton Administration's trade negotiations with Japan aimed at allowing more U.S. goods to be sold in that country]: In a nutshell, I have a feeling the Clinton people have become like the proverbial mouse trapped in a corner by a cat. They don't know which way to run.

Los Angeles Times,
2-11:(A)5.

Lloyd N. Bentsen
Secretary of the Treasury
of the United States

3

[On Asia's economic boom]: Here is some [numbers] I think hit home. In Asia—excluding Japan—they will spend a trillion dollars in infrastructure of all types in the next decade . . . If I were 30 years younger, I know what market I'd want to be in. I'm from Texas; I'm used to big. But it is difficult to comprehend how big that market is and how those economies are transforming . . . Asia is a continent that economically could be larger than Europe and the United States combined within the next 50 years. By the year 2000, even leaving Japan out, some 75 million Asian households will have incomes comparable to middle-income Americans. We are talking about econo-

mies that make up half of the world's output . . . To keep growth up, there has to be financing behind it. The Asians have high savings rates; I admire them; I am envious of them. But they are not that high to pay [for their economic expansion plans]. Corporate retained earnings won't do it. Borrowing at the local bank won't do it. They need outside capital.

To business people,
Los Angeles, Calif., March 18/
The New York Times, 3-19:1,18.

Sandy Berger
Deputy Assistant to President
of the United States Bill Clinton
for National Security Affairs

4

[Defending U.S. President Clinton's decision to renew most-favored-nation trade status for China despite that country's continuing negative record on human rights]: [The President had to decide whether to sever] a $40-billion [trade] relationship that has enormous importance to the security and economic [interests of the U.S., or] whether we pursue human rights better through a policy of contact, of engagement, in which we press the human-rights agenda but not through threatening to sever the entire relationship.

Broadcast interview/
"Good Morning America,"
ABC-TV, 5-27.

Bill Bradley
United States Senator,
D-New Jersey

5

[Although economic] growth alone will not democratize China, it creates a fluid political and social environment and the emergence of a class of prosperous Chinese—all of which fuel democratization. Evidence from South Korea and Taiwan shows that prosperity breaks down old controls and generates demands for improved political and social conditions.

Time, 6-6:26

.Anson Chan
Chief Secretary of Hong Kong

1

[Supporting changes in Hong Kong's government that would expand democratic rule with an eye toward the 1997 date when Hong Kong comes under Chinese control]: The Legislative Council stands on the brink of one of the most momentous decisions in its history. It is paramount that there is confidence both in Hong Kong and internationally that the rule of law will continue after 1997, and that is best assured by an electoral system that is free and fair.

Hong Kong, June 30/
The New York Times,
6-30:(A)4.

Chan Heng Chee
Director, Institute of
Southeast Asian Studies
(Singapore)

2

[Criticizing U.S. lecturing to Asian nations about human rights and democracy]: For the first time, there is an open debate going on between Asia and America [on these issues]. There is an aggressive Western agenda [the U.S. is] putting forth on democracy and human rights, and this has provoked a response from us . . . Human rights is used to justify so many other fights that it's beginning to lose its validity as an argument.

The Washington Post,
4-22:(A)33.

Jean Chretien
Prime Minister of Canada

3

[On his policy of increasing Canada's trade with China, despite that country's negative record on human rights]: If I were to say to China, "We are not dealing with you anymore," they . . . would not feel threatened by Canada. I'm the Prime Minister of a country of 28 million people. He [Chinese leader Jiang Zemin] is the President of a coun-try with 1.2 billion . . . Am I supposed to tell the President of China what to do?

The Christian Science Monitor,
3-25:9.

Warren Christopher
Secretary of State
of the United States

4

[On whether the U.S. would accept North Korea having even one nuclear weapon]: I don't see that at the present time, because our goal is to have that peninsula be nuclear-free. That's the goal we're pursuing and I do not see an acceptance of that. I do not see us sort of relaxing and finding nuclear weapons in the hands of North Korea. It would not be something that we would find an agreeable phenomenon by any means.

Interview, Jan. 5/
USA Today,
1-6:(A)15.

5

[On China]: I would say, from our standpoint, the progress they've made on their economy, while laudable, does not excuse the failure to make progress on the human-rights record. A number of people have said, "Look, they're doing so well on the economy, you ought to forget about the human-rights record." That's not my position. It's not [U.S. President Clinton's] position.

Broadcast interview,
Geneva, Switzerland/
"Meet the Press,"
NBC-TV, 1-16.

6

[Criticizing Japan's reluctance to heed U.S. desires that it open up its markets to U.S. products]: For the world's two largest economies, agreeing to disagree is not good enough. We must not allow a situation to persist that might eventually erode public and political support for our overall relationship . . . We cannot let political dead-

(WARREN CHRISTOPHER)

lock or bureaucratic inertia or outdated thinking stand in the way.

Before Keizai Doyukai business group, Tokyo, Japan, March 11/ The New York Times, 3-11:(C)1.

1

[If the Chinese are at all forthcoming on improving human rights,] I would look forward to a situation in which (MFN) is continued [by the U.S.], but continued on a basis where its renewal can be more routine than it's been over a period of the last four years. Depending on the nature of the progress made, we are prepared to work out techniques that will achieve that result. If there is progress, I think we can all look forward to the time when human rights and [the MFN issue] is put away from the center of the relationship.

Before American Chamber of Commerce, Beijing, China, March 13/ The Washington Post, 3-14:(A)14.

2

[Saying China would not interfere with U.S. efforts to keep North Korea from acquiring a nuclear arsenal]: I think China has the same interest that we have in having a non-nuclear peninsula. I would say that if we work at it carefully and patiently in the United Nations and bring the Chinese along, that they will not block the imposition of sanctions [against North Korea]. That's maybe a little different than agreeing to them, but they'll not block them,

Broadcast interview/ "Face the Nation," CBS-TV, 3-20.

3

[On North Korea's belligerent attitude and its possible development of nuclear weapons]: We've

made it clear to North Korea that it must become a responsible member of the international community or that community will have no choice but to pursue other options. Our commitment to South Korea's security remains firm. We're prepared to take all necessary steps to insure that the North does not misread our determination to deter aggression.

Before Senate Foreign Relations Committee, Washington, D.C., March 22/ The New York Times, 3-23:(A)4.

Bill Clinton
President of the United States

4

[Announcing the lifting of the U.S. trade embargo against Vietnam that was enacted following the Vietnam war of the 1970s]: From the beginning of my Administration, I have said that any decisions about our relationships with Vietnam should be guided by one factor and one factor only—gaining the fullest possible accounting for our prisoners of war and our missing-in-action. We owe that to all who served in Vietnam and to the families of those whose fate remains unknown. Today I am lifting the trade embargo against Vietnam because I am absolutely convinced it offers the best way to resolve the fate of those who remain missing and about whom we are not sure . . . Whatever the Vietnam war may have done in dividing our country in the past, today our nation is one in honoring those who served and pressing for answers about all those who did not return. This decision today, I believe, renews that commitment and our constant, constant effort never to forget those until our job is done.

At White House ceremony, Washington, D.C., Feb. 3/ The New York Times, 2-4:(A)6.

5

[On the failure of the U.S. and Japan to agree on how to increase U.S. penetration of the Japanese marketplace]: [Japan's markets] still remain

(BILL CLINTON)

less open to imports than any other [major nation's. Japan still] screens out many of our products, even our most competitive products. [But] it is better to have reached no agreement than to have reached an empty agreement.

News conference,
Washington, D.C./
Time, 2-21:41.

1

[Saying he is renewing China's most-favored-nation trade status, despite the continuing negative human-rights record in China and despite criticism of the decision by many in the U.S.]: That linkage [between MFN and human rights] has been constructive during the past year, but I believe, based on our aggressive contacts with the Chinese in the past several months, that we have reached the end of the usefulness of that [linkage] policy ... We need to place our relationship into a larger and more productive framework ... To those who argue that in view of China's human-rights abuses we should revoke MFN status, let me ask you the same question that I have asked myself over and over these last few weeks as I have studied this issue and consulted people of both parties who have had experience with China over many decades: Will we do more to advance the cause of human rights if China is isolated, or if our nations are engaged in a growing web of political and economic cooperation and contacts?

Washington, D.C., May 26/
Los Angeles Times,
5-27:(A)16.

2

[On North Korea's possible development of nuclear weapons]: This is an issue which is very important to the long-term security of the United States. The question of a country that belongs to the non-proliferation regime deciding to become a nuclear power, the prospect that a nuclear capacity could be transferred, either by design or by accident, to other countries or to rogue groups—

this is a very serious thing for our long-term security. And we have spent a lot of time to make sure we are firm and deliberate.

News conference,
Washington, D.C., Aug. 3/
The New York Times,
8-4:(A)10.

3

[On the just-signed agreement between the U.S. and North Korea aimed at defusing the dispute over North Korea's possible development of nuclear weapons]: [It is] a good deal for the United States. The United States and international inspectors will carefully monitor North Korea to make sure it keeps its commitments. Only as it does so will North Korea fully join the community of nations.

News conference,
Washington, D.C., Oct. 21/
The New York Times,
10-22:7.

Barber B. Conable
Former President,
International Bank
for Reconstruction and
Development (World Bank)

4

[On whether the U.S. should try to block World Bank loans to China because of that country's human-rights record]: The U.S. cannot organize the World Bank when everyone else in the world wants to deal with China up to their smiling chops.

U.S. News & World Report,
5-30:41.

Dalai Lama
Exiled former ruler of Tibet

5

[Saying China is increasing its suppression of Tibet]: Time is running out. [China's intent] is to suppress [Tibetans] completely and in the mean-

(DALAI LAMA)

time to increase the Chinese population [in Tibet] so that in a few years' time, the Tibetans become insignificant in their own land. Some of my friends call this the "Final Solution" of the Tibet issue.

Interview,
Dharamsala, India/
Los Angeles Times,
5-13:(A)11.

1

If something happened today to me, or my life were to cease, if the Tibetan people want another reincarnation or want another Dalai Lama, then certainly my reincarnation, my rebirth will take place among Tibetans. And not among Chinese [who now rule Tibet]. Because the real purpose of reincarnation is continuing the previous life's work. That means while we are outside [Tibet], if I pass away, then certainly if the Tibetan people want another reincarnation, they will find it among Tibetans, and not in Chinese hands. But if death takes place at the time when we have already returned to Tibet [after its liberation from Chinese control], and there is some kind of freedom there, I have officially stated that the Tibetan people should decide whether the institution of the Dalai Lama should continue or not. If people feel there's not much relevant about this institution, then it will automatically cease. That's no problem.

Interview,
Dharamsala, India/
Los Angeles Times,
5-15:(M)3.

Mou-Shih Ding
Taiwanese Ambassador
to the United States

2

[Calling for the UN to allow Taiwan to join that organization]: The ROC's participation in the

United Nations would enhance that organization's relevance in today's environment. We believe it would also lend credibility to the body as a truly representative global forum. And it could significantly bolster its assets. My government would be prepared to make fair and equitable contributions to the United Nations' resources and its international missions. My country's bid for participation does not challenge the Peking [Chinese] authorities' place in the United Nations, but simply asks for a recognition of reality and fairness by the world community for the 21 million people of the Republic of China on Taiwan. We ourselves acknowledge that our jurisdiction does not currently extend to the Chinese mainland, just as that of the Peking authorities does not extend to Taiwan. While we are firmly committed to the eventual reunification of China, we are entitled in the interim to equal representation in international organizations like the UN. Our participation would not perpetuate or institutionalize the present de facto division of China; the precedents already set by UN membership of East and West Germany prior to unification and by North and South Korea refute that notion. To the contrary, our simultaneous involvement in this and other international forums will actually help facilitate communication and cooperation across the Taiwan Strait. This, too, serves everyone's interests.

Interview/
Nation's Business,
October:56.

Robert J. Dole
United States Senator,
R-Kansas

3

[Criticizing U.S. President Clinton's handling of the problem of North Korea's possible development of nuclear weapons]: North Korea, determined to possess a nuclear capability, is offered an ever-expanding bundle of concessions [if it will

(ROBERT J. DOLE)

stop nuclear development]—as if it is another poor, Third World country misunderstood by the West.

At Conservative
Political Action Conference,
Washington, D.C., Feb. 10/
The Washington Post,
2-11:(A)14.

Joycelyn Elders
Surgeon General
of the United States

1

[On the controversial sentence of caning for an American teenager convicted of vandalism in Singapore]: When we go into a society, I think we have to abide by the rules and regulations of that society. I'm opposed to beatings of anybody. I'm absolutely opposed to beatings . . . [But] you break the laws, you have to pay. If someone from China came over here and broke our laws, they would have to abide by what our laws are, wouldn't they?

Interview/
The Washington Post,
5-6:(A)23.

Gareth Evans
Foreign Minister of Australia

2

[Calling for U.S. renewal of most-favored-nation trade status for China, despite China's poor record on human rights]: We support the continuation of unconditional most-favored-nation status for China. [As for the human-rights situation there,] the better course is to work through international human-rights forums or bilateral dialogue and engagements. Our position [on trade] is very firmly and clearly on the record. We support MFN for all who seek it—not as a privilege but as a normal basis for trade. [Revoking China's MFN status would adversely affect Hong Kong, which] would cause high unemployment, reduction of economic growth and resumption of quite a de-

gree of tension inside Hong Kong, none of which we see as being desirable to the larger regional state of affairs.

News conference,
Canberra, Australia, March 9/
The Washington Post,
3-10:(A)34.

Leslie Gelb
President,
Council on Foreign Relations
(United States)

3

[On U.S. policy toward North Korea, which the U.S. wants to see denuclearized]: What's needed there now is a forthright expression of our goal—the denuclearization of the Korean peninsula; an articulated willingness to trade improved relations and economic assistance as the means to get the North to play ball; a sternly delivered reminder that we stand by our pledge to defend the South—with the specifics left purposely vague; and then an intense but completely private diplomacy.

Time, 5-30:48.

Richard A. Gephardt
United States Representative,
D-Missouri

4

[Saying U.S. companies should expand their operations in Asian countries such as Thailand, Indonesia and China]: The amount of Japanese investment in these countries is staggering, much more than ours. All five Japanese car manufacturers are in Thailand, for example; we have no one there. In terms of competing, we are AWOL. We need to encourage our companies to be more aggressive . . . to be concerned more about American investment. Half of the world's population is in Asia.

The Christian Science Monitor,
2-23:18.

Vo Nguyen Giap
Chairman,
National Institute for
Development Studies (Vietnam);
Former Minister of
Defense of North Vietnam

1

My vision of [Vietnam's] future is based on the perspective of the past. In the past, our greatest challenge was the invasion of our nation by foreigners. As long as foreigners dominated us, we could not determine our own destiny, nor could we deal with our most pressing problems. Now that Vietnam is independent and united, we can address our biggest challenge. That challenge is poverty and economic backwardness. Vietnam is a poor country, but its people are rich in spirit. My vision of the future is one in which the rich spirit of the Vietnamese people will cause our nation to prosper.

Interview,
Hanoi, Vietnam/
Los Angeles Times,
1-9:(M)3.

Newt Gingrich
United States Representative,
R-Georgia

2

[On the current confrontation between the U.S. and North Korea over that country's possible development of nuclear weapons]: I think [U.S. President Clinton] recognizes this is the most dangerous foreign-policy problem he's faced so far in his term, and I think on our side there's a "Be cautious, be firm but don't rush into anything right this minute" kind of mood.

Washington, D.C.,
June 15/
Los Angeles Times,
6-16:(A)11.

Goh Chok Tong
Prime Minister
of Singapore

3

[Arguing against Western trade sanctions against China aimed at improving human rights in that country]: When China becomes powerful in 20 or 30 years' time, there is no reason why China should behave kindly toward the West. That's our worry: China may want to flex its muscles, and then it will be a very troublesome world.

Los Angeles Times,
5-28:(A)14.

Susan Greenhalgh
China specialist,
University of California, Irvine
(United States)

4

[On China's new law aimed at preventing births of children with genetic diseases or abnormalities by banning marriages likely to produce such children and by encouraging abortions of such children]: They're trying to achieve an $800 per capita income by the turn of the century. And that's what's driving their population policy. The state treats people like commodities—like refrigerators.

Newsweek,
11-28:36.

Tsutomu Hata
Prime Minister of Japan

5

[On U.S.-Japanese trade talks aimed at allowing more U.S. products to be sold in Japan]: I am absolutely confident we will find a way. Japan is determined to open its markets, and the U.S. is just as determined to sell here.

May 24/
Los Angeles Times,
5-25:(D)2.

ASIA AND THE PACIFIC

Kim R. Holmes
Vice president and director
of foreign-policy and defense studies,
Heritage Foundation (United States)

1

The fact is, democracy is *not* the new organizing order. If I were [U.S.] Secretary of State, I'd [say] that in deciding our foreign policy for a certain country, the question is not whether that country is democratic but whether it has a pro-Western foreign policy. In Asia, you have countries that are pro-Western but not necessarily democratic. I was just in China, and it's clear that in the next 10 or 15 years the People's Republic will evolve into an authoritarian mix of capitalism and socialism. It's not going to be democratic. [But] it's going to be increasingly capitalist.

Panel discussion,
Washington, D.C./
Harper's, January:63.

Hong Guodong
Director,
China Research Center
on Aging

2

How to better provide and care for the aged is a big problem for China. Respecting the old is a traditional value in China. However, this belief is decaying. Younger people tend to seek pleasure for themselves and care less for the old. Perhaps this is the price a nation pays for modernization.

The Christian Science Monitor,
6-29:12.

Morihiro Hosokawa
Prime Minister of Japan

3

If I cannot deliver on my promise of political reform [in Japan], I have no intention whatsoever of clinging to the Prime Minister's post . . . Without political reform, we cannot hope that economic stimulus measures could succeed. Without politi-

cal reform, it will be impossible to realize administrative or [budgetary] reform, or reform and opening of our economy and society. The people's loss of confidence in party and parliamentary politics will become decisive, and it is perfectly clear that Japan will lose completely the trust of the international community.

At political rally,
Tokyo, Japan, Jan. 27/
Los Angeles Times,
1-28:(A)5.

4

[Denying that Japan would go nuclear if North Korea develops nuclear weapons]: There have been reports in the last few days that Japan might change its [non-nuclear] policy should North Korea arm itself with nuclear weapons. I wish the people who write such reports would come to Japan and talk to our people. Then they would realize how deeply we feel about this issue.

At Georgetown University,
Washington, D.C., Feb. 11/
The New York Times,
2-12:4.

Anwar Ibrahim
Deputy Prime Minister
of Malaysia

5

The Americans show a continued presence and concern in the [Asian] region. And we do welcome it. The whole question is whether their military presence should be pronounced or not. While we don't discount the fact that the Americans need to have a continued presence, we don't accept the idea of the need for a superpower. We don't consider countries in the region as a threat to our security. For instance, to use the [military] buildup in China as a reason to continue the U.S. presence, that certainly is not welcome.

Interview/
World Press Review,
January:35.

Shanmugaram Jayakumar
Minister of Law
and Foreign Affairs
of Singapore

1

[On criticism in the U.S. of a Singapore court's sentence of caning for an American teenager convicted of vandalism]: The issue at stake is not on the caning penalty, but a broader one: whether a country should not respect the right of another country to enact and enforce its laws within its jurisdiction, even though one may disagree with that law, so long as such law is applied without discrimination and after due process of law. To put it another way, can a country insist that its national who has committed an offense abroad be exempt from the laws of the country asserting jurisdiction because the value system or criminal-justice system of the accused's country disapproves [of] the law that he has violated or the penalty he would face? This is a fundamental issue. If today we [in Singapore] are told that we are not entitled to cane, then tomorrow we will be told that we cannot enforce the death penalty, and on some other day that we cannot enforce some other law . . . Singapore's approach to law and order is based on two basic principles. Firstly, we believe that the legal system must give maximum protection to the majority of our people—who are law-abiding—from a small number of criminals, miscreants and juvenile delinquents. We make no apology for clearly tilting our laws and policy in favor of the majority. Secondly, arrested persons have rights to due process of law. But when found guilty, offenders must be punished sufficiently so that they and others will be deterred from repeating the offense.

Before
Interpacific Bar Association,
Singapore, May 5/
The Wall Street Journal,
5-9:(A)12.

Mike Jendrzejczyk
Washington director,
Human Rights Watch/
Asia

2

[Criticizing U.S. reluctance to sanction China for its human-rights abuses]: From our point of view, this is the worst-case scenario, that the Chinese feel there is no price to be paid whatsoever for continued political repression in the name of guaranteeing social stability.

Los Angeles Times,
7-25:(A)4.

Chalmers Johnson
Professor emeritus,
University of California,
San Diego;
Authority on Japan

3

[Saying career government bureaucrats in Japan are the real power there, not the Prime Minister]: They [the U.S. Clinton Administration] need to understand that the Japanese Prime Minister is never able to do anything. The Japanese government is a puppet, and they need to talk to the puppeteers.

Los Angeles Times,
7-25:(A)4.

Sidney Jones
Executive director,
Human Rights Watch/Asia

4

[Criticizing U.S. President Clinton's renewal of China's most-favored-nation trade status despite the continuing negative human-rights record in China]: Clinton has left his Administration looking vacillating and hypocritical, while the Chinese leadership, by contrast, has emerged as hard-nosed, uncompromising and victorious. We're deeply disappointed by this decision.

May 26/
Los Angeles Times,
5-27:(A)16.

Kang Sok Ju
Chief North Korean negotiator
in talks with the United States

1

[On the just-signed agreement between his country and the U.S. aimed at defusing the dispute over North Korea's possible development of nuclear weapons]: [The agreement is] a very important milestone document of historic significance [that will end the dispute] once and for all. [It will resolve] all questions of the so-called nuclear-weapons development by North Korea [that have caused] such unfounded concerns and suspicions. We have neither the intention nor the plan to develop nuclear weapons.

Geneva, Switzerland, Oct. 21/
The New York Times,
10-22:7.

Mickey Kantor
United States Trade Representative

2

[Explaining the U.S. Clinton Administration's decision to abandon its "all or nothing" stance in trade negotiations with Japan in favor of a "take what you can get now and deal with the rest later" attitude]: You have got to be realistic. We can't predict what is going to happen in every area. When you are ready to reach an agreement on a particular sector, you should go ahead and finalize that and continue to move forward on the other areas. We are not going to wait to open up everything until we make deals in all sectors. But—let me be very clear—we don't intend to stop with just one or two sectors, either. We see the framework negotiations as a continuing process.

Interview,
Paris, France, June 6/
The New York Times,
6-7:(C)14.

3

[On the government of new Socialist Japanese Prime Minister Tomiichi Murayama]: I think we have to be careful, cautious, realistic and prag-

matic as we deal with these Japanese officials under a situation where we face the fourth Japanese government in less than a year.

Washington, D.C., June 29/
Los Angeles Times,
6-30:(D)2.

Robert A. Kapp
President, United States-China
Business Council

4

[Arguing against a proposal by human-rights groups that U.S. business in China adopt a code of conduct aimed at bettering the rights situation there]: The impetus of laying on the American business community a corporate code of conduct simply gives credence to the idea that business is morally responsible for the human-rights situation in China. We don't accept that . . . There is a great uneasiness [in the business community] about notions of codes of conduct. First, it becomes a process of public shaming. It is very easy to say things that sound good. Number 2, the advocates of heavy economic pressure against China, to compel China to change its domestic political behavior, believe they are dealing with universal values. That is one of the explanations for what I believe is a cavalier approach to national sovereignty.

The New York Times,
5-24:(C)2.

Islam Karimov
President of Uzbekistan

5

We favor an American presence in Uzbekistan and Central Asia as a guarantor of our democratic development, but you've got to help us, rather than assume moralistic poses [about the human-rights situation]. We will build democratic institutions—but keeping in mind our own special circumstances. Do you think it was possible to create other political parties in a state long-dominated by the Communist Party [and the now-defunct Soviet Union]? We aligned ourselves by the stars atop

(ISLAM KARIMOV)

[Moscow's] Kremlin, and you suddenly expect us to have a democratic state in only two years? Why should this be a stumbling block in relations with Uzbekistan?

Interview/Time, 7-25:43.

Bob Kerrey
United States Senator,
D-Nebraska

1

Our price for normalization [of U.S. relations with Vietnam] should be freedom for the people of Vietnam. We fought a war there for freedom. I want Vietnam to know Americans are prepared to come back there proud and with their heads up. I'm not talking about [Vietnam] having elections soon, but I believe Vietnam is in a position to change its human-rights policies.

Interview, Jan. 10/
Los Angeles Times,
1-11:(A)10.

Kim Young Sam
President of South Korea

2

I am sure that [North Korea is] intent on acquiring nuclear weapons, but I don't think that there is any crystal-clear evidence that they have already acquired them. Unfortunately, we cannot trust any promises or pledges they make. In our experience, they abruptly broke all of them. It is also our experience that if you make concessions toward the North, then they come up with another demand for concessions, rather than making a positive response. So it is difficult to imagine that you can give something to North Korea and expect the same substantial concessions to be made in return. This is exactly the difficulty the U.S. is experiencing now in its dialogue with the North. It is difficult to deal with North Korea patiently, but I think time is on our side. Even if North Korea can develop nuclear weapons clandestinely,

that route will lead to its self-destruction. The most important thing in all of this is to persuade North Korea to open its doors and participate in the international community.

Interview,
Seoul, South Korea/
Time, 3-28:42.

3

I would like to create a society where the rule of democracy and the rule of law make a difference, and we are moving in that direction. Whether it is factory workers or business leaders, they find the society we are now creating is much more comfortable. For example, business leaders used to have to donate as much as one-third of their profits to the military regime. They don't have to do this anymore. I tell them, "If you have extra money that you would like to spend, don't give it to me; give it to your own employees."

Interview,
Seoul, South Korea/
Time, 3-28:43.

Kim Young Soon
Aide to North Korean
President Kim Il Sung

4

[Saying his country is not preparing for war despite recent tensions with South Korea and the West]: Why should we prepare for war to destroy our whole nation? For 40 years, we have built monuments of reconstruction and a strong economy . . . We don't want to destroy all that.

Interview/
USA Today, 4-15:(A)4.

Lane Kirkland
President, American Federation
of Labor-Congress
of Industrial Organizations

5

[Criticizing U.S. President Clinton's renewal of China's most-favored-nation trade status despite

(LANE KIRKLAND)

the continuing negative human-rights record in China]: [Clinton's decision] sends a clear message to the world: "No matter what America says about democracy and human rights, in the final analysis profits, not people, matter most" . . . America should be standing with the Chinese people, not their oppressors.

May 26/
Los Angeles Times,
5-27:(A)16.

Le Mai
Deputy Foreign Minister
of Vietnam

1

When talking of human rights, Vietnam and other developing countries feel the United States considers itself as a model for the world, imposing its way of living and thinking on other nations. They are always reminding the Vietnamese people [that] they are dealing with a superior power. Sometimes we feel the United States doesn't treat us on an equal footing.

Interview, Feb. 16/
The New York Times,
2-19:5.

2

The U.S. should see relations with Vietnam as part of its overall strategy, and go in a stronger manner toward a new relationship with Vietnam. To have problems with Vietnam over a war 20 years ago is unexplainable . . . [And] no country is perfect on the question of human rights. If the United States holds human rights [in Vietnam] as a condition [for good relations], it should hold it as a condition for all countries.

Interview,
Hanoi, Vietnam/
USA Today,
3-7:(A)8.

Patrick J. Leahy
United States Senator,
R-Vermont

3

[Criticizing North Korea's handling of an incident involving the shooting down of a U.S. helicopter over its territory, which killed the pilot, and its refusal to release the co-pilot]: This is going to make a lot of people [in the U.S. Congress] wonder just what kind of nuclear deal we have [the recent agreement in which North Korea pledged not to develop nuclear weapons and to open its facilities for foreign inspection]. If they can't handle a very simple, though tragic, thing like this helicopter incident with any openness and decisiveness, how are they going to handle anything as enormously complex as a nuclear-power agreement?

USA Today,
12-23:(A)6.

Lee Kuan Yew
Former Prime Minister
of Singapore

4

One reason why growth is likely to last for many years in East Asia—and this is just a guess—is that the peoples and the governments of East Asia have learned some powerful lessons about the viciousness and destructiveness of wars. Not only full-scale wars like in Korea, but guerrilla wars as in Vietnam, in Cambodia and in the jungles of Malaysia, Thailand, Indonesia and the Philippines. We all know that the more you engage in conflict, the poorer and the more desperate you become. Visit Cambodia and Vietnam; *the world just passed them by.* That lesson will live for a very long time, at least as long as this generation is alive.

Interview/
Foreign Affairs,
March-April:121.

(LEE KUAN YEW)

1

I know that the present generation of Japanese leaders do not want to project power. I'm not sure what follows when leaders born after [World War II] take charge. I doubt if there will be a sudden change. If Japan can carry on with its current policy, leaving security to the Americans and concentrating on the economic and the political, the world will be better off. And the Japanese are quite happy to do this. It is when America feels that it's too burdensome and not worth the candle to be present in East Asia to protect Japan that [Japan] will have to look after its own security. When Japan becomes a separate player, it is an extra joker in the pack of cards.

Interview/
Foreign Affairs,
March-April:123.

2

[On Singapore's success as a multi-ethnic society]: From my own experience, I would say, *make haste slowly.* Nobody likes to lose his ethnic, cultural, religious, even linguistic identity. [But] to exist in one state, you need to share certain attributes, have things in common. If you pressure-cook, you are in for problems. If you go gently, but steadily, the logic of events will bring about not assimilation, but integration.

Interview/
The Washington Post,
4-7:(A)26.

3

[Saying the U.S. should not attempt to impose sanctions or otherwise intimidate China because of that country's negative human-rights record]: You will [then] end up with a very hostile China, one which you'll have to live with as an adversary and will not be your partner in keeping the world peaceful and stable. [That would drive up U.S. defense budgets and cause] problems in

the Middle East with the export [by China] of all kinds of weaponry and nuclear fissionable material.

Interview, Australia/
The Washington Post,
4-22:(A)33.

Li Lanqing
Vice Prime Minister of China

4

[Criticizing the U.S. for trying to get China to improve its human-rights record]: China is a country that attaches importance to human rights. Although we have not yet acceded to the Universal Declaration of Human Rights, we do support these documents. Due to differences in history, religious beliefs and the level of economic development, countries cannot have exactly identical concepts of human rights. That is where the differences and the problem between our two countries lie. We are most concerned about our right to development and subsistence. We have to support 22 percent of the world's population on 7 percent of the world's arable land. At the same time, we are striving to improve the living standards of our people. That is what the Chinese government and people care about most at this stage . . . We are reasonable people, but you [the U.S.] had better refrain from interfering in the internal affairs of China, because we are a people with a strong sense of pride. We are ready to conduct a dialogue with you on the question of human rights, but one should not link irrelevant matters with [economic] trade.

Interview, Beijing, China/
Time, 3-28:43.

Li Peng
Prime Minister of China

5

[On U.S. pressure aimed at improving human rights in China]: History has already proven that it is futile to apply pressure against China. China will never accept U.S.-style human rights.

March 12/Time, 3-21:47.

(LI PENG)

1

Even when [China's] economy is developed and our country becomes rich and powerful, we will never claim hegemony [over other Asian nations] and will always maintain friendly relations based on equal rights.

Tashkent, Uzbekistan,
April 19/Los Angeles Times,
4-20:(A)12.

2

[Saying foreigners should not listen to dissidents in China who criticize the country's human-rights situation]: Foreign statesmen will surely make mistakes in their decisions if they base their understanding of China merely on the words or views of a tiny number of Chinese, and ignore the interests and wishes of all other Chinese people.

To visiting former
U.S. National Security
Affairs Adviser
Zbigniew Brzezinski,
Beijing, China/
The New York Times,
5-19:(A)1.

Winston Lord
Assistant Secretary for
East Asian and Pacific Affairs,
Department of State
of the United States

3

[On U.S. efforts to get China to improve its human-rights record]: It's not a matter of talking about American values or Chinese values. We're not telling China to be like America. We're talking about universal rights. And arbitrary arrests or torture. It's got nothing to do with normality. There are universal rights in the UN charter.

Time, 3-21:47.

4

No [U.S.-Japan economic] strategy is going to work miracles when they [the Japanese] have four or five governments in the course of a year. We really don't feel we had a fair test of our approach on the economic issues because of the constant changing of the Japanese political leadership.

Interview/
Los Angeles Times,
7-25:(A)4.

5

If anyone gives you flat assurances or predictions or analyses of what's happening in North Korea, immediately distrust him or her.

Washington, D.C./
Los Angeles Times,
7-29:(A)5.

David Marshall
Former Chief Minister
of Singapore

6

In the very marrow of our bones [in Singapore], the concept is supremacy of society over the individual. We've been cribbed and cabined and confined by the concept of absolute respect for authority, whereas you [in the U.S.] have been free to develop freedom of spirit. But with the emphasis on the individual, tragically in the United States it has meant fragmentation and the loss of moral values . . . Despite what we owe the United States, we've been encouraged to sneer at you. I don't . . . [But in promoting human rights in Asia,] the danger is [America's] lack of understanding of other people and your adolescent impatience with us. [It is better to adopt] a more modest profile and more friendly approach to what you see as our blemishes. You don't apply surgery to pimples.

The Washington Post,
4-22:(A)33.

Dave McCurdy
United States Representative,
D-Oklahoma

7

Just achieving the short-term goal of [international] inspections [of North Korea's nuclear

287

(DAVE McCURDY)

facilities] falls short of the ultimate strategic goal—
to ease the North back into the community of nations so that it doesn't implode or explode.

U.S. News & World Report,
2-28:21.

Mike McCurry
Spokesman for the Department
of State of the United States

1

[On North Korea's downing of a U.S. helicopter which was flying in the North's airspace]:
The American people are clearly very concerned
about the fate of [the] two crewmen. The American people will in some sense form a judgment
about North Korea based on how North Korea re-
sponds to our repeated requests for more information and more details about the incident . . . We
clearly want an early resolution to this matter and
a full accounting. This is a very high-priority matter for the United States government.

Washington, D.C., Dec. 19/
The New York Times,
12-20:(A)3.

Zubin Mehta
Music director,
Israel Philharmonic Orchestra;
Former music director,
New York Philharmonic Orchestra

2

[On his current visit to India, where he was
born]: I walked down the street where I used to
live, and what did I find? A Baskin-Robbins
[American ice-cream store]! We used to say Japan
had grown wealthy with all its industry and commerce, but lost its soul. Now the same thing is happening here. So you have to wonder, what is India
going to do to preserve its soul?

Interview, Bombay, India/
The New York Times,
12-6:(B)4.

George J. Mitchell
United States Senator,
D-Maine

3

[Criticizing U.S. President Clinton's renewal
of China's most-favored-nation trade status despite
the continuing negative human-rights record in
China]: I disagree with the decision . . . The experience of recent years has been that each conces-
sion to the Chinese Communist regime encourages its intransigence, and I believe this will be
the unfortunate result of this decision. It will con-
firm for the Chinese Communist regime the success of its policy of repression on human rights
and manipulation on trade. It is likely to produce
a result that is the opposite of what [President
Clinton] intends.

May 26/
Los Angeles Times,
5-27:(A)16.

Walter F. Mondale
United States Ambassador
to Japan

4

[Lamenting the resignation of Japanese Prime
Minister Morihiro Hosokawa because of an ethics scandal]: I'm very sad. I liked Hosokawa, I
consider him a friend, and I feel very sorry for
him. Here is a guy who offered a new Japan. He
appealed to the young; he had a Kennedy-esque
appeal; he talked about political reform, opening
Japan to the world, finally responding to the consumers. There was such hope. Here was the fresh
political persona, coming from prefectural politics, and ending up in charge of a system that
needed so many changes.

April 8/
The New York Times,
4-9:5.

Tomiichi Murayama
Prime Minister of Japan

5

[On worries by some about his being of the
Socialist Party]: I know people are worried about

(TOMIICHI MURAYAMA)

my government, both inside and out of Japan. My job is to do the best I can to get rid of those worries . . . The Socialist Party has changed considerably already. The word "socialism" does not appear in the latest Socialist Party platform. We are now capable of keeping abreast of the times.

News conference,
Tokyo, Japan, July 1/
The New York Times, 7-2:5.

Madhav Kapur Nepal
General secretary,
Communist Party of Nepal

1

[On his Communist Party, which was victorious in the just-held elections in Nepal]: We don't have to go by the word of Marx or Lenin or Mao. It is we who are the leaders of Nepal, and it is we who know what is best. As they used to say in Eastern Europe: "Just because it rains in Moscow, do we have to carry an umbrella?"

Interview,
Katmandu, Nepal, Nov. 20/
The New York Times,
11-21:(A)6.

Sam Nunn
United States Senator,
D-Georgia

2

[Saying the U.S. should not take away China's most-favored-nation trading status because of that country's negative human-rights record]: We have to understand here the stakes are very high. Let's keep the pressure on human rights, but that is not our top priority. Our top priority has to be, in that region of the world, to prevent [nuclear] proliferation, to prevent the nuclear arms race . . . I think using total cutoff on MFN is too heavy a weapon, particularly when we have the other stakes in northeast Asia.

Broadcast interview/
"Meet the Press,"
NBC-TV, 1-30.

Michel Oksenberg
President, East-West Center
(United States)

3

[Saying Chinese leader Deng Xiaoping's failing health is causing Chinese officials to act tough toward the U.S. in anticipation of a realignment in the government]: No one dares be anything but a strong nationalist in these circumstances. I think in each major dimension of relations with China, one can expect to see recalcitrance as Chinese leaders and the various contestants for power position themselves to make sure they don't lose their nationalist bona fides.

The New York Times,
12-19:(A)3.

Ichiro Ozawa
Chief strategist for Japanese
Prime Minister Tsutomu Hata

4

Japan would obtain not a single benefit from arming itself with nuclear weapons. Japan would be viewed with suspicion by all the world. And with nuclear weapons, would Japan be able to ensure its security? Not at all.

Tokyo, Japan, June 14/
Los Angeles Times,
6-15:(A)6.

Chris Patten
Governor of Hong Kong

5

[On China's scheduled takeover of Hong Kong in 1997]: I have never sought to deny that [China] can come in and throw out the Legislative Council, the directly elected local government and [other democratically elected] bodies that have been created [in Hong Kong]. [But] I don't think that will be widely regarded as a very effective way of winning people's minds and hearts. And I think the rest of the world will inevitably see China's assumption of international responsibilities very much through the prism of how it deals

(CHRIS PATTEN)

with Hong Kong and how it behaves in Hong Kong ... I hope we will be able to make at least some progress in convincing Chinese leaders that this hugely precious community, representing as it does 23 percent of Chinese GNP, succeeds not just because of some capitalist equation but because its way of life helps to sustain its prosperity as well as its prosperity helping to sustain its way of life.

Interview,
Hong Kong, July 13/
The New York Times,
7-14:(A)3.

William J. Perry
Secretary of Defense
of the United States

1

[On North Korea's nuclear-weapons program]: I know they're lying when they say they're not developing a nuclear program ... The dangers are going to be compounded two or three years from now when [their] plan is finished ... and they're producing bombs at the rate of a dozen a year.

Broadcast interview/
"Meet the Press,"
NBC-TV, 4-3.

2

[On U.S. policy regarding nuclear-weapons development by North Korea]: Our policy right along has been oriented to try to keep North Korea from getting a significant nuclear-weapons capability. [As for the possibility they may already possess one or two atom bombs,] we don't know anything we can do about that. What we can do something about, though, is stopping them from building beyond that.

On flight returning to U.S.
from visit to countries
of the former Soviet Union/
Time, 4-11:58.

3

I know that some in China believe that the United States regards China as a threat, or at least a future threat. As Secretary of Defense of the United States, I can assure you that those who make these arguments don't understand American defense policy.

To Chinese Army officers,
October/
U.S. News & World Report,
11-14:85.

Nicholas Platt
Former United States Ambassador
to the Philippines

4

[On the U.S. Clinton Administration's apparent de-emphasis on Asia after coming into office with an aggressive Asian agenda]: Every Administration comes to power feeling it has to change something. And often, what they feel they have to change doesn't need to be changed. The fact that they [the Clinton Administration] are going back to [former President George] Bush's policy toward Asia doesn't make them look good. But it doesn't make me feel bad.

Los Angeles Times,
7-25:(A)4.

Clyde V. Prestowitz, Jr.
President, Economic Strategy Institute
(United States)

5

[On recent tough talk by the U.S. Clinton Administration about Japan opening up its markets to American products]: Have we called their bluff? Have they called ours? I don't know. All I know is that both we and the Japanese have to begin to seriously re-analyze the whole relationship. It has become like a bad marriage, and only by starting over and trying to put it on a different footing is it going to work. It is long overdue.

The New York Times,
2-12:4.

(CLYDE V. PRESTOWITZ, JR.)

1

[On the resignation of Japanese Prime Minister Morihiro Hosokawa because of an ethics scandal]: Hosokawa's fall demonstrates the fallacy of the view that somehow a new political leader was going to emerge, be the savior, change the Japanese system, resolve the trade conflicts with the U.S. and spare us [Americans] having to take difficult measures to solve the problems. The power center [in Japan] remains the bureaucratic mandarins and big-business cartels, who do not want to see the kind of change we are advocating.

April 8/
The New York Times,
4-9:5.

P. V. Narasimha Rao
Prime Minister of India

2

[Addressing Pakistan on the subject of Kashmir]: With you, without you, in spite of you, Kashmir will remain an integral part of India.

Independence Day address,
New Delhi, India, Aug. 15/
Los Angeles Times,
8-16:(A)6.

Alan Romberg
Authority on Asia,
United States Institute of Peace

3

[On possible U.S.-led foreign economic sanctions against North Korea to protest that country's refusal to permit international inspections of its nuclear facilities]: I think if we actually get to [strong economic] sanctions, we [could] probably dig in for a very long haul. North Koreans do not respond well when they are cornered . . . They respond pretty well when they are cornered with a reasonable way out, at least as perceived by them . . . Both sides have an obligation to look at the situation and see if we can't, consistent with each of our sets of principles, step back from the cur-

rent impasse and find a constructive way out . . . It's very important to keep on trying.

The Christian Science Monitor,
6-13:4.

J. Stapleton Roy
United States Ambassador to China

4

[On human rights in China]: If you look at the 150 years of modern China's history since the Opium Wars, then you can't avoid the conclusion that the last 15 years are the best 15 years in China's history. And of those 15 years, the last 2 years are the best in terms of prosperity, individual choice, access to outside sources of information, freedom of movement within the country and stable domestic conditions . . . [If U.S. Secretary of State Warren Christopher] were to recommend next May that we should extend [China's MFN trade status with the U.S.] without conditions, that would not remove human rights from our foreign-policy agenda with China. We would expect to still continue an active human-rights dialogue with the Chinese, and we would continue to expect to see significant progress on human-rights issues.

Interview, Beijing, China/
The New York Times,
1-1:5.

Brent Scowcroft
Former Assistant to
the President of the United States
(Gerald Ford and George Bush)
for National Security Affairs

5

[Criticizing the U.S. Clinton Administration's apparent policy of accepting that North Korea may develop a few nuclear weapons but not to allow more than that]: The consequences around the world [of even a few North Korean nuclear weapons] will be disastrous . . . A small number of nuclear weapons is not fundamentally a military weapon, but a terror weapon designed to intimidate. So the difference between an "insignificant"

(BRENT SCOWCROFT)

number and a "significant" number may defy close analysis.

Time, 4-11:58.

Paul Simon
United States Senator,
D-Illinois

1

[Criticizing the new U.S. policy of very limited increases in economic contacts with Taiwan, while still keeping strict curbs on political contacts]: [These changes are only] small steps and this was an opportunity for truly significant, constructive and realistic adjustments [in increasing Taiwan's status with the U.S.] . . . Many of the terms of our relations with Taiwan were outdated long ago. Today, they seem like offical pettiness.

Sept. 7/
Los Angeles Times,
9-8:(A)4.

Suharto
President of Indonesia

2

[Saying the West should not hold Asian nations to the same high human-rights standards as exist in Western countries]: We are people of the East, so we must use Eastern standards. We cannot don Western clothes because they are too big. It would make us look like scarecrows.

Speech/
Los Angeles Times,
5-28:(A)14.

William Taylor
International security analyst,
Center for
Strategic and International Studies
(United States)

3

[Criticizing North Korea's holding of the co-pilot of a U.S. helicopter it shot down over its territory]: Pyongyang has been playing the helicopter incident for all the propaganda value it can get. [There is a] pattern [in which North Koreans] take the South and the U.S. to the brink over major and minor incidents . . . If they don't release [the co-pilot soon], look out. The Republicans in [the U.S.] Congress and the American public are going to come after [U.S. President] Clinton. You can only humiliate Americans for so long.

USA Today,
12-23:(A)6.

William Warwick
President, AT&T China

4

The choices for American companies like mine are stark. Either we establish a major presence in the China market, or we forget about being a global player, forget even about being able to define our market in what is increasingly an interdependent world economy.

The Washington Post,
3-14:(A)14.

Gerry Adams
President, Sinn Fein party
of Northern Ireland

1

[On the ethnic violence in Northern Ireland over British rule there]: Sinn Fein doesn't advocate violence. We don't advocate armed struggle. We have suffered from the violence. I want to see an unarmed strategy. I want to see a situation where the IRA ceases activities. But the people who are looking down their guns at us are saying, well, you can't talk to us unless you renounce violence. To me it's all meaningless, it's all platitudes. There is nothing in my political life, or in fact in my other life, that gives me any reason to trust the British. I think every Republican [who wants Northern Ireland to reunite with Ireland] wants peace. But they are not war weary. They don't want to just give up.

Interview,
Belfast, Northern Ireland/
Time, 8-1:40.

2

[On the IRA's newly announced cease-fire in the ethnic conflict in Northern Ireland]: The struggle [against British rule] is not over. The struggle has entered a new phase.

Newsweek, 9-12:19.

Sergio Balanzino
Deputy Secretary General,
North Atlantic Treaty Organization

3

[On Russia's joining NATO's Partnership for Peace program]: This is a defining moment in shaping the security of our continent. We must not repeat the mistakes of Europe's past. Our main objective remains a new Euro-Atlantic order of security with the active participation of Russia.

Brussels, Belgium,
June 22/
Los Angeles Times,
6-23:(A)1.

Alexei Belov
Deputy Chief of Police
of Moscow, Russia

4

The Italian mafia is a kind of kindergarten in comparison to the organized crime we have now in Russia.

World Press Review,
August:5.

Silvio Berlusconi
Prime Minister of Italy

5

[On suggestions that his new government has Fascist elements in it]: In Italy there is no such thing as nostalgia for a period [the Fascist era in World War II] that we consider to be completely buried in the past and having been condemned by history.

News conference,
Rome, Italy,
June 2/
The New York Times,
6-3:(A)6.

6

[Criticizing Northern League leader Umberto Bossi for bolting from the coalition Berlusconi formed earlier this year that enabled him to become Prime Minister]: Sovereignty belongs to the people, and no one has the right to carry it away. Whoever works against the will of the voters, for whatever reason and at whatever time, offends the spirit and soul of the democratic Constitution. Bossi has put not only my patience but also that of the government to a great test. He behaves like someone with a double personality, or triple, or even quadruple.

Before Italian Parliament,
Rome, Italy, Dec. 21/
The New York Times,
12-22:(A)6.

Tony Blair
Member of British Parliament;
Labor Party Shadow Home Secretary

1

The [British] Labor Party—in common with most left-of-center parties in the last 20 or 30 years in Europe—has undergone a considerable amount of change. Not changing its basic principles but updating those principles for the modern world. The argument between public versus private sector is really a dead argument within the Labor Party. Socialism is a word I know that has a particular meaning in the United States, [but] socialism to most of us within the Labor Party is a basic set of values; it's a view of society and the individual and the belief that individuals prosper best within a strong and cohesive society and community. And that value system is what the modern Labor Party is about rather than economic prescriptions that may have been fine for particular generations or have some historical connection with certain perspectives about socialism but don't really represent the Labor Party as it is today.

Interview, London, England/
Los Angeles Times,
6-12:(M)3.

Tony Blair
Leader, Labor Party of Britain

2

I shall not rest until, once again, the destinies of our [British] people and our [Labor] Party are joined together again in victory at the next general election—Labor in its rightful place, in government again. [The task] is a mission to lift the spirit of the nation, drawing its people together, to rebuild the bonds of common purpose that are at the heart of any country fit to be called one nation. You [Conservatives] have had your chance. You have had 15 years to get it right. If you can't change this country for better after 15 years, you never will. It is time for you to go.

Accepting the Labor Party leadership,
London, England, July 21/
Los Angeles Times, 7-22:(A)6.

David L. Boren
United States Senator,
D-Oklahoma

3

[Saying the new openness in Russia since the demise of the Soviet Union has made U.S. intelligence-gathering there more difficult]: It used to be that if you know what 100 people were doing and saying to each other, you knew what was happening in Russia. Now we have to monitor a far greater range of decision-makers. We're getting indigestion from the amount of information we have.

U.S. News & World Report,
3-7:32.

Zbigniew Brzezinski
Counsellor, Center for Strategic
and International Studies
(United States);
Former Assistant to the President
of the United States (Jimmy Carter)
for National Security Affairs

4

[Saying the U.S. Clinton Administration is too attached to Russia and its President, Boris Yeltsin, despite signs of increasing Russian nationalism and hard-line rhetoric]: Our approach . . . has been characterized by sloganeering, wishful thinking and a romantic attachment to Russia. I think the Administration is beginning to realize that its policy is floundering, is unsound, but is very reluctant to face that fact.

Los Angeles Times, 3-8:(A)8.

Rocco Buttiglione
Leader, Popular Party of Italy

5

[In Italy,] there has not yet been an adequate rethinking [of Fascism]. And it's not an issue for the professors. It touches the soul of the whole nation. In the absence of this debate, the risk remains that forms of totalitarianism will return.

Sept. 15/
The Christian Science Monitor,
9-28:14.

Barbara Cartland
British author

1

[On scandals rocking the British Royal Family]: If we lose the Royal Family, then what would there be for people to see? A rather dull little island.

U.S. News & World Report,
10-17:30.

Warren Christopher
Secretary of State
of the United States

2

[On the desire of former Soviet-bloc countries to become members of NATO]: I don't think it's realistic to think of immediately admitting new members to NATO. There's been a good deal of talk, and you've heard [Polish] President Lech Walesa say why not admit Poland immediately. I think they really misunderstand our Constitutional process in the United States . . . Before we put our security perimeter out to the end of Slovakia or Poland, there will be a major debate here . . . The [proposed] Partnership for Peace [program] gives every nation [that wants entry into NATO] an opportunity to participate in the planning and exercises to show that they have the capacity of resources, and the interest, to become members. They'll be judged by the NATO members as to whether they have qualifications for membership. This is a military alliance, and nations will only enter on a *quid pro quo* basis.

Interview, Jan. 5/
USA Today, 1-6:(A)15.

3

[On nationalist Vladimir Zhirinovsky, whose party won a large vote in the recent Russian election, and whose extreme views have concerned many in the West]: He is obviously a significant phenomenon. He captured . . . about 16 percent of the seats in the Parliament. It's probably accurate to describe that as primarily a protest vote. As

we're seeing more and more public-opinion polls, that vote seems to have been based more on economic considerations than nationalism . . . I think people were not voting for all the rather bizarre ideas he's put forward, but that he was a vehicle by which they could express their pain and suffering from the dramatic changes taking place [in Russia].

Interview, Jan. 5/
USA Today, 1-6:(A)15.

4

[On U.S. aid to Russia]: Seventy-five percent of the aid is going to the private sector or non-governmental organizations; only 25 percent goes to the central governments. Of that 25 percent, virtually all of it goes to privatization [efforts], which itself is very important for the people of the country. So it's our determination . . . to have virtually all of the aid go to the people. That's why 75 percent of it goes to the non-governmental organizations in the thought that this will get the aid down to the grass roots, down to the people.

Before Senate Foreign
Operations Subcommittee,
Washington, D.C.,
March 2/
The Washington Post,
3-3:(A)28.

Tansu Ciller
Prime Minister of Turkey

5

We [Turks] fought Iraqi aggression in the [1991 Persian] Gulf war. We still support the embargo against Iraq, despite the burden on our economy. We have tried to integrate our economy with the European Union. But still we are rejected. Over the same period, Spain, Portugal, and Greece entered the EU and got billions of dollars in aid. Our people have started questioning.

Interview, Ankara, Turkey/
U.S. News & World Report,
6-6:52.

Bill Clinton
President of the United States

1

[Saying Eastern European countries should not be granted NATO membership while some current members object]: We don't want right now in 1994 to draw a new line across Europe which will make the very people we're trying to support be, in effect, more insecure . . . I think it's important to emphasize that we view it not as putting a limit on NATO membership, but as opening the door to fuller partnership. I think it clearly will lead, ultimately, to some more countries coming into NATO at some point in the future.

Interview, Washington, D.C., Jan. 5/
Los Angeles Times, 1-6:(A)6.

2

[On Vladimir Zhirinovsky, a Russian nationalist whose party received a large vote in recent Parliamentary elections despite his radical views]: I wouldn't say it scares me, but it concerns me. . . A lot of the bad guys that have been elected in history got elected for reasons that didn't have anything to do with their most outrageous claims. And yet, they did what they said they'd do when they got in. So it is a concern.

Interview,
Washington, D.C., Jan. 5/
Los Angeles Times,
1-6:(A)6.

3

The core of [U.S.] security remains with Europe. That is why America's commitment to Europe's safety and stability remains as strong as ever. That is why I urged NATO to convene this week's summit. It is why I am committed to keeping roughly 100,000 American troops stationed in Europe, consistent with the expressed desires of our allies here. It is not habit, but security and partnership that justifies this continuing commitment by the United States.

At NATO summit meeting,
Brussels, Belgium, Jan. 9/
The New York Times, 1-10:(A)4.

4

My Administration supports European union. We recognize we will benefit more from a strong and equal partner than from a weak one.

At NATO summit meeting,
Brussels, Belgium, Jan. 9/
The Christian Science Monitor,
1-12:3.

5

This period may decide whether the states of the former Soviet bloc are woven into the fabric of transatlantic prosperity and security or are simply left hanging in isolation as they face the same daunting changes gripping so many others in Europe. These pivotal decisions ultimately rest with the people who threw off Communism's yoke. They must make their own decisions about their own future. But we in the West can clearly help to shape their choices, and we must summon the political will to do so. The task requires a steady and patient effort, guided by a strategic star that points us toward the integration of a broader Europe. It also requires a fair amount of humility, understanding that we cannot control every event in every country on every day. But if we are willing to assume the central challenge, we can revitalize not only the nations of the East, but also our own transatlantic relationship.

At NATO summit meeting,
Brussels, Belgium, Jan. 9/
The Washington Post, 1-10:(A)11.

6

We must build a new security for Europe. The old security was based on the defense of our bloc against another bloc. The new security must be found in Europe's integration—an integration of security forces, of market economies, of national democracies. The purpose of my trip to Europe is to help lead the movement to that integration and to assure you that America will be a strong partner in it . . . I have proposed that we create the Partnership for Peace. This partnership will advance a process of evolution for NATO's formal enlargement. It looks to the day when NATO will

296

(BILL CLINTON)

take on new members who assume the alliances' full responsibilities . . . The Partnership for Peace will not alter NATO's fundamental mission of defending NATO territory from attack. We cannot afford to abandon that mission while the dream of empire still burns in the minds of some who look longingly toward a brutal past. But neither can we afford to draw a new line between East and West that could create a self-fulfilling prophecy of future confrontation.

At NATO summit meeting,
Brussels, Belgium, Jan. 9/
The Washington Post,
1-10:(A)11.

1

Do I intend to work with [Russian] President [Boris] Yeltsin as long as he embodies Russian democracy and as long as he is the choice of the majority of the people of Russia to be the President? Of course. There is no other [Russian] President. There may be some people who wish someone else was President of the United States, but I am the only U.S. President you have right now. That's not the same thing as saying that I'm all there is to American democracy. I am not.

At "town meeting,"
Moscow, Russia, Jan. 14/
The New York Times, 1-15:4.

2

Support of the United States for reform in Russia does not flow from a sense of charity or blind faith. Our policy is based on our clear American interests clearly pursued.

News conference,
Washington, D.C., Feb. 25/
Los Angeles Times, 2-26:(A)21.

3

[On the growing nationalist movement in Russia and the hard-line rhetoric of some newly elected members of the Russian Parliament]: Is it possible that we will re-create the Cold War? In one re-

spect, it is unlikely for sure, and that is the nuclear respect. [But] somewhat more likely [is that] the Russian people will turn to leaders who will say the best way to go for the future is . . . the reimposition of some sort of empire. The United States has worked with and supported [Russian] President [Boris] Yeltsin because we believe that he followed policies supporting democracy, supporting reform and supporting respect for the territorial integrity of Russia's neighbors—all three things. This is still our policy. We are interested in supporting those things.

To reporters,
Washington, D.C., March 7/
Los Angeles Times, 3-8:(A)8.

4

[On criticism of new Italian Prime Minister Silvio Berlusconi, whose party has been linked with Fascism]: For a number of reasons, some parties that take part in democracies have their roots in the past. But things change. I'm thinking like an Italian citizen and I'm saying—he was elected. Let's see if he knows how to do his job. Let's give him a chance and support him.

Italian broadcast interview/
The New York Times, 6-2:(A)3.

5

[On the D-Day landings in 1944]: Here on this quiet plateau . . . we honor those who gave their lives for us 50 crowded years ago. Today, the beaches of Normandy are calm. If you walk these shores on a summer's day, all you might hear [is] the laughter of children playing on the sand, or the cry of sea gulls overhead, or perhaps the ringing of a distant church bell . . . the simple sounds of freedom barely breaking the silence. Peaceful sounds. Ordinary sounds. But June 6, 1994, was the least ordinary day of the 20th century. On that chill dawn, these beaches echoed with the sounds of staccato gunfire, the roar of aircraft . . . came the soldiers out of their landing craft and into the war, away from their youth and toward a savage place many of them would . . . never leave . . . Millions of our GIs did return home . . . But on

(BILL CLINTON)

this field are 9,386 who did not . . . They were the fathers we never knew, the uncles we never met, the friends who never returned, the heroes we can never repay. They gave us our world. And those simple sounds of freedom we hear today are their voices speaking to us across the years.

At Omaha Beach,
Normandy, France,
June 6/
USA Today, 6-7:(A)3.

1

Our trans-Atlantic alliance clearly stands at a critical point. Militant nationalism is on the rise, transforming the healthy pride of nations, tribes, religious and ethnic groups into cancerous prejudice, eating away at states and leaving their people addicted to the political pain-killers of violence and demagoguery. We see the signs of this disease from the purposeful slaughter in Bosnia to the random violence of skinheads in our nations.

Before French National Assembly,
Paris, France, June 7/
The New York Times,
6-8:(A)4.

2

[On disagreements between the U.S. and Russia]: Russia is still a democracy. Russia is still pursuing economic reform which is critical to the kind of political stability that will lead to a responsible partnership. There will always be some areas of difference between us. These things are to be expected in the relationships of great nations that have a lot of irons in the fire. I'll watch them. I'll work on them. I'll do whatever is necessary to protect our interests.

News conference,
Miami, Fla.,
Dec. 11/
The New York Times,
12-12:(A)6.

Antonino Cuffaro
Italian Senator

3

[Criticizing the inclusion of neo-Fascists in the new government of Italian Prime Minister Silvio Berlusconi]: We are facing not a renewal, but a return to Fascists who are still heirs of a dictatorship that brought the country to war . . . They are trying to show they are different, but [they] can't succeed however hard they try.

May 18/Los Angeles Times,
5-19:(A)6.

Fabrizio Del Noce
Italian legislator

4

[On the recent election victory of the Forza Italia party, to which he belongs]: The voters saw us as the only really new thing since 1945. And we only promised concrete, physical things because the polls said that's what Italians wanted: jobs, health care, pensions, the fight against the Mafia. These were the main issues, instead of the abstract debate by the former Christian Democrats and the former Communists. And now you can see that after three or four years of crisis, there's a new optimism. You see the restaurants and shops filling. [But] if we can't keep our promises within two years, we probably won't have another chance.

The New York Times,
5-10:(A)7.

Tamas Deutsch
Vice president, Alliance
of Young Democrats of Hungary

5

[On Hungary's economic woes of the last several years since abandoning Communism for the free market]: All former Communist countries have problems with their economies. [But] the previous 40 years of Communism was more responsible for these problems than the last three or four years.

Los Angeles Times, 1-29:(A)9.

Robert J. Dole
United States Senator,
R-Kansas

1

[On the recent arrest in the U.S. of an American CIA employee on charges of spying for the Russians]: [This] threatens the foundation of our relationship with the new republic of Russia. [The U.S. has] moved perhaps too far, too fast in assuming that changes in Russia [aimed at reform] have permanently altered the international landscape.

Before the Senate,
Washington, D.C./
Time, 3-7:39.

Dzhokhar M. Dudayev
Leader of Chechnya, Russia

2

[On Chechnya's drive for independence, including fighting the Russian military's current assault on the region]: We have to strike them from the rear, deal them a strong blow. This is the centuries-old tactic of the mountain people. Strike and withdraw, strike and withdraw, to exhaust them until they die of fear and horror.

Russian broadcast interview,
Dec. 13/
The New York Times,
12-15:(A)8.

Elizabeth II
Queen of England

3

[On the inauguration of the English Channel Tunnel between England and France]: To rejoin what nature separated some 40 million years ago has been a recurring dream of statesmen and engineers for several centuries. This is the first time in history that the heads of state of France and Britain have been able to meet each other without either of them having to travel by sea or air.

At inaugural ceremony,
Calais, France, May 6/
Los Angeles Times, 5-7:(A)6.

Padraig Flynn
Director of Social Affairs,
European Commission

4

[On the aging of Europe's population and the drop in birth rates]: Europe has been getting older since the turn of the century, but the effect on our quality of life may really start to show in the next few years. If we don't get some of the 20 million unemployed people back to work soon, it will be hard to finance our welfare systems.

The Washington Post,
1-20:(A)19.

Giorgio Galli
Professor of political history,
University of Milan (Italy)

5

[On the aftermath of the just-announced resignation of Italian Prime Minister Silvio Berlusconi]: The ideal solution would be [an interim] coalition of all major political parties led by a prestigious personality . . . This government alternative could provide a new institutional structure for Italy, one in favor of more regional autonomy and a less bureaucratic centralized power.

The Christian Science Monitor,
12-23:6.

Robert M. Gates
Former Director of
Central Intelligence
of the United States

6

[On the recent arrest in the U.S. of an American CIA worker who is charged with spying for the Russians, even though the Cold War is supposedly over]: With the Cold War over, there may have been the expectation that this kind of [spying] wouldn't go on any longer. [But] there are a number of us who have been warning for quite some time that, even after the collapse of the So-

(ROBERT M. GATES)

viet Union, the Russians continued to spy . . . It may serve as a useful reminder that we may not be fast friends yet.

World Press Review,
May:15.

Franz-Olivier Giesbert
Editor, "Le Figaro" (France)

1

France has always loved reform but hated change. That is why, unlike a lot of other nations, we feel the need occasionally to make a revolution, good or bad, so as to decompress.

Los Angeles Times,
2-25:(A)1.

Paul Goble
Russia specialist,
Carnegie Endowment for
International Peace (United States)

2

[Saying Russian President Boris Yeltsin is alienating many Russians because of his decision to use the military to forcefully put down the independence movement in the Chechnya region]: Yeltsin has alienated much of the intelligentsia, a good hunk of his army, and lost his political clout. This is the end of our hopes for a democratic, free-market Russia . . . The Russian people don't want insubordination from the regions, but they also don't want body bags. Yeltsin's only supporters appear to be ultra-nationalists like Vladimir Zhirinovsky and the [U.S.] Clinton Administration.

USA Today, 12-23:(A)6.

Al Gore
Vice President of the United States

3

[Saying the U.S. must support reform in Russia]: The struggle to erase Communism's scars and ensure democracy's success is not their struggle alone. It must also be our struggle. It is the fight of a lifetime, our lifetime. It is the story of a century, our century.

Speech,
Milwaukee, Wis.,
Jan. 6/
USA Today, 1-7:(A)4.

4

[On a cease-fire in Northern Ireland's ethnic conflict announced last week by the IRA]: The American people have a dream that this peace process will succeed. It is right at the top of our foreign-policy agenda. [U.S.] President Bill Clinton and I stand ready, as do all the American people, to support our British and Irish friends in their efforts to achieve peace. The President and I commend those who have worked so diligently over the past 25 years to achieve what at times seemed impossible to find—a way to peace . . . Each side stands only to lose by further violence. Both can gain the promise of a better, more prosperous future for their children through a just and lasting peace.

At Shannon Airport, Ireland,
Sept. 7/
Los Angeles Times,
9-8:(A)11.

Pavel S. Grachev
Minister of Defense of Russia

5

[Saying the Russian military is in poor condition]: Not a single army in the world is in such a catastrophic state. I ask you to take this as a warning . . . For the sake of the country's security, think about this [defense] budget. We must frankly ask ourselves the question: "Do we need an army?" If so, it is a sin to keep it in poverty and half-starved.

Before Russian Parliament,
Moscow, Russia, Nov. 18/
The New York Times,
11-19:4.

Gregor Gysi
Member of German Parliament

1

[On how the former East Germany, where he is from, is fairing after reunification with West Germany]: I accept the political freedom, the legal order and the democratic possibilities that this [western] system offers. But I also maintain that people in eastern Germany have lost important rights, and that in this society there is much social injustice and much that needs to be fundamentally changed. We are not facing the global social, ecological and cultural challenges that confront us. So for me there are still very good reasons to be anti-capitalist.

Interview/
The New York Times,
6-29:(A)4.

Herbert A. Henzler
Chairman, German branch,
McKinsey & Company,
consultants

2

You could say, wouldn't it be great if the Germans had new industries, like the service industry or whole new enterprises springing up like we see in the United States. But I don't see that because we [Germans] don't have a lot of owner-entrepreneurs. We don't have the thousands of guys who start something and fail and get up again. If you fail in Germany, you've often failed for a lifetime.

Los Angeles Times,
8-9:(A)12.

Roman Herzog
Chief Justice of Germany;
President-elect of Germany

3

[Asking for greater understanding between the western and eastern parts of the now-united Germany]: To the citizens of the former Federal Republic [West Germany], of whom much sacrifice is being asked, I would say that this is the result of a historical injustice [the post-war split-up of Germany] which happened to fall on the Elbe border. To those in the new states [what used to be East Germany], please understand that you are not a burden to us but a windfall. You bring much with you, experiences that we in the west did not have, in a world where many things were more humane than they were with us.

Speech, May 23/
The New York Times,
5-24:(A)6.

Richard C. Holbrooke
United States Ambassador
to Germany

4

For almost five decades in the post-war period, the relationship [between the U.S. and Europe] was basically military. The departure of the troops from Berlin represents the beginning of an emphasis on trade and economics.

Time, 9-19:51.

John Hume
Member of British Parliament
from Northern Ireland;
Leader, Social Democratic
and Labor Party

5

[Urging the IRA and Sinn Fein to accept the recent British-Irish peace declaration for Northern Ireland and enter into talks to end the ethnic violence there]: It will require from the republican movement, given the experience that its members have been through, one of the greatest acts of moral courage of this century. But at the end of the day, it is moral courage that gives real leadership and that creates truly historic opportunity . . . Let us commit ourselves to spilling our sweat and not our blood.

Jan. 4/
Los Angeles Times,
1-5:(A)4.

(JOHN HUME)

1

[Saying pro-British loyalists in Northern Ireland should honor the cease-fire recently proclaimed by the IRA]: If they refuse to do so, we shall witness a strange spectacle: loyalist paramilitaries, who want British troops to stay in the province, confronting them in our streets. Such a situation would be difficult for the people of Britain to understand.

Sept. 5/
The Christian Science Monitor,
9-7:3.

Josef Janning
Deputy director,
Research Group on European Affairs,
University of Mainz (Germany)

2

Europe right now is a glass that is both half empty and half full. While Western Europe, including the former Fascist powers, has succeeded in becoming modern and democratic in its organization, we are still archaic in our pattern of reaction to new European conflicts. That leaves us vulnerable to our past.

The Christian Science Monitor,
6-8:9.

Douglas H. Jones
Chief of United States
diplomatic mission in Berlin, Germany

3

It is not reassuring that more progress is not being made toward guaranteed civil rights for foreigners [immigrants and refugees] in Germany ... How can those minorities remain anything but conspicuous, underprivileged targets of anger and frustration if they have no chance to become assimilated on an equal basis with Germans if they so choose, or to have their own cultural distinctiveness protected from attack if they do not? If Germany is not a racist society, why is its nationality law, which was written in 1913, predicated upon race? Public attitudes toward minority communities in Germany are ambivalent at best.

Speech, Oranienburg, Germany/
The New York Times, 4-19:(A)5.

Karl Kaiser
Chairman,
German Society for Foreign Policy

4

[On the necessity for Germany to take more responsibility in world affairs]: Inevitably after reunification, [Germany] can no longer be a consumer of stability and prosperity primarily produced by others, but now must carry the burden of producing it. But it is a long, difficult and indeed domestically controversial process of how a country that emerged precisely with a purpose to abstain from world politics now is to take part.

The Christian Science Monitor,
10-26:8.

Islam Karimov
President of Uzbekistan

5

[On the now-independent former republics of the Soviet Union]: Once the people in Russia, Ukraine and Belarus experienced crisis and hardships [after independence], they started to have doubts about whether they needed independence at all. The more hardships crop up on the way to reform, the more ground Bolshevik forces gain. A major danger for us in Uzbekistan is the possible re-emergence of the Communist Party. We are going through the same crisis that [every other former Soviet republic] is, but our people have not attained the level of political sophistication of Europe or even of Russia. Should a Bolshevik show up at a street corner again and promise to give the people back everything they used to have, they might be tempted to follow him. But we will see that it never happens here. An important factor is that we have rejected shock therapy. We have protected the young, the old and the poor. Ask anyone in the streets. They will tell you that no one has been left out.

Interview/Time, 7-25:43.

Kurt Kasch
Senior vice president,
Deutsche Bank (Germany)

1

[On Germany's economic problems, brought on by unification and other factors]: Germany is at a fork in the road. We have the ability to change, and even to change without much pain. But the question is whether we are willing to do it. All we need to do is work and save a little more, and consume and spend a little less . . . [But] political leadership has failed at every level. The Christian Democrats are tired and the Social Democrats are weak. Many say they will join in a "grand coalition" after the election this year. That would be a marriage of the lame and the blind. It would be a government in constant internal strife, and would only increase this feeling of alienation that is spreading across Germany.
Interview, Berlin, Germany/
The Atlantic Monthly,
February:33.

Klaus Kinkel
Foreign Minister of Germany

2

[On a decision by the German Supreme Court and Parliament to allow the German military to take part in multinational missions]: Even after the ruling, we will stick with our established culture of restraint. Normality in foreign and security policy does not mean playing world policeman . . . The military mission must be fulfillable, and the military components must be part of a convincing concept for a political solution.
Before German Parliament,
Bonn, July 22/
Los Angeles Times, 7-23:(A)6.

Vaclav Klaus
Prime Minister of the Czech Republic

3

We are in favor of European integration, and by integration I mean the free exchange of people,

goods, ideas, labor, capital. We can't be an island of non-participation. The problem is that the idea of integration has slowly shifted toward something else, toward the idea of unification. Most Europeans started with the idea that the primary entity is the state and the secondary, derived entity can be European integration, not the other way around.
Interview,
Prague, Czech Republic/
USA Today, 11-25:(B)4.

Helmut Kohl
Chancellor of Germany

4

In Germany [today], two-thirds of the population was born after Hitler. I see the role of my generation as explaining to the younger ones how it was [during the Nazi era], bearing witness to the good things their parents' generation did as well as the bad—not denying the past at all.
Interview, Bonn, Germany/
The New York Times,
3-15:(A)6.

5

[Saying Communists who were part of the resistance movement against Adolf Hitler during World War II should not be honored at a memorial to resistance fighters]: To entirely understand the lasting meaning of German resistance for the present and future, we may not limit ourselves to the question of what it was aimed *against*. We have to ask ourselves what the people who took part in it were *for*. The inheritance lies in the *what for*.
At commemoration of Germans
who resisted the Nazis
during World War II,
Berlin, Germany, July 20/
Los Angeles Times, 7-21:(A)9.

6

[On the narrow re-election victory of his Christian Democratic Party-led coalition]: We will continue the coalition [government]. It will be difficult, but that's the way life is. I am not a fair-

(HELMUT KOHL)

weather Chancellor . . . A close result has one advantage—it imposes more discipline.

Oct. 16/
The Washington Post,
10-17:(A)1.

Vyacheslav V. Kostikov
Press Secretary to
Russian President Boris N. Yeltsin

1

[On U.S. President Clinton's current visit to Moscow]: I wish he would stop in the street and talk to people. He would see that Russia is a psychologically open society, [not as it was in the 1960s when] people were dressed in gray coats and Russian-made suits that all look alike . . . Imagine an American President on Russian television back then [Clinton is due to speak on Russian TV during his visit]—simply impossible! Now there is even no need to negotiate with Russians the topic of his speech.

Interview,
Moscow, Russia, Jan. 11/
Los Angeles Times,
1-13:(A)13.

Mical Kovac
President of Slovakia

2

I would like this [new Slovak] government to succeed in raising the political credibility of Slovakia abroad. It should be able to persuade the politicians and the banks and the businessmen that Slovakia wants to be a stable, democratic country, a country that wants to join Europe's political and economic structures.

After swearing-in
of his new government,
Bratislava, Slovakia,
March 16/
The New York Times,
3-17:(A)6.

Vladimir Kozhemyakin
Member of
Russian Parliament

3

[On the emergence of a more assertive and nationalist Russian foreign policy]: I've been saying for more than a year that a certain new stage is inevitable. People feel not anti-Americanism, but a certain desire to prove that [Russia] is independent, is great, has its own policy. This is something that Americans should treat as natural and inevitable and not endangering the relationship. But I wouldn't say the Russian bear is rising. There's no strength left in the bear.

The Washington Post,
3-1:(A)1.

Andrei V. Kozyrev
Foreign Minister
of Russia

4

There is internal strife in Russia. There is a party of war, new imperialists, even Fascists. Two days ago, I was so outraged by their attacks against me in Parliament that I called them all "political bastards." They had called me a traitor for signing the Partnership for Peace [with NATO]. I felt I had the right to answer them in kind. Such healthy debate and lovely talk! There is a total lack of political culture in the whole space of the former Soviet Union. The typical Soviet mentality was to take up your rifle and grab power. We were brought up with this idea. "One day Comrade Lenin did it, so you too can seize a gun and establish a paradise on earth." Now there is more than one Comrade Lenin in our areas of ethnic conflict. After they take up their rifles, they ask for peacekeeping forces, which really means, "Be with me and help me defeat the other side. If you don't, you're imperialists." That is why we ask—beg—for an international presence.

Interview/
Time, 7-11:44.

Anatoly Krasikov
Spokesman for Russian President
Boris N. Yeltsin

1

I'm personally convinced that the time of NATO is passing, because NATO is the concrete product of an absolutely concrete, specific epoch, the epoch of confrontation. Now some new structures should be created—which one, I don't know. I think no one knows.

Washington, D.C., Sept. 28/
Los Angeles Times,
9-29:(A)13.

Leonid M. Kravchuk
President of Ukraine

2

Everyone should understand that Russia will never agree to be on the sidelines of the world. They could not renounce their 1,000-year history.

To reporters and diplomats,
Kiev, Ukraine, March 1/
The Washington Post,
3-2:(A)22.

Alexander A. Kreder
Historian,
Saratov University (Russia)

3

Until this very day, initiative is punished [in Russia]. People who take the initiative are not thought of well. I am conscious all the time, at the university, that I must show that I am not proud. It's instinctive. I know one must be modest. If I had money, I would buy a second-hand [car]. I would feel more comfortable that way.

Los Angeles Times, 8-23:(A)6.

Denis Lacorne
Political analyst, National Political
Science Foundation (France)

4

[France is] a very centralized state, and that creates a certain fear. In the United States, when

something goes wrong, it might cost a company or university president his job. But in France, It goes right up to the government.

Los Angeles Times,
2-25:(A)13.

Catherine Lalumiere
Secretary General,
Council of Europe

5

[On the recent increase in xenophobia, nationalism and intolerance in Europe]: We must ask ourselves why Europe has such difficulty establishing the very values it promotes as its own. It's as if we on this old continent are still convulsed by the question, "Who am I?," and its corollary, "Who are you?"

The Christian Science Monitor,
3-9:1.

Richard G. Lugar
United States Senator,
R-Indiana

6

[Suggesting caution on U.S. aid to Russia]: We have to get over the idea, I think, that [the U.S. Russian relationship] is a partnership. This is a tough rivalry, and that is an important distinction to make. These are tough people with whom to deal. And we're not going to be involved in handouts.

Broadcast interview/
"Meet the Press,"
NBC-TV, 2-27.

Alexander Lukashenko
Candidate for President of Belarus

7

[On his receiving the largest share of the vote in the first round of Belarus's Presidential elections]: What happened today came as a sensation only to those who refused to face the truth about our country. The poor and deprived people for the first time had a chance to elect somebody like them to this supreme post, and the people spoke.

To reporters,
Minsk, Belarus, June 24/
The New York Times,
6-25:3.

Paolo Macry
Professor of contemporary history,
University of Naples (Italy)

1

In Milan and elsewhere in central and northern Italy, the efficiency of public services is much higher than in Naples, precisely because throughout central and northern Italy the political parties didn't have to win consensus in this way, because they had a much more solid history behind them . . . [In Naples,] there were no controls of any kind. There wasn't a regulatory plan. There were no building regulations, and those that existed were violated. Probably Naples must in some way be radically rethought as a city. I'm aware that today it's difficult to think of demolishing buildings, but in Naples there's a population density that's absolutely irreconcilable with a civil standard of living.

Interview, Naples, Italy/
The Christian Science Monitor,
6-29:10.

John Major
Prime Minister
of the United Kingdom

2

[On the IRA's just-announced cessation of the use of violence in its fight to end British rule in Northern Ireland]: If [Gerry Adams, leader of the IRA's political arm, Sinn Fein] were to say tonight, "This statement is unambiguous," that the violence has ended for good, then within three months we could start talking with Sinn Fein on how to go forward with the peace process.

BBC interview, Aug. 31/
Los Angeles Times, 9-1:(A)8.

Patrick Mayhew
British Secretary for
Northern Ireland

3

[On ending the ethnic violence in Northern Ireland over British rule]: People say to me, "Are you optimistic?" I don't think that's a rational thing to be anymore . . . What people ought to be concerned about is whether you have sensible grounds for being hopeful. And I have. What are we trying to achieve? We are trying to help the people of Northern Ireland find a less antagonistic way of living together . . . The future of Ireland, Northern Ireland, is going to be decided by the consent of the people who are affected by it—the principle that coercion, violence can't have any place in that; the principle that everyone is welcome to come to the table, provided they have a democratic mandate and are committed to peaceful methods. If you wish to back up your arguments with a bomb or a bullet, you exclude yourself. When I walk the streets of Northern Ireland, and I talk with the people in the factories and shops wherever I go, I find people wanting their politicians to talk. [There is] great impatience now with the occupancy of ancestral trenches and the shouting of tribal hostilities. So that's how I see it. I can't give you a time scale, but I'm privately confident that we are going to succeed.

Interview, Boston, Mass./
The Christian Science Monitor,
4-13:4.

Viktor N. Mikhailov
Minister of Atomic Energy
of Russia

4

[Saying Russia should keep the plutonium it developed during the Cold War, rather than getting rid of it as the U.S. wants it to do]: We have spent too much money making this material to just mix it with radioactive wastes and bury it . . . The 21st century will belong to nuclear power.

Interview, Moscow, Russia/
The New York Times,
8-19:(A)6.

Slobodan Milosevic
President of Serbia (Yugoslavia)

1

Ah, the [foreign] media war against Serbia. They have produced *mountains* of lies! And the average American *believes* media. They are not informed at all. [Yugoslavia] is a moral failure not only of journalism, it is as well, indirectly, a moral failure of democracy. You know, practically, what happened was Yugoslavia was disintegrated with the pressure of different foreign factors which were following their interests. They supported disintegration, they supported secession! And in the same time, they have punished loyalty to your home country. Who is guilty [according to the media]? All who are fighting for integration, for preservation of integrity to their country, were punished.

Interview,
Belgrade, Serbia (Yugoslavia)/
Vanity Fair, June:129.

Musa Mirzhuyev
Military adviser to
Dzhokhar M. Dudayev,
leader of Chechnya, Russia

2

[On the Russian government's military assault on Chechnya, which is seeking its independence]: The Russian empire was never capable of using a scalpel. It has always barged into other people's gardens with a bear's claw.

Dec. 19/
The New York Times,
12-20:(A)1.

Francois Mitterrand
President of France

3

[In France today, there are urban areas marked by] ugliness, hate, tedium, anger and delinquency. Many suffer a lot. Beware of revolts when reason is swept aside.

February/
The New York Times,
3-19:3.

Dominique Moisi
Deputy director,
Institute for
International Relations (France)

4

Unless there is a major catastrophe in Europe, America is not interested. There is no European policy in [the U.S. Clinton] Administration. It is difficult to see America as the answer to European problems.

U.S. News & World Report,
6-6:49.

5

[On the ethnic animosities and wars that have broken out in Eastern Europe following the collapse of Communism there]: Communism was a freezer. It simply froze old hatreds [that were there already]. Unfortunately, the hatreds thawed before the European Union was strong enough to provide a concerted response in the absence of real American leadership in Europe.

The New York Times,
11-26:4.

Richard M. Nixon
Former President
of the United States

6

Some say the Cold War is over and Russia lost. That is not true. The Communists, the Soviet Communists, lost the Cold War. But democratic Russia, under the courageous leadership of [President] Boris Yeltsin, gave the knockout blow to Soviet Communism.

At reception
at residence of U.S. Ambassador,
Moscow, Russia, March 10/
The Washington Post,
3-11:(A)19.

7

There is no question that since the [recent Russian] elections there has been a much more assertive position [by Russia] toward Ukraine and

(RICHARD M. NIXON)

other countries [in the C.I.S.]. I do not say that most of the leaders go along with the position of [Russian nationalist legislator Vladimir] Zhirinovsky and other extremist leaders. But there is no doubt sometime in the future there will be occasions when the U.S. will have to look at Ukraine and look at Russia and say, "Who do we choose?"

News conference,
Kiev, Ukraine, March 16/
Los Angeles Times,
3-17:(A)4.

Emil Pain
Adviser to Russian President
Boris N. Yeltsin

1

[Saying many Russians are against President Yeltsin's decision to invade Chechnya, which is trying to become independent of Russia]: There are two Chechen conflicts in Russia. One is in the North Caucasus [in Chechnya itself], the other in Moscow. The one in Moscow is even more dangerous.

The New York Times,
12-17:4.

Sergei Parkhomenko
Russian political journalist

2

[Saying Russian President Boris Yeltsin is isolated and out of touch with the country]: It's not just a palatial style of living. It's palace politics. He's steadily losing contact with the world.

U.S. News & World Report,
11-7:52.

Volker Ruhe
Minister of Defense of Germany

3

We [the German military] are all too well-prepared for the most unlikely case—an invasion from the East—but we are poorly prepared for the most likely case: an intervention somewhere in the world. The Bundeswehr [the German military] must become a lot more flexible.

The Christian Science Monitor,
10-26:9.

Alexander V. Rutskoi
Former Vice President of Russia

4

[There is a] deterioration of our nation. Cynicism, immorality, lying, theft have become everyday phenomena. But patriotism is held to be . . . extremism . . . I should make it clear that I do not accept radicalism and demagoguery. I feel close to those who love the fatherland, who say that Russia deserves a superpower role . . . As for [controversial nationalist politician Vladimir] Zhirinovsky, if my positions conflict with his in any respect, I think we can come to an agreement.

World Press Review,
July:26.

5

Any Russian who talks about restoring the Soviet Union has no respect for his own country. We've had enough of a milk-cow-style union, where the head is in Russia grazing, and the milking goes on in other republics.

Time, 7-25:43.

6

I am for the rebirth of Russia within the borders of the [old] Soviet Union, but only through the free will of the people. Russia has the possibilities to live without the others [the now-independent former Soviet republics]. But I'm not sure the others could live without [Russia's] natural gas and other resources.

To reporters/
The Christian Science Monitor,
8-17:3.

Antonis Samaras
Former Foreign Minister of Greece

1

[On Greece's concern about a threat from the former Yugoslav republic of Macedonia, now an independent state]: This is not a phantom fear but a reality. It is not a problem with the present Skopje [Macedonia]; that is ridiculous. We are concerned for the future potential combination of forces in this region. There are three expectations: a Greater Bulgaria, a Greater Albania and a Greater Serbia. And always with Turkey looming in the back.

Interview, Athens, Greece/
The New York Times,
4-23:7.

Rudolf Scharping
Leader, Social Democratic Party
of Germany

2

Right-wing radicalism [in Germany] has economic and social causes. Sometimes it's encouraged by reckless political behavior. Whoever sets fire to other people's homes or churches or synagogues is a crook and belongs in prison. And it would be good if every politician in Germany would clearly say so.

The Washington Post,
4-11:(A)10.

Brent Scowcroft
Former Assistant to the President
of the United States
(Gerald Ford and George Bush)
for National Security Affairs

3

[On recent revelations of continued Russian spying in the U.S., and vice versa, despite the end of the Cold War]: [The U.S. and Russia have an] evolving relationship. We are in a position to do Russia grievous harm. In the case of the British, for example, we could do them great harm and they could do us great harm, but there is no conceivable circumstance under which anyone could be-

lieve that could happen. There is, thus, no reason for [the British] to conduct intelligence operations here or us there.

Feb. 22/
The Washington Post,
2-23:(A)12.

John M. Shalikashvili
General, United States Army;
Chairman, Joint Chiefs of Staff

4

[Urging former Soviet-bloc countries to accept membership in a Partnership for Peace plan with Western militaries, rather than pursue full membership in NATO at this time]: I absolutely reject the argument that this is just simply some sort of facade. When the day comes when we wish to speak about extending [NATO] membership, our militaries will already have the joint procedures . . . that are absolutely vital to making an alliance like NATO work. I think it's important to understand that we are evolving away from the notion of asking the question whether there should be an extension of [NATO] membership. We are much more now speaking about the issue of how and when.

To Eastern European reporters,
Washington, D.C., Jan. 3/
The Washington Post,
1-4:(A)12.

Eduard A. Shevardnadze
Chairman,
Supreme Soviet of Georgia

5

[On the difficult transition to democracy in Russia]: I still believe it is going the way it should. Real democracy cannot be born without serious struggle. How can viable democracy be created in a militarist country overnight? [Russian President Boris] Yeltsin is trying to form democratic institutions by using a certain kind of authoritarianism. This is necessary in a transitional period.

Interview/Time, 7-25:42.

(EDUARD A. SHEVARDNADZE)

1

[On the threat of Russian imperialism now that the Soviet Union is no more]: It's impossible to restore the empire. This isn't the 19th century. All states of the world are now interdependent. In spite of very painful local processes, there is one big universal logic [of independence]. The disintegration of the Soviet Union was a manifestation of this logic. It could have occurred in a different form or at a different pace, but it had to happen. This process is irreversible. Georgia may lose out on some things. There will be difficulties. But ultimately, a new relationship will be built among these [former Soviet republics which are not independent] countries, probably the kind of relationship that exists in Europe, where there is positive cooperation in economics, science and so on. Russia must understand that its empire will never be restored and must encourage and support the building of the new independent states.

Interview/Time, 7-25:42.

Dmitri K. Simes
President, Nixon Center
on Peace and Freedom (United States)

2

[On U.S.-Russian relations]: I would say we're seeing the worst relations since 1984. We're seeing a fundamental worsening of the relations, which reflects not domestic Russian circumstances, not the Republican Congressional victory [in the recent U.S. elections], not Bosnia, but trends in Russia that once again make it a serious power with nationalist interests and an increasingly assertive manner.

The New York Times,
12-8:(A)6.

Jean Kennedy Smith
United States Ambassador
to Ireland

3

[On U.S. President Clinton's decision early this year to grant a visa to Gerry Adams, head of

Sinn Fein, the political arm of the Irish Republican Army, despite his organization's use of violence in its dispute with Britain]: I supported the President's decision. President Clinton is totally engaged in the peace process [in Northern Ireland], more than any other American Administration. I can't believe [Adams] doesn't have a commitment to peace. If he doesn't come through, he will be very isolated by the United States government and the people . . . [The conflict in Northern Ireland] affects generations of children who grow up without a grandfather. I don't see how people can inflict such pain on anybody.

Interview,
Dublin, Ireland/
The New York Times,
7-29:(A)5.

Alexander Smolensky
President, Stolichny Bank (Russia)

4

[Saying those in Russia who think President Boris Yeltsin is isolated and out of touch are underestimating him]: He reminds me of Czar Ivan the Terrible, who pretended to be dead, then opened his eyes and—zzzttt—lopped off the heads of the boyars who had already started celebrating. It's only an illusion among the public that [Yeltsin] is an idiot who sees nothing, hears nothing.

U.S. News & World Report,
11-7:52.

W. Richard Smyser
German social scientist

5

[On the German economy]: The basic problem is that it's an economy that is brilliantly geared to make the products of the late 19th and early 20th century—chemicals, machine tools, steel. Those are the things on which you can build a great industrial establishment, and they did. The only trouble is, what happens when the world economy changes under you? The question is whether the Germans can deal with this challenge quickly

(W. RICHARD SMYSER)

enough. Because the rest of the world isn't going to say, "Oh, yes, Germany, take your time!" We're talking about 10 years at the most . . . The German economy, being dominated by banks, is therefore dominated by bank thinking. And banks are not venturesome in Germany. They're not like these crazy Americans who will invest millions in start-up ventures despite knowing that four in five will go bust. But that fifth one . . . Ahh!

The Washington Post,
8-9:(A)12.

Richard Staar
Scholar, Stanford University
(United States)

1

[On the conflict between Russia and Chechnya, which is pushing for independence]: The only thing the Russians and the Chechens have in common is a mutual hatred.

U.S. News & World Report,
12-26:24.

Carole Beebe Tarantelli
Italian legislator

2

The situation [in Italian politics] is so fluid that people have lost their historical memory. Italy has been through the most incredible two years since [the] Tangentopoli [bribery scandal] came up. The whole Italian political class has been arrested and put in jail for kickbacks, and the two ruling parties have virtually disappeared.

Vogue, November:218.

Dmitri Timashkov
Colonel, Russian armed forces;
Spokesman for the Russian command
in Wunsdorf, Germany

3

[On the final pullout of Russian troops from Germany]: We [originally] came here not because

we wanted to attack Germany, but because Germany attacked us [in World War II] and invaded our territory all the way to Moscow. Later on, two worlds based on two different ideologies developed. Maybe one proved better and more successful. But we feel that we fulfilled our role here. We managed all of our conflicts in a peaceful way, and we are partly responsible for the fact that there was no war in Europe for 45 years, no World War III. This is a time for us to work together for the future instead of arguing about who did what in the past.

Interview, Wunsdorf, Germany/
The New York Times, 3-4:(A)6.

Jacques Toubon
Minister of Culture of France

4

[Criticizing the trend in France of foreign, mainly English, words creeping into the vocabulary]: Nowadays, people think everything modern or young comes from foreign words. It is a trend from high school. I think we should try to show our young people that by using the word *decontracte*, instead of "cool," they are saying the same thing. Television is imposing a cultural model made in the U.S.A. For example, the trend at the moment is to play street basketball, and this leads to children dressing like the American basketball players, walking like them and using the same vocabulary. This phenomena has always existed, but I think this may cause our society to break down into tribes. The ultimate risk would be that our Republic, our common thing, disappears. There is a lot at stake here.

Interview, Paris, France/
Los Angeles Times, 7-10:(M)3.

Lech Walesa
President of Poland

5

[Saying Russia's fear of having NATO members on her borders should not prevent NATO from accepting former Soviet-bloc countries, such as

(LECH WALESA)

Poland, into the organization]: There is Russia, which threatens; there is the organized West, which is afraid [of Russia's reaction]; and there are those of us in the middle who say: There's nothing to be afraid of; one should only try to increase the potential of Western Europe, both physically and technically. We understand the reasons why the West, and particularly the United States, is so concerned about Russia's reaction. [But] we are also concerned about Russia's reaction.

The New York Times,
1-11:(A)6.

1

[On his current unpopularity in Poland]: If I was very polite, if I didn't provoke everybody, if I didn't work hard, my position would be different. These are signals of my hard work—entering into conflict situations in order to solve them.

Interview/
The New York Times,
7-6:(A)5.

2

I remember [that U.S. President Clinton said] that his agenda focused on America and the economy . . . [But] I don't think that the top people from any other [U.S.] Administration have made as many visits to Europe, including to Poland. But at this time of reforms and revolutions in Europe, the needs are even greater. So our expectations exceed even this great American activism.

Interview/
Newsweek, 7-11:33.

3

[On Nazi atrocities against Poland during World War II]: We do not give absolution to the murders in Warsaw, but we do not pass those feelings upon the German nation [of today]. Blood and hatred are a curse of the 20th century; may they disappear in the past along with it.

At ceremony marking
50th anniversary
of the Warsaw Uprising,
Warsaw, Poland, Aug. 1/
Los Angeles Times, 8-2:(A)6.

Bernard Weill
Director of personnel,
Peugeot Company (France)

4

[Saying European welfare-state benefits will have to be cut to sustain economic competitiveness]: As workers get older, they want better treatment, but the reality of the market is that you either become more productive or you lose jobs. That's why many industries, not just automobiles, are turning toward robots to perform tasks better and more cheaply than humans . . . Old people can protest all they want, but in the long run our societies simply cannot sustain the present level of benefits they enjoy. The Golden Boys and Golden Girls will have to get by with less and less in the years to come.

The Washington Post,
8-8:(A)12.

Hans Westphal
Chairman,
Babcock-Borsig AG (Germany)

5

[On his and other German manufacturing companies' need to cut back on employee perks and restructure because of the country's faltering economy]: We're in the same situation in the manufacturing industry in Germany now that the Americans were in the early 1980s. Why are we so far behind? Because beginning in 1982 we had a boom period that lasted nearly 10 years. That time was used by American manufacturers to restructure and be more aggressive, while we were riding the wave. We became too fat, too heavy, and we didn't do the homework that we needed to do to be com-

(HANS WESTPHAL)

petitive in the future . . . We Germans have lost the monopoly of being better educated than most of the world. We've lost the monopoly we once had on advanced technology. And we've lost the ability to be flexible and react to change quickly. We have not understood that we're a Mickey Mouse player in global competition.

Interview, Berlin, Germany/
The Washington Post,
2-22:(A)1,12.

1

We [in Germany] are living in a dream world because we believe we can maintain high prices and high salaries while making low-tech products. But the world is telling us that we cannot. Why should anybody buy a steel tube at a higher price just because it's made in Germany? No good reason.

The Washington Post,
8-9:(A)12.

Boris N. Yeltsin
President of Russia

2

The time when our country considered itself a besieged fortress and was in confrontation with the rest of the world is over. It is more than military power that determines a country's fitting place in the world.

Before Russian Parliament,
Moscow, Russia, Jan. 11/
The Washington Post,
1-12:(A)13.

3

[Agreeing with U.S. President Clinton's proposal to have former Soviet and East European nations join in a "Partnership for Peace" with NATO, rather than granting them full membership in NATO]: I think that the initiative of President Bill Clinton and also of some Europeans not to accept countries into NATO on a case-by-case basis, but to proclaim all of them to be partners in maintaining peace and security is a good formula, because drawing one more line, dividing all into white and black anew, no, this won't do.

News conference,
Moscow, Russia, Jan. 14/
The New York Times,
1-15:4.

4

As long as I am the President, I will defend and protect the course of economic transformation. [But] our task is to find a reasonable balance between the pace of reform and the social cost.

Before Russian Parliament,
Moscow, Russia, Feb. 24/
USA Today, 2-25:(A)5.

5

It is our duty to make the year 1994 the year of close attention to the problems of the people of Russian extraction living in neighboring states [that used to be part of the defunct Soviet Union]. When it comes to violations of the lawful rights of people of Russia, this is not an exclusive internal affair of some country, but also our national affair, an affair of our state.

Before Russian Parliament,
Moscow, Russia, Feb. 24/
The New York Times,
2-25:(A)4.

6

[Saying NATO should not accept for membership former Soviet-bloc Eastern European countries while not accepting Russia]: While respecting the sovereign rights of states and organizations, Russia is opposed to the expansion of NATO with various countries of the European continent, but without Russia. This is a path of new threats to Europe and the world. Russia is not a "guest" in Europe; she is a full-fledged participant in the European community.

Before Russian Parliament,
Moscow, Russia, Feb. 24/
The New York Times, 2-25:(A)4.

WHAT THEY SAID IN 1994

(BORIS N. YELTSIN)

1

[Criticizing former U.S. President Richard Nixon for visiting with Yeltsin's chief opponents during Nixon's current trip to Russia]: Nixon met [former Russian Vice President Alexander] Rutskoi and [Communist leader Gennady] Zyuganov here while the most interesting thing is that he had been coming here to meet me. How can one do this—come to a country and search for dark spots? No. After this, I will not meet him. And the government will not meet him. Let him know that Russia is a great country and you cannot play around with her like that.

To reporters,
Moscow, Russia,
March 9/
The Washington Post,
3-10:(A)33.

2

I'm an optimist. I believe that, no matter what, reforms [in Russia] cannot and will not be reversed, no matter who crows like a rooster to prove the opposite . . . The Communists will remain, like in any other country. But they will gradually change to what they are in [the U.S.]—small groups that preach Communism. Our people are fed up with Communism, so the Communists will just be a minor hindrance in Parliament. Maybe sometimes they will hold the odd rally—but in the framework of the law, because we will no longer allow them to take to the streets.

Interview,
Moscow, Russia, April/
Newsweek, 5-2:47.

3

[On the economic reforms in his country]: Before, everything was planned very precisely [under the Communist system]. Every nail was registered and everyone knew where it was to be sold and for how many kopeks. Then suddenly there was this transition to a free market, free trade, free prices. What they called profiteering before they

now call private enterprise: buying cheap and selling for a higher price, at a profit. Those who are unable to work honestly are, doubtless, attracted by such a situation. They get a chance to obtain money illegally, sometimes committing crimes, murdering people, taking bribes, corrupting officials and so on. But I am convinced that as the economic and financial situation stabilizes, crime will drop. As slight positive changes take place in the economy, as people grow psychologically accustomed to [the] market, and as all government structures try to combat crime, all this inevitably leads to a decrease in crime.

Interview,
Moscow, Russia, April/
Newsweek, 5-2:47.

4

The main peacekeeping burden in the territory of the former Soviet Union lies upon the Russian Federation.

At United Nations,
New York/
Newsweek, 10-10:42.

5

[On his decision to use military force to put down the independence movement in the Chechnya region of Russia]: The Russian people have for a long time justly rebuked us for indecision, for a lack of political will, for the reluctance to restore order to the territory of the Chechen republic, an integral part of Russia. The extremely complicated situation required the gravest decision—to use the [Russian] armed forces on the territory of Chechyna . . . Remember, the outrage of gangsterism on the Chechen land is a dangerous threat to the whole of our country. Your [Russian soldiers'] kin could even be among its victims. I understand that it is not easy for soldiers today. It is not easy for the Minister of Defense and the Minister of the Interior either. You [soldiers] are in difficult conditions; you are not praised by the mass media. But I call on you to do everything you can to fulfill this task . . . [This is] defending the unity of Russia. This is the indispens-

(BORIS N. YELTSIN)

able condition for the existence of the Russian Federation. Not a single territory has the right to withdraw from Russia.

Broadcast address,
Moscow, Russia,
Dec. 27/
The New York Times,
12-28:(A)1,4.

Viktor Yerofeyev
Russian author

1

[On the crime and aggressive atmosphere in Moscow since the Soviet Union collapsed]: This is not the same city it once was. It is a completely barbarian life we are living. There are no moral values, no family values, no religious values. Nothing at all. Before, it was fear [of Soviet authorities] that kept people in line; but when it vanished, there was nothing.

The Washington Post,
4-2:(A)14.

Wolfgang Zeitlmann
Member of
German Parliament

2

[On the influx of immigrants in Germany]: With the collapse of the Iron Curtain, Germany's situation has changed drastically. We're no longer a border state with a hermetically sealed eastern frontier. We're in the middle of Europe, adjacent to countries with economies in much worse shape than our own. That has created an irresistible sucking effect. Every oddball in Eastern Europe wants to cook his soup in this land of high living standards and good economic prospects, and Germans aren't used to it.

U.S. News & World Report,
5-16:42.

Vladimir V. Zhirinovsky
Member of Russian Parliament;
Leader, Liberal Democratic Party
of Russia

3

[Criticizing U.S. President Clinton for ruling out meeting with Zhirinovsky, the top vote-getter in Russia's recent election, when Clinton visits Russia shortly]: All of you in the West have become rotten and moldy. That is why you are afraid that a new honest and brave man has emerged in Russia. You want us to be weak and to rot together with you . . . I want to tell [Clinton] that we should have good, normal relations and he should not be afraid to meet me. He should not show that he is such a coward. He should meet me personally, and I will tell him everything. There is only one party in this country [Zhirinovsky's party], tell him that. Some President of the United States of America he is! Let him play his saxophone back home instead of coming here to meet with nobodies!

Shchelkovo, Russia, Jan. 6/
Los Angeles Times,
1-7:(A)1,11.

4

[On threats of Western air strikes against Serb positions in Bosnia during the current ethnic war there]: I want to warn all governments of Western countries that bombing any towns in Bosnia means declaring war on Russia. Let them not forget that the Russian army is still in Europe and it may stay there a long time.

News conference,
Belgrade, Yugoslavia, Jan. 30/
The Washington Post,
1-31:(A)12.

5

[To Bosnian Serbs who are threatened by NATO bombing in the current ethnic conflict in the Balkans]: Don't worry, brother. We [Russians] will protect you . . . If a single bomb falls on Serbia [positions in Bosnia], we will consider that an attack on Russia . . . Once we punished France; 50 years ago we did the same to Germany. Now the same treatment awaits anyone who mistreats the Serbs.

> *At rally,*
> *Bijeljina, Bosnia,*
> *Jan. 31/*
> *The Washington Post,*
> *2-1:(A)16.*

1

[On suggestions he may become Russian President by 1996]: The leader and the party are one and the same. This regime [of Russian President Boris Yeltsin] is in its final agony. And when a sick man is lying on the operating table, you need a single doctor, not a team of consultants.

> *At conference of his*
> *Liberal Democratic Party,*
> *Moscow, Russia/*
> *The New York Times,*
> *4-5:(A)6.*

2

[On his controversial, outspoken views]: If I behave like the good-natured intellectual I really am, I won't get votes. It's war out there, and I'm out to win . . . It's the sorry state of affairs in this country that forces me to take so tough a stand to avert something even worse. If there were a healthy economy and security for the people, I would lose all the votes I have.

> *Interview,*
> *Moscow, Russia,*
> *July 1/*
> *Time, 7-11:40, 42.*

3

The world is on the edge of a war. If something happens in Russia, that's where it will start. Everything here will come to an end, and the army will stage a coup. In order to feed a hungry and angry Russian population, we'll have to expand. Where? I say south, others say west. We already have soldiers [in Europe]. Another 300,000 and we'll remake Europe so it has Russian characteristics. We won't invade you ourselves; we'll send the Turks and the Arabs. That's how we'll destroy "white" Europe. Then we'll finish off the Arabs . . . Do you know why poor people rebel? Because they are robbed! You [in the West] all have warm, cozy houses. What do you expect of poor people? They'll just take that house and live in it. You're the ones who made us poor! You want us to leave this planet! We can't take any more!

> *Interview,*
> *Moscow, Russia/*
> *Vanity Fair,*
> *September:83.*

Peter Zwack
Former Hungarian Ambassador
to the United States

4

[On the success of former Communists in the just-held election in Hungary]: The nostalgia for [the Communist era] in this country is enormous. People want less corruption, more law and order and a government that takes care of them . . . The present [non-Communist] government has succeeded in making socialism popular in just four years, something the Communists couldn't do in 45 years.

> *The Washington Post,*
> *5-9:(A)12.*

THE ETHNIC CONFLICT IN THE BALKANS

All of the quotations in this sub-section relate to the ethnic civil war which broke out following the self-declared independence in 1992 of the Yugoslav republics of Bosnia-Herzegovina and Croatia. In this conflict, Bosnian Serbs, with support from Yugoslav Serbs, aim to conquer Muslim territory in Bosnia to form a larger Serbian-ruled area. The fighting has also involved Croatia.

Morton I. Abramowitz
President,
Carnegie Endowment
for International Peace
(United States)

1

The United States has to decide whether it is going to continue to be a pseudo-moralizer [about the war] or lead the West in resolving one of the most profound political and moral crises of our time.

The New York Times,
2-8:(A)8.

Yasushi Akashi
Ranking United Nations
representative in
Bosnia-Herzegovina

2

[On the limited use of UN-sanctioned NATO air strikes against Bosnian Serb positions]: We [at the UN] are in a very sensitive and delicate situation. If we did not act, we would be viewed as incompetent and spineless. But if we acted too vigorously, we could provoke an escalation leading to tragic consequences. We try to tread this narrow path.

Nov. 21/
The New York Times,
11-22:(A)6.

3

If we [the UN] leave [Bosnia], the suffering of civilians, particularly in the Muslim enclaves and in Sarajevo, may be of such tragic proportions that there would be a cry for a reintroduction of an international force, whether dressed in green or white. The conflict would sharpen and may spill out of Bosnia. Cleavages between the United States and Russia would be exacerbated. There would be a major destabilization in Europe.

The New York Times,
12-10:5.

Madeleine K. Albright
United States Ambassador/
Permanent Representative
to the United Nations

4

The objective of peace cannot be achieved by diplomacy alone. Our [the West's] diplomacy must be backed by a willingness to use force when that is essential in the cause of peace. For it is only force plus diplomacy that can stop the slaughter in Sarajevo and break down the stalemate [at the peace talks] in Geneva . . . We are entering uncharted waters. Cooperation between the NATO and the United Nations is essential—not only for the citizens and other safe areas in Bosnia but also for the precedent it will set for the future of collective security.

At United Nations,
New York, Feb. 14/
The New York Times,
2-15:(A)4.

Kofi A. Annan
Undersecretary General
of the United Nations
for Peacekeeping Operations

1

[Criticizing the U.S.—which does not have ground forces in Bosnia—for implying the UN is not doing all it can to end the conflict]: I believe the UN is being made a scapegoat. Of course, we do have a scapegoat function. But it is absolutely unfair when member states do not want to take the risks—when they do not want to commit the resources—but blame the UN for failure to act.

To reporters,
United Nations,
New York, Nov. 28/
The New York Times,
11-29:(A)4.

2

Even in situations where there is no peace to keep, properly organized and properly led [UN] peacekeepers can make major contributions. In the case of [the Balkans conflict], they have fed several million people. They have been able to protect several safe havens. When we talk of [the besieged city of] Bihac, we forget what the UN troops have done in Sarajevo. They have protected Srebrenica. They have made major sacrifices in Gorazde. These are not mean achievements.

Interview/
The New York Times,
12-5:(A)6.

Francis Briquemont
Lieutenant General,
Belgian armed forces;
Commander, United Nations
forces in Bosnia-Herzegovina

3

[Saying UN resolutions on the conflict don't have teeth]: I don't read the Security Council resolutions anymore because they don't help me. There is a fantastic gap between the resolutions of the Security Council, the will to execute those resolutions and the means available to commanders.

The New York Times,
1-20:(A)4.

George Bush
Former President
of the United States

4

[Criticizing U.S. President Clinton's reluctance to take the lead in intervening militarily in the war]: The United States can't wait for somebody else to decide what we have to do. If I had sat around and waited before Desert Storm [1991's U.S.-led war against Iraq's invasion of Kuwait] for the Congress to come along, [Iraqi President] Saddam Hussein would be in Riyadh [Saudi Arabia] today, and we would be paying 10 bucks for oil.

Newsweek, 2-21:15.

Jimmy Carter
Former President
of the United States

5

[Addressing Bosnian Serb leader Radovan Karadzic]: I cannot dispute your statement that the American public has had primarily one side of the story [the Muslim side]. [Carter's current visit with the Bosnian Serbs will provide] one of the rare chances to let the world know the truth.

Pale, Bosnia, Dec. 19/
The New York Times,
12-20:(A)6.

Warren Christopher
Secretary of State
of the United States

1

[Criticizing the actions of Bosnian Serbs]: [They are to blame for] a tangle of lies and misleading statements that seldom have been equaled. [This conflict is] the largest human tragedy in Europe since the descent of the Iron Curtain.

April 18/
The New York Times,
4-19:(A)4.

2

[Calling for U.S./NATO air strikes against Serb positions in Bosnia]: [The U.S.] just can't turn our back [on Bosnia]. I feel very strongly that this is a time when even a cautious Secretary of State, which perhaps I'll always be, feels the need to vindicate United States leadership and to take a strong robust position to ensure that this conflict does not spread and to ensure that we maintain the credibility of NATO as well as our own forces.

At Senate Appropriations
Subcommittee hearing,
Washington, D.C., April 21/
The Washington Post, 4-22:(A)41.

3

If you lift the [U.S.] arms embargo [against the Bosnian Muslims], then you have to ask the question: Can the Bosnians defend themselves? Probably, the question is no—at least, certainly, not right away. So you start a bombing campaign [against the Serbs] to help [the Muslims]. But no military expert that I know of feels that a bombing campaign will be successful. But the United States, having caused the withdrawal of UNPROFOR, lifting the arms embargo, starting a bombing campaign, would have its commitment made. Our national interest would have been engaged there. And I think we would probably have to vindicate that interest by then putting in ground troops.

Broadcast interview/
"This Week With David Brinkley,"
ABC-TV, 12-4.

Vitaly Churkin
Deputy Foreign Minister
of Russia

4

[Criticizing Bosnian Serb actions]: It's about time for Russia to stop all negotiations with the Bosnian Serbs. The time for talking is over. The Bosnian Serbs must understand that by dealing with Russia, they are dealing with a great power and not a banana republic. Moscow must decide if it can allow a group of extremists to use the politics of great Russia for achieving its own goals. Our answer is clear—never.

Moscow, Russia, April 18/
The New York Times,
4-19:(A)4.

Bill Clinton
President of the United States

5

[The warring factions are] going to have to make up their own mind to quit killing each other. I don't think that the international community has the capacity to stop people within that nation from their civil war until they decide to do it.

Washington, D.C., Jan. 24/
Los Angeles Times,
1-25:(A)8.

6

Our nation has clear interests at stake in this conflict. We have an interest in helping to prevent a broader conflict in Europe that is most compelling. We have an interest in showing that NATO, history's greatest military alliance, remains a credible force for peace in post-Cold War Europe. We have an interest in stemming the destabilizing flows of refugees that this horrible conflict is creating. And we clearly have a humanitarian interest in helping to prevent the strangulation of Sarajevo and the continuing slaughter of innocents in Bosnia. These interests do not justify unilateral American intervention in the crisis, but they do

(BILL CLINTON)

justify the involvement of America and the exercise of our leadership.

To reporters,
Washington, D.C., Feb. 9/
Los Angeles Times,
2-10:(A)6.

1

It is difficult to analogize this conflict from the point of view of the U.S. and the United Nations to others which occurred during the Cold War and which had some sort of Cold War rationale, some of which sometimes broke down. It's important not to be too arrogant about our ability to totally dictate events so far from our shores.

News conference,
Washington, D.C.,
April 22/
Los Angeles Times,
4-23:(A)18.

2

[On criticism that his policy regarding the conflict is indecisive]: [Those critics have] simplistic ideas that sound good on bumper stickers but that would have tragic consequences. [The Administration's policy] is not quick; it is not neat; it is not comfortable. But I am convinced, in a world of interdependence where we must lead by working with others, it is the right path. Our Administration will not walk away from this Bosnian conflict. But we will not embrace solutions that are wrong. We plan to continue the course we have chosen—raising the price on those who pursue aggression, helping to provide relief to the suffering and working with our partners in Europe to move the [warring] parties to a workable agreement.

At. U.S. Naval Academy
commencement,
May 25/
Los Angeles Times,
5-26:(A)14.

William J. Crowe, Jr.
United States Ambassador
to the United Kingdom

3

I have an obligation to try to explain what I think the American perception of Bosina is—essentially that it's a European problem but also that the Bosnian Serbs are the aggressors, that we have countries [in the Balkans], no matter how fledgling they are, that have been recognized, and now the aggressors are trying to upset those boundaries and have committed a lot of atrocities. Whether it is right or wrong, many Americans believe that the [Western arms] embargo [against the Bosnian Muslims] unduly helps the aggressor against the aggrieved, and that we would be better off—though it would not be a perfect answer—if we lifted the embargo and, in the trite phrase, made the playing field level.

Interview,
London, England/
The New York Times,
11-28:(A)6.

Milovan Djilas
Author;
Former Vice President
of Yugoslavia

4

[Saying the reign of Communism in Yugoslavia after World War II and its leader Josip Broz Tito put a lid on ethnic hatreds among the various groups within the country]: The reality is that the Communists defeated Serbian and Croatian nationalism as well as the Nazis. Yugoslav Communism alone resolved the national question after World War II. Tito was acutely aware of this, and to the end he was afraid that Yugoslavia might break up [which it finally did in 1992, leading to the current conflict].

The New York Times,
11-26:4.

Radoje Djukic
Minister of Small Business
of Serbia (Yugoslavia)

1

[On the commercial outlook for his country after the UN lifts economic sanctions imposed because of Serbia's role in the Balkans conflict]: This country is going to be a tiger in Europe. Everyone knows our products are good. Once the sanctions are lifted, a lot of people will want to buy from us—even if they think we're monsters.
The Christian Science Monitor,
11-23:9.

Michael Dugan
General (Ret.),
and former Chief of Staff,
United States Air Force

2

[Criticizing the recent limited NATO air strikes against Serbian forces laying siege to Gorazde, Bosnia]: There has been no plan, just an ad hoc response. No military power applied in this kind of fashion is going to have much of a political impact. There are few examples in history where raids have had a significant impact, and these two or three attacks do not qualify as a good raid.
The New York Times,
4-19:(A)5.

Lawrence S. Eagleburger
Former Deputy Secretary of State
of the United States

3

[On recent U.S./NATO air strikes against Serbian positions in Bosnia]: It's a piddly little sort of pop on the nose.
Newsweek, 4-25:19.

Nabil A. Elaraby
Egyptian Ambassador/Permanent
Representative to the United Nations

4

The continuation of the [conflict] in Bosnia and Herzegovina and the inability of the [UN] Security Council to take decisive and immediate measures to rectify that situation puts a big question mark on the credibility of the Council in its capacity as the custodian of international peace and security. It also puts the whole United Nations system and the contemporary international system in the balance.
At United Nations,
New York, Sept. 23/
The New York Times,
9-24:6.

Jonathan Eyal
Director of studies,
International Institute
for Strategic Studies (Britain)

5

The Yugoslav war has revealed Western institutions as bungling, incompetent and powerless. We [in the West] thought we could bark and people in the Balkans would listen; but they defied us and found us naked. The message that sends is terrible. The only question now is how violent the Bosnian war will be and how far will it spread.
The New York Times,
11-26:4.

Ejup Ganic
Vice President
of Bosnia-Herzegovina

6

[Asking the U.S. to unilaterally lift the arms embargo imposed by the UN against Bosnian Muslims]: We want the change because we are dying. We are not asking for your troops to fight [against the Serbs] for us on the ground. That is our job and our task. But please, do not combine any more big words with small deeds.
Before U.S. Senate
Foreign Relations Committee,
Washington, D.C.,
June 23/
The New York Times,
6-24:(A)6.

WHAT THEY SAID IN 1994

Newt Gingrich
United States Representative
R-Georgia

1

[Calling for the UN to lift its arms embargo against the Bosnian Muslims so they can defend against the Serbs]: I think the United Nations has proven itself a failed instrument in Bosnia. It won't allow the Bosnians to defend themselves and it hasn't defended the Bosnians.

Broadcast interview/
"Meet the Press,"
NBC-TV, 4-24.

Newt Gingrich
United States Representative, R-Georgia;
Speaker of the House-designate

2

[The U.S. should send its former Joint Chiefs of Staff Chairman, General Colin Powell,] to visit Belgrade and to visit the Bosnian Serb leadership and to say to them: "If you launch a general offensive [after UN forces leave Bosnia], we [the U.S.] would reserve the right to use air power against every position you have, against every command-and-control center, against every position everywhere. We would reserve the right to take you apart, and we would do it in three to five days, and we would paralyze your capacity to function as a society. And we're telling you to just back off and accept an armed truce." And I would do it all with air power, but I would do it like Desert Storm [the 1991 U.S.-led offensive against Iraq in the Persian Gulf war]. I would not engage in this nonsensical "you shoot one missile at us, we'll drop one bomb."

Broadcast interview/
"Meet the Press,"
NBC-TV, 12-4.

Al Gore
Vice President of the United States

3

[Defending recent U.S./NATO air strikes against Serbian positions in Bosnia]: The fact is

when the United Nations has said something in the past, the Serbs and others have sometimes doubted it. I don't think they doubt it now.

Newsweek, 4-25:19.

Lee H. Hamilton
United States Representative,
D-Indiana

4

I think almost certainly you have to have a more robust reaction by NATO and the United States here. There's been a real humiliation of both organizations, and we simply cannot take the kind of brutality that we have seen from the Serbs in [the Bosnian city of] Gorazde without some kind of response.

The New York Times,
4-20:(A)4.

Steny H. Hoyer
United States Representative,
D-Maryland

5

For two years now, we have looked the [Bosnian Serb] aggressor in the eye and said, "If you go one step further, we will take definitive action [against you]." And they took some steps, and we backed up. There is an old, old, historical lesson: Tyrants never respond to weakness.

Los Angeles Times,
6-10:(A)7.

Douglas Hurd
Foreign Secretary
of the United Kingdom

6

If they [Bosnian Serbs] want to have a settled future, if they want to reconstruct towns and villages, if they want to see some decent standard of living for themselves and their children, if they want a place in Europe and the world, then they'll

(DOUGLAS HURD)

need to settle. Because they're not going to achieve any of those things by hanging on to land which they now occupy by force.

News conference,
London, England, April 25/
Los Angeles Times, 4-26:(A)7.

1

We don't see a military victory for one side or another in this war, and we are not involved in helping one side or another to a military victory, as we think that is impossible.

Nov. 21/
The New York Times,
11-22:(A)6.

Alija Izetbegovic
President of Bosnia-Herzegovina

2

What shall be the result of the war in Bosnia, which is now being prolonged due to a mixture of incapability, hesitation and sometimes even ill will of the West? The result shall be a discredited United Nations, a ruined NATO, Europeans demoralized by a feeling of inability to respond to the first crisis after the Cold War.

At conference on European security,
Budapest, Hungary, Dec. 5/
The New York Times,
12-6:(A)4.

Josef Janning
Deputy director,
Research Group
on European Affairs,
University of Mainz (Germany)

3

The true lesson of the conflict is the return of *Realpolitik* [in the world], of nations and their clients, and of balance-of-power strategies. It's the defeat of order based on norms and principles like democracy, human rights and non-aggression.

The Christian Science Monitor,
2-23:18.

Alain Juppe
Foreign Minister of France

4

I say today that the obstinacy of some and the demagogy of others risk setting the Balkans ablaze tomorrow. I am still ready to do everything I can to prevent such a development, but my duty, alas, is to say that it [is] no longer improbable . . . [And there are] governments [such as the U.S.] that want to give us [Europeans] lessons when they have not lifted a little finger to put even one man on the ground [in Bosnia].

Before French National Assembly,
Paris, France, Dec. 7/
The New York Times, 12-8:(A)1.

Radovan Karadzic
Leader, Bosnian Serbs

5

The sufferings of the divided Serbian people have gone on for 600 years. One can hear the moans of the parts separated from the whole, and the whole yearns for its separated parts as orphans long for their mothers and a mother longs for lost children. For 600 years, the Serbs have lived with reminiscences of their past glory and lost greatness . . . Serbia is a world miracle. Serbia is a model for countries and nations. Serbia is a creation of the Lord. It is a rock on which empires and world orders break. Serbia is something great. Its greatness is measured by the hatred of its enemies.

World Press Review,
May:18.

6

[Criticizing an international proposal to end the conflict by dividing Bosnia among the Serbs, Muslims and Croats according to a specific map outline]: The contact group [proposing the plan] is playing with fire. It is clear that they want to foist on the victorious [Serbian] side in this war, on the victorious army, the Serbian army, humiliating conditions to end the war. If the map is not changed, we should definitely go our own way. We should stop all cooperation with this entire

(RADOVAN KARADZIC)

worldwide mafia concerning our problem. We should deny the right of anyone in the world community to dictate to the Serbian states.

Interview, July 1/
The New York Times,
7-2:3.

1

If NATO or the United States want to assist the United Nations [to leave Bosnia], then they should not approach Serbian territory. We would not attack them, but if they approach Serb territory and are hostile to us, there would be a big war between us. There will be another Vietnam.

Interview, Dec. 9/
The New York Times,
12-10:5.

Ivo Knezevic
Minister of Information
of Bosnia-Herzegovina

2

[Criticizing what he says is a UN position that Bosnian Muslims should accept the victories of Bosnian Serbs]: The problem is that the basic aim of the [UN] mission from the beginning has been to see us [Muslims] capitulate. All their calculations have been based on this assumption. We've blown all their plans because we do not accept this. This is why we have become such an irritation to the power brokers of the world.

Los Angeles Times,
5-28:(A)8.

3

[Criticizing UN peacekeeping operations in his country]: Not a single objective of this [UN] mission has been achieved, because it is compelled to remain neutral in the face of an obvious aggression [by the Serbs]. For UNPROFOR troops, overseeing our people's suffering has become a matter of jobs [for themselves]. We don't want to sound unfair or ungrateful for their endeavors and the

aid that we do receive, but the negative aspects of this mission are now dominating.

Interview, Sarajevo, Bosnia/
Los Angeles Times,
6-22:(A)8.

Richard G. Lugar
United States Senator,
R-Indiana

4

[The U.S. Clinton Administration has] been hoping that Bosnia would go away, disappear from the front pages and the TV news. But surely [President Clinton] knows now that it won't. [In responding to the conflict,] he must take a leadership role he doesn't want, that he's uncomfortable with, that's risky, because he's the only person in the world who can do it.

The New York Times,
2-8:(A)8.

Michael Mandelbaum
Foreign-policy specialist,
School of Advanced
International Studies,
Johns Hopkins University
(United States)

5

[On U.S./NATO threats to use air strikes against Serb positions that are firing on Sarajevo]: It's bombing as therapy. Therapy for us [in the West], that is; proof that we've done *something* at last—even if the Serbs simply move their heavy weapons and strike elsewhere, or hunker down till the dust clears.

Time, 2-21:29.

John McCain
United States Senator, R-Arizona

6

[Arguing against increasing the use of U.S. air power against Bosnian Serbs]: If the President [Clinton] succeeds in securing NATO agreement

(JOHN McCAIN)

for this more extensive use of air power, I fear that we will become further enmeshed in incremental escalation until such point where we face a choice between deploying American ground troops or withdrawing in abject defeat.

April 20/
Los Angeles Times,
4-21:(A)13.

Slobodan Milosevic
President of Serbia (Yugoslavia)

1

[Criticizing the Bosnian Serbs for not accepting an international plan to end the ethnic conflict in Bosnia by partitioning the country and officially recognizing Bosnian Serb areas]: All explanations that the Serbian people [in Bosnia] would be threatened by accepting the peace plan become senseless and absurd when one considers they are refusing a secure border guarantee by the international community; they are refusing a border across which no grenades can fly and over which nobody would be killed. They are rejecting peace at the moment when their Serbian republic has been recognized over half of Bosnia and Herezegovina's territory, and when their acceptance of peace would bring about the lifting of sanctions against those [the Yugoslav Serbs] without whom they cannot exist . . . Their decision to reject peace cannot be in the interest of the people by any criteria of truth and justice. It can only be in the interest of war profiteers and in the interest of those people whose conscience is not clear, who are afraid of peace—in the event of which all their wrongdoing would come to light.

Aug. 4/
The New York Times,
8-5:(A)5.

George J. Mitchell
United States Senator, D-Maine

2

[Criticizing those members of the U.S. Senate who want the U.S. to unilaterally defy the UN-imposed arms embargo on Bosnian Muslims]: [British, French and other allied peacekeeping forces on the ground in Bosnia] are doing what we [the U.S.] have been unwilling to do. Their men are being killed. Their men are being wounded. Their countries are spending hundreds of millions of dollars to try to bring about a resolution to this conflict. And here we are [ready to supply arms to the Muslims and thus widen the war and endanger those allied troops], preaching at them, insulting them, telling them, "You've got to do what we say."

Before the Senate,
Washington, D.C., June 24/
The New York Times, 6-25:2.

Daniel Patrick Moynihan
United States Senator, D-New York

3

[Saying the West should intervene militarily in the conflict and the UN should lift its arms embargo against the Bosnian Muslims]: We are in the process of shredding the entire legal order we put into place at the end of World War II . . . [The Yugoslav republic of Serbia has in effect] invaded another country [Bosnia], a member of the United Nations, in violation of the [UN] Charter. Then they have specifically associated themselves with genocide, in violation of the genocide treaty, of which we [the U.S.] are a member, and is our law; and in [the city of Gorazde, they have violated] the fourth Geneva convention on the treatment of civilians during wartime.

Broadcast interview/
"This Week With David Brinkley,"
ABC-TV, 4-24.

Leon E. Panetta
Chief of Staff to President
of the United Stated Bill Clinton

4

[Dropping a U.S. push for the use of NATO air strikes against the Bosnian Serbs]: Our only hope is that at some point the parties recognize

(LEON E. PANETTA)

that there's no use continuing the kind of carnage that's going on there at the present time.

Washington, D.C., Nov. 28/
The New York Times,
11-29:(A)1.

William J. Perry
Secretary of Defense
of the United States

1

[On the possibility of U.S./NATO air strikes against Serb forces around Sarajevo]: If air strikes are Act One of this melodrama, what is Act Two, Act Three and the conclusion of the melodrama? . . . It's a two-track process, peace negotiations and air strikes. The air strikes . . . allow us to reduce the level of carnage and violence that was going on in Sarajevo by raising the price for anybody that wants to shell that city, dramatically raising the price. And secondly, they illustrate firmness and resolve and solidarity in NATO, and therefore by that means they help the peace process along.

Broadcast interview/
"This Week With David Brinkley,"
ABC-TV, 2-13.

2

The Serbs have [now] occupied 70 percent of [Bosnia]. There's no prospect, as I see it, of the Muslims' winning that back . . . NATO is prepared to respond with air strikes [against the Serbs] if the United Nations asks them. [But] the United Nations has not been asking for air strikes, and therefore we are really powerless to conduct air strikes to influence that situation. I should say, though, that even if they were to ask for air strikes, the air strikes cannot determine the outcome of the ground combat.

Broadcast interview/
"Meet the Press,"
NBC-TV, 11-27.

Malcolm Rifkind
Secretary of Defense
of the United Kingdom

3

[Criticizing those in the U.S.—which does not have ground forces in Bosnia—who blame the British and French for blocking the use of NATO air strikes against the Bosnian Serbs]: I think that when we have thousands of brave British soldiers—some of whom have lost their lives in Bosnia—giving their all to help the cause of peace, it ill becomes people in the countries that have not provided a single soldier on the ground to make that kind of criticism.

Interview, Nov. 28/
The New York Times,
11-29:(A)4.

Michael Rose
Lieutenant General,
British Army;
Commander of United Nations
forces in Bosnia

4

[A pullout of UN forces from Bosnia would lead to] a nightmare scenario. If we go, who is going to feed the 2.7 million people here who are totally dependent on aid? Who is going to push the peace process? The cease-fire in Sarajevo would unravel. Even in central Bosnia, where there is already a political agreement, there is the risk that everything would come unstuck.

Interview/
Los Angeles Times,
5-24:(H)3.

5

[On calls for increased use of force by the UN in the Bosnian conflict]: If someone wants to fight a war here on moral or political grounds, fine, great—but count us out . . . I'm not going to fight a war in white-painted tanks.

Newsweek, 10-10:19.

Muhamed Sacirbey
Bosnian Ambassador
to the United Nations

1

[On the Bosnian Muslim military force's readiness to fight the Bosnian Serbs]: We're not engaged in this for military victory. But we have learned that successful actions on the battlefield are the best diplomacy.

Newsweek, 2-14:23.

Raymond Seitz
United States Ambassador
to the United Kingdom

2

[On U.S. policy on Bosnia]: We have [a] disconnect. For example, we are rather warlike in the air, whereas the people on the ground are trying to be peacekeepers. We say we're not going to put any troops in. But we tell people they need to secure the peace. Then we vote not to raise the [spending] ceiling at the UN . . . It just throws these people off over here [in Europe]. We need a little more patience, a longer sense that history begins before the arrival of the first CNN crew.

Interview/
U.S. News & World Report,
5-16:39.

Haris Silajdzic
Prime Minister
of Bosnia-Herzegovina

3

[Saying the U.S. should intervene militarily against the Bosnian Serbs]: The answer is, use force . . . Otherwise, this is going to be a very, very long and bloody "peace." [Use] air strikes. When they [Serbs] kill innocent people, they should be punished for that, and they will not stop until they are punished.

Broadcast interview/
"Meet the Press,"
NBC-TV, 4-3.

4

All we [Bosnian Muslims] ask from the United Nations and NATO is to protect our borders. The Serbs are attacking across the Croatian border from a United Nations-protected area. Their tanks are effectively enjoying United Nations protection while Bosnia still has an arms embargo imposed on it. This is completely absurd.

Nov. 21/
The New York Times,
11-22:(A)6.

Srdjan Trifkovic
Bosnian Serb representative
to the United Kingdom

5

[When Bosnia broke away from Yugoslavia in 1992,] it was the intention of the Muslims [in Bosnia] to disregard Serbian aspirations, reducing them to the status of an irrelevant and despised minority. Armed resistance was the only way.

Newsweek, 3-21:45.

Boris N. Yeltsin
President of Russia

6

My suggestion [is] that we, the leaders of Russia, the United States, the European Union, the United Nations, should come to some neutral European country and invite all the Yugoslav [Serb, Muslim, Croat] leaders. We should put them around a negotiating table and get them to sign a peace treaty. There's no other solution, because the Muslims tell Americans, "No, *we're* not provoking it." The Serbs tell us, "No, *we're* not starting it." In fact, it's hard to understand who is starting it and who is responding. Even the UN peacekeepers that are right there cannot quite figure it out. That's why I suggest this, and I believe it would be the best way out for Yugoslavia and the entire world if the leaders of the countries involved sorted it out.

Interview,
Moscow, Russia, April/
Newsweek, 5-2:47.

WHAT THEY SAID IN 1994

Jovan Zametica
Adviser to Bosnian Serb leader
Radovan Karadzic

1

Our message is simple. We Serbs wish to live together as Serbs in one state, under one roof. We don't want to be forcibly incorporated as national minorities in hostile states.

Newsweek, 3-21:45.

The Middle East

Yasir Abed-Rabbo
Director, information department,
Palestine Liberation Organization

1

[On the recent massacre of Palestinians by an Israeli settler]: During the past [Israeli-Palestinian peace] negotiations, the Israeli side was stressing the Israeli security requirements. This massacre has proved that security is a Palestinian need mainly, and for this reason, without having real guarantees for the security of the Palestinian people, I don't think the resumption of the talks, even in Washington, will lead to a successful result.

Feb. 25/
Los Angeles Times,
2-26:(A)8.

Yasir Abed-Rabbo
Minister of Information
of the Palestinian Authority
(the governing entity of the
now self-ruled areas of
Gaza and Jericho)

2

[On the implementation of the Israel-PLO agreement allowing Palestinian self-rule in Jericho and Gaza]: We and the Israelis have completed the first stage of what we agreed to almost a year ago. It was a very difficult test, but our success is giving a very strong impetus to the peace process throughout the region. I won't say it can't be stopped, but even the doubters now want to join in.

Paris, France, July 7/
Los Angeles Times,
7-8:(A)14.

Mohsen abu Ayta
Official of Hamas Islamic
Resistance Movement in Gaza

3

[On PLO leader Yasir Arafat's visit to Gaza after implementation of last year's Israel-PLO

mutual-recognition agreement allowing Palestinian self-rule in Gaza and Jericho, an agreement Hamas doesn't support]: We are not going to stand in front of these emotional crowds who are welcoming Arafat, because some people like him. But at the same time, we will not let anybody say that we quit or stood aside. We are keeping silent, because we know this agreement will fail. We must let the people enjoy these emotional times. Let us bide our time . . . I think of the agreement as a very nice meal. Nice and tasty, good smell. But inside, it's full of poison [for the Palestinian people]. When the people eat this meal, they are going to get a very big stomachache.

Los Angeles Times,
7-6:(A)6.

Bassam abu Sharif
Senior adviser to
Palestine Liberation Organization
chairman Yasir Arafat

4

[On the effect on Palestinian-Israeli peace negotiations of the recent massacre of Palestinians by a Jewish settler]: There will be no more two stages of a settlement. There will be one stage: dismantling [Jewish] settlements [in the occupied territories], ending occupation, normalizing relations. Condemnation, apology, sorrow [by Israel] means nothing. It means nothing. What means something concrete is a serious step toward peace . . . And dismantling settlements built illegally is an indispensable step.

Los Angeles Times,
3-2:(A)8.

Joseph Alpher
Director, Jaffee Center for
Strategic Studies,
Tel Aviv University (Israel)

5

[Israel's enthusiasm for peace negotiations with the Arabs] is highly dependent on Israelis'

329

(JOSEPH ALPHER)

sense of personal security. If they do not feel secure, the peace process will fail.

U.S. News & World Report,
10-31:46.

Yasir Arafat
Chairman,
Palestine Liberation Organization

1

[On the PLO responsibility for running Gaza and Jericho as part of last year's Israel-PLO mutual-recognition agreement]: For us it is easier because the PLO is more than just an organization. We are responsible for the whole life of our people. We have a parliament representing Palestinians everywhere; no revolution ever had a parliament. We have democracy. We have established universities, schools and hospitals. We have a political department, one of the strongest in the Arab world.

Interview/Time, 1-3:42.

2

[On whether the recent massacre of Palestinians by an Israeli settler will negatively affect Israeli-Palestinian peace talks]: What kind of peace are you talking about, if the crimes and killings against our people do not stop? This will have a serious impact, not just on the negotiations, but on all aspects and at all levels.

Feb. 25/
Los Angeles Times,
2-26:(A)8.

3

[Demanding an armed international peace-keeping presence to protect Palestinians in the Israeli-occupied territories following the recent massacre of Palestinians in Hebron by an Israeli settler]: Who will give me the guarantee—give it to my people—that there will be no [further] massacres? And what will give our people tranquillity, security and peace? Slogans? They will not

forget. You have seen the fury of our people, of the Arab peoples, the Islamic nation. The [international] armed presence is basic . . . [As for last year's Israel-PLO peace agreement,] for the first time the furious masses in Hebron slashed my photos [after the massacre]. For the first time! [Israeli Prime Minister Yitzhak] Rabin has one opposition [Israel's Likud Party]; I am facing Palestinian opposition, Arab opposition, Islamic opposition, Christian opposition. Be fair. From the beginning [of the peace agreement], I am paying the price of the peace.

Interview, March 5/
Newsweek, 3-14:32.

4

The Israeli settlements [in the occupied West Bank and Gaza] have always been . . . a major obstacle on the road to peace. Today, and I say it with regret, they have become an alternative to peace. Peace cannot be achieved . . . as long as these extremist hotbeds lie at every corner of the road.

Speech,
Strasbourg, France, April 13/
Los Angeles Times, 4-14:(A)10.

5

[Saying arms are going into the hands of Jewish settlers in the occupied territories where an Israel-PLO agreement will allow Palestinian self-rule]: Guns! Guns are flowing into the territories. Those Jewish settlements are powder kegs, and the Palestinian factions are arming themselves too. I will not approve any agreement [with Israel] that does not provide adequate means to assure law and order and protect human life. I will not preside over another Somalia.

Interview,
Tunis, Tunisia/
Vanity Fair, May:18.

6

[On the Israel-PLO agreement on implementing Palestinian self-rule in Jericho and Gaza]: If this step needs great courage to complete it after

(YASIR ARAFAT)

long decades of war and violence, then the coming steps will need even greater courage and deep vision. Our peoples have struggled for a very, very long time to witness this day . . . We must all realize that all those who are lovers of peace must consider the seriousness of this step to see that it is carefully executed and implemented.

At signing ceremony
for the agreement,
Cairo, Egypt, May 4/
Los Angeles Times,
5-5:(A)6.

Hafez al-Assad
President of Syria

1

[Addressing U.S. President Clinton, and denying that Arab guerrilla groups fighting Israel are terrorists]: Who says that working to liberate Arab land can be classified as terrorism? Did you [Americans] not fight whom you considered to be an occupier? Were George Washington and his comrades terrorists?

At meeting with Clinton,
Geneva, Switzerland, Jan. 16/
The New York Times,
1-19:(A)8.

2

Syria seeks a just and comprehensive peace with Israel as a strategic choice that secures Arab rights, ends the Israeli occupation [of Arab land] and enables our peoples in the region to live in peace, security and dignity. In honor we fought, in honor we negotiate, and in honor we shall make peace. We want an honorable peace for our people and for the hundreds of thousands who paid their lives in defense of their countries and their rights. There is hardly a home in Syria in which there is no martyr who fell in defense of his country, nation and of Arab rights. For the sake of all those, for their sons, daughters and families, we want the peace of the brave—a genuine peace which can

survive and last—a peace which secures the interests of each side and renders all their rights.

News conference,
Geneva, Switzerland, Jan. 16/
The New York Times,
1-17:(A)6.

3

I stressed to [U.S.] President Clinton [in recent talks] the readiness of Syria to commit itself to the objective requirements of peace through the establishment of peaceful, normal relations with Israel in return for Israel's full withdrawal from the Golan [Heights] to the line of June 4, 1967, and from the south of Lebanon.

News conference,
Damascus, Syria, Oct. 27/
The New York Times,
10-28:(A)5.

Tarik Aziz
Deputy Prime Minister of Iraq

4

[Criticizing the U.S. Clinton Administration for its hostile attitude toward his country and Iran]: Amateurs! . . . They have this foolish policy of dual containment. That's just a theory put on paper—but in practice, who is being contained? First of all, Iran is not contained by any means. Iran can buy whatever it wants from all over the world. It has money. It has borders. It has ports. There is no containment on Iran. And even Iraq is not contained . . . A nation is not a bunch of chickens to put in a cage and contain it and feed it, give it the small amounts of food you would like to give it. This is very arrogant and shallow kind of thinking . . . I don't know what's behind this obsession in the position of the United States. They have been just wasting their time and efforts and money trying to achieve what they cannot achieve. The Iraqi people are not going to change their government because some people in the [U.S.] White House or the State Department don't like their government.

Interview, New York, N.Y./
Los Angeles Times, 4-10:(M)3.

Ahmed Bahar

Director, Islamic Association,
charity organization

1

[Criticizing the lifestyle of many officials of the PLO, which will administer the newly self-ruled area of Jericho and Gaza]: The PLO leaders live in hotels and villas. They drive nice cars like Mercedes. They have friendly relations with these Arab dictatorships. These PLO officials say they are Muslims, but they do not act like Muslims. They drink and carry on, but most of all they do not give the money they have to the poor. They neglect those who are suffering.

The New York Times,
3-8:(A)9.

Ehud Barak

Lieutenant General and Chief of Staff,
Israeli Defense Forces

2

Syria has 4,000 tanks, 700 fighter planes and missiles such as Scud Bs and Cs, which include binary chemical warheads more advanced than those of the Iraqis. It's possible to reach all of Israel with them. Viewed from a historical perspective, a long stalemate [in Israeli negotiations with Syria] makes another confrontation very probable. This doesn't mean there is a timetable, or that nothing can be done; but in a historic sense, it starts a countdown. You don't know if it will take place in two or five years; the nature of the confrontation is unknown, as is who else will be involved.

Interview/
U.S. News & World Report,
12-26:51.

Yossi Beilin

Deputy Foreign Minister of Israel

3

[On last year's Israel-PLO agreement allowing Palestinian self-rule in Jericho and Gaza]: There are many problems down the road, but I believe all of them are surmountable, all of them

. . . I'm not saying Israel is ready to compromise on Jerusalem now, but I think that since we are ready to go a very long way with the Palestinians for many other issues, we can solve the problem of Jerusalem too, [when each side] understands the "red lines" of the other side.

To reporters,
Jerusalem, Israel,
July 7/
Los Angeles Times,
7-8:(A)14.

Zine Abidine ben Ali

President of Tunisia

4

[Addressing PLO leader Yasir Arafat, who has been based in Tunisia the last 12 years, on his impending return to live in now-Palestinian-ruled Gaza]: Go home in peace. All our congratulations to Palestine on the occasion of your triumphant return. And all our congratulations too to her valiant people upon the return of her combatants. Now, by the grace of God, there will be no more wandering, no more exile. Goodby, until we meet again in Palestine.

Farewell ceremony,
Tunis, Tunisia,
July 11/
Los Angeles Times,
7-12:(A)1.

Ted Galen Carpenter

Authority on the Middle East,
Cato Institute (United States)

5

[On the U.S. program of flying patrols over Northern Iraq to protect Kurds from the Iraqi government]: This mission is a little like the Energizer [battery] bunny: It keeps on going and going and going with no clear destination. It's so diffuse, so ill-defined, I'm not sure what our policy in Iraq is.

USA Today, 4-15:(A)3.

Warren Christopher
Secretary of State
of the United States

1

[On PLO chairman, Yasir Arafat]: He is the indispensable figure [in the Palestinian-Israeli peace process]. He is a political leader, but he is also the flag and *The Star-Spangled Banner* all wrapped into one person.

Before House
Appropriations Committee,
Washington, D.C., March 1/
Los Angeles Times, 3-2:(A)8.

2

[Saying the U.S. wants to continue the international economic sanctions against Iraq, despite increasing pressure from other nations to ease them]: Our resolve to defend this interest against aggression from any quarter is as strong today as it was when the United States led the coalition effort to liberate Kuwait from Iraq's aggression [in 1991]. We remain vigilant and determined. We are conscious that the region is far from free of threats.

News conference,
Riyadh, Saudi Arabia, April 27/
Los Angeles Times, 4-28:(A)8.

3

[On the Israel-PLO agreement on implementing Palestinian self-rule in Jericho and Gaza]: We live in an age of political wonder, where old hatreds are giving way to new hopes. With leadership, vision and courage, peace between old enemies is possible . . . We're here today because unspeakable acts of violence could not still the voices of peace, or weaken the resolve of the peacemakers.

At signing ceremony
for the agreement,
Cairo, Egypt, May 4/
Los Angeles Times, 5-5:(A)6.

4

[On the current peace talks between Jordan and Israel]: This ancient land's cries for peace are finally being heard. To a troubled world, you send forth a simple message that exalts our vision and strengthens our faith—that the scars of war can be healed, the divisions of memory can be overcome, peace between Arab and Jew can be made.

At opening ceremony
for the talks,
South Shuneh, Jordan, July 20/
Los Angeles Times, 7-21:(A)1.

5

[On recent terrorist bombings of Israeli and Jewish targets in Buenos Aires and London]: The killers involved in those terrible incidents must not—we will not let them—succeed. Groups like Hezbollah that wreak havoc and bloodshed must be defeated. And Hezbollah's patron, Iran, must be contained . . . Iran is an international outlaw, yet some nations still conduct preferential commercial relations with Iran and some take steps to appease that outlaw nation. They must understand that by doing so, they make it easier for Iran to use its resources to sponsor terrorism throughout the world.

Before House
Foreign Affairs Committee,
Washington, D.C., July 28/
The New York Times,
7-29:(A)1,2.

6

In an environment of genuine and comprehensive peace [between Israel and Syria], in which there'll be no place for terrorists on Israel's borders, we can look to the day when relations between Syria and the United States will improve.

At Georgetown University,
Oct. 24/
The New York Times,
10-25:(A)3.

Bill Clinton
President of the United States

7

During our meetings, I told [Syrian] President [Hafez] Assad that I was personally committed to

(BILL CLINTON)

the objective of a comprehensive and secure peace that would produce genuine reconciliation among the peoples of the Middle East. I told him of my view that the agreement between Israel and the PLO constituted an important first step by establishing an agreed basis for resolving the Palestinian problem. I also told him that I believe Syria is the key to the achievement of an enduring and comprehensive peace that finally will put an end to the conflict between Israel and her Arab neighbors. . . . I believe that President Assad has made a clear, forthright and very important statement on normal peaceful relations [with Israel]. Now, in order to achieve those relations, a peace agreement has to be negotiated in good faith and carried out. But [his] is an important statement—the first time that there has been a clear expression that there will be a possibility of that sort of relationship.

News conference,
Geneva, Switzerland, Jan. 16/
The New York Times, 1-17:(A)6.

1

[On the recent massacre of Palestinians by an Israeli settler]: On behalf of the American people, I condemn this crime in the strongest possible terms. I am outraged and saddened that such a gross act of murder could be perpetrated, and I extend my deepest sympathies to the families of those who have been killed and wounded. Extremists on both sides are determined to drag Arabs and Israelis back into the darkness of unending conflict and bloodshed. We must prevent them from extinguishing the hopes and the visions and the aspirations of ordinary people for a life of peaceful existence.

Washington, D.C., Feb. 25/
Los Angeles Times, 2-26:(A)11.

2

[On the just-signed peace declaration between Israel and Jordan]: It takes but a minute or two to cross the River Jordan, but for as long as most of

us can remember, the distance has seemed immense. The awful power of ancient arguments and the raw wounds of recent wars have left generations of Israelis, Jordanians and Palestinians unable to imagine, much less build, a life of peace and security. Today King Hussein [of Jordan] and [Israeli] Prime Minister [Yitzhak] Rabin give their people a new currency of hope and the chance to prosper in a region of peace.

News conference,
Washington, D.C., July 25/
The New York Times, 7-26:(A)5.

3

[On the signing of the Israeli-Jordanian peace declaration]: [The U.S.] will support leaders whose boldness and wisdom are creating a new Middle East. Today I have reaffirmed to [Israeli] Prime Minister [Yitzhak] Rabin that as Israel moves forward in the peace process, the constant responsibility of the United States will be to help ensure its security. I have also reaffirmed to [Jordanian] King Hussein my determination to assist Jordan in dealing with its burden of debt and its defense requirements.

News conference,
Washington, D.C., July 26/
Los Angeles Times, 7-27:(A)6.

4

[On his forthcoming trip to the Middle East]: I will visit Syria, because it is my judgment that the visit will further the goal of an ultimate peace agreement between Israel and Syria. And until that is done, we will never have comprehensive peace in the Middle East.

News conference,
Washington, D.C., Oct. 21/
The New York Times, 10-22:1.

5

[On the signing of an Israel-Jordan peace agreement]: [With today's signing,] we break the chains of the past that for too long have kept you [Israel and Jordan] shackled in the shadows of strife and suffering. You will take the hatred out

(BILL CLINTON)

of [your] hearts and you will pass along to your children the peace of a generation . . . Now you must make this peace real—to turn no-man's land into everyman's home, to take down the barbed wire, to remove the deadly mines, to help wounds of war to heal, open your borders, open your hearts.

At signing ceremony
for the agreement,
along Israel-Jordan border,
Oct. 26/USA Today,
10-27:(A)3.

Abba Eban
Former Foreign Minister
of Israel

1

[On the current improvement in relations between Israel and Jordan]: The task of leadership is not to follow public opinion blindly, but to lead public opinion; and both [Israeli] Prime Minister [Yitzhak] Rabin and [Jordanian] King Hussein are doing this . . . We never would have reached the agreement with Jordan unless we had reached the agreement with the Palestinians [last year]. And we won't have peace with Syria unless we cherish the Palestinian and Jordanian agreements.

Aug. 8/
The New York Times,
8-9:(A)3.

Saeb Erekat
Member,
Palestinian Authority
(the governing entity of the
now self-ruled areas
of Gaza and Jericho)

2

I have mixed feelings, to be honest with you [about Palestinian self-rule in the previously Israeli-occupied Gaza and Jericho]. On the one hand, it really is a good feeling to see that the Palestinian flag is flying in the skies of Jericho. But at the same time you have to keep in mind what we are

beginning—the road ahead is really a difficult one. There are enormous challenges facing us. It is time to plant rather than to harvest . . . What happened here is a step of just one centimeter in a journey that will be a hundred kilometers long.

Los Angeles Times,
5-14:(A)13.

3

[Saying there is a lack of funds for the new Palestinian administration of Jericho and Gaza]: The situation is very, very serious. Our institutions are brand new, and they need money to operate and meet the people's needs. Without money, they won't function. The whole effort could fail for the lack of start-up funds . . . We were born without a penny, and we are told that our ability to cope will test our readiness to govern ourselves. In a sense, this is right—if we can run Gaza and Jericho without cash, we are miracle workers. Instead of real help, we are getting one [foreign] delegation after another, flying in first-class and business-class from around the world, spending money on hotels and meals that we could use to pay salaries, and then telling us they will make a recommendation after the summer.

Los Angeles Times,
5-31:(A)1,8.

Mahdi Abdul Hadi
Palestinian political scientist

4

[On the Israel-PLO agreement on implementing Palestinian self-rule in Jericho and Gaza]: Peace should never become so prosaic that it will be reduced to municipal chores like street repairs and trash collection. But we will be measured and tested by our ability to give our children an education, to improve health care, to create jobs . . . Political power is always to be used for betterment.

May 4/
Los Angeles Times,
5-5:(A)7.

Hamad Youssef Hammadi
Minister of Information
of Iraq

1

[On the UN embargo against Iraq, which began following 1991's Persian Gulf war]: One day or another, these sanctions will go. Because there is a lot of pressure now on the American Administration. The American Administration does not want to admit failure, but it is cornered . . . Even if it comes to the worst case, a vote in the [UN] Security Council, and the U.S. uses the veto, the others will not comply. Politically, maybe. But not technically. If the U.S. uses the veto, the British or the French or the Russians will say, "This embargo is not a Council action, it is an American action." They will deal with Iraq, even if there is an American boycott.

Interview/
Los Angeles Times,
9-7:(A)6.

Jesse Helms
United States Senator,
R-North Carolina

2

This whole [Israel-Syria] peace process over there is a fraud, and you'd better look carefully at what's going on. Syria doesn't want peace. They want the [Israeli-occupied] Golan Heights. They want access to the pocketbooks of the American taxpayers . . . [As far as U.S. aid to Israel is concerned,] we need to find out what it would cost us to protect our interests in that region—oil and everything else—if there were no Israel. What I'm saying is, let's don't give them foreign aid. Let's give them compensation out of the [U.S.] defense budget.

Broadcast interview,
Washington, D.C./
"Evans & Novak,"
CNN-TV, 11-18.

Ahmed Abdul Karim Hih
Senior diplomat,
foreign ministry of
the Palestine Liberation Organization

3

[On the transfer of hundreds of PLO officials from Tunis, Tunisia, to Jericho and Gaza, which, under Israeli-PLO agreement, will now be administered by Palestinians]: Everybody is worried about the future. The future of the people, and the future of the PLO. From Tunis to where? From outside to inside, but where? Nothing is clear. In a few days, the Palestinian police will find themselves face to face with the people who led the uprising for seven years. It will not be easy. I think the matter of implementing this agreement, it is different than signing the agreement. To sign it was almost impossible. And to implement it, it will be unbelievable!

Los Angeles Times, 5-24:(H)5.

Bruce Hoffman
Co-director, Center for Terrorism
and Conflict Studies,
St. Andrew's University (Scotland)

4

[On the recent spate of terrorist attacks against Jewish targets while peace agreements are being signed between Israel and Arabs]: Perhaps the most dangerous time is still ahead as the peace process is actually implemented and as barriers between Mideast states come down. As peace takes hold, terrorists will have even more to lose and more motivation to demonstrate their capacity as spoilers.

Los Angeles Times, 8-1:(A)6.

Stefani Hoffman
Specialist on the former Soviet Union,
Hebrew University (Israel)

5

There is a desire on the part of the Russians to maintain a sphere of Russian interests rather than just be a vassal of the West. They see the

(STEFANI HOFFMAN)

Middle East as an area where they can show their independence.

The Christian Science Monitor,
4-25:3.

Hussein ibn Talal
King of Jordan

1

[On last year's Israel-PLO mutual-recognition agreement allowing Palestinian self-rule in Jericho and Gaza]: Initially there was a great deal of enthusiasm and hope within Israel and the Arab world. But none of us has shown the capabilities to deal with the challenges . . . The sad part was that an agreement was made without filling in all the details. As a result, there has been a delay. In the meantime some terrible things have happened in the region. We can't afford to have this . . . I believe the Arab-Israeli problem is the root cause of instability in this region. If that is adequately resolved, it will contribute greatly toward decreasing the tensions, the frustrations and the anger and despair. With peace, there will be the breaking of a new dawn as far as the quality of life of people is concerned. Almost every eruption in this area that has occurred in recent history had Palestine as the objective in some form or another. It has been the ladder to power of adventurers time and again. We have to address it.

Interview,
Time, 4-18:43.

2

[On his planned meeting with Israeli Prime Minister Yitzhak Rabin]: If the meeting between me and the Israeli Prime Minister is a price to change the picture of this country, I will not hesitate at all and I consider it a service for my country, which is facing threats from all directions.

Before Jordanian Parliament,
Amman, Jordan, July 9/
The New York Times,
7-14:(A)4.

3

[After signing an Israeli-Jordanian peace declaration]: I come before you today as a soldier who seeks to bear arms solely in the defense of his homeland, a man who understands the fears of his neighbors and who wishes only to live in peace with them.

Before joint session
of U.S. Congress,
Washington, D.C., July 26/
Los Angeles Times,
7-27:(A)6.

4

[On Islamic terrorists who are suspected of being responsible for recent violence against Jewish and Israeli targets in Buenos Aires, London and elsewhere]: [The terrorists are] enemies of life, enemies of human relations between human beings, enemies of hope, enemies of security, enemies of what should be normal among people. Nothing irritates me more or is more painful to me than to witness and see acts and attitudes attributed to Islam that have nothing to do with Islam, my faith and my religion.

News conference,
Washington, D.C., July 26/
Los Angeles Times,
7-27:(A)6.

5

[On the signing of an Israel-Jordan peace agreement]: This is peace with dignity; this is peace with commitment; this is our gift to our peoples and the generations to come . . . All of us have suffered for far too long. [U.S.] President Clinton, you have been our partner; you have been our friend; you have given us your support. No one will ever forget this day, and in particular we will always remember the fact that you personally came to be with us here on this most happy of occasions at the end of a chapter of darkness and the opening of a book of light.

At signing ceremony for the agreement,
along Israel-Jordan border,
Oct. 26/USA Today, 10-27:(A)3.

John Paul II
Pope

1

[On the legitimacy of the existence of Israel]: It must be remembered that Jews, who for 2,000 years were dispersed among the nations of the world, had decided to return to the land of their ancestors. This is their right.

Interview/
Los Angeles Times,
4-4:(A)4.

Sayed Kamal
Palestine Liberation Organization
ambassador to Egypt

2

[On Palestinian demands for protection following the recent massacre of Palestinians by an Israeli settler]: As a Palestinian official who has consistently supported the peace process even before the Oslo [PLO-Israeli peace] agreements last year, I am certain the whole edifice of peace that we built so far will collapse if we were to go back to the negotiating table without guarantees insulating Palestinians from what has become regular abuse by armed Jewish settlers in the West Bank and Gaza. It is a matter of overwhelming Palestinian—indeed Arab—popular demand. We can feel the pressure for action in the occupied territories. We can see it here [in Cairo] and in every Arab capital. What we need is waterproof measures of containment to be imposed on those settlers which insulates Palestinians from them. Ever since last Friday [the massacre], this is a binding popular demand. It is so strong that no Palestinian leader, including [PLO chairman Yasir] Arafat himself, can ignore it at this point.

Interview,
Cairo, Egypt,
March 10/
The New York Times,
3-11:(A)4.

Marwan Kanafani
Spokesman,
Palestine Liberation Organization

3

[On PLO leader Yasir Arafat's return to live in now-Palestinian-ruled Gaza]: When you look at his holster [which Arafat still wears as part of his military uniform], you miss his briefcase, and in the briefcase are the plans for Gaza's economic development . . . The struggle for Palestinian independence [from Israeli rule] has always been fought on many levels, in many arenas, on many battlefields. But we are very clear that the place today is Gaza, and the crucial test will be jobs. We know this, and it is our priority, our top priority.

To reporters,
Gaza Strip, July 12/
Los Angeles Times,
7-13:(A)8.

Ali Khamenei
Spiritual leader of Iran `

4

The Westerners are admitting that Iran's Islamic slogans and ideas have transformed Egypt, Algeria and some other places in the world. This is considered a great threat to Western capitalism. Therefore, Islamic Iran, which possesses a powerful weapon like the dynamism of its ideas, logic and words of justice, does not need to resort to terrorism.

The New York Times,
8-3:(A)3.

Kare Kristiansen
Nobel Prize jurist

5

[On her resigning as a Nobel jurist to protest the awarding of a shared Nobel Peace Prize to PLO leader Yasir Arafat]: Mr. Arafat is not in any way worthy of this prestigious prize. His past is too tainted with violence, terrorism and bloodshed, and his future too unpredictable.

U.S. News & World Report,
10-24:18.

Robert Kupperman
Senior adviser,
Center for Strategic
and International Studies
(United States)

1

[On the Middle East-based Hézbollah Islamic group, which many suspect was responsible for recent bombings of Jewish targets in Latin American]: Hezbollah is mainly engaged in terrorism in Europe and the Middle East, but it has migrated to Latin America. There are a lot of Israelis [in Latin America]—a lot of targets—and it's a springboard to the United States . . . The purpose behind the [latest] bombings is that Hezbollah wants to show it has a long arm and can reach anywhere.
Los Angeles Times,
8-4:(A)6.

David Levy
Former Foreign Minister
of Israel

2

[Criticizing Israel's Prime Minister, Yitzhak Rabin, for signing the Israel-PLO peace agreement, in light of PLO leader Yasir Arafat's recent speech which some have interpreted as being belligerent toward Israel]: What is becoming clear is that we have a naive government. Whoever heard the Prime Minister and understood his demand [for reaffirmation from Arafat of the peace agreement] understands that he was misled and did not see and did not read the map correctly.
May 23/
Los Angeles Times,
5-24:(A)14.

Abdul Salam Majali
Prime Minister of Jordan

3

[On the current peace talks between himself and Israeli Foreign Minister Shimon Peres]: [The talks are] vital and critical moments which historians shall cherish and poets shall relish. They will

be recorded in the annals of history in block letters, for they separate the age between peace and war, construction and destruction, and even life and death.
At opening ceremony for the talks,
South Shuneh, Jordan, July 20/
Los Angeles Times, 7-21:(A)12.

Alfred Moses
United States Ambassador to Romania;
Former president,
American Jewish Committee

4

[The Saudi Arabian government wants Iraqi President Saddam Hussein] wiped off the face of the earth, [and] they are critical of the United States for not finishing the job [during the Persian Gulf war] in 1991 and want to see it finished now. [And] they are not concerned with the dismemberment of Iraq.
U.S. News & World Report,
10-24:26.

Hosni Mubarak
President of Egypt

5

[On the Israel-PLO agreement on implementing Palestinian self-rule in Jericho and Gaza]: A historical move toward peace in the land of peace has started. Caravans are on the move. It is now time to plant roses in place of barbed wire and land mines.
At signing ceremony
for the agreement,
Cairo, Egypt, May 4/
Los Angeles Times, 5-5:(A)7.

Sari Nasr
Professor of sociology,
Jordan University

6

[On the recently signed peace treaty between Israel and Jordan]: [As far as the Palestinians are

(SARI NASR)

concerned,] it's all talk [about economic gains for them from the treaty], and economic gains don't really compensate for the injustices that lurk at the bottom of the matter, which is the Palestinian problem.

USA Today, 10-28:(A)4.

Jacques Neriah
Former Senior Adviser
on Arab Affairs to Israeli
Prime Minister Yitzhak Rabin

1

[On the current instability in the now-Palestinian-ruled Gaza]: This is a turning point. The walls in the street leading to [PLO leader Yasir] Arafat's office are painted with [Palestinian] graffiti calling for his assassination. He has become vulnerable. We are now entering a period of semi-instability during which the opposition will be testing him at every opportunity.

The New York Times,
12-3:4.

Benjamin Netanyahu
Leader, Likud Party of Israel;
Former Deputy Foreign Minister
of Israel

2

[Criticizing the Israel-PLO agreement on implementing Palestinian self-rule in Jericho and Gaza]: This is a black day for the state of Israel, and one of the most difficult days in the history of Zionism. [Israeli Prime Minister Yitzhak] Rabin will be able to say, "In Cairo [where the agreement was signed], I established the Palestinian state, the Palestinian terrorist state."

May 4/Los Angeles Times,
5-5:(A)6.

3

[Criticizing the forthcoming visit by PLO leader Yasir Arafat to Gaza and Jericho, now un-

der Palestinian rule following last year's Israel-PLO mutual-recognition agreement]. This is a national embarrassment [for Israel], allowing a murderer to enter Gaza and Jericho. The [Jewish] people feel this is a humiliation. With this visit of Arafat, the countdown begins toward a Palestinian Arab state whose goal is the destruction of Israel.

June 29/
Los Angeles Times,
6-30:(A)12.

4

[On his Likud Party's approval of a recent peace declaration between Israel and Jordan, despite Likud's criticism of the Israeli Labor Party's granting self-government to the PLO in Jericho and Gaza last year]: In contrast to the impression that the [Labor] government tries to create—that there is among the people a camp of supporters of peace [Labor] and a camp of enemies of peace [Likud]—the reality is the reverse, and we're proving that here today.

Before Israeli Knesset (Parliament),
Jerusalem, Israel, Aug. 3/
Los Angeles Times, 8-4:(A)8.

5

[Criticizing the awarding of the Nobel Peace Prize to PLO leader Yasir Arafat, who is sharing it with Israeli Prime Minister Yitzhak Rabin]: The fact the prize is given to the person who invented international terrorism, the archmurderer who says he decided to stop killing for a while and whose men killed seven Israelis this year, this fact turns the prize into a farce.

Newsweek, 10-24:21.

6

[Addressing U.S. President Clinton]: [Jerusalem is] a united city, under Israeli sovereignty, and it must remain so. I . . . hope that one day, Mr. President, it will be your policy, the policy of the United States.

Oct. 27/USA Today,
10-28:(A)1.

Sari Nusseibeh
Palestinian political scientist

1

[On the difficulties so far encountered by Palestinians in governing the newly self-ruled Gaza]: Certainly, if you go to Gaza today, unlike during the *intifadah*—uprising against Israel—at least you see some kind of satisfaction on the faces of the people there. The satisfaction of being free, at least in some sense, of the Israeli soldiers . . . [But] this is a situation of people who have come suddenly to take over things that have to be created, and that's extremely difficult. And to compound the difficulty, of course, we had no financial means in order to make things run. Israel has not made things easy. The international community has not made it easy. The international community has asked us to be perfect and to [create] perfect financial institutions in order to receive the funds that were promised us. But we can only become perfect if we start, but we can't start as perfect institutions.

Interview/
The Christian Science Monitor,
12-7:9.

Ehud Olmert
Mayor of Jerusalem, Israel

2

If an Arab wishes to purchase land and build in west Jerusalem, I have no objection. Likewise, I must respect the right of every Jew to live anywhere in Jerusalem . . . Jerusalem will, one day, be negotiated over. [But] one does not negotiate the essence of Jewish history.

Interview/
World Press Review,
March:34.

Ori Orr
Chairman, Foreign Affairs
and Defense Committee,
Israeli Knesset (Parliament)

3

[On the Israel-PLO agreement on implementing Palestinian self-rule in Gaza]: The main question now—a big, big *if*—is whether the Palestinians can control the area, whether they can provide the education, the health care, the jobs, what Gaza needs. This agreement succeeds or falls on this. If the Gaza refugees don't see some kind of light ahead, and improvement in their miserable lives, they will pick up the knife, the gun again . . . The main problem before us is the PLO's ability to rule.

May 4/
Los Angeles Times,
5-5:(A)7.

Shimon Peres
Foreign Minister of Israel

4

[On just-concluded peace talks between Israel and the PLO in Cairo]: We could have gone the Bosnian way—to shoot, to fight, to kill. Instead, we went our way—to agree to find common grounds, to tell the Palestinian people, tell the Israeli people, that we are serious, we are credible; we are not looking for images and public relations; we are looking for real peace for all children in the Middle East, Arabs and Jews . . . Before we came to Cairo, [PLO] chairman [Yasir] Arafat said that he would respect the security needs of Israel, and surely we cannot compromise on our security. On the other hand, we have announced that we shall do whatever we can to introduce an air of dignity and respect for the Palestinians. I know the people of Israel are seriously and deeply interested in making peace a reality. I'm convinced that historically and morally we do not want to be the dominating force of the Palestinian people.

Cairo, Egypt, Feb. 9/
Los Angeles Times,
2-10:(A)10.

5

[On the Israel-PLO agreement on implementing Palestinian self-rule in Jericho and Gaza]: [PLO] chairman [Yasir] Arafat, our partner in a very difficult journey: We did it! Once we had a

(SHIMON PERES)

dream before we had a map. Now we have a map and a dream together. For almost half a century, we experienced blood and hatred, terror and war. Today, we declare that the conflict is over. We [Israelis] don't want to be the generals, the judges or the police of the Palestinian people . . . Today, we welcome you, the Palestinian people, as neighbors.

At signing ceremony
for the agreement,
Cairo, Egypt, May 4/
Los Angeles Times,
5-5:(A)7.

1

[Saying low public support in Israel for peace negotiations with the Arabs will not deter the government from its determination to continue such talks]: A politician must have a certain capacity to look ahead. You don't always need to look backwards, content upon just collecting compliments. I'm not impressed by this. I know people that are so afraid to be unpopular that they are paralyzed. Who needs them? . . . I'm convinced there is a stream of history that even the public polls cannot stop.

Interview/
U.S. News & World Report,
7-11:39.

2

[Welcoming an announced easing of the Arab economic boycott against Israel by Saudi Arabia and Persian Gulf countries]: [This is] an additional move in dismantling the walls of hatred and separation and boycott. [The nations involved in the boycott] hurt themselves. The boycott has had a negative effect on the Arab countries as well because today markets are more important than countries, and if you put limits to trade you limit your own capacity to trade in a changing world.

To reporters,
Jerusalem, Israel, Sept. 30/
The New York Times,
10-1,6.

Lester Pollack
Chairman, Council of Presidents
of Major Jewish Organizations
(United States)

3

[Expressing his disapproval of a U.S. Clinton Administration hint that it would not veto a UN resolution backed by the PLO that, among other things, states that Jerusalem is part of Israeli-occupied Palestinian territory and not part of Israel itself]: I reminded [U.S. Secretary of State Warren Christopher] that any deviation on [long-standing American policy that Jerusalem is not Palestinian territory], any deviation on that, would be of serious concern to the Jewish community. He assured me there was no change in policy. He made abundantly clear that any effort to prejudge the status of Jerusalem would be met with opposition from the U.S. government.

March 11/
The New York Times,
3-12:5.

Yigal Pressler
Brigadier General,
Israeli Armed Forces;
Adviser on terrorism
to Israeli Prime Minister
Yitzhak Rabin

4

[On the recent bombing of a Jewish community center in Buenos Aires, Argentina]: The answer to attacks of the type that occurred in Argentina is not defensive activity. Another fence, another roadblock, another guard will not help. The countries of the world must cooperate intensively to foil Iranian and Islamic terrorism. It is essential to penetrate them, to collect intelligence, to uncover intentions and to foil attacks. Cooperation among countries should be tightened, and this matter must take on significance and importance.

July 19/
Los Angeles Times,
7-20:(A)10.

William B. Quandt
Professor of government,
University of Virginia;
Former specialist in
Middle Eastern affairs,
National Security Council
of the United States

1

The chances of [an Israeli] peace with Syria being negotiated and carried out are better than they've ever been. There is logic in this piece of the puzzle falling into place. Now [that] there is [an Israeli] peace with Egypt and Jordan, it rules out the option of an all-Arab war, and [Syrian President Hafez] Assad doesn't want to remain isolated. The only serious military threat to Israel is from Syria. If [Assad] can end that threat, the Arab-Israeli war is essentially over, and the state of Israel is secure.

Interview/
Los Angeles Times,
10-30:(M)2.

Yitzhak Rabin
Prime Minister of Israel

2

[On last year's Israel-PLO mutual-recognition agreement allowing Palestinian self-rule in Jericho and Gaza]: I knew that the key for any meaningful movement toward peace was with either Syria or the Palestinians. Through my explorations done quietly, I concluded that there would be a better chance to do it with the Palestinians. And I realized that everything is dictated by the PLO. What we did in recognizing them would have been unheard of four years ago. I believed that I had to do something which is not expected.

Interview/Time, 1-3:41.

3

[On last year's Israel-PLO mutual-recognition agreement allowing Palestinian self-rule in Jericho and Gaza]: What we are trying to create here is peaceful coexistence between two entities who do not much love each other. Geographically they

are mixed up; they criss-cross one another daily by vehicles. There is no line that divides. We have to create the confidence that will allow this unique interim arrangement to work. The real problem is to what extent the PLO will have the ability to take over what we are ready to give them and to fulfill their commitments. The PLO has never been responsible for running the life of a large community . . . Let the Palestinians run their affairs, create a situation in which no Israeli soldier will have to maintain public order, whether in Gaza or the West Bank. Let's give it to the Palestinians, as long as there is security for us [Israelis]. No more occupying another people.

Interview/Time, 1-3:42,44.

4

[On Syrian President Hafez Assad's statement that he is ready for normal relations with Israel]: Normalization was also mentioned by the Syrians in the past. The problem is what is the concept of peace and what is the timing for achieving peace and what price Israel will have to pay.

Jan. 17/
The New York Times,
1-18:(A)4.

5

I believe the Zionism of today is not judged by how we expand the territory under Israeli sovereignty. I believe the real Zionism is the return to Zion of most of the Jewish people from all over the world to build up a society that can serve as an example of traditional Jewish values coupled with Western civilization.

The Christian Science Monitor,
1-25:7.

6

[On whether the recent massacre of Palestinians by a Jewish settler in the occupied territories will be a roadblock to continued Israel-PLO peace negotiations]: I expect the Palestinians not to let this terrible and horrible Jewish murderer achieve his goal. [The killer] went to the holy place in Hebron not just to kill Palestinians, but to achieve

(YITZHAK RABIN)

a political goal; to kill the peace and to kill the negotiations with the Palestinians. I understand the pain, the sorrow, the agony of the Palestinians . . . But I expect them—I refer to their leadership—to understand that delaying the negotiations will bring more difficulties . . . Once [a peace] agreement is signed, we have to stick to it. There may be terrible events on both sides, from people or organizations who oppose the whole negotiations between the PLO and Israel. We have to cope with them and . . .do the utmost to prevent them from reaching their main goal: halting and undermining the negotiations.

Interview,
Jerusalem, Israel/
Newsweek, 3-14:34.

1

For us, peace, important as it is, cannot prevail without security. Israel will be very forthcoming in its quest for peace [with the Palestinians], but it will not compromise on its security . . . I must clarify to our Palestinian partners: The feeling of loss and sorrow in the wake of the Hebron tragedy [in which a Jewish settler massacred Palestinians in a mosque] will not change our fundamental positions regarding the security of the state of Israel and its citizens, including the Jewish residents [in the occupied territories]. We have no intention of compromising on security matters. Our security is your security and the basic guarantee of the success of peace.

Before American Israel
Public Affairs Committee,
Washington, D.C., March 15/
The Washington Post,
3-16:(A)25.

2

[On Israeli-Syrian relations]: We feel that the window of opportunities that opened after the [1991 Persian] Gulf war is narrower than we thought. Time is running out. Therefore, 1994 has to be the year of great decisions in the peace pro-

cess . . . [Syrian] President [Hafez] Assad said that Syria had made a strategic choice for peace with Israel. That was encouraging. Peace with Syria has always been our strategic choice. We recognize the importance of Syria to a comprehensive peace in the area . . . We know that as we engage in serious and authoritative negotiations, the point will come where painful decisions will have to be made. The promise of peace and its genuine benefits for all Israelis justifies making such decisions vis-a-vis Syria. We will not compromise on our security, but we will stand ready to do what is required of us if the Syrians are ready to do what is required of them.

News conference,
Washington, D.C., March 16/
The New York Times,
3-17:(A)4.

3

For 27 years, we [Israelis] have ruled another people [the Palestinians in the occupied territories] who do not want us to rule over them. For 27 years, Palestinians in the territories get up in the morning—Palestinians who today number 1.8 million men and women—and nurse their burning hatred for us as Israelis and as Jews. Every single morning, they get up to a difficult life, which is not exclusively but [partially] our fault. We cannot deny that continuing to rule over a people foreign to us, who do not want us, has inflicted a painful price—the price of neverending conflict between us.

Before Israeli Knesset (Parliament),
Jerusalem, Israel, April 18/
The New York Times,
4-19:(A)4.

4

[Saying he would dismantle Jewish settlements in the Golan Heights if that is required for a peace agreement with Syria]: My foremost consideration regarding the Golan Heights is the security value. But if we need to evacuate settlements for the sake of peace, I was in favor of that and I will be in favor of it. Peace is for me a more im-

(YITZHAK RABIN)

portant value for the future security of Israel than a group of settlements.

Before United Kibbutz Movement,
April 21/
The Washington Post,
4-22:(A)45.

1

[On the Israel-PLO agreement implementing Palestinian self-rule in Jericho and Gaza]: I turn to the people, the Palestinian people, our neighbors. A hundred years of animosity has created hatred between us. We have killed you, and you have killed us. Thousands of our graves, thousands of your graves are the painful signposts in your history and in our history. Today, you and we stretch out our hands to each other. We begin a new count. The people of Israel hope that you will not disappoint us. Let the future flourish. It is hard to forget the past, but let us get over these scars and use this historic, important day so that the past will not be repeated, so that we will go to a future which is a future without fear, without the eyes of frightened children, without pain. Alive, where we will be able to build our house, plant our vineyard, each alongside one another.

At signing ceremony for the agreement,
Cairo, Egypt, May 4/
The New York Times, 5-5:(A)8.

2

[Accusing the political right in Israel, which criticizes last year's Israel-PLO peace agreement, of using the actions of anti-Israel Islamic militants as justification of its opposition to the agreement]: The extreme right in Israel celebrates the bloodshed by the terrorist murderers of extremist Islam, trying to use the Israeli victims as a lever against the agreement. The extremist murderers of Islamic Holy War and Hamas are the tool of the extreme right in Israel.

At Israeli Labor Party meeting,
July 3/
The New York Times, 7-4:1.

3

[On the recent bombing of a Jewish community center in Buenos Aires, Argentina]: The world community must actively organize operations, cooperate both with respect to secure intelligence and in actions against the extremist Muslim terrorist groups. If this is not done, I fear that we will be victimized each time that those who wish to attack do so . . . They have these capabilities, and they are deployed around the world . . . This again underscores the commonality of Jewish fate. It obligates the countries in which Jews live to take appropriate steps for increasing security for Jews, certainly in those countries where a radical Islamic terrorist infrastructure exists.

July 19/
Los Angeles Times,
7-20:(A)10.

4

[After signing an Israel-Jordan peace declaration]: I, who served my country for 27 years as a soldier, say to you . . . today we are embarking on a battle which has no dead and no wounded, no blood and no anguish. This is the only battle which is a pleasure to wage; the battle for peace . . . The Middle East that was a valley of the shadow of death will become a place where it is a pleasure to live. We live on the same stretch of land; the same rain nourishes our soil; the same hot wind parches our fields. We find shade under the same fig tree. We savor the fruit of the same green vine; we drink from the same well.

Addressing Jordanian King Hussein,
before joint session of U.S. Congress,
Washington, D.C., July 26/
Los Angeles Times, 7-27:(A)6.

5

[Saying Syria must signal its readiness to make peace with Israel by some gesture, as did the PLO and Jordan which recently signed agreements with Israel]: Syria has to do something. It needs public diplomacy, it needs public utterances that will bring the people of Israel to be convinced that Syria is eager to have peace. I'll give you an

(YITZHAK RABIN)

example:[The late Egyptian President Anwar Sadat came to Jerusalem. Believe me, he broke down all the walls between Egypt and Israel by the mere fact that he came there. Even without signing a peace treaty, we had a trilateral meeting in Washington [recently] in which the President of the United States, the King of Jordan and myself shook hands, were together openly. We haven't seen anything of this kind, not even on a smaller scale, by Syria.

To reporters, Taba, Egypt,
July 31/
Los Angeles Times, 8-1:(A)8.

1

[On the status of Jerusalem as Israel's capital in light of recent peace agreements and negotiations between Israel and the PLO and Jordan]: This government, like all those which preceded it, believes that there are no disagreements in this chamber over the eternalness of Jerusalem as the capital of Israel. The whole, unified Jerusalem was and will be until the end of time the capital of the Israeli people, under Israeli sovereignty, a center for the longings and dreams of every Jew. [Jerusalem] is not to be bargained for.

Before Israeli Knesset (Parliament),
Jerusalem, Israel, Aug. 3/
Los Angeles Times, 8-4:(A)8.

2

[On the signing of an Israel-Jordan peace agreement]: From this podium, I look around and I see the Arava. I see only a desert. There is almost no life here. There is no water, no wells and not a spring, only mine fields . . . Our generation and the next, we are the ones who will transform this barren place into a fertile oasis . . . The peace that was born today gives us all the hope that the children born today will never know war between us and their mothers will know no sorrow.

At signing ceremony for the agreement,
along Israel-Jordan border,
Oct. 26/USA Today, 10-27:(A)3.

Hashemi Rafsanjani
President of Iran

3

[On the recent Israeli-PLO mutual-recognition agreement allowing Palestinian self-rule in Jericho and Gaza]: We do not consider it a peace plan, for this plan tramples upon the rights of the Palestinian people. [But other than] declaring our views, [Iran will not engage in] practical interference, executive action, or the physical prevention of developments.

News conference, June 7/
The Christian Science Monitor,
6-29:19.

Saadi Mahdi Saleh
Speaker of Iraqi Parliament

4

We [Iraq] don't have a problem [with Kuwait] in the sense the Americans think [in light of Iraq's invasion of Kuwait in 1990]. We have recognized Kuwait as an independent state. We are cousins. We might get angry with each other, and yet we can come to good terms later. The Arabs are like one nation, one family. We don't have a problem as far as the sovereignty of Kuwait is concerned, and we are ready to negotiate with the Kuwaitis [on the issue of borders] in the sense that each party will have its right.

Interview/
Los Angeles Times,
9-8:(A)10.

Paul E. Salem
Director, Lebanese Center
for Political Studies

5

[On Syria's domination of Lebanon and Lebanon's possible signing of a peace treaty with Israel]: Everybody will know it was not really the Lebanese who signed—it was really the Syrians on our behalf. It helps deflect the political tension, and that's a factor for political stability. We have zero power, and so you might expect that in a zero-

(PAUL E. SALEM)

sum game we lose everything. But that's not reality. The negotiations [between the Arabs and Israel] are leading toward a new Middle East, a Middle East of contacts and relations and networks, not a carving up of states. Lebanon will remain a state. Technically, on paper, it will remain independent. And gradually, Lebanon will in fact become independent as Syrian influence recedes over six or seven years. In this system, a country like Lebanon stands to gain a lot, because Lebanon is one of the only states ready now for the new system, in terms of having a political system that is open, a free economy, good relations with the West, experience in trading and markets.

Los Angeles Times,
7-25:(A)6.

G. Henry Schuler
Director, energy and
national security program,
Center for Strategic
and International Studies
(United States)

1

The very existence of close military and personal relationships [between the U.S. and unpopular Middle East leaders] exacerbates the internal tension [in those countries]. And in every one of those instances [when countries threw out those leaders in the past], the successor regime adopted oil [-export] policies that were confrontational, and resulted in oil shocks [in the U.S.].

The Christian Science Monitor,
1-28:2.

Nabil Shaath
Chief Palestinian negotiator
in peace talks with Israel

2

[On the recent massacre of Palestinians in the town of Hebron by a Jewish West Bank Settler]:

The real obstacle to peace is and is always going to be the settlers. There is nothing more explosive. These people are armed to the teeth, in Hebron in particular. They are the most extreme hatemongers.

Cairo, Egypt/
The New York Times,
2-26:5.

Nabil Shaath
Minister of planning
of the Palestinian Authority
(the governing entity
of the now self-ruled areas
of Gaza and Jericho)

3

[Saying that between Gaza and Jericho, the two Israeli-occupied areas now under Palestinian control, Gaza is the more important]: Jericho is a town of 15,000 people, and we took it [in last year's agreement with Israel] as a symbol for the West Bank. Gaza has almost one million people. It is the country, the place and the people—it is everything. Jericho is a symbol, and Gaza is a reality.

To reporters,
Cairo, Egypt, June 29/
The New York Times,
6-30:(A)4.

Yitzhak Shamir
Former Prime Minister
of Israel

4

[Criticizing the return of PLO leader Yasir Arafat to formerly Israeli-controlled Gaza, which is now under Palestinian rule]: The arrival of Arafat in the land of Israel symbolizes the start of the destruction of Israel and its being turned into a Palestinian state.

U.S. News & World Report,
7-11:38.

WHAT THEY SAID IN 1994

Joseph J. Sisco
Former Under Secretary of State
of the United States

1

There is no immediate outlook that [Syrian President Hafez] Assad is going to make peace with Israel. The gap on key issues is still significant. He continues to insist on total [Israeli] withdrawal from the Golan Heights, and Israel insists on a full peace that includes diplomatic relations, open borders, economic interaction and actual cooperation. Hard negotiations are ahead, and there is absolutely no breakthrough.

Interview/
Los Angeles Times,
10-30:(M)8.

Strobe Talbott
Deputy Secretary of State-designate
of the United States

2

[On his former view of Israel being a liability to U.S. security interests]: I do want to set the record straight on the question of my view of Israel as a strategic asset. On that I have simply changed my opinion . . . Israel is a very special country in the world, by virtue of its people, by virtue of the circumstances that brought about its birth. My core beliefs are also that we [the U.S.] have a special obligation, for reasons not only rooted in our moral obligation to Israel, but also rooted in our geopolitical interests, to support the security of Israel.

At Senate Foreign Relations
Committee hearing
on his nomination,
Washington, D.C., Feb. 8/
The New York Times,
2-9:(A)7.

Hassan al-Turabi
Spiritual leader of Sudan

3

Arab governments are collapsing. They know it. Even [PLO leader Yasir] Arafat knows that this latest peace deal [with Israel] is only an act of necessity. The Arabs are changing from below. Arab nationalism is finished and the Islamic spirit is rising in places like Saudi Arabia. This is one of the consequences of the [1991 Persian] Gulf war.

Interview,
Khartoum, Sudan/
The New York Times,
12-6:(A)7.

Mahmoud al-Zahar
Leading official of Hamas
(Arab anti-Israeli organization]

4

Everyone wants a civil war here [in now-Palestinian-ruled Gaza]. Israel wants it. America wants it. But what makes them think anyone here will fight for [PLO leader Yasir] Arafat and his peace treaty [with Israel]? Is there anyone in Gaza who does not realize that Israel still occupies 40 percent of the Gaza Strip with settlements and troops to protect the settlements, that it controls our shorelines, that its surveillance planes patrol the skies, as you can see them now, that Arafat himself needs permission by Israel to leave and come, and that we are locked up here periodically under curfew whenever Israel feels like it? Do you think Gazans are going to fight for those arrangements, which are the result of the agreement Arafat has negotiated with his Israeli friends?

Interview, Gaza/
The New York Times,
12-3:4.

PART THREE

General

Jane Alexander
Chairman, National Endowment
for the Arts of the United States

1

If we [at the NEA] can maintain an advocacy role, which hasn't happened in 12 years, then people will begin to understand the value of the arts. They will see what the arts can do to revitalize towns, to help children, to help us maintain our competitive edge in business. People say that artists should make money on their own. I say tell that to a choreographer who makes $5,000 or $6,000 a year, whose work has no commercial potential but which enriches lives.

Interview, Washington, D.C./
The New York Times,
3-23:(B)5.

2

We in the art world are not necessarily in the business of making controversial art. But art is not necessarily *without* controversy. No one's conception of art is going to be acceptable to everybody ... I've seen society change so much since the '60s and early '70s, and still we have the Endowment and still we have art. I don't know where art is going to go in the future, so I can't hypothesize about whether I would still want to be at the NEA if it got into any issue of morality. All I want to do is make sure that art is available to all Americans in a participatory way, whether you engage in the art process yourself or you're an audience member.

Interview/
"Interview" magazine,
July:41.

3

People have strong feelings about what the arts should do. And the arts are very visible. In most of the agencies in the government, the American public could not tell you what's going on. But in our case, when certain organizations or individuals choose to isolate specific works of [NEA-supported] art they don't find appealing, or that

they find offensive, then it gets picked up by the media, because it excites people. And that's just what art should be doing—it should move people, be able to make them think and wonder. But I want to stress that at the NEA we have two criteria that our panels look at when making grants—artistic excellence and merit.

Interview,
San Francisco, Calif.
Los Angeles Times,
10-2:(M)3.

Richard Avedon
Photographer

4

Art isn't art because someone uses a paintbrush. Photography is either good or bad, and when it's good it's like any art that's good. It becomes Art.

Interview/
Vogue, February:286.

Fernando Botero
Colombian painter and sculptor

5

The artist is no longer a chronicler of his time, as Canaletto, Goya and Velazquez were. We have television, the movies and photographs for that. The question now is of language. Those who say that figurative painting is all over because of photos are mistaken. The inner world of the artist cannot be photographed. He is a chronicler of *his* world, not that of the landscape.

Interview/
World Press Review, June:48.

Bill Clinton
President of the United States

6

At a time when our society faces new and profound challenges, when we are losing so many of our children and when so many people feel in-

WHAT THEY SAID IN 1994

(BILL CLINTON)

secure in the face of change, the arts and the humanities are fundamental to our lives as individuals and as a nation.

> *Announcing the revitalization*
> *of the President's Committee*
> *on the Arts and the Humanities,*
> *Washington, D.C., Sept. 19/*
> *The New York Times, 9-20:(B)2.*

David Cole
Attorney, Center for
Constitutional Rights

1

[Criticizing the NEA's "decency" standard for its arts funding]: When artists apply for funding, knowing they are subjected to these vague standards, they are chilled in their freedom of expression. The ultimate effect is for artists to back away from anything controversial . . . To allow government to use words like "decency" as a basis for allocating money for speech is very dangerous. It could allow the government to control the content of books in libraries and the content of public-TV shows . . . The current [NEA] Chair may not use it that way, but the next one might.

> *During court session on*
> *NEA funding and in interview,*
> *Pasadena, Calif., Feb. 3/*
> *The Washington Post, 2-4:(C)2.*

Philippe de Montebello
Director, Metropolitan Museum of Art,
New York, N.Y.

2

[On museums that lend their collections to other museums for a fee]: If the special cases [of loans-for-cash] start to multiply, you will eventually arrive at a norm . . . When institutions begin to regard the collections as being in the service of development and the budget—a commodity to be loosely and frequently traded in exchange for funds—then I have a problem.

> *The Wall Street Journal,*
> *7-21:(A)12.*

Federico Fellini
Motion-picture director

3

Every creative process is like an operation to uncover one's personality. For this reason, any work, be it a book, a picture, music, or a film, can be considered a means to free oneself from an obsession. The liberation is in realizing the obsession and giving it form . . . For every creative person, fantasy has certain aspects of obsession. Being unable to free oneself from these fantasies is a kind of torture.

> *Interview/*
> *"Interview" magazine,*
> *January:76.*

John E. Frohnmayer
Former Chairman,
National Endowment for the Arts
of the United States

4

[On whether the new Republican majority in Congress will gut the NEA]: I'm not sure that they will, willy-nilly, rush to rip apart the Endowment. My guess is that when they take a close look at it, they will recognize two things: One, the Endowment does contribute significantly to mainstream America; and the second is that the endowments [which the NEA makes to artists and art organizations] more than pay for themselves in terms of their stimulation of tax dollars. When you lay out that argument, it's a very Republican thing.

> *Los Angeles Times,*
> *12-25:(Calendar)93.*

Maria Guerra
Mexican art curator

5

In Mexico, we have a pictorial tradition of painting. And now it's a pity, because there are so many good painters there, but they believe that they are not allowed to think. In the art schools in Mexico, the teachers tell the student, "Don't think! Let the brush think for you" . . . I want to restore

(MARIA GUERRA)

the faith of painting in Mexico . . . I want to broaden the way people look at art in Mexico. It's a very interesting and exciting time there in terms of having alternative ways of showing work outside of galleries and official venues where you are obliged to organize exhibitions that are compromised.

Interview, Los Angeles, Calif./
Los Angeles Times, 6-29:(F)8.

Howard Hodgkin
Painter

1

My work is ultimately all about feeling; but so often, seeing a movie or a play or reading a book, I've found that there's some tremendous emotion, but it's not turned into art. You can put any kind of passion or feeling that you want into a work of art, as long as it *has* become a work of art, and has not remained some huge stain of grease which is feeling.

Interview, London, England/
Harper's Bazarre,
December:186.

Jacob Lawrence
Painter

2

[On suggestions that his paintings have a child-like simplicity and are Cubist in style]: The very beauty of art is that everyone has the right to see what they see in it. But I'd have to say that I never actually looked at Cubism. I had been painting this way long before I was exposed to Modernism. If you think about it, you could almost call children's art or African art Cubist, and they didn't look at Picasso. Children pare things down to the emotional and formal essentials; images aren't edited by logic but are laid down directly, powerfully, in their simplest form.

Interview, Washington state/
The Christian Science Monitor,
2-4:13.

It's too bad that one of the first things to go in our schools is the art programs. You know, when there's an economic situation, music, dance, theatre and visual arts are the first things to be cut, while sports gets all the attention and the money. Sports are certainly important, but we stress them so much at the expense of art, leaving out young people who don't have the physical strength for sports, or the interest. After all, civilizations are remembered because of their art. No. I don't think the powers-that-be realize how very valuable arts activities are, how important art is in many ways, from training your mind to your spirituality. Arts education feeds into so many areas. Just in the visual arts, you involve yourself with chemistry, materials, with learning to see and translate and it's the same thing with music, dance and theatre. You can't always put this into words, but many people think art is a frivolous discipline. It's far from that.

Interview, Seattle, Wash./
Booklist, 2-15:1049.

Fran Lebowitz
Author

4

If people don't read, you have the kind of culture—and I use the word very loosely—that we have now. I think television turned out to be exactly as bad as the most irritating and pedantic intellectuals of the '50s said it was going to be.

Interview, New York, N.Y./
The New York Times,
8-12:(B)8.

Dmitri Likhachev
Russian literary historian

5

Russian culture is truly a great culture because it has made global achievements in art, literature and music, [in] painting, the Russian avant-garde . . . Russian culture can't go from great to small. But real Russian culture can be crushed [by de-

WHAT THEY SAID IN 1994

(DMITRI LIKHACHEV)

clining government subsidies since the fall of Communism]—if the libraries are destroyed and if there is general illiteracy.

Interview, St. Petersburg, Russia/
Los Angeles Times, 2-19:(A)1.

Constance Lowenthal
Executive director,
International Foundation
for Art Research

1

[On the increase in stolen art treasures from Eastern Europe since the end of the Cold War]: These countries are hemorrhaging their heritage. The devastating combination of open borders, the need for hard currency and a ready and unscrupulous market in the West makes for a recipe of cultural disaster.

The New York Times,
4-12:(B)1.

Roger Mandle
President, Rhode Island
School of Design

2

I am firmly on the side of thinking that the arts, inherently and externally, have moral values. An artist has thought about creating a composition, about balance, and he or she has eliminated extraneous ideas and forms. In their thought, they have confirmed it to have values. I suppose you could argue that in creating a bomb or hand grenade that all extraneous weight has been removed, and that therefore it will fall just the right way with just the right amount of explosive. But what is left in the wake of the bomb is very different from an encounter with a work of art. With the bomb, there is nothing you can count as having life-reinforcing values.

Interview, Providence, R.I./
The Christian Science Monitor,
4-18:17.

Martin Mawyer
President, Christian Action Network

3

The NEA repeatedly refused to accept responsibility for subsidizing outrageous performances and programs which have surfaced over the years. It is precisely this attitude that has the Endowment on the ropes today.

Daily Variety,
7-20:15.

Nikita Mikhalkov
Russian motion-picture
director

4

[On the cutbacks in support of the arts in Russia]: The situation is absolutely monstrous. It's monstrous because culture is seen as an appendage that will return by itself when the people are fed and clothed and shoed . . . [But] culture is the mother of the people, and if we lose it and the people are left orphaned, we will not be forgiven.

Moscow, Russia/
Los Angeles Times,
2-19:(A)12.

Adolfo V. Nodal
General Manager,
Cultural Affairs Department
of Los Angeles, Calif.

5

[On the NEA's announced cuts in funding for the arts]: I'm disappointed that it's happening now under [NEA Chairman] Jane Alexander's tenure. You would hope that at this point under the Clinton Administration, with Jane as a leader, that the leadership could be found to make sure we don't continue to demonize artists. Obviously, it's the same old game.

Los Angeles Times,
12-25:(Calendar)6.

Andrew Oliver

Director of Museum Programs,
National Endowment for the Arts
of the United States

1

[On museums that lend their collections to other museums for a fee]: There is no reason why museums shouldn't charge for the use of their assets. If you have a shortage of funds, why not send something on tour?

The Wall Street Journal,
7-21:(A)12.

Christine Robbins

Executive co-director,
New Langston Arts

2

[On the NEA's announcement that it will cut $1.65-million in arts funding]: Any move by the NEA in the last six years can easily be construed as being motivated . . . to avoid controversy. If this [cut] had happened in 1990, there would have been an outcry in the [arts] community. I'm not seeing that happen this year, which is disturbing to me. It's the frog being [slowly] boiled in water.

Los Angeles Times,
12-25:(Calendar)6.

Peter Selley

Spokesman for Sotheby's,
British auction house

3

[Defending Sotheby's against criticism for its selling artifacts from British traitor and Soviet spy Kim Philby]: We do not side with Napoleon when we sell material related to him, nor embrace free love when we sell D. H. Lawrence material.

Newsweek,
8-1:17.

Beverly Sills

Chairman-designate,
Lincoln Center, New York, N.Y.;
Former opera singer

4

Probably the greatest difficulty we are going to face [in fund-raising for Lincoln Center] is that there are social problems today that didn't exist 15 years ago. Fifteen years ago you may have been competing with another arts organization. Today when you're trying to raise money you find that companies have other obligations: the homeless, AIDS, teenage pregnancy, drugs. It's a major job to convince people that the arts are not a frill. But look at what Lincoln Center has done for the West Side, for the restaurants, apartment buildings, office buildings and employment in the area. Lincoln Center has been a huge octopus, and its tentacles keep spreading and spreading.

Jan. 24/
The New York Times,
1-25:(B)2.

Isaac Stern

Violinist

5

The arts have to be a continuing effort, a fight for the minds and the freedom of our children, and not just a social adornment. I have a feeling that while it is not the Number 1 priority for the [U.S. President Clinton] White House, they know this and are prepared to back it.

The New York Times,
3-23:(B)5.

Gore Vidal

Author

6

All the arts seem to be on hold. Walt Whitman said that to have great poets, you must have great audiences. I think that holds true in all the arts. If there aren't people who can appreciate it, art withers and dies. Epic poetry is finished. The masque is gone, the verse play is gone, the serious novel is

(GORE VIDAL)

going. Novels by lawyers and thrillers by Stephen King should not have driven out serious books, but they have.

Interview, Italy/
Modern Maturity,
April-May:62.

Harold Williams
Director, the Getty Trust

1

[On the possibility that the new Republican majority in Congress will curtail or eliminate the NEA]: The Federal government plays a very significant role in today's world in articulating what's important to this country. I guess what I worry about most is what message comes out of Washington about the importance of culture in this nation, and the importance of the arts and humanities to what we call a civilized society. I don't believe the issue is Federal funding. That's my sense of it—it's something more profound.

Los Angeles Times,
12-25:(Calendar)93.

Allen Alter

Foreign editor,
"Evening News," CBS-TV

1

We assumed during the Cold War that there was a secure market for international news. Now [with the Cold War over] it's difficult to figure out who our clients [the audiences] are and what foreign stories they want, if any.

Columbia Journalism Review,
July-Aug.:28.

Christiane Amanpour

Correspondent,
Cable News Network

2

I never editorialize. I never express my personal opinions. I mean, no one elected me, and I am not an academic. I don't pretend to give history lessons. I only report what I see. [But] what does it mean to be completely unbiased? If I were covering the Holocaust, would I have to say, "Oh, the poor Nazis; maybe they have a point"?

Interview, Paris, France/
Vogue, March:246.

Roone Arledge

President, ABC News

3

[On TV's star news anchors, such as ABC's Diane Sawyer]: Diane Sawyer is one of a handful of people in TV news—like Peter Jennings, Ted Koppel or Barbara Walters—who are able to make or break a franchise in news. Diane can do newsmagazines. She can do hard news. She's intelligent. She's a personality. She is someone whose presence on a news program makes a difference. It's like putting [basketball star] Michael Jordan into the game. You want to watch what she does.

Los Angeles Times,
8-7:(Calendar)7.

David Bartlett

President, Radio-Television
News Directors Association

4

[Saying a current trend at some TV stations to downplay violent-crime stories on their newscasts may not be a good idea]: In some cases, good journalism demands that we disturb our audiences.

Time, 6-20:55.

Joanna Bistany

Vice president, ABC News

5

[On "star" journalists in TV news]: In order to be a "star" in news, you have to have intellect, journalistic ability, drive and something called presence. Ted Koppel, Peter Jennings, Barbara Walters and Diane Sawyer all have it. It's not just a matter of performance on the air—you have to be a journalist who elicits confidence and credibility.

Los Angeles Times,
2-21:(F)13.

Wolf Blitzer

White House correspondent,
Cable News Network

6

[On the Washington press corps' eagerness to meet singer Barbra Streisand after one of her concerts]: We are little children. We get excited when we meet big stars.

Newsweek, 5-23:17.

Tina Brown

Editor,
"The New Yorker" magazine

7

[On the reduced amount of fiction in *The New Yorker* since she became editor in 1992]: One piece of fiction a week is right for the reading rhythms of our times. In the press of modern life, readers

(TINA BROWN)

are much less luxurious with their time and one has to edit a magazine for real life rather than ideal life. I don't think we will get people to read more than one piece a week.

The New York Times,
6-20:(C)5.

Robert C. Byrd
United States Senator,
D-West Virginia

1

[Criticizing TV reporters]: They have absolutely no sense of shame, no sense of propriety. They are like the buzzards . . . Apparently no excess, no savagery—no respect for others, no limits on behavior—is too much in the chase for headlines or air time.

Before the Senate,
Washington, D.C./
The Washington Post,
3-3:(C)1.

Connie Chung
Anchor, CBS News

2

Real-life stories have more appeal to people than fiction. My husband [who hosts a TV talk-reality show] said not long ago that his ratings were better than his competition—the soap operas—and when people asked him why, he said it's because the people are finding the real-life soap-opera stories more watchable than the fictional soap-opera stories. And they *are* similar.

Interview, New York, N.Y./
Vanity Fair, August:130.

Eleanor Clift
White House correspondent,
"Newsweek" magazine

3

[On criticism that she is a cheerleader for the Clinton Administration]: There's no penalty for

an individual reporter who is perceived as being too tough. But the reporter who is perceived as being soft is immediately delegitimized, portrayed as being in the tank. It's not comfortable to be singled out as someone who is somehow a cheerleader. That's the last thing any reporter wants to be considered. What I've said [in reporting on the White House] holds up under the banner of fair analysis.

The Washington Post,
4-4:(B)1.

Hillary Rodham Clinton
Wife of President of the United States
Bill Clinton

4

We have to ask ourselves, "Has the exhaustive and perhaps excessive coverage [by the news media] of violence contributed to the increasing alienation and dysfunctional behavior on the part of our children and youth? And does news coverage engender so much cynicism that they grow up with no faith in their institutions?"

Speaking by satellite
from the White House
to a conference
at Stanford University,
March 4/
The New York Times,
3-5:9.

5

If the press becomes the handmaiden of the political right, which it is becoming—from the so-called liberal press all the way to the attack dogs of the right wing—then you can't expect people to have any trust in what they read or see. And if they can't trust what they read or see, how can they make the decisions that are essential to keeping our democracy going?

Interview,
Washington, D.C./
Vanity Fair,
June:159.

Walter Cronkite
Former anchor, CBS News

1

I think it's clear today that anybody who wants to be well-informed has got to be multimedia; you can't ignore any part of the media. You've got to watch television; clearly, you can't ignore it. As for the daily newspaper, I'd like to think that people choose papers of a serious vein if [they're] lucky enough to have access to one of the major ones. A lot of local newspapers today are pretty sketchy in the amount of material they provide. They're trying to come into television's backyard by trying to meet the public's short attention span with these one-line headline items, and today's news all in one little box. So you need something more than that for your background information. You're not going to get a lot of background from television, but unfortunately a lot of newspapers today don't give you a lot of background either. So it's necessary to go to good opinion journals and to books . . . I think there's a superficiality in both the media and the public. They're feeding each other's touch-and-go outlook on the world. There's a lot of information but not a lot of understanding. We're almost being over-communicated *at* not communicated *with*.

Interview,
Boston, Mass./
The Christian Science Monitor,
3-17:16.

2

"Presentation" became dominant as the [technological] capabilities [of TV news broadcasting] increased, to the degree that in a lot of cases I felt the importance of the stories was lost. We went for the stories that could be illustrated and left alone the ones that required careful examination through text. This distorted the whole value of television news, to my mind. And distorts it to this day. I'm afraid—and I said this early on—that those who expected to be fully informed by television expected what could not be, and the fact that television was being accepted as the principal news source by a greater and greater percentage of our population was creating considerable difficulties for the democracy. An uninformed democracy is dangerous. Thomas Jefferson told us that the country that expects to be ignorant and free expects what never can and never will be. We are perpetuating ignorance by making television news so easily assimilated that people do not go to print any longer. This is dangerous.

Interview,
New York, N.Y./
American Heritage,
December:44.

Everette Dennis
Executive director,
Freedom Forum Media
Studies Center,
Columbia University

3

[On ABC's new contract with broadcast journalist Diane Sawyer that pays her a salary of $7-million]: The bidding for her services [among the various networks] is simply a further recognition that news is a profit-making enterprise. ABC wouldn't have paid her this salary if they didn't think she would generate profits for the network.

Los Angeles Times,
2-21:(F)13.

Gregg Easterbrook
Contributing editor,
"Newsweek" magazine

4

[Supporting the idea of news organizations paying sources for their cooperation]: I don't see why professional reporters should be the only ones to profit from producing news. We in the press seem to think [people] should surrender their privacy and submit to our embarrassing questions so that we can make money off it.

Columbia Journalism Review,
July-Aug.:46.

Betty Friedan
Author;
Women's-rights advocate

1

We [women] are still largely invisible in the [news] media, still subject to symbolic annihilation, despite our increasing numbers in politics and the workplace.

The New York Times,
4-13:(A)10.

Gerald Garcia
Editor, "The Houston Post"

2

[On minorities attaining high positions in the news media]: The bottom-line question is, do the predominantly white males who own and manage the media want to make the commitment in money, training, hiring and promotion for people to succeed them who will be different from them? The answer, so far, is a resounding no.

USA Today, 7-26:(A)2.

Gabriel Garcia Marquez
Colombian author

3

To be a journalist, you need a strong cultural base and a lot of practice. You also need a good deal of ethics. There are so many bad journalists who, when they have no news, invent it.

Interview/
World Press Review, July:48.

Hunter George
Vice president,
Thomson Newspapers (Canada)

4

[On newspapers being available in high-tech form on personal computers]: At this point, you'd have to say there is no compelling demand for the information a newspaper provides to be transmitted in electronic form. People prefer the printed word. They do not like to read off a TV.

Los Angeles Times,
1-17:(A)11.

Rebecca Greer
Senior articles editor,
"Woman's Day" magazine

5

[On writing for magazines]: What [many] writers don't consider is the reader: What's in it for the reader? We've seen a shift in topics because [magazines] must keep up with the times. We do more on working women, for example, because more of our readers are working. But writers don't give much thought to the readers' lives ... Basically, many writers just want to write about their own lives and opinions.

Interview/Writer's Digest,
September:39.

Bernard Gwertzman
Foreign editor,
"The New York Times"

6

[At *The New York Times*,] we have been quietly and not so quietly urging more and more stories on economic affairs for the foreign report. Every correspondent must make a major effort to become literate in economic affairs, to be able to write about macroeconomic trends such as monetary policies, as well as on micro stories such as new business in former Communist states . . . [There is a] need to demystify global economic news the way we dejargonized nuclear-strategic news during the Cold War.

Columbia Journalism Review,
July-Aug.:28.

Seymour Hersh
Journalist

7

[Arguing against news organizations paying sources for their cooperation]: We never did it at *The New York Times*. We used to fly people in and put them up at a good hotel and feed them, give them a free phone and all that. But just paying someone for information is a rational no-no.

Columbia Journalism Review,
July-Aug.:46.

William Hilliard
President and editor,
Portland "Oregonian"

1

It was not the intent of our Founding Fathers that the First Amendment be held in abeyance through one's adolescence. If the American newspaper establishment fails to defend free speech for high-school and college journalists, how can we claim it for ourselves?

Before American Society
of Newspaper Editors,
Washington, D.C., April/
Columbia Journalism Review,
July-Aug.:12.

Serge July
Editor, "Liberation" (France)

2

The French have a passion for magazines. On a per-capita basis, they are the world's largest buyers of magazines but only the 28th-largest buyers of newspapers. They read magazines because society is treated in a sophisticated and exhaustive way. That's why the reconquest of the daily press must pass through magazines.

Interview, Paris, France/
The New York Times,
10-3:(C)7.

Marvin Kalb
Director,
Barone Center on the Press,
Politics and Public Policy,
Harvard University

3

[Saying press coverage of the Whitewater scandal, which allegedly may involve President Clinton, has been excessive]: Without any significant legal evidence linking the President to any criminal activity, everyone and his uncle in the press is on board this train, and they are riding to a destination that is utterly unknown to them. There is a rushing to judgment that is unprofessional and

distasteful. The press is going to have a lot to answer for when this is over.

The Washington Post,
3-12:(A)1.

Jon Katz
Media critic,
"New York" magazine

4

In the last 10 years, the [TV] networks have gone to the old Hollywood star system for visible female personalities [in their news divisions]. It's like what MGM did with Jean Harlow—making stars out of glamorous women rather than letting them do serious journalism. But that's the way you create a journalistic superstar now—build big mythologies about them and their careers, and promote them heavily.

Vanity Fair, August:93.

Murray Kempton
Newspaper columnist,
New York "Newsday"

5

[On writing a column]: You make a bad choice [of topics] in the morning. Then you get back to the office at 4, and you hope you don't have to stick with the morning's bad choice.

Interview, New York, N.Y./
Los Angeles Times,
5-23:(E)5.

Ron Konecky
Journalists' agent

6

[On the high salaries being negotiated for star broadcast journalists]: [Agents have] been very helpful for the industry, certainly in bringing news talent up to par [salary-wise]. There was a time when it was tawdry for anyone in news to ask for more money.

Los Angeles Times,
11-13:(Calendar)3.

WHAT THEY SAID IN 1994

Charles Kuralt
Correspondent, CBS News

1

Anyone who has intimations of fame or immortality chose the wrong career in TV news. This business is so fast and fleeting, I don't think anything lasts for very long.

Interview/
The Christian Science Monitor,
4-11:16.

Andrew Lack
President, NBC News

2

[On salary negotiations with the agents of news anchors and reporters]: It's taking more time than I like. We're in a competitive business in which talent negotiations have become a sort of *mano a mano*. [Agents are] not ashamed to ask for the moon [for their clients] and they wait you out until you give them the stars and the sun. I'm only saddened when I remember that journalism is supposed to be a calling.

Los Angeles Times,
11-13:(Calendar)3.

Robert Lichter
Co-director,
Center for Media and Public Affairs

3

The culture of national journalism is cosmopolitan, socially liberal, secular, and in that sense out of touch with a lot of middle-American concerns. Washington correspondents and New York-based network producers look at ordinary people the way anthropologists view primitive tribes.

The New York Times,
4-16:7.

Dale Rogers Marshall
President, Wheaton College (Mass.)

4

[On the popularity of TV news personalities as college commencement speakers]: Television

newscasters are role models for our students. It says something about the centrality of the media in our time.

The New York Times,
5-21:6.

James Michaels
Editor, "Forbes" magazine

5

[Saying editors should not refrain from involving themselves in trying to improve reporters' articles]: I think most newspapers take the attitude today that the reporter knows best. I don't think that young reporters necessarily do know best. I think I learned something in the last 50 years about covering stories and about the world, and I don't think there's anything wrong with me injecting my view into the reporters' heads and even asking them to inject it into the story.

Interview/
The Wall Street Journal,
6-7:(A)15.

Bill O'Reilly
Host, "Inside Edition,"
Fox-TV

6

[Supporting the payment of money to sources by TV news and tabloid shows]: The networks are making millions off news programs. Why shouldn't the common man participate in that? It's capitalism at its finest.

Columbia Journalism Review,
July-Aug.:46.

Tony Podesta
Political strategist

7

[On TV coverage of government corruption]: People get indicted on the *Today* show, tried on CNN and sentenced on *Nightline*.

U.S. News & World Report,
11-7:36.

Peter Prichard
Editor, "USA Today"

1

Much of the so-called legitimate news media ... run things that they wouldn't have run years ago just because peoples' standards have changed and the level of acceptability is different then it was in 1955. It's far more acceptable to talk about things that people didn't talk about before.

Los Angeles Times,
2-17:(A)18.

George Putnam
Broadcast journalist

2

We have the greatest [TV news] technology in the history of the world. But I frankly don't think our present-day reporting has kept up with the technology. With present-day technology, an independent or local station is as effective as any network in the history of mankind . . . But as far as the reporting is concerned, I'm very disturbed by [such things as] tabloid journalism—the fact that hard news is suffering, that I tune in a news report in the evening and get as much as eight or 10 minutes of shootings and stabbing and rapes. All of that titillation and much of it trivial. Scandal, a numbness, a kind of a loss of feeling about what blood truly is, about what life truly is, what the human truly is, all lost in kind of a world of make-believe that crosses over into actuality.

Interview/
Los Angeles Times,
7-21:(F)10.

Marilyn Quayle
Wife of former Vice President
of the United States Dan Quayle

3

[On the ridicule her husband received in the media when he was Vice President]: It was painful because it was not understandable. There were people in the press who certainly knew better—people who had followed his career in the Senate

and knew the substantive nature of the man. I think everyone wants to believe what they read and what they see. But to have the realization that there's this press out there that doesn't care for the facts—then you've really lost something . . . *The Washington Post* is genetically incapable of being fair to us. I can't pick up a newspaper or watch the evening news and believe anything I see or read. And that's hard to deal with.

Interview,
Washington, D.C., May 6/
The Washington Post,
5-10:(B)1,3.

William Raspberry
Political columnist,
"The Washington Post"

4

One of my great discoveries is that on virtually every public controversy, most thoughtful people secretly believe both sides. They will espouse one side and suppress the other, depending on what company it puts them in . . . Some people find it infuriating, but I'd rather agonize in print about my views about capital punishment than say it's wrong under all circumstances. I try to invite people out of their boxes, at least for 750 words [in a column].

Upon winning the Pulitzer Prize
for commentary, April 12/
The Washington Post,
4-13:(A)13.

Jay Rosen
Professor of journalism,
and director of Project on
Public Life and the Press,
New York University

5

[On what "journalistic objectivity" is]: It is the value of fairness, which is extremely important. It's the ethic of restraining your own biases, which is also important . . . It's the idea that journalism can't be the voice of any particular party

(JAY ROSEN)

or sect, which is also important. All those things are very honorable, very important. What is insidious and crippling about objectivity is when journalists say: "We just present you with facts. We don't make judgments. We don't have any values ourselves." That is dangerous and wrongheaded . . . I don't think the kind of bias journalists are usually accused of—ideological bias, personal animus—is generally worrisome. Far more subtle and more dangerous are the conventions of journalism: the ways in which journalists go about dividing the world, framing public life for us, picturing the world of politics. There are values and assumptions hidden in those decisions that are extremely important to name and to debate, and I think, at this point, to change.

Interview/
The New York Times,
12-12:(C)7.

Diane Salvatore
Senior editor,
"Redbook" magazine

1

[On writing for *Redbook*]: [There should be a] chemistry between writer and story. We approach it as a marriage—we want to know that the writer is qualified, but we must also sense that the writer brings a unique perspective to the story, something that makes it a *Redbook* story. We've been learning how critical this matchmaking process is . . . It's harder to break into *Redbook* than it was three years ago. To jump out of that slush pile is harder. We have a much higher standard than before. Thorough and conscientious reporting is a must, but we also want writing that is stylish and fresh, writing that knocks the breath out of you. The bottom line is that these days, we're interested in more experienced writers.

Interview/
Writer's Digest,
September:40.

Diane Sawyer
Anchor, ABC News

2

[On whether she is worth her $7-million salary]: It's not as if you wake up in the morning and say, "Boy, do I deserve it!"—because you know you don't. But we're in a marketplace where these salaries are paid. The money is there; it's like something you look at. You look in the closet door and say "Oh, my" and go off and do what you've been doing for 15 years. I didn't get into this business for the money—I got into it for the work.

Interview, New York, N.Y./
Los Angeles Times,
8-7:(Calendar)7.

Liz Smith
Newspaper gossip columnist

3

Just like bad money drives out good money, bad gossip drives out good gossip. Gossip has been totally vitiated today by this explosion of interest in it, especially by television, which has made it worse than ever. There's nothing wrong with gossip, but when it's sensationalized to death, it changes. [TV's] *A Current Affair*, for example, has had a profound effect on newscasts, forcing them to be jazzier and less concerned with real news. And when shows pay for stories, people will do anything for the money—such as releasing hospital records, which is despicable.

Interview/
Modern Maturity,
Sept.-Oct.:65.

Alice Turner
Fiction editor, "Playboy" magazine

4

[On fiction in magazines such as *Playboy*]: Fiction is kind of a nuisance. It's labor intensive. The ad sales guys don't see the point. They would cut it out if they could, except for the fact that it adds a certain respectability.

The New York Times,
6-20:(C)5.

R. Emmett Tyrrell
Editor, "The American Spectator"

1

[On journalists who criticize his magazine's hard-hitting style]: These journalists are all too goddamn timid. I've been lectured to on the standards of journalism by all these second-rate journalists. Well, let me tell you, I've read journalism in this country for over a quarter of a century and there is no such thing as journalism standards.

Interview,
McLean, Va./
Esquire, June:89.

Sanford J. Ungar
Dean, School of Communication,
American University

2

[On a Los Angeles TV station's incorrect report about evidence in the forthcoming murder trial of former football star O. J. Simpson]: Every time something like this happens, the mainstream media take one step closer to the tabloid press, and the public has another reason to be cynical about what it reads and sees.

The Washington Post,
9-29:(A)12.

Literature

Edward Albee
Playwright

1

If you are going to learn from other writers, don't only read the great ones, because if you do that you'll get so filled with despair and the fear that you'll never be able to do anywhere near as well as they did that you'll stop writing. I recommend that you read a lot of bad stuff, too. It's very encouraging.

Interview/
The Writer, April:3.

2

Payoff? Who needs payoff? You write because you're a writer and it's your responsibility to communicate. And if you're a responsible citizen, you do it.

The Writer, June:3.

Margaret Atwood
Author

3

I think when you're actually writing, you're really involved with every page as you're doing it. If you stop to wonder whether you're going to please a bunch of theoretical people, or your publisher for that matter, you might as well just give up because you can never know in advance how people are going to respond to something. You can't second-guess the reader in that way.

Interview,
Chicago, Ill./
Booklist, 1-15:898.

Rick Bass
Author

4

[On writing]: Show, don't tell. Writing and reading are acts of discovery. "Telling" robs a story of the feel of discovery.

Writer's Digest,
August:25.

Charles Baxter
Author

5

[As a writer,] if you're suffienctly chameleon-like, you can slip into somebody's skin temporarily and slip out again. It's not so miraculous or strange a thing to do. I think we all have potential possible selves, and writing stories has something to do with letting them get free . . . I've written characters I haven't liked, but never a character I couldn't imagine myself being.

The Writer, May: 5.

Louis Begley
Author

6

Of course, everything in a serious novel comes out of a writer's life, inevitably. Where else would it come from? . . . Words lead one on. A word will come into one's head, and one wants to do something with that word, and pretty soon there is a sentence. And all the things that are inside you go into that sentence.

Interview,
New York, N.Y./
Publishers Weekly,
5-2:278.

Doris Betts
Author

7

I feel I'm by nature a short-story writer and that I've been trying to learn to write novels. People are by temperament inclined to one form or the other. The short-story writer has a fast metabolism, never returns library books on time, doesn't carry umbrellas in case it might rain; whereas the novelist writes longer sentences and has a different breathing rate.

Interview/
Publishers Weekly,
4-25:43.

Harold Bloom
Professor of humanities,
Yale University;
Professor of English,
New York University

1

I am very unhappy with current attempts throughout the universities of the Western world, by a group I have called "the school of resentment," to put the arts, and literature in particular, in the service of social change. The utility of literature is to teach us not how to talk to others, but how to talk to ourselves. And the function of the critic is to make one aware both of the sorrows and of the very occasional and rather perilous glories of what it means to be condemned to talk to oneself. A proper use of Shakespeare and Dante and Tolstoy and Cervantes and the other writers of the very highest order is to teach us both to fill out and to temper that conversation with ourselves.

Interview,
New Haven, Conn./
Newsweek, 10-10:75.

Stephen G. Breyer
Judge, United States
Court of Appeals
for the First Circuit;
Associate Justice-designate,
Supreme Court of the United States

2

[Saying he likes to read Shakespeare]: He's a little bit archaic—you know, the language—but if you put in the time . . . you see every different kind of person . . . every different situation there is in the world . . . and you see the whole thing in poetry.

Newsweek, 7-25:15.

Christopher Buckley
Author

3

I love to write. It's pretty great when it works. I was an only child with a lot of time to kill. I

suspect a lot of writers are only-children or only-children become writers because it's a way of being alone.

Interview, New York, N.Y./
The New York Times,
6-30:(B)4.

Peter Burford
Publisher and editor,
Lyons & Burford, publishers

4

[On publishers' deciding whether or not to publish a submitted manuscript]: I know that it hurts writers' feelings that a decision is made so quickly about something that they've invested so much energy in, but it has to be made quickly. It's not because we don't like books and respect them and respect the authors' work; it's because our sense of what will succeed and what will fail on our list is very finely honed. And I think that is true of editors generally. It's almost always easy to decide whether something's worth considering or not. We're not on the fence for very long.

Interview/
Writer's Digest,
February:45.

Robert Olen Butler
Pulitzer Prize-winning author

5

A good relationship [for an author] with an editor should be like love-making: "That feels good, no, a little higher, a little over to the left . . ." In love-making there is the inevitable mutual adjusting of the experience, which is absolutely necessary to the process.

Interview/
Publishers Weekly, 1-3:61.

Ethan Canin
Author

6

I wanted to write without tricks and jazzed-up language, which I can do, but it's harder to write

(ETHAN CANIN)

plain English and to write stories that have plots and make sense, or, as Flannery O'Connor said, that are "inevitable and surprising." That was my challenge to myself: to write a regular story that sounded like a true story and that would hold up to second and third reading. You need a challenge to keep you going when you sit down to write because it's so miserable. It's like, "Can I run 12 blocks today? Can I run past the water fountain and go two more blocks?"

Interview,
New York, N.Y./
The Wall Street Journal,
3-22:(A)12.

Grace Cavalieri
Host, "The Poet and the Poem"
radio program

1

The poet is one of the most meticulous people there could be as far as thought processes go . . . the kind of person who creates order instead of making a mess of thought.

The Writer, June:3.

Denise Chavez
Author

2

Writing for me is a healing, therapeutic, invigorating, sensuous manifestation of the energy that comes to you from the world, from everything that's alive. Everything has a voice and you just have to listen as closely as you can. That's what's so exciting—a character comes to you and you can't write fast enough because the character is speaking through you. It's a divine moment.

Interview,
Las Cruces, N.M./
Publishers Weekly,
8-15:77.

Ron Chernow
Biographer

3

At the outset, a biographer feels swamped by the material and wonders how the wilderness of random facts can be tamed into the formal garden of a book. Early in my research, I tend to jot down information with a nervous, indiscriminate pen. What finally simplifies matters is the emergence of the central theme, which becomes the glue, the binding agent, for the book. Once you find that principal focus, the material quickly divides itself into the essential and the superfluous. The panic subsides. Then you can climb back in from the window ledge.

Interview/
The Writer, October:10.

Lucille Clifton
Poet

4

My writing comes through my caring. It is my response to what the world is about. Poetry didn't start in the academy. Poetry was the human's response to seeing that one was connected to something larger than oneself.

Radio interview,
"The Poet and the Poem"/
The Writer, September:3.

Michael Crichton
Author

5

[On how technology will affect how literature is written and the form in which it is presented]: There's a tremendous amount of baloney being dished up about the future. But I don't think there is any doubt that books will change enormously, or any reason to be nostalgic. The ability to add sound, graphics animation and layers of text will alter the experience of what a book is, and I can't wait.

The Wall Street Journal,
3-21:(R)7.

Clive Cussler
Author

1

Some days I write two pages, some days I write six. I'm not prolific at all. Hopefully, it adds up finally to a book, and I can type "The End." And then it's like being paroled from prison.

Interview,
Paradise Valley, Ariz./
Publishers Weekly,
7-11:59.

Robertson Davies
Canadian author

2

[Journalism] teaches you [as an author] to write more concisely and to get busy and write when you must, instead of just sitting around waiting for the inspiration, which isn't going to come.

Interview,
Toronto, Canada/
The New York Times,
12-15:(A)4.

Peter De Vries
Author

3

I write when I'm inspired, and I see to it that I'm inspired at nine o'clock every morning.

The Writer, June:3.

E. L. Doctorow
Author

4

[On the future of today's conglomerate-owned publishing companies]: I have always maintained that as long as a generation of classic book people was in charge of editorial questions, the line would be held. Good editors today form a kind of Sierra Club of literary ecology. What this will mean 20 years from now, when they're all gone or retired, I simply don't know.

Interview, New York, N.Y./
Publishers Weekly, 6-27:52.

5

The more I see of business, the more I realize how lucky I am to be in something that requires just one person in a room with the door closed.

Interview,
New York, N.Y./
Publishers Weekly,
6-27:52.

6

Being a motion-picture reader was a wonderful apprenticeship for a writer. For three years I got my hands on everything that was being published. Seeing how much bad stuff was coming out gave me great confidence.

The Writer, September:3.

Rita Dove
Poet Laureate
of the United States

7

There is an incredible hunger out there. I feel it. There's a hunger for poetry . . . It's a feeling that [people] don't have a way of connecting with the soul and telling someone else about it without it sounding hokey. Which isn't to say poetry is going to cure all their ills, but it really does reflect a terrible tragedy in our culture. We tend to close off our souls, and it just isn't cool to talk about it, to talk about having an interior life . . . [Poet W. H.] Auden said poetry makes nothing happen. Okay. Poetry may not change the world. But it can change a heart, and it can change a moment— a heart *in* a moment. That's a lot. I still remember reading Sylvia Plath's *Daddy* for the first time in college. Just realizing the anger she had, that she could have all this anger and hate toward her father and write it in a poem—I think that changed my life. Not that it freed me to hate someone, but to see that we have all these competing feelings and can express them in poetry.

Interview,
Charlottesville, Va./
The Washington Post,
4-22:(C)1,2.

Timothy Findley
Canadian author

1

We as a society keep missing the wonder and resource of great literature. [Instead of reading the classics,] we look to the thin application of the answers to human life found in the televised world. That has become our reading of the time. But it doesn't deliver the way literature does.

Interview/
Publishers Weekly,
4-11:42.

Carolyn Forche
Poet

2

[On her being called a "political poet"]: [There has been a cyclic debate peculiar to the United States concerning the relationship between poetry and politics . . . And I felt that the debate wasn't a useful one, that the grounds were reductive and simplistic and unhelpful to anyone who wanted to think about the responsibility of citizens, much less writers . . . There was no notion that language might be inherently political or perhaps ideologically charged whatever the subject matter and even when the person isn't aware of [it].

Interview/
The Christian Science Monitor,
4-20:20.

Gabriel Garcia Marquez
Colombian author

3

I don't read my books, out of fear, because when I begin reading, I take out my ballpoint pen. I begin to make corrections, and I don't stop. I've made a rule never to change a book after its first edition. That's why I go through so many versions and corrections.

Interview/
World Press Review,
July:48.

Newt Gingrich
United States Representative,
R-Georgia;
Speaker of the House-designate

4

[Saying that, because of criticism by some fellow Republicans and from Democrats, he will forgo the $4.5-million advance he was to receive from the publisher of two of his forthcoming books]: No less than 23 current Senators, plus Vice President Al Gore, have published books while in Congress. Those include party leaders [George] Mitchell and [Robert] Dole, and they run the gamut ideologically from Claiborne Pell and Barbara Boxer to Bill Cohen and Jesse Helms. So I just want everybody to understand [that] when we went into this, we frankly thought we were doing everything that was correct . . . [But] sometimes you hear things and something you haven't quite gotten suddenly becomes clear. And I realized that we really owed it to every person who was on the [Republican Party 1994 election] team to say to them, "We don't want anyone at any level to think we're taking any advantage" [to cash in on such things as the book deal because of the Republican election victory].

News conference,
Marietta, Ga., Dec. 30/
The New York Times,
12-31:6.

Allen Ginsberg
Poet

5

[On the current renewed interest in his work, which flourished during the "Beat Generation" of the 1950s]: There's a reappraisal of the literary value of the Beats in general I think. People are starting to realize that we weren't just a star that exploded long ago, and that we've continued to write all these years—aside from [Jack] Kerouac and [Neal] Cassady, very few of us fell by the wayside. We have a good longevity record compared with most of the academic poets who killed themselves by drinking. We just smoked a little

(ALLEN GINSBERG)

grass instead of totally knocking out our livers with booze, and the ones of us who died young were the alcoholics.

Interview,
Los Angeles, Calif./
Los Angeles Times,
2-16:(F)1.

David Halberstam
Pulitzer Prize-winning
author and journalist

1

I don't believe writers who say they never read their reviews. First off, anyone who says that probably isn't telling the truth. Second thing, I think you learn from reviews . . . If you're going to be a professional, you have to listen. It goes with the territory.

Interview/
The Writer, March:2.

Pete Hamill
Author

2

I write every day, one thing or another. I usually don't function very well in the morning. I get most of the serious writing done from 7:30 p.m. to 2:00 a.m. . . . Basically I write at night because of the peace and quiet. If it's baseball season, I can work with the ballgame on—because it's got no plot. And I'll play music that has to do with whatever it is I'm writing. One of the things I learned . . . was how useful music can be to trigger memory.

Interview, New York, N.Y./
Publishers Weekly, 1-10:39.

Robert Hass
Poet

3

Lyric poetry as an art form is nearer to and more capable of rendering the inner life, conscious-

ness, in a fresh way, than any other art form, except possibly music. Painting can do certain things, and novels can do certain things, and they can do them in powerful ways. But everybody talks, and everybody has internal lives, and finally that's the subject matter of poetry.

The Writer,
December:3.

James Kelman
Scottish author;
Winner, 1994 Booker Prize
for fiction

4

[On his controversial style of writing, which uses the language of working-class Glasgow, Scotland]: In order to fight against the [normal] house style, you have to justify every single comma. Every comma in my work is *my* comma. Every absence of a comma or full stop or semi-colon or colon is *my* absence. You have to be much more precise and bloody pedantic. You have to revise and revise and proof at every bloody stage to insure that everything's spot-on, especially because you're working in what other people regard as inconsistent ways, so you have to be really sure. You have to trust the fact that you're a writer.

Interview,
Glasgow, Scotland/
The New York Times,
11-29:(B)2.

Barbara Kingsolver
Author

5

Beginning [to write] a novel is always hard. It feels like going nowhere. I always have to write at least a hundred pages that go into the trash can before it finally begins to work. It's discouraging, but necessary, to write those pages. I try to consider them pages -100 to zero of the novel.

Writer's Digest,
August:25.

Galway Kinnell
Poet

1

Writing a poem is like making an artifact. It is making something physical out of words. There is a wholeness to a poem, as with a vase. There is also a sense of talking to someone, the reader. But we all have such different ideas of what poetry is. To me, poetry is somebody standing up, so to speak, and saying, with as little concealment as possible, what it is for him or her to be on earth at this moment. In no other art can we do that directly in words. That may be why so many people are writing poetry. They want to say what it is for them to live now. Poets are not, as they used to be, a special breed, set apart.

Interview, New York, N.Y./
Publishers Weekly, 12-5:56.

Judith Krantz
Author

2

You know, it's not an insult to be accused of writing "page turners." That's the critics' term for best-sellers. Of course they're not literature. They're commercial. But they're high-end commercial.

Interview,
Los Angeles, Calif./
"W" magazine,
April:44.

Anne Lamott
Author

3

[On her new book, a manual for writers]: Writing can help make sense of the world and give you direction and company and solace. Everyone who wants to write should get to. But many people are so burdened by perfectionism, and by this fantasy that published writers must know what they are doing every step of the way, that I wanted to sort of help them to find the crumbs that would bring them to that path of getting a little work done

every day for the rest of their lives, whether they get published or not.

Interview,
San Rafael, Calif./
The New York Times,
12-1:(B)4.

Fran Lebowitz
Author

4

The act of writing puts you in confrontation with yourself, which is why I think writers assiduously avoid writing. The number of alcoholic writers makes a lot of sense because if you're going to be face to face with yourself, maybe it's better that you don't recognize that person.

Interview, New York, N.Y./
The New York Times,
8-12:(B)8.

5

Until I was about 7, I thought books were just there, like trees. When I learned that people actually wrote them, I wanted to, too, because all children aspire to inhuman feats like flying. Most people grow up to realize they can't fly. Writers are people who don't grow up to realize they can't be God.

Interview, New York, N.Y./
The New York Times,
8-12:(B)8.

6

[On being a well-known writer]: Anyone's public image is a cartoon. It's comprised of one or two elements of your personality that have been exaggerated for commercial purposes, for you or the media to exploit. And those are the things that stick in people's minds. I once wrote a piece called *Children: Pro or Con?* It's half things *against* children, half things *for* children. People only remember the half that is against.

Interview/
"Interview" magazine,
November:66.

Rhoda Lerman
Author

1

I love good writing. It's music to my ears. I was brought up in a musical household. Everyone played cello. A truly great sentence has music coming out of it. I read my stuff aloud to myself. It has to "sound" right.

Interview,
Cazenovia, N.Y./
Publishers Weekly, 8-1:61.

Barry Lopez
Author

2

I'm always writing. There's no difference for me between my life and my work; they're completely of a part, totally related. I'm reading when I get up in the morning and I'm reading when I go to bed at night. I'm walking and traveling and doing all that feeds my work during all my waking hours. And I'm certain that during my sleeping hours, stories gestate.

Interview/
Publishers Weekly,
9-26:42.

Walter H. Lorraine
Vice president and director
of the children's book department,
Houghton Mifflin, publishers

3

I think it's going to be a good number of years before electronic or interactive books really change things. I can remember sitting with an author, having one of these conversations about CD-ROM and the interactive facet of it, and the author said, "Why would I want that? I wrote this book because I wanted to make a statement about the way I feel about things. I don't want the reader to tell me what I feel." I don't see things changing that radically that soon. One of the most important parts of a book is the enthusiasm of the author. Does that come across electronically? I always publish

authors rather than titles. It's a particular person's ideas that you're communicating to somebody else. That's why we read. To see the way the other guy sees it. To see things through another person's eyes. Anyway, that's how the books I've seen involved with function. Ever since I've been around, there have been predictions about the death of the book. But here they are still going along pretty strongly.

Interview/
Booklist, 6-1:1827.

Colleen McCullough
Author

4

[As a writer,] never regard your work as sacred, not to be assaulted by the opinions or suggestions of your editor. Even Nobel laureates can benefit from the comments of a good editor. Remember that your editor is the one critic of your work who can matter to you, for your editor is the only professional critic who sees your work in preparation, rather than in the final form of a book.

Writer's Digest,
August:25.

David W. McCullough
Member, editorial board,
Book-of-the-Month Club

5

[On the Book-of-the-Month's editorial board, which will be dissolved at the end of this year after almost seven decades]: The books that we selected weren't always the expected best-sellers, but what we honestly thought were the best books we'd read that month. More and more, the focus shifted to predicting what was going to be on the best-seller list. I think idiosyncratic qualities are falling out of publishing in general, and the industry is becoming financially conservative, focused on sure things and not wanting to take risks.

Interview/
The New York Times,
7-1:(B)2.

Patrick F. McManus
Author

1

Write out of the reader's imagination as well as your own. Supply the significant details and let the reader's imagination do the rest. Make the reader a co-author of the story.

Writer's Digest,
August:25.

Barbara Mertz
Author

2

I become somewhat testy when people ask where I "get" my ideas. Expressed in that fashion, the question implies that ideas can be ordered, singly or by the dozen, from a catalogue. Ideas aren't "got." They grow like a coral reef, by slow accretion, starting with a single, simple concept—a one-liner, one might call it. Gradually, this basic premise develops details—a specific setting, the names and personalities of the characters, various plot devices. When enough material has built up, the structure rises out of the murky depths of my subconscious and becomes visible as a possible plot.

Interview/
The Writer, February:3.

Walter Mosley
Author

3

If you're writing a scene, you're writing about one particular thing that's going on, whether it's a conversation, a murder, sex between two characters, whatever. But to write that scene, there may be 99 other things going on at that time that are assumed, and you have to know about every one of them. I find that when I'm unhappy with what I've done, most of the time what's happened is that one or two of those things that needs to be assumed has crept into the writing.

Interview, New York, N.Y./
Publishers Weekly, 5-23:67.

Barbara Mujica
Author

4

The short story allows the writer to concentrate on a single problem, on a single aspect of the character's personality, on a single conceit. It not only "allows" these restrictions, it imposes them.

The Writer, December:3.

V. S. Naipaul
Author

5

[On author-publisher relations]: An author lives with editors who don't read him, publishers who don't read him, booksellers who don't read him. You need someone who reads the work well—I'm using "read" in the technical way—someone who reads beautifully and sensitively. Writers need this. But you also need to be published aggressively. Sometimes it's difficult to combine the two.

Interview, New York, N.Y./
Publishers Weekly, 6-6:45.

John Nichols
Author

6

I never lack thoughts for a project, always have some ax to grind. Things percolate a lot, and when I sit down to work it just comes out, though it's often very different from what I've been thinking. I do the first draft very quickly, then rewrite—and rewrite, and rewrite—trying to find the story, kind of by trial and error. I love the revision process, dwelling on lines, words—that final stage is really writing.

Interview, Taos, N.M./
Publishers Weekly, 2-14:69.

Tim O'Brien
Author

7

[Writing non-fiction is] much easier than fiction by a long shot: just look at the world and write

(TIM O'BRIEN)

about it. On the other hand, it's real hard to be honest in non-fiction. You have to force yourself.

Interview/
Booklist, August:1991.

Camille Paglia
Author

1

The moment I have to read a novel, it's very tedious to me, because even with a writer like Brett Easton Ellis, who has a sharp, sadistic style, I think there's a kind of concealed liberal ideology there. It has this artsy sound to it; the authentic speech rhythms are gone. I'm more interested in the great stars' autobiographies, in literary and celebrity biographies; that's what I read. Non-fiction has absorbed the varieties and styles of fiction.

Interview, Washington, D.C./
Publishers Weekly, 11-28:40.

Joseph Parisi
Editor, "Poetry" magazine

2

[On the increase in poetry competitions and poetry prize awards]: Poets today are probably doing better [financially] that in all of history. Despite the romantic myths, I don't think poverty is conducive to creativity.

U.S. News & World Report,
10-10:20.

Richard North Patterson
Author

3

Write about what you care about and understand. Writers should never try to out-guess the marketplace in search of a salable idea; the simple truth is that all good books will eventually find a publisher if the writer tries hard enough. And a central secret to writing a good book is to write one that people like you will enjoy.

Writer's Digest, August:25.

Gary Paulsen
Author

4

I tried at one time writing with a tape recorder and having it transcribed—and I couldn't. I couldn't because I have to see it. Even the type of word processor I use makes the screen look like a page of typing. I have to see how it will look on a typewritten page. Exactly the same. I have to see how it will look for the drama of it and the way that it will go into the reader. And I don't do it grammatically. I'm not concerned with grammar as much as I am with artistic effect . . . The way it looks on the page fits into what the prose says and how it says it.

Interview/
Writer's Digest, July:44.

Octavio Paz
Mexican poet;
Winner, 1990 Nobel Prize
in Literature

5

When I read the poems I wrote when I was an adolescent, I can see what I was trying to do even though I did not succeed. You start by imitating others, there is lack of clarity, there are many reasons to fail. But there is a seed that slowly grows.

Interview, Paris, France/
The New York Times,
6-11:13.

Margot Peters
Biographer

6

You could say that there is a similarity between the detective and the biographer. To the biographer, the "victim" is the subject; and while you are not searching for a murderer, you are trying to unravel a life, to understand motivation. At the same time, you interview "suspects" in order to analyze their relationship with the subject, which further reveals the subject himself.

Interview, Lake Mills, Wis./
Writer's Digest, March:36.

Reynolds Price
Author

1

That's basically what I always wanted an editor [at a publishing house] to be: someone who [only] tells me that a character's eyes change from brown to blue in the course of the book. And I want someone who is really going to fight for the book within the house, to see that the book is taken as seriously as it deserves to be by production and design and especially publicity and sales. I need a good publisher more than an editor; I've never been able to work with someone looking over my shoulder.

Interview, Durham, N.C./
Publishers Weekly, 5-9:52.

R. A. Salvatore
Author

2

I think it was Robert Cormier who told me this: "Character is the most important ingredient to any fiction story. A good plot with lousy characters makes a lousy book; but a mediocre plot with strong characters makes for enjoyable reading." That advice makes sense. If I've got a hero who nobody cares about, no matter what jeopardy I might put him in, my readers will not be on the edge of their seats. But if they love this hero, they'll feel every pain he or she feels and sing out in triumph if he or she prevails.

Writer's Digest, August:25.

Mark Salzman
Author

3

The idea persists that writers exist in a vacuum, [that] they're geniuses and no one dares touch their work. [But] I benefit enormously from my friends and editors and my wife, who reads all my drafts. It would be great to be a completely independent genius. That not being the case, I'm more than glad to acknowledge help.

Interview, Pasadena, Calif./
Publishers Weekly, 1-17:358.

Charlie Smith
Author

4

Writers become writers because they're readers. Regular folks respond to something they've seen out in the world; writers are the ones who respond to something they've seen on the page. And a writer wants to *do* that thing he's seen on the page.

The Writer, October:3.

Richard E. Snyder
Chairman, Paramount Publishing

5

[On the current trend toward mergers and downsizing of book publishers and the release of fewer new books]: It's happening not just in publishing but in corporate America. Under the old system, there wasn't enough profitability or efficiency. The law of economics always prevails, and it finally prevailed in publishing.

The New York Times,
1-24:(C)6.

Stephen Spender
British poet

6

[On his persuading a publisher to cancel a novel he says mirrors too closely an autobiographical work he wrote many years ago]: I don't bear [the novel's author] any ill will. I'm 85 and on the brink of my grave, so I try to be benevolent. The people to criticize are the publishers. They don't seem to have editors who save young writers from making these bad mistakes.

Feb. 16/The Washington Post
2-17:(A)39.

Charles Spicer
Senior editor,
St. Martin's Press, publishers

7

[On publishers' decisions whether or not to publish a submitted manuscript]: It's tough for

(CHARLES SPICER)

first-time authors, and it's tough for non-first-time authors. Publishing is a very difficult business. It's a hard business to make money at. Yet, I really do believe a good book will win out.

Interview/
Writer's Digest,
February:42.

Gore Vidal
Author

1

Fewer and fewer [young people] are addicted to reading. If they don't get into it from the time they are 10 or 12 years old, they'll never enjoy reading. And if you don't *enjoy* reading, there goes literature . . . Literature takes a skill beyond just listening. You have to know how to read; you have to be able to take a line of prose—it's a bridge between you and the mind of the writer—and become as one with the other end of that prose. A great writer can do that for you, and a great reader can do that for any writer. If you get a great reader and a great writer, you have a kinetic energy that is very powerful.

Interview,
Italy/
Modern Maturity,
April-May:62,63.

Cynthia Voigt
Author

2

When I'm writing, I feel as if I have a responsibility to the story, and the story tells me if I'm doing it wrong. The story is my touchstone, not anything else. Which assumes, of course, that the story has, in some Platonic universe, already been written. And we all know it hasn't. Or so we think. It's almost an odd way of disclaiming responsibility. But I know I'm doing something wrong if I find myself thinking not about the story, but about

whether this is acceptable, what will be said, whether anybody will want to read it, what if nobody wants to read it.

Interview,
Maine/
Publishers Weekly,
7-18:226.

Theodore Weesner
Author

3

When I first started to write, I knew what I was after, but there were times when I couldn't make it happen. Now [at age 59] it seems that the words come very quickly, and that's reassuring and pleasant. I know some writers who absolutely run out of gas by their late 40s. I feel more desire and more interest now than I have ever felt in my life. I'm into another novel now, and it's part of a planned trilogy. There's nothing I'd enjoy more than to stay here all day at this table, look at the water down there, watch the snow fall outside and write my stories on these little pads of yellow paper.

Interview,
Portsmouth, N.H./
Publishers Weekly,
12-12:47.

Tobias Wolff
Author

4

I work every day, at least six hours a day. Sometimes the pace is glacial. It takes me about three months to get a story to the point where I really like it. When I am working at the top of my form, I see things differently, and there's an excitement that comes when things become clear to me that were not so clear before. I can think of no other word for what happens than revelation.

Interview,
Syracuse, N.Y./
Publishers Weekly,
10-24:46.

Virginia Euwer Wolff
Author

1

[On how she began to write books]: I just sat down and wrote one day . . . I had never taken a writing course, and I had never finished a short story. I just decided I would sit down and write a novel. You know, "where angels fear to tread." I do everything "where angels fear to tread." I believe that's how our best writing gets done. I had a whole bunch of impulses and half-witted perceptions coming out of me, just coming out my ears; so I sat down and let stuff pour out onto the typewriter.

Interview/
Booklist, 3-1:1250.

Drew E. Altman
President, Henry J. Kaiser
Family Foundation

1

[On the controversy over President Clinton's health-care plan and the competing plans]: The group that is most likely to be helped least—at least as the discussion stands now—is the working middle class . . . which is a little surprising, since it was the rise of middle-class concern that put this issue on the front burner in the first place.

Los Angeles Times,
8-5:(A)1.

2

[On the fear the public has about government involvement in the health-care system as it applies to President Clinton's health-care plan]: It's a huge issue because "bureaucracy" and accusations that a plan is a "big government" plan have become almost nuclear weapons. And critics [of the Clinton proposal] have been tremendously successful in instilling fear and skepticism about the government's ability to reform the health-care system.

Los Angeles Times,
8-16:(A)16.

Helen Alvare
Director of planning and information,
National Conference of Catholic Bishops

3

[Criticizing having abortion included in President Clinton's health-care benefits proposal]: [Health-care] reform should be judged primarily by how it treats the most marginalized and helpless members of society: the poor, the uninsured, the undocumented and the unborn. Genuine reform must begin from a conviction that healing, not killing, is a service owed to all human beings. [To mandate that abortion be included as a health-care benefit would] assault the consciences of millions of Americans.

Christianity Today, 4-25:40.

Bruce N. Ames
Biochemist,
University of California,
Berkeley

4

Much of cancer is built in; a good part of it is due to aging. If you plot cancer versus age, you'll see that in 60 million years, evolution took us from short-lived creatures like rats, where a third have cancer by the age of 3, to long-lived creatures like humans, where a third have cancer by the age of 80. There's very little human cancer until after the age of 30; then it increases with age.

Interview/
The New York Times,
7-5:(B)5.

Richard K. Armey
United States Representative,
R-Texas

5

[On President Clinton's health-care reform plan]: Clinton can't pass his bill. Members of Congress cannot go home and defend a vote for a nightmarish bureaucratic infrastructure or job-killing mandates like those in the Clinton bill.

Interview/
The New York Times,
1-3:(A)7.

Scott Ballin
Executive director,
Coalition on Smoking
OR Health

6

[On the reported adverse health effects of cigarettes]: I can't think of another product that, faced with the scientific evidence which is associated with tobacco, could remain a legal product on the market and almost completely exempt from regulation.

Time, 4-18:61.

Gary L. Bauer
President,
Family Research Council

1

[Criticizing new government-sponsored TV ads promoting the use of condoms to reduce the risk of AIDS transmission]: Is there an American who tunes into prime-time TV who hasn't already gotten the message about condoms? I think there is another political agenda here. I think it is more about pushing the envelope on explicitness of sexual matters during prime-time TV than concerns about the disease. I would urge the CDC to have the courage to be creative in telling Americans that abstinence outside of marriage is the best way to prevent transmission.

Jan. 4/
Los Angeles Times,
1-5:(A)10.

Robert Bell
Chairman, department of
molecular cancer biology,
Duke University

2

Signal transduction is the single most important unifying concept in modern-day biology and medicine. These are the pathways that get screwed up in a lot of diseases. Once we have the wiring diagrams, we'll be able to be good technicians and fix them.

U.S. News & World Report,
3-28:66.

Arnold Bennett
Media director, Families USA

3

[Supporting President Clinton's health-care reform plan]: Of course we're for universal coverage. No one is backing away from that. But the message is that this plan means no American will ever again have to worry about losing their insurance. When you talk about "universal coverage," people start to worry about paying for someone else. When you talk about "losing" insurance, it sounds like something that will protect them.

The New York Times,
7-28:(A)12.

Neal Benowitz
Professor of medicine,
University of California,
San Francisco

4

[Saying nicotine in tobacco is addictive]: What maintains tobacco use is nicotine. No one smokes cigarettes without nicotine. There are a lot of semantics about addiction . . . But the majority of people who want to stop smoking can't.

Aug. 2/
Los Angeles Times,
8-3:(A)10.

Steve Bercham
Spokesman, Pharmaceutical Research
and Manufacturers of America

5

[Defending drug companies from criticism that they mislead doctors when pushing sales and use of the drugs they manufacture]: The issue here is making sure that physicians know about how to use medicines. We play a vital role in that. Who knows the drug better than the drug companies?

Los Angeles Times,
7-27:(A)12.

Robert J. Blendon
Chairman, department of health
policy and management,
Harvard School of Public Health

6

[Health-care reform] is something the country wants Congress to act on. When you ask Americans what government should do first, health care is number one. Health care looks fixable . . . Unfortunately, complex plans [such as President Clinton's] require a very high level of trust of po-

(ROBERT J. BLENDON)

litical leaders, because you basically have to say, "Look, I can't understand this, but I trust you." And Clinton doesn't have that level of trust.

Interview,
Boston, Mass./
AARP Bulletin, May:20.

1

[On a study he worked on showing one in five American families had problems paying their medical bills, despite most of them having health insurance]: The problem is that many people's insurance is not as deep as they think, and their medical bills are not being paid for adequately by insurance. You do not have absolute security. The real message of our survey is uncertainty: You think your insurance is going to cover you and the answer is, maybe you're right . . . We believe that we're having a national health debate because of the reduction of benefits that people are experiencing. You're covered for less. You're paying more. And you're nervous about what is going to happen in the case of large medical bills.

The New York Times,
5-12:(A)1,16.

David E. Bonior
United States Representative,
D-Michigan

2

[Saying members of Congress are wary about voting on health-care reform legislation]: We've got to contend with people keeping one eye on the Senate and the Senate keeping one eye on us. Plus, the emotional issues involved here—mandates, revenues, abortion, employment issues—these are really hot items all by themselves. When lumped together, they really create a caldron of difficulties.

Los Angeles Times,
7-18:(A)12.

3

[On a new health-care plan proposed by House Democrats]: This is not the [President] Clinton bill. Our plan cuts bureaucracy, cuts the cost to taxpayers, cuts the "alliances" that everyone calls big government, cuts the automatic price controls, cuts red tape, and cuts the burden on small business.

Washington, July 29/
The New York Times,
7-30:6.

David L. Boren
United States Senator,
D-Oklahoma

4

[On his decision to support a Republican-sponsored health-care reform plan rather than President Clinton's plan]: My action today should not be viewed as any opposition to the President's goals, but as the best way to move them forward . . . If we do not form a bipartisan consensus soon and we don't begin to work on a bipartisan basis within the Senate Finance Committee, we will lose health-care reform.

May 4/
Los Angeles Times,
5-5:(A)22.

Lawrence Bossidy
Chairman, AlliedSignal, Inc.

5

[On the various health-care reform plans being talked about in Washington]: I think the [President] Clinton plan is clearly overdone, and it's not going to be one of the options. It's not going to come up for consideration, so I won't spend any time on it. I think the final bill is apt to be a very modest bill where universal coverage is one of the "aspirations." I hope that there's no damage done. A lot of companies have effective health-care-management programs. By and large, if there's any bill at all it will be modest.

Interview, July 18/
USA Today, 7-19:(B)4.

John B. Breaux
United States Senator,
D-Louisiana

1

[On health-care reform proposals]: Liberals want to do everything all at once and hope they got it right; and conservatives want to do nothing and take a long time to do it. I'm trying to take one step at a time and make sure we get it right. When you're in the middle, you get beat up by both sides.

The New York Times,
8-16:(A)10.

Lonnie R. Bristow
Chairman, board of trustees,
American Medical Association

2

It is a gross conflict of interest for a physician to treat an individual patient and have to worry about the needs of society [for cost cutting].

U.S. News & World Report,
4-25:39.

Lee P. Brown
Director,
White House Office of
National Drug Control Policy

3

Getting the media to understand the [illegal-] drug problem is probably the Number 1 domestic problem. They have a role to play in helping educate people. Some 160,000 kids don't go to school every day because they're afraid. If you look at health care, the soaring costs can be related clearly to the drug problem. If you look at the workplace, we're less productive because of substance abuse. If you look at public housing, people are terrified. Any aspect of our life today is impacted by the drug problem. Unless we get a handle on drugs, we won't have things we want, like family, like work, like community.

Interview/
USA Today, 6-30:(A)11.

4

Marijuana, as you know, is a controlled substance. Our position is that it should remain a controlled substance. We feel that way because it is a potentially dangerous psychoactive drug, with strong links to medical problems and negative, or at least high-risk, behavior among its users.

The Atlantic Monthly,
September:94.

Lovola W. Burgess
President, American Association
of Retired Persons

5

[Saying her organization is not endorsing President Clinton's health-care reform plan]: The Clinton plan is the nearest to what we are looking for, but it falls short in a number of ways. We are concerned about the financing. We don't know if the proposed cuts in the growth of Medicare and Medicaid would provide enough money to help finance the President's plan. We fear that doctors would be less willing to see Medicare patients if their fees are cut.

Interview, Feb. 24/
The New York Times,
2-25:(A)1.

Robert C. Byrd
United States Senator,
D-West Virginia

6

[Saying the country can't afford a large-scale health-care reform plan]: We just can't do it; we have to restrain our appetite. Our national heart is large, but our national pocketbook, sadly, is small.

Aug. 18/USA Today, 8-19:(A)4.

Arthur L. Caplan
Director, Center for Biomedical Ethics,
University of Minnesota

7

[On moves to restrict smoking]: As people start to think about sharing the cost of health care

(ARTHUR L. CAPLAN)

with their neighbors, they start to wonder why they have to share that cost if their neighbor smokes. If their neighbor smokes, drinks, has multiple sex partners, is a fat couch potato, they begin to say: "I don't want to pay the price of that person's lifestyle." And smoking is at the head of this particular parade of vices because we know so much about its impact on health.

Los Angeles Times,
3-26:(A)20.

Dorothy Caruso-Herman
Former nurse practitioner;
Co-founder, Hospice Nurses Association

1

I don't think physicians should be threatened [by nurse practitioners]; NPs are not trying to take away their role. Nurse practitioners do pick up a lot of things. NPs are much more aware psychosocially, more conversant and take more time with patients. Physicians are threatened that a nurse practitioner might make a decision that would not be what they would make. They have a corner on the market and never wanted to accept the fact that the nurse was never more than their handmaiden. I see the nurse and nurse practitioner and well-trained physician assistants moving into the area, in effect, of middle management, with physicians as upper management. More partnerships, less hierarchy—neither threatens the other.

Los Angeles Times,
7-25:(B)5.

Christine Cassel
Professor of medicine
and public policy,
University of Chicago

2

People feel that if they go to the doctor and don't walk out with five tests and a prescription, they haven't had a good visit.

Newsweek, 6-27:31.

William Castelli
Director, Framingham (Mass.)
Heart Study

3

[On the findings of the study he directed, which spanned four decades of monitoring the people of Framingham, Mass.]: Most people who get heart attacks and strokes [today] don't die. They live. This is how our country is going broke, paying for the bypass operations, angioplasties and truckloads of medicines needed to keep people with cardiovascular diseases alive. Hospitalizations for coronary disease have actually increased, not declined. We have to look at the whole picture, not just pat ourselves on the back because death rates have fallen. We have a long way to go in preventing these diseases.

The New York Times,
1-5:(B)7.

Bill Clinton
President of the United States

4

I want to make this very clear. If the [health-care reform] legislation you [Congress] send me does not guarantee every American private health insurance that can never be taken away, you will force me to take this pen, veto that legislation, and we'll come right back here and start over again.

State of the Union address,
before joint session of Congress,
Washington, D.C., Jan. 25/
The New York Times, 1-26:(A)1.

5

I have said that I cannot sign—and indeed would have to veto—a bill that pretended to reform the health-care system without providing a system by which everyone is covered. Because—unless everyone is covered—there is no cost control, there is no end to cost-shifting, there is no real security and there is no balance in the system.

Before American Society
of Association Executives,
Washington, D.C., March 8/
Los Angeles Times, 3-9:(A)11.

(BILL CLINTON)

1

[On his plan for health-care reform]: When I put my ideas out, I made it clear that I was very flexible on how to get there, how to solve this problem, which is a system that costs too much and does too little, and that we ought to find a way to cover the American people just the way every other advanced country has covered all their people.

To Congressional leaders,
Washington, D.C., June 15/
The New York Times,
6-16:(A)10.

2

[Providing health insurance to all Americans] goes to the heart of whether we can get out our own economic house in order. It goes to the heart of whether we can make government work for ordinary people. It goes to the heart of whether we can empower people to view change as a friend instead of an enemy. Unless we can provide coverage for every American in a reformed system which focuses on both quality and control of costs, the deficit will grow, your costs will continue to grow and undermine productivity, and more and more Americans will lose their coverage or be at risk.

Before Business Roundtable,
June 21/Los Angeles Times,
6-22:(A)12.

3

[Calling for guaranteed health insurance for everyone]: The politicians have it. The wealthy have it. The poor have it. If you go to jail, you have it. Only the middle class doesn't have it, and I don't think that makes much sense.

Speech, Greenburg, Pa., July 15/
The New York Times,
7-16:7.

4

[On his health-care reform plan]: We know we're not going to get right at 100 percent [cover-

age], but we know that you've got to get somewhere in the ballpark of 95 percent or upwards . . . [And] I would not rule out a health plan that didn't have an employer mandate in it, if we knew that we were moving toward full coverage and we had some evidence that it would work . . . All I ask in the closing weeks of this debate is that we take the political air out of the balloon and ask ourselves what will work for ordinary Americans.

At National Governors'
Association conference,
Boston, Mass., July 19/
Los Angeles Times,
7-20:(A)1,9.

5

[On criticism that, in a recent speech to state Governors, he backed away from some key elements in his proposed health-care reform plan]: I have been saying for four weeks [that] we have agreed to dramatically change this plan. We're going to string it out, we have to have a longer phase-in, we have to have less bureaucracy, we have to have totally voluntary small-business [health] alliances, and we have to give a bigger break to small business to get them to buy into it . . . That is exactly what I said to the Governors; that is exactly what I've been saying for the last three or four weeks.

News conference,
Washington, D.C., July 22/
The New York Times,
7-23:8.

6

[On health-care reform]: I have seen no one yet who has come up with a better idea than shared responsibility between employers and employees for private health insurance in our private health-care system. I desperately want a bipartisan bill. I have reached out to members of the [Republican] Party . . . But every time I have reached out, they have moved further away . . . Let us discard politics. And let our focus be simply this: What will work? I have no pride of authorship; nothing would please me more than if somebody else's name, a

(BILL CLINTON)

hundred names, four hundred names, five hundred names in both houses of Congress would be on a health-care bill.

At ceremony commemorating
enactment of the Americans
With Disabilities Act,
Washington, D.C., July 27/
Los Angeles Times, 7-28:(A)18.

1

We're fighting for health-care reform not just for those who don't have health insurance—but for those who do have it and who could use it and *lose* it because they have to change jobs, because someone in their family gets sick, because they simply have to pay too much for it. They deserve better, and we're fighting to see that they get it. We want to guarantee private, not government, insurance for every American. The plan I originally proposed has been changed [in Congress], and much of it for the better. The proposals before Congress are less bureaucratic. They're more flexible. They provide more protection and support for small business. They contain a reasonable phase-in time over a period of years to make sure we get it right. No bureaucrat will pick your doctor. You can keep your own plan or pick a better one. This approach controls government spending but relies on competitive forces in the free market to restrain the growth of private health-insurance premiums. Much of it has changed for the better, but one rock-solid principle remains: private insurance guaranteed for everyone. We know it will work.

News conference,
Washington, D.C., Aug. 3/
The New York Times,
8-4:(A)10.

2

[On health-care reform]: At one time when we started this debate, and I said I wanted universal coverage, many members in Congress stood up and clapped, of both parties. At one time there

were two dozen Republican Senators on a bill to give universal coverage to all Americans; they have all abandoned that bill. We have reached out to them, as was our responsibility, to try to work together in a bipartisan fashion; and every time we've done it, they have moved away. So the questions now should shift to them. Are we going to cover all Americans or not? Are we going to have a bill that provides health-care security or not? If you don't like our approaches in the Senate and the House, what is your alternative? That's what I hope we'll see.

News conference,
Washington, D.C., Aug. 3/
The New York Times,
8-4:(A)10.

Hillary Rodham Clinton
Wife of President
of the United States Bill Clinton;
Former Chairman,
White House Task Force
on National Health Care Reform

3

I have this old-fashioned idea that young people ought to help pay for old people and healthy people ought to help pay for sick people, because at some point we're all going to be sick and we're all going to be old. And I see people beginning to understand that they don't lose anything by trying to help somebody else. In fact, they gain more security. If everybody is secure, we are all better off. Instead of fighting over who gets this particular [medical] procedure because I can afford it and you can't, if all of us can afford it, there will be more of it for everybody.

Interview/
Modern Maturity,
Feb.-Mar.:69.

4

We're confusing the fact that we [in the U.S.] have the finest physicians and hospitals in the world with the fact that we have the stupidest financing system for health care in the world. The

(HILLARY RODHAM CLINTON)

financing system is becoming the tail that wags the dog. The insurance companies are in charge and pick and choose who they cover.

To health-care professionals,
Philadelphia, Pa., Feb. 4/
Los Angeles Times, 2-5:(A)21.

1

If we do not act [on health-care reform], two groups of Americans will continue to be secure—the very rich, who will be able to afford whatever health care they need, and the very poor, who . . . will be on government assistance. Everyone else . . . will be even more insecure than they are today.

USA Today, 6-30:(A)4.

2

[On the Clinton Administration's health-care reform plan]: You know, this part of the country [the West] was settled by people who got on wagon trains and went out not knowing exactly where they would end up. When we began this health-care crusade, I sometimes felt like I was on a journey that I did not know exactly where it would end up either. But every day that went on I became more and more convinced that if the American people had a chance to vote themselves, there would be no question about the outcome. And if we give our energy, our hearts, our souls to the next few weeks and make it clear that the American people want what the members of Congress have—guaranteed health insurance paid for with an employer-employee shared responsibility system—we will get it for every single American.

At rally, Portland, Ore., July 22/
Los Angeles Times, 7-23:(A)26.

3

[On health-care reform]: If you start out with those of us who are insured, our numbers are going down. We have fewer people insured in the workplace than we did five years ago. We've lost about five million people who used to be insured . . . So the status quo is a declining one in terms of coverage for those of us [who] are insured. It's also one in which costs continue to increase and choice decreases. So even if we are able to retain our insurance, most of us are paying more for the same insurance than we used to have. If we're not paying more, then we've given up choice of physician and health plan as our employers have tried to control costs. So we're really being caught in a squeeze play. If we're still hanging onto our insurance, it is either costing us more or it is decreasing the coverage or the choices available to us . . . All of us who are not rich enough or poor enough to get guaranteed insurance are one job away from health insurance being taken away. One layoff. One divorce. One sickness away. So everyone who is currently insured, I would like to ask them to ask themselves: "Am I free to leave my job with insurance and go into the job market not knowing whether I will be able to get insurance? Am I free to leave my job because I or someone in my family has a pre-existing condition?" . . . I'd like people to ask themselves: "Suppose I were divorced and I'm the dependent spouse on my spouse's policy—how long could I afford the extension of insurance before it ran out?"

Interview, Washington, D.C./
USA Today, 8-8:(A)8.

4

[Criticizing those who she says are opposed to Democratic Party health-care reform proposals]: [There is a] small core of people [who are] ideologically opposed [to health-care reform], who think nobody should get anything from anyone else. [They are the same people] who drive down highways paid for by government funds [and who] love the Defense Department . . . But they have a different mind-set when it comes to social policy and trying to be a compassionate and caring nation. [They are] pulling the strings of others . . . and inflaming people . . . making charges of socialism and that the government is going to take over health care.

Interview,
Washington, D.C., Aug. 9/
The Washington Post, 8-10:(A)5.

(HILLARY RODHAM CLINTON)

1

When people keep asking me if I'm going to give up on health-care reform [because of the failure of the Clinton Administration to get reform passed this year], my answer is always the same: Why would I give up on America or the American people? I am the result of privilege. I am the result of good health. I am the result of a great education. Why would I not want to do what I could in any small way to make it possible for others to have the same opportunities that I have had over my lifetime? We must have the courage to keep going. If this were easy, somebody else would have done it.

At George Washington University
School of Medicine, Sept. 29/
Los Angeles Times, 9-30:(A)18.

2

[On the failure of the Clinton Administration to get its health-care reform plan passed by Congress this year]: We knew we would have to move off of mandatory [health] alliances and the forum of the [insurance-] premium cap and the size of the benefit package. We anticipated doing that. [But] we never adequately got across to people, and we were then painted as being inflexible or unwilling to negotiate, when that is how we saw the whole process. What we were not willing to do is negotiate and get nothing in return, to give up on chunks of a coherent plan.

Interview, Washington, D.C./
The New York Times,
10-3:(A)9.

3

Groups that profit from the existing [health-care] system are extremely well financed and powerful, and they have launched a very effective campaign over the last year and a half to confuse people and to make people afraid [of the Clinton Administration's health-care reform plans]. The opponents [of change] say, "You're trying to get the government to take over the medical system."

Totally untrue, but it scared people. Or we're going to take away your choice of doctor. Totally untrue, but people don't know who to believe. And if you're sitting at home, you see an eight-second television news story where somebody in the Administration says, "We're going to preserve your choice of doctor." Then you see very well-produced ads that run around the news, and then you get a mailing. How do you know what to believe?

Interview, Washington, D.C./
Ladies' Home Journal,
November:274.

Jim Cooper
United States Representative,
D-Tennessee

4

[On the Clinton Administration's failure to get its health-care reform bill passed this year]: I think the Administration's key mistake was not being bipartisan. They only had one Republican in America supporting their approach . . . Partisan approaches are doomed to fail on any major issue. What was the [Thomas] Jefferson quote? "Great initiatives cannot be built on slender majorities." You have to have a consensus.

The New York Times,
9-27:(A)13.

Mario M. Cuomo
Governor of New York (D)

5

I think many of the people in the country misperceive the rationale for universal [health-care] coverage. They think it is purely a matter of compassion and concern for 36 to 37 million uncovered people. And that leads some of them to believe that you are asking the covered people to give up wealth for the benefit of the uncovered people, when the better rationale is: In order to protect the covered people—at least eventually—you have to get the uncovered people into coverage, because they're receiving health care, but it's too expensive and the burden of that expense falls on the shoulders of the premium-payers, which is the rest of us.

Washington, D.C., July 26/
The New York Times,
7-27:(A)15.

John C. Danforth
United States Senator,
R-Missouri

1

[On the struggle in Congress and the White House on health-care reform]: It's like lava flowing down the side of a volcano. Fluid and hot.

U.S. News & World Report,
7-4:30.

Tom Daschle
United States Senator,
D-South Dakota

2

[Criticizing the idea that proposed Democratic health-care reform plans would result in too much government involvement in the health-care system]: There ought to be some regulatory framework. And if it isn't the government who creates that regulatory framework, who does? Do we just turn over the entire system to the insurance sector for them to do whatever they wish? Do we turn it over to the doctors, the hospitals? How would it be if we let the airlines run the entire system without any kind of oversight and regulatory control with the FAA, one of the most if not the safest air-controlled system in the world today? How would it be if our banking system did not have a regulatory framework? How would it be if we simply threw the entire system of highways open to the private sector and let them design roads for whatever choices there may be without some kind of framework? . . . But to say that in a banking system, in an air-traffic-control system, in a highway system we've got an entire system run by the government is a gross exaggeration and an overstate-

ment. So I would hope that we could have an opportunity to talk about these [health-care] issues with proper characterization, a recognition that, indeed, we must have the kind of framework that we've been able to acquire in other parts of our economy, in other parts of our system; and I certainly hope that, ultimately, when we pass the [health-care reform] legislation that I know we can pass in the coming weeks, that it will recognize the importance of a private-sector system in an appropriate governmental framework.

Before the Senate,
Washington, D.C., Aug. 15/
The New York Times,
8-16:(A)11.

Richard J. Davidson
President,
American Hospital Association

3

[Criticizing proposed cuts in Medicare spending as a way to finance health-care reform]: In its quest for universal [health-care] coverage, Congress looks to Medicare as a huge source of money, a bottomless well. The Medicare cuts in the [House] Ways and [Means] Committee bill are a farce. If Congress is serious enough to make a commitment to assure universal coverage, it should be serious enough to make the tough choices to pay for it. Members of Congress ought to quit kidding themselves. You cannot finance health-care reform on the backs of hospitals and doctors who serve the elderly, or else you will harm the quality of care.

July 13/
The New York Times,
7-14:(A)9.

Richard K. Davidson
Chief executive,
Union Pacific Railroad

4

The crowd I run in, there is clear opposition to the [U.S. President] Clinton [health-care] plan,

(RICHARD K. DAVIDSON)

and it is solidifying. People are thinking of the negatives, the big-brother role for government, the hidden costs, the taxation, that sort of thing. They fear big-government solutions.

The New York Times,
5-10:(C)1.

Brennan Dawson
Spokesman, Tobacco Institute

1

The studies examining smoking in the workplace, in 12 out of 14 cases, do not show an increased [health] risk for non-smokers. In order to regulate any substance, OSHA has an obligation to demonstrate a significant risk or hazard, and that has not been done with environmental [second-hand] tobacco smoke.

March 25/
The New York Times,
3-26:5.

Richard Daynard
Professor of law,
Northeastern University

2

[On proposed Federal legislation putting more regulations on smoking in public places and possibly on levels of nicotine in cigarettes]: No one wants to make people hooked on cigarettes suffer. We just want to make sure they are not followed by future generations.

Time, 3-21:62.

Christopher DeMuth
President,
American Enterprise Institute

3

It is fashionable at the think tanks to wring our hands over the legislative sausage factory on Capitol Hill. Yet this year's health-care [reform] debate has—so far—been a model of serious de-

liberation. A great heap of terrible legislative proposals has been rejected, in defiance of well-organized political and media promotion, having been discovered by the public and the Congress to be unsound and worse. That serious threats to the vitality of American medicine have been averted is genuine progress. To be sure, many positive and badly needed reforms have been lost in the shuffle—but maybe only postponed. The year has not been a waste of time but a time of public education, which with any luck will have laid the groundwork for better proposals and policies to come.

At health-care conference,
Washington, D.C., July 28/
The Wall Street Journal,
7-29:(A)12.

Christopher J. Dodd
United States Senator,
D-Connecticut

4

[Saying the chances are poor that a health-care reform bill will be passed before this fall's elections]: Time is the 101st Senator. He is the ally of the people who want to do nothing.

Newsweek, 9-5:21.

Robert J. Dole
United States Senator,
R-Kansas

5

[Criticizing President Clinton's health-care reform plan]: The Administration is attempting to sell price controls and global budgets and government monopolies as answers to very real problems. They call us [critics of the plan] naysayers and nitpickers because we oppose turning one-seventh of the economy over to the Federal government.

Before
American Hospital Association,
Washington, D.C., Jan. 31/
The New York Times,
2-1:(A)10.

(ROBERT J. DOLE)

1

The [U.S.] health-care system may not be perfect, but it is the best in the world. It needs repair, but I'm not certain that it needs a complete and total overhaul and certainly not a complete and total takeover by the Federal government . . . How do you get [to President Clinton's proposal for universal coverage]? How much does it cost? Is it 91 percent coverage, 92 percent, 95 percent? Is it Ivory Soap? What is it? . . . I have no trouble with everybody being covered in America. The issue is how do we do it and how much does it cost. And I suggest that between getting it done right and getting it done fast, many of us would prefer getting it done right.

At National Governors' Association
conference, Boston, Mass., July 19/
Los Angeles Times, 7-20:(A)9.

2

[Criticizing the Clinton Administration for the way it is handling the health-care reform debate]: One day they attack me. The next day they attack employers. The next day it's insurance companies. It's politics as usual at the White House. They are looking for enemies instead of solutions.

July 26/
The New York Times,
7-27:(A)15.

3

[Saying health-care reform should be pursued slowly, without the major changes to the system proposed by the Clinton Administration and other Democrats]: The American people are going to insist, they are insisting, that we not rush to judgment . . . If you want to see a health-care "crisis," go to Sarajevo [Bosnia, during the current ethnic conflict there], or go somewhere in Rwanda. We don't have a crisis in America. But it is a serious problem, and it ought to be addressed.

At American Enterprise Institute,
Washington, D.C., July 28/
The New York Times, 7-29:(A)8.

4

[On Vice President Al Gore's criticism of Republican health-care reform proposals and his favoring of the various Democratic programs announced by President Clinton and Senator George Mitchell and Representative Richard Gephardt]: I suggest to the Vice President, instead of criticizing our plan, maybe he ought to decide which plan he is for. Is he for the original Clinton plan or for the Clinton-Gephardt plan or the Clinton-Mitchell plan or for some other plan? Perhaps we could have another secret [Democratic Party] task force we have not heard about. Maybe they could draft a new plan over the weekend.

Before the Senate,
Washington, D.C., Aug. 4/
The Washington Post,
8-8:(A)9.

5

[On charges by Democrats that Republicans have not cooperated in a bipartisan manner to reform health care]: I've attended all the hearings. I went to the bipartisan retreat. I've been to two Republican retreats. We've had dinner at the White House. But we never got down to serious talk about bipartisanship. [From the Democrats] it was always, "If you accept our package, or maybe minor changes, we'd be happy to talk to you." So I don't know what else we [Republicans] could have done.

Interview/
USA Today, 8-8:(A)8.

6

I can't remember a piece of legislation receiving as much media coverage as [President Clinton's health-care] bill. It was discussed and debated and dissected in town-hall meetings and kitchen-table discussions across the country. And something happened as the weeks and months went by. Despite the fact that the President and the First Lady had the full use of the White House bully pulpit, and despite the fact that they are both very

(ROBERT J. DOLE)

eloquent, public support for the Clinton plan did nothing but go down and down and down.

Before the Senate,
Washington, D.C., Aug. 9/
The New York Times, 8-10:(C)19.

1

[Disagreeing with Senate Majority Leader George Mitchell's charge that Republicans are responsible for the failure of Congress to pass President Clinton's health-care reform bill this year]: I think the American people, after all the debate and discussion, understood [the bill] and wouldn't buy it. It's just too complex, too bureaucratic, too expensive . . . Senator Mitchell blames Republicans for everything except the [small] plane that [recently] crashed into the White House. [In the Democratic health-care plan, the American people] feared an overdose of government control. We saw democracy in action. That's what happened. That's the way it is supposed to work.

Sept. 26/
The New York Times,
9-27:(A)1.

Rudiger Dornbusch
Professor of economics,
Massachusetts Institute of Technology

2

[President Clinton's health-care reform plan is] recklessly expensive, murderously ineffective, and . . . the means are so far away from economics that they are frightening.

The Christian Science Monitor,
1-13:9.

David Durenberger
United States Senator,
R-Minnesota

3

On both sides [of the health-care issue] there are extremists who demand that what they want be it; and that's why it seems to me the progress in

health-care reform in the Congress of the United States to date has been total chaos.

USA Today, 6-27:(A)4.

Joycelyn Elders
Surgeon General
of the United States

4

If I could be the "condom queen" and get every young person who is engaged in sex to use a condom in the United States, I would wear a crown on my head with a condom on it! I would!

USA Today, 2-4:(A)11.

5

The Medicaid system must have been developed by a white male slave owner. It pays for you to be pregnant and have a baby, but it won't pay for much family planning. White male slave owners wanted a lot of healthy slaves, people to work. We don't need slaves anymore. We need healthy, educated, motivated children with hope. We need to really invest in family planning.

Before National Family
Planning and Reproductive
Health Association,
Washington, D.C., Feb. 25/
The New York Times, 2-26:7.

6

If reproductive choice is to be a reality in our country, reproductive choice must include access to the latest, most effective means of contraception . . . The fundamental problem remains [that] the price of [contraceptives such as] Norplant and Depo Provera is too high in this country for a large portion of working poor women to realize contraceptive equality. With 57 percent of all births in the country considered unplanned or unwanted, we need to insure that the newest, most highly effective methods of contraception are not priced beyond the reach of a majority of American women.

Before House Subcommittee on Regulation,
Business Opportunities and Technology,
Washington, D.C., March 18/
The New York Times, 3-19:8.

Maura Ellis
Spokeswoman, R. J. Reynolds
Tobacco Company

1

[On criticism that cigarette advertising, such as the "Joe Camel" ads, influence young people to smoke]: Every study will show the overwhelming influence on kids who start smoking is peer pressure and family influences. Children from homes where their parents are smokers tend to have a higher [smoking] rate. And since these ads have been in place, the number of kids who smoke has continued to decline.

Winston-Salem, N.C./
Los Angeles Times,
2-21:(D)2.

Alain C. Enthoven
Professor,
Graduate School of Business,
Stanford University

2

[Criticizing President Clinton's health-reform plan]: Price controls don't and won't work, and therefore the first thing Congress should do is delete pages one through 1,342 of Clinton's 1,342-page bill.

Before American Insurance Association,
New York, Jan. 12/
Los Angeles Times, 1-13:(A)8.

3

[The health-care reform bill that will be passed] will put us on a path that will eventually—in six to eight years—get to universal coverage, provided we define universal coverage reasonably. By that, I mean something like 95 percent. There will always be some people whose lifestyles and behavior do not fit in with enrollment in a health plan—the homeless and some young people who never believe they ever will be sick. There will always have to be a public-provider system of last resort. [And] I presume undocumented aliens will not be covered by this plan.

Interview/
Los Angeles Times, 3-27:(M)3.

Jack Faris
President,
National Federation
of Independent Business

4

I think what we're hearing from the President [Clinton] is that he must have a health-care [reform] bill this year. He is out now trying to get anything he can so that it can still be "Clintonesque."

USA Today, 7-25:(A)4.

Dianne Feinstein
United States Senator,
D-California

5

The best way to achieve health-care reform is to take it step by step [instead of doing it all at once] . . . One side wants too much, the other wants nothing. Our aim is to bring the two leaders [Democrat and Republican] together and say, "We can do *something* now."

News conference,
Washington, D.C.,
Aug. 19/
Los Angeles Times,
8-20:(A)1.

Richard Fenigsen
Retired Dutch physician
and opponent of euthanasia

6

[On the liberal euthanasia laws in the Netherlands]: The euthanasia movement actually promised liberation by death from the power of medicine. [But instead,] the power the doctors increased immensely. Doctors determine how euthanasia is practiced, they establish the diagnosis, they inform the patient if they want, they decide whether to report it to the authorities—and most cases are not reported.

U.S. News & World Report,
4-25:36.

Tom Fitzgerald
Spokesman,
Brown & Willaimson
Tobacco Corporation

1

[Defending his company against charges by FDA Commissioner David Kessler that it developed a high-nicotine tobacco plant to make it easier to "hook" people on smoking]: Contrary to what Dr. Kessler said, there was nothing secretive about the development of Y-1 tobacco. He has totally blown the issue out of proportion. What Dr. Kessler called "manipulation" [of nicotine content] was an effort on our part to lower tar levels in our brands and provide the taste that consumers were expecting. We've used a variety of domestic-and foreign-grown tobaccos to provide the unique recipes that go into each cigarette blend. Y-1 was a blending tool for flavor . . . What we have here is an agency [the FDA] with an agenda—and their agenda is to acquire jurisdiction over tobacco so it can regulate it out of existence.

June 21/
Los Angeles Times,
6-22:(A)11.

Richard A. Gephardt
United States Representative,
D-Missouri

2

[Criticizing Republicans for opposing President Clinton's health-care reform plan]: Every time we [Democrats] try to lift people up, they say it's socialism, it's big government, it's tax and spend. Now that the Democratic Party is trying to fix the crushing health-care crisis, we're hearing the same rehashed, time-worn, discredited rhetoric. [Republican Representative] Newt Gingrich says that guaranteed [health-care] coverage is, I quote, "socialism, now or later, and a dictatorship on health care."

At National Press Club,
Washington, D.C., Feb. 4/
The New York Times,
2-5:7.

3

[Blaming Republicans for the Clinton Administration's failure to get its health-care reform bill passed this year]: With few exceptions, Republicans cannot look their constituents in the eye and say that they made a good-faith effort to give health security to every American. Next year we will have to figure out if there is a more modest and incremental way to pursue the same goals. I don't know if there is or not.

The New York Times,
9-27:(A)13.

Sheldon G. Gilgore
Chairman,
G. D. Searle & Company;
Chairman-elect,
Pharmaceutical Manufacturers
Association

4

[On the higher prescription-drug prices in the U.S. than in other countries for the same product]: The fact of the matter is, prices in the United States are higher than in the United Kingdom or France or Germany or Italy or Spain. We cannot deny that they are higher. But you cannot fuel the research engine that discovers and develops new drugs on the profits that you make in countries outside the U.S.

Interview, January/
The New York Times,
2-3:(A)9.

Newt Gingrich
United States Representative,
R-Georgia

5

[Responding to Democratic Congressman Richard Gephardt's accusation that Republicans are blocking health-care reform]: I think it is very sad to see Gephardt reduced to a [President] Clinton level of dishonesty. [Despite Republicans repeatedly offering to work with Democrats on health legislation,] what they [Democrats] mean by bipartisan is us caving in. [Republicans are resisting] selling out your principles to pass one bill.

Interview, June 16/
The New York Times,
6-17:(A)1.

James F. Glenn
Chairman,
Council for Tobacco Research;
Chief of staff, University of Kentucky
Medical College

1

I reject your premise that we [at the Council for Tobacco Research] are a biased organization [in favor of the tobacco companies], I reject the premise that smoking causes cancer, and I reject the inference that our activities have been to obscure the truth. On the contrary, they've been dedicated to developing scientific truth. No one has been able to demonstrate that smoking causes any diseases.

Before House Health and
the Environment Subcommittee,
Washington, D.C., May 26/
Los Angeles Times, 5-27:(A)4.

John Glenn
United States Senator, D-Ohio

2

[On the possibility that risky or improper radiation, medical or other testing on humans, such as occurred in the Cold War era, is still being conducted by the Federal government]: I am calling for a government-wide review of all testing programs—from drug tests at FDA to military tests at DOD—to determine if any improper experiments on humans persist to this day. We need to know from the [Clinton] Administration that they are doing everything possible to assure that no improper testing . . . continues. No other answer is acceptable . . . We know that radiation testing—presumably with informed consent—continues

within the government. But do we know, with 100 percent certainty, that testing without consent does not continue to this day somewhere deep in the bowels of the Federal government?

News conference,
Washington, D.C., Jan. 6/
Los Angeles Times,
1-7:(A)20.

Marvin Goldman
Professor emeritus of
radiological science and radiobiology,
University of California, Davis

3

[Saying medical advances that resulted from radiation experiments on human beings during the Cold War should not be ignored in the current ethical debate on that testing]: The ethics of [the testing] is very disturbing to me. There's a lot of angst and emotion. [But] the scientific data are valid. It's against the public interest to just ignore them. If a fact exists and it is an important fact that I need to know, I will use it. You're not punishing the ill-doer by ignoring the observation. You're going to quote me on this and it will look awful.

Interview/
The New York Times,
1-1:7.

Peter C. Goldmark, Jr.
President, Rockefeller Foundation

4

[Universal coverage is] the political imperative everybody agrees on [for a health-care reform plan]. Whatever passes, there will be a conspiracy among Democrats and Republicans not to plot out its costs honestly. It will be passed with some salami-like phases, and that will make the political victory for everyone a lot more diminished. During the 1990s, we'll be in an almost continuous agony of health reform. It was up like an Epiphany, but it will be dragged out like a soap opera.

Interview/
Los Angeles Times, 3-27:(M)3.

Al Gore
Vice President
of the United States

1

[On health-care reform]: It's important to understand what group of Americans universal coverage is aimed at. The poor have many programs, [and] because of the Medicaid program, they have health care. The wealthy can do very well buying their own health insurance.[But] middle-income families are the group that are at risk of losing their insurance.

Broadcast interview/
"Meet the Press,"
NBC-TV, 7-24.

2

[Criticizing Republican Senator Robert Dole and his Party for trying to block health-care reform plans initiated by the Democrats]: If Bob Dole and the special interests win, millions of Americans will lose. Bob Dole used to support a mandate [for employers to pay for their workers' health insurance]; now he doesn't. He used to support universal coverage, now he doesn't. He used to want health-care reform this year; now he says he would rather wait.

Aug. 4/The Washington Post,
8-8:(A)9.

Bill Gradison
President, Health Insurance
Association of America

3

[On the Clinton Administration's failure to get its health-care reform bill passed this year]: [It] failed to read the lessons of history on health reform. We're likely to get to universal coverage more quickly a step at a time rather than in one fell swoop. Regrettably, all or none often means none. It takes time to build consensus for any major legislative proposal. It took six years to pass a crime bill. It took more than six years to pass Medicare and Medicaid . . . We are going to do a lot of introspection around here in the weeks ahead.

I've sent signals to the White House that after they finish beating up on us [in the insurance industry], if that's what they choose to do, we'd like to examine ways to work more harmoniously together than we did in the last year or two, when they chose unwisely to demonize the health-insurance industry.

The New York Times,
9-27:(A)13.

Phil Gramm
United States Senator,
R-Texas

4

[On charges that Republicans are fighting against President Clinton's health-care reform plan for political reasons]: If we were viewing it as a political issue, we would be cheering Bill Clinton on in his effort to socialize medicine, because the passage of anything like [the] Bill Clinton [health plan] would guarantee us [Republicans] victory in 1994 and 1996, because the American people are going to hate it.

News conference,
Washington, D.C., June 30/
USA Today, 7-1:(A)8.

5

[On the health-care reform debate in the U.S.]: I can hardly believe my ears when the health-care system of the United States of America is compared unfavorably to the health-care systems of Canada, Great Britain and Germany. Last year more people died in Canada waiting to get into the operating room than died on the operating table. People all over the world under government-dominated systems are dying because health care that is readily available in America is not available in those countries . . . We have, in the United States of America, the greatest health-care system in the history of the world. In the last 25 years, 90 percent of all the pharmaceuticals, 95 percent of all the medical procedures, 90 percent of all the routine miracles that we expect every time we go to the doctor, every time we go to the hospital, they

(PHIL GRAMM)

have all been developed by Americans. It is very interesting to me that so many of my colleagues, when they think of medical perfection in the world, look to the north to Canada; and yet I notice when they and people they love get sick, they never ever go to Canada to try to get well. And yet on any given day in America, in any referral hospital . . . [you] will find that those referral wards are full of rich or politically powerful Canadians. They're full of people who have an opportunity to look socialized medicine in the face in Great Britain and Germany and have found that face to be an ugly, uncaring face. And they have come to the United States of America to get health care. Now, that may not tell some people anything, but it tells me something. And that is we have a lot to lose in this debate as well as a lot to gain. I am not going to support tearing down the greatest medical-care system in the history of the world to rebuild it in the image of the Post Office.

Before the Senate,
Washington, D.C., Aug. 11/
The New York Times,
8-12:(A)11.

1

[On health-care reform]: When we talk about 37 million Americans last year who didn't have health insurance on at least one day, over 75 percent of those people, by some studies, didn't have health insurance for one reason: They changed jobs. And when you change jobs in America, you lose the insurance through the employer you're with and you don't get insurance on the new job until, generally, you've been there for 30 days. We can solve 75 percent of the problem of people not having insurance on a provision that as far as I know every single member of the Senate supports: Make it easier for people to change jobs without losing their health insurance. That was in the two bills I introduced. It was in the bill that Senator [Robert] Dole introduced. It's in the [Senator George] Mitchell bill. It's in the [President] Clinton bill. It's in the [Representative Richard] Gephardt

bill. It's in everybody's bill. That's not what we're debating here. Every bill that has been introduced, as far as I'm aware, deals with the problem of permanence.

Before the Senate,
Washington, D.C., Aug. 11/
The New York Times,
8-12:(A)11.

2

[Comparing the health-care reform plan submitted by Republican Senator Robert Dole with that submitted by Democratic Senator George Mitchell]: The big difference is that the Dole bill seeks to reform health care by promoting a more-efficient system. It can help working people by paying part of their premiums—not as much as the Mitchell bill, but the Mitchell bill has 18 new taxes; the Mitchell bill has 40 new government regulatory agencies; the Mitchell bill has over 100 unfunded mandates.

Before the Senate,
Washington, D.C., Aug. 15/
The New York Times,
8-16:(A)11.

Mark Green
Public Advocate
of New York, N.Y.

3

The irrefutable medical evidence [about the dangers of] second-hand [cigarette] smoke has been the booster rocket launching the anti-smoking movement into orbit.

Time, 4-18:60.

Karel Gunning
Secretary,
Dutch Physicians' League

4

[Criticizing the liberalized euthanasia law in the Netherlands]: We believe that once you make it so easy to kill people, you start on a slippery slope. It is very dangerous. Even if a baby is go-

(KAREL GUNNING)

ing to die soon, every baby needs care and love. We say doctors should help patients, relieve their suffering—that's what the government should encourage.

The New York Times,
12-23:(A)3.

Robert B. Helms
Director of health-policy studies,
American Enterprise Institute

1

[On whether a heath-care reform plan will be passed soon that provides universal coverage]: No. But there are lots of ways that people will make it look like we are getting universal coverage. We will not be able to pass universal coverage because of economics. You've got to pass tax increases or hide taxes through some kind of mandates, such as employer mandates. You would have to have huge government subsidies to get universal coverage, and I don't think Congress can afford it.

Interview/
Los Angeles Times,
3-27:(M)3.

Jimmie Holland
Chief of psychiatry,
Memorial Sloan-Kettering
Cancer Center,
New York, N.Y.

2

[Saying modern technology has given patients opportunities and difficult responsibilities to decide which treatments to request for their conditions]: We have created a climate which says that the good patient is the most consumer-oriented, who gets the most information and makes the most informed decision. Patients feel a tremendous obligation to make judgment oneself.

The New York Times,
1-27:(A)1.

Edward F. Howard
Director,
Alliance for Health Reform

3

[Saying he doubts most members of Congress will vote against comprehensive health-care reform because of a controversial provision covering abortions]: Ultimately, for most members, there is no single issue that's worth risking the social legislation of a generation. I just don't know how many members there are who will stake out a single issue and then go over the cliff for it.

Los Angeles Times,
7-14:(A)10.

Harold M. Ickes
Deputy Chief of Staff to
President of the United States
Bill Clinton

4

[On President Clinton's declared aim of universal coverage as a key part of any health-care reform plan]: The President is insisting on universal coverage. There was no backing off on that . . . [But] you can have a phase-in period. The questions are whether the phase-in period is a reasonable amount of time and whether at the end of the process everyone is covered.

Interview, June 15/
Los Angeles Times,
6-16:(A)1.

Ada Jacox
Professor of nursing,
Johns Hopkins University

5

[Recommending the use of larger doses of drugs to relieve pain in cancer patients]: Unrelieved pain can produce unnecessary suffering, limit physical activity, decrease the appetite, reduce the amount of sleep and increase the fear of cancer, all of which reduce the patient's ability to fight the disease . . . The edict to "just say no to drugs" applies to the illegal use of controlled sub-

(ADA JACOX)

stances. It has no place in the minds and language of cancer patients and the health professionals who care for them.

March 2/
The Washington Post,
3-3:(A)3.

Peter Jahrling
Senior research scientist,
United States Army
Medical Research Institute
of Infectious Diseases

1

[Saying not only animals, but people too, are responsible for bringing foreign diseases into a country]: If you're a monkey imported from the Philippines, your first stop when you hit this country is a quarantine facility. If you're a free-ranging adult human being, you just go through the metal detector and you're on your way.

Time, 9-12:69.

Kirk B. Johnson
Senior vice president
and general counsel,
American Medical Association

2

[On charges that doctors who own a financial interest in diagnostic equipment tend to order too many tests for their patients]: If you have the equipment at your fingertips and you operate it yourself, you have complete confidence in the results, and you're more likely to use it. I'd rather go to a doctor who has his own machine and will feel free in a close case to use it. The economics of medicine are such that blatant over-utilization is going to make a physician's practice uncompetitive.

April 12/
The New York Times,
4-13:(A)11.

Lloyd Johnson
Researcher, survey on drug use
conducted by Institute
for Social Research,
University of Michigan

3

[Saying teenage use of illegal drugs has been rising after a decline in the late 1970s and early '80s]: These are disturbing findings . . . It's an early warning to all sectors of society that the improvements of the last decade can't be taken for granted. Each generation of American youth is naive about drugs and has to learn the same hard lessons.

The Washington Post,
2-1:(A)1.

James W. Johnston
Chairman,
R. J. Reynolds Tobacco U.S.A.

4

[What the] anti-tobacco industry wants is prohibition [of smoking]. We hear about the addiction and the threat. If cigarettes are too dangerous to be sold, then ban them. Some smokers will obey the law, but many will not. People will be selling cigarettes out of the trunks of cars, cigarettes made by who knows who, made of who knows what.

Before House Health and
the Environment Subcommittee,
Washington, D.C., April 14/
The New York Times, 4-15:(A)10.

5

[On the controversy over smoking]: All you need to do is ask and honestly answer two simple questions. First, would you rather board a plane with a pilot who just smoked a cigarette or one with a pilot who just had a couple of beers or snorted cocaine or shot heroin or popped some pills? Second, if cigarettes were addictive, could almost 43 million Americans have quit smoking, almost all of them on their own without any outside help?

The Washington Post,
8-1:(A)3.

Yale Kamisar
Professor,
University of Michigan Law School

1

[On controversial pathologist Jack Kevorkian's involvement in "assisted suicides" of persons with serious medical conditions]: There is growing support for assisted suicide, but I don't think people realize that the distinction between assisted suicide and active euthanasia is very thin. If you oppose active euthanasia, you should take your stand now. What Kevorkian does is 98 percent euthanasia and two percent assisted suicide.

May 3/
The Washington Post,
5-4:(A)2.

Nancy Landon Kassebaum
United States Senator,
R-Kansas

2

[On President Clinton's health-care reform plan]: The public has grown increasingly confused about the complexity of this issue, and those who are opposed have managed to create further seeds of doubt. The public worries about the cost and about the ability to have choices in the system. I'm just finding growing opposition. The question becomes: Should we do interim steps like insurance reform? It seems more likely we will approach it that way. If I had to make a prediction: Something less than a comprehensive approach will be designed in incremental steps. It will be portrayed as containing enough of what the President wanted so he'll declare victory.

Interview/
The New York Times,
1-3:(A)7.

Neal Kassell
Neurosurgeon, University of Virginia

3

[On technological advances that aid in surgery]: Half the time you spend in the operating room is finding out where you are, and separating what's normal from what's abnormal. Now that work is being done on a computer, and with it will go a lot of the uncertainty of surgery. Procedures will be much quicker, more simple, less dangerous and less invasive . . . If you want to blow something up in Baghdad [Iraq, such as the U.S. did in the Persian Gulf war in 1991,] you get your imagery [via military technology], your diagnostic test. Next you do the routing of the mission planning, then navigation. It's no different than planning how to take a tumor out with the least collateral damage. We owe a lot to the end of the Cold War and the release of technology like this.

Interview/
The Washington Post,
8-15:(A)3.

David Keene
President,
American Conservative Union

4

[On health-care reform]: This particular issue impacts everybody. And while voters may not have a sense of the intricacies, everybody has a sense of what they want and don't want. And I think that gives Republicans an advantage because as the debate has gone on, voters have soured on the Democratic [Party] approach that the government can take care of everything.

Los Angeles Times,
8-16:(A)5.

Jack Kemp
Former Secretary of Housing
and Urban Development
of the United States;
Former United States
Representative, R-New York

5

[Criticizing President Clinton's health-care reform plan, which was spearheaded by First Lady Hillary Clinton]: Health care amounts to 14 percent of our GNP—a lot of money. It is the size of

(JACK KEMP)

the Italian economy. And the President turned it over to his wife.

Newsweek, 2-7:15.

Sheldon King
Former chief administrator,
Cedars-Sinai Medical Center,
Los Angeles, Calif.

1

[Criticizing President Clinton's proposal to reduce certain Medicare payments to hospitals]: I admire what President Clinton is trying to do [reduce the government's health-care costs]. But to say that hospitals can take all these cuts and provide care for everyone without the quality suffering, that is patent nonsense.

Los Angeles Times,
3-28:(A)14.

Lane Kirkland
President, American Federation
of Labor-Congress
of Industrial Organizations

2

[Any health-care reform plan that] fails to provide universal coverage and an employer mandate . . . is not genuine reform and will not solve the critical and fundamental problems of our health-care system.

Aug. 19/Los Angeles Times, 8-20:(A)10.

James Klein
Executive director,
Association of Private Pension
and Welfare Plans

3

[On the health-care reform plans being offered by President Clinton, Senator George Mitchell and Representative Richard Gephardt]: Folks who are saying that the Mitchell bill isn't as bad as the Clinton or Gephardt bill are asking the wrong ques-

tion. [The question should be,] is it better or worse than the current system with all its flaws? Business, both large and small, is increasingly of the view that it is worse than the current system and shouldn't be allowed to go through.

At City Club,
Washington, D.C., Aug. 9/
The Washington Post,
8-10:(A)4.

Christopher Klose
Spokesman,
National Agricultural
Chemicals Association

4

[Criticizing suggestions that pesticides in food can be dangerous to consumers]: [Pesticide levels in produce are] impossibly small. The American public has a right to be protected from the kind of food-scare-of-the-week that is seemingly popping up like mushrooms.

USA Today, 5-19:(A)1.

Gerald P. Koocher
Chief psychologist,
Children's Hospital,
Boston, Mass.

5

[On the psychological effects of chronic illness]: When you're dealing with the emotional consequences of chronic illness, you need someone to help you cope with real-life problems triggered by the diagnosis of chronic illness. Lots of people are living and living longer with chronic illness, but the medical profession is ill-equipped to help them cope with it. [In people with chronic illness,] self-image is permanently altered, people worry about being stigmatized, their angry feelings are buried so they can cope with day-to-day problems, they fear isolation and abandonment, and they feel out of control, as if they were coming unglued.

The New York Times,
6-8:(B)7.

C. Everett Koop
Former Surgeon General
of the United States

1

It's a funny thing, but even though I was an appointee of the [Ronald] Reagan and [George] Bush Administrations, I have had my closest relationship with the Clinton White House. I think [First Lady Hillary Rodham Clinton] is a remarkable woman, and I think her health-care [reform] plan, while not perfect, is the best of what I've seen offered.

USA Today,
5-16:(D)2.

William Kristol
Chairman, Project for
the Republican Future

2

The vast majority of Republicans are united behind targeted [health-care] reforms and are united in opposition to a government overhaul of the health-care system. It may be politically incorrect, but I am confident it is a political winner.
USA Today,
5-25:(A)4.

3

[On the Clinton Administration's failure to get its health-care reform bill passed this year]: Clinton's [reform] plan failed because of its very nature. He thought the middle class would accept an expansion of government in return for quote health security, and I think he radically underestimated the American people's mistrust of big-government liberalism. He thought he was elected to carry forward, to enact the final piece of the New Deal, Great Society agenda, and it turns out the American public is more interested in reversing course now rather than continuing that course.
The New York Times,
9-27:(A)13.

Thomas Lauria
Assistant to the president,
Tobacco Institute

4

I think that since the '60s, studies have shown that cigarette smoking has been linked as an important risk factor for emphysema, heart disease, lung cancer and other serious problems . . . [But] there are a certain amount of adult consumers who want to enjoy tobacco products. And like those who drink alcohol or who enjoy high-risk sports activities, it is really up to the individual adult to determine what's appropriate for their own conduct.

Time,
4-18:62.

5

[Criticizing proposed legislation that would increase FDA regulation of tobacco]: [The tobacco industry has] a longstanding opposition to the FDA's regulation of a product that is not a food, not a drug and not a cosmetic. [This legislation would usher in] a new era of prohibition.
June 13/
Los Angeles Times,
6-14:(A)21.

Mathew H. M. Lee
Medical director,
Rusk Institute
of Rehabilitation Medicine,
New York University
Medical Center

6

Pain is very subjective. It's an experience that's unique to each one of us. In the epidemiology of pain—why it does or doesn't occur—you find a different environment in each person. And that's why one person will say "Ouch" and someone else won't say anything at all.
Interview/
Newsweek,
10-10:(Supplement)13.

WHAT THEY SAID IN 1994

Philip R. Lee
Assistant Secretary for Health,
Department of Health
and Human Services
of the United States;
Director,
U.S. Public Health Service

1

[Criticizing the reluctance by many doctors to use larger doses of drugs to relieve pain in their cancer patients]: We're always reading about the over-use of technology and over-treatment. [But] I can't overemphasize enough that in cancer pain, under-treatment is the problem.

To reporters, March 2/
The Washington Post,
3-3:(A)3.

Eugene Lehrmann
President, American Association
of Retired Persons

2

[Supporting the health-care reform bills now being proposed by the House and Senate Democratic leadership]: We have been waiting a long time for this to happen. Now is the time for us to strike. Although neither bill is perfect, we conclude that these bills provide the foundation for comprehensive health care for all Americans. If either bill is defeated, health-care reform will be dead for years to come.

Washington, D.C., Aug. 10/
Los Angeles Times,
8-11:(A)1.

Jay Levy
AIDS researcher,
University of California,
San Francisco

3

[On the complexity of the AIDS virus]: There aren't *many* reasons why progress against AIDS is so difficult, but they are very *big* reasons . . . I don't know where AIDS is going. But if we don't

stop it soon, it may spread beyond all our imagining.

Interview/
Los Angeles Times,
8-8:(A)13.

Connie Mack
United States Senator,
R-Florida

4

[Saying many senior citizens in his state are concerned that Democratic Party proposals for health-care reform would cap Medicare spending]: What they are afraid about is that, when you put a cap on how much can be spent, somebody has to give up something. What we are talking about is the potential damage that can be done to the best health-care system in the world.

Broadcast
Republican Party
discussion program,
Aug. 1/
Los Angeles Times,
8-2:(A)14.

Ira C. Magaziner
Senior Adviser for
Policy Development
to President of
the United States Bill Clinton;
Former Manager,
White House Task Force
on National Health Care Reform

5

[On the "alliances" which are part of President Clinton's health-care reform plan]: The alliances are designed to end discrimination in the marketplace. It is not right that because of your age or health status you pay more [for insurance]. If you want to achieve an end to discrimination, you need a large pool [which the alliances would provide].

Los Angeles Times,
2-19:(A)22.

(IRA C. MAGAZINER)

1

[On the Clinton Administration's failure to get its health-care reform bill passed this year]: Although [opponents of reform] failed to convince the American public that the fundamental [Administration] goals of universal coverage and cost containment were wrong, they succeeded in scaring and misleading the public that the bills proposed by the President and various Congressional committees would threaten what they like about their own health care. They scared the public—confusing them about whether they would be able to see their own doctor and whether the health-care system would turn into a giant government bureaucracy. It is interesting to note that despite the hundreds of millions of dollars spent to defeat health-care reform, support for the President's goal of universal coverage remains strong.

The New York Times,
9-27:(A)13.

Wendy Mariner
Professor of health law,
Boston University

2

[On doctors who ask their Medicare patients to pay extra fees to them above what Medicare pays]: There is no reason on God's green earth for patients to agree to pay more unless they are worried that their physician is going to refuse to treat them otherwise. In effect, the doctors are saying, "I reserve the right to charge you whatever I want at any time." And that's unconscionable.

The New York Times,
2-15:(B)8.

Theodore R. Marmor
Professor of public policy
and management, Yale University

3

In terms of either interference with professional practice or the amount of both form-filling

and administrative expense, the American health-care system is by far the most administratively complex and costly in the advanced world, while our government role is weakest.

Los Angeles Times,
8-16:(A)16.

Jim McDermott
United States Representative,
D-Washington

4

[Supporting a "single-payer" health-care plan]: As somebody who had practiced medicine for 24 years, I had the experience of seeing people wrestle with financial fears at a time when they were in a health-care crisis. It's a national disgrace. It doesn't happen anywhere else in the world. It shouldn't happen here.

The New York Times,
2-5:7.

5

[Criticizing the "alliances" which are part of President Clinton's health-care reform plan]: You are looking at the beginning of a monstrous and potentially powerful agency . . . a massive bureaucracy erected to hide a government program. It's not at all clear who they will answer to, and I fear they will be accountable to no one.

Los Angeles Times,
2-19:(A)22.

Lorrie McHugh
Spokeswoman on health issues
for President of the United States
Bill Clinton

6

[Criticizing the National Federation of Independent Business for not supporting President Clinton's health-care reform plan, which includes mandates that business pay 80 percent of employees' insurance costs]: I don't think anyone underestimates the power the NFIB has in influencing the debate. [But] this is the same organization that

(LORRIE McHUGH)

has opposed anything that would help working Americans: minimum wage, family and medical leave, worker safety law. They have a strong grassroots organization that's capable of scaring people.

The New York Times,
4-26:(A)16.

Walker Merryman
Vice president,
Tobacco Institute

1

[On recent and proposed taxes, bans and other efforts to reduce tobacco use]: What's happened in the last month is an extraordinary, probably unprecedented confluence of events. There's never been a time when there have been so many things leveled against us . . . [But] no one should underestimate the ability or willingness of this industry to very vigorously defend itself.

Los Angeles Times,
3-26:(A)20.

Lynn Mills
Spokesman,
Michigan Right to Life

2

[Criticizing a jury's acquittal of Dr. Jack Kevorkian, who was charged with violating Michigan's law against assisted suicides]: That jury has just unleashed the floodgates. There is going to be no stopping him or other doctors who believe that they are God.

May 2/
The New York Times,
5-3:(A)1.

C. Ben Mitchell
Director of biomedical and life issues,
Southern Baptist Conference

3

[Criticizing having abortion included in President Clinton's health-care benefits proposal]: By making abortion a requirement of the comprehensive benefits package, health-care reform of the President's variety would compel every [religious] denomination and local congregation to either fund abortion or else break the law [by refusing to pay into the system] and suffer the penalties. Every congregation, as an employer, would be required to take money from the offering plate and offer it up to abortionists.

Christianity Today,
4-25:40.

George J. Mitchell
United States Senator,
D-Maine

4

[On his health-care reform proposal]: The bill does not provide for a government-run health-insurance system. It is a voluntary system which builds upon the current private insurance market. Indeed, under my bill one of the largest government programs—Medicaid—would be virtually abolished. And 25 million Americans who are now in the Medicaid program—a government program—would be taken out of that program, which would be virtually abolished, and would be encouraged to purchase private health insurance in the same system of insurance payment and coverage that most Americans are now in. So not only is it not a government-run program, it is just the opposite. It is a private program, a voluntary system in which citizens are encouraged and assisted in the purchase of health insurance.

Before the Senate,
Washington, D.C., Aug. 15/
The New York Times,
8-16:(A)11.

5

I think the elderly should be the most concerned [about the failure of Congress to pass health-care reform legislation in 1994], because, in the last few years, Senate Republicans and a few Senate Democrats have proposed caps on Medicare and Medicaid as a way to deal with the

(GEORGE J. MITCHELL)

Federal budget problem . . . If we don't act on health-care reform and health costs, not just in the society as a whole but as a part of the Federal budget, the pressure will increase dramatically for such caps. [And] I think they're likely to pass in the absence of meaningful health reform that includes some effective cost control.

Interview, Washington, D.C./
AARP Bulletin,
December:16.

Mike Moore
Attorney General
of Mississippi

1

[On Mississippi's suit against tobacco companies aimed at getting reimbursed for the state's expenses in providing medical care for smoking-related illnesses]: This lawsuit is premised on a simple notion: You caused the crisis; you pay for it. The free ride is over. It's time these billionaire tobacco companies start paying what they rightfully owe to Mississippi taxpayers. It's time they quit hooking our young people on nicotine delivered through the dirty needle of cigarettes and other tobacco products . . . While I cannot bring [those who died from smoking-related diseases] back, I can spare Mississippi taxpayers from paying medical bills that are the tobacco companies' responsibility. I fully intend to make the tobacco companies pay for their sins.

The New York Times,
5-24:(A)8.

John J. Motley
Vice president,
National Federation
of Independent Business

2

[On his group's opposition to President Clinton's health-care reform plan]: We made the decision to fight this health plan earlier than al-

most anybody else did. One of the things that enabled us to be so successful on this is that we got our message out long before the calliope of voices on the issue was able to drown us out . . . Our strength is that we have a large membership that is homogeneous in that it represents Main Street businesses in this country who are struggling to keep the doors open.

Interview/
The New York Times,
7-6:(A)10.

3

[On the Clinton Administration's failure to get its health-care reform bill passed this year]: The left killed health-care reform by overreaching, by not being willing to accept a consensus approach, by not trying to put together a proposal in the middle of the political spectrum. The seeds of the demise of the President's proposal were sown in the very early days of the Administration, within the task force that drafted his proposal. The left in this debate, the real liberals, were able to seize control of the creation of the proposal. They seriously overreached and developed a proposal that was too large and too expensive, that gave too big a role to the government, and that simply couldn't pass.

The New York Times,
9-27:(A)13.

Daniel Patrick Moynihan
United States Senator,
D-New York

4

[On President Clinton's expressed desire for a health-care reform plan that includes universal coverage]: I think a bill that took you a long way toward universal coverage, and declared universal coverage to be the policy of the United States to be achieved in a time certain, that fits his conditions.

Broadcast interview/
"Meet the Press,"
NBC-TV, 6-19.

WHAT THEY SAID IN 1994

Ralph Nader
Lawyer; Consumer advocate

1

[Criticizing President Clinton's handling of health-care reform]: Clinton ducked the issues that need to be addressed in terms of quality health care, accountability to patients, consumers, and the financing of it. How we ever developed a system that holds the President responsible for the unemployment rate but not accountable for environmental or health-care issues . . .

Interview/
The Christian Science Monitor,
1-25:14.

Norman J. Ornstein
Fellow,
American Enterprise Institute

2

[On the now-being-formulated health-care reform bill]: I can't think of a bill this important that passed by only a vote or two. You may have some close votes along the way on amendments or procedures, but in the end, Senators just don't feel comfortable passing something this big unless everyone's on board—you'll either get 70 votes, or you'll get 40.

Newsweek, 5-23:45.

Leon E. Panetta
Chief of Staff to President
of the United States Bill Clinton

3

[On speculation that President Clinton, in a speech at the National Governors Conference, may have backed away from his long-stated position of having a health-care reform plan with universal coverage and employer mandates]: The President's bottom line is what it's always been—guaranteed health coverage for every American. And that's what he said to the Governors today. Are we willing to discuss ways to guarantee universal coverage? Absolutely. Are we changing the goal? Absolutely not.

July 19/Los Angeles Times,
7-20:(A)9.

Steve Parrish
Senior vice president
and general counsel,
Philip Morris U.S.A.

4

[Criticizing the arrogant attitude toward him and other tobacco executives by members of a House subcommittee before which they testified on smoking]: They asked us to come and present the facts on issues. If that's true, why aren't we afforded the same fairness and courtesy that other witnesses appearing before a committee are entitled to get? I've never need anything like this. It's outrageous.

Washington, D.C.,
April 14/
The New York Times,
4-15:(A)10.

William Paul
Director, Laboratory of Immunology,
National Institute of Allergy
and Infectious Diseases;
Director-designate,
Office of AIDS Research,
National Institutes
of Health of the United States

5

[Arguing against a "Manhattan Project"-style crash program against AIDS]: If we were to invest our money in a crash program, we would have to be very wise in choosing, because we could easily make the wrong decision. The consequence of [choosing wrongly] is that we would fall behind. It's not yet clear where the great push should be. Most people don't understand that most of the things scientist do *don't* work. Those of us who have done it our whole lives know that. Others are not completely attuned to that—they don't understand the frustration of trying something and not getting it quite right. That's why a Manhattan Project won't work. We could end up *not* doing things where the greater opportunities lie.

Los Angeles Times,
3-16:(A)5.

Mark Pauley
Health economist,
Wharton School of Business,
University of Pennsylvania

1

I think most people think that if you spend less on health care, you just spend less. But every dollar we spend is [a health-care worker's] income, and in this case it's frequently the income of someone who doesn't have very many other choices. If we cut health-care spending, we are going to have to create some other job programs. And at minimum we have to make sure that it is something just as valuable as the spending we are replacing.

The Washington Post,
2-28:(A)11.

Ross Perot
Industrialist;
1992 independent
Presidential candidate

2

[Criticizing President Clinton's proposed health-care reform plan]: Everybody is being programmed day after day to believe that government is going to give you free candy. There is no free candy. Somebody has to pay for it . . . So far I haven't seen any evidence that the government really knows how to run health care . . . We look after people who cannot look after themselves, [but] history tells us that the least effective way to do that is to send your money to Washington.

Before United We Stand America,
Dallas, Texas, Feb. 4/
Los Angeles Times, 2-5:(A)20.

Richard J. Pollack
Executive vice president,
American Hospital Association

3

[Criticizing President Clinton's health-care reform plan]: Hospitals are prepared to talk about how much we spend on health care. We are prepared to talk about targets and goals. But we will

not talk about global budgets that are imposed from the top down based on an arbitrary number pulled out of thin air. We will not talk about a global budget enforced by a rate-setting guillotine tied to the Federal budget process.

The New York Times,
2-1:(A)10.

Ronald Pollack
Executive director,
Families USA

4

Most Americans are not [medically] uninsured, but most Americans are afraid of losing their insurance. Generally, people act out of self-interest, not out of altruism. So if you want them to care about health reform, you don't talk about the uninsured, you talk about people who have lost their insurance.

The New York Times,
7-28:(A)12.

David Pryor
United States Senator,
D-Arkansas

5

[Criticizing pharmaceutical companies for their high drug prices]: Their prices are unconscionable, and they simply can't justify them. This is not like lipstick or perfume. These are drugs that people need to live, and now [the companies] are trying to brainwash Congress into believing that if they do not allow them to continue to set their own prices, they will give up trying to find a cure for cancer, for AIDS, for Alzheimer's.

The New York Times,
3-7:(A)12.

Dennis Rehberg
Lieutenant Governor of Montana

6

[On state spending for hospitals]: The problem with AIDS is: You got it, you die. So why are we spending money on the issue?

Newsweek, 12-26:85.

Uwe E. Reinhardt
Professor of political economy,
Princeton University

1

Health care is a special thing, especially when you're aching. That's when people are most vulnerable and need the most dignity. If you tell me the uninsured *do* get care, I always ask, "On what terms? Do the terms have dignity? Are the people health-care beggars?" I grew up a pauper in a tool shed [in Germany]. But when we were sick we had dignity because we had rights that came with our insurance card. We had the right to be treated respectfully because the doctor was paid, whether he was treating me or a rich kid. Health care plays a social role. It's not a consumer good; it's a quasi-religious commodity.

Interview, Washington, D.C./
Modern Maturity, Nov.-Dec.:67.

John H. Robinson
Scientist, R. J. Reynolds
Tobacco Company

2

The premise that nicotine in cigarettes is addictive at any level is incorrect . . . Intoxification [is an] essential element [of addiction, and] smokers do not smoke to become intoxicated; and they do not experience withdrawal symptoms in any way comparable to those experienced by true addicts . . . If smokers are not addicted, why then do they continue to engage in a behavior that has such well-publicized risks associated with it? The simple answer is smokers obviously enjoy smoking.

Aug. 2/Los Angeles Times,
8-3:(A)1,10.

Dan Rostenkowski
United States Representative,
D-Illinois

3

[On health-care reform]: With 37 million [uninsured] people, I don't think members [of Con-

gress] can afford to go home without solving the availability-of-insurance argument and how we're going to pay for it. We have to educate the American people. We have to tell them, "You're going to get what you're willing to pay for."

Interview/
USA Today, 2-23:(A)11.

4

Critics who say that a government health program will inevitably combine the efficiency of the Post Office with the compassion of the Internal Revenue Service seem to be sadly ignorant about [the success of] Medicare. I think the American people know better.

At Harvard School
of Public Health, April 22/
The New York Times,
4-23:10.

5

[Saying broad tax increases may be required to pay for health-care reform that provides universal coverage]: [We will not find the] tens of billions of dollars [needed each year from the] health fairy [or] by simply tweaking our tax laws and making adjustments that are only visible to the most sophisticated—and richest—taxpayers. I don't have the optimistic view . . . that the [Clinton] Administration does [that large tax increases wouldn't be necessary]. I think that this is a major problem and that if we're serious about it, that we have to belly up to the bar and we have to ask the American people just how serious they are about it.

At Harvard School
of Public Health, April 22/
The Washington Post,
4-23:(A)8.

John C. Rother
Director of legislation and public policy,
American Association of Retired Persons

6

Congress will pass a bill assuring health security to every American. Congress will make

(JOHN C. ROTHER)

modifications to the substance, financing and timing of [President Clinton's health-care reform plan]. But the final product will closely approximate the full scope of the Administration's proposal.

Interview/
The New York Times,
1-3:(A)7.

Warren Rudman
Co-chairman,
Concord Coalition;
Former United States Senator,
R-New Hampshire

1

[On whether a health-care reform plan will be passed providing universal coverage]: Not now. The cost is higher than anybody is willing to assume. You cannot pick up costs of coverage for 35 million people and figure they will be absorbed by osmosis. Without any new taxes, I don't see how you're going to fund universal coverage.

Interview/
Los Angeles Times,
3-27:(M)3.

Rick Scott
Chairman, Columbia/
HCA Healthcare Corporation

2

Hospitals have high fixed expenses because of all the equipment and skilled professionals you need to run them. Any time you can make a hospital busier, you can increase your cash flow and reduce your average costs per patient while also improving quality. When you get sick, go to a busy hospital. That's the one that always has everything you need, from the specialists to the equipment, because it can afford them.

Time, 3-21:59.

Robert Sedler
Professor of Constitutional law,
Wayne State University

3

[On a jury's acquittal of Dr. Jack Kevorkian, who was charged with violating Michigan's law against assisted suicides]: It sends a message to prosecutors that juries in Michigan are not willing to convict a doctor who helps a terminally ill person implement a decision to hasten inevitable death. And it sends a message to politicians that if you vote [for] a new law criminalizing such conduct you may face political retribution.

May 2/
The New York Times,
5-3:(A)1.

P. John Seward
Chairman,
American Medical Association

4

[On the Clinton Administration's failure to get its health-care reform bill passed this year]: The main reason that health-system reform didn't pass is simply the complexity of the nation's health-care system, and the complexity of the solutions proposed. Rather than blaming interest groups, the Administration or Congress, we have to learn lessons from this exercise. We never thought it would be a simple job. The issues are very complex. They do not lend themselves to simple answers.

The New York Times,
9-27:(A)13.

Donna E. Shalala
Secretary of Health
and Human Services
of the United States

5

[On whether Congress will pass a universal-coverage health-care bill this year resembling that proposed by President Clinton]: Absolutely, Congress will pass legislation guaranteeing universal coverage. From the farmers in Iowa to the small-

(DONNA E. SHALALA)

business people in Florida to the working folks in Wisconsin, everyone is sending the Administration and Congress the same message: "We want the security of knowing that our family and friends will have health-insurance coverage that can never be taken away." The bill that eventually passes will parallel the Administration proposal quite closely.

Interview/
The New York Times,
1-3:(A)7.

1

AIDS is often thought of as a hopeless problem. There has been pessimism and despair as the number of infected people continues to rise. Today, we are here to talk about solutions. Let me be very clear. Every new HIV infection is a needless infection. We have the knowledge and the technology to prevent the sexual spread of HIV. What we have lacked until now is the political will. Because we have been to timid to talk openly about the prevention tools that are really at our disposal.

News conference,
Washington, D.C.,
Jan. 4/
The Washington Post,
1-5:(A)18.

Robert Shope
Epidemiologist,
Yale University

2

[On creating new vaccines, for example for each strain of flu]: First we have to discover something new is happening. Then we have to find a manufacturer willing to make a vaccine. Then the experts have to meet and decide what goes into the vaccine. Then the factory has to find enough hens' eggs in which to grow the vaccine. There are just a lot of logistical concerns.

Time, 9-12:69.

Benjamin Shwachman
Anesthesiologist;
Former president,
Medical Association
of Los Angeles County, Calif.

3

Nurse practitioners should think of practicing in the same light as physicians do: Proceed with great fear. Restrict yourself and accept the fact that you can't do it all; and to the extent you want to do more, you should go back for more training. There is no shame or harm in being supervised [by a physician]. No one's trying to stop nurse practitioners from working. The main thing is that the patient get the best from everybody.

Los Angeles Times,
7-25:(B)5.

Mark Siegler
Professor of medicine,
and director of the Center
for Clinical Ethics,
University of Chicago

4

[On the current debate on the ethics of radiation testing on human subjects during the Cold War]: I think the reason we're seeing so much focus on these radiation experiments is that they involve a large number of government departments and agencies that were pursuing these research programs for other than traditional purposes. It's not just an outcry against medical research but against government secretness and the way the government might use the medical establishment.

The New York Times,
1-1:7.

Arlen Specter
United States Senator,
R-Pennsylvania

5

[On a chart prepared by the Republicans to show the complexity of President Clinton's health-care reform plan]: If a picture is worth a thousand

(ARLEN SPECTER)

words, a chart is worth more than a hundred agencies.

USA Today,
1-28:(A)13.

1

[On health-care reform proposals]: 86.1 percent of Americans [now] have the best care in the world. I don't think we should change that basic system.

Newsweek,
6-27:34.

Fortney H. "Pete" Stark
United States Representative,
D-California

2

The magnitude of over-ordering of tests by doctors who own an interest in an X-ray or MRI practice is staggering. We are talking about billions of dollars of waste and abuse.

April 12/
The New York Times,
4-13:(A)11.

3

[Criticizing complaints from hospitals about a proposed bill that would cut Medicare spending as a way of financing health-care reform]: Hospitals have always looked at Medicare as a bottomless pit to pay them. I'm dumbfounded by the hospitals' terribly narrow and parochial attitude. One would think they might have some interest in the health of the community at large and not just in their own self-interest. This bill is a good deal for hospitals that are well-managed. It's not too good a deal for hospitals that want to make a huge profit off sick people.

July 13/
The New York Times,
7-14:(A)9.

James S. Todd
Executive vice president,
American Medical Association

4

[Criticizing plans to allow Blue Cross health-insurance companies to become for-profit organizations]: We think this is very bad to have the delivery of health care in the hands of profit-making organizations. [For such companies,] healthy profits become more important than healthy patients.

June 29/
The New York Times,
6-30:(C)7.

Laura D'Andrea Tyson
Chairman,
Council of Economic Advisers
to President of the United States
Bill Clinton

5

We've make the case . . . that in order to have effective cost containment [in health care], over time you need to have universal [health insurance] coverage. Without it, people are served in inefficient and expensive ways, and the cost of treating them are shifted to those who are paying for [health insurance].

Interview/
USA Today, 8-3:(B)2.

Henry A. Waxman
United States Representative,
D-California

6

[On proposed legislation that would ban smoking in all buildings used by the public, a measure favored by President Clinton and by six U.S. Surgeon Generals who testified before a House subcommittee]: This is the first time that any Administration, Democrat or Republican, has supported comprehensive, nationwide restrictions on smoking. This hearing is the first time that six Surgeon Generals have appeared before Congress on any issue. This hearing marks a turning point.

(HENRY A. WAXMAN)

The national mood has changed. The American public has awakened to the dangers of environmental tobacco smoke and is demanding tough Federal action.

*At House Health and
the Environment
Subcommittee hearing,
Washington, D.C., Feb. 7/
The New York Times,
2-8:(A)10.*

1

[On moves to ban smoking in all public places]: I think non-smokers finally realize they just don't want to put up with other people's smoke in public places anymore. Before, it was just a nuisance and they felt that smokers should have their rights as well. But now that you know you're going to be poisoned by somebody else's smoke, you feel there's no excuse for it anymore.

*Los Angeles Times,
3-26:(A)20.*

Charles O. Whitley
*Lobbyist, Tobacco Institute;
Former United States Representative,
D-North Carolina*

2

[Arguing against proposals from anti-smoking activists to ban nicotine from cigarettes]: If you take away from tobacco the thing, one of the main qualities of tobacco, there's not much left. That's like advocating alcohol-free spirits; look at their market share; it's not much of a marketable product. [Nicotine] is a natural part of tobacco and the tobacco experience, and if you take it all out you totally change the character and the nature and certainly the flavor and the taste of a cigarette.

*Interview, March 25/
The New York Times,
3-26:5.*

Joshua M. Wiener
*Senior fellow,
Brookings Institution*

3

[On U.S. health-care reform plans]: If [government] subsidies [for insurance] are limited to very low-income people, you don't solve the problem of the uninsured. If subsidies are not so limited, they become very expensive, and it will be attractive for employers to drop coverage. Employers will ask why they should pay for health insurance if the government will pay for it . . . If you reform the health-insurance market so that everyone can get coverage, many sick and disabled people will come into the insurance pool, raising the price.

*The New York Times,
6-24:(C)18.*

Steve Wilkins
*President,
Oxford Health Plans (HMO)*

4

[On doctors who originally spurned HMOs but who now want to join them and are refused]: When I hear all the complaining, it reminds me of the story of the Little Red Hen. When she asked the other animals to help her plant grains of wheat, they said no; when she asked them to help water them, they said no. But when they grew and she made them into bread, they wanted to eat it. And she said: "No, you were not involved in making this."

*The New York Times,
6-25:9.*

Harris Wofford
*United States Senator,
D-Pennsylvania*

5

In yesterday morning's *Washington Post*, one of my Republican colleagues was quoted as saying that health care is too important—get those words—health care is too important for this Con-

(HARRIS WOFFORD)

gress to pass a reform bill now. Instead of acting, he says, we should commission a study—a study! We've had years of studies, mountains of studies. We don't need another study to tell us what is wrong with this system; we need the backbone to fix it. Not after the next election; not sometime in the next century; now! Health care delayed is health care denied . . . If members of this Congress want more time to study, let them study what it's like to be a middle-class American caught up in the health-insurance mess. Let them study what it's like to try to buy insurance on the open market without the help of their employers . . . The problem with the present system of health insurance is that so much of it is phony. You pay and pay and then just when you need it, it isn't there . . . I've heard members of Congress say that "doing nothing on health care doesn't hurt me at all." Well, it should. It should hurt every one of us if we fail to act, because it sure is going to hurt the American people and the American economy.

Before the Senate,
Washington, D.C., Aug. 11/
The New York Times,
8-12:(A)11.

Sidney M. Wolfe
Director, Public Citizen Health
Research Group

1

[On the difficulty in enforcing a ban on smoking in the workplace]: In most health regulations involving protecting workers from pollution, you can say the pollution is being caused by the company; whereas here, the pollution is also being caused by the workers. In many ways, the workplace smoking bans will be daunting to enforce,

especially if they involve workers reluctant to rat on their co-workers.

Los Angeles Times,
8-8:(A)9.

2

[Saying doctors should improve their bedside manner]: A doctor can't get away with being a technical whiz and an impersonal jerk.

Newsweek, 12-5:23.

Steffie Woolhandler
Associate professor of internal medicine,
Harvard University

3

The drug-company salesmen are trying to convince physicians that for every human problem the answer is the latest new drug. So much money is spent on miseducation of physicians by drug companies. Too little is spent on spreading real scientific information about drugs.

Los Angeles Times,
7-27:(A)12.

Kevin Zeese
Vice president and counsel,
Drug Policy Foundation

4

[Calling for an end to the ban on using marijuana for medical purposes]: It's time we stopped making criminals out of seriously ill Americans by denying them a medicine that obviously helps. The ban on medical marijuana is inconsistent with the research of marijuana's effectiveness and inconsistent with the feelings of patients and doctors throughout the country.

Los Angeles Times,
1-6:(A)13.

The Performing Arts

David E. Bonior
United States Representative,
D-Michigan

1

[Criticizing U.S. House Speaker-designate Newt Gingrich's $4-million book contract with a publisher owned by Rupert Murdoch, who is trying to get the U.S. Congress to grant his Australian company the right to own U.S. TV stations]: Last week, Newt Gingrich threatened to shut down public broadcasting [by stopping government funding]. This week, we learn that Newt's cut a sweetheart deal with the most notorious foreign news corporation in the world. Is this Newt Gingrich's idea of renewing American civilization: to silence [PBS's] Big Bird and Mr. Rogers while turning the airwaves over to foreign companies?

News conference,
Washington, D.C., Dec. 22/
The New York Times,
12-23:(A)10.

David Brugger
President,
Association of America's
Public Television Stations

2

[Criticizing incoming Republican House Speaker Newt Gingrich's stated desire to eliminate government funding of PBS]: If he has any fair examination of our services, we will see that in fact public TV exemplifies the Republican agenda . . . Rather than "eating taxpayers' money," public broadcasting attracts $5 from supporters for each Federal dollar. [Whether or not the new Republican-controlled Congress will cut Federal public-TV funding] all depends on whether the 180 million people who use our services let their representatives know that the 80 cents they spend a year on public broadcasting is the best media buy they make.

Daily Variety, 12-9:3.

James W. Carey
Professor of journalism,
Columbia University

3

[Public television is] a treasure . . . It provides a public space in which minority audiences of all kinds can find programming that exists nowhere else, that has no room on commercial networks . . . [And PBS has been the] major innovative, entertainment and educational program producer for children . . . Children are a minority audience, and no one has shown an interest, except a commercial one, in them except public broadcasting.

The New York Times,
12-17:9.

Dick Clark
Entertainment producer

4

There is so little live television [today. When there is a live program on,] people look to see if there will be an accident, a surprise, something unexpected. Anything that's live these days draws a big audience because we're satiated on prepared material.

Interview/
Los Angeles Times,
2-7:(F)1.

Bill Clinton
President
of the United States

5

[On the effect on young people of violence in TV programming]: Because there are so many young people today who spend too much time in front of the television and have too few other things to do—or because they don't have parental super-

(BILL CLINTON)

vision—the cumulative impact of it is to make people almost subconsciously more prone to violence.

Interview/
U.S. News & World Report,
5-2:47.

Glenn Close
Actress

1

There's a facile morality on TV that offends me. And I think the surfeit of information—the noise, the voices, the manic hype—that's poured over us every day is adding to our anxiety level, to the endemic depression in this country, a feeling of inertia, of helplessness. And I think the cult of celebrity fostered by the media is adding to this negative, vicarious life.

Interview/
Cosmopolitan,
February:234.

Walter Cronkite
Former anchor,
CBS News

2

[I] predicted that the day would come when [TV] news would garner just as good a rating as entertainment [programs], because entertainment would drop in the ratings. There would be a point where it would make more economic sense to do news in prime time than to do entertainment. I said that in a speech ten years ago. Well, it's happened, and now we've got this profusion of magazine programs. I thought that with those we would finally get in-depth presentation of matters of great importance to the democracy. Unfortunately, we see that in most cases they go tabloid.

Interview,
New York, N.Y./
American Heritage,
December:44.

Patrick Duffy
Actor

3

[On whether or not he wants recognition as an actor, such as winning an Emmy, in the TV work he does]: *Dallas* won two Emmys [in its long series run]. One was for film editing; there's a biggie. Barbara Bel Geddes won, I think the second year of the show, and that was because she was a great film star doing a TV show. We were the Number 1 show, God knows, for how many years in a row, but you couldn't win an award. So I learned long ago that kind of recognition, as good as it is, is not why I go to work. I go to work because somebody asked me to work. If I were to have left *Dallas* and said the next thing I want to do is something that gets [a] degree of recognition, then you take a whole different approach to what you pick as work; to be quite honest, with rare exceptions, those shows don't stay on the air. My *raison d'etre* is to work. That's why I looked at everything that was offered me the minute *Dallas* was off the air and I took something. I go to work with the best of what's available and then I will make that my job.

Interview,
Los Angeles, Calif./
Los Angeles Times,
2-4:(F)21.

Ervin S. Duggan
President,
Public Broadcasting Service

4

Public broadcasting properly understood is the very essence of what I would call democratic elitism. It makes the highest and best accessible to everybody no matter how poor or how remote. To me that is the wonderful thing about America. We are obliterating the walls that separate the elite from everybody else.

Interview/
Emmy, August:64.

415

WHAT THEY SAID IN 1994

Richard Frank
President,
Academy of Television Arts
and Sciences

1

Through TV we got to know all about [the ice-skating scandal involving] Tonya [Harding] and Nancy [Kerrigan], the fictional drama of *NYPD Blue*, and also the real-life drama of a lone Ford Bronco [in the O. J. Simpson murder case]. Much about TV is not perfect, but there is so much that is extraordinary that brings us together. TV is something we all share and take for granted; we rarely take time to appreciate its wide-ranging impact.

Daily Variety, 9-12:25.

George Gilder
Senior fellow,
Discovery Institute

2

[On the TV of the future, which may enable viewers to choose what they want to see when they want to see it]: You're looking to a possible future with one channel, which has whatever you want on it. In other words, all your first choices. Think of it as text, and you've got the picture. Just as you buy your own books, your own magazines, you receive your own mail, you will receive your own video and multimedia when you want it . . . The availability of [pornography] is already a problem. It probably can be managed by parents who focus on it, but it still will be a problem. The world is still hovering out there with all of its seductions and offenses, and I don't think government regulation can stifle it. But you will have much more, much better programming available for every family.

Christianity Today, 2-7:42.

Michael Grade
Chief executive,
Channel 4 TV (Britain)

3

[Saying his company does not believe in programming by popularity polls]: Go and ask the public what they'd like to see, and they'll say: more shows like *Roseanne* or *Cheers*. That's useless. Do you think Shakespeare walked up and down outside the Globe Theater, asking the crowds what they fancied seeing next? Television programs are living, organic things, not commodities.

Interview, London, England/
Los Angeles Times,
9-30:(F)14.

David Hall
Program director,
KFI radio, Los Angeles, Calif.

4

If talk radio is moving away from anything, it's public service. And it's definitely moving toward entertainment. I think in the old days, people used to do topics because they felt they had to be done. Now they do topics just because they're fun to do. But a show still needs to have as much information for it to really have some bite and some substance. It can't just be entertainment, but it can't just be information either.

Los Angeles Times,
6-24:(F)22.

Reed E. Hundt
Chairman,
Federal Communications Commission

5

I do not think we should deny that TV violence hurts our children. The overwhelming majority of Americans already believe TV violence is a serious problem . . . Any business makes a big mistake when it ignores the views of its customers. [If the FCC is authorized to enforce TV anti-violence laws that may be passed,] we will do whatever we can to win those lawsuits for the government.

Before National Association
of Television Program Executives,
Miami, Fla., Jan. 24/
The Christian Science Monitor,
1-28:17.

(REED E. HUNDT)

1

You [in the TV industry] need not settle for reflecting the worst in us. You can help us take care of our children, instead of playing to some degree a role in harming them . . . We might argue . . . that just as courts have found that the First Amendment does not permit a person to avoid punishment for shouting "fire" in a crowded theater, so it does not preclude Congress from protecting children from [TV] programming that inflames young minds . . . If a TV sitcom can sell soap, salsa and cereal, then who could argue that TV violence cannot affect to some degree some viewers, particularly impressionable children? . . . Don't ask yourselves what is the minimum you can do to reduce violence on TV—or what it would take to keep Congress from legislating changes in your business. Ask instead what is the most you can do on the information highway to improve education for children and help adults find a better way of life.

Before National Association
of Television Program Executives,
Miami, Fla., Jan. 24/
Daily Variety, 1-25:1,18.

2

No one wants to see government trying to micromanage cable [TV] or any other industry. Government should not dictate content or tell cable whether to add or subtract channels or design business or marketing techniques. Similarly, government should not tell telephone companies how to increase productivity under price caps or design business or marketing techniques. In short, government policy is to foster competition, not to do business management.

At Big Picture Media Conference,
New York, N.Y., April 12/
Daily Variety, 4-13:12.

3

We [the FCC] don't do censorship [of TV] and we don't want to. That's not our job and none of the Commissioners feel that they should be in that line of work. On the other hand, we do have a Congressional mandate relating to indecency, and we are concerned about the impact of TV violence. In my case, the latter comes from a reasonably thorough amount of investigation. I've met with psychologists, parents' groups, teachers' groups, U.S. Senators and Congressmen on the issue. I've read a lot of the research and believe that there's a real problem with too much violence on TV. It does affect behavior and attitudes, particularly of children. It's not the *only* thing that contributes to violence in the United States, it's not the *most* important contributor, but it is something that those involved in TV can do something about. In fact, I'm very impressed with what the television community has already done, and I'm rather optimistic that private industry is going to be able to address TV violence on its own without the need for legislation.

Interview/
Emmy, August:75.

4

We want to make sure that we continue to have a viable, free over-the-air broadcast industry. There's a social contract between the public and the broadcast industry—TV and radio—that, I think, the partners to that contract want to see maintained . . . It is something that I think is part of our national community, and it helps to weave the fabric of our national culture together. I believe that it's very likely that cable penetration will grow, but that doesn't have to take away from the strength of broadcast TV . . . It's very important that free over-the-air television be a viable economic proposition on a stand-alone basis. And if new revenue streams are necessary to achieve that goal, then we're delighted to have the broadcasters think about how to get those new revenue streams.

Interview,
Washington, D.C./
The Wall Street Journal,
9-9:(R)9,10.

WHAT THEY SAID IN 1994

(REED E. HUNDT)

1

I think there is a balance between being concerned about the text of television and being loath to regulate content. I do not want to see us [in government] regulate content. But on the other hand, part of the social contract between broadcasters and the public is that broadcasters do take some responsibility for the effects of broadcasting on the public. I think that it is demonstrable that excessive violent content in television programming does have behavioral effects. It causes people, particularly children, to develop cultural attitudes that are negative, that tolerate aggression, that are more likely to endure through later life and lead to, overall, a more violent society. It would be wrong for anyone to suggest that content of television is the major cause of violence in society. I don't think anyone says that. We have problems of unlawful gun usage, drugs and other social ills. Content on TV is much, much lower on the list of factors. But it's not totally off the list, and if the programmers and broadcasters who are responsible for putting violence into TV shows were to consider the possible effects of their decisions on the children, I think they would be more reluctant to load up their shows with violence.

Interview, Washington, D.C./
The Wall Street Journal,
9-9:(R)9.

Charlayne Hunter-Gault
Broadcast journalist, PBS-TV

2

[On minorities in TV news operations]: When I look at . . . the way the world is changing, hear the rhetoric of station managers and news directors, especially in public television, which has always talked a good game—well, all I can say is that public television is resting on its past laurels. In the system's prime hours, its principal [public-affairs] programs are anchored by white males.

Interview, New York, N.Y./
Los Angeles Times,
7-31:(Calendar)78.

Jon Katz
Media critic,
"New York" magazine

3

[On the lower journalistic standards of prime-time TV newsmagazines]: These shows are about popular culture, family life, gender, crime and celebrity. There's a huge appetite for that in America. It doesn't mean the public is stupid. It means [that mainstream] journalism is not reflecting the appetites of the people.

Newsweek, 4-11:65.

Ted Koppel
Host,
"Nightline," ABC-TV

4

[On television]: We now communicate with everyone and say absolutely nothing. We have reconstructed the Tower of Babel, and it is a television antenna.

At Catholic University
commencement/
The New York Times,
5-21:6.

Gerald Levin
Chairman,
Time Warner, Inc.

5

I can't speak about the big picture for our business and pass over the ill-considered actions taken by the FCC to enforce a second round of regulation on the cable [TV] industry. It's bewildering to me how a Commission that preaches growth of new technologies—creation of jobs, the rebuilding of our international competitiveness and the re-engineering of government bureaucracy to make it more efficient—can with one action negate all these goals.

At Big Picture
Media Conference,
New York, N.Y., April 12/
Daily Variety, 4-13:12.

Shari Lewis
Children's television personality

1

[On the difficulty in getting good children's programming on TV]: There have been years when I have had seven shows optioned and not sold one, because the people at the networks are mothers and fathers, they're nice people, they'd like to put on quality, they would like to put on wholesome stuff, but they have to be competitive. Until two years ago [even] the [PBS] member stations didn't want to put on any more programming for young children, nor did they want to put on anything that was considered soft or gentle.

Interview, New York, N.Y./
The Washington Post,
4-4:(B)7.

Edward J. Markey
United States Representative,
D-Massachusetts

2

[Criticizing proposals by the incoming Republican Congressional majority to stop government funding of the Corporation for Public Broadcasting]: I think they're going to find enormous resistance on a bipartisan basis from those who understand the critical role that public broadcasting plays. It's the most family-oriented network on television, and there is no close second.

The New York Times,
12-17:9.

Leslie Moonves
President,
Warner Bros. Television

3

In television, casting is almost everything. It may be more important than the script, because television is such a people medium. Very rarely will a good script get by with bad casting . . . [But] my concern can't solely be the best actor. I'm looking for people who are "attractive." That's part of the crass commercialism the studios and the net-

works have to look at. I have to think, "Am I going to have a *TV Guide* cover in six months, and what's that going to look like?"

Interview/
The New York Times,
4-6:(B)4.

Mary Mulvihill
Executive director,
National Parenting Association

4

Anything that they [TV networks and cable channels] can possibly do to reduce violence [in their programming] is good. Because, let's face it: It's not grandma or grandpa telling the stories anymore, it's TV. And programmers need to start appealing to the best instincts in both adults and children.

The Christian Science Monitor,
2-1:3.

Terry Rakolta
Founder, Americans
for Responsible Television

5

[Criticizing TV violence]: We have these huge media conglomerates now that own newspapers, television stations and movie companies. Soon there will be only two or three people who control everything that we see and hear; and those people will be accountable to only shareholders and bottom-line profits. And there are no signs of [TV] violence really letting up. Producers know sex and violence sells . . . We're not saying that entertainment violence is the only reason for violence in America . . . But you certainly cannot talk about violence in America without discussing the entertainment industry. I don't think a child picks up a gun and just starts shooting. There's been a lot of imprinting done before that . . . The conflict resolution on television is almost always to use a gun.

Interview/
The Christian Science Monitor,
4-25:17.

Michael Robinson
Media and political scholar

1

It takes so little money to produce political TV shows that it is viable if it has one of two things—a few people willing to kick in bucks, or a sliver of an audience that advertisers find attractive.

Los Angeles Times,
3-17:(A)5.

Forest Sawyer
Host, "Day One," ABC-TV

2

[On the lowering of journalistic standards for prime-time TV newsmagazines]: [Operating in prime time means that] you sometimes dance with the Devil, I guess. We're perfectly aware we have to survive. A story that has strong journalistic value but might not "play" [attract a large audience] is not one we're going to put on. That's realistic.

Newsweek, 4-11:64.

Tom Selleck
Actor

3

The entertainment industry should shoulder some of the responsibility for where we've gone with all this violence and sleaziness on TV. It desensitizes us to the violence, especially violence where there's no consequence for the act or [where] the hero is the most violent element. The thing kids need to know foremost is that there are consequences for their acts.

Interview/
Ladies' Home Journal,
March:54.

Paul Simon
United States Senator,
D-Illinois

4

[Saying the TV industry's initiative to have its violence content monitored is a step in the right direction toward limiting violent programming]: [The initiative is] a real turn in our culture . . . If you get old television films and movies out, you will see that smoking is a very common habit, heavy drinking is very common. We have changed, and in the process we have changed our culture. The same thing is starting on violence. It does not mean that immediately viewers are going to see any dramatic change. But broadcast [TV] has already moved significantly, and cable is moving also.

News conference,
Washington, D.C., Feb. 1/
The Washington Post,
2-2:(A)1.

5

[Saying government should have a role in regulating violence and pornography on TV]: It's a difficult thing for a parent to monitor, and it's difficult to know what are the good programs and what are not the good programs. Second, if Johnny or Jane goes next door to play, you're a pretty unusual parent if you can control what's on at the neighbors. And finally . . . we have a lot of single parents who are . . . just struggling to get by. Having a chance go monitor their children in a significant way is almost beyond their capacity.

Christianity Today,
2-7:42.

Howard Stringer
President,
CBS Broadcast Group

6

[On the problem of excessive violence in TV programming]: [U.S.] Senator [Paul] Simon in particular has approached the problem more methodically and thoughtfully. He's convinced us [in the TV industry] that rather than just sit around and argue about whether TV causes violent behavior, we should look at our schedule and just try to do good programming . . . [Today] the baby-boomers are embracing family values [in TV pro-

(HOWARD STRINGER)

gramming] with all the enthusiasm that they embraced drugs in the '60s.

The Washington Post,
5-2:(B)7.

Ted Turner
Chairman,
Turner Broadcasting System

1

[On gratuitous violence in TV programs]: You know that everything we're exposed to influences us—our teachers, our parents. Those films influence us and the TV programs we see influence us. The weaker your family is, the more they influence you . . . The problems with families in our cities are catastrophic—but when you put violent programs [before] people who haven't had a lot of love in their lives, who are angry anyway, it's like pouring gasoline on the fire.

Interview, Atlanta, Ga./
Los Angeles Times,
4-3:(Calendar)9.

Jack Valenti
President, Motion Picture Association
of America

2

[The entertainment industry] must . . . act as if TV is indeed a factor in anti-social behavior . . . Our industry must confront one indispensable truth: Each of us has to be more responsible for what we create . . . We in the creative community have an obligation to be responsible for what we conceive, accountable only to our lucid, moral instincts.

Before National Association
of TV Program Executives,
Miami, Fla., Jan. 27/
Daily Variety, 1-28:1.

Lindsay Wagner
Actress

3

The best thing about television is its potential and that at times it's willing to do meaningful pieces. A certain amount gets through each year . . . [But] I find it ironic that there's a children's show where heroes are set up to spend their whole time physically fighting the bad guy and that's how they solve problems. Then, at the end of the show, a two-minute skit tells children not to fight. Children should see how to resolve a problem. You just don't tell them to work it out. You show them how someone works through a problem and how violence can be avoided.

Interview/
Los Angeles Times,
8-5:(F)21.

Peggy Wehmeyer
Religion correspondent,
ABC News

4

Television is primarily visual. If you show a bunch of people sitting in a meeting, you lose viewers immediately. People just don't watch talking heads. It has to be visual.

Interview/
Christianity Today,
8-15:16.

MOTION PICTURES

Robert Altman
Director

1

[On the French effort to limit the showing of American movies in their country in an effort to spur France's own film industry]: The French stand is very justified, because I think they're struggling. But it's a losing battle. I think the idea of saying that people's interest lies in the land mass they live in is redundant, because we live in bands of airwaves around the globe. I supported the French position in the GATT thing [to limit importation of U.S. films] very strongly, but I think it's just a Band-Aid on the wound, because there's just too much money involved in it.

Interview/
"W" magazine, April:92.

Lindsay Anderson
Director

2

[On the late director John Ford]: Aggressive and defensive in equal measure, he was gentle and irascible, bloody-minded and generous, courageous, uncompromising and endlessly evasive. He could be kind and he could be cruel. He was an artist, strictly professional, obstinately personal.

Los Angeles Times,
7-3:(Calendar)5.

Marvin Antonowsky
Authority on
motion-picture marketing

3

Stars can only enhance a movie that people want to see in the first place. If people don't like what a movie is about—or think they've seen it before—they just won't go. Star or no star.

The New York Times,
7-28:(B)1.

Richard Attenborough
Actor, Director

4

It's my concern that movies that are granted any stature whatever nowadays tend to be imbued with cynicism, with brutalities. The pornography of violence and all that. Well, fine. I don't say for one second they shouldn't be made. But for an audience, particularly an upcoming [young] audience, to assume that's what movies are, that's the staple diet, and if you go to movies that's what you're going to encounter, that's another thing. So the one thing you don't do is go *en famille*. You have to examine carefully what you take your family to. And the phrase "family movie" has terrible connotations; you're yawning before you start. But I do think there's room for—what else do you call it—family entertainment. Films where you go in and won't be affronted or horrified, because there are other elements: fantasy, magic, love, jollity, kindliness, warmth, concern of one human being for another. Say what you will about *Miracle on 34th Street* [the new family-oriented movie he's appearing in], I can take my grandchildren to it. If I had a maiden aunt, I could take her. Or my ma and pa if they were alive. And you go *en famille*. I think there's room for that.

Interview, London, England/
Los Angeles Times,
11-13:(Calendar)42.

Margaret Atwood
Author

5

[On writing film screenplays]: Movies can't do figurative language. There are certain things you can do with pictures, and certain things you can do with words; what you're missing in movies is that level of metaphoric connection that you have in writing . . . The writer is a very low-down cog in the film-making machine. If the screenplay

(MARGARET ATWOOD)

is awful, the movie can't be good; but even if the screenplay is great, the movie can still be awful. So much depends on so many different individuals, accidents, contingencies, things beyond your control. There's so much money involved. There's so much more freedom in writing [books]; you're in control, and if you don't like something, you can just crumble it up.

Interview,
Chicago, Ill./
Booklist,
1-15:899.

Marty Bauer
President,
United Talent Agency

1

This town [Hollywood] is about ego and power . . . I don't think Hollywood is open to outsiders normally, because people don't like change. It's very easy to be a player in Hollywood . . . But the question is, how do you become a successful player? And that depends on whether or not you can function with the power in an effective way.

Los Angeles Times,
8-17:(F)4.

Harry Belafonte
Entertainer

2

We're still plagued by an [entertainment] industry unwilling to make films of historical substance. They're unwilling to focus primarily on anybody of color, because they don't consider these films bankable. The philosophy still is "keep it light, be entertaining." As a consequence, we're entertaining ourselves into utter apathy.

Interview,
San Francisco, Calif./
Los Angeles Times,
8-7:(Calendar)40.

Tim Burton
Director

3

[On being a director]: Because of the nature of the technical problems that arise [in making a movie], I can't imagine that anybody could walk into it feeling like it's a picnic. Those are the people who should be hauled away. It's like the idea of finding a completely happy person somewhere in the world. It's an incredible responsibility because of the money involved even on a low-budget film; you should care 1000 percent, and if you care 1000 percent you go through a lot of emotions. Studios don't realize that, and they should a little bit. They're giving you money and then torturing you. I'm trying to do what they want as well—come up with a good movie that some people might like. That's anybody's impulse. There's a little *too much* torture involved, in my opinion.

Interview/
Film Comment,
Nov.-Dec.:63.

Glenn Close
Actress

4

I find being a movie actor a ridiculous position to be in. When people recognize you, a look comes on their face that I find mortifying—like they're not looking at a human being here. All the shyness comes out in me. And I don't deserve that separation just because my face is blown up on a big screen. That's my work, not me.

Interview/
Cosmopolitan, February:234.

5

The characters that I have played have helped me explore my own life. Because if you are confronted with a certain character, you have to find what areas in yourself will make that character real. And it's all part of learning about the landscape of the heart.

Interview, Los Angeles, Calif./
Vogue, November:180.

Joan Collins
Actress

1

I think one should immerse oneself in the part onstage, but I don't think one should take it home. Do you know the wonderful story about Dustin Hoffman and Laurence Olivier when they were doing [the film] *Marathon Man*? Dustin, who is the complete American method actor, said to Olivier, "I just can't feel it today. I just don't feel that I can become this character. What am I going to do?" And Olivier said, "Why don't you try acting, dear boy?"

*Interview, London, England/
The Daily Telegraph (Britain),
1-16:(Review)3.*

Tom Cruise
Actor

2

[For an actor,] "image" ... is something that's created by the press, by different audiences on particular movies. All actors go up against this. It's frustrating, actually. Incredibly frustrating. But as an actor, you don't allow yourself to get locked into that. I feel for actors, because I know they hear all the time how they can't do it: "Well, you don't look the role." There's not a lot of imagination.

*Interview/
"Interview" magazine,
November:104.*

Allen Daviau
Cinematographer

3

[Criticizing the practice of motion-picture companies, and others who hold the copyrights, to alter films through technical means to make them more salable to TV and other media]: Something gets edited, speeded up, colorized, panned and scanned; this is the very first scratch on what's coming up. The same techniques that are emerging on the digital domain create great opportuni-

ties in the making of films, and those techniques can be utilized to alter films beyond recognition.

*Panel discussion/
Daily Variety,
4-27:26.*

Daniel Day-Lewis
Actor

4

[On his approach to acting]: Basically, it's just common sense. Any person who wants to understand a life and to borrow that life for a while, there are various means by which you do that. The reason I get involved with things in the first place is the *life* [the character]. It's not the idea of making a film that appeals to me; it's the idea of discovering a life which is fascinating to me. It's not like an exercise in self-flagellation or some kind of willful act of dedication that leads one to work in that way. If you're going to explore a life, the easiest way to explore it is from within, by holding onto it, and not sort of wandering in and out of it and wearing it one moment and slinging it off the next. [But] this is all junk, because I'm talking about something I don't really understand.

*Interview,
New York, N.Y./
Los Angeles Times,
1-2:(Calendar)28.*

Richard Donner
Director

5

[On the poor reaction by critics to one of his past films, *Radio Flyer*]: I was destroyed by the reaction to that film. You have no idea how it hurts. It tears you up inside and out and it affects your relationships, everything. It could have destroyed me. [But] as hurt as [his wife] Lauren was by the reaction to that film, she helped me through it. We never like to use the expression "It's only a movie" because it never is; it's a year out of your life. But there was a point at which Lauren said to me: "It's

(RICHARD DONNER)

only a movie. We've got to move on." And she was right.

Interview/
The New York Times,
5-24:(B)2.

Faye Dunaway
Actress

1

[On the role of the washed-up actress Norma Desmond in *Sunset Boulevard*, which she is playing on the stage and which is based on Billy Wilder's original movie]: I'm going to play her as 50, the age she was in the movie. I think there's something that Wilder was trying to say about a 50-year-old woman in Hollywood that does not apply to a 50-year-old woman in any other walk of life. You can be a great journalist when you're 50; you can be a Senator when you are 50. You can be almost anything, except a model or an actress.

Interview, Los Angeles, Calif./
Los Angeles Times,
6-5:(Calendar)9.

Amy Ephron
Screenwriter

2

[Arguing against the practice of using several writers, rather than one, to write a screenplay]: The really great movies have tended to be written by one person. They're less homogenized, have better characters and a much clearer vision. Writing is not a communist enterprise.

Los Angeles Times, 2-9:(F)1.

Joe Eszterhas
Screenwriter

3

I've always felt the writer of a piece deserves to be compensated as well as directors and actors

[are]. In the case of an original screenplay, it is the writer's vision up on the screen.

Los Angeles Times,
5-19:(D)13.

Federico Fellini
Director

4

I never make films to compete [for awards]. I won hundreds of prizes; you can see them in my home and office, stashed in corners, wherever my wife put them. [But] I never cared much for prizes, because I never made films for others but for myself . . . to release an obsession that left me no other choice. Perhaps my shooting time has always taken too long because I had difficulties releasing my child, my idea. I always felt a kind of psychological resistance to seeing my films afterward and rarely did, simply because I did not care about them anymore. The child had left the house. It remaind my child, part of my family, but my interest went to the birth of the next one.

Interview/
"Interview" magazine,
January:110.

Colette Flesch
Director General,
Cultural Affairs Department,
Executive Commission
of the European Union

5

Europe has no alternative but to develop an coherent global strategy if it wants its [entertainment] industry to survive and develop. It is in this context that the Commission . . . aims at presenting both governments and professionals with options, not to increase protectionism, but to give a new dynamic perspective to the European audiovisual sector.

At media seminar,
Brussels, Belgium, March 25/
Los Angeles Times,
3-26:(D)1.

Jodie Foster
Actress, Director

1

When I was a kid, my mom said, "Actors aren't very smart. And you're smart, so you don't want to be an actor, because that's what dumb people do. Acting is a hobby, it's a way to make money to provide you with the opportunity to do other things" . . . I think I realized eventually that it wasn't the craft that wasn't engaging, it was me playing safe, and that it was my responsibility to etch out the intellectual and spiritual aspects in the material . . . To a certain extent, you either have it or you don't [as an actor]. A lot of what some of the acting schools cater to is how to make actors who don't have it . . . passable. When the truth is they don't really have access to something that's an unschooled skill. That's half the battle, this unschooled skill.

Interview, Los Angeles, Calif./
Vanity Fair, May:171.

2

[On the lack of good scripts for women]: This business is so risk-averse because of the tremendous amount of money that's spent. So what's the first thing that you're going to put out there? Male-driven movies like *Speed*. That's the least risky thing you can do. I'm surprised that there are *any* movies made with women.

Interview, Los Angeles, Calif./
The New York Times,
12-12:(B)4.

Jean-Luc Godard
Director

3

[Saying his films are complex in a scientific sense]: [A century ago,] scientists believed the atom was the ultimate matter. Then they discovered that in one atom there are many things, and in one of those there are many *more* things, and so forth . . . In films, we are trained by the American way of movie-making to think we must understand and "get" everything right away. But this is not

possible. When you eat a potato, you don't understand each atom of the potato!

Interview, New York, N.Y./
The Christian Science Monitor,
8-3:12.

4

To have a good script is very rare. To have this is not only to have a story, but to have a *subject*—a meaning, a belief in something. American pictures usually have no subject, only a story . . . A pretty woman is not a subject. [Actress] Julia Roberts doing this and that is not a subject. JFK is not a subject—the relationship between a [late President John] Kennedy and the American people *may* be a good script when you know the subject and try to explore it.

Interview, New York, N.Y./
The Christian Science Monitor,
8-3:12.

Conrad Hall
Cinematographer

5

[In the 1950s,] cinema was still so new, so young, so innocent. It wasn't, as now, driven by the motor of marketing. We don't tell stories any more with the joy and the passion and the sensibilities we used to tell them with.

Daily Variety, 2-24:20.

Tom Hanks
Actor

6

[As an actor,] the cinematic image [of yourself] is something you carry into every job you do. You can't change it, because if you try to change it, you're making a false choice. In all honesty, Robert De Niro is Robert De Niro. He carries that cachet with him every time he appears before the camera. Spencer Tracy, the same thing. Every time anyone has ever done this, they've had *that thing*. The people who have washed out over time are the people who really didn't have much

(TOM HANKS)

of some sort of cachet that bled through. That's dictated by something that is utterly beyond our power, utterly past our ability to make it metamorphose. It's this confluence of energies that says *You!*, as opposed to *him*. I think that has happened to me without question. I think that's fate.

Interview/
Vanity Fair,
June:153.

Gale Anne Hurd
Producer

1

There's an interesting psychological profile of people who come to Hollywood. They're insecure and unstable. And they'd be insecure and unstable anywhere. And what do they do? They choose the most insecure and unstable place to work, a place where the average executive stays in a studio job for 18 months, where you're only as good as your last movie. They've created an environment where they play out their worst fears and never, ever, feel safe and secure and comfortable. That's the pathology of the place.

Interview,
Hollywood, Calif./
The New York Times,
5-3:(B)1.

Jeremy Irons
Actor

2

I don't think actors should accept a [British] knighthood. Actors should be jesters, not the court. They should be the ones kicking against the system . . . Actors should be—dangerous.

Interview,
London, England/
"W" magazine,
March:90.

Tommy Lee Jones
Actor

3

[Saying actors should be interested in the experiences of other people]: For an actor, that's a handy skill or point of view to take. Other people's experience is important. That's one of the best things about being an actor. I have a real interest in people—for entirely *selfish* reasons. I don't forget anything . . . Actors are better off if they don't park themselves at the center of the universe so that the world revolves around them, you know? Many people live in a universe that is constructed in this manner. It's no place for a good actor.

Interview/
Film Comment,
Jan.-Feb.:31.

John Landis
Director

4

What defines a good movie? Well, in reality, a good movie is a movie that's tremendously profitable. That's the real definition according to [the trade paper] *Daily Variety* and the studios. Well, as you well know, there are a lot of terrible movies that make a fortune and more really good movies that fail. So this is schizophrenia of a very high order. Everyone's talking out of both sides of their mouth—especially when you have studio heads at the AFI yakking about the great art of film and meanwhile they want to make *Ace Ventura: Pet Detective 12.*

Interview/
Daily Variety, 5-24:26.

George Lucas
Director

5

[On the effect of new technologies on the making of movies]: Sure, I think you can make "cookie-cutter" movies with computers, and I'm certain some people will start doing that. Talent is expensive and, at the same time, thinking is hard.

WHAT THEY SAID IN 1994

(GEORGE LUCAS)

But computers or no computers, movies will always be about storytelling. I think you're going to find that the things that are worthwhile will involve the slightly psychotic state of a writer that produces the most interesting things to watch. If you take the "twist" out of movies, you've lost the interest of your audience.

Interview/
The Wall Street Journal,
3-21:(R)20.

Alexander Mackendrick
Former director

1

Boy, do I get a lot of trouble with these young students learning about direction. There is a misconception that's awfully hard to get out of their systems that the director shows the actors what to do. If you have any sense, you do nothing of the sort. You watch what the actor is going to do anyway and then you help him. You never tell the actor where to go or—most fatally—how to read a line. If you do that, what you get is the actor imitating you, which is the last thing you want. You want to find out how the actor plays the character. Then you have to study *him*. What you're looking for is the instinctive and intuitive impulses of the actor in the character.

Interview, Los Angeles, Calif./
Film Comment, May-June:42.

Shirley MacLaine
Actress

2

So many men [in the film industry] don't have a clue what to do with the feminine in themselves. And a lot of women feminists don't either. So [when making films] you tend to avoid it, and you'd rather go to action, mystery, high-tech, fantasy. But where are the stories about *us*? Not *women*—people. Although I think there should be many more women in positions of leadership [in

Hollywood], those that are there now are not making this any better.

Interview,
Malibu, Calif./
Ladies' Home Journal,
May:82.

Louis Malle
Director

3

Often, in [making a] film, you're under so much pressure about money and time that it's completely artificial. You would think that with $45-million you could do anything you want, and sure you have big sets, big cranes. But to have the courage to say, "Well, I don't feel that scene, I don't see it," and do it again—you can only do that in small-budget films with small crews and actors who are not paid half a million dollars a day. That puts you, as a director, on the same level as a novelist or a painter. Most of the time, you're dealing with these huge machines that almost run without you, and trying to pretend, like [Jean] Cocteau said, that you're the organizer, when really you don't know what's going on.

Discussion,
New York, N.Y./
Vogue, November:182.

Steve Martin
Actor, Comedian

4

One of the biggest mistakes Hollywood makes in looking at a script is that inevitable question: "Will people like the character?" But they equate likability with someone never doing anything unlikable. It becomes Mr. Bland—almost like a hostile guy when it's really the foibles that make him good and human. I like it when a character is selfish or has a flaw that makes him more real than if he is Mr. Nice Guy.

Interview/
Los Angeles Times,
12-18:(Calendar)87.

Marcello Mastroianni
Actor

1

[On why he would not want to direct a film]: I tell you. Very simple. [To direct,] you have to have so much confidence. You have to believe in yourself so—what's the word?—strongly. Then you have a script. Then, maybe, in some circumstances, you have a mistress. And she says, "Maybe there's a part for me?" Then you have a producer. And he tells you what *he* thinks. Then *he* has a mistress. Maybe there's a part for her? [To be a director,] you have to believe in yourself so much, and have so much confidence. I do have, just enough to be an actor.

Interview, Paris, France/
Vanity Fair, November:201.

Mike Medavoy
Former chairman,
TriStar Pictures

2

There's no question that the public makes movie stars, and that's easy enough to determine looking at an actor's track record. [But] no one has ever had an absolutely unblemished career, and people who are "bankable" one year can get cold fast. But stars are unquestionably a magnet for audiences, and are worth their weight in gold if you've got a good picture.

Daily Variety, 7-28:7.

Jeanne Moreau
Actress

3

[On the popularity of American movies in Europe, which some see as a threat to European culture]: Nobody forces the European audiences to see American films. When I see them, I am rewarded. Even the B films. There's so much energy, so much craft. And if there is a weakness on the part of the Europeans, it is a self-indulgence.

Interview,
Beverly Hills, Calif./
The New York Times,
1-3:(B)2.

Ennio Morricone
Composer of music
for motion pictures

4

The true mark of a film composer is to find the path which serves his dignity as a composer, and serves the public and the producer, but especially serves the director. This conditioning does not impede the composer. It may take off or explode and ensure his creativity with this new freedom, found above the obligations of the film.

Interview, Los Angeles, Calif./
Los Angeles Times, 6-23:(F)8.

Liam Neeson
Actor

5

[On his role in the film *Schindler's List*, which brought him an Oscar nomination]: *Schindler's List* was a curse and a blessing . . . Every script that came my way [afterwards], I was comparing it to *Schindler's List*. Doing that film made me aware of the importance of what you say on a 20-foot screen that 20 million people are going to see. There's a responsibility. It's not that I wanted to play good guys all the time. But it made me wary of doing a piece of trash just because it had a large budget. Not that there's anything wrong with entertainment, and Hollywood will churn that out regardless. It's just that I was suddenly made aware of the responsibility I have as an actor.

Interview,
Fort William, Scotland/
Los Angeles Times,
11-20:(Calendar)5.

Paul Newman
Actor

6

I remember when you had a stable of actors at a studio and you started with the first scene, and then you shot the second scene, and then you shot the third scene, and finally on the last day of shooting you shot the last scene. Now you shoot the

(PAUL NEWMAN)

last scene the week after you've started, and people get shuffled in and out because they've only got nine days and everything is out of sequence. And how the film comes together in some semblance of emotional buildup is something of a puzzle. You go on instinct a lot. You take the plan, the script, and eliminate the organization, and maybe it works better that way.

Interview,
Westport, Conn./
Los Angeles Times,
12-18:(Calendar)40.

1

[Movies are] certainly the theater of the senses now, as compared to the theater of the mind. They escalate the sensory impact of films now, the noise of them, the violence of them, the sensuality of them, and where will it end? In the Westerns of the '30s, the sheriff shot the villain at the finish. Now he's not even remotely right unless he has 88 corpses at the beginning of the picture, just to show that he has the proper intentions. It's a score card: sheriff, 344 bad guys; bad guys, 12 good guys; a few offside penalties.

Interview,
Westport, Conn./
Los Angeles Times,
12-18:(Calendar)46.

Mike Nichols
Director

2

What happens with [making] movies is that you start out with material that really turns you on, and what's exciting is making this scene work and then that one. Then, somehow, the externals take over. They get stronger and stronger. You make a few more movies, something is a hit. Is the next one a hit? It gets real . . . Then there are all these people after a while. There's [producer] Joe Levine, and Joe Levine has all these *feelings* about *The Graduate*, and he wants *another* one.

You're not alone anymore; you're not *just* doing your work.

Interview, New York, N.Y./
Vanity Fair, June:78.

Gregory Peck
Actor

3

So much of the Establishment movie-making [today] is calculated as really light entertainment, including the violence and the special effects. It is basically light entertainment, extremely well done—*technically*. But you [the audience] don't carry anything away with you. Maybe you had a couple of hours, like a ride at Magic Mountain [amusement park], that took you over the hills and rode you around. *Jurassic Park* is maybe the best example of that kind of movie. But the most recent ones I liked were *Belle Epoque* and *Like Water for Chocolate*. They are passionate to tell a story that they are in love with and to play those characters.

Interview, Los Angeles, Calif./
Los Angeles Times, 6-2:(F)10.

Frank Pierson
President,
Writers Guild of America

4

[Arguing against the right of motion-picture companies, and others who hold the copyrights, to alter films through such processes as colorization, time compression and other technologies to make them more salable to TV and other media]: It's not simply the damage that is done to the reputation of the artist [the original film-maker]. It is the whole concept of intellectual property which is the underpinning of all copyright law— that is, to secure to the artist the right to participate in whatever flows from the creation of his work . . . The country was not only enriched in an artistic sense, but also enriched literally in the commercial sense by the growth of an industry based upon intellectual property. Now that concept is utterly violated if the works that are cre-

(FRANK PIERSON)

ated under the copyright laws are systematically subverted and reduced in value or altered to the point that they do not any longer represent what the artist intended.

Panel discussion/
Daily Variety,
4-27:26.

Marc Platt
President, TriStar Pictures

1

[Saying the film industry is adjusting to the public's desire for less graphic gore and violence in movies]: As always, studios and film executives are sensitive to what plays in the marketplace. [His studio's forthcoming movie, *Mary Shelley's Frankenstein,*] given the nature of the material and inherent creepiness, could run the gamut of very graphic gore. Even three years ago, the same movie might have been more graphic. [But] we made sure that there is no part of the movie where you want to cover your eyes.

U.S. News & World Report,
5-9:42.

Sydney Pollack
Director

2

[Arguing against the right of motion-picture companies, and others who hold the copyrights, to alter films through such processes as colorization, time compression and other technologies to make them more salable to TV and other media]: Motion pictures are made by people—not legal entities. And if motion pictures are art, and I believe there is no question about that, then who, for heaven's sake, is the artist? Clearly the artist or artists are those people whose [original] choices define the shape and texture, the style and tone of what is art. After all, that is what art is made of.

Choices. A series of choices—first imagined, then implemented. Change the choices and you change the impact and therefore the value of the work of art.

Daily Variety 4-27:23.

Frank Price
Former chairman,
motion-picture division,
Columbia Pictures

3

[On being head of a major studio]: It's like playing poker: When you like a job, they have to pry you away from the table—even if you don't win every hand. Whenever I felt overly stressed, I reminded myself that it's easier than writing. It's "let's put on a show" . . . and getting paid to do it . . . I'd like to know what the drawbacks are. Anyone who complains about the stresses is a fool. The pay and the perks are good. You have fun lunches with [Barbra] Streisand and [Robert] Redford. And it's sort of like being head of a small country. Though I rarely used the plane, I was met at the airport and commanded a certain amount of deference. Things go your way—period.

Interview/
Los Angeles Times,
12-18:(Calendar)54.

Robert Redford
Actor

4

The [film] industry has become more centralized, more costly and more formulaic. It's so much about the "opening weekend," about volume. You watch certain films and say, "Why did that get made? How'd they spend that kind of money on that film?" And you realize that there's an assembly line moving through the industry—a product line. So many personalities and directors making films now bring with them a mentality honed by

their work in television. Their style is more overt, like [TV] sitcoms or the funny-paper pages. "Okay, folks, here's a tale that can be told in four panels."
"Interview" magazine,
September:111.

Ivan Reitman
Director

1

Movies, if you'll excuse the cliche, involve action. I'm always thinking of life beyond the frameline [of the camera]. For whatever reason, I've made a number of films that have outlandish premises. I find the way to make those work is to make sure that it feels that it's really going on, that there's a real truth to the world. Not just a truth to the world of the two or three characters that you're looking at within the frameline, but that if somehow the camera wandered by accident to the right or to the left, you would believe in the reality of the situation . . . [of] life going on every-where you can imagine. Little things that don't jump out and take focus from what one intends to, but which subconsciously give you a sense of the world.
Interview/
Daily Variety, 11-18:41.

2

I couldn't make a film with despicable [char-acters]. I have villains, but my movies have the kind of people we'd all like to be. Go back to any of my films . . . and you know when you get right down to the bottom there's a good person there with the right heart who's going to do the right thing at the right time. I could never make a movie like *Short Cuts* or the [Quentin] Tarantino mov-ies; they're great films but have a very black out-look on life. My outlook is the opposite. I keep looking for that thread of decency that keeps us as humans special.
Interview/
Los Angeles Times,
11-20:(Calendar)85.

Julia Roberts
Actress

3

I have a hard time finding scripts that I really like, and I'm 26 years old. The bulk of material written is about youngerish people, because it's easier, because as we get older our life situations become more complex. We're not as frivolous. You know, you just can't write some sort of silly tale about a 40-year-old woman. This is a woman who has done things, who maybe has kids, who's maybe loved four or five different people profoundly in her life. And I think that's probably a lot more difficult to write a clever story around than it is to write a story about a 21-year-old girl who doesn't give a s——, and will sort of go with whatever and be with whomever.
Interview, New York, N.Y./
Vogue, June:168.

Alan Rudolph
Director

4

I don't look at [making a movie] as [a] risk, because the real risk is for anybody who puts up the money. I mean, what am I gonna risk [as a director]? Somebody doesn't like me? Well, I learned from the beginning: You make a film and then you duck. That's basically the posture of movie-making. The problem in American busi-ness, but certainly Hollywood, is if you're not a success, you're a failure. That's basically the atti-tude. And I don't believe in it. So there's no risk for me whatsoever.
Interview,
Santa Monica, Calif./
American Way, 12-1:66.

Susan Sarandon
Actress

5

I think life is so much bigger than my craft [acting] that I would rather invest my genius in my life. It has many more challenges, many more

(SUSAN SARANDON)

surprises. It may even demand more from the imagination. I mean, I don't know how full a cup you [as an actor] can bring to a project if you're not living a life. If you're not drawing from real life, then all you're doing is rehashing images you've seen in films. Even the images of yourself.

Interview,
New York, N.Y./
Los Angeles Times,
7-17:(Calendar)39.

Robert Shaye
Chairman,
New Line Cinema

1

[On excessive costs in the motion-picture industry]: There's kind of a duplicitous and obscure business process where people lie a lot. It's greed. I mean it goes to things like an actor doesn't want to go on a big publicity tour in Europe unless you give extra things on top of it. How's about a car? How's about some jewelry? And it makes you gag. [But] on the other hand, you don't want to mess up your international customers. But it gets to the point where you say: "Wait a second. This is wrong, It's just wrong."

The New York Times,
12-29:(B)1.

Steven Spielberg
Director

2

Getting an Oscar has never been a goal of mine. But anyone who is nominated [and] who denies that it's not a goal at that moment is loopy.

After receiving best-director
and best-picture Oscars
for "Schindler's List,"
Los Angeles, Calif.,
March 21/
Los Angeles Times,
3-22:(F)1.

Sylvester Stallone
Actor

3

[What spells success in motion pictures] is the perfect blending of men and material. But I don't think anyone's ever going to accept me in a comedy—ever, ever, ever. I'm a commodity. If you go to the store and grab a can of Stallone, [and] you open it up and see [comic actor] Steve Martin—you don't want that.

U.S. News & World Report,
5-9:46.

Oliver Stone
Director

4

The camera for me is an actor. If it were in this room, there'd be three people. The camera's view of what we do is what a third participant's relationship is to the scene, so it really is not a recording device—it's a participant. In other words, you cannot tell me that's a fourth wall—I don't accept it. Once the camera's in the room, you have to deal with it; it's not like we're secretly here. You have to have an attitude toward the camera, otherwise you're just doing TV.

Interview/
Film Comment, Jan.-Feb.:37.

5

In order to make movies, you have to be an optimist. Because by the time the glint in your eye becomes a reality, you have to have constancy and belief. I think I'd probably do something else or just retire if I were a pessimist. Right now, I still believe the world is an adventure.

Interview, New York, N.Y./
"Interview" magazine,
September:135.

Barbra Streisand
Singer, Actress

6

I want to make movies. Directing is what I love. It is about having a complete vision . . . hav-

(BARBRA STREISAND)

ing a dream. It is waking up in the morning or looking at something in the street or at somebody's face and thinking, "Turn the camera on that." It involves everything I love to do . . . including dealing with people on a psychological level, trying to get the best out of them. It's about going toward the real emotion, getting a moment of truth on the screen. That is what really interests me . . . all the aspects of putting something together.

Interview, Detroit, Mich./
Los Angeles Times,
5-23:(F)7.

MUSIC

Tony Bennett
Singer

1

I never sing songs I don't like. Frank Sinatra is the one who told me, "Just stay with good songs." That philosophy sustained me no matter what the fashion was, whether it was rock or disco or rap. If there's not a sense of timelessness, I don't go near it.

Interview,
San Francisco, Calif./
USA Today,
3-25:(D)1.

2

[Saying his audiences appreciate that he has stuck to traditional popular music]: They tell me they like the fact that I didn't change. I'm not trying to sing rock music to them. I'm not trying to "connect" with them. I'm just doing what I've always done, and they see someone who's never given in—like a fighter who never took a dive.

Newsweek, 5-2:56.

Carlo Bergonzi
Opera singer

3

[On the opera singers of tomorrow]: Students no longer have the patience to study for three or four years. They're all in a hurry. And even the ones who do study for all that time often arrive at the opera house for auditions with roles they're not vocally suited for. You know, you can become a star in one week if you're in the right place at the right time. But you need something to carry you from there.

Interview,
New York, N.Y./
The New York Times,
4-16:8.

Richard Bonynge
Opera conductor

4

I think young [opera] singers are more prepared today. There are a lot of serious artists out there—Americans, yes, but also French and Italian—who provide a great deal of enjoyment in this repertory. The danger is with singers who think "How much sound can I make?" rather than "How beautiful or expressive a sound can I make?" The reason I underline technique is because a good technique allows you to do what you want when you want to do it. But technique is only a means to an end. In bel canto, the end is expression. You don't have to turn cartwheels or sing on your stomach to be dramatic. The drama is in the music.

Interview/
Opera News, 1-22:16.

Deborah Borda
Executive director,
New York Philharmonic Orchestra

5

We [the orchestra] strive to integrate ourselves into the community and to give back what we can. But we need to find out what our role should be. Can a symphony orchestra really be expected to make up for what's happened to musical education in the public schools? I seriously question the premise that an orchestra should be a social-service institution.

Interview/
The New York Times,
2-15:(B)2.

Dick Clark
Entertainment producer

6

[On the music industry today]: Nothing about the talent has changed. The business has changed.

(DICK CLARK)

It's now owned by five or six multinational corporations, run by people who deal very much with the bottom line. Breaks for new [talent] are negligible. There's so much money invested in the well-known names, perpetuating their careers and recouping the investment, that you and I, if we just started now, would have a steep uphill battle. In the old days, you'd find a guy who managed the business out of his garage, and you'd be the star, the mainstay.

Interview/
Los Angeles Times,
2-7:(F)10.

Van Cliburn
Pianist

1

I do everything from the heart, from personal conviction. If you try to find love by charting a course, you'll never find it. Everyone at [the] Juilliard [School] scoffed when I chose to play unfashionable Liszt or even Tchaikovsky and Rachmaninoff. And you can't imagine how they teased and ridiculed me for always beginning a performance with the national anthem.

Interview,
Fort Worth, Texas/
The New York Times,
3-3:(B)4.

2

You carry with you all your experiences on stage and you build on that. Each performance is a rehearsal for the next one. Whatever I play in public I like, and if I learn something, it's not to play for this week or that week, but forever.

News conference,
Beverly Hills, Calif./
Los Angeles Times,
7-3:(Calendar)7.

William S. Cohen
United States Senator,
R-Maine

3

[On music, such as "gangsta rap," which glorifies violence]: I don't consider myself a prude, but when I hear these messages aimed primarily at black men, about what they should do to black women, it concerns me. If you say something long enough, the boldest possible lie becomes the truth . . . How do you get back family values at a time when you are glorifying the dehumanization of women and heroizing images of those who are propagating violence as a way of life? I don't know how you legislate that.

Interview/
The Washington Post,
5-10:(A)1,4.

Barbara Cook
Singer

4

The most difficult thing [for a singer] to learn is that just feeling what we're feeling is enough. Most people, especially if they're 18 or 20, can't imagine that their own mundane life experience is important enough to expose it. They figure they have to be Barbra Streisand. They can't imagine that all they have to do is just *be.* Now, that ain't easy to do, because as soon as we start growing up, we realize we have to protect ourselves constantly to get through life. We don't even know we've put on all this armor. But what I'm [as a singing teacher] asking people to do is stand there and take all the armor off. And it's very difficult for people to understand that armor is useless onstage . . . Safety lies in the thing that seems most dangerous—letting people see your emotional stuff. Because everybody's got the same stuff—but very few people are given the gift to communicate it. When I hear a singer who allows me to come in emotionally, they've got me. Because the most fascinating thing on earth to people is another person.

Interview/
Opera News, October:44.

Bruce Crawford
President,
Metropolitan Opera Association,
New York, N.Y.

1

There are many critics, both here and abroad, who think that American musical institutions are run as businesses, with financial considerations coming first and artistic ones second. These critics also allege that the basis for much private support stems more from personal gain through public exposure than from a serious interest in music. They further believe that this crass and shortsighted motivation inevitably leads to unsophisticated, bland repertory and a breakdown of standards. They deplore the increasing number of people listening to wonderful *old* music, while *new* music and less traditional fare are performed only under pressure. They like to cite Europe as a better model: More adventurous musical fare is available there, since there is no reliance on private funding, which instills a conservatism on the American cultural scene. [But] the situation is a lot more complex . . . Quality and diversity have been and will be more dependent on artistic and managerial leadership and vision than on the specific nature of a financial support system. The advantages and disadvantages of private versus public funding will continue to be debated. If there are a few certainties in the opera world, I recognize these: 1) opera will continue to be an expensive art form; 2) income from ticket sales will never cover the cost of the production and presentation of opera; and 3) one way or another,the taxpayer will continue to pay for opera in societies that believe opera companies and opera houses are important cultural assets and, indeed, national treasures.
Speech to
Metropolitan Opera patrons, June/
Opera News, November:44,45.

Christoph von Dohnanyi
Music director, Cleveland Orchestra

2

[Comparing live recordings made during a regular concert with recordings made in a sound studio]: For me, a live recording is a kind of snapshot . . . of what you feel at the moment. A studio recording is more like a portrait.
Interview, Shaker Heights, Ohio/
The Wall Street Journal,
2-28:(A)12.

Hugues Gall
Director, Geneva Opera (Switzerland);
Director-designate, Paris Opera (France)

3

What I am proud of here in Geneva is that after 15 years I will have presented 122 different operas, and for not one moment was the budget surpassed. And remember, 10 years ago the budget was twice what it is now. I like rules. I play the game with the cards I am given.
Interview, Geneva, Switzerland/
The New York Times, 8-4:(B)2.

Charlie Haden
Jazz musician

4

There are so many things you can learn [from music]. It teaches humility, and if you pick up on that, it's a type of humility that's very special. Music teaches that you'll not be allowed to play music unless you're humble. It teaches about being in the moment you're in and that there's no yesterday or tomorrow, there's only right now. And in that moment you have to see your insignificance and unimportance to the rest of the universe before you can see your significance or importance. The secret of playing music in a powerful and beautiful way is to have humility.
Interview, Los Angeles, Calif./
Down Beat, August:17.

Herbie Hancock
Jazz musician

5

I've been around for a long time in jazz, and I realize that I had the great opportunity to inherit

WHAT THEY SAID IN 1994

(HERBIE HANCOCK)

the influence of the masters like Miles [Davis] and Bill Evans. If I start naming them, there will be a long list. I have heard fans who have put me in this "legend" category. I don't think that way. I'm sitting in this chair right here, so from my perspective I'm a musician who hopes to be inspired enough to inspire others, to be somewhere along the chain of influences that encourages constructive values like passion, sensitivity and joy to emerge from music.

Interview,
Beverly Hills, Calif./
Down Beat, June:20.

Julio Iglesias
Singer

1

[As a singer,] whatever I provoke in my public is not something I study. When something happens naturally, you don't have to think about it. What I know is that when I was playing soccer, I loved the biggest stadiums. I didn't distinguish if it was females or males in the stands. I distinguished the heat of the applause. As I singer, I don't know whether it's a man reacting or woman. I don't know about that. I just want the heat.

Interview, New York, N.Y./
The Wall Street Journal,
6-22:(A)12.

Mark Lamos
Opera stage director

2

[On working with opera stars]: Some directors say, "Oh, those cows!" But they're superhuman, larger than life, sometimes *much* larger. And somehow you have to get turned on—rather than off—by those facts. Using performers' temperaments and personalities strongly informs my approach. I'm an actor myself, and the actor is the one left holding the aesthetic bag. Not to allow people to bring their ideas and temperament to the

work is to limit energies that can be very useful. Read the reviews! When something gets panned, everybody gets panned. If it gets praised, everyone gets praised. You are *one*!

Interview/
Opera News, 1-8:15.

Vincent La Selva
Music director,
New York Grand Opera

3

I find an element of singing in most symphonic music. I view Mozart as a singer, Beethoven too. When you look at a score by Mozart, you see a lot of symbols, but not what he was *saying*. He said so much more than you can see, and I attempt to hear his voice when I approach his music. We too often get bound to the printed page and stick with that alone. But Mozart must have been a wildly expressive person. He used to yell and scream at rehearsals, not about technical perfection but about expression. As a conductor, this is where my instinct and insight come in. I think of what expression is there, and how it sings.

Interview/
Opera News, June:20.

Zubin Mehta
Music director,
Israel Philharmonic Orchestra;
Former music director,
New York Philharmonic Orchestra

4

India [the country of his birth] doesn't need Western music, as Japan and China do. Because, unlike the Japanese and the Chinese, Indians have maintained a passion for their own classical music. Every nook and cranny in India has its own music, so Western classical music in India will always be for a relatively small number of aficionados.

Interview, Bombay, India/
The New York Times,
12-6:(B)4.

Steven Mercurio
Principal conductor,
Opera Company of Philadelphia

1

I almost always have a great rapport with musicians. They just want you to help them. It's one thing to bark at the clarinet player, "You're a bar late!" He *knows* that. The question is, what can you tell him so that he can hear where he was wrong and get it right the next time? Being a good leader doesn't mean you have to scream and yell. It means that the players will follow you off the edge of the earth because they have such confidence that you know the score, that you have both the skill and temperament to dictate the score to them . . . Because they're in the pit, opera orchestras sometimes feel they're not appreciated, not the focus of attention. You have to convince them how essential they are to the success of the performance.

Interview/
Opera News, June:10.

Ennio Morricone
Composer of music
for motion pictures

2

A composer who does not do his own orchestrations, it's a serious defect to consider him a composer 100 percent. Either he's not capable, or he's lazy, or he's capable but he doesn't love his own profession—three negative things that make him a halfway composer. I am confronted in what I say by the consideration of the great composers of centuries ago. Beethoven and Bach and Stravinsky and Mozart—they didn't have arrangers, orchestrators.

Interview, Los Angeles, Calif./
Los Angeles Times, 6-23:(F)8.

Magda Olivero
Former opera singer

3

It has always been easy for me to enter a character. I often think I don't deserve to be praised for my interpretations, for it all came so naturally. Whenever I hear music, I am immediately transported into another world. Even now, when I listen to music I have sung onstage, I feel a violent emotion welling up inside me. If I cannot release that emotion by singing, my head starts to spin, my blood pressure soars, my hands go cold. Even when I was young, music gave me access to emotions and experiences of which I had no direct knowledge.

Interview/
Opera News, 3-19:14.

Regina Resnik
Opera singer

4

The [opera] profession has turned out to be a *huge industrial machine*, with p.r. and media, videocassettes and recordings, learning quickly and singing quickly, pushing and being afraid that your youth is over˙. . . Young singers today know nothing about style—*nobody knows*, and the music industry of today is not interested. They're interested in taking a work like the present [Metropolitan Opera production of] *Lucia* and turning it inside out, just to be different. Everything's in a big grab bag, and the younger singer—I'm sorry to say—has blown it. Not that these things didn't exist in my time. But it's heavy now. The profession is not going to make life easy [for] the young opera singer. They're in the Olympics all the time.

Interview, New York, N.Y./
Opera News, 12-10:24.

John Scofield
Jazz guitarist

5

Playing good is so much a mental attitude. Over the years, the most amazing musicians I've met have had a kind of joyous attitude. Maybe the music happens because everybody's "up" for it. You spend your whole life going back and forth between different ways of thinking about and approaching this imperfect art form.

Interview/
Down Beat, April:18.

Leonard Slatkin
Music director,
St. Louis (Mo.) Symphony Orchestra;
Music director-designate,
National Symphony Orchestra,
Washington, D.C.

1

[On his "audience-friendly" approach, which includes talking to the audience before a performance]: We are in competition with all the other events that the public could go to in a given day or evening—movies, sports, sitting at home. We're in a competition for that individual and, on a very basic level, for that dollar. I think of it as drawing people into what we're doing, bringing them more into play with the performance itself . . . I find that a lot of people enjoy having more information via the program notes or what I would have to say . . . I do it as I see it's necessary for the enjoyment of the performance, something that takes the audience further along in a piece of music.

Interview,
St. Louis, Mo./
The Christian Science Monitor,
4-15:17.

Rise Stevens
Opera singer

2

I was very fortunate to spend most of my career performing in operas with librettos by Hofmannsthal, Da Ponte, Meilhac and Halevy—who could argue with them? I never wanted to change a word. They were the best and still are, I think. I know some people dislike tragic endings in opera and would prefer happy ones, but I think when these operas were composed people lived that kind of life. They had an acceptance of fate and the harshness of life that we don't have today. Everyone today tries to think about life more joyously.

Interview/
Opera News,
12-10:29.

Barbra Streisand
Singer, Actress

3

Why am I so affected by things that are written [about her] that aren't true? Why can't I let it roll off my back? Because the truth is what I rely on as an actress, as a singer, as a director. I think that any performer knows his or her work has to be based on the truth if it's to communicate to the audience. If I'm truthful to the moment while I'm singing, it works; if I'm not, the audience feels that. So the truth to me is all-powerful.

Interview, Los Angeles, Calif./
Vanity Fair, November:193.

Yuri Temirkanov
Director,
St. Petersburg Orchestra (Russia)

4

An orchestra is like a living organism. It needs to be in touch with its progenitors . . . Youth has to study with somebody.

Los Angeles Times,
2-19:(A)12.

Jean-Yves Thibaudet
Pianist

5

[Saying that, although he is a classical musician, he also likes pop music]: I think music is just music. If you like music, you have to love all kinds of music. Which also should go the other way. All those young kids who love pop music should also like classical.

Interview, New York, N.Y./
Los Angeles Times, 4-29:(F)15.

Mel Torme
Singer

6

[On his pop and jazz singing with symphony orchestras]: Generally speaking, it is a tremendous thrill to work with symphony orchestras. I mean, I

(MEL TORME)

write all of the arrangements, so to stand up there and hear 80 or 90 people play what you put down on paper—it's the closest thing to being God I can think of.

Los Angeles Times,
7-3:(Calendar)6.

Jose Van Dam
Opera singer

1

[On today's young opera singers]: They are in too much of a hurry to sing the big roles. [Today] if you tell young people they must study up to six years, then sing for about 10 years without making a big name, they say, "No, it's too difficult; I won't do this." When I was in Geneva singing small roles in *Wozzeck* and *Meistersinger*, I said to myself, "Someday I will sing those [major] roles, but not at 25." You can do it, but it's dangerous—you could end up finished at 30.

Interview,
Brussels, Belgium/
Opera News, 1-22:12.

Joseph Volpe
General manager,
Metropolitan Opera,
New York, N.Y.

2

The responsibility of the general manager [of the Metropolitan Opera] is to keep a balance between the striving for artistic excellence and the business needs of the Met. I believe it was [the late Met manager] Rudolf Bing who said: "Every artistic decision is a financial one, and every financial decision is an artistic one."

Interview/
Opera News, September:14.

THE STAGE

Edward Albee
Playwright

1

[On winning his third Pulitzer Prize for drama]: Of course, I'm surprised and delighted. But then I'm surprised when I don't win awards, too. Every artist has many lives and deaths and you really can't afford to think too much about it. There's never been much of a link between quality and popular acceptance, so you just keep on doing it on the assumption that you're doing good work . . . I want to reach as wide an audience as possible but, alas, on my own terms. I don't want to compromise or over-simplify just to give myself the illusion of accomplishment. You start lying, telling half-truths, well, what's the point? Ascribe it to my arrogance—an arrogance that any artist in the United States has got to have to survive—but I can't really approach my work in any other way.

Interview,
Houston, Texas, April 12/
Los Angeles Times,
4-21:(F)1,6.

2

[Saying American dramatic theater is healthy around the country, though not on Broadway]: [Drama] occurs Off-Broadway, Off-Off-Broadway, in the regional theaters, in the university theaters. But the people who are misinformed into thinking that Broadway is the home of drama in America, they just don't get to see it.

Interview,
Houston, Texas, April 12/
The Washington Post,
4-13:(D)8.

3

Plays are about people that are not getting along with each other terribly well. Situations that are wrong. Most serious plays, good plays, are about something that's wrong that should be corrected.

The Writer, October:3.

Jane Alexander
Chairman,
National Endowment for the Arts
of the United States

4

It's unrealistic to expect to get more public money [for the arts] in this time of widespread budget-cutting, so a practical partnership between the commercial sector and non-profit groups is essential in the future . . . [Non-profit theater companies] are the proving ground for many of the most well-known and acclaimed stories and dramas in America, and the crucible for many of our playwrights, screenwriters, directors and actors. [Therefore,] we need the help of the commercial theater sector and its sister industries in film and television to support a movement to reinspire theater in New York and across the country.

At Showbiz Expo
East conference,
New York, N.Y., Jan. 6/
The New York Times,
1-7:(B)1.

Emanuel Azenberg
Producer

5

[Saying it has become financially more viable to produce a major play Off-Broadway than on Broadway]: Off-Broadway, 400 seats at $40 makes me a smash. On Broadway, 400 seats at $55 closes me down. You tell me—what makes sense?

The New York Times,
11-21:(A)1.

Mikhail Baryshnikov
Ballet dancer

1

One reads these things about ballet becoming obsolete and all that. If we're in a bit of an empty state now, it's nothing to cry about, because it's normal for the time. There's certainly not much excitement happening—a bit of a choreographic vacuum, that's for sure. No outstanding classical ballet choreographers. In the last few years the most interesting work has come from modern choreographers like Mark Morris and Twyla Tharp, who do pieces for classical companies. Uneven pieces sometimes, but more interesting somehow than the things the "classical" choreographers are doing. Especially because, in comparison, modern-dance choreographers are so creative—Trisha Brown, Paul [Taylor], Merce [Cunningham], Twyla—astonishing creativity!

Interview/
Dance Magazine, March:41.

2

The professional choreographer-dancer relationship is also very much a personal relationship. There's a danger of becoming *too* familiar—then it becomes like an old lover, and choreographers lose interest in you. That's why just to be with one or two choreographers all the time is dangerous: Too much of *you* is bad for *them.* If they want to do something for you as a dancer, it should be their choice always. *Their* priority, not just "Oh, please do a piece for me!" It doesn't work that way. Yes, you can sometimes approach a person, but you never can twist their choreographic mind to do something for you.

Interview,
Dance Magazine, March:42.

Darcey Bussell
Principal dancer,
Royal Ballet (Britain)

3

[As a dancer,] it's easy to work on your technique and to get things right. But to be able to portray a person you're not while you're dancing is hard. To be believable to the audience is very hard. You want them to be wrapped into the whole plot, like at the cinema.

Interview/
Dance Magazine,
September:48.

Jeremy Collins
Principal dancer,
American Ballet Theater
and San Francisco Ballet

4

[On cutbacks in company seasons]: Layoffs [for dancers] are awful—for everyone. They remind us that we're losing precious time and precious ground. Dancers need to dance. Taking class is not a substitute. You must be onstage to get better and build momentum. But being on a constant round of gigs isn't good, either. You need to be with a company for rehearsal periods, for learning new roles and pushing creative boundaries. And in order to fit everything in, you're willing to "red-eye it," adjust to sleeping on a night flight, performing on arrival, and red-eyeing it back. You also learn how to sleep sitting up in air terminals during layovers. We're more like alley cats. We fend for ourselves.

Interview/
Dance Magazine,
March:61.

Garth Drabinsky
Producer

5

[On his extravagant staging of revivals of past hit shows on Broadway]: You have to apply an innovative vision to the restoration of these shows. They have to be made larger than life and brought up to audience expectations. There's only one way to restore "The Last Supper," and that's impeccably.

Interview, Toronto, Canada/
The New York Times,
11-1:(B)1.

Robert Egan
Producing director,
Mark Taper Forum,
Los Angeles, Calif.

1

To be in the theater, one's commitment has to be evangelical. For any of us in the theater, there's never going to be a financial reward. You've got to believe in something else about theater that's collegial, that's spiritual, that's intellectual, that's political.

Interview,
Los Angeles, Calif./
Los Angeles Times,
1-23:(Calendar)74.

Alessandra Ferri
Ballerina

2

Art is an expression of the world inside us; there cannot be any separation between the woman in the street and the woman on the stage. My life is one with my art. I really don't know what I would have done on the stage had I not spent time meditating on my life as a woman.

Interview,
Milan, Italy/
Dance Magazine,
April:56.

Jeremy Gerard
Theater critic, "Variety"

3

Scratch a Hollywood producer, director or actor and you will undoubtedly find an emigre from the theater. TV and movies still get most of their talent from the live theater, and many of the most successful in their craft return regularly to the theater for artistic replenishment. Audiences, of course, have known all along that the live theater is one of the last remaining places to find nourishment for the soul.

Daily Variety,
2-8:16.

John Guare
Playwright

4

[On the stage]: It's the oldest art form. As Herb Gardner says, it's the only medium without knobs . . . You don't have to turn anything. It's just you and them [the audience]! The directness, the nakedness of just coming into one room where at one end of it is them and the other end is you, and the object of it is to tell each other, to get into the deepest part of each other . . . It's to say, "Okay, you know what I want to do? I want to get into your dream life" . . . [With TV,] you're in your own home. You are comfortable. And you are free to flick it off. You [the audience] are in the driver's seat. But when you go to the theater, we have to get ready and leave our house and travel *at a specific time*, to be there at eight o'clock, and join a group of strangers, and lose ourselves in that group of strangers. And on the other side of the room, well, there is nothing more extraordinary or addictive to a writer or actor than making a roomful of strangers laugh at the same time, or making them silent at the same time. In the theater, what's happening on the stage is the boss. The stage is even above us often. We look up at it.

Interview,
New York, N.Y./
Lear's, January:11.

Nicholas Hytner
Director

5

I think the megamusicals are over. Because, in the end, the only way a new one can be better than the one before is for it to be *bigger*. And there's a limit. I wasn't aware of that when I was doing *Miss Saigon*, and bigger it certainly was! But I would say that everything that's good in that show is small, and everything that's not good is *huge*.

Interview/
Vogue,
March:250.

Julie Kent
Principal dancer,
American Ballet Theater

1

I think the music carries you away when you're onstage. I'm not thinking anything technical when I'm out there. I'm just thinking the music, especially in something like the second-act pas de deux in *Swan Lake*. I think it's pretty rare that you can lose yourself in a role onstage. But if you can take yourself to that level where you become a character, I think that's what people are really touched by—that kind of energy connection with the audience when they can believe a story because they know *you* believe it.

Interview/
Dance Magazine,
February:69.

Tony Kushner
Playwright

2

There may not be any *great* playwrights writing right now, nobody on the level of [Eugene] O'Neill or [Tennessee] Williams, but I think there are more *interesting* playwrights writing right now than at any other point in American history.

The Writer,
September:3.

Jiri Kylian
Choreographer,
Netherlands Dance Theater

3

On occasion I am asked to give some of my older works to [other dance] companies, and sometimes it feels like being in purgatory. It feels like you are doomed to seeing your own work in endless perpetuation. I don't want to see the old babies anymore; I want to see the young babies. And all choreographers are the same. It is very unjust to the old works. But I also find interesting that our idea of our older works completely changes; it is never the same. As you grow older, your ex-

perience changes, and every time you look at your works, you see them differently, although they stay the same. A work that you just created you don't really understand well. I do not really understand my work, fundamentally, because much of it is done through instinct, and I cannot really understand my instincts.

Interview/
Dance Magazine,
November:61.

Louis Malle
Director

4

They always said that once the talkies [sound motion pictures] came in the thirties, that was the end of the theater; but actually the theater resisted extremely well. [But today]—I don't know if it's television, or it's 30 years after television—but suddenly it seems there's this mysterious illness [in the live theater]. People lose money, shows close. The economy of the theater is really bad.

Discussion,
New York, N.Y./
Vogue,
November:184.

Steve Martin
Actor, Comedian

5

[On his recent experience working on a play]: Working on a play is more like group writing. It's watching the thing unfold, and seeing the possibilities. It's like stand-up [comedy] only in that you are working off the audience. Compared to movies, the process is very different. With a movie, you shoot it, spend $25-million on it, and then they test it to see if it works. With a play, you write it, test it, and then decide whether you want to spend the money to produce it.

Interview,
Beverly Hills, Calif./
American Way,
12-1:99.

Arthur Miller
Playwright

1

In other parts of the world, it's accepted that, of course, a play is written because the author has something to say about the world. [But U.S. critics complain] when anything departs from pure entertainment, or when an author has any viewpoints on society or politics.

Interview, New York, N.Y./
The Christian Science Monitor,
4-26:12.

2

[On the lack of success of recent serious plays on Broadway, such as his *Broken Glass*, which will have only a short run]: *Broken Glass* must close after some 10 weeks in New York because the costs of running are greater than the receipts. This despite many sellouts . . . Some plays fail because they are failures. This play, as a play, is precisely what I wanted it to be and is beautifully performed. Its audiences, I dare say, have been spellbound. The conditions of non-musical theater production in New York are what have failed, not *Broken Glass*. In a city of so many millions, mine was the only straight play to have been initiated on Broadway. We used to have a crisis; we are now in post-crisis, in catastrophe . . . We will not subsidize serious theater. We insist on theater-for-profit. And this is the theater we have. There is only one problem: Where is it?

Interview,
Roxbury, Conn./
Los Angeles Times,
6-19:(Calendar)9.

Paul Newman
Actor

3

You can't have good theater without good audiences; just as you can't have good literature or good pictures without good audiences. And I don't know where the audiences are now. I think there are just two straight plays on Broadway.

Many of the theaters are dark [closed for lack of product]. But you've got all these wide-eyed [young actors] coming out of Yale, Juilliard, Northwestern, and now the Actors Studio has a course at the New School. What the hell are they going to do?

Interview, Westport, Conn./
Los Angeles Times,
12-18:(Calendar)46.

Eric Overmyer
Playwright

4

I tell them [his playwriting students] they shouldn't outline a play and plot it through to the end. If they do, nothing surprising will happen. There's a quote attributed to [the late artist Pablo] Picasso that I use: "A painting is a revelation of a discovery, not the culmination of a plan." I let the play lead me.

Interview/
The New York Times,
12-5:(B)3.

Georgina Parkinson
Ballet mistress,
American Ballet Theater

5

[On teaching ballet]: I don't ever want to make the mistake of expecting anybody to approach anything the way *I* did. You allow them [her dancers] to contribute as much as possible rather than inflict the way *you* thought about it. I will suggest, and if they haven't come up with anything better, they might accept what I say for now and rethink it later . . . All I can do is advise and help out and suggest. But hopefully, it'll be their decision. Then you see their choice, not mine. And ultimately, I like watching their performance, for what they do really is show their implicit trust, and so together I think we make something.

Interview/
Dance Magazine,
June:42,43.

Harold Prince
Director

1

[On his being an "elder statesman" of the theater]: There's a success quotient that doesn't figure into the computation anymore. I want to work for the pleasure of making theater. It makes the work purer because you're saying, "Do I like it? Does the show work for me?" Not, "Is the show going to be a hit at the box office? Am I going to get hired next year?"

Interview, New York, N.Y./
The Wall Street Journal,
9-29:(A)12.

Anthony Randazzo
Principal dancer,
San Francisco Ballet

2

When someone sees me on the stage, my goal is for that person to think he's seeing a natural activity. Whether it's the story, or a feeling of texture, color or poetry. I'm hoping the observer will receive the experience in a comfortable way. The opposite of this is when a speaker stutters or when a dance looks uncomfortable and shows strain or trips. My goal is to show movement that is seamless and seems to make sense. That's the way it should be.

Interview/
Dance Magazine,
January:62.

Lynn Redgrave
Actress

3

[On performing on the stage]: I think it's courageous for any of us to get up there every night, to go out on your own and say, "Watch me"— even though we love it. And the longer one does it, the standards are higher. You always fear failure. I have to fight back fear every time: "Maybe tonight I'll blow it."

Interview, Los Angeles, Calif./
Los Angeles Times,
12-18:(Calendar)57.

Chita Rivera
Actress

4

You don't want to shove anything down an audience's throat. You make your statement as clearly as you can, and you allow the intelligence and the emotions of the audience to come their distance. They must find it—that shock of discovery. Theater is a very intelligent form. Even when it's noisy and robust, it still is the meeting of the theatrics and the audience.

Interview/
Dance Magazine,
February:80.

Neil Simon
Playwright

5

[On his plans to open his next show in an Off-Broadway theater, rather than on Broadway as he has in the past]: It's not just economics. When I was a kid, going to a movie comedy wasn't that different from going to a play. Broadway [today] is trying to outdo itself with bigger and bigger shows. Now it's all special events and revivals. People are used to what they see in the movies. Young writers don't even aim their material for Broadway anymore. The last hope is Off-Broadway.

Daily Variety, 10-20:14.

Barbra Streisand
Singer, Actress

6

[On her starring in the Broadway musical *Funny Girl* in the 1960s]: When we were changing *Funny Girl* every night [before the Broadway opening], I loved it . . . I would eat Chinese meals before I went on; nothing bothered my stomach. That's what I love . . . the experimentation. But once they froze that show on Broadway, I was in prison. I had to do the same thing over and over.

Interview, Detroit, Mich./
Los Angeles Times, 5-23:(F)1.

447

Robert Whitehead

Producer

1

[On the lack of success of recent serious plays on Broadway, such as Arthur Miller's *Broken Glass*, which had only a short run]: It's a comment on the theater. A play of this depth has a tough time right now. It has to do with the kind of taste that has been generated by an endless mass of television: It's Las Vegas time.

Los Angeles Times,
6-19:(Calendar)9.

Paul A. Allaire
Chairman, Xerox Corporation

1

It's appropriate that my thought . . . comes from the practice of quality. And it can be summarized in one word, a Japanese word, *kaisan*. It means continuous change for the better. It's based on the belief that no matter how good we are today, we must be better tomorrow. Competition in all walks of life is an ever-present reality. And change—unprecedented change—is the way of contemporary life.

At Clarkson University
commencement/
USA Today, 5-19:(A)13.

Woody Allen
Actor, Writer, Director

2

[On how he imagines he will die]: [Maybe] just slipping away in my sleep. I think sleep would be best. That's the nicest thing you could wish a person. You know, it's been said that I'm cynical about life. But if you think about it, what else can you be in a world where the kindest thing you can say to someone is, "I hope you die in your sleep"?

Interview,
New York, N.Y./
Esquire, October:90.

Richard K. Armey
United States Representative,
R-Texas

3

Freedom works. If you like peace more than freedom, you lose.

U.S. News & World Report,
12-12:52.

Alan L. Bean
Former American astronaut

4

Certainly riding a rocket to the moon is the biggest kick you can have. But when I paint, I get the same feeling that I got when I flew in space well. Certainly the view isn't as good, but the best part of life is internal.

Interview,
Houston, Texas/
The New York Times,
7-20:(A)10.

Harry Belafonte
Entertainer

5

If I were to pick one word that's the most strategic to human interchange and human thought, it would be the word *difference*. But people are so afraid and intimidated by difference. Many people are manipulated to be intimidated by it. Many people manipulate it for evil ends. Others embrace difference so we can understand more about each other. It is in difference that we find the opportunity to learn, to love and to serve. It is in difference that we find the center to our own humanity.

At International House,
University of California,
Berkeley/
Los Angeles Times,
8-7:(Calendar)40.

Tony Bennett
Singer

6

My heroes in life are Pablo Casals, Picasso, Duke Ellington, Eubie Blake, Fred Astaire—they worked until the end of their lives. You should never stop the flow. There's never been a day in my life that I've felt like throwing in the towel, no matter how rough it was. I love to entertain people. Fred Astaire said, "All I ever tried to do was knock people outta their seats." That's what I'm trying to do.

Interview,
San Francisco, Calif./
USA Today, 3-25:(D)2.

Bennett Berger
Professor of sociology,
University of California, San Diego

1

There's a nostalgia for "community," this kind of vaporous thing that the old folks had that must have been better. But people forget that there's always a price that comes with the freedom of modern times. Part of that price is a degree of alienation.

Mother Jones,
May-June:24.

Joseph Bernardin
Roman Catholic Archbishop
of Chicago, Ill.

2

The demands of the ego are unrelenting, and its desires are insatiable. Some of our greatest writers have shown, in vivid characterizations, the frustrations and suffering that come from clinging to the ego and its needs.

At Marquette University
commencement/
USA Today, 6-8:(A)11.

George Bush
Former President
of the United States

3

[On life after the Presidency]: Well, for one thing, I find that I no longer win every golf game I play.

Newsweek, 12-26:60.

Charles
Prince of Wales

4

[I believe] strongly in the importance of well-tried principles, of those more familiar things in life, which help to anchor us in the here and now and give meaning and a sense of belonging in a world which can easily become frightening and hostile . . . [There is a] misnamed fashion for what people call "political correctness," which amounts to testing everything, every aspect of life, every aspect of society, against a predetermined, preordained view, and rejecting it if it doesn't measure up, so that people feel intimidated and browbeaten, not daring to stand up and disagree, or voice a contrary opinion, for fear of being considered old-fashioned or plain reactionary.

Before Newspaper Society,
London, England, May 4/
The Washington Post,
5-6:(B)7.

5

[Humorously supporting a campaign for a plain, non-bureaucratic English language]: It was when I was still a juvenile future constitutional figurehead substitute that I first became sensitized by my mother-tongue abuse awareness.

U.S. News & World Report,
12-5:50.

Eugenia Charles
Prime Minister of Dominica

6

[As Prime Minister,] nobody is satisfied with anything you do, because everyone has a different notion of what should have priority. And also there's always the opposition barking at you. They want to take your place, so they have to fight, whether they like it or not, with whatever you do. But this is easier to bear because you know their motive. It is more difficult when you think you are doing things for people to really help them in their development, in their way of life, and they don't like it.

Interview/
Essence, September:74.

Warren Christopher
Secretary of State of the United States

7

Somebody once said that what I've done in my life has been based on kind of a pontoon grid,

(WARREN CHRISTOPHER)

where one thing has led to another. My clerkship with [Supreme Court] Justice [William] Douglas was tremendously important in this regard. I remember Justice Douglas telling me: "Christopher, get out into the stream of history and see what happens." I've tried to follow that advice.

Interview/
"Interview" magazine,
November:74.

Bill Clinton
President of the United States

1

God has endowed us as individuals with inalienable rights . . . The state exists by our consent solely to advance freedom and security and prosperity for all of us as individuals. That is still a radical idea in the world in which we live, developed by Locke and Montesquieu, put into practice in my country by Jefferson and Madison. It has toppled tyrants; it has drawn millions to our country's shores.

At NATO summit meeting,
Brussels, Belgium, Jan. 9/
The Washington Post,
1-10:(A)11.

2

There is no greater tribute to give to those who have gone before than to build for those who follow. Surely, that is the timeless mission of freedom and civilization itself.

At Oxford University,
England, June 8/
Los Angeles Times, 6-9:(A)1.

3

The challenges our generation faces are different than those our parents faced. They are problems that in many cases lack pressing drama. They require quiet and careful solutions. And if we meet them well, our reward will not be stunning moments of glory, but gradual and real improvements in the lives of our people. We must find the will to unite around these opportunities of peace, as previous generations have united against war's life-or-death threats and oppression's fatal grip. To the courage that enables men and women to drop behind enemy lines, face down rumbling tanks or advance freedom's cause underground, we must add a new civil courage—the energy and optimism and patience to move forward through peaceful but hard and rapidly changing times.

Before Polish Sejm (Parliament),
Warsaw, Poland, July 7/
The New York Times, 7-13:(A)5.

Hillary Rodham Clinton
Wife of President
of the United States Bill Clinton

4

What's most important is how power is used, not the gender of the person who uses it. There are good uses of power, and there are dangerous uses of power. And women are just as capable as men of using and abusing power. I don't think there is a style of power that is particular to women. I like when men and women use power to bring people together to solve problems and reach collective goals.

U.S. News & World Report,
6-6:72.

Glenn Close
Actress

5

Like everybody else, I've known thwarted love—probably the most painful thing I've gone through in my life. To have no outlet . . . even for your lust if that's what you're feeling at the time. And I honestly don't know what that pain is. It literally is a pain in your heart. What chemical makes your heart ache? You can't breathe, you can't sleep. Every minute is an hour, several hours. But you learn your best lessons through pain—and your heart can withstand a huge amount of pain, again and again. Yet you shouldn't be profli-

(GLENN CLOSE)

gate with your spirit. The soul is a very delicate entity.

Interview/
Cosmopolitan,
February:147.

Hume Cronyn
Actor

1

All the cliches say that as you grow older, you grow wiser. I don't feel one damn bit wiser! Wisdom is not concomitant with age. I've met some extremely stupid people who, as they've hardened and grown older, have become more selfish, intolerant, vindictive, driven to outrage easily, and they dwell in their disappointments. But a kind of acceptance isn't easily arrived at. I'm talking about graceful acceptance, a recognition of your own foibles, your own limitations, and I'm not talking of physical limitations. Somehow to make peace with the fact that you, like the trees, plants and landscapes, are going through and inevitable process.

Interview/
Modern Maturity,
July-Aug.:81.

Dalai Lama
Exiled former ruler of Tibet

2

I still believe that human nature is basically good and benevolent. If we let the negative overpower us, we will only be faced with destruction.

Israel/
The New York Times,
3-26:4.

E. L. Doctorow
Author

3

Communities appear temporally rather than spatially. They form as circumstances demand, and when the emergency is over people go back to their semi-estranged mood. Communal expressions that really matter on a day-to-day basis are probably made by people who have no thought of community. A surgeon who only wants to make money and live well and has a lousy bedside manner still contributes. The Korean grocer on the [American street] corner who works hard trying to survive may feel a foreigner, but the store is a contribution to the neighborhood. I don't know if you can ask for more.

Interview/
Mother Jones,
May-June:23.

Jurgen Dongas
German economist

4

In public opinion, there is a certain tyranny of the status quo. Many people think the alternative to the status quo is a curse.

The Christian Science Monitor,
9-21:10.

Kirk Douglas
Actor

5

Old age gives you wrinkles, but the worst wrinkles are the wrinkles inside of you, the wrinkles on your soul . . . To be old is to shrivel up and do nothing. But to be young is to keep creating, to keep blooming, to do something.

Interview/
Los Angeles Times,
3-16:(F)9.

Joycelyn Elders
Surgeon General
of the United States

6

We need to speak out to tell people that sex is good, sex is wonderful. It's a normal part and healthy part of our being, whether it is homosexual

(JOYCELYN ELDERS)

or heterosexual. There are certain times and places where sex is inappropriate, but just because it is inappropriate does not mean that it's bad.

Interview/
The Washington Post,
3-19:(A)13.

Federico Fellini
Motion-picture director

1

I consider independence the most important thing in one's life. If you have that, no one can blackmail you or corrupt you with money, flattery or promises. Just to be yourself and realize that what you're reaching for is what matters.

Interview/
"Interview" magazine,
January:110.

Stuart Fischoff
Media psychologist,
California State University

2

For everyone who is going to become a celebrity today, there is an unwritten contract: The minute you put yourself in the spotlight, you become a target for the weirdos of society.

Newsweek, 1-17:46.

John Kenneth Galbraith
Economist

3

[On what occasions he lies]: When silence no longer saves someone I love from acute distress; when praise of intelligence and beauty will be well received and, always, quite harmless.

Interview/
Vanity Fair, July:140.

Allen Ginsberg
Poet

4

I don't think love dies—it just gets buried under bad experience and incommunicability, or people go mad, suffer money woes, get caught up in a war. But if you look to your dreams, you'll find the original love tears, throbs and grief remain completely intact. The emotions remain in the body, the mind and the heart, and they often come out in dreams.

Interview,
Los Angeles, Calif.
Los Angeles Times,
2-16:(F)9.

Al Gore
Vice President
of the United States

5

I believe that sympathy and compassion are revolutionary forces in the world and that they are working now. For my part, in the 25 years since my Harvard graduation, I have come to believe in hope over despair, striving over resignation, faith over cynicism.

At Harvard University
commencement, June 9/
The New York Times,
6-10:(A)11.

Mark Green
Public Advocate
of New York, N.Y.

6

There are two qualities that any successful person needs, certainly in politics, perhaps in other fields as well: authenticity and energy. Sometimes phonies can make it, and sometimes lazy people can make it, but they are the exceptions.

Interview,
New York, N.Y./
Lear's, March:14.

Michael Huffington
United States Representative,
R-California

1

Government can't teach kids values . . . Most of the social problems we have today—drugs, alcohol abuse, teenage pregnancy, welfare—if we want to solve those problems, it gets back to the families of those kids spending time with the children while they're young. Reading with them at night, making sure they do their homework, teaching them virtues like hard work, courage, compassion, responsibility and faith. That part is really up to the family, not to the Federal government. We're just spending billions and billions of dollars that is going to waste. It's not helping the taxpayers, and it's not helping the recipients, either.

Interview/
Los Angeles Times,
10-30:(M)5.

Andrei A. Laptev
Former Soviet
economics professor

2

I don't think a superpower is defined by the number of its missiles or tanks or the amount of steel cast, the standards we used to beat our chests with pride. A superpower is measured by what it gives its people.

Los Angeles Times,
8-23:(A)6.

Tom Lasorda
Baseball manager,
Los Angeles "Dodgers"

3

I've learned that tough times never last, but tough people do. In every lifetime, doors are going to close. I look to open doors.

Interview/
USA Today, 5-20:(C)6.

Fran Lebowitz
Author

4

[I] have always said that I prefer the company of the average child to the company of the average adult. The level of creativity that a child needs to get through each day is tremendous, far more than any artist as an adult has to muster. Children lead rigorous lives. I'm 43. I have been out of school since I turned 17, and there has not been a single Sunday night since then that I haven't thought, Well, at least you don't have to go to school tomorrow morning.

Interview/
"Interview" magazine,
November:66.

Lee Kuan Yew
Former Prime Minister
of Singapore

5

The liberal, intellectual tradition that developed after World War II claimed that human beings had arrived at this perfect state where everybody would be better off if they were allowed to do their own thing and flourish. It has not worked out, and I doubt if it will. Certain basics about human nature do not change. Man needs a certain moral sense of right and wrong. There is such a thing called evil, and it is not the result of being a victim of society. You are just an evil man, prone to do evil things, and you have to be stopped from doing them. Westerners have abandoned an ethical basis for society, believing that all problems are solvable by a good government, which we in the East never believed possible.

Interview/
Foreign Affairs,
March-April:112.

6

[On countries' importing culture from other countries]: You should not abandon your basic pattern of culture, because there is a real danger of "deculturalization"—of losing your own basic

(LEE KUAN YEW)

values without absorbing the essence of the other culture. Culture does not consist of only customs, norms, external manifestations. There's an inner spirit to it, which holds a set of values into a coherent whole . . . A culture is something that develops indigenously from within a family, to a tribe, to a clan, to a society, into a civilization. It comes with mother's milk. It's how people have been able to protect their integrity over the millennium.

Interview/
The Christian Science Monitor,
4-27:24.

Jeanne Moreau
Actress

1

I'll be 66 in January. What should I do? Shoot myself? I've never worried about age. If you're extremely, painfully frightened of age, it shows. Life doesn't end at 30 . . . I try to see aging as a privilege. Aging allows me to do anything I want. It gives me freedom to speak up and tell the truth. You see the pain in women about getting old, and it's not only the actresses. But I just worry about being alive, taking care of my life. I mean, I'm an actress but also a woman. The actress keeps the woman and the woman keeps the actress. The whole aim of my life is to say: "Beware. Don't be trapped by what people expect of you. Just go your own way."

Interview,
Beverly Hills, Calif./
The New York Times,
1-3:(B)2.

Paul Newman
Author

2

I can't think of anything that gets better with aging. I'm not mellower, I'm not less angry, I'm not less self-critical, I'm not less tenacious. Maybe the best part is that your liver can't handle those

beers at noon anymore. I can't think of the worst part either. I don't know what's changed. Oh, you can't get to the [tennis] net as quickly. So what? It's not of consequence.

Interview,
Westport, Conn./
Newsweek, 12-19:62.

Mike Nichols
Motion-picture director

3

People always say, "One day at a time." As if we had a choice. They say, "Living well is the best revenge." Living well is exhausting, bone-crushing work that I've decided isn't worth it. Living simply is more like it. In the end, when the opportunity for revenge presents itself, you have better things to do.

Interview,
New York, N.Y./
Vanity Fair, June:82.

Michael Novak
Resident scholar,
American Enterprise Institute

4

There are two types of liberty: one, pre-critical, emotive, whimsical, proper to children; the other, critical, sober, deliberate, responsible, and proper to adults. Alexis de Tocqueville called attention to this alternative early in *Democracy in America*; and at Cambridge, Lord Acton put it this way: Liberty is not the freedom to do what you wish; it is the freedom to do what you ought . . . It is this second kind of liberty—critical, adult liberty—that lies at the living core of the free society. It is the liberty of self-command, a tolerable mastery over one's own passions, bigotry, ignorance and self-deceit. It is the liberty of self-government in one's own personal life. For how, James Madison once asked, can a people incapable of self-government in private life prove capable of it in public?

Upon receiving 1994 Templeton Prize,
May 5/The Wall Street Journal,
6-28:(A)18.

Charles Nuckolls
Anthropologist,
Emory University

1

We've stripped away what our ancestors saw as essential—the importance of religion and family . . . People feel they want something they've lost, and they don't remember what it is they've lost. But it has left a gaping hole.

Newsweek,
11-28:55.

Octavio Paz
Mexican poet;
Winner, 1990 Nobel Prize
in Literature

2

Our democratic capitalist society has converted Eros into an employee of Mammon. Profit, gain and the extraordinary materialism of our society are weakening the human condition.

Interview,
Paris, France/
The New York Times,
6-11:13.

Uwe E. Reinhardt
Professor of political economy,
Princeton University

3

America developed schools of public affairs, schools of health administration, schools of management much earlier than most other countries. So out came all these policy wonks who specialize in dealing with complicated issues. It's not inconceivable that the reason things are complicated is that we have an over-supply of people to whom complexity is a livelihood, and who think everyone else is like them.

Interview,
Washington, D.C./
Modern Maturity,
Nov.-Dec.:68.

Werner Riedel
Director of the organization
that sponsors the Jugendweihe
coming-of-age ceremony
in Germany

4

[Addressing 14-year-olds]: Today is an important event in your life. Today you finish that long and peaceful part of your life that we call childhood. You are becoming young men and women. Yes, you're big now. Your knowledge and your choices deserve to be taken seriously. At 14, you can't write letters to Santa Claus and expect your parents to grant your every wish. You have to do your own thinking about how to fulfill yourselves. If you want to be strong tomorrow, you have to begin taking responsibility for yourself today. You have to reject violence, racism and anti-foreigner feelings. You have to respect the environment, and not treat our Mother Earth as if we have a second or third one in our pocket. You have to read good books, go to the theatre and the cinema, to galleries and museums . . . For the girls, I wish you nice boys, and for the boys, I wish you nice girls—but please, there's no hurry.

At Jugendweihe
coming-of-age ceremony,
Berlin, Germany, May/
The New York Times,
6-11:5.

John M. Shalikashvili
General,
United States Army;
Chairman,
Joint Chiefs of Staff

5

[On the job of his dreams]: To own a country hardware store. To sit outside in the sun with my blue apron, waiting for a customer to come by. To rummage through little bins looking for a particular bolt a customer might want, and, once found, to go back out to my bench in the sun.

Newsweek, 9-19:19.

Alan B. Shepard, Jr.
Former American astronaut

1

[On looking at Earth from space during his moon mission in 1971]: I remember being struck by the fact that it looks so peaceful from that distance, but remembering on the other hand all the confrontation going on all over that planet, and feeling a little sad that people on planet Earth couldn't see that same sight, because obviously all the military and political differences become so insignificant seeing it from that distance.

Interview/
The New York Times,
7-20:(A)10.

Hedrick Smith
Journalist

2

The notion that *everybody* is a player is crucial. It's definitely true in the effective corporations and schools today, and it is certainly true in all of our foreign competitors that are any good. If you're not a player, if you can't speak up, if you can't become an agent for change within your own environment—that environment, that company, that school is going to be in trouble somewhere pretty soon down the pike. If you're in an organization that is not open to genuine change, it's going to be in trouble some time in the next five years. Better you know it now than wait until it happens. And either start to make the changes within the organization or get out.

Interview/
American Way, 1-4:48.

Jacques Toubon
Minister of Culture of France

3

We support the concept of linguistic pluralism. If, one day, all mankind spoke in one language, or rather in one international code, this would lead to a dramatic impoverishment of culture and cultural exchange; and, finally, it would mean a regression of humanity. I do not think having everybody speak English or American English would be a sign of progress. On the contrary, progress is when each individual expresses his identity through his culture and through the language that is its foundation.

Interview,
Paris, France/
Los Angeles Times,
7-10:(M)3.

Ted Turner
Chairman,
Turner Broadcasting System

4

When I was first getting going, people fell out of their chairs laughing. The TV station I bought was going bankrupt; I couldn't afford to buy a network affiliate. The smaller you are and the bigger you aim, the more hooting and hollering you're going to get. That's not just true of me. If you're at McDonald's making $1 an hour and you say, "I'm going for $1.10," nobody's going to doubt you. If you've got a dollar and you say, "I'm going to build a multibillion-dollar corporation that is going to rival the networks," then they're going to hoot at you.

Interview, Atlanta, Ga./
Los Angeles Times,
4-3:(Calendar)83.

Desmond M. Tutu
South African Anglican Archbishop;
Winner, 1984 Nobel Peace Prize

5

You know, evil is real. Many people think it is a figment of our imagination. Evil is not just impersonal. Evil is directed. And evil does want to spoil the good thing that God wants to see happen. In many ways, we are involuntary collaborators with evil. Those who want to gain political power will often appeal to the baser sides in all of us.

Interview/
American Way, 10-1:61.

Richard von Weizsacker
President of Germany

1

If you see the solution to problems like racism and violence only in stricter laws, tougher police measures and stringent political speeches, you are mistaken. It isn't police or laws that determine how people behave and think. Teachers, parents and even the media have much greater influence, and should be aware of the role they have to play.

Interview/
The New York Times,
5-18:(A)4.

Cornel West
Professor of religion and director
of Afro-American studies program,
Princeton University

2

[Look] at young people these days. I think we can see quite clearly that they are creatures of a market culture, much more than you and I. You and I are deeply affected by it; but we grew up, we were socialized and acculturated, at a moment in which civic institutions played an important role in transmitting to us non-market values like love and care and concern and the community and loyalty and so forth; whereas young people [today] find themselves in a much more atomized society and much more individualistic society, a society that evolves much more around buying and selling and promoting and advertising at every level than we did. Now, we both were affected by the market values of a capitalist society, but the degree to which market forces now permeate and saturate life is, I think, much more so than it was when we were coming along. Therefore, more and more young people find it very difficult to envi-

sion a life beyond the pervasive hedonism and narcissism and privatism of our moment.

Interview/
Humanities,
March-April:6.

Pete Wilson
Governor of California (R)

3

[On the late U.S. President Richard Nixon]: I will always remember him for . . . the quality that great fighters have. They call it heart. Heart is what let Richard Nixon climb back into the ring time and again when almost anyone else would have thrown in the towel. It was his heart that taught us the great lesson of Richard Nixon's life: to never, ever give up. To him, it was no disgrace to fight and be beaten. The only disgrace was to quit. And he never did.

At burial ceremony for Nixon,
Yorba Linda, Calif, April 27/
Los Angeles Times,
4-28:(A)15.

Judy Woodruff
Anchor, Cable News Network

4

What is most important is that you single out the area you want to contribute to . . . and you work just as hard as you can in that area . . . You may not get rich. For a while, you may barely make ends meet. But at the end of most days, you will feel fulfilled . . . and you won't be so burdened with worrying about how much more you wish you were earning.

At Duke University
commencement/
USA Today, 5-19:(A)13.

Patriarch Bartholomew

Spiritual leader
of world's Orthodox Christians

1

[On the desecration last year of his church's tombs in Turkey, where he is based]: Have we not suffered enough without being at all to blame, except that we are Greek by origin and Orthodox in faith, and because of this—being a minority, that is—we are regarded as a negotiable crowbar in the relations between neighboring and allied countries? Is it not enough that so few of us have remained here because of this last point?

The New York Times,
2-7:(A)7.

Gary L. Bauer

President,
Family Research Council

2

[Criticizing liberals who are against prayers in public schools]: The liberals are screaming about "religious differences," but there was not one ounce of that sensitivity when it came to some things like sex education . . . We are trying to right the balance [by allowing school prayer. For years] it has been a brutal battle to get even the most minor accommodation of our most deeply held views.

The New York Times,
11-19:8.

Anthony Bosco

Roman Catholic Bishop,
Greensburg, Pa.

3

People speak of the priesthood as a right, but that's a misperception. The church has to call you, and the mere fact of someone saying "I believe I am called" has to be ratified by the church.

Christianity Today,
7-18:53.

William Cleveland Bosher, Jr.

Superintendent of Public Instruction
of Virginia

4

[On permitting voluntary prayer in schools]: Even though I strongly believe schools should not be used to teach a dogma, I believe young people should be permitted under the realm of free speech to acknowledge who and what they are, including a faith. Being compelled to pray a prayer is offensive, but being compelled to hear a prayer from other students is an opportunity to understand their faith and culture.

Interview, Richmond, Va./
The Washington Post,
3-10:(Va.)3.

Joan Brown Campbell

General secretary,
National Council of Churches

5

[On a planned organization of religious people opposed to what is knows as the "religious right" or "religious conservatism"]: Our concern is that the radical right lays claim to the fact that they uniquely speak for people of faith in this country, in essence that "God is on our side." We feel we must come together as an interfaith group and say to this country [that] there is an alternate religious voice.

The New York Times,
7-14:(A)11.

Bill Clinton

President of the United States

6

Over several years, the leaders of the evangelical community [in the U.S.] have gotten more and more identified with the conservative wing of the Republican Party. Some of those same people have made abortion and homosexuality the litmus test of whether you're a true Christian. Certainly these are not the most-mentioned issues in the

WHAT THEY SAID IN 1994

(BILL CLINTON)

Bible, but they're the things that have become the litmus test, and if you're wrong on them, it's almost like saying you're a fraud, you can't really be a Christian.

Interview, Washington, D.C./
Christianity Today, 4-25:27.

1

Since I've been here [as President], I've spent a lot more time than I ever have in my life reading religious books, books by people I've come to know and respect. And it's made a huge difference, actually, in enduring what is the pretty significant isolation of this job.

To religion journalists,
Washington, D.C., Oct. 3/
The New York Times,
10-4:(A)11.

Hillary Rodham Clinton

Wife of President of the United States
Bill Clinton

2

[The media] don't know what to do with religion or faith. They don't know what to do with spirituality. And so they try to denigrate it or poke fun at it because they're scared of it. You have to feel sorry for people like that . . . Both on a personal level and a social one, there has been a turning away from some of the deeper values that are part of the human experience in our culture.

Interview, Washington, D.C./
Working Woman, June:82.

3

One of the differences I have with some of the denominations is the idea that one's Christianity is sealed at the moment that you accept Christ as your Savior and become in whatever ways are open to you a practicing Christian. I think that is a never-ending challenge. And I believe that every day I fall short of what I should be achieving.

Interview, Washington, D.C./
Newsweek, 10-31:25.

Charles Colson

Founder, Prison Fellowship ministry;
Former Special Counsel
to the President of the United States
(Richard M. Nixon)

4

[Saying Roman Catholics and Protestant evangelicals must work together]: We have differences. Nonetheless, on the ancient creeds and the core beliefs of Christianity we stand together. Christianity is besieged on all sides—by a militant nation of Islam, by pantheists who have invaded many areas of life, including the church through the New Age movement, and by the aggressive secularism of Western life. If we can't stand together, we have very little chance to make a common defense of our truth and our world view.

Interview,
New York, N.Y., March 29/
The New York Times,
3-30:(A)8.

Michael Dine

Physicist, University of California,
Santa Cruz

5

[On the relationship between science and religion]: I view religion as dealing with a moral dimension, and on that science is silent.

Newsweek, 11-28:59.

Joycelyn Elders

Surgeon General of the United States

6

I am very eager for churches to go out and really help dysfunctional families get the services they need for people to survive. How can you moralize about the issue when children are hungry, cold and abused? People should not just sit around and talk about their religion. They should live the life of a Christian. Judaism teaches the same thing. So does Islam.

Before National Family Planning
and Reproductive Health Association,
Washington, D.C., Feb. 25/
The New York Times, 2-26:7.

Willis Elliott
Theologian,
United Church of Christ

1

The feminization of Christianity represents the greatest upheaval in the church since the Reformation.

Newsweek, 11-28:62.

Matthew Freeman
Research director,
People for the American Way

2

[On the possibility of the new Republican-controlled Congress passing legislation allowing prayer in public schools]: Who is going to decide whether something is sufficiently non-sectarian or non-proselytizing? Then there is the whole question of the impact of watered-down prayers. Prayers are meaningful. Prayers are specific. This whole question goes to how people go about worshiping their gods.

The New York Times,
11-19:8.

Ira Glasser
Executive director,
American Civil Liberties Union

3

[Criticizing House Speaker-to-be Newt Gingrich's desire to allow prayers in public schools]: Voluntary prayer is an Orwellian phrase. What Gingrich wants is government-sponsored prayer.

The New York Times,
11-19:8.

Barry M. Goldwater
Former United States Senator,
R-Arizona

4

If they [the Christian right] succeed in establishing a religion as a basic Republican Party te-

net, that could do us [Republicans] in . . . Thomas Jefferson rode his horse around the 13 Colonies to try to keep us from having a national religion. Mixing religion with politics doesn't work.

Interview, Phoenix, Ariz./
U.S. News & World Report,
12-26:35,38.

Billy Graham
Evangelist

5

America is not a Christian country. It's a secular country in which many Christians dwell. We are made up of all the religions of the world. We have thousands of mosques in America. We are a pluralistic society, so I could not say that Christianity has become too Americanized. If it became Americanized, I would fear for the future of Christianity.

News conference,
Tokyo, Japan/
Christianity Today,
2-7:47.

6

I used to say take a newspaper in one hand and a Bible in the other and go preach the gospel. Today I'd say take a television set and a radio— you have to be relevant.

Interview,
Wheaton (Ill.) College/
Christianity Today,
6-20:55.

7

[On being onstage during his evangelical appearances]: I'm always afraid. Afraid that I may give the wrong word to someone and that it might affect their eternal destiny. I feel every time I go to that platform that I'm unworthy to be there. I often wish that the platform would just open up and let me drop through.

Interview,
North Carolina/
Life, November:116.

Philip Hefner
Theologian;
Director, Chicago Center for
Religion and Science

1

[On the relationship between science and religion]: I see a turnaround in which many scientists are [now] saying we can integrate science into an existing religion, a personal philosophy of life, or New Age beliefs.

Newsweek, 11-28:56.

Howard W. Hunter
President, Church of Jesus Christ
of Latter-Day Saints (Mormons)

2

[On disagreements within the Mormon Church on social and structural issues]: I pray that we might treat each other with more kindness, more courtesy, more humility and patience and forgiveness. To those who have transgressed or been offended, we say, "Come back." To those who are hurt and struggling and afraid, we say, "Let us stand with you and dry your tears."

News conference,
Salt Lake City, Utah, June 6/
The New York Times,
6-7:(A)12.

William H. Keeler
Roman Catholic Archbishop
of Baltimore, Md.;
President, National Conference
of Catholic Bishops

3

We in the church stand with the unborn and the undocumented, the poor and the vulnerable, the hungry and the homeless, in defense of human rights and human life. Our advocacy does not fit ideological or partisan categories, for our witness is not politically correct, but unfailingly consistent.

Before National Conference
of Catholic Bishops,
Washington, D.C., Nov. 14/
The New York Times,
11-15:(A)10.

Frances Kissling
President, Catholics for a Free Choice

4

[Criticizing the Catholic Church for not putting women in more responsible positions in the church's operations]: What you have is a group of well-meaning men who believe in their own goodness and see themselves as representatives of a church which has a drive toward justice and they have an automatic inclination to justice. We're saying they're flawed human beings with the same shortcomings and weaknesses other employers have.

The New York Times,
11-17:(A)10.

Beverly LaHaye
President, Concerned Women
for America

5

[On the possibility of the new Republican-controlled Congress passing legislation allowing prayer in public schools]: I don't know what magician is going to write this language. But it's going to be interesting to see. We have a huge problem on our hands here. Prayer is not supposed to divide people but to bring them together. So if prayer is going to be the big battleground, maybe we should sit back and take a long look at it.

The New York Times,
11-19:8.

Roy Larson
Member of the staff,
Center for Religion
and the News Media,
Northwestern University

6

Living in a secular world is like living in an astrodome with a roof over the top. The temperature is always 70 degrees and the grass is always green. Even in a place that holds 70,000 people, you feel claustrophobic. You need to breathe some fresh air.

Newsweek, 11-28:53.

Peter Mason
Anglican Bishop of Kingston,
Ontario, Canada

1

We as a church have become increasingly is-sue-driven, have lost our sense of worship and Christian community, and have found ourselves drained of energy to maintain our ongoing church life.

At "Essentials '94" conference,
Montreal, Canada, June/
Christianity Today, 8-15:49.

Robin Munro
Hong Kong director,
Asia Watch

2

[On China's crackdown on foreigners' reli-gious proselytizing in that country]: I think what these detentions and expulsions show is that the regulations issued by the [Chinese] authorities last month do indeed signal an increased crackdown on unofficial church movements in China . . . This shows the depth of the [Chinese] authorities' fear and anxiety about the rapidly developing unoffi-cial Christian movement across China, which they see as a threat to the society and to the [Chinese Communist] Party.

Los Angeles Times,
2-17:(A)13.

David Novak
Professor of Judaic studies,
University of Virginia

3

[On U.S. President Clinton's mentioning of his religious faith during talks and speeches]: It's important, because what Clinton has done . . . is he's insisted that all religious rhetoric doesn't lead to a right-wing position . . . It means a religious point of view is not the province of people on the right and that a secular point of view isn't the prov-ince of people on the left.

The Washington Post, 3-10:(A)30.

Michael Novak
Resident scholar,
American Enterprise Institute

4

The last respectable bigotry in the United States is against evangelicals and [religious] fun-damentalists. It seems perfectly acceptable to ut-ter insulting language about them amongst people who would be ashamed of uttering the same sort of language about anybody else. The country will get over that; usually, once you begin to point out a form of bigotry, some of the more fair-minded people begin noticing it, too, and start to correct it. This one will be harder to correct, but the cor-rection will come.

Interview/
Christianity Today, 10-24:31.

Ronald L. Numbers
Professor of history
of science and medicine,
University of Wisconsin, Madison;
Authority on religion

5

[There is a] reduced cultural authority of evangelicals in American society. The evangelicals of the 1920s saw themselves slipping somewhat but still felt powerful enough to prevent what they regarded as an anti-religious notion creeping into the public schools. In recent years, there have been no illusions among evangelicals that they could monopolize the curriculum. And so now they would be very happy to settle for equal time in the public schools. I think this also reflects a phenom-enon that we've seen occasionally in American history. When a group loses the moral authority to convince the public to behave or think a certain way, there is a tendency to go to the courts. We saw that with Prohibition earlier in the century, and we see that now. If you can't convince Ameri-cans that they should take creationism seriously, then you go to the state legislatures and mandate that high-school students should learn creationism whenever they learn evolutionism.

Interview/
American Heritage,
November:113.

Ralph Reed, Jr.
President, Christian Coalition

1

[Saying school-prayer is not the most important issue for his organization when the new U.S. Congress convenes next January]: I want to make it perfectly clear that this is not our top priority. I, for one, don't think we'll turn the country around by having public acts of piety. Our priorities are tax relief and welfare reform.

The New York Times,
11-19:1.

Jay Alan Sekulow
Chief counsel,
American Center for Law and Justice

2

[Supporting a Constitutional amendment that would allow prayers in public schools]: We talk a lot about tolerance in America. What about being able to tolerate 30 seconds of a prayer you don't agree with?

The New York Times,
11-19:8.

Desmond M. Tutu
South African Anglican Archbishop;
Winner, 1984 Nobel Peace Prize

3

We tend to turn the Christian religion into a religion of virtues, but it is a religion of grace. You become a good person because you are loved. You are not loved because you are good.

Interview, New York, N.Y./
The Christian Science Monitor,
10-26:13.

Herbert D. Valentine
Presbyterian minister;
Chairman, Interfaith Alliance

4

[Criticizing conservative religious extremists]: Religious extremism is being used as a weapon to attack politicians, to censor classroom textbooks, to cut back school breakfast programs, to promote discrimination and to mislead voters. The message of the radical right is that there is only one way to think and live to be a good Christian.

July 14/
Los Angeles Times,
7-15:(A)25.

Rembert Weakland
Roman Catholic Archbishop
of Milwaukee, Wis.

5

It is becoming clearer and clearer that committed Catholics are very committed, very involved [in the church]. And then there are the others. They go to Mass irregularly and they say they are Catholics on a census, but that is about it.

Interview/
The New York Times,
6-1:(A)14.

Peggy Wehmeyer
Religion correspondent,
ABC News

6

Religion is probably one of the most significant forces in our society. It shapes, molds and makes us who we are as a culture. It motivates people at the deepest level of their being to do the things they do and make the decisions they make. To ignore the religious dimension of culture and society is to leave a huge hole in the picture. ABC [News] has recognized this. They're saying, "We've got to find a way to grapple with this dimension of life, even if it is personal, even if it is sometimes abstract and hard for journalists to visualize. We can no longer ignore it." Look at Bosnia, look at Northern Ireland. How can you ignore religion in those situations?

Interview/
Christianity Today,
8-15:16.

Patricia Wittberg
Church sociologist,
Indiana University

1

[On the sharp decrease in the number of Roman Catholic nuns in the U.S., as well as the decrease in younger nuns]: My generation—I'm a baby-boomer—is disproportionately under-represented, nuns between 35 and 50 years old. That's one generation next to missing. The next generation, the baby-busters, is missing. That's two whole generations that are not there.

Los Angeles Times,
2-21:(A)22.

Giancarlo Zizola
Writer specializing
in coverage of the Vatican

2

[On Pope John Paul II's current health]: For many years, papal illnesses were taboo. And there still exists one of the most constant beliefs of the Vatican, according to which the Pope enjoys the best possible health until the moment he dies.

The New York Times,
9-24:5.

Science and Technology

Mark Albrecht
Former Executive Secretary,
National Space Council
of the United States

1

Every commission that looks at NASA comes to the conclusion [that] the core problem is the high cost of the [space] shuttle. We have billions to spend on the space station, yet do nothing about launch costs. It's a national disgrace.
Newsweek, 4-11:31.

Edwin "Buzz" Aldrin
Former American astronaut

2

While the moon circled the Earth 50 times from 1968 to 1972, a dozen Americans had the good fortune to briefly visit its dusty surface. We will one day walk on Mars in the spirit of wonder that sets our species apart.
USA Today, 7-15:(A)15.

Neil A. Armstrong
Former American astronaut;
First man to walk on moon in 1969

3

During the Space Age, we have increased the knowledge of our universe a thousandfold. [But] we leave you much that is undone. There are great ideas undiscovered, breakthroughs available to those who can remove one of truth's protective layers. There are places to go beyond belief.
At White House ceremony
commemorating 25th anniversary
of first moon landing,
Washington, D.C., July 20/
Los Angeles Times, 7-21:(A)15.

4

[On why he doesn't talk very much in public about his walk on the moon in 1969]: Pilots take no special joy in walking. Pilots like flying.
Newsweek, 8-1:17.

Barry Diller
Chairman, QVC, Inc.

5

The most relevant example to me of the rush to judgment [in new technologies] involves those dreaded words: the information superhighway; the 500-channel universe, the dawn of a new era, two trillion words juiced up to truck up all the possibilities, and then—thud. It's as if it was going to take place in an hour and a half.
At American Magazine Conference,
Laguna Niguel, Calif.,
Oct. 24/
The New York Times,
10-25:(C)18.

Charles M. Duke, Jr.
Former American astronaut

6

[On his being on the moon during the Apollo 16 mission in 1972]: We could see all the way across the valley to the horizon, and it was breathtaking. I looked out on this valley that was unspoiled, pristine, quiet, immense, and I felt a part of it. It was majestic and we were the only two people who had ever seen it. [At the time,] I didn't rub my chin and ponder the origins of man. It was yahoo, here we are!
Interview/
The New York Times,
7-20:(A)10.

Kevin Elliot
Project leader,
New Media Research Laboratory,
Banff Center for the Arts (Canada)

7

Everybody talks about an "information highway," but nobody has the faintest idea what's going to be on it. It has to get easier to make the content, or it won't get done.
World Press Review,
July:43.

Bill Gates
Chairman, Microsoft Corporation

1

There are certainly a lot of [technology] visionaries . . . Just a ton of people are speculating about the future. That's pretty easy as long as you set a time frame out far enough. Although I get visibility, there are lots of smart people doing this stuff. I'm writing a book about the "information highway," and publishers told me there are 20 other people writing books about it. I put my money where my mouth is because I really do have to think time-frame. Even if I'm totally right about this highway being a great thing and it doesn't happen, say, for 10 years, then I'm spending way too much [money] at an early stage. But if it does happen, say, within five years, then the urgency we're showing is well-placed.

Interview/
USA Today,
7-18:(B)3.

John Glenn
United States Senator, D-Ohio;
Former astronaut

2

We should all feel a sense of history to have been a part of the first generation to step away from the Earth [via the space program]. The space station is the next step we need to take.

USA Today,
7-15:(A)15.

Daniel S. Goldin
Administrator,
National Aeronautics
and Space Administration
of the United States

3

Humanity is going to go to space. Learning to live and work in space is a necessary step, and the [proposed] space station will help us learn these things.

Newsweek, 4-11:31.

Mark Green
Public Advocate
of New York, N.Y.

4

Technology is a powerful centrifugal force, but it is spinning us away from each other. The more people have PCs at home and the more there's cable [TV] so you can watch one of your 100 stations—unlike 20 years ago, when 90 percent of Americans watched just three stations—the more it divides us [as a community].

Interview,
New York, N.Y./
Lear's, March:16.

Phillip D. Hammer
Physicist, Ames Research Center,
National Aeronautics and
Space Administration
of the United States

5

As science broadens, there are just more and more questions we discover we need to ask. The effort is worth all the trouble and time. It contributes to basic understanding. Of everything.

Interview,
Nashville, Tenn./
The Washington Post,
1-29:(G)9.

Stephen Hawking
British mathematician
and astrophysicist

6

Computer "viruses" should count as life . . . It says something about human nature that the only form of life we have created so far is purely destructive. We've created life in our own image.

At Macworld Expo,
Boston, Mass., Aug. 2/
USA Today,
8-3:(A)1.

Torrence Johnson
Project scientist for
the Galileo spacecraft,
Jet Propulsion Laboratory,
Pasadena, Calif.

1

[On the chances of the Earth being hit by a large comet, such as is about to happen to Jupiter]: Just about one in 10-50 million years. But you've got to remember that for every one of those big ones out there, there are thousands of small [comets]. In fact, in 1908, a relatively small body, much smaller than the thing that's going to hit Jupiter, managed to enter the Earth's atmosphere and blew up over Siberia. The effects of that looked very much like the explosion of a hydrogen bomb. If it had occurred over Moscow, I assure you, you would have read about it in your history books.

Interview/
USA Today,
7-14:(A)13.

Michio Kaku
Physicist, City University
of New York

2

Most people think of physicists as people who wear white smocks and work with tuning forks or study friction. But in fact, we make our living discovering things that blow people's minds.

U.S. News & World Report,
5-9:59.

Edward Kolb
Physicist,
Fermi National
Accelerator Laboratory

3

The easiest thing in science is to find what you are looking for.

Newsweek,
11-28:56.

Leon Lederman
Nobel Prize-winning physicist

4

[To many people,] science is forbidding, makes the eyes glaze over. Intellectuals who excel in humanities tend to feel frustrated that they're incapable of following scientific revolutions, so they try to cover it up by calling science value-free: It's experimental, it's dehumanizing, it's cold, it has no social values. That's nonsense, of course. Science has beauty and symmetry and elegance and deep cultural significance.

Interview/
Modern Maturity,
June:61.

Peggy Noonan
Author; Former speechwriter
for former President
of the United States Ronald Reagan

5

This new technology is riding us; we are not riding it. Because we *can* be in touch instantly, we feel that we *must* be in touch instantly. I know people who think they must fax me directions to a meeting that is three weeks away!

The New York Times,
4-25:(B)4.

Kevin O'Leary
President,
SoftKey International, Inc.

6

[Saying computer software companies will need to merge in order to survive]: If you look back at any industry, such as the cereal business or the automotive business in the '30s, they all ultimately consolidated down to five to 10 companies, and I believe in the next decade you will have only 10 software companies . . . In the last two years, we've moved from an industry that sells primarily to businesses, to an industry that's going through a violent change to becoming a commodity. Software is becoming no different than a

(KEVIN O'LEARY)

videotape or a record album or a paperback book, and not all of us are ready for that change . . . In the overall industry, you're either consolidating, you're being consolidated, or you're evaporating. There's no steady state of being small. [Generally speaking,] everybody under $50-million in sales is talking to somebody.

Interview,
Cambridge, Mass./
The Christian Science Monitor,
6-28:9.

Fredric Paul
Features editor,
"Electronic Entertainment"
magazine

1

In five years, there won't be much of a difference between regular audio CDs and multimedia interactive experiences. It will be all points on a continuum, different levels of the same thing. You can take it on whatever level you want. You can sit and listen and watch or you can go deeper . . . It's whatever you're in the mood for.

The Christian Science Monitor,
3-14:15.

Joseph G. Perpich
Vice president for grants
and special programs,
Howard Hughes
Medical Institute

2

[On his organization's $86-million grant to a number of universities for their science programs]: We're seeing a profound change in the way many college students learn science. Literally hundreds of colleges and universities are quietly developing new approaches that attract more students to science while maintaining vigor and quality.

The New York Times,
10-4:(A)8.

Emiel Petrone
Vice president of marketing,
Philips Consumer Electronics

3

[On the unexpectedly slow acceptance of recent consumer electronic products and services]: To convey to people what the notion of "interactivity" is is very difficult. It's not the kind of product category where you wake up and say, "Hey, it's 9 o'clock and I haven't interacted yet." To establish a new product category in consumer electronics is more than one or two [product] shows. We haven't even scratched the surface.

Los Angeles Times,
1-6:(D)2.

Robert B. Reich
Secretary of Labor
of the United States

4

Technological changes have diminished the role of labor, especially unskilled labor, in the modern factory. The most striking [technological] change in the workplace has been the brash arrival of the computer. In 1984, about 25 percent of American workers used computers on the job. Last year, almost 47 percent did. Contrary to the myth that computer-literate youngsters are running circles around their technophobic elders, 50 percent of workers between the ages of 40 and 54 use computers at work.

Interview/
USA Today, 9-2:(B)3.

Louis Rossetto
Co-founder, "Wired" magazine

5

The changes [in communications technology] going on in the world now are literally a revolution in progress, a revolution that makes political revolution seem like a game. It will revolutionize how people work, how they communicate, and how they entertain themselves, and it is the biggest engine for change in our world today. We're

(LOUIS ROSSETTO)

looking at the end of a 20- or 30- or 40-year process, from the invention of tubes to transistors to
fiber-optic and cable to the development of cable
networks, until we've reached critical mass today.

Interview,
San Francisco, Calif./
The Atlantic Monthly,
September:62.

Bruce Ryon
Analyst, Dataquest, Inc.

1

[On the unexpectedly slow public acceptance
of recent consumer electronic products and ser-
vices]: For a lot of this stuff, the expectation out-
stripped the reality. I think there was an assumption that the technology could do what they [the
developers and manufacturers] wanted it to—and
the fact is, it's really very complicated.

Los Angeles Times,
1-6:(D)2.

Michael Stricklin
Professor of communications,
University of Nebraska

2

[Saying those with access to computers and
technology will be better off in the high-tech world
of the future]: Those who are on the peaks have
access. The ones in the valley don't. The poor will
always be with us, and that is true with the information highway.

Los Angeles Times,
1-11:(A)18.

Edward M. Szynaka
Director, Pasadena (Calif.)
Public Library

3

Twenty years ago, it was much easier to describe libraries. But nowadays we give out bits of

information that change people's lives, as opposed
to only handing out great books to read. In Alvin
Toffler's *Future Shock*, he describes how we'll all
have to become accustomed to the "dynamic"
quality of technology. As we've all grown more
dependent upon information, it also has turned into
a utility much like water and electricity. In the future, the library will be a resource and a center for
the "information poor." The people who succeed
will know how to obtain, use and utilize this information.

Interview/
Los Angeles Times,
7-25:(B)5.

Don Valentine
Managing partner,
Sequoia Capital

4

[On the predicted "information highway"]: I
don't understand the hullabaloo. Can you imagine a more frivolous way to spend billions, hooking up people's homes so that kids can compete
playing Marioworld? The information highway is
a buzzword, created by public-relations people and
folks at the White House who want to be seen as
technology visionaries. To me, it doesn't mean
anything . . . [The telephone companies] want to
grow. They want to get into unregulated industries, including entertainment. Movies over the
phone lines. Mega-billion-dollar mergers. They've
been seduced by Hollywood. Look at other industries that were massively deregulated, where companies started screwing around in businesses they
didn't understand and had no experience in. The
airlines. The savings and loans. Now you have
wreckage everywhere. Why will it be any different with the phone companies [and the information highway]? Ten years from now, there is going to be a lot of embarrassment over who wrecked
the telephone companies.

Interview/
Newsweek,
4-11:53,54.

Watts Wacker
Spokesman, Yankelovich Partners,
public-opinion analysts

1

Currently, about 10 percent of households engage in electronic [home] shopping. We predict that by 1996, 40 percent of households will engage in electronic shopping . . . Americans are losing their technophobia. More and more of them view technology as a tool to make life easier.

Los Angeles Times,
1-18:(D)3.

Albert Wheelon
Former chief executive officer,
Hughes Aircraft Corporation;
Former member,
1993 Presidential
Space Station Commission

2

[On the U.S. space-station program]: The science value is wildly exaggerated . . . It's a jobs program plain and simple.

Newsweek,
4-11:30.

Sports

Henry Aaron
Former baseball player,
Atlanta "Braves"

1

[On his 1974 surpassing of Babe Ruth's all-time home-run record]: April 8, 1974, really led up to turning me off on baseball. It really made me see for the first time a clear picture of what this country is about. My kids had to live like they were in prison because of kidnap threats, and I had to live like a pig in a slaughter camp. I had to duck. I had to go out the back door of the ballparks. I had to have a police escort with me all the time. I was getting threatening letters every single day. All of these things have put a bad taste in my mouth and it won't go away. They carved a piece of my heart away.

Interview, Atlanta, Ga./
The New York Times,
2-5:33.

2

[On a possible baseball strike]: This game is for the fans, not for the owners or the players. The fans came out to see the Babe [Ruth] and they came to see me and they come to see Ken Griffey, Jr. [The fans are] the ones to be hurt by a strike, along with the groundskeepers, the ticket-takers, the peanut vendors. The people . . . Something's going on I don't know about if a strike can really hurt those multimillionaire owners or players who make $45,000 every two weeks.

Interview, Atlanta, Ga./
The New York Times,
8-5:(B)16.

Albert Applin
Vice chancellor,
United States
Sports Academy

3

Sports mirror society. In our achievement-oriented society there is the urge to be Number 1. And competitive sports mirror this, including the violence that can result from that urge. Until society resolves its underlying problems, sports will reflect all of society's problems . . . There is trickle-down in sports. The highest level of pro sports sets the example for all the other levels. When former heavyweight fighter Mike Tyson talks about driving a guy's nose into his brain, that type of mentality is sure to trickle down to the next level. It happens in all sports. Fighting is now commonplace in baseball, and it wasn't 20 years ago. The epitome of violence today is hockey . . . The irony is that sports were introduced in the late 1800s to help violent juvenile delinquents because they had been alienated by the industrial revolution. Now it seems sports pushes some young people toward violence.

The Christian Science Monitor,
1-6:2.

Al Arbour
Former hockey coach,
New York "Islanders"

4

Coaching is aggravation. You give the players aggravation and they give it back.

Los Angeles Times,
6-28:(C)2.

Charles Barkley
Basketball player,
Phoenix "Suns"

5

I've never been a big fan of [NBA] expansion. It just makes people pay to see bad teams. Fans already get screwed enough . . . The league isn't that good anymore. Top to bottom, the talent isn't there. There are five good teams. There are three or four middle-of-the-road teams. The rest are real bad. The league has just deteriorated. We've had some bad general managers drafting bad players.

The Washington Post,
5-2:(C)8.

Bobby Brown
President,
American (baseball) League

1

[On the new three-division system in the major leagues, which has produced a situation in which some teams with poor records are very much in contention]: You look at the four teams in the [American League's] West [division]. The records look pretty punk, but at the same time the race is getting pretty close. The fans in those four cities look at their teams and say they're not doing well, but at least they have a shot. Maybe that's what the people want.

June 27/
The New York Times,
6-28:(B)12.

John Chaney
Basketball coach,
Temple University

2

Take what they're doing in the name of gender equity. They're cutting back on scholarships in men's football, basketball and track, and adding them in women's sports like badminton, crew and synchronized swimming. Everybody knows that sports are cultural, and that the effect of that is to take opportunity away from black men and give it to white women. Where's the justice in that? If we had proper minority representation in the NCAA, you wouldn't see that sort of thing. They talk about raising academic standards [for athletes], but why should the elite schools make the rules for places like Temple? And why should black people have to apologize for wanting to develop the talents we have? If you have success in one area—like basketball—you have something you can build on and, maybe, transfer to other areas. Transfer—that's the key. You may start a trip hoping to get to New York, but even if you only make it to Newark it doesn't mean the trip is wasted. It's the work you do along the way that counts.

Interview, Philadelphia, Pa./
The Wall Street Journal, 2-7:(A)10.

Robert Cialdini
Sports psychologist,
Arizona State University

3

The successes and failures of sports teams are felt as personal successes and failures by their fans.

Newsweek, 1-17:47.

Fred Claire
General manager,
Los Angeles "Dodgers"
baseball team

4

[On the current major-league baseball players' strike, which may be long enough to put an end to the season]: In 25 years with the *Dodgers*, I have never seen anything like this. This thing has thrown everybody off stride. None of it makes any sense to me. Clearly there are no winners in this situation and I'm not sure there ever will be. There's no reason to go into specifics, because there's more than enough blame to go around. All I can say for certain is, there's a lot of ground to make up, a lot of damage to recover from. Both players and management have a bigger job to do than just end this strike eventually. There's the rebuilding of the game itself to think about. A great deal of damage has been done to the game of baseball, and somehow people's faith has to be restored.

Interview,
Albuquerque, N.M., Sept. 13/
Los Angeles Times,
9-14:(C)8.

Bill Clinton
President of the United States

5

[Calling into question baseball's antitrust exemption in light of the current players' strike against team owners which has prompted an early end to this year's baseball season]: [Baseball's antitrust exemption should be re-examined] if this has just turned into another business in America . . . We have [prematurely] ended what could have

(BILL CLINTON)

been the best baseball season in 50 years . . . I don't see how we can avoid a serious examination of it.

To reporters,
Washington, D.C.,
Sept. 14/
Los Angeles Times,
9-15:(C)6.

Jerry Coleman
Former baseball player

1

Pitchers have become sort of sectionalized. There are starters, set-up men, middle relievers, long relievers, closers. When I was playing [in the 1940s and '50s], we'd say, "Let's take this [pitcher] apart in the sixth, in the third at-bat." Now you never get the chance, because he's gone by your third at-bat. The bullpen has become so important. A team almost *has* to have a closer . . . The art of pitching has extended the game. I think basically pitching is not as good as it was; it's not that the hitting has gotten so much better. I think there are a lot of inexperienced, not-very-cagey pitchers out there, and the balls are flying out all over the place.

Interview/
Newsweek,
8-22:55.

Len Coleman
President,
National (baseball) League

2

We have to create a greater focus on the game for the fans so they can enjoy the game and not have to hear as much rhetoric about the business aspects of baseball. We have to understand that the business of our game *is* the fans.

Ebony, June:117.

Ben Crenshaw
Golfer

3

[On the possibility of golfers being accosted or attacked by fans, in light of recent attacks on athletes in other sports]: When you hear something like this, you think about the danger out here [on golf courses], but then you have to go about your business. Let's face it; we're probably the most approachable professional athletes. Every day, we walk through the crowds, brush up against them. You can't worry about it. You just have to put it out of your mind.

Jan. 6/USA Today,
1-7:(C)2.

Walter Cronkite
Former anchor, CBS News

4

[On the forthcoming 25th anniversary of the first manned landing on the moon]: We learned that man can damn well do anything he sets his mind to do. And the challenge was to keep this lesson in front of us. If we could get to the moon, we should be able to solve *any* problem on Earth. That's what the moon shot said to us.

Los Angeles Times,
6-28:(E)1.

Joseph N. Crowley
President, National Collegiate
Athletic Association

5

Today, intercollegiate athletics has become the arena in which the issues of fairness, equity and opportunity are being examined. All of us involved in intercollegiate athletics—executive officers, other administrators, the teachers in the classroom and the teachers on the court—should welcome this challenge. Athletics and the academy have often been the leaders in social progress. We can and must be again.

San Antonio, Texas, Jan. 11/
The New York Times, 1-12:(B)9.

Mike Dunleavy
Basketball coach,
Milwaukee "Bucks"

1

The way the money [player salary] structure has changed [in the NBA] within the last couple of years has changed things a great deal, as far as players coming into this league making the kind of money they do and knowing their future is secure, instead of establishing themselves like the players of old. [In the old days,] you carried bags, and you carried the 24-second clock. Now it's, "If I don't like it, I'm going to take my ball and go home."

Los Angeles Times,
5-14:(C)6.

Harry Edwards
Sociologist

2

[On teams that lose in football's Super Bowl]: You get to the Super Bowl—you've struggled up this mountain, everything is on the line—then all of a sudden, you find it slipping away from you. It's like an illness and you literally feel your life running out of the soles of your shoes . . . If you get into a situation where you have a recurrent history of losing [in the Super Bowl] . . . it's like *Night of the Living Dead* . . . Even though you're the second most successful team in the NFL, you have died.

Broadcast interview/"75 Seasons:
The Story of the National
Football League,"
Turner Network Television, 9-13.

Donald Fehr
Executive director,
Major League (baseball)
Players Association

3

[On the possibility of a players' strike during this season]: It's extremely difficult to visualize the players playing out the season with no agreement in circumstances in which the [team] own-

ers could just impose the salary cap or whatever else they wanted to do off-season and tell the players they could go on strike in November if they wanted to . . . We have never seen a cap which would do anything but lower salaries. It would be impossible for me to envision owners proposing a cap that would increase player salaries. The one group that has the most experience with it, the basketball players, can't wait to get rid of the cap. They feel it has lined the owners' pockets at the expense of their [the players'] fair market value.

News conference,
Chicago, Ill., June 16/
The New York Times,
6-17:(B)15.

4

[On the possibility of a players' strike this season]: No one wants this. No one wants the fans to sit through another work stoppage, but any fan who has followed the last 18 months understands that this is not a fight of the players' choosing. I have never seen a situation in which a day after the [team] owners finally make their proposal, their chief negotiator is predicting a strike. I mean, there's a pattern to it, and I think it's obvious that some management people still believe they can break the union and hope to provoke a strike. But the players won't be provoked until there's no other option.

News conference, July 11/
Los Angeles Times,
7-12:(C)5.

5

[On the premature ending of this year's baseball season due to a players' strike]: History isn't written by contemporaries. And if it is, it usually isn't very good. It seems to me I can predict pretty well what the scholars will say 50 to 75 years from now about labor relations in baseball the last 20 years. What they'll say is, you had a cartel [the team owners] that was exempt from antitrust laws and was used to doing whatever it wanted to whomever it wanted under whatever conditions it wanted. You also had a [players'] union that didn't

(DONALD FEHR)

want to let them do that. But as a result of the [owners'] special privileges, they provoked eight work stoppages. I expect historians will say somebody should have understood that the antitrust laws are there for a reason.

Sept. 14/
Los Angeles Times,
9-15:(A)20.

Mary Joe Fernandez
Tennis player

1

[On what makes a top tennis player]: I think it's mostly mental. They know they should be there, at the top, and everybody at that level pretty much plays well all the time. I'm working on that aspect of my game—the visualization or mental aspect. Because in the end, getting there is really about belief, about just having a little more faith in yourself.

Interview, Miami, Fla./
"Interview" magazine,
June:87.

Bill Fitch
Former basketball coach

2

[On his experience in rebuilding mediocre basketball teams]: I'm always interested in a challenge . . . That's how I've made my living [rebuilding teams]. It's hard work. You've got to have a plan and you've got to follow it. If they do that, nothing's impossible. I've seen too many teams rise from the ashes.

Los Angeles Times,
7-28:(C)7.

Raymond Floyd
Golfer

3

[Saying he gets into a personal "zone" when he is on the course]: I feel like I'm going half speed.

I'm not hitting the ground very hard when I walk. I'm aware there are people around but I don't see them. I might talk to the player I'm walking with, but I don't know it. I'm alone and at ease.

Los Angeles Times,
5-14:(C)2.

Mike Gartner
President, National Hockey League
Players Association

4

[On the labor strife between team owners and players in the NHL]: I think there wouldn't be anything worse to alienate the fans than not having hockey at all. If you see baseball and what's happened in baseball [this year's players' strike that led to an early end to the season], the national pastime of the United States, [fans] turned it off in a heartbeat. What do you think is going to happen to hockey?

Los Angeles Times,
9-30:(C)7.

Bill Giles
Owner, Philadelphia "Phillies"
baseball team

5

[On the new three-division realignment of baseball's major leagues]: Only a couple of teams in the American League don't [at this date] have some glimmer of hope and, in the National League, there are about eight or 10 teams with still a decent chance [to win their divisions]. Basically, fans hope their team can get into the World Series. The whole purpose of realignment was to give more teams a chance.

USA Today, 7-1:(C)2.

Sid Gillman
Former football coach

6

You have today [in football] seven quarterbacks who can do it all: Montana, Marino, Young, Moon, Aikman, Elway and Kelly. I mean guys who

(SID GILLMAN)

have both a great brain and a great arm. Everything an offensive coach does is aimed at giving his team an advantage—say, single coverage on a wide receiver downfield—but if the quarterback can't recognize and seize it, it's down the drain. Given the choice between an arm and a brain, I'll take the brain. There were guys who threw the ball better than John Hadl, my quarterback with the [San Diego] *Chargers*, but not many who could out-think him.

Interview/
The Wall Street Journal,
9-30:(A)12.

David Halberstam
Pulitzer Prize-winning
author and journalist

1

When I was a [baseball fan as a] boy, I brought a complete innocence to the game. These [players] were the first heroic figures of my life, the first men whom I had read about and heard about over the radio and then beheld with my own eyes. Not surprisingly, I saw them and their deeds in mythic terms ... Now I am older and more skeptical and, because I have written two books on baseball, I have a far better sense of the players themselves; that their skills, supreme in this one small area of human endeavor, are often accompanied by fears and anxieties in other aspects of life, which frequently makes them surprisingly vulnerable. It does not so much shrink them as make them more mortal, which is probably a healthier thing. It's not so much that Joe DiMaggio has gone away, and that America is thereby diminished; it is more that in the end he was a great centerfielder and a great hitter, which is at once far more than enough, and yet a great deal less than the myth.

Interview/
Newsweek,
8-22:56.

Orrin G. Hatch
United States Senator, R-Utah

2

[Saying he is in favor of repealing baseball's antitrust exemption because of the current contract dispute between team owners and players]: I am fast becoming convinced that the majority of the owners are trying to break the Players Association. I do not want to become involved in collective-bargaining negotiations, but I'm starting to believe, like many people, that these negotiations are not being done in good faith.

Interview, Dec. 23/
The New York Times,
12-24:1.

Orel Hershiser
Baseball pitcher,
Los Angeles "Dodgers"

3

[On the current major-league baseball players' strike, which may be long enough to put an end to the season]: This is all uncharted waters, but history shows the players have stayed together better than almost any other union. There's such a kinship and unity among players because of career length, of what it took to get here ... and all the different things that bring baseball players together. I don't think people would cross the line.

Sept. 13/
Los Angeles Times,
9-14:(C)8.

Edward Hirt
Social psychologist,
University of Indiana

4

Women athletes are an interesting mix of perceptions. Do you view them as *athletes*, in the same context as males? Or do you view them as *women*, in terms of their femininity? That doesn't happen with men.

Newsweek,
1-17:46.

Roy Hodgson
Coach of Swiss soccer team
at 1994 World Cup matches

1

[Saying victories in sports tend to make players and fans look for greater victories]: There's an old Swedish saying, that no tree grows to heaven. But that's not true in the sports worlds. In the sporting world, trees are expected to grow to heaven.
June 22/
Los Angeles Times,
6-23:(C)9.

Walt Hriniak
Hitting coach, Chicago "White Sox"
baseball team

2

Good hitters are made, not born. God-given talent isn't enough. Show me a good hitter and I'll show you a guy who works hard at his hitting.
Interview,
Chicago, Ill./
The Wall Street Journal,
5-27:(A)6.

Kelly Hrudey
Hockey player,
Los Angeles "Kings"

3

[On the labor strife between owners and players in the NHL]: Not only are we employees and players, we're fans. Ask any player if he watches games and he'll tell you, "Tons of them." That's what's upsetting [about the current player-owner problems]. I truly believe some of the people who make the decisions aren't fans. Just executives trying to make money . . . I don't think people are fooled by rich people owning big businesses [hockey teams], saying they're losing money. With the economy and the climate of the world we live in, [people] are more business-wise now.
Interview/
Los Angeles Times,
9-30:(C)7.

Michael Jordan
Baseball player,
Chicago "White Sox";
Former basketball player,
Chicago "Bulls"

4

[On playing baseball compared with basketball]: I've been in situations where I've had bad nights. As an athlete you want to come back and have a better night the next night. The difference is, you've got to still be patient coming back the second night in this game [baseball]. In basketball, you can be more aggressive, go out and create your own opportunities. Here, you can't come out and be impatient and swing at anything.
Interview,
Sarasota, Fla.,
March 3/
The New York Times,
3-4:(B)14.

George Karl
Basketball coach,
Seattle "SuperSonics"

5

I know I'm not well liked in the league. I used to think: screw perceptions. [But] the thing is, right or wrong, in this business you're only what you're perceived to be.
Newsweek, 3-14:65.

Jeff Klein
Sports editor,
"The Village Voice"
(New York, N.Y.)

6

There exists a common misconception that baseball is full of byzantine strategies that only the most sophisticated observer can grasp. That just isn't true. Baseball tactics are simplistic compared to football.
Newsweek, 12-5:64.

Tom Lasorda
Baseball manager,
Los Angeles "Dodgers"

1

I want to be remembered as a guy who loved the *Dodgers*, loved baseball, a guy who went day-in, day-out to spread the word of the *Dodgers* and baseball . . . I was called the greatest ambassador for baseball that we have. That, for me, is the ultimate compliment. Nothing else can compare.

Interview/
USA Today, 5-20:(C)6.

John Madden
Football commentator;
Former NFL coach

2

It's hard to be [a football-team] owner. An owner has to have a big ego. It's easy to stay in the background with a big ego when you're losing, but a lot tougher when you're winning Super Bowls. Winning is a great deodorant, but sometimes it's got problems. Sometimes, it's not enough of a deodorant.

The New York Times,
3-30:(B)9.

Don Mattingly
Baseball player,
New York "Yankees"

3

I don't think that, as a player, you can worry that if we don't play well this year, then the manager is going to get fired. He takes on that responsibility when he comes to a big-league club . . . We [players] can't worry about that. It's just like he prepares and prepares and prepares us. At one point, you have to let the players go. It's up to us . . . If he gets fired, he can go anywhere he wants. Well, not anywhere he wants, but there are other situations. If you don't ever put yourself on the line [as manager], you'll never get axed. But you got to put yourself on the line.

New York, N.Y., April 8/
The New York Times,
4-9:33.

Tim McCarver
Sportscaster, ABC Sports;
Former baseball player

4

I see a lot of things [in baseball today] that I didn't see when the game was played with more rigid regard for the way the game should be played. Today the game is played by better athletes—I don't think there's any question about that—but that doesn't mean players play the game better. A lot of things they do defy common sense . . . It's a shoot-from-the-hip society, and the society is reflected in the way the game is played. It's also an indictment of [the players'] stays in the minor leagues. It's not the instructors' fault. [It's because] the players aren't there long enough. When players come up [to the majors] now, they still have a lot to learn. There's more teaching now at the big-league level than there used to be.

Interview/
Newsweek, 8-22:55.

Tony Meola
Goalkeeper of United States
soccer team at
1994 World Cup games

5

[As a goalie,] you understand in every game you're the hero or the goat. That's part of the training. You have to enjoy the mystique because there's no place to hide.

Newsweek, 7-11:54.

Mike Moore
President, National Association
of Professional Baseball Leagues

6

[On the increase in attendance at minor-league baseball games since the current players' strike against the major leagues started]: It's important to keep perspective. We [in the minors] were having healthy increases [in attendance already] . . . but the major-league strike has been icing on the cake. People need a baseball fix. It's a family tra-

(MIKE MOORE)

dition. They find ways to get to baseball games and have fun.

USA Today,
8-23:(C)1.

Chuck O'Connor
Principal attorney for
baseball-team owners
in contract negotiations
with players

1

We [the owners' side] haven't been the ones talking about litigation [to end the strike impasse]. We've been trying to negotiate a new agreement [with the players]. I still believe this will be resolved in a room that contains a bargaining table and not in a courtroom or the halls of Congress. Unfortunately, the [players] union is more disposed to and more comfortable in the environment of litigation and legislation, not negotiation.

Dec. 27/
The New York Times,
12-28:(B)10.

Peter O'Malley
Owner, Los Angeles "Dodgers"
baseball team

2

[Saying baseball-team owners should offer to make the currently striking players union a partner in various aspects of the game]: Even if we can't agree on the formula, there's no reason we can't let them in on the ground floor now. There's so much going on in the area of TV, licensing properties and the Commissioner's office that now is the time to give the union a meaningful presence and not just that of a potted palm. There's no downside to it.

Los Angeles, Calif.,
Sept. 28/
Los Angeles Times,
9-29:(C)1.

Steve Palermo
Special assistant to the chairman
of Major League
Baseball's Executive Council;
Former umpire

3

[On calls for shortening the playing time of baseball games]: I don't think the problem is shortening the game; I think the problem is with the pace of the game. That's why everybody is addressing time and they're looking at their clocks. In all other sports, there is a clock you look at. In football, there is the buildup to the two-minute warning. In baseball, there is no warning. It could strike at any time.

April 7/
USA Today, 4-8:(C)3.

Carl Peterson
General manager,
Kansas City "Chiefs"
football team

4

[On the football playoffs]: If you play a team you haven't played during the season, you may have something sprung upon you. But not with teams that know each other [such as in the playoffs]. The key for success in the playoffs is experience, playoff experience. This really is a third season, with the intensity, the speed seemingly higher than the regular season.

USA Today, 1-7:(C)4.

George Raveling
Coach of United States
basketball team at
1994 Goodwill Games

5

[On the improvement in basketball playing in countries around the world]: Americans need to understand that these other countries are efficient at basketball. We [in the U.S.] don't see a lot of international basketball other than the Olympics, so we don't get a chance to appreciate Italian

(GEORGE RAVELING)

basketball, Brazilian basketball, Croatian basketball. There are a lot of countries that play good basketball.

St. Petersburg, Russia, July 27/
Los Angeles Times, 7-28:(C)4.

Richard Ravitch
President,
major-league baseball-team owners'
Players Relations Committee

1

[On the possibility of a players' strike this season over such issues as a cap on players' salaries, as put forth by team owners]: I hope the union is responsive to our underlying needs. The owners will lose between $125-million and $150-million this year. The disparity in revenue among the clubs is becoming greater. There is no alternative to the owners' need to change the system. It would be an act of self-immolation on the part of the union to strike for a long time, thinking the owners will capitulate as they have in the past. It won't happen this time.

News conference,
July 11/
Los Angeles Times,
7-12:(C)5.

2

[On current contract talks with the players union]: We began these negotiations by saying to the players, "We've got to know what it's going to cost us to play ball. Work with us; talk with us; let's develop a system that will enable us to know that." We were told to make a proposal, and we finally did. That was for a sharing of revenues on a percentage basis. We made it clear we didn't think that was the only way we could achieve our objective and welcomed any ideas the union had. We got none. All we heard was a cry for more, more, more. It isn't going to fly.

New York, N.Y., July 18/
USA Today, 7-19:(C)3.

[On the current players' strike]: This has all the elements of a Greek tragedy, but the fans have to remember that the [team] owners didn't go out on strike and didn't force the players to go out. We didn't make some kind of radical or off-the-wall proposal. We asked [the players] to consider the same system that is working in football and basketball, and we guaranteed the same billion dollars in compensation they are receiving now, with a chance to receive considerably more if revenue continues to grow as it has in recent years ... The union's contention that the owners forced the strike so that they could implement their proposal is nonsense. Implementation doesn't solve anything. Collective bargaining does. We can implement from now to kingdom come, but we can't force the players to sign and we can't force them to play. We do have a Constitution in this country.

Sept. 13/
Los Angeles Times,
9-14:(C)8.

Dan Reeves
Football coach,
New York "Giants"

4

[Expressing misgivings about new offensive rules intended to increase scoring]: I don't think we should be so worried about offense as much as we should be about exciting football. What was our most exciting game last year? It was the Phoenix game at home, of course, where we kicked the field goal at the end to win it. Fans want excitement and I'm not sure that means more scoring. We've got to watch the balance between offense and defense, and I think these rules swing too much for the offense. The coaches weren't really involved in this. No one asked us. But the owners, it's their teams, and if they want it, I guess they get it.

Orlando, Fla., March 22/
The New York Times,
3-23:(B)9.

Robert B. Reich
Secretary of Labor
of the United States

1

[Saying he, as Labor Secretary, has no authority to order striking baseball players back to work]: There is no power under Federal law to order the [team] owners to reopen the ballparks and for the players to play ball. This is not a national economic emergency. They have local economic consequences, certainly, and there are hardships for local retailers, vendors, parking attendants, etc. But this isn't like a national transportation strike or a fuel stoppage in which the Federal government has power to order the parties to resume production. The cost here is less tangible. It's measured in the sad faces of my sons.
Interview, Sept. 8/
USA Today, 9-9:(C)8.

Pat Riley
Basketball coach,
New York "Knicks"

2

[On playing in the NBA finals]: Somewhere, you have to say to yourself, "I never want to go back to the thought that I wasn't part of a championship team." To me, that's misery. It's playing your whole career and making a lot of money, getting a lot of prestige, a lot of recognition, but knowing for the rest of your life you never . . . will get the chance to walk together forever as champions. They can never, ever, take that away.
Houston, Texas,
June 20/
The New York Times,
6-21:(B)14.

Kyle Rote, Jr.
Former United States
soccer player

3

We [in the U.S.] can make a mistake in allowing the formula of soccer success to be defined as having a high-profile, nationally televised league like the National Basketball Association or the National Football League. Soccer *is* successful. It's like softball. We don't have a pro softball league, but softball is a great sport. Soccer may just be one of those sports you enjoy watching.
Interview, Boston, Mass./
The Christian Science Monitor,
7-6:13.

Nolan Ryan
Former baseball pitcher

4

[Saying there is a backlash by fans against players' high salaries]: Baseball is a form of entertainment. I think more people relate to ballplayers, having played the game themselves, and that's why they're singled out. [But] you don't see anyone complaining about an actor making $20-million or $30-million a year.
News conference,
Washington, D.C., Aug. 18/
USA Today, 8-19:(C)4.

Ryne Sandberg
Baseball player, Chicago "Cubs"

5

[Saying he is retiring from baseball, despite having a very lucrative contract, because of his own dissatisfaction with his performance]: The money has never been a big part of my thinking or why I played the game. It's not the thing that motivated me . . . I am not the type of person who can be satisfied with anything less than my very best effort and my very top performance. I am not the type of person who can leave my game at the ball park and feel comfortable that my future is set regardless of my performance. And I am certainly not the type of person who can ask the *Cubs'* organization and Chicago *Cubs'* fans to pay my salary when I am not happy with my mental approach and my performance.
News conference announcing
his retirement, Chicago, Ill., June 13/
The New York Times, 6-14:(B)10.

Bud Selig
Owner, Milwaukee "Brewers"

baseball team;
Acting Commissioner of Baseball

1

We've got to have a system [in baseball] that ties [player] salaries to revenues. The NBA and NFL have one, and it should be our turn. Things are too unpredictable now. The small-market teams are fighting for their lives, and I think the fans are tired of the constant player-club acrimony over money. It's in everyone's interest to get this resolved on a sensible basis . . . I'm as much a traditionalist as anyone. I wish we could turn back the clock to the 1950s, when a box seat cost $2.50 and there were teams in Ebbets Field and the Polo Grounds. But wishing won't make it so.

Interview/
The Wall Street Journal,
3-18:(A)12.

2

[On the premature ending of this year's baseball season due to a players' strike]: You would have to be naive, insane or all of the above not to think that we haven't been scarred [in the eyes of the fans]. There are no winners in this. Both sides [owners and players] failed on so many fronts. I mean, it's almost impossible to articulate the sense of sadness and poignancy I feel today . . . Were we willing to negotiate with the [players'] union? Of course; but the union never responded to our need for cost certainty and a system that would control the growth of salaries. At this point, there's no sense getting into a debate over who has been the most intransigent.

News conference, Milwaukee, Wis.,
Sept. 14/Los Angeles Times,
9-15:(A)20,21.

David Stern
Commissioner,
National Basketball Association

3

[On recent changes in the basketball rules of play]: It's arguable that more vigilance in enforcing existing rules would bring the same results, but sometimes you need to redefine things for emphasis. Habits of officiating get formed, and they're hard to break. It's like in baseball, where the strike zone keeps shrinking even though its rule-book definition stays the same. Maybe they [the people who run baseball] ought to have another go at that.

Interview, New York, N.Y./
The Wall Street Journal,
10-28:(A)12.

4

[On basketball's cap on player salaries]: It's a cap, in a way, and if I were a player, and that's all it was, I'd be against it. But you could just as easily call it a floor on salaries or a cap on owner profits. It's a formula for sharing certain revenues the league takes in, with at least 53 percent going to the players. I think it's been an important part of the success we've had.

Interview,
New York, N.Y./
The Wall Street Journal,
10-28:(A)12.

Peter Thomson
Australian golfer

5

I've always said that if your grandmother can't enjoy it, it's not a great golf course. I have begun to rate golf courses by the number of balls you need. For instance, if a course is a one-ball course, assuming it has all the usual features, I think it's a great course. But a 12-ball course I think is rubbish. That's my basic criticism of Jack Nicklaus [-designed] courses. They are very much like the man himself, very serious and lacking in humor.

Interview/
Los Angeles Times, 7-6:(C)2.

Peter V. Ueberroth
Former Commissioner of Baseball

6

[On the early ending of this year's baseball season due to a players' strike]: Baseball games

(PETER V. UEBERROTH)

are won and lost because of errors—and this will go down as the biggest "E" of all. 1994—the season that struck itself out.

Los Angeles Times,
9-15:(C)6.

Herschel Walker
Football player,
Philadelphia "Eagles"

1

As a young [player], I basically took a vacation when I wasn't carrying the ball. Now I understand the game better, see it from different angles. The more different things I do, the more I want to do. Getting off a good block gives me as much of a kick as a 20-yard run used to.

Interview/
The Wall Street Journal,
12-9:(A)10.

Bill Walton
Basketball commentator,
NBC Sports; Former player

2

[On the NBA playoffs]: Everything changes now. Once you get this deep in the playoffs, this is the time where the great ones separate themselves from the good ones, and the average ones just wilt away in the heat of the moment. This is a time when you find out a lot about the real strengths of players. Sometimes you find out that a lot of them don't understand how to carry themselves in times like these. They don't understand how big the moment is.

USA Today, 5-20:(C)9.

Lenny Wilkins
Basketball coach,
Atlanta "Hawks"

3

[On his coaching style]: I tell guys from the beginning that this is the way it is here, and I define their roles. I don't treat anyone special. Everybody knows the parameters, and I don't make allowances for anyone, because it'll come back and bite you later on. Everyone is accountable for his own actions. Players know what to expect, but I also try to utilize their individual talents. I don't have a system that is rigid, except for the fact that you have to play defense.

Interview/
USA Today,
12-27:(C)1.

Ted Williams
Former baseball player,
Boston "Red Sox"

4

[Saying he doesn't think there will be a baseball players' strike this year]: The present players are in the most enviable, luckiest situation an athlete could be in. I don't think there will be a strike . . . This game is too important for a squabble like this . . . I think the level heads are going to smooth it out.

At autograph appearance,
Newton, Mass./
The New York Times,
7-29:(B)17.

The Indexes

Index to Speakers

A

I

J

M

T

U

W

Wacker, Watts, 471
Wagner, Lindsay, 421
Walesa, Lech, 311-312
Walker, Herschel, 484
Walker, Vaughn R., 81
Wallace, George C., 52
Wallop, Malcolm, 150
Walton, Bill, 484
Wardlaw, Kim McLane, 159
Warwick, William, 292
Washington, Craig A., 150
Waters, Maxine, 52
Wattenberg, Martin J., 198
Watts, Gary, 122
Waxman, Henry A., 411-412
Waybourn, William, 52
Wayne, Stephen, 198
Weakland, Rembert, 464
Weber, Vin, 150
Weesner, Theordore, 377
Wehmeyer, Peggy, 421, 464
Weill, Bernard, 312
Weinberg, Daniel H., 211
Weinstein, Harris, 198
Welch, John, 91
Wertheimer, Fred, 150, 199
West, Cornel, 212, 458
West, Darrell, 199
Westphal, Hans, 312-313
Weyrich, Paul M., 199
Wheelon, Albert, 471
White, Robert, 273
Whitehead, Ralph, 199
Whitehead, Robert, 448
Whitley, Charles O., 412
Whitman, Christine Todd, 52, 150, 200
Whittman, Marshall, 53
Wiener, Joshua M., 412
Wilhelm, David C., 200
Wilkins, Lenny, 484
Wilkins, Roger, 53
Wilkins, Steve, 412
Willetts, David, 212
Williams, Harold, 356

Williams, S. Linn, 112
Williams, Ted, 484
Willie, Charles, 123
Wilson, Pete, 39, 81, 150, 212, 236, 458
Winn, James, 123
Winsten, Jay, 81
Wirth, Timothy E., 237
Wirthlin, Richard, 200
Wittberg, Patricia, 465
Wofford, Harris, 39, 412
Wolfe, Sidney M., 413
Wolff, Tobias, 377
Wolff, Virginia Euwer, 378
Woodruff, Judy, 458
Woolhandler, Steffie, 413
Woolsey, R. James, 237, 273
Wright, Wendy, 53
Wyld, Tom, 81
Wyss, David, 112

Y

Yablonsky, Lewis, 81
Yankah, Kojo, 249
Yellen, Janet L., 112
Yeltsin, Boris N., 313-314, 327
Yerofeyev, Viktor, 315
Young, C. W. "Bill," 91

Z

Zahar, Mahmoud al-, 348
Zaleznik, Abraham, 62
Zametica, Jovan, 328
Zartman, I. William, 250
Zedillo (Ponce de Leon), Ernesto, 260
Zedlewski, Edwin, 81
Zeese, Kevin, 413
Zeien, Alfred M., 62
Zeikel, Arthur H., 62
Zeitlmann, Wolfgang, 315
Zemans, Frances, 159
Zhirinovsky, Vladimir V., 315-316
Zizola, Giancarlo, 465
Zwack, Peter, 316

Index to Subjects

A

Abortion—*see* Women
Acceptance of own limitations, 452:1
Acquired immune deficiency syndrome (AIDS)—
    see Medicine
Acting/actors:
    Actors Studio, 446:3
    age aspect, 425:1, 432:3, 455:1
    bankable aspect, 429:2
    as center of universe, 427:3
    characters, 423:5, 424:4, 428:1
    a commodity, 433:3
    common-sense aspect, 424:4
    confidence, self-, 429:1
    dangerous, should be, 427:2
    and directors, 428:1
    dumb/smart, 426:1
    earnings/pay, 482:4
    fear aspect, 447:3
    greed aspect, 433:1
    heart, landscape of, 423:5
    home, taking role, 424:1
    image, 424:2, 426:6
    immersing oneself, 424:1
    jobs, lack of, 446:3
    journalists meeting with, 357:6
    life, drawing from, 432:5
    the method, 424:1
    other people's experience, use of, 427:3
    recognition aspect, 415:3
    recognized, being, 423:4
    responsibility aspect, 429:5
    safe, playing, 426:1
    same thing over and over, 447:6
    schools, 426:1
    stage/theater, 444:3, 444:4, 446:3, 447:3,
      447:4, 447:6
    stars, 357:6, 422:3, 429:2
    system, kicking against, 427:2
    television, 415:3, 419:3
    truth aspect, 440:3
    women/actresses, 425:1, 426:2, 428:2, 432:3,
      455:1
    young/new, 446:3
    See also specific actors

Acton, Lord, 455:4
Adams, Gerry, 306:2, 310:3
Adulthood, 456:4
Advertising—*see* Commerce
Afghanistan, 237:2
Africa, pp. 238-250
    borders, national, 247:1
    Communism/Marxism, 245:3
    democracy/elections, 241:5, 242:2, 246:3
    development aspect, 244:4
    economy/business, 238:2, 241:6, 245:3, 246:4
    education/academic aspect, 246:4, 248:4
    hopeless continent, 246:4
    leadership/dictators, 239:4, 246:2, 246:4,
      247:6, 248:4
    pessimism, Afro-, 244:4
    political aspect, 246:3, 246:4
    telecommunications industry, 241:6
    relations with:
      Europe, 247:1
      South Africa, 238:2, 238:6, 239:4, 244:4,
        247:3, 247:6, 248:2
    See also specific African countries
Age/youth, 377:3, 452:1, 452:5, 455:1, 455:2
    See also Acting
Air transportation—*see* Transportation
Albania, 309:1
Alcohol—*see* Medicine: drugs
Alexander, Jane, 354:5
Algeria:
    Islam, 338:4
    journalism, 245:5
    relations with:
      France, 242:1, 246:1
      Iran, 338:4
Alienation, 450:1
America/U.S., pp. 34-40
    anyone can be anything, 37:2
    average person, cult of, 37:2
    breakdown of, 38:2, 137:2
    charitable, Americans as, 210:4
    Christian country, 461:5
    citizenship, 39:6
    civilization, maintenance of, 36:5
    community, sense of, 34:2, 34:5, 35:1, 35:2

---

*Many references to Bill Clinton are not listed in this index due to the numerous routine mentions of his name throughout the book. Only references that are specifically about him, personally or professionally, are listed here.

Defense/military *(continued)*
peacekeeping/humanitarian use of, 89:5, 90:3, 91:2
peacetime deployment, 83:7
personnel, quality of, 90:1
place in world, determination of, 313:2
policy, understanding of, 290:3
political aspect, 89:6, 90:4
prepositioning, strategy of, 89:1
President (U.S.)/Commander-in-Chief aspect, 84:5, 86:1, 86:5, 90:4, 266:1
press coverage during wartime, 85:3
readiness/preparedness, 83:7, 86:2, 90:1
Reagan, Ronald, aspect, 84:5
regional conflicts, fighting in, 88:4
research and development, 84:1
revamping of, 231:6
scandals, 83:4
Tailhook, 89:2
See also "friendly-fire" accidents, *this section*
Secretary of Defense, U.S., 137:6
society at large, link with, 84:4
spending/budget/cutbacks/downsizing, 83:2, 83:3, 83:5, 83:6, 84:1, 84:2, 85:1, 85:4, 85:5, 85:6, 86:2, 86:3, 86:4, 87:4, 87:5, 88:4, 91:1
superpowers—*see* Foreign affairs
technology aspect, 84:2, 86:4, 88:5, 399:3
television coverage during wartime, 85:3
tests on humans during Cold War, 394:2
two wars, fighting of, 85:4, 88:2
United Nations control of U.S. forces, 91:2
volunteer force, 84:4
war production, World War II, 88:3
weapons compatibility, 84:3
women aspect, 83:1, 88:1, 88:7, 89:2
de Klerk, Frederik W., 248:2
Democracy, 43:3, 120:5, 122:3, 134:7, 137:3, 142:4, 149:3, 149:4, 157:5, 270:3, 274:1, 359:2
See also Foreign affairs; Freedom
Democratic Party (U.S.):
abortion aspect, 52:1
accomplishments, failure to communicate about, 175:3

Democratic Party (U.S.) *(continued)*
campaign-finance reform, 199:3
Clinton, Bill, aspect, 162:3, 162:5, 175:5, 180:6, 183:3, 185:1, 186:1, 192:3, 200:2
New/Old Democrat, 175:6
re-election challenge by other Democrats, 189:4
Congress aspect, 143:1, 165:1, 169:1, 186:3, 192:5
See also Republican Party: Congress: election victory
conservative/right aspect, 162:3, 196:4
crime aspect, 78:4
economy:
spending/budget, 94:2, 98:5
taxes, 95:3, 191:5
election of 1992, 169:1
election of 1994, 180:5, 183:3
See also Republican Party: Congress: election victory
extremism, 164:4
families aspect, 204:3
foreign-affairs aspect, 220:4, 232:2
government, role of, 141:5
Haiti aspect, 263:1, 272:1
health-care aspect—*see* Medicine: reform
history, rewriting of, 194:4
liberal/left aspect, 173:4, 272:1
moderate aspect, 162:3
national/local aspect, 180:6
New/Old Democrat, Bill Clinton as, 175:6
public attitude toward, 164:4
purists, nomination of, 186:1
Reagan, Ronald, aspect, 174:4, 194:4
Republican Party aspect, 178:2, 181:3, 184:4
endorsement of Democratic candidates, 179:2, 179:3, 198:3
sound like Republicans, Democrats who, 163:3
treatment of Republicans, 160:3
See also Reagan, Ronald, *this section*
scandals, 186:5
See also Whitewater, *this section*
sleaze factor, use of, 174:4
social-welfare aspect, 201:1, 211:1

E

F

I

K

N

Nuclear power—*see* Energy
Nuclear weapons—*see* Defense

O

O'Connor, Flannery, 367:6
Oil—*see* Energy
Olivier, Laurence, 424:1
One thing leading to another, 450:7
O'Neill, Eugene, 445:2
Opera—*see* Music

P

Pacific—*see* Asia
Pain, 451:5
    See also Medicine
Pakistan, 233:2, 291:2
Palestinians:
    economic aspect, 339:6
    Gaza, 330:4
        See also Israel: Palestinians: peace
    Hamas, 329:3, 345:2
    Hezbollah, 333:5
    Jericho—*see* Israel: Palestinians: peace
    massacre by Israeli/Jewish settler in Hebron,
        329:1, 329:4, 330:2, 330:3, 334:1, 338:2,
        343:6, 344:1, 347:2
    Palestine Liberation Organization (PLO):
        Arafat, Yasir, 329:3, 332:4, 333:1, 338:2,
            338:3, 339:2, 340:3, 341:4, 341:5,
            347:4, 348:3, 348:4
            Nobel Prize, 338:5, 340:5
        lifestyle of officials, 332:1
        Muslims aspect, 332:1
        terrorism, 338:5, 340:5
        See also Israel: Palestinians: peace
    security aspect, 329:1, 330:3, 338:2
    state, 340:2, 340:3, 347:4
    terrorism, 338:5, 340:2, 340:5
        See also Hamas, *this section;* Hezbollah,
        this section
    West Bank, 330:4, 338:2
        See also Israel: Palestinians: peace
    relations with:
        Iran, 346:3

Palestinians *(continued)*
    relations with (continued)
        Israel—*see* Israel
        Jordan, 339:6
        U.S., 348:4
Panama:
    Canal, 259:3, 259:5
    Democratic Revolutionary Party, 258:4
    elections, 251:5
    Noriega, Manuel Antonio, 251:5, 258:4, 269:5
    refugees from Haiti, acceptance of, 255:3
    world's deposed leaders, taking in of, 251:3
    relations with:
        Haiti, 255:3
        U.S.:
            Bush, George, aspect, 266:1
            invasion of 1989, 251:5, 258:4, 269:5
            treatment by U.S., 255:3
            See also Canal, *this section*
Panetta, Leon E., 173:3
Paraguay, 257:2
Pataki, George, 179:3
Peace, 451:3
Pell, Claiborne, 370:4
Perot, Ross, 162:4, 171:4, 189:1
Persian Gulf war of 1991—*see* Middle East
Philby, Kim, 355:3
Philippines, 285:4
Philosophy, pp. 449-458
Phoniness, 453:6
Picasso, Pablo, 353:2, 446:4, 449:6
Plath, Sylvia, 369:7
Player, being a, 457:2
Poetry—*see* Literature
Poland, 295:2, 311:5, 312:1, 312:2, 312:3
Police—*see* Crime
Politics, pp. 160-200
    abortion aspect, 52:1, 184:5
    ambition, 143:4
    approval, politicians' need for, 143:4
    authenticity/phoniness aspect, 453:6
    bad things for a good end, doing, 197:4
    baser side, appeal to, 457:5
    black aspect, 53:2
    book contracts for politicians, 370:4,
        414:1

Religion/church *(continued)*
  Christianity/Catholicism *(continued)*
    the Bible, 51:2, 459:6, 461:6
    challenge, never-ending, 460:3
    China, 463:2
    Christian Coalition, 464:1
    commitment, 464:5
    conservative/right (political)—*see* conser-
      vative/right *elsewhere in this section*
    helping people, 460:6
    homosexuals aspect, 459:6
    Islam aspect, 460:4
    issue-driven, 463:1
    litmus tests, 459:6, 464:4
    New Age movement, 460:4
    nuns, 465:1
    Orthodox, 459:1
    the Pope, 465:2
    the Vatican, 465:2
    virtues/grace, religion of, 464:3
    women/feminism aspect, 461:1, 462:4
    working together, Catholics and Protestants,
      460:4
  conservative/right (political) aspect, 160:1,
    164:2, 168:2, 172:2, 185:3, 188:3, 194:6,
    196:2, 200:1, 459:5, 459:6, 461:4, 463:3,
    464:1, 464:4
  creationism, 463:5
  cultural authority of, 463:5
  desecration of tombs, 459:1
  education/schools aspect, 463:5
    See also prayer, *this section*
  evolutionism, 463:5
  freedom of, 133:3
  health-care reform aspect, 404:3
  helping people, 460:6
  homosexuals aspect, 51:2, 459:6
  importance/significance of, 456:1, 464:6
  Islam/Muslims, 238:3, 242:1
    Algeria, 338:4
    Christianity aspect, 460:4
    Egypt, 338:4
    France, 246:1
    helping people, 460:6
    international challenge, 224:1
    Iran, 338:4

Religion/church *(continued)*
  Islam/Muslims *(continued)*
    Middle East/Arab countries, 348:3
    militancy, 460:4
    Palestine Liberation Organization (PLO)
      aspect, 332:1
    Saudi Arabia, 348:3
    terrorism, 337:4, 342:4, 345:2, 345:3
    See also Balkans war
  Judaism/Jews, 42:6, 43:1, 188:3, 460:6
    See also Israel
  liberal/left (political) aspect, 459:2, 463:3
  morality aspect, 460:5
  Mormons, 462:2
  national religion, 461:4
  New Age movement, 460:4, 462:1
  political aspect, 461:4
    See also conservative/right, *this section;*
      liberal/left, *this section*
  prayer in schools, 36:4, 177:6, 182:4, 459:2,
    459:4, 461:2, 461:3, 462:5, 464:1, 464:4
  preaching/proselytizing, 461:6, 461:7, 463:2
  President (U.S.) aspect, 460:1
  press/media aspect, 362:3, 460:2, 464:6
  priesthood as right/calling, 459:3
  Republican Party (U.S.) aspect, 160:1, 168:2,
    185:3, 196:2, 200:1, 459:6, 461:4
  science aspect, 460:5, 462:1
  secularism, 362:3, 460:4, 461:5, 462:6, 463:3
  television aspect, 461:6
  Turkey, 459:1
Reno, Janet, 71:2, 174:6
Republican Party (U.S.):
  abortion aspect, 52:1, 162:1
  blacks/minorities aspect, 185:5
  campaign-finance reform, 199:3
  Clinton, Bill, aspect, 175:2, 180:4, 194:5
  cohesion, 198:3
  combativeness, 138:2
  come together, ability to, 196:3
  Congress/House/Senate:
    attitude in, 138:2
    election victory/control/majority, 37:1,
      86:3, 92:4, 93:2, 100:4, 130:2, 134:4,
      135:2, 140:4, 141:2, 141:5, 142:7,
      143:1, 144:6, 145:5, 147:3, 149:6,

S

T

Virtues, 454:1

W

Walesa, Lech, 295:2, 312:1
Walters, Barbara, 357:3, 357:5
War, 285:4
   See also Foreign affairs: ethnic/local conflicts;
   and specific wars
Washington, D.C.:
   Mayoral election, 162:6
   rivers, 125:4
   *References to Washington, D.C., as seat of the
   Federal government are too numerous and
   non-specific to list in this section*
Washington, George, 331:1
Washington, Martha, 135:4
Watergate—*see* Politics: ethics
Welfare—*see* Social welfare
West, the U.S.—*see* America
Whitman, Walt, 355:6
Wilde, Oscar, 48:1
Wilder, Billy, 425:1
Williams, Tennessee, 445:2
Wilson, Pete, 197:2
Winfrey, Oprah, 156:4
Wisdom, 452:1
Women/women's rights:
   abortion:
      biological aspect, 43:4
      China, 280:4
      clinics/doctors, protection of/violence
         against, 41:1, 41:2, 45:3, 46:2, 46:5,
         48:4, 49:3, 51:1, 51:5, 53:3
      conservative (political) aspect, 47:3, 184:5
      Democratic Party (U.S.) aspect, 52:1
      family-planning aspect, 42:4, 47:2
      insurance coverage for, 379:3, 381:2, 397:3,
         404:3
      international/worldwide right to, 46:1, 47:4
      liberal (political) aspect, 47:2, 47:3
      morality aspect, 42:4
      pill (RU-486), 42:3, 51:3
      political aspect, 52:1, 184:5
      promotion of, 42:4
      Reagan, Ronald, aspect, 52:1, 184:5

Women/women's rights *(continued)*
   abortion *(continued)*
      religious aspect, 42:4, 43:4, 47:2, 53:1,
         404:3, 459:6
      Republican Party (U.S.) aspect, 52:1, 162:1
      Roe v. Wade Supreme Court decision, 41:3,
         47:3, 48:2, 52:1, 53:1, 184:5
      Surgeon General (U.S.) aspect, 44:5
      U.S. policy, 46:1
   acting/actresses, 425:1, 426:2, 428:2, 432:3,
      455:1
   age aspect, 455:1
   black aspect, 436:3
   choices, 44:3
   conservative/right aspect, 44:3
      See also abortion, *this section*
   crime victims, 77:4
   economics/workplace/wages aspect, 42:1,
      47:5, 49:2
   education/schools/colleges aspect, 47:5, 118:2,
      119:2, 119:3, 119:4, 122:1, 473:2
   equality/equity, 45:4, 47:5, 48:2
   in government, 52:5
      in Congress, 146:5, 148:5
      First Lady—*see* Presidency, U.S.
      Governor, running for, 191:3
      running for political office, 51:4, 191:3
      White House, in key positions at, 132:6,
         146:3, 148:6
   harassment, sexual:
      Clinton, Bill, aspect, 49:5, 185:2
      Tailhook scandal, U.S. Navy, 89:2
   hatred, self-, 51:4
   journalism aspect, 360:1
      anchors, 361:4
   judges, 151:1
   labels, 52:5
   lawyers, 152:1, 159:1
   military aspect, 83:1, 88:1, 88:7, 89:2
   money aspect, 50:6
   motion-pictures aspect, 428:2, 432:3
   music aspect, 436:3
   power aspect, 51:4, 451:4
   religion aspect, 461:1, 462:4
   Republican Party (U.S.) aspect, 44:3, 185:5
   role in life, 44:3

Women/women's rights *(continued)*
    sports aspect, 473:2
    stereotypes, 44:3
    taking charge of own affairs, 50:6
    violence, domestic, 77:4, 80:5, 157:2
    welfare aspect, 201:6
Woodward, Vann, 36:1
Work, 449:6, 458:4
    See also Labor
Wright, Wilbur/Orville, 214:1
Writing—*see* Literature

Y

Yale University, 446:3
Yeltsin, Boris N.—*see* Russia

Yourself, being, 453:1
Youth—*see* Age
Yugoslavia/Serbia:
    Balkans war, 320:4, 321:1, 325:1, 325:3
    breakup of, 320:4
    Communism, 320:4
    economy, 321:1
    greater Serbia, 309:1
    journalism aspect, 307:1
    sanctions against, 321:1, 325:1
    United Nations (UN) aspect, 321:1

Z

Zhirinovsky, Vladimir V.—*see* Russia
Zimbabwe, 246:2
Zyuganov, Gennady, 314:1